Fielding's
PEOPLE'S REPUBLIC OF CHINA
1987

by
Ruth Lor Malloy and Priscilla Liang Hsu

Fielding Travel Books
c/o Willow Morrow & Company, Inc.
105 Madison Avenue, New York, N.Y. 10016

Fielding's
PEOPLE'S
REPUBLIC
OF CHINA
1987

Current Fielding Titles

Red Guides—updated annually

FIELDING'S BERMUDA AND THE BAHAMAS 1987
FIELDING'S CARIBBEAN 1987
FIELDING'S DISCOVER EUROPE: OFF THE BEATEN PATH 1987
FIELDING'S ECONOMY CARIBBEAN 1987
FIELDING'S ECONOMY EUROPE 1987
FIELDING'S EUROPE 1987
FIELDING'S MEXICO 1987
FIELDING'S PEOPLE'S REPUBLIC OF CHINA 1987
FIELDING'S SELECTIVE SHOPPING GUIDE TO EUROPE 1987

Blue Guides—updated as necessary

FIELDING'S AFRICA: SOUTH OF THE SAHARA
FIELDING'S AFRICAN SAFARIS
FIELDING'S ALL-ASIA BUDGET GUIDE
FIELDING'S EGYPT AND THE ARCHAEOLOGICAL SITES
FIELDING'S EUROPE WITH CHILDREN
FIELDING'S FAMILY VACATIONS USA
FIELDING'S FAR EAST
FIELDING'S HAVENS AND HIDEAWAYS USA
FIELDING'S LEWIS AND CLARK TRAIL
FIELDING'S MOTORING AND CAMPING EUROPE
FIELDING'S SPANISH TRAILS IN THE SOUTHWEST
FIELDING'S WORLDWIDE CRUISES 3rd revised edition

Acknowledgments

It is impossible to mention by name the hundreds of people who helped with this guide; people met on trains, in airports, and in hotels; business travelers, students, foreign residents, diplomats, travel agents, airline officials, and, of course, tourists. Each contributed generously of their experiences traveling or living in China.

I am particularly indebted to the patient guides and officials of the China International Travel Service and other Chinese travel and tourism agencies. Especially noteworthy were Xiao Yuzhen and Yu Zhengwen of China's National Tourism Administration, both of whom went far beyond the call of duty to help. Thanks also are due for the generous hospitality given to me by the National Tourism Administration and by Chinese travel agencies in Beijing, Chengde, Guangzhou, Quanzhou, Shanghai, Xiamen, and Yantai, and by the Great Wall Hotel in Beijing.

C.I.T.S. is responsible for most of the Chinese translations, and Z. M. Li for most of the art.

For this edition, I am especially grateful to the Canadian China Society, particularly Kaicene Cheng, Betty McWhinnie, Molly Phillips, Priscilla Tsao, and Ross Willmot. A special thank you goes to Harry Campbell and William Small for reading parts of the typescript and offering suggestions.

I also appreciate the help of Nancy Langston Brain, Lauren Flattery, Ursula Franklin, Vigor Fung, Marion Heidel, Katharine B. Hockin, Agnes Y. Lor, Gary Lum, Linda, Martin, and Terry Malloy, David Mitchell, Dora Nipp, Ted Stannard, Michael True, and editors Eunice Riedel and Randy Ladenheim.

Words cannot adequately express the outstanding contribution of Priscilla Liang Hsu, who traveled all over China sending back reports not just on tourism developments, but also on such topics as Chinese opera and calligraphy. She organized the Chinese characters for the "Food" and "Destinations" sections, arranged for typesetting, and reviewed the typescript. Without her, this book would not be as useful or as stimulating.

Ruth Lor Malloy

Up-to-Date Information

The logistics of tourism everywhere are constantly changing, especially in China, where new hotels are opening at a furious pace. Yet information about these hotels and the new regulations is difficult to obtain, frequently discovered only upon asking.

Because travelers need information on China as current as possible, we offer the benefit of our resources *free* to owners of *Fielding's People's Republic of China* for one time only.

For a sample copy of our most recent newsletter with the latest information and changes that have come to our attention, *please send the following coupon and US$1 (or equivalent) for postage and handling.* Copies of our newsletter are available without coupon by mail for US$5 (or equivalent) each. We will try to send it to you by return mail, but please allow one month at the most for an answer (postal services being what they are). If we are unable to reply by your deadline, your coupon or check will be returned so you can use it again at a future time.

The newsletter is published quarterly beginning in Autumn 1986.

GOOD FOR ONE COPY

of Ruth Lor Malloy's most recent newsletter
on China's tourism and hotels,
to be used with the 1987 edition of
Fielding's People's Republic of China.

Coupon valid to December 31, 1987

Your deadline:_____

Please check information needed.

( ) Information **not already** in this book on hotels in China, including
telephone numbers, addresses, descriptions, evaluations, and current price
of at least a standard double in F.E.C.s—where these are available.
Noted will be the hotels that have informed us in writing that they will
reconfirm reservations by telex.

( ) Latest information **not already** in this book on visas, customs,
credit cards, and currency; new flights, travel from Hong Kong, cities
open to foreign visitors, important new tourist attractions with evaluations (if possible). Also travel tips, important address changes, etc.

( ) Latest prices: A sampling of prices for food, film, hotel laundry,
taxis, souvenirs, C.I.T.S. service charges, etc.

Photocopies or facsimiles of this coupon will be ignored.

Please make checks or money orders payable to Ruth Lor Malloy,
570 Windermere Ave., Toronto, Ont. M6S 3L8, Canada.

Name: (please type or print)_____

Address:_____

_____

( ) Please indicate here if you would like to receive information on
how to order a subscription, and copies of newsletters you have missed.

CONTENTS

xii　*Contents*

List of Cities Open to Foreign Tourists

Municipalities Directly Under Central Government

Beijing   Shanghai   Tianjin

Hebei Province

Qinhuangdao
Shijiazhuang
Chengde
Baoding
Tangshan
Handan
Zhuoxian

Shanxi Province

Taiyuan
Datong
Linfen
Yuncheng

Inner Mongolia Autonomous Region

Huhhot
Baotou
Erlianhot
Manzhouli
Tongliao
Hailar
Dongsheng
Xilinhot
Zalantun
Dalateqi

Liaoning Province

Shenyang
Dalian
Anshan
Fushun
Dandong
Jinzhou
Yingkou
Fuxin
Liaoyang
Benxi
Tieling
Chaoyang
Panjin

Jilin Province

Changchun
Jilin
Yanji
Siping
Laoyuan
Tonghua
Baicheng
Antu

Heilongjiang Province

Harbin
Qiqihar
Daqing
Jiamusi
Mudanjiang
Jixi
Hegang
Qitaihe
Yichun
Wudalianchi

Jiangsu Province

Nanjing
Suzhou
Wuxi
Lianyungang
Nantong
Changzhou
Yangzhou
Zhenjiang
Xuzhou
Huaiyin
Yancheng

Zhejiang Province

Hangzhou
Ningbo
Shaoxing
Wenzhou
Jiaxing
Huzhou
Jinhua
Shujiang
Putuo

Anhui Province

Hefei
Wuhu
Huangshan
Bengbu
Tunxi
Maanshan
Anqing
Huainan
Huaibei
Chuzhou
Chaohu
Shexian
Fengyang
Jingxian
Jiuhuashan

Fujian Province

Fuzhou
Xiamen
Quanzhou
Zhangzhou
Chongan

Jiangxi Province

Nanchang
Jiujiang
Jingdezhen
Yingtan
Jinggangshan
Ganzhou

Shandong Province

Jinan
Qingdao
Yantai
Taian
Weifang
Zibo
Jining

Henan Province

Zhengzhou
Kaifeng
Luoyang
Anyang

Xinxiang
Xinyang
Nanyang
Puyang
Pingdingshan
Wenxian

Hubei Province

Wuhan
Yichang
Shashi
Xiangfan
Xianning
Danjiangkou
Huangshi
Jingmen
Ezhou
Shiyan
Jiangling

Hunan Province

Changsha
Hengyang
Yueyang
Xiangtan
Zhuzhou

Guangdong Province

Guangzhou
Foshan
Zhaoqing
Shenzhen
Zhuhai
Shantou
Haikou
Zhanjiang
Zhongshan
Jiangmen
Shaoguan
Huizhou
Chaozhou
Sanya
Meixian
Dongwuan
Gaoyao
Qiongshan
Dingan

INTRODUCTION

WHY GO TO CHINA?

—Because it is historically and culturally one of the richest countries in the world, and many of its ancient buildings have been restored for all to enjoy.

—Because China has some of the world's most spectacular natural scenery.

—Because what is happening now to the Chinese people is vital and exciting—a recent openness to the outside world in which you, the foreign visitor, can play a part. Here is a drama of immense importance to human history—will China, with its tremendous population of more than one fifth of mankind, achieve its goals of modernization by the year 2000? Can she do this with a minimum of social damage before any adverse reaction to current policies takes place?

—Because the banquet food is rarely duplicated anywhere. Where else can you get dishes shaped like phoenixes or swans or rabbits? And today the art of the great master chefs is being passed on.

—Because you can see for yourself its time-honored handicrafts being made; for example, 45 balls within balls, each intricately carved and free-moving.

—Because you can experience a culture very different from your own, and yet in many ways similar.

—Because foreigners have influenced the development of China and traces of that history can still be found and studied.

—Because if you are of Chinese ancestry (in this life or previous lives), you can look for your roots and especially help in the development of your ancestral land.

—Because China is available for the first time in recent history to tourists, and who knows when it may be closed to tourists again?

BACKGROUND

China is a country that has infuriated yet tantalized the rest of the world for centuries. Its arrogant indifference, the wealth and divine right

1

of its emperors have intrigued generations of curious people everywhere. In more recent years, its fanatical adherence to an alien ideology has continued to mystify. Even today, people around the world are asking, "Is it or isn't it?"

China started out as a nation over 2200 years ago. The thousands of years of relative isolation since then allowed the Chinese to indulge in and develop their unique Confucian-based culture until the 19th century. At that time, more advanced technology and greed encouraged many European countries and Japan to grab power and territory in China. The Chinese reacted to foreign victories with bewilderment, various anti-foreigner rebellions, and then, in 1911, with a republican revolution. After a period of embarrassing national disintegration, first under the war lords and then during civil war and Japanese invasion, the country was finally reunited in 1949 under the Communists.

In spite of several drastic setbacks, China has moved ahead since that point to a period of relative prosperity and freedom.

The Chinese people, up until very recently, have been 80% agricultural. Attachment to land has colored their thinking and behavior. Their religion, their loyalties, and their efforts have always been based on pragmatism.

Before 1950, China's economy stemmed primarily from a feudal system, land rented to peasants in return for a percentage of the crops. Landlords ideally had responsibility for the welfare of their serfs, on whom they were largely dependent for their wealth. Although the system was abused frequently, owning land was the goal of millions.

China became a Communist country in 1949. Heady with victory, the Communist leaders embarked on a series of programs religiously following the theories of Mao Zedong, the man who had led them to power. But the Chinese leaders were pragmatists first. When something didn't work, they tried something else.

The Communists started out with a land-to-the-peasants program, and then to collectivization, to communes, and to communes with private plots. During the Cultural Revolution, private plots were abolished, to be reinstated and encouraged later. In the 1970s, it was apparent that even that system was not meeting the needs of the people.

In the early 1980s, an economy largely based on the family replaced that of the communes. Most counties adopted the Responsibility System, whereby rural inhabitants rent land or machines. The government receives an agreed share in the produce while villagers can keep or sell the surplus. Anybody can also work on projects such as handicrafts, livestock, and vegetables, which they can sell for their own gain. These you will see on sale in "free markets." Families and collectives have opened up hotels, restaurants, and factories. It would seem that China has almost come around full circle, with the government replacing the feudal landlords. But has it?

Under the new economic system, the government no longer determines all that is grown or produced and how much; the market now affects most production directly. Many peasants have been working furiously and are making more money than they ever have before. Many villagers now have higher incomes than most salaried city dwellers.

At present, China is thus undergoing another revolution. For the first time, many villages are earning less than 50% of income from agriculture. Over the next few decades even more mechanization of agriculture and urban growth should develop, especially as new airfields, resort complexes with golf courses, new factories and schools eat into existing agricultural land.

The revolutionary slogans of nationalistic self-sufficiency and personal sacrifice of the fifties and sixties have now given way to international cooperation and modernization.

The new economic policies also include the opening up of many cities to foreign investment. A concerted effort to attract foreign money has been made in the coastal areas, with a series of regional development zones extending from Dalian in the north to Beihai city in the south, and especially in Shenzhen, Guangzhou, Shanghai, Dalian, and Tianjin. Here foreign investment particularly is being encouraged, and harbors, roads, and telecommunications added to or improved. Factories, office blocks, hotels, and workers' quarters are shooting up everywhere. Some of these areas have or will soon have International Direct-Dial (IDD) telephones and international airports.

The effects of the new economic policies are apparent everywhere, as you can see by the many construction cranes wherever you go. A battalion of private souvenir merchants greet you at almost every tourist attraction. Relatively expensive Hong Kong–made clothes hang for sale in front of stores and in the free markets. Groups of former peasants are building hotels, paving roads, and constructing bridges, playgrounds, libraries, and schools. In some areas, you can see a great deal of new peasant housing, some of luxury size.

The one-child birth control program continues to keep the population from overwhelming the economy. The population of China (including Taiwan, Hong Kong, and Macao) is 1.046 billion, and the leadership hopes it will stay below 1.2 billion. The program has recently drawn criticism from abroad because of abortions ("28% of all pregnancies" end in abortion, according to the *Wall St. Journal*) and suggestions of *widespread* female infanticide (which China has denied).

Problems to be studied include the psychological effect of a child with no siblings but masses of doting aunts, uncles, and grandparents; and the financial support of the growing proportion of elderly people. Recently signs have indicated that birth control regulations may loosen up a bit, especially in the countryside and among minorities, where controls have been less strict, anyway, than in the cities. With the economy based on family enterprises, more children are needed to help out.

You can see the relaxing of the puritanical Maoist ethic in the new freedom to enjoy life. Without the hours spent in political meetings studying the works of Chairman Mao, people now have more leisure. Instead of saving their money for the development of the country, they are eating out in restaurants, and couples are ordering bigger and more elaborate wedding feasts. People are buying videos, color televisions, washing machines, refrigerators, and mopeds. A few private citizens have even bought cars and trucks! But are they so concerned about acquisitions that they are forgetting about sensitivity to others?

Life is less serious now. Lively dance parties are held in every city. Many men and women wear high-heeled shoes and sunglasses, and the women are adding some glamour to their lives with permanent waves, lipsticks, and colorful dresses. A beauty contest has even taken place in Guangzhou! And Chinese tourists flock everywhere in China, a few even traveling outside the country.

Whereas anything foreign was considered counterrevolutionary before, today musicians like Wham! and John Denver, innumerable foreign symphony orchestras and dance groups, and artists like Robert Rauschenberg have helped to stimulate an interest in foreign culture. New also is the more mature approach to history, some credit being given to the help of the Nationalists in fighting the Japanese invaders, for example. While before only revolutionary themes could be expressed in the arts, today Marx is treated as a human on stage, and nude models have been used in art classes. References to human sexuality are gingerly appearing for the first time in recent literature and stage plays—but nothing like elsewhere in the world. In the late 1970s, none of this could have been predicted.

After decades of drabness, China is beginning to look more cheerful. It is a nice change.

The current revolution has also affected education. Previously, the government decided solely through examinations who would be paid to go to university and what jobs those graduates would take later. Today, some new colleges are being built where students pay fees, choose their own subjects, and find their own jobs after graduation. At least one U.S.-style private university is operating in China (Huanghe University in Zhengzhou) with English as the medium of instruction. Some universities with U.S. ties are granting MBAs. Thousands of Chinese students also have been encouraged to study abroad, not all with government funding. The country's leadership is aware that the former system cannot supply the expertise to modernize the country before its goal, the year 2000.

With any new system come abuses and inequalities: a few resentful, less ambitious, and less successful people have tried to sabotage those developing the economy and getting personally rich in the process. Black-market currency merchants, some disguised as hawkers, have proliferated. Some government officials, no longer needing approval from Beijing for purchases using foreign exchange, have gone overboard and imported automobiles, foreign television sets, mopeds, etc. While China's foreign exchange reserves rose to a record high early in 1984, ranking her eighth in the world, this foreign spending spree brought on China's first foreign exchange deficit since 1981, later that same year. In March 1985 the government had to again impose restrictions, and it has been threatening to stop issuing foreign exchange certificate (F.E.C.) because F.E.C.s are out of control. Beijing city bus drivers went on a kind of strike, working only half time because taxi drivers were getting five times more pay than they did. Commuters suffered, as they had to fight even more to get on fewer buses. And then there were the rising prices!

China's leaders are concerned about these adverse economic and social changes and, if things go too far, probably would not hesitate to put some clamps on other areas as well.

On the surface, the Chinese may appear to be moving quickly toward capitalism. This confusion makes a visit to China now particularly intriguing. Have they or haven't they abandoned Communism, or Marxism, or Marxist-Leninism, or whatever they've been following? Some theoreticians argue that it is only Mao Zedong's own brand of Marxist-Leninism that they have abandoned. Among other heresies, Mao based his revolution on the peasants rather than industrial workers. And does the government still control the means of production? Why don't you check that one out for yourself?

These are just a few of the changes. When you go to China in the late 1980s, you will see many others. It is an exciting time to go, and you will experience history being made. But you have to be alert to what is going on.

See also "Milestones in Chinese History."

TOURISM

Traveling in China is still not like visiting anywhere else in the world. Prepaid group tourism is the best way to go and should continue to be so until the late '80s, when enough hotels are open and computers are operating to meet the needs of individual travelers. As it is, in past years arrangements for individual travelers were still occasionally being canceled enroute in favor of groups. During the very busy seasons, China International Travel Service (C.I.T.S.) curtailed its programs for individuals. Except for the new joint-venture hotels, one could not even get a reply to a request for a reservation, and even the group tours couldn't be guaranteed specific hotels. During the high tourist season, hotels were jammed in Beijing, Guangzhou, Guilin, Shanghai, Luoyang, Dunhuang, and Xi'an. Confirmed hotel reservations were essential.

In 1985, about 18 million visitors entered China, of whom over 80% were Hong Kong and Macao compatriots. (Since Hong Kong only has about 5 million people, this probably means that many were making more than one trip to China during this period.) China is aiming for 5 million noncompatriot visitors by 1990, and 10–12 million by the year 2000.

China has continued upgrading her tourism facilities. Since 1978, when she really started trying to attract foreign exchange, she has been particularly obsessed with building hotels and renovating ancient temples. She has spanned valleys with cable cars and imported minibuses. She has been extending railway lines, asphalting highways to tourist attractions, and building and upgrading airports. More luxury tourist ships are being added to her fleet, particularly on the Yangtze River. She has been expanding her airlines and air routes, and improving telecommunications. The pace is moving so furiously that keeping track of all of these changes is impossible.

But, generally, the results are great!

One is now beginning to hear of projected hotel room surpluses in the biggest cities, especially Guangzhou.

Hotel construction will continue through the 1980s—everything from fancy, international-class joint ventures to tiny pensions owned and operated by cooperatives, temples, and families. The first luxury-class hotel appeared in 1978, but so far China has not produced any hotel that meets international five-star standards, though she has come close. Some of her hotels at first glance are equal to or better than those in New York City or Toronto or London. Some lobbies are huge and elegant, rivaling the best of Manila and Bangkok. Staff members are smartly dressed in beautifully Hong Kong–tailored uniforms or silk *cheong samschipaos*. Beijing's Great Wall Hotel is not the only one serving "jet-fresh prime U.S. beef."

However, poor maintenance and lack of professionalism still plagues the industry; for example, at one luxury hotel in Beijing some cooks gave the impression they were deliberately sabotaging efforts to improve. One day, my poached eggs arrived perfect (towel-dried before being put on toast); however, the next day the croissants arrived white and raw. Inquiries revealed that the cooks had been sent for training in North America. When they discovered the comparatively fabulous salaries of cooks there, they lobbied for higher wages upon their return to China. With no other trained staff available to replace them, management could not discharge them.

Top hotels also have problems of getting imported supplies and equipment, like fixtures. In some hotels, the faucets in public washrooms were stolen and could not be readily replaced. They remained unusable for months.

At another relatively new hotel where most foreign tourists were billeted in Shanghai, I found attendants sleeping on dining tables at 5:30 a.m., opaque rusty water in the bathtub, and tacky carpets. Be prepared for the unpredictable!

But one must remember that China has come a long way since

1978. Before then shower curtains were unknown and attendants spoke no English and barged into rooms without knocking. Guests had to carry their own luggage, and no hotel had 24-hour hot water or any air conditioning. You couldn't get anything to eat except at fixed meal hours. An attendant in an Overseas Chinese hotel then responded to a complaint about a rat in a room with "It's the season."

For long-time China travelers, having the option of luxury hotels in many cities has been especially welcome. For these, you *can* make hotel reservations relatively easily through airlines, travel agents, and hotel chains before you go. But standards generally still remain uneven. As recently as 1985, foreign guests at the old Renmin Hotel in Xi'an arrived to find dirty linen on their beds—because replacements "aren't dry yet." Fortunately for foreigners, that hotel is being downgraded and will not be used for foreigners once new hotels there have opened. Incidents like this should be protested.

The number of tourist destinations open to foreigners continues to expand, especially as hotels of higher standards are being opened. Travel permits for open cities are no longer required.

English-speaking tourist guides are now available for hire at some important tourist sites.

Government travel agencies have been making a great effort to be helpful where they can. But a sharp increase in the number of tourists have curtailed many of C.I.T.S.'s regular services, including the booking of train tickets.

Still, a few years ago, a Canadian who bought a cheap five-day ski package from China Sports Service was met by a car in Harbin and a retinue of three escorts. She was taken to buy some warm down ski clothes and thick boots at a store in the city at reasonable prices. After a night at the Swan Hotel, she took a 7-hour train ride to Yabuli. There, an open truck took her to a hostel one hour away. Fortunately she was in the cab, but other tourists (mainly from Hong Kong) had to ride in the cold. The next day a truck drove her five minutes away to the slopes. She was able to rent skis with safety bindings (no brakes). The two tows, a poma and a rope tow, were not operating at the time. (I've been assured that they are working now.) Her retinue of three carried her skis, boots, and a stool up the hill for her!

The training of guide-interpreters continues, and standards are rising. But the shortage continues.

A private travel agent for foreigners has opened in Beijing so recently that no one knows how efficient it is.

One can now use certain credit cards to pay for hotel rooms and not just to obtain cash. This service was temporarily suspended in 1985 in Beijing by the Bank of China, so you still cannot count on it entirely. American Express cards are now accepted, for example, only in 55 hotels in 30 cities.

Tourist visas take about a week, except in Hong Kong, where they can be obtained in 24 hours. In some Chinese cities one need only show up from abroad at the airport with a confirmed hotel reservation to get a transit visa, renewable up to a month. Mini-F.I.T. packages for individuals are available for some cities, but travel agents in North America needed six to eight weeks to obtain one.

C.I.T.S., the main government tourist office for foreigners, is becoming more decentralized. Tours and visas can be arranged more cheaply through some provincial travel and tourism offices, mainly for prepaid groups. Getting information about tourism has improved, and more C.I.T.S. branches are answering more letters than before, with many more brochures. But many C.I.T.S. branches still do not answer letters, especially those in English. Their interpreters are too busy. The National Tourism Administration's attempt to publish a much-needed, up-to-date list of hotels in China was stalled by sluggish printers. Information about changes in regulations take a long time to reach travel agents and ticket sellers, unless they subscribe to *China Daily*.

CAAC (China's civil aviation administration) has shown improvement, but is still not up to international standards, especially in its domestic operations. Payment now can be made in traveler's checks as well as cash, but still not by credit card. In the mid-1980s, travel agents abroad complained that CAAC did not even acknowledge requests for reservations on domestic flights if seats were not available, and that flights were canceled without notice. But CAAC is currently being restructured and computerized domestically. Its efficiency should improve early in 1987 if all goes well. Forty airlines have applied for licenses to operate in China, including two with American financing.

CAAC also has an archaic accounting setup. The country is divided up into six administrative regions. While one can book flights within one of these regions easily, an individual traveler from Shanghai wanting to go to Harbin, for example, can only buy a ticket for Beijing at CAAC in Shanghai. Then the traveler had to go into downtown Beijing to the CAAC office to buy a ticket on the Beijing-Harbin sector, necessitating an overnight stay in the capital. Such a ticket could not even be bought at the Beijing airport! This inconvenience is in the process of being remedied.

CAAC *in the past* has bumped off some confirmed passengers, flown only in perfect weather, stopped for lunch and dinner on long flights, and spewed white mist on passengers on antique, Soviet-built Anonovs at certain altitudes. Passengers have flown in some propeller-driven planes, too, on some routes. Passengers waiting for delayed flights were never given progress reports and nothing more than tea. Stewardesses rarely smiled and sometimes did not even check seat belts or seat backs, or give any safety lectures. Military aircraft and military airports were pressed into service during heavy tourist seasons or in bad weather.

Some of these medieval practices have been phased out, but residues remain, especially on routes to isolated cities. Some confirmed passengers on a delayed flight even in 1984 had to argue to get free overnight billeting with meals in a hotel. This happened after a full day of waiting at the airport for their flight, without progress reports or complimentary food.

Stewardesses smile more frequently now, and give the impression of wanting to help. They are dressing more smartly; they used to wear baggy khaki uniforms. Toilets on some recent flights have been neglected, though.

The new economic policies and the resulting competition have given birth to some excellent new restaurants. Joint-venture restaurants, especially in Guangzhou, have also contributed to improved standards. More services should become available. Hotel-booking services currently serving only Chinese customers could start helping foreigners too.

A recent trend has been the development in several cities of theme parks with reproductions of ancient buildings. The classic novel *Dream of the Red Chamber (Mansions)* seems to be a favorite. Resort complexes with golf courses are being built even in that most hallowed of spots: the Ming Tombs north of Beijing. Employees in period costume offering ancient-style food, accommodation, and transportation are proliferating all over, with varying degrees of success. Whole streets are being renovated in Song, Ming, or Qing architecture.

The bad news is that with a few exceptions (notably the hotels), the toilets are still smelly and clogged. At least one visitor is convinced that he got parasites from eating on an excursion boat on Guilin's famous Li River in 1985. I have also seen dishes on these boats washed in water where buffaloes wallow.

Some of the beautiful new buildings have shown signs of poor materials and workmanship, cracks in the walls appearing less than a year after opening. The tendency in many Chinese hotels seems to be a complete renovation project every few years, closing sections of the hotel, rather than a continuous cleaning job whenever dirt appears, as is done now in the joint-venture hotels. A dramatic example of poor craftsmanship was the relatively new museum in Changsha built to house the artifacts from the Han tomb. The ceiling of one of the new rooms was falling down over the still intact 2100-year-old casket. Today's builders have obviously lost their ancestors' art.

Improving workmanship and staff training have been tackled since the late 1970s, but the demand for trained workers has exceeded the supply.

"It doesn't seem to be so much their not wanting to help," said one two-time Beijing visitor. "It's just that they don't know how to help." Many hotel floors and bathtubs still look filthy. If the dishwasher on the Li River boat were asked about her cleaning practices, I imagine her surprised answer would be, "We've always washed our dishes in the river and none of *us* has gotten sick from it."

Some hotels operate their own airport and tour buses now.

Beijing has a tourism college, but its president has been quoted as saying that no teacher had ever worked in a hotel or tourism installation before. Guangzhou has a tourism-management college at Zhongshan University. Other schools also have courses. But setting up high-level tourism training schools is a step in the right direction. That and an army of honest health inspectors should solve many problems.

The age of the individual traveler has dawned. While most tourists still go in tour groups, a growing army of intrepid F.I.T.s, including persistent backpackers, have invaded China, especially since 1984 (when taking advantage of the black market in currency made for a cheap travel experience). This, coupled with the loosening of restrictions on local Chinese travelers in addition to the increased tourism from abroad, has been taxing all transportation systems and hotels. Foreign business-men have also been taking up much hotel space. In some cities Chinese citizens can now legally provide board and lodging for foreign friends and relatives—a great opportunity for people-to-people contact. Tickets on planes and trains are still hard to get in high season, but more rail-way lines and railway cars are being built.

Some enterprising entrepreneurs have gone into the ticket-scalping and free-lance portage businesses at airports and railway stations, but you cannot always count on it and may still have to carry your own bag. However, one must be very careful of taxi drivers now. No longer can you relax knowing your driver will honestly calculate your fare even if he doesn't have a meter. You should settle on a fare before you get in. The world has caught up with China!

But *officially* still *no tipping, no gambling, and no prostitution!*

NOTE

Fielding's People's Republic of China was written for all tourists in China: those on their own and those on escorted tours. It is for business people, foreigners living there, Overseas Chinese and Hong Kong, Macao, and Taiwan Compatriots—anyone wanting to make the most of opportunities in this fascinating country. This guide has been designed to help visitors plan their trips, and to give them an idea of what to expect. It should help you orient yourself, travel around China independently, and make decisions about where to stay, how to get there, and what to do and see. For those on escorted tours, it should give a broader picture of the places you are visiting and the options you have.

Here also are as many Chinese characters as we could get for the names of hotels, restaurants, stores, and tourist attractions. You can communicate by pointing to them so non-English speakers will know where you want to go.

Over 240 cities, counties, towns, and villages are now available to foreign tourists. We have presented what we feel are the most important. Many of the minor destinations are listed as side trips from the larger cities, especially provincial capitals.

Since we couldn't put over 240 names on one map, we have put the names of many of the cities mentioned in this book on maps of the six tourist regions. After each city name in "Destinations" is the region. If you want to find out what other places of interest are in the area, consult that particular map as well as the text on the provincial capital.

China is now producing a great deal of travel literature of its own. We encourage you to supplement the information here with what is available in China, especially the Cartographic Department maps and the China City Guides series.

Please do not consider any guidebook as the only source of information about a country. A guidebook should stimulate your interest as well as give you a lot of essential facts. So please ask many questions in China about what you are experiencing. Only then will you learn, and in learning, enjoy.

Fielding's People's Republic of China is one in a series of six China guides written by Ruth Lor Malloy since 1973 under a variety of titles. Each one has been updated, expanded, and improved over its predecessor. This is the first one written in collaboration with Priscilla Liang Hsu.

Pinyin spellings: In 1979, China adopted the pinyin system of romanizing its language based on the Beijing pronunciation. This was no easy decision since the language is monosyllabic and the word *ma,* for example, can have at least four totally different meanings depending on the tone. China's newly published literature in English has been using this system. However, many older history books were written in the old Wade-Giles romanization, and in China itself, many historical names like Chiang Kai-shek and Dr. Sun Yat-sen can be found in either form of romanization. We have used the spelling most commonly found now in China.

We have also tried to include the English terminology and new spelling for place names because you will hear both. This might look cumbersome, especially with the Chinese characters; however, we hope all this effort will be helpful to you. The names of dynasties are in the new spelling. A glossary and charts are in the "Quick Reference" section to help straighten things out.

In cases where both the old and new spellings are used, the operative one is the new spelling.

Important to know is that pinyin is phonetic and that "X" is like *sh* as in *she,* "Q" is like *ch* as in *cheek,* "Zh" is like *j* as in *jump,* and "Z" like *z* as in *zero.* See also *How to Pronounce Chinese Letters* in "Quick Reference."

Another confusing area has been whether words like Hong Qiao should be together as one or separated into two words. The tendency now is to combine place names into one word even though they can be very long. Shijiazhuang, for example, would be easier to pronounce if separated into Shi Jia Zhuang, but is found written both ways.

Avoid confusing the provinces Hunan and Henan, Jiangxi and Jiangsu, Shaanxi and Shanxi, Hubei and Hebei, and the cities Jilin and Jinan, the many Hengshan Mountains, and Taishan (in Guangdong) and Taishan (in Shandong). And there is still no standard translation for important place names; for example, Lingyan Si in Jinan has been translated Magic Cliff or Intelligent Rock Temple in different pieces of Jinan tourist literature. It could be difficult to figure out just what is being described.

The imperial dating system has always been used in China: "in the fifth year of the Emperor Hongwu." We have compromised here by giving specific dates and/or the dynasty name or the number of "years ago." Dynastic identification is important because it puts events into context. Some dynasties are more important than others and we hope you will gradually learn them and not have to turn to the "Quick Reference" every time they come up.

From the first Sunday in April to about the second Sunday in September, China is on daylight savings time. Be sure to clarify exact departure and arrival times of trains, ships, and planes.

Note also that the information in this book is as accurate as could be compiled at press time. The situation in China is so fluid that changes will have taken place by the time you visit. When in doubt, ask. And should you find things different, please let us know so we can make changes for future editions. A handy form is in the back of the book.

The travel agencies, hotels, restaurants, and other enterprises listed here free of charge *should* be able to help you. As far as we can see they are reliable, but a mention in this book is not necessarily a recommendation.

Have a great trip!

THE BASICS

WHERE IN CHINA?

First of all, you must decide where in China you want to go. China is full of choices. It is a big country, the third largest in area in the world. It has huge mountains and small mountains, deserts and tropical rain forests, and the second lowest saltwater lake in the world. It has 5000-year-old neolithic sites and pandas in the wild. Among its many ethnic minorities are the Tibetans, who live on the roof of the world and have fascinated people for centuries with their unique customs and religion.

No other country has such variety and vitality, and such a long, continuous history. No other country has such a wealth of temples, pagodas, ancient palaces, gardens, mountains, and elaborate tombs. China has so many valuable cultural relics that one can actually get indigestion from seeing a fraction of what it has to offer.

Careful choices are important if you want to be continually thrilled and surprised. The third set of 500 unique *arhats* can get very boring unless you know what to look for.

The ideal is to take several two-week trips rather than one trip a month long. This gives you a chance to do some digesting and reading in between. Many visitors, unfortunately, have to take longer trips, their perceptions dulled by fatigue toward the end.

Keep in mind your physical capabilities. The most strenuous places to visit are the Silk Road, Inner Mongolia, and, especially, Tibet.

To help you plan your itinerary, make a list of your priorities. If you want to join an existing group tour, see if you can find one that fits. Here are some suggestions. Take one city from any of the following groupings in which you are interested. Take two cities if you want to see more of any particular item. Yes, the hard part is choosing; China has over 240 places open to visit! You have to study a long menu.

If time and money are short, try to confine yourself to one tourist region, such as North China or West China. Staying in one area is cheaper and less time-consuming than hopping all around the country.

13

General interest

For details, see "Destinations." If you can only visit one city, it must be Beijing. Then, in order of priority, Xi'an, and Suzhou or Kunming.

Ancient capitals: Best to visit are Xi'an and Beijing; then Luoyang, Chengde, Chengdu, Nanjing, and Shenyang; and finally Anyang, Hangzhou, Kaifeng, Datong, and Suzhou. Well-preserved imperial palaces still only in Beijing, Chengde, and Shenyang.

The Great Wall: Best near Beijing; also impressive at Shanhaiguan and Jiayuguan. See "Great Wall."

Impressive city walls: Nanjing, Kaifeng, and Xi'an.

Imposing imperial tombs: Ming dynasty—better near Beijing, but also the first one in Nanjing. Qing dynasty—most impressive in Zunhua, but also in Shenyang and Yixian (see "Zunhua"). Qin, Han, and Tang dynasties in Xi'an. The famous Qin Army Vault Museum is visited from Xi'an. Song dynasty near Zhengzhou, but not worth making a special trip.

Important Buddhist sites: Xi'an, Luoyang, and Beijing. Impressive temples with 500 arhats are in Beijing, Suzhou, Chengdu, and Kunming. The most important Lama temples are, of course, in Tibet, but there are also some exciting ones in Chengde and Beijing. The *Four Sacred Buddhist Mountains are Putuo Shan (Ningbo), Jiuhua Shan (Hefei), Wutai Shan (Datong), and Emei Shan, with many old temples. For **martial arts fans,** Shaolin Temple is reached from Zhengzhou.

Cave temples: The best are in Luoyang, Datong, and Dunhuang. Also impressive: Dazu, Lanzhou, and Leshan.

The *Four Important Taoist Temples: Baiyun Monastery in Beijing, Qingyang Monastery in Chengdu, Taiqing Monastery in Shenyang, and Shangzhen Monastery in Suzhou. For the mythology, there's Yantai, Lushan, and Yueyang.

Important Confucian sites: Best is Qufu, hometown of the sage. Beijing has the second largest temple, now the city museum.

Most important cities with Jewish history: Kaifeng and Shanghai.

Important mosques: Guangzhou, Quanzhou, Beijing, Hangzhou, Yangzhou, and Xi'an.

Neolithic site museums: Xi'an and Zhengzhou. After 1987, also Lanzhou.

Primitive man: Peking Man (Zhoukoudian—see Beijing); Maba Man (see Shaoguan).

Shang dynasty sites: Zhengzhou and Anyang.

Foreign imperialist history: Very little in museums, but much European architecture in Tianjin, Shanghai, Wuhan, Beijing, and Qingdao. Some in Xiamen and Guangzhou (Canton). Among the 46 treaty

*Traditional Chinese evaluation.

ports were also Zhenjiang, Ningbo, Fuzhou, Xiamen (Amoy), Nanjing, Jiujiang, Shashi, and Chongqing.

Best ancient history museums: Beijing, Shenyang, Xi'an, Zhengzhou, and Wuhan.

24 cities of historical or revolutionary importance protected by the State Council: Beijing, Chengde, Datong, Nanjing, Suzhou, Yangzhou, Hangzhou, Shaoxing, Quanzhou, Jingdezhen, Qufu, Luoyang, Kaifeng, Jiangling, Changsha, Guangzhou, Guilin, Chengdu, Zunyi, Kunming, Dali, Lhasa, Xi'an, and Yan'an. In some cases, whole streets of ancient buildings are being preserved.

Most important revolutionary sites: With good museums—Beijing, Yan'an, Shaoshan, Nanchang, and Jinggang Shan.

Other unusual structures worth seeing: Hengshan for the Temple in Mid-air; Lhasa for the Potala.

Memorable boat rides: The Yangtze Gorges, the Li River from Guilin, and the Grand Canal.

Limestone formations: Very impressive caves in Guilin, but also good at Yixing, Nanning, and Zhaoqing. The Stone Forest at Kunming is celebrated.

Seaside resorts: Beidaihe, Qingdao, Zhongshan, and Shenzhen.

Well-preserved ancient cadavers and their belongings: In museums. The best is in Changsha of a 2100-year-old noblewoman. Also Zhenjiang and Jingzhou. Large mummy collection in Urumqi. A few mummies near Turpan.

Best classical Chinese gardens: Summer Palace and Beihai Park in Beijing, the Yu Garden in Shanghai, and many gardens in Suzhou and Hangzhou.

Gorgeous mountain scenery: Guilin—tame; Lushan Mountain, Chengde, and Jinggang Shan—a little rough, but you can drive around there; Taishan Mountain (a 4-hour climb, but cable cars available); Huang Shan (cable car in 1987?), Emei Shan (cable car), and Hua Shan—very rugged. Then there are the Himalayas in Tibet and Xinjiang!

Handicraft Factories: Carpets (Tianjin), ivory and jade carving and cloisonne (Beijing), silk weaving (Hangzhou), Persian-type carpets (Urumqi), etc. See list under most destinations and "Shopping."

Camel and pony rides, and yurts: Hohhot, and Silk Road.

*Three Most Famous Hot Springs: Anshan, Conghua, and Weihai.

*Three Most Eminent Halls: Tian Kuang Hall in Tai'an; Taihe Hall in the Imperial Palace, Beijing; and the Dacheng Hall in Qufu's Confucius Temple.

*Five Great Mountains: Taishan, Hengshan (Hunan), Hengshan (Shanxi), Huashan, and Songshan.

Dream of the Red Chamber Theme Parks: Shanghai, Beijing.

For Those with Special Interests

Musicians should be interested in the bronze chime bells in Wuhan and the Chinese musical instruments factory in Suzhou.

Plant lovers can visit botanical gardens: Lushan, Guangzhou, Nanjing, Hangzhou, etc.

Hot-air ballooning and gliding: Anyang.

Sports: Mountaineering—Seven peaks, including Qomolangma (Everest) are open. **Skiing**—Not well developed yet, but tows in Harbin and Jilin. **Scuba diving**—In Zhanjiang and soon in Hainan Island. **Golf**—In Zhongshan, Shenzhen, and soon in Shanghai and Beijing.

Visits to ancestral villages and relatives: See "Special for Overseas Chinese."

Steam locomotives: Factory in Datong; museum in Shenyang.

Performing panda: Shanghai Acrobats and Circus.

Pandas in a wildlife preserve: Wolong, near Chengdu; Baishuijiang Nature Reserve in Gansu province.

Sister Cities: Many foreign cities have "friendship links" with specific Chinese cities, and you may want to include yours in your itinerary. For example, Melbourne and Tianjin, Edinburgh and Xi'an, Toronto and Chongqing, Chattanooga and Wuxi. Ask your city hall.

As a rule of thumb:

—The cradle of Chinese civilization was along the Yellow River (Zhengzhou, Anyang).

—The Silk Road went west from Xi'an. See *Silk Road*.

—The western imperialists controlled areas along the Yangtze River, and also Changsha. They were active on the east coast between Liaoning province and Hainan Island. The Japanese controlled Northeast China, then known as Manchuria, and, later, most of urban China.

—Most national minorities live mainly in the west, north, and southwest parts of China, especially Guangxi, Yunnan, Guizhou, Sichuan, Xinjiang, Tibet, and Inner Mongolia. Turkish-related Moslem minorities live primarily in Xinjiang, Qinghai, and Gansu.

—The earlier migrations of Chinese to America and Australia in the 19th and early 20th centuries originated from Guangdong province; the migrations to Southeast Asia originated largely from Fujian, but also from Guangdong.

—**The 14 Coastal Cities** earmarked in 1984 for accelerated development are Beihai, Dalian, Fuzhou, Guangzhou, Lianyungang, Nantong, Ningbo, Qingdao, Qinhuangdao, Shanghai, Tianjin, Wenzhou, Yantai, and Zhanjiang. **Special Economic Zones:** Shenzhen, Xiamen, Shantou, and Zhuhai. The Yangtze and Pearl river deltas—including Guangzhou—part of southern Fujian province—including Xiamen, Zhangzhou, and Quanzhou—and the Liaodong and Shandong peninsulas are also S.E.Z.s. Direct international flights to many of these cities have started or will probably be available by 1988.

—**The Ten Most Popular Tourist Attractions in China,** the result of a poll in the mid-1980s by Chongguo Luyou Bao, China's tourism magazine: Great Wall, Guilin, West Lake (Hangzhou), Imperial Palace (Beijing), Suzhou Gardens, Huangshan, Yangtze Gorges, Sun-Moon Lake (Taiwan), Imperial Summer Resort (Chengde), and the Qin Army Vault Museum (Xi'an). Runners-up were: Lake Taihu (Wuxi), Summer Palace (Beijing), Taishan Mountain (Tai'an), Emei Mountain, Lushan, Huangguoshou Falls (Guiyang), Mogao Grottoes (Dunhuang), Lake Tianchi (Urumqi), Potala Palace (Lhasa), Seven Star Rock (Zhaoqing), and Huashan Mountain.

WHEN TO GO?

If you care about the weather, the best time to visit is May–June or September–October, but these, of course, are the times when most people like to travel. If you go then, you could run into crowds and delays, even if all reservations are confirmed. You could also try April or November and hope for good weather. Do consult each city listed under "Destinations." South China is chilly but fine in January. Kunming has spring temperatures most of the year.

It is important to remember that the Chinese do not heat their buildings as warmly as foreigners do in winter. South of the Yangtze there is no heat at all, except in tourist hotels, even though it can be very chilly. If the cold bothers you, avoid Northeast China, Inner Mongolia, Northwest China, Tibet, Qinghai, and any mountains in winter, especially around the lunar new year (around late January or early February). Even in Guangzhou at that time you need a top coat and a sweater. Avoid the lunar new year especially in Guangzhou and Fujian, as hotels and trains are full of Overseas Chinese visitors and prices are at their highest. Industrial pollution is particularly bad in winter too. But most tour agencies give discounts in such low seasons!

The hottest time of the year is usually July and early August. Traditionally, the "three furnaces" of China are Nanjing, Wuhan, and Chongqing. There's also Nanchang. Almost all hotels, but few other buildings, are now air-conditioned. Most tourist buses and some taxis are air-conditioned. This is the time to put mountain or seaside resorts at the end of a hot tour.

In late spring, April–May through the summer, rain and high humidity make south China (including Guangzhou and Guilin) quite oppressive, but the greenery is lush and beautiful. Inner Mongolia and the Silk Road have a problem with sandstorms in spring and autumn.

As a rough gauge, China extends from the same latitude as James Bay in Canada to south of Cuba. Beijing is at almost the same latitude as Philadelphia, and Guangzhou as Havana. Take altitude into account: the higher, the colder. Winter begins in early November.

Other things to consider when planning dates:

—If you are interested in visiting schools, factories, and offices, avoid vacations and holidays. People wanting to do business should avoid the national holidays.

—If you want to see a festival like the Third Moon Market or the dragon boats, consider those dates.

For dates of holidays and some festivals, see "Quick Reference."

HOW TO GO?

Take your pick. The group tour is *not* the only way to go, but it could be cheaper, with less hassle.

Groups and Individuals

On a prepaid tour This is the easiest way to visit China. Just book with a good travel agent and most of your problems are solved. You can choose one of the set tours offered by a travel agent or you can have one custom-made. The average size of a tour is about 20 people, but you could have as few as one. Special Tours for Special People of New York City says "Individual programs for 10 to 21 days based on a minimum of two to eight people are now becoming the ideal way to see China." Of course, the fewer people you have, the more expensive the rate per person can be.

China prefers prepaid tours. They use scarce staff interpreters more efficiently and are given preference. Even groups of four pay-as-you-go individuals run the risk of being downgraded or having their reservations canceled in favor of a full-scale prepaid tour group.

By ordering and paying in advance, groups, rather than individuals, are more likely to get what they want. For example, a group can book a helicopter in Sichuan to go to Jiuzhaigou, and do the trip in a day. A party of two could also book the helicopter, but if it isn't already going there, the rate for two would be prohibitive to all but the richest tourists. Some of the tours listed in this book, such as cooking and taiqi lessons, are not generally available to one or two individual tourists, but a group can book them, and if there is space left over, then the individuals who happen to be there at the time might be able to pay their share and tag along.

By hiring a professional tour leader, tourists do not have to bother about getting permits, making reservations, and all the annoying and time-consuming things you will see in the chapter on getting around.

Basically all prepaid tours are treated the same in China except for the quality of the hotel. You can choose between "regular" or the more expensive "deluxe" rooms. If the price of the same tour still differs from one agency to another, it could be because (1) more restaurant meals are included (rather than hotel meals); (2) there is an orientation session on China, and perhaps a full-time guide, who has more than a superficial knowledge of Chinese history and culture; (3) more than one agency is getting a commission; try to book from the wholesaler; (4) one agent is getting a bigger commission; (5) a luxury tourist ship rather than a ferry is guaranteed on the Yangtze; (6) the tour has been organized through a provincial tourism agency, which offers cheaper tours that are more limited in scope than those of C.I.T.S. national office.

Prepaid tourists can usually choose what they want to see in each city from a set list. You have to pay extra for any "optional tours." Some tourists complain of the time spent in making group decisions; others are happy to have a choice. If you just want to see China, a general-interest tour is ideal. If you want to visit schools, several factories, or hospitals, better take a special-interest or Friendship association tour. Or you could make sure schools, factories, or hospitals are included in your tour.

Group tours are also flexible insofar as you can choose to avoid most of the group activities. If you want to sleep in a different hotel from the one assigned, you can in some cities. But you might have to pay extra. Just be sure to tell your group leader so no one will look for you.

But you usually have to travel from city to city with the group, or at least in and out of the country with it. Each group has one "group visa" and individual passports are not stamped at the border. The only way you can leave the country without your group is to have a new visa stamped in your passport.

Some group tourists have been able to acquire individual visas once inside China. You have to convince the authorities that you have a very good reason and probably some clout to make the change. For example, some professors have stayed behind for lectures, and of course, if you are sick, arrangements can be made. Chinese guides have been very reluctant to make changes except for business people once an itinerary is set up. But some foreign travel agency representatives have dutifully done the job. You might have to take time off from your tour to face the bureaucracy yourself.

Overseas Chinese tour groups are usually given individual visas in the first place so members can visit relatives after the tour is over.

Tour groups can be fun if you have the right people. But a tendency does develop to look inward toward your own group, and to regard the Chinese as "them" as opposed to "us." As soon as group members start joking about the "natives," you've crossed the line and have truly become a group tourist. If you are visiting China to meet Chinese people and learn about the country, you do have to make an effort to break free from your groupiness. Do venture out into the streets alone. Lounge in parks especially on Sundays. A lot of students are waiting to practice their English on you. You might even be invited to someone's home.

Luggage for C.I.T.S. foreign tour groups is not usually opened by Chinese Customs, but that of Overseas Chinese might be. The total weight of group luggage to be flown is usually added together and averaged.

On a cruise Among the cruise lines that have included China are Holland America Cruises, Lindblad Travel, Inc., P&O Line, and Cunard Line. You usually pay extra if you want a guided tour at ports of call. See also "Yangtze Gorges" and *Fielding's Worldwide Cruises* by Antoinette DeLand.

On a minipackage C.I.T.S. offers prepaid packages that include travel tickets, hotel accommodations, and breakfast. You sightsee on your own or, *if available,* book sightseeing tours locally. It is an ideal compromise for business people and those who want the flexibility of scheduling their own time, as well as the assurance of a place to sleep. Minipackages are available for many cities, including Beijing, Fuzhou, Guilin, Guangzhou, Hangzhou, Harbin, Jinan, Kunming, Nanjing, Qufu, Shanghai, Suzhou, Tai'an, Tianjin, Xi'an, and Wuxi.

As a pay-as-you-go traveler Many foreigners, especially those with time to spare, have traveled China happily and successfully on their own. Some backpackers have loved it, not minding the dormitory accommodations and delays. Backpackers should take along the Lonely Planet guidebook. Travelers with bigger budgets have an easier time. The international-class luxury hotels all have travel desks, and bookings are made with less difficulty now. If a group tour is not scheduled in a city, you can always hire a taxi.

On-your-own traveling is not, however, as easy in China as in Europe. If you can't speak Chinese, you can get around with this guidebook. See also "Getting Around."

As a traveler of Chinese ancestry People of Chinese ancestry can choose to travel either under C.I.T.S., China Travel Service (C.T.S.), or any other travel agency. You can travel individually, paying as you go, or in a group. If you go to ancestral villages or homes of relatives in places not normally open to foreign visitors, you need an alien permit. Arrangements can be made with C.T.S. or a knowledgeable Hong Kong tour agency like United (Taishan).

C.I.T.S. guides do not usually know anything about places in Fujian or Guangdong, where many Overseas Chinese (O.C.) have relatives. However, C.T.S. doesn't have many English-speaking staff members.

Chinese missions abroad have a quota of individual visas for Overseas Chinese. It is possible to get a visa from one within a week or, in Hong Kong, in one working day. Early in 1985, regulations permitting Overseas Chinese to buy train and plane tickets more cheaply than Foreign Friends were announced. However, no one selling tickets knew anything about it in mid-1985. By the time you arrive, the order should have filtered down through the bureaucracy, so ask about it.

An Overseas Chinese is anyone with a Chinese surname, face, or the address of a relative and/or an ancestral village in China, and either a foreign or Chinese passport. Those with a Chinese ancestor who have a Chinese name but do not look Chinese might be able to convince authorities that they qualify. Overseas Chinese have successfully argued for lower rates in hotels, which could be 10–50% of those for other foreigners. Don't be shy about asking, especially in off seasons and in hotels with low occupancy rates. Much depends on the clerk at the registration desk.

Overseas Chinese are regarded as family and are especially welcome in China. You can take in duty-free many kinds of gifts for relatives—but because Hong Kong Chinese have spoiled it for everyone by smuggling pornographic literature and video tapes, etc., into China, Customs tend to look more closely at your luggage.

It is possible to take a non-Chinese spouse, children, and a close friend to China and stay in cheaper Overseas Chinese hotels or take cheaper C.T.S. tours. It is possible to live with relatives in China or have relatives stay with you in your hotel. See also "Special for Overseas Chinese."

As a Hong Kong, Macao, or Taiwan Compatriot Hong Kong and Macao Chinese who have reentry permits to Hong Kong or Macao can enter China the same way Americans enter Canada. They can just buy a ticket and get on some means of transportation. Taiwan Compatriots are especially welcome but may get into trouble with Taiwan authorities upon their return home unless they buy a document (2 photos required) in Hong Kong. This document is stamped instead of a passport. Travel arrangements can be made through China Travel Service or any travel agency that deals with it.

On business The usual procedure here is to communicate with a trade officer at a Chinese mission abroad, your mission in China, or your own government's department of trade. They will all probably tell you to contact a Chinese trading corporation. If the Chinese are interested in what you want to buy or sell, they will send you an invitation that will give you a visa from a Chinese mission. A travel agent can do all the bookings.

Business people can usually take their spouses and travel individually in China, not just for negotiations, but afterward as tourists. You can discuss the logistics with your host trading corporations or deal with a Chinese travel agency once in China. You can also take time off from a prepaid tour to visit a trading corporation. See also "Special for Business People."

As a foreign student, scholar, or foreign expert Foreign exchange students studying in China are usually there as the result of an agreement between governments or educational institutions. Information on these exchanges can be obtained from the United States Information Agency in Washington, DC, or from the Council on International Educational Exchange, New York. In Canada, contact the Association of Universities and Colleges of Canada in Ottawa. Other countries have their own counterparts.

Most exchange students are already university graduates and stay up to two years. The home government pays transportation to and from China and gives spending money. The Chinese government pays tuition, the cost of accommodations, and a small stipend. It is possible to save money and also to travel around the country during vacations.

Some universities and colleges abroad have bilateral arrangements with their counterparts in China, and information can be obtained from schools in your home country.

"Self-supporting" foreign students are also accepted at an increasing number of schools in China; prospective students can apply directly. These students should be aware that academic credits for courses studied in China may not be equivalent to those studied in their home countries.

Foreign students have lived in guesthouses in rooms sometimes described by students at Beijing University as "cold and small" with little if any privacy. Many have hot tap water only two hours a day. Students at some other universities might fare better. Food is usually of higher standard than that of Chinese students, but with less meat than in the foreigner's home country.

Students learn a great deal about China and the Chinese language. Courses and teaching methods in Chinese institutions, however, are not as rigorous as in Western countries. Students do get closer to Chinese people than most other foreigners.

Chinese missions abroad and foreign missions in China should have information on studying in China. Ask for the *List of Specialties in Chinese Universities and Colleges Open to Foreign Students* from the cultural and educational officer.

Scholarly visits are also arranged by government agreement, but much is being done privately now, bilaterally between institutions or directly by scholars themselves. In the United States the U.S. Information Agency, for example, sponsors the Fulbright program, which makes it possible for a limited number of American scholars to teach American studies in Chinese universities. U.S.I.A. also finances the National Program, which helps American scholars and professionals lecture and do exploratory research in China for one to three months.

The Committee on Scholarly Communication with the People's Republic of China (C.S.C.P.R.C.) have developed programs with the Chinese Academy of Sciences, the Chinese Academy of Social Sciences, the State Council on Education, and the Chinese Association for Science and Technology.

The C.S.C.P.R.C.'s activities include a program for American graduate students, postdoctoral students, and research scholars to carry out long-term study or research. This is in affiliation with Chinese universities and research institutes. There are also short-term reciprocal exchanges of senior-level Chinese and American scholars, bilateral conferences, and an exchange of joint working groups in selected fields.

In Ottawa, Canada, contact the Social Sciences Research Council and the Humanities Research Council for information.

People who are going to China in other capacities can also make valuable professional contributions in China. Specialists and professionals can give lectures or demonstrations to their Chinese counterparts if invited to do so.

If you're thinking of getting financial compensation, forget it. If you're thinking of helping China in exchange for a deeper insight, as well as business or academic contacts, do offer to lecture—if you have anything worthwhile to say, that is. Don't expect anything more than a "thank you" and, if you're in business, probably a tax write-off for part of your expenses (if you can convince your tax people that you were actually making business contacts in China).

Full-time **foreign experts** and **teachers** have been hired by the Bureau of Foreign Experts of the State Council on Education and other bodies in Beijing and elsewhere. Increasingly, individual universities and colleges have been doing their own recruiting without going through Beijing, a much faster route. One teachers' college hired a foreign teacher itself but couldn't get permission for the foreign exchange for his airplane ticket until two months *after* he arrived! The eager teacher paid his own way and so far, I haven't heard if he has been reimbursed.

Many teachers hired by China specialize in a foreign language with one- or two-year contracts. The great need is for English language teachers and teachers of middle-level technology and managerial skills. In recent years, there have been more than 9000 foreign teachers working in China.

Long-term experts should receive a contract giving them their transportation paid from home and back, as well as home leave, after the first year and then every other year, for a month or so. The stipend ranges from about ¥500 to ¥1000, with a few getting as much as ¥1,500 a month, depending on qualifications. An M.A., for example, has received ¥700–750. Fifty percent of one's salary can be taken out of China in foreign currency. Certain categories of experts also receive free accommodation, free medical care, transportation to and from work, and a month's vacation in China. The salary for foreign experts is frequently ten times that of local teachers, so no complaints, please.

Foreign *teachers* (as differentiated from *experts*) are usually locally hired and do not get the same benefits as experts. *Teacher-students* occasionally teach part-time and study part-time.

Foreigners working in China have been advised by one teacher assigned to Nanjing "to know how to say 'no,' since the Chinese will often pile work on them. I would also suggest, if possible, getting advice from someone who has taught in China prior to one's assignment, and bringing as many teaching materials as possible, including textbooks. Warm clothes for winter and a commitment from the university about sufficient heat for housing are essential. . . . Some foreign experts have had a terrible time with the cold.'' Ask any branch of a China Friendship Association for the names of teachers with experience in China.

As a consultant Foreign companies also send experts to China in connection with their own projects. These make the most money and live more comfortably.

The Canadian Executive Service Overseas (C.E.S.O.), Toronto, sends recently retired Canadians to work as volunteer consultants to industry, institutions, and governments in developing areas such as China. Other countries and some companies probably have similar programs.

Many foreign workers and students get taken on sightseeing tours for free, but more likely at much cheaper rates than regular tourists. Do read *China Bound: A Handbook for American Students, Researchers and Teachers,* published by the C.S.C.P.R.C. and the National Association for Foreign Student Affairs, Washington, DC. The N.A.F.S.A. has literature available on education in China as well.

While some foreigners live without (horrors!) a refrigerator and air conditioning—and the minimal heat gets turned off on March 15 no matter what the weather—many are pleased with the experience. Some are not. Working in a developing country is the best way to learn how most of the world has to live and how very privileged those in the developed world are. In addition to the cheaper travel, foreign residents benefit from learning that perishable foods can be kept on balconies in cold weather and perhaps under a continuously wet rag in summer. They learn that silk jackets can be made for ¥15, and other such secrets, previously known only to the Chinese. They do make some Chinese friends, especially if they live outside of Beijing.

The standard of living of foreign experts and students has risen over the years.

As a casual student Many provincial travel and tourism offices are now offering courses in cooking, martial arts, acupuncture, and other Chinese arts, but primarily for groups. Several colleges and universities offer six- to eight-week summer Chinese language courses, for students 16 to 45 years of age, 55 for teachers. Some of these schools also give spring and autumn courses. Some of the schools are in Beijing, Shanghai, Tianjin, Nanjing, Wuhan, Jinan, Xiamen, Hefei, and Guangzhou. Information can be obtained from Chinese missions abroad.

One should not expect to learn Chinese or any other language in eight weeks. Nor can one learn taiqi in a day. It would be better to start learning such skills before you go to China, and expect polishing from the short course.

As a job hunter Tourists can try to pick up a job while traveling in China, but don't count on it. If you want to live in any particular place and are an experienced teacher, you could start by asking C.I.T.S. or any college or university if teachers are needed locally. If that's not your line, talk with business people about job possibilities. Good English-speaking secretaries are in short supply. But check out work regulations and income tax for foreigners first. Local hires might be paid Chinese-level salaries.

For medical treatment Some provincial travel and tourism agencies, for example Wuxi, offer tour packages for treatment in Chinese sanitariums.

As a property buyer Foreigners and Overseas Chinese can now buy resort, residential, and business property in some Chinese cities. Contact a Chinese mission or the municipal office in the city of your choice. Advertisements frequently appear in Hong Kong newspapers. Many Overseas Chinese have retired in China, especially in the south.

On a convention Many cities can now handle hundreds of convention visitors. Some of the new or renovated hotels have simultaneous translation facilities. Contact C.I.T.S. or any travel agent specializing in China for information.

As a journalist Contact a Chinese mission or Xinhua, the New China News Agency, if it is represented in your country. You could also contact the Information Office of the Foreign Ministry, Beijing.

Special tours The important thing to remember is that C.I.T.S. and C.T.S. tours are set up primarily for tourists. They cannot be expected to understand the needs of travelers primarily interested in meeting Chinese Christians, for example, or doctors wanting to meet their counterparts in China. The needs of doctors and scientists could be met by some travel agents. Or you could contact the Foreign Affairs Department of the Chinese Academy of Sciences yourself. Mountain climbers should contact the Chinese Mountaineering Association, and school groups, China Youth Travel Service. Sports teams wanting to play Chinese teams, or individuals wanting a ski package or parachuting should go through China Sports Service. Unusual requests like the Hong Kong-Beijing Motor Rally (34 cars, and 3400 km, first held in 1985) have taken several years to arrange. Most, however, can be worked out more quickly. A good travel agent experienced with China knows how. For religious groups, see also "Religion."

If you have any other questions, it might help to consult an experienced travel agent, a Chinese mission, or a China Friendship Association. Yes, you can write an organization in China directly with a good chance of getting a reply—but don't count on it.

In dealing directly with China, the best way to communicate is by Telex. Letters can take up to three weeks from North America. They do arrive more quickly if addressed in Chinese, and are answered more quickly if written in Chinese. If you telephone China, be sure to have a Mandarin-speaking person with you in case no one understands English at the other end of the line.

For Addresses, see "Important Addresses and Information."

Should You Take Your Children?

I took my five-year-old for a five-week visit in 1973, my seven-year-old to visit relatives in 1978, and my nine-year-old on a group tour in 1979. I even took a reluctant teenager on an eight-destination tour. I was glad I did, but then, this depends on the child. A year later, the teenager went back to China on her own with her school to work on a commune!

I did not use a baby-sitter because the younger children accompanied me to evening movies and theatrical performances. Chinese dance dramas are easy for a child to understand, and acrobats and puppets are fun for all ages. The younger children did find the traditional operas boring, so unless you're sure of lots of action, skip them.

I would not take a child just to be left with a Chinese-speaking baby-sitter unless the child understood Chinese.

At communes and factories, many willing hands kept the children amused while grown-ups talked. The children were interested in seeing how things were made. Guilin, with its caves, mountains, and boat trip was ideal. My nine-year-old found the 2100-year-old cadaver in Changsha fascinating.

The Chinese love children and are intrigued by those different from their own. You may have to protect children with blond hair and blue eyes, for instance, from being overly fondled. Tour-bus drivers bought mine popsicles; cheeks were pinched. In restaurants they disappeared with waiters to be shown off to the cooks.

Two of them became sick with bad colds, but doctors took care of them. They were well in a couple of days, missing only one day of the tour. Two of them lived with relatives. The seven-year-old had a ball learning how to bring up water from an open well, washing his own clothes by hand, and tending a wood cooking fire. It took awhile to adjust to the smelly outhouses, but he managed.

The neighborhoods where we lived with family were full of other children, and in spite of initial shyness and the language barrier, they made friends. Strangers on the street and in buses would stop and try to talk to them. Barriers of formality melted right away, and I'm not the only one who has gotten a room in an overcrowded hotel because "my child is very tired."

Food was a problem. One lived only on scrambled eggs and *char siu bow* (steamed barbecued pork buns). Hamburgers are now easier to find. Baby food in jars for infants and disposable diapers have arrived at Friendship Stores, but may not always be available at the time and place you want them.

CHOOSING A TRAVEL AGENT

You can deal directly with C.I.T.S. in Hong Kong or China (time-consuming) or work through a travel agent at home. Do not hesitate about bothering agents. They make their money from commissions. Sometimes a travel agent will discount, especially if you buy packages. And yes, you can save money organizing your own tour group. The more people you have, the cheaper it is, but also the more headaches.

In dealing with a travel agent, consider seriously the following, especially if these apply to your situation.

How experienced is the tour organizer with tours to China? In other words, has the wholesaler established good relationships with tourism officials in China so you will get the best rooms and services for your money? The Chinese do their best for people they know and trust. If a tour organizer sends a lot of tours to China, and has been doing so for several years, then the organizer is in a stronger position than some company organizing only a few groups.

Does the agent know enough to advise you what to do in the event of a plane cancelation in a city where no hotel rooms are available? Would he warn you that the late plane from Beijing arrives in Xi'an after most restaurants are closed?

For prepaid tours with set itineraries especially

How many of your desired destinations are offered? How many days will you have in each place? Does the price include the Dazu sculptures in Chongqing, for example, or do you have to pay extra?

Do the dates fit your own schedule, weather preference, and Chinese holidays?

What is the price? Why is it different from another organizer's with the same cities and same number of days? What are you paying for? Usually the price includes visa fee, group transportation (be sure you establish if this is from your home or from your first point in China), hotel accommodation (double or single occupancy?), three meals and beverages a day, sightseeing, group transfers, transporting one piece of luggage (maximum 20 kg per person?), and admission tickets to tourist attractions and cultural events. Does the price include all the taxes and service charges along the way? Will you be traveling with a guide-interpreter? (Groups of over six people qualify for an escort.)

Are the hotel rooms "regular" or "deluxe," and do you get a refund if a deluxe room is not available? Are the trains soft or hard class? Are the airplanes first or economy class?

Price quotes do not usually include passport fees, laundry, hair-dressing, taxis, postage, long-distance telephone calls, excess baggage, medical, and other expenses of a personal nature. Nor do they include insurance or expenses for changes in the itinerary, or prolonged tours "due to unforeseen circumstances." Ask about those "unforeseen circumstances.'' These could include plane cancelations, overbooking, and arriving at the airport after the plane leaves. Tour escorts have been known to pay for minor "extras," but will you be expected to pay on the spot or at the end of the tour for any substantial changes? If not, get it in writing. Ask about these, health insurance, and cancelation insurance. Health insurance is especially recommended.

What language will the guides speak? For example, a tour booked in Japan may only have Japanese-speaking guides, while some tours booked in Hong Kong are in English. Or a tour might be in Beijing dialect and you expected Cantonese.

Do you get a group visa or an individual visa? Some tours allow longer time for individuals to visit relatives or negotiate business, etc.

How many people are in the group? How old? Sexes?

How much is the deposit and when do you pay in full? Are departures guaranteed? What refund do you get if the tour is canceled? Should you buy cancelation insurance? What happens if you have to leave partway through the China portion? Will you get a prorated refund?

Will you be able to see everything you want?

Does the tour operator offer the Yangtze Gorges tour on a regular public ship or on a luxury, air-conditioned tourist ship? Which would you prefer? See "Yangtze Gorges."

All tours are subject to changes in itinerary by the Chinese, so don't blame your travel agent. These changes should become less frequent as China acquires more hotels, trains, and airplanes. Prices, too, are subject to change.

Travel agents China International Travel Service now has representatives in New York City, Tokyo, London, Paris, and Frankfurt who should be able to answer travel questions. If you can't find an experienced agent, here are some suggestions. Most of these can also make arrangements for individuals.

U.S.A. *American Youth Hostels:* Bicycle tours; *China Passage, Inc.; Club Med:* Resort in Guangdong; *Kuo Feng:* one of the largest for both O.C. and Foreign Friends (F.F.); *Lindblad Travel, Inc.:* More comfortable than most tours, since Lindblad has invested capital to improve services in China. General interest and off-beat tours like the Wolong Nature Preserve and Tibet to Kathmandu by land. Luxury cruise ships on the Yangtze. Uses some of the best hotels; *Mountain Travel:* General- and special-interest tours. Treks in Northwest China. Wolong Nature Preserve and Everest. Birdwatching in Northeast China. Mountaineering. Tibet to Nepal overland; *Pacific Delight Tours:* Special and general interest; *Silkway Travel and Trading:* Visas and packages for groups and individual travelers; *Society Expedition:* Special-interest tours on art, history, and archaeology, with qualified lecturers; *Special Tours for Special People, Inc.:* One of the most experienced special-interest organizers. Has close relationship with Chinese educational, medical, scientific, and technological institutions. Can arrange individual travel, but not for tourists; *Voyages Jules Verne:* Train tours between Hong Kong and Britain, including a unique one along the Silk Road.

Canada *Blyth & Co.* for off-beat tours. Knows about cross-country skiing in China. Special-interest tours. Also *East Asia Travel Service, P. Lawson, Pan-Pacific Travel Service,* and *Tin-Bo Travel Service Ltd.*

Hong Kong See "Getting There."

Australia *Friendly Travel, Viva, Marco Polo, Travman, Bannink's World Tours,* and *Cathay Pacific Airways.*

China Friendship Associations all over the world can give information on travel to China and their own study tours. Some of these associations can organize tours for individuals. They also entertain visiting Chinese delegations and students, teach English, collect books for China, show movies, and provide lecturers on China. Addresses can usually be obtained through the Cultural Affairs Officer at a Chinese mission. With information quoted from their letters, some examples follow.

Australia-China Friendship Society offers "15 tours a year, mostly of 23 days duration, all escorted by experienced tour leaders. No more than 24 people on any tour. As we are a friendship organisation our society is non-profit making and consequently our prices are lower than other similar commercial tours. Our tours are aimed at promoting greater understanding of China and we try to give a great deal of information to prospective travellers and to encompass as wide a range as possible of Chinese life, history and culture while on tour."

The *Federation of Canada-China Friendship Associations* had 18 tours in 1986, some specializing in minorities, performing arts, Silk Road, art and archaeology, Shandong, medicine, art and photography, naturalists, and Tibet. One of their tours takes in the Great Wall, the dragon boat festival at the original site, and the Yangtze. Some include Hainan Island and tropical Yunnan.

The *Associazione Italia-Cina* had 44 group tours in 1985, some visiting Tibet and Hainan Island.

The U.S.-China Peoples Friendship Association was "the first tour wholesaler to deal with China ten years ago. . . . Our tours are limited to approximately 15 passengers and recognized by Chinese guides as 'friendship groups' and we feel we receive additional considerations. In addition to the typical tourist stops, our tour leaders are free to include nurseries, communes, etc. Also, if the participant has any special interests he may ask the tour leader to request a special event for him in China. We do this on a much larger scale, of course, with our special interest groups like dentists, psychologists, train-lovers, criminal justice specialists, retired university personnel, textile artists, and folk dancers."

See also "Getting Around" and money-saving travel tips in "Budget."

BEFORE YOU GO

Book as much of your itinerary as possible beforehand. Complex international bookings are not as easy to make in China as in other countries. Domestic flights, trains, and ferries in China will be booked by C.I.T.S. if you go in a prepaid group, but individuals may have to wait until they arrive in China. If possible, get as many visas as you need.

Ask your agent if the flights are nonstop. Do you care? Is there an extra charge for stopovers? A day in Paris? You've always wanted to see Kyoto! Budget airport taxes, taxis, and a hotel. Is going via Hong Kong really the cheapest? Maybe it's better via Karachi. How far away is the Taj Mahal? What about going by land to Lhasa from Kathmandu?

A stopover in Taiwan is no problem now. The only complication might be Taiwan Customs objecting to any China-made goods you are carrying with you into Taiwan. These might be seized and put into bond at the airport.

By air Every travel agent has a book with the current schedules of every major airline in the world. In some cases, you pay less through an agent because a good one should know about cheaper flights like the excursion fares, off-season discounts, and charters of *all* airlines. On the other hand, each airline understandably prefers to sell you space on its own planes.

A travel agency can tell you when airlines fly between China and the other places you want to go. It can also tell you which ones have direct flights. Airlines do not fly all routes daily; some fly once a week. So you must plan your schedule carefully. Give your agent a list of stops you want to make before and after China, and how long you want to spend in each place. Suggest several options. Your agent should be able to work out a satisfactory itinerary. See also CAAC in "Getting Around" and "Introduction."

China's airlines now fly direct, nonstop, from the following cities to China, unless otherwise indicated. Because of reciprocal arrangements, at least one airline of another country also flies the same route.

Addis Ababa to Beijing (1 stop)
Bagdad to Beijing (2 stops)
Bangkok to Guangzhou; to Beijing (1 stop)
Bucharest to Beijing (1 stop)

Frankfurt to Beijing (1 stop)
Hong Kong to Beijing, Guangzhou, Hangzhou, Kunming, Shanghai, Tianjin, and Xiamen
Karachi to Beijing
Kuwait to Beijing (1 stop)
Los Angeles to Beijing (2 stops); to Shanghai (non- and 1 stop)
London to Beijing (2 stops)
Manila to Guangzhou; Beijing (1 stop); Xiamen
Moscow to Beijing
Nagasaki to Shanghai
New York to Beijing (2 stops); to Shanghai (1 stop)
Osaka to Shanghai; Beijing (non- or 1 stop)
Paris to Beijing (1 stop)
Pyongyang to Beijing
Rangoon to Kunming
Rome to Beijing (1 stop)
San Francisco to Shanghai; Beijing (1 stop)
Sharjah to Beijing
Singapore to Guangzhou; Shanghai: Beijing (1 stop)
Sydney to Guangzhou; Beijing (1 stop)
Tokyo to Beijing; Shanghai
Vancouver to Shanghai
Zurich to Beijing (1 stop)

CAAC has announced that it will also open services with Argentina, Brazil, the German Democratic Republic, Mongolia, Nepal, and Turkey, and provisional service between Bangkok and Kunming. In addition, international services to some of the 14 Coastal Cities should commence before 1988.

By ship: Regular passenger ships sail from Hong Kong. These are not luxurious, but they are adequate. A ferry now plies between Kobe, Japan, and Shanghai.

By land: The only land routes open to west China are from Nepal and Pakistan, with possible delays due to mountain landslides. Chinese officials have been talking about a railway line through northwestern Xinjiang province linking up with the Soviet railway system across the border, but that won't be for a while! Going overland via the old Silk Road has been done, but is not generally advised, as that route is not developed.

By train from Moscow and Ulan Bator, Mongolia, to Beijing, from Pyongyang, Korea, to Beijing, and from Hong Kong to Guangzhou. A train line exists from Hanoi, but China is not on good terms with Vietnam.

By bus from Hong Kong and Macao to various points in Guangdong and Fujian provinces.

For travel via Hong Kong, see "Getting There."

FORMALITIES

Passport. If you haven't got a passport valid for your trip and preferably three months afterward, get one. You can't travel without it. Give yourself plenty of time to get a copy of your birth certificate, photos, etc. Contact your closest passport office or consulate, or consult your travel agent.

A **China tourist visa** can be obtained from any Chinese consulate in a week. A frequent traveler can obtain a multiple-entry visa. A Chinese passport holder living abroad does not need an entry and exit visa.

China has started issuing **transit visas** at some of its international ports, valid for seven to ten days, and renewable for a month. The traveler must have a confirmed hotel reservation, valid passport, photo, and visa fee. He also fills out the form mentioned below. These cities now include Beijing, Fuzhou, Guilin, Hangzhou, Kunming, Shanghai, Tianjin, Xiamen, and Xi'an, and the visa fee is cheaper here than elsewhere.

Also, if you go to Hong Kong, travel agents there can usually provide anyone a visa in 24 hours or less (for a service charge). Tourist visas from the Visa Office of China's Foreign Ministry are cheaper. See "Getting There."

Travel agents usually obtain one visa for a prepaid group tour, but you have to enter and leave China with your group unless arrangements are made inside China. You do have to give your travel agent your passport number and other such information.

Overseas Chinese with Chinese passports do not need any visas at all for entry or exit. Nationals of South Africa, the Vatican, Israel, and South Korea are not usually allowed into China.

An **"Alien's Application Form for Entry or Transit Visas"** requires one or two photos and the following information. It would save time if you had all the facts beforehand: Name, Nationality (state change, if any), Marital Status, Sex, Date and Place of Birth, and Passport Number, issued by and valid until . . . It also asks Present Occupation and Place of Work, Present Address, Telephone Number, Purpose of Journey, and Destination in China.

Also required are: date and place of departure from your home country, date and port of entry into China, where from and by what means of transport; date and port of exit from China, and by what means of transport; what country will you proceed to after leaving China? Whether entry permit to that country has been obtained?

The "Name and address of your sponsor in China" is usually C.I.T.S., but it could be whatever Chinese agency is organizing your trip, the hotel where you have a confirmed reservation, or a friend in China who has invited you. The form goes on to ask for accompanying family members (name, sex, age, nationality, and relationship to applicant); previous occupation (give post, name of organization, place, and time); relatives and friends in China (name, nationality, present occupation and place of work, address and relationship to applicant); ever been in China? (If so, state place, time, and purpose of stay).

Sometimes, especially if booking by mail, a photocopy of the first four essential pages of your passport is required.

Overseas Chinese will win Brownie points if they add their Chinese name in Chinese. **In case of unexpected delays,** give yourself a few more days in China than you think you need.

Your visa will be almost entirely in Chinese and will admit you to any international airport or seaport in China and to any of the cities currently open to foreign visitors without a travel permit within the time limit mentioned. The date of expiry is written on it. If you want to stay longer, you can apply in China for an extension.

The visa stamped in your passport will probably mention your status in China: tourist, business, etc. Formalities should be simplified even more in the future.

Other visas may be required for countries in which you will be traveling. They are not necessary for countries where you change planes, as long as you stay in the transit section of the airport. They may be necessary for train travel, such as through the Democratic Republic of Germany, Poland, the U.S.S.R., and Mongolia, all of which have missions in Beijing. But do you want to spend precious time there getting visas? Consult your travel agent, who can obtain visas by mail or courier. Individual visas are processed more quickly and cheaply if you take your passport to a country's mission yourself.

Shots. You will need a certificate of immunization only if you are in a cholera or yellow fever area just prior to visiting China. Otherwise, no shots are required for China. However, if you are going to be living in the countryside, or any place where hygiene is minimal, consult the health department in your home city. At press time, immunization against typhoid, tetanus, polio, and hepatitus B (three doses in a period of six months) was recommended. In south China, once-a-week pills against malaria are recommended wherever mosquitos are thick at night. Most tourists do not have to worry about this, but those going off-the-beaten-track should think about it. The health department or your travel agent should know if immunization is required for the other countries you will be visiting.

Plan your budget See "Local Customs and Emergencies" and "Budget."

Chinese customs regulations Check through the customs regulations in "Important Addresses and Information" to see what you can and cannot take into China.

Hotel reservations Your travel agent can take care of reservations, but if you want to do it yourself, phone your airline or the relevant hotel reservation system. For example, for the Sheraton Hotel in Beijing, phone the closest Sheraton to you. Reservations can be made before you go only at the top, expensive hotels. No reservations can be made confidently for the cheaper hotels except through C.I.T.S. or a travel agency.

Write ahead to people you want to meet, giving yourself at least 30 days for an answer if by mail. Do ask for their telephone numbers so you can call when you arrive. Most people could arrange their schedules to fit yours. Chinese friends and relatives should also be able to take time off with pay from their jobs to visit and even sightsee with you. If you receive no reply, it could mean they are not interested, or you have the wrong address, or they are terrible letter writers. Sorry, I can't decide for you.

China does go through occasional xenophobic periods and your Chinese friends especially might get into a lot of difficulty explaining your relationship to them. Recent years have been all right. If you get replies welcoming you to China, then you can make plans to meet. If you have only a couple of days in their city and do not know your exact itinerary ahead of time, you could telegraph them after you arrive in China. See "Local Customs" on looking up specific Chinese citizens.

Overseas Chinese in particular may want to write to ask what their relatives would like you to bring them. Don't be surprised if they ask for a refrigerator, video, and moped. Other relatives abroad could help pay for expensive gifts. If you cannot afford these, take a less expensive present and they will (or should) be happy to see you anyway.

Usually, Chinese relatives just want you and your foreign passport for use as a courier. Only Overseas Chinese with foreign passports can import certain desirable goods duty-free. Hong Kong and Macao are set up for such shopping. You can either bring the goods in with you (the store or a travel agency supplying the transport), or you can just pay and carry the receipt and have it stamped by Chinese Customs officials at the border. It depends on the availability of the "gifts" in China. Your relatives can pick up the goods later in an Overseas Chinese store in China. I have never had trouble being reimbursed and I have carted sewing machines and bicycles on the train from Hong Kong! **But make sure reimbursement and in what terms are understood.** You have already saved them 30–50%!

At this stage, Overseas Chinese should start collecting the names of relatives, particularly of ancestors, born in China. The name of your ancestral village is essential. Usually you should refer only to your father's family. No one cares about maternal lines! The names should help people in your village place you. The welcome if they can establish a connection is better than if they can't. The names, of course, should be written in Chinese. Take as much documentation as you can: a letter in Chinese from your family association, your father's or grandfather's old passport or head tax receipt, or whatever. One O.C. who didn't look Chinese was accused by C.T.S. and C.I.T.S. of forging these, but never mind. He did get some 50% discounts in a few hotels. See also "Special for Overseas Chinese."

Overseas Chinese in particular should use both their Chinese and English names on correspondence and refer to themselves by the Chinese one, especially if they travel with C.T.S. The Chinese remember Chinese names more easily. If you don't know how to write your name in Chinese, learn. If you don't have a Chinese name, get one. It doesn't have to be legal, but it will make things easier for you as you travel around China. Just be sure you know how it is pronounced in both your family dialect and *pu tung hua* (standard Chinese).

In case of emergency, inform people at home how you can be reached in China. Give **copies of your itinerary,** with your tour number and travel agent, to key people. If you are with a C.I.T.S. tour, your friends can telephone the C.I.T.S. branch wherever you are in China and ask that you be told to telephone home. The tour number and itinerary are important to help locate you. Your friends could also try the airline if you took an airline tour. The mission of your country in Beijing, Shanghai, or Guangzhou might also be able to help. If you are traveling on your own without a set itinerary, an advertisement could be placed in *China Daily* asking you to phone home. This means you have to read *China Daily*. Outside of the big cities, it arrives several days late.

If you are not on a prepaid tour, it is best to schedule a **mail or cable pick-up** at your embassy, or at one of the big hotels (whether or not you are staying there). Ask at the desk or look for a bulletin board. American Express now has client mail service in Beijing.

Also leave your **passport number** with whomever does your banking, in case money has to be cabled to you through the Bank of China. Photocopy the essentials of your passport in case of loss and carry this copy with you in a separate place as you travel. Take extra **passport pictures** in case you need them on the trip.

Since letters could take up to 15 days to reach you, quicker if by "express" or courier, it is best to tell friends not to write unless your trip is longer than that.

Consider buying **health insurance** in case of serious illness or accident, and **travel insurance** in case you lose anything.

Essential up-to-date information If you are wondering before you go if any particular city is unsafe to visit due to floods, earthquakes, war, or civil disturbances, phone the State Department in Washington, (202) 632–6300; the Citizen Emergency Center, (202) 632–5225; or consult the Travel Advisory bulletin, found at every American consulate abroad (American Citizens' Services). You don't have to be American to get information.

Learn some Chinese If nothing else, learn to read numbers. Then at least you will know dates in museums and street numbers.

If you're going to live with friends or relatives and they're Cantonese, Fukienese, or Shanghainese, they probably speak this dialect at home. If you're traveling around China, however, it would be more practical to learn Mandarin, *pu tung hua,* which is understood all over the country.

The same Chinese characters are also understood throughout China. The characters used today have been simplified since 1950, and Chinese people living abroad do not know the revisions unless they have kept up with the changes. Just make sure that whoever teaches you the characters gives you the new script and the pinyin romanization. The new script is used in "Useful Phrases." It might be good to memorize some of these phrases so you can communicate.

As in any country, the more of the local language you learn, the cheaper your expenses will be. In the meantime, use the "Useful Phrases." The standard of English spoken in China is improving daily, but it is still poor.

I don't speak much Chinese but traveled alone and had a good time even without an interpreter. Unlike the French, the Chinese try very hard to understand attempts to communicate. Draw pictures and try charades. Point at the characters in this book. At hotels, look for individual travelers, especially in restaurants, many of whom are lonely and delighted to make friends. Some of these speak Chinese and could interpret for you.

The more you try to speak Chinese, the more friends you'll make, and the more you'll enjoy China.

Learn about China To get the most out of your trip, learn something about China before you go. There is a dizzying list of good books on China. Here are only a few suggestions. See "Bibliography" for details.

The more you know about most countries, the better you will enjoy going there. A statue may be striking, but it becomes more meaningful if you know it's the "warrior woman," made famous in American literature by Maxine Hong Kingston. A building in a park in Lhasa becomes the movie theater built by Heinrich Herrar where the German refugee showed the eager young Dalai Lama his first movies. A peaceful street in Beijing becomes the fortress for terrified foreigners caught in a noisy, life-death siege at the turn of the last century. A tranquil lake is the site of an American missionary compound during the Northern Expedition, its idealistic residents fighting the attempts of the U.S. Navy to take them to "safety."

Armed with background knowledge, you can also be sensitive to internal conflicts and avoid unwise activities like taking sides on human rights issues. You will be able to understand the people you meet—what do they really mean by inviting you to dinner? Are they just being hospitable? Or do they want you to help get the son into a school abroad?

And how can you, too, develop your own *guanxi* (connections) so you can get what you want?

Books: If you know nothing about China, start out with a **general history** like Brian Catchpole's *A Map History of Modern China,* which is extremely easy to read (high-school level), half maps and diagrams, the rest text. You can graduate from that to *China, Yesterday and Today,* a paperback that you might want to take with you for background. This covers the history of China, its political life, agricultural policy, etc.

Good bedside reading and very informative are *The Wise Man from the West,* about Matteo Ricci's unsuccessful attempts to convert China to Christianity 400 years ago, and *Son of the Revolution,* an autobiography of a young Chinese who grew up on the wrong side of the political fence and married his American teacher. *Son of the Revolution* is imperative for anyone wanting to get an insider's look at today's system, how the various campaigns since Liberation have affected the kind of people that you will be meeting, and how some Chinese circumvent the rules and stifling bureaucracy.

Fascinating is the *Soong Dynasty,* about the Chinese Christian who was educated in America, and whose children controlled China's economy for several decades. Daughter Soong Ching-ling eloped with Dr. Sun Yat-sen and worked and died (1981) in China. Her sister Soong Mei-ling married Chiang Kai-shek and fled with him to Taiwan.

Also readable, especially if you go to Shanghai, is Noel Barber's *The Fall of Shanghai,* about its 1949 takeover by the Communists.

You might want to read about all the **cities** to which you will be going—in addition to this guide, that is. Write to the C.I.T.S. branch in those cities and hope for an answer and a brochure. If those cities are ancient capitals, then look into dynastic history. Raymond Dawson's *Imperial China* is another book to carry along—a good index and lots of juicy gossip about the likes of Tang Empress Wu and her boyfriends. If you are going to Hangzhou, the classic is *Daily Life in China* by Jacques Gernet, with a map of the city in 1274—if you want to look for changes.

For Beijing, read any biography of the Ming or Qing emperors and that of Empress Dowager Cixi (Tzu Hsi) and *her* boyfriend. For Tibet, read Heinrich Herrar's two books, his classic *Seven Years in Tibet* and the recent sequel.

Han Suyin's autobiographical trilogy *The Crippled Tree (1885–1928), A Mortal Flower (1928–1938),* and *Birdless Summer (1938–48)* are good background for those periods. She grew up in Chengdu. Her earlier *Destination Chungking* is for those who will be going there too. It is set during the Japanese war when Chiang Kai-shek was a hero to her.

People interested in **history** could consider China's interpretation of her own events in *An Outline History of China,* compiled by Tung

Chi-ming, which covers from 500,000 years ago to 1949. For **British involvement** in China, there's George Woodcock's *The British in the Far East,* about the bad, old, but interesting imperialists like Captain Charles "Chinese" Gordon. For **U.S. involvement,** there's John Fairbank's *The United States and China.* If you're interested in missionaries, try Pat Barr's *To China with Love.*

For more **recent history,** see Schram's or Hollingworth's biographies of Mao Tse-tung, and especially Edgar Snow's *Red Star Over China,* which not only relates the history of the Long March but has the only autobiography dictated by Mao. Don't let the Chinese tell you that Yang Kai-hui was his first wife. According to Snow, Mao had four—his first was a village girl whom he ignored.

Then there are the **personal accounts** of people who lived in China, notably Chen Yuan-Tsung's *The Dragon's Village,* a good picture of land reform in a poor village in western China in the early 1950s. Jack Chen's *A Year in Upper Felicity* and Ken Ling's *The Revenge of Heaven* are both set during the Cultural Revolution. For more details on that painful period, Jean Daubier has published *A History of the Chinese Cultural Revolution* and Roxanne Witke has written *Comrade Chiang Ching,* one of the best books about Chairman Mao's widow.

Among the modern **Western novels,** the Communists used to say that Pearl S. Buck romanticized China too much and did not make political analyses, but a lot of the flavor of old China is in *The Good Earth* and *Pavilion of Women,* if you can find them. *The Sand Pebbles* by Richard McKenna was better as a movie, but is worth reading or seeing, for a good story and Northern Expedition background. It tells of an American gunboat engineer and a missionary woman in Changsha and the Yangtze in 1925. (Remember Steve McQueen and Candice Bergen?)

If you're interested in **Chinese arts and crafts,** I would take along Margaret Medley's *A Handbook of Chinese Art,* Michael Sullivan's *The Arts of China,* or C.A.S. Williams's *Outlines of Chinese Symbolism and Art Motives.* These are all excellent reference books, profusely illustrated, that will help you appreciate the architecture, symbols, mythology, and customs of China. But do keep in mind that Williams's was written before Liberation.

Look up back issues of magazines like *China Reconstructs* and *China Pictorial,* which have articles about many of the places you will be visiting, descriptions of Chinese movies and plays, and Chinese arts and history. The glossy magazines *China Tourism* and *Shanghai Hotels and Tourism* should inspire you.

Chinese **periodicals** can usually be found in bookstores in many Chinatowns. In the United States, the best-stocked store for China books is China Books and Periodicals, Inc. Write for a catalog. In Hong Kong, there's the Joint Publishing Co., Peace Book Co., and Commercial Press.

Many western periodicals now have their own correspondents in Beijing, and you should keep your eyes open for news reports about China before you go. Updated travel information can be found in Hong Kong's *Asia Travel Trade. China Daily,* Beijing's English language newspaper, is printed also in New York City, San Francisco, and Hong Kong, and available by subscription. It usually reaches Toronto, for example, only four days old, much faster than a letter from China.

You can pick up the very good Cartographic Department **maps** and China City Guides after you get there. One exists for every major city. They are inexpensive and describe the tourist attractions in some detail. However, you may want to see where you're going before you get there, and China Books and Periodicals, some travel book stores, and Chinese book stores abroad may carry them. Chinese publications are considerably cheaper in China.

The **National Committee on U.S.-China Relations** has a briefing kit for US$20 tailored for individual travelers to China. It can recommend lecturers. The China Friendship Associations can also recommend lecturers, and some branches have copies of Chinese periodicals in their libraries. Talk also to old China hands, contacted through these groups.

Videos of tourist attractions can be borrowed from Chinese missions, and film festivals do show Chinese **films** occasionally, some of which are no longer available in China. My favorite is the sentimental *Memories of Old Peking.* For good historical background, look for some China-made joint-venture movies. Attempts have been made to depict authentic clothing, architecture, and lifestyles, and some have been photographed at the actual site. Try to find movies like *Power Behind the Throne, The Burning of the Summer Palace* (see "Beijing"), and *Shaolin Temple.* The Lu Xun classic, *The Story of Ah Q* was filmed in Shaoxing. You could try also to find an abridged copy of *Marco Polo,* filmed for television in China.

The only foreign-made movie I can recommend about China is *The Sand Pebbles* (although filmed in Taiwan). In the 1980s, Chinese-made movies have been very good technically and no longer drip with propaganda.

Learn about your own country This is indispensable in your preparation for China if you want to see factories and schools there. Visit a factory at home and take notes so you can compare with China's such things as incentives to work, unions, employee benefits, maternity leave, child care for working mothers, job security, automation, and so forth.

When was the last time you were in a school? Find out what subjects are taught at what level, how discipline is maintained, how many students are in a class, and about "open" classrooms. What about teacher qualifications, incentives to learning, and slow learners? Who makes the decisions as to what subjects are taught? How many computers does the school have? Audio-visual equipment? Take your notes with you, and in China, ask similar questions, point by point. With good facts on hand, you can also help to clear up Chinese misconceptions about your country.

Helping out If you are thinking of inviting **relatives or friends** to join you as immigrants or students, it has been increasingly possible to do so. Check before you go with the China desk in your government's foreign office, or your country's immigration office. You can also ask for information at your country's consulate in China.

Getting permission is a long process and you should not expect all procedures to be completed during a short trip. A new regulation says that local public security bureaus must notify Chinese citizens applying for a passport of their decision within 30 days in cities and 60 days in the countryside.

See also "Gifts" and "Special for Overseas Chinese."

Check your own Customs regulations Best write for a booklet. Find out what you cannot take back into your own country. Dried mushrooms and dried beef have been confiscated. Some kinds of fruits and plants are forbidden; orchid plants grown without soil are permitted entry only in some instances. Certain animal products are forbidden or restricted; for example, the United States will allow only "a couple of" pieces of ivory, and no crocodile or alligator, leopard, or tiger products, as these are endangered species. China has sable, mink, fox, and wolf fur coats and hats for sale, also. See page 108.

Canada says no elephant ivory whatsoever.

In many countries, coin and stamp collections, antiques (over 100 years old), and "works of art" (one of a kind—not factory-made copies) are duty-free. Be sure to get a certificate of proof at time of purchase. Canada has allowed sculptures duty-free if valued over $75.

Some items may be duty-free but liable to sales tax in Canada. You will need to keep receipts for purchases in China. The red wax seal on an antique is China's proof that the vase or incense burner is over 100 years old, but you have to convince a customs officer.

Before you leave your own country, register valuable items such as cameras and expensive jewelry with Customs, especially if these items look new. This is to avoid a hassle with customs officials on your return. You don't want to pay duty on items you've had for years.

For the United States, obtain a booklet from the U.S. Customs Service. Americans are allowed a duty-free exemption of $400, with payment of 10% on the next $1000 worth of goods, even though items like uncut gems are normally dutiable at 2.3%. If you are planning to do a lot of shopping, it would be wise to consult the Customs regulations and tax rates before you go. For example, the tax rate on carvings from Hong Kong is lower than the tax rate on carvings from China. You can mail gifts worth US$50 or less, but the receiver cannot accept more than one duty-free parcel in one day.

Canada has a duty-free personal exemption on $100 worth of goods after 48 hours absence or more, and a duty-free exemption once every calendar year of Can$300. These exemptions have to be claimed on separate trips. You may send duty-free gifts from abroad to friends or relatives in Canada, each gift valued at no more than Can$40. These must not be alcoholic beverages, tobacco, or advertising matter. Be sure to enclose a gift card. The cost of shipping, however, may exceed the cost of the duty.

For more detailed information, please contact your local customs office. It is easier to get the information before leaving. Diplomatic missions abroad do not always have the latest regulations.

Comparison shopping If you are a serious shopper intent on bargains, I suggest doing some research and keeping notes.

First of all, many goods you can buy in China are available abroad, and one traveler sadly related how the painted eggs she bought there were the same price as the ones she found later in a Washington store. So look around at home, especially in local Chinatowns, where prices are usually cheaper than in fancy curio shops.

On the whole, however, the choice for bargains is really between Hong Kong and China. Serious shoppers should try to spend several days in Hong Kong going and returning. The China-made products available there are frequently priced cheaper than in China in order to attract the foreign exchange. Hong Kong prices sometimes can be even better than buying at the factories in China.

WHAT TO TAKE

Besides the items mentioned in the last chapter, such as passport, ticket, money, gifts, reference books, etc., here are some more suggestions. But weigh each decision carefully. Do not take anything you're not going to use.

If you're going in a tour group, you're usually allowed one suitcase. You should also have a **carry-on bag** for overnight train rides (your big bag may not be accessible) and airplanes.

If you're not in a tour group, remember that CAAC, China's main domestic airline, is very lenient about hand-carried luggage, but strict about its 20-kg limit on checked bags. It does not charge excess baggage rates if you arrived in China with a heavier allowance. But other travelers have to pay, so put books and other heavy items in your carry-on bag.

Also keep in mind the lack of porters. This is usually no problem with tour groups, but independent travelers should be prepared to carry their own luggage in some train stations, perhaps up and down a flight of steps, to a taxi. Porters and trolleys are available in some but not all train stations and airports. Even if you are being met, you may be embarrassed if your guide offers to carry your luggage. Consider a set of **luggage wheels.**

Consider also the strength of your bag. Visitors report that some bags have been damaged in handling. See also *CAAC* in "Getting Around."

Money Be aware that only a few credit cards are accepted in China at press time, some of them with a 4% surcharge. Only some of the top international hotels and a few stores accept certain credit cards. Phone American Express, Visa, MasterCard, or whatever you use, and ask if its card is accepted in China. If so, be very specific. Ask which hotels. Can you get cash? Will there be a surcharge? This area is changing so rapidly for the better that up-to-date information is impossible for us to print. But be aware also that the Bank of China, for a period in 1984–85, suspended credit card payments for Beijing hotels, except for Japanese cards. **Do not depend entirely on credit cards.**

At press time, personal checks are not generally accepted, but some are with a specific credit card; checks of companies and embassies established in China are accepted if known to the person cashing the check; it takes five banking days to cable money to you in China, assuming everyone does his job right; you might ask your embassy to help you cash a personal check, but don't count on it. At this writing, aside from the Hongkong Bank in Shenzhen, no foreign bank had a branch in China that could cash checks or change money. This is changing, of course, so check with your bank before you go. Most of the foreign bank branches will be in the Special Economic Zones. Many banks have representatives for liasion and consultation, but few can do actual banking.

This all means, of course, that you should take enough cash and traveler's checks. You get less Chinese currency for cash than for traveler's checks. The Bank of China R.M.B. traveler's checks, which you can buy wherever there is a Bank of China (New York, Hong Kong, London, Luxembourg, and Singapore) have only been valid for six months. They might save you from the fluctuations in the exchange rate, but at this writing, the value of Chinese currency was decreasing against many foreign currencies. If this is still the case, you make less money buying and holding on to them. See also "Budget."

Clothing From early November to late March, north China, including Beijing, is bitterly cold, sometimes with snow. I even froze in Beijing one May; two sweaters and a top coat were barely enough. Many of the buildings are not heated and many foreigners complain of the cold even in hotels.

The Chinese sometimes lend heavy, padded jackets to visitors who didn't anticipate the cold, but you should take along your own coat plus long thermal underwear and heavy slacks. Thermal socks and underwear, warm boots, and *hot water bottles* are in order too.

I suggest you do as the natives do: plan on layers of warm clothing and a lightweight top layer. This is better than one thick, heavy coat that would only be excess weight in the warmer south. Down coats and jackets are on sale in cold weather, sometimes at half the price you would pay at home. They are ideal if you are staying a long time.

The rainy season is March to May in the south, with rain or drizzle almost every day. After it starts getting hot, a trench coat or plastic raincoat will feel like a sauna. You could buy a cheap umbrella then. The Chinese sell plastic sandals, which are great for rain, but they may not have big enough sizes for Western feet.

All of lowland China is hot in July. Sundresses on foreign women in tour groups are common now in big cities. In smaller towns, especially if you are alone, please cover your shoulders. The more you deviate from what the Chinese wear, the more they will stare at and surround you, a most oppressive experience on a hot day or when you're tired.

Generally speaking, most Chinese women wear trousers, loose-fitting blouses, sweaters, and jackets in winter, and, increasingly, skirts or long shorts and blouses, always with short sleeves, in summer. For men, slacks and loose-fitting white shirts are worn in the summer even in offices. In winter, they wear layers of sweaters and Mao jackets or Western-style jackets. Everyone wears padded coats.

The new, with-it generation is dressing more colorfully, and even men wear high heels. Jeans are fashionable at dance parties. A few younger Chinese tourists have been seen in felt hats, Western suits, and ties—but don't let any fad intimidate you. For the first time in their lives, many people, especially those traveling on vacation, are dressing any way they want to!

At banquets, cocktail parties, embassy receptions, and other formal occasions, Chinese men, particularly high officials, show up in Western suits and ties, or well-tailored Mao jackets. Black-tie occasions are rare. Foreign men should dress equally well, but women should dress modestly, as Chinese women don't usually wear elegant clothes.

If you are invited to dinner, you could ask your host if what you have on is all right. Should men wear ties? How fancy is the restaurant? Your host may be pleased you asked, and dress accordingly himself. Women should not hesitate to wear some makeup, but, again don't overdo it, or you'll have other people at the table wondering if your eyelashes and hair are real. Does everyone in Australia have blue eyelids? Some younger Chinese women are beginning to wear makeup themselves. Go easy on the jewelry too.

Wearing cosmetics, jewelry, and bright colors (except for children) has been frowned on from Liberation until recently. Doing so led to hours of interrogation and even imprisonment during the Cultural Revolution. People who wore them then were considered self-indulgent, bourgeois, and counter-revolutionary. People in tight trousers then sometimes had them torn off in the streets. Long hair was seized and shorn off. It is understandable why the older generation hesitates about changes.

At less formal banquets, both Chinese men and women wear loose-fitting short-sleeved shirts and loose-fitting trousers, coming as they do from work. Going home and coming back to a restaurant on a bicycle after changing into something more dressy just isn't practical. Chinese officials have not been bringing their spouses to banquets, but this is changing.

For business, you should dress as you would in your own country if you want to impress people; otherwise dress casually. Most government offices are dumpy and tacky until you reach near the top.

Tourists should dress for comfort, with good walking shoes. You will be on your feet a lot and climbing stairs. You may even climb rough stone paths, treacherous for high heels. Sneakers are ideal. Please, no short-shorts; you might be thought of as sexually promiscuous. The natives are going to stare at you anyway, even if you are Overseas Chinese, so if you want to minimize the attention, wear conservative colors—dark blues and grays. White is the color of mourning, so brighten it up with colored ribbons or something.

Laundry is done in one day at all hotels if in by 8 a.m. Not all hotels have dry cleaning. Don't expect high-class service. The Chinese do an adequate job, but if your dress is special, covered with "pearls" or such, they could ruin it. It would be wise not to take your most expensive clothes to China, and to wash delicate clothes like underwear by hand yourself.

You can take drip-dry clothing if you want to do your own laundry, and in some luxury hotels clothes lines are provided, but don't count on it. Take your own. I found that even lightweight clothes took two days to dry in humid Guangzhou, except in air conditioning. In the humid south, too, anything but predominantly cotton mixtures were stifling hot.

One feels compelled to dress up, however, in the new international-class hotels, where the clothes of staff members look better than that of the average Chinese and government official. But some tourists do lounge around the fancy lobbies in shorts and Hawaiian shirts, so wear what you feel most comfortable in.

Toiletries Take your favorite brands of shampoo, toothpaste, shaving cream, soap, sanitary napkins or tampons, if you wish. You will probably be able to buy China's equivalent of all of these in hotels and Friendship Stores in big cities, but not always when you want them in a hurry. The quality is quite good and has been improving. Foreign-brand toiletries are beginning to appear in Friendship Stores even in small towns and especially in the luxury hotels. Some are made in China as the result of joint ventures. Otherwise, prices are higher than in their country of manufacture. If you're adventurous, you might want to experiment with Chinese brands. The lemon shampoo is acceptable. The ginseng toothpaste is weird, but it might improve your sex life. Sandal-wood soap smells heavenly. It can be used to make drawers smell nice at home.

Finicky people have taken a disinfectant or scouring powder for the bathtubs, and their own towel. If you care about fine clothes, take a small plastic bag of detergent or a small bottle of Woolite.

Shortwave transistor radios are still needed to get the BBC, Voice of America, or Radio Australia world news. Better hotels have radios in the rooms, but not short-wave. You can receive news hourly from Radio Beijing in English. In the three largest cities, you can buy the current day's edition of *China Daily* (for market reports, local television schedules, NFL football scores, and some Chinese and world news). About two days late are the *Asian Wall St. Journal* and *International Herald Tribune.* Also available are *Time, Newsweek,* and the *Far Eastern Economic Review*.

Photography See "Customs Regulations." You can buy Kodak film, usually Kodacolor, in China, but it is cheaper and you have more choice if you import your own supply. Kodak film is available all over the country, but the prices are cheaper if you pay in F.E.C.s. Color print film can be processed in many cities, but the quality may not be as good as at home except in the top cities. If you're going to be in Hong Kong afterward, best have films processed there, as prices are considerably cheaper than in America. Masterprint in Hong Kong does great enlargements and Kodak stores are usually reliable.

Be sure to take extra camera batteries, flash cubes, video tapes, and Polaroid film if needed, since these are not readily available in China. If you run out, Guangzhou and Beijing have some available in special stores, but the button-shaped batteries are hard to find.

Maps and books See "Learning about China" in the previous chapter for books to take with you. Some foreign books are available in China, but titles are limited. Even if you are on an escorted tour, you may not get a knowledgeable guide.

You can usually buy a good tourist map in English in each city. A Chinese-English dictionary is superfluous if you have a bilingual person with you most of the time. For wandering around on your own, I have tried to anticipate most needs in the "Useful Phrases" in this book.

Medicines and vitamins Take what you will need; exact Chinese equivalents may be hard to find. The Chinese do have antibiotics, cold tablets, and cough syrups. Chinese traditional medicines are frequently effective, so if you're adventurous, you might rely on those after you arrive. A few Chinese pharmacists can fill basic western prescriptions, but don't count on it. You may want to take Lomotil in case of upset stomach.

Gifts are not essential, but because of the "no tipping" policy, you may want to leave an expression of your appreciation or a souvenir of your visit. This is one area that has been changing for the worse in the last few years. Chinese people are no longer satisfied with ballpoint pens, panty-hose, and souvenir pins as gifts. Some taxi drivers now are keeping the change without protest.

So what should you give, if anything?

Trade, commerce, and other officials dealing with foreigners have been accepting television sets for several years now, and some are reported asking shamelessly for videos, computers, and mopeds. There is no guarantee that an expensive gift will get you what you want, and the intent could prove counterproductive.

The danger is that from time to time, campaigns rage against corrupt officials who use their positions for personal gain. Don't encourage corruption. Chinese jails aren't as nice as those at home. And Chinese legal rights aren't the same either. Capital punishment has been imposed for corruption.

Usually, inviting an official to a banquet to celebrate a deal, or to thank especially helpful people, is sufficient.

It is not imperative to take gifts to schools, and certainly not to factories and communes that you visit for a few hours. The factories and communes will make money from your purchases. But schools do not usually receive any material compensation for the disruption caused by visitors. If you want to leave a souvenir of your visit, give **general gifts** like books and pictures that everyone can enjoy. Giving to a few individuals may antagonize the others. One tour group collected ¥20 for a youth palace in Beijing. If you want to do the same, ask your host to buy some treats or equipment for the children.

Since people everywhere are studying English and other foreign language, give **books.** Textbooks, good supplementary reading books, and objective histories of Asia would be great. *The Soong Dynasty* is easily read and enlightening. Agatha Christie is fun. Edgar Snow is popular. Please, no sexy novels! Books from museums are great. C.I.T.S. guides have written to ask for "best-sellers," Chinese-English dictionaries and thesauruses. Books about your country are fine, particularly if you have a sister-city or sister-province relationship with China.

"Talking books" on cassettes are good for learning English and are lighter to carry. Most guides and schools have access to cassette players. Since you may be carrying music tapes anyway for dance parties, you could give some of these as gifts just before you leave.

You could take **posters and educational materials** for schools, novelty toys like Frisbees, and unusual (for China) **sports equipment** like a boomerang, hockey sticks and pucks where there's ice, or a baseball and bat. As football has been seen on television in China, a football would probably be much appreciated. Don't forget to demonstrate their use. The Chinese already have basketball, Ping-Pong, and soccer. China is so short of teaching materials, especially in science, technology, and languages, that the Chinese should appreciate everything you can give them—educational movies (16 mm is okay), taped English lessons and, if possible, tape recorders to match. Books on space and the history of flying come immediately to mind. As souvenirs of a visit, a geological delegation might want to give labeled rock specimens; a solar energy group may want to give a simple model.

Group gifts are difficult to organize on general-interest tours, where you might meet your fellow travelers for the first time on a plane across the Pacific. So don't worry about gifts. But **special-interest** and **Friendship tours** are different. Again, it's up to you. You may want to write ahead to the schools where you will be spending *more* than just an afternoon. Ask what they need. If the gift needs duty-free customs clearance, give the institution your date and point of entry so the papers will be ready for you. Do not be surprised if you get a list of books worth US$50,000. Never mind; take only what you can afford. The Chinese are used to spending very little money for locally printed books; they think books are cheap everywhere. See Chinese Customs in "Important Addresses and Information."

Just don't be turned off by a request for expensive presents. In all fairness, the Chinese really do not know the value of money outside China. When you get there just say something like, "I'm sorry I could only get these. They are just a fraction of what I wanted to bring." That should satisfy them. If it doesn't, don't feel guilty. Don't encourage greed. You did your best. Besides, some cheap pirated foreign textbooks are now available in China.

For **guides,** surprisingly, the best gifts are reference books on *China.* Many get their spiels from old copies of *Nagel's* and you might want to leave behind this guide. Yes, guidebooks with lots of good photos from your own country are also important. C.I.T.S. is eager to improve its services and would like to see what other countries offer tourists.

Officially, tour guides are not allowed to receive gifts, but no one quibbles about inexpensive things. Guides will usually knock themselves out trying to help you anyway. You could pick up a carton of cigarettes (State Express is a favorite), and pass packs around to **drivers,** but that would be encouraging cancer, wouldn't it! How about chocolate bars, or wouldn't that rot their teeth! What about cute novelties, oversized pencils, bouncing things for decorating their buses? Ballpoint pens have become too common! You can give lipsticks and other cosmetics to women.

If you are going to Lhasa, Tibetans appreciate photos of the Dalai Lama.

If you are visiting **foreign residents** in China, do write and ask what would be best to take them, especially if they are living in isolated communities away from the big cities and fancy hotels. Many are teaching English, so as many relevant books as you can possibly carry would be helpful. They also appreciate hard-to-get snack foods: instant dried soups, cheeses, popping corn, Cheese Curls, instant coffee and tea bags, and Mom's homemade cookies. Around your holiday times, take traditional spices, condiments, and treats like cranberry sauce, Christmas spices, Sunkist oranges, delicious apples, the makings for minced meat and pumpkin pies. China has all kinds of fruit, a limited variety of vegetables, and many meats, but there's nothing like goodies from home. If you are flying to the north from the south, pick up some tropical fruit, like litchis, in Hong Kong or Guangzhou.

Museum pieces. The next suggestion is entirely my own, so don't blame anyone else for it. So many things were stolen from China by looting foreigners in the old days that as a gesture of friendship and support for the current policy of openness to foreigners, some visitors may want to return Chinese relics if they have any. These, of course, must have historic value, which could be simply the act of returning them. The British once returned a sword belonging to one of the Taiping princes. It is now in the Taiping museum in Nanjing. I think old photos of foreigners in China (against recognizable Chinese backgrounds), important old documents, and missionary clothes and old military uniforms would be most welcome. A museum official in Zhenjiang said she was eager to get anything like that.

You really should write ahead of time to the Bureau of Historical Relics in Beijing *and* directly to the museum in the city relevant to the relics. Give details and ask if they would be interested in receiving the relics as a gift. Keep in mind that China has a problem of too many historical objects, but something unique and significant would be appreciated. Also be aware that captions on exhibits from imperialist times might be written in anti-imperialist jargon. The Chinese are currently moving away from such bitterness, and your gift should help.

I once asked a guide at the Beijing Museum of Chinese History about this idea, and she laughed in my face, saying, "No one would give up anything that valuable!" I hope someone will prove her wrong. Co-author Priscilla Hsu is collecting information on the availability of items of this nature and looking into possible museum sites in China. Please let her know if you have anything you would like to give, but please *do not* send it yet. Write to her at Box 4726, Beijing, China, or to Ruth Malloy, c/o Fielding's People's Republic of China, William Morrow and Co., 105 Madison Ave., New York, NY 10016, U.S.A.

Your next problem is getting gifts into China without paying duty. See *Customs Regulations* in "Getting There."

Miscellaneous If you're fussy about coffee and tea, take in your favorite brands, powdered cream, sugar, and a spoon. Chinese coffee tastes different from ours. Chinese hotels provide cups and a big thermos of hot water every day. Take prunes if traveling makes you constipated. A jackknife is handy for cutting fruit for snacks and a flashlight imperative for caves, museums, dark houses, and late-night walks. (Drivers of motor vehicles do not always turn headlights on at night, and many streets have ditches and potholes with no warning signs.) Cheap jackknives and flashlights can be bought in China too. Do you need a portable hair dryer? an iron? (Consider voltage.)

Take a money belt to hold valuables if you will be sleeping on boats or trains. If you're fussy about your cigarettes or liquor, take some in with you. China has some foreign cigarettes and liquor, but maybe not your favorites. Cocktails and beer are not served on airplanes. Visitors are usually pleased with the local beer, but find the wine very sweet. In many hotels you now find ice (made from boiled water, I hope). Chinese brandy and vodka have been described as "outstanding," and of course there's *maotai*. But these are all a matter of taste. Yes, Coca-Cola is available locally, but not all varieties.

Take instant soups, crackers, hot chocolate mix, instant cereal, things to munch on, and a can opener. You may get tired of Chinese food.

During the rainy season you might be bothered by mosquitoes, if, for example, you're staying with a family or in an isolated rural guesthouse. Also take insect repellant then. Hot water bottles are great for hotels that have little or no heat in winter. Hot water from thermoses is easily available.

For people who want to do unusual things, and are not on a whirlwind tour, yes, take your paints, or if you want to be able to say you ice-skated in China, take your skates. Take your alpine skis or at least your boots if you're going to Jilin or Harbin in winter. (You can rent these there, too, but the skis available have safety straps but no brakes.) Take cross-country skis if you're staying any length of time in snow country, the northeast. Trails are not developed yet, so you're pioneering. Blyth and Company can tell you about it. The only scuba diving is in Zhanjiang, and possibly Sanya on Hainan Island. Some Hong Kong dive shops are tied in with the sport in China, so you can get information from them before you go. Keep in mind that the Chinese are very concerned about the safety of visitors and your guides may hover around you protectively.

If you're big on bicycling and staying any length of time, buy a bicycle in China or take one in with you. Chinese bicycles usually have one gear. You can sell it when you leave if you want.

Think of everything you need before you go and try to be as self-sufficient as possible. If goods are sent in by mail, a hefty duty may have to be paid at a hard-to-find government office.

Voltage Chinese appliances are 220V and have either two-, or more commonly, three-pronged plugs (with straight or slanted prongs). Some hotels have adapters and transformers, but not all. Your 110V North American electric razor and hair dryer may not work, except in the luxury hotels. You may want to pick up 220V electronics in Hong Kong.

GETTING THERE (AND BACK)

The prepaid traveler with a human guide does not have to worry about logistics. Read the sections on *Border Formalities, Adjusting Your Watch,* and *Leaving China,* but just glance at the rest of this chapter to see what you're missing.

The do-it-yourself traveler does have to read most of it.

Via Hong Kong While many travelers go directly from their own country into China, many more enter China via Hong Kong. This is because flights from North America and Britain are usually cheaper to Hong Kong, even with the added cost of air travel to Beijing. It is cheaper still to go into China and take the plane from Guangzhou to Beijing (but you lose a day). That long flight is calculated with "domestic" rates, and not the more expensive "international."

Because hundreds of thousands of Hong Kong Chinese and many foreign residents travel to China yearly from Hong Kong, competing travel agents there have developed a high degree of expertise. They are usually the first to upgrade services. Many have direct connections with individual tourism officials in China with whom they share a common language. Hong Kong is also loaded with professional China watchers, China-related banks, and experienced business people who can give advice.

While its prices have risen over the years, Hong Kong is still one of the bargain cities of the world, with its tax-free and duty-free jewelry, cameras, watches, and radios, and its relatively cheap shoes and clothes. It is a good place to stock up on camera film, video tapes, snacks, down coats, dried-food gifts for relatives, and locally published China guidebooks. Books published abroad and cosmetics are more expensive in Hong Kong. But a good selection of China books is available.

Bargains are also to be found in the stores primarily stocked with goods from China. Some of these stores, like Yue Hwa, China Products, and Chinese Merchandise Emporium, should have up-to-date lists of what Overseas Chinese can take into China duty-free. They will even pack and ship purchases to the railway station or provide a truck into

China if you give them a couple of days' notice. Prices are "fixed," but they will give you a 10% discount card if you ask and show a passport, and argue that you are "only in town a couple of days before going to China, and will be buying a lot of things." (Try the Overseas Chinese Service Department, usually on the top floor.)

In the smaller owner-clerk stores, you can haggle. Prices will go up automatically because you are a foreigner, so if there's no one else around, try your hand at this fine art. See *Gems and Jewelery in Hong Kong—a Buyer's Guide.*

Avoid money changers. You get better rates at banks.

Hong Kong was taken from China by the British during and after the Opium Wars. It will revert back to China in 1997. Urban areas are extremely crowded because of the refugees from China. You can feel some of the flavor of old China there, especially in isolated island villages or in the New Territories—the tiny temples, colorful incense-smoked festivals, elaborate weddings with brides dressed in red, and funerals with wailing mourners clad in sackcloth and white. It is a good introduction to the contrasts of new China next door, and it might be good for you to talk with refugees from China—why did they risk their lives to leave? Welfare agencies can help you contact them, or just ask around. China is beginning to practice again many of the old Chinese customs you will see here—but not so elaborately.

From Hong Kong to Guangzhou: Three **hovercrafts** daily (two at 8:45, and one at 10 a.m.) make the 3-hour trip. One departs from Guangzhou at 12:45 and two at 2 p.m. These are recommended because the maximum 68 passengers each means shorter queues; however, you can't see much of the scenery.

Jet-foils leave at 8:30 and 9:30 a.m. and take 3 hours. Sometimes the 8:30 one is canceled if not enough passengers book. The return trip leaves Guangzhou at 2:15 and 2:30 p.m. These are more spacious than hovercrafts and have toilets.

Overnight ferries, either the *Xing Hu* and *Tien Hu,* leave Hong Kong and Guangzhou nightly at 9 p.m. No sailings on the 31st of any month. The trip is comfortable in air-conditioned deluxe cabins (2 and 4 passengers), though some people have found the cabins stuffy and the bathrooms badly maintained. No announcements are made in English. A duty-free store is on board. The early morning arrival means you've saved a night in a hotel room and you have a full day in China ahead of you.

Most ships leave Hong Kong at Tai Kok Tsui, near the Yaumati Typhoon Shelter in Kowloon. This is a convenient ferry ride from Blake's Pier in Central. A smaller ferry takes passengers out to the big ships. Ferries dock at Zhoutouzui, on Guangzhou's south shore. Customs and immigration sometimes take over an hour to clear if they have 500 or so passengers.

Because the ships are on a river, stability is good except during typhoons. Seasickness is not usually a problem.

Four air-conditioned **through-trains** leave Hunghom Railway Station in Kowloon (near East Tsimshatsui hotels) daily at 8:25 a.m., 1:05 p.m., 2:35 p.m., and 5:29 p.m. for the 3-hour ride. Best buy tickets in advance, but you can also buy them at the train station on the day of departure—if any are left.

Frequent **electric trains** zip to the border at Lo Wu and passengers walk across the covered bridge to Shenzhen. This way is not recommended unless you like waiting in railway stations, or standing on trains or in lines. No toilets are on the Hong Kong trains, which leave Hunghom railway station in Kowloon or Kowloon Tong MTR Station. An electric service all the way to Guangzhou is being planned.

Planes leave for the 35-minute trip to Guangzhou at least three times a day.

A **bus** departs every other day on even-numbered days at 7 a.m. (6-hour trip), returning from Guangzhou on odd days. This trip should improve with the opening of a new highway soon.

Other destinations from Hong Kong By air, see "Before You Go" for Chinese airlines. Hong Kong has Cathay Pacific and Dragonair, also flying to China.

By ferry:

—to **Shanghai,** about every eight days on the S.S. *Hai Xing* or S.S. *Shanghai,* a 2½-day voyage. See also "Shanghai."

—to **Xiamen,** on the M.S. *Gulangyu,* six times a month.

—to **Zhuhai** (about an hour), **Shekou** (about 30 minutes), **Jiangmen** (about four hours), and to **Wenzhou** and then by bus to **Guilin.**

—to **Hainan Island.**

Contact the China Merchants Steam Navigation Co., 152–155 Connaught Rd., C.; tel. 5–430945. For Zhuhai, see Zhuhai Tours. For Xiamen, try Yick Gung Shipping and Enterprise Company Ltd.

Depending on the class, going by ship could be the cheapest and most direct way to get to these cities from Hong Kong. Buses could be cheaper, but are not as comfortable. Avoiding Guangzhou saves time and hassle too. Services are basic. Lineups to disembark start early.

On the overnight ships, no regard for sexes is considered in the assignment of cabins, but you might successfully protest. Meals are usually very early. On the bigger ships, the pools may be unswimable.

By buses: regularly to **Shantou, Xingning, Xiamen,** and **Fuzhou.** Some routes may have an overnight hotel stop.

Bus Companies:

For Shenzhen, Shantou, Guangzhou, Xiamen, and Fuzhou: The Motor Transport Company of Guangdong and Hong Kong, Ltd., 152–155 Connaught Rd., C.; tel. 5–420871. Departing from Chatham Rd., Kowloon.

For Shenzhen and Guangzhou: Handsome Tour Service Ltd., Room 1004, Mohan Building, Hankow Rd., Kowloon; tel. 3–666527.

As services are continually being improved and opened to more cities, it is best to ask the Hong Kong Tourist Association for up-to-date information. It has offices conveniently located at the Star Ferry pier in Tsimshatsui, Kowloon, and in the Post Office building beside the Star Ferry on the Hong Kong side. Ask about taxis to Shenzhen.

Most **Hong Kong travel agents** listed here should be able to book some or all of these. Most can get you an individual visa within three working days, or, for a higher service charge, within 24 hours or less. These agents can book you on a variety of prepaid tours to China, and some are content to get you just a visa and a train or ferry ticket.

A few Hong Kong travel agents, but not those listed here, have given the industry a bad name because of unreliable service. Worse are the ones who take your money and disappear. The following have been in business for years, and I have used some of them myself. If any of them fail you, please let me know and I will certainly take them off the list in future editions. Tell us also if you have found others reliable.

If you try a travel agency on your own, make sure it is a member of the Hong Kong Tourist Association. If it does anything questionable, then you have the association to intercede for you. Always telephone first for information and tell the agency where you got its name. Having learned of it through this book, they are answerable for any mistakes to me. They should do their best for you. You in turn are adding to my influence with them. This is a lesson in Chinese *guanxi*.

Since the price of visas, tours, and train tickets can vary from agent to agent, do also ask about prices and services.

China International Travel Service (H.K.) offers group tours for individuals in English, individual visas, hotel bookings, and ship and CAAC tickets. Other languages are offered if booked for a whole group. C.I.T.S. is primarily for Foreign Friends. Booking by mail is possible. Write for a list of tours and prices if only to compare with what you are being offered elsewhere.

China Travel Service (H.K.), the granddaddy of them all, is primarily for Overseas Chinese and Compatriots, and is cheaper than C.I.T.S. if you qualify. Foreign Friends, children, and spouses can also go, but only with an Overseas Chinese. C.T.S. provides the same services as C.I.T.S., but its tours are usually in Cantonese or Mandarin, not English. Bookings by mail accepted.

China Youth Travel, like C.I.T.S. and C.T.S., is an official travel agency under the General Administration of Travel and Tourism of China. It arranges tours of interest to and in conformity with the studiousness and vitality of young people the world over. Special tours are offered for professional groups like medical doctors, nurses, lawyers, and teachers to broaden contacts and exchange knowledge/experiences with their

Chinese counterparts. For youth, it arranges general sightseeing, but also visits to schools, communes, and national minorities. It also arranges seminars with university students and scholars, summer camps, cycling expeditions, cultural studies, and performing arts troupes.

Club Med can put you in touch with its resort just across the border in China.

Crosspoint Tours (China Explorations) has "pioneered and specialised in bicycle tours and special tour programmes since 1981." Tours to Huangshan, Mongolia (camels), and Xi'an, etc.

Hong Kong Student Travel Ltd. offers conventional package tours, but also individual arrangements. Commune living in Taishan, Guangdong (for a minimum of two).

International Tourism has tours to Zhongshan and Guangzhou via Macao.

Rosalind Henwood is a general agent who specializes in cheaper air fares anywhere. Ask for Rosalind or Elena.

Silkway Travel Ltd. seems to do everything for F.F. and O.C. groups and individuals. Visa service. They told me it was cheaper to take a Chinese-speaking friend than to pay the high per diem rate for an all-inclusive individual tour for one. I like that kind of agent. They can also help find residential or office space, acupuncture courses, or a place to bury your grandfather in China.

Travel Advisers Ltd.: All kinds of tours and services.

Travellers' Hostel is my own favorite for budget travelers.

United (Tai Shan) Travel represents Taishan County, Guangdong province, in Hong Kong. Recruits U.S. university students to study in China. Visas in six hours during office hours, with a one-month maximum validity, which can be extended anywhere in China. Books hotels. Ask for Sydney Chee.

Voyages Jules Verne has train tours between London and Hong Kong with sightseeing stops in Beijing and six other cities. Also has unique train trip along Silk Route.

The **Visa Office of the Chinese Ministry of Foreign Affairs** issues visas at the cheapest prices. This is not a travel agent, but the equivalent of a Chinese consulate.

Via Macao This Portuguese territory on the other side of the Pearl River delta can be reached after a 50-minute jetfoil ride from Hong Kong. It is also a free port, its prices lower than Hong Kong's because rent and labor costs are less. But its shopping selection is not as vast. Noted for its gambling casinos and good Portuguese food, it might be closer than Hong Kong for some ancestral villages.

The Portuguese traders lived in Macao from the 16th century, but went seasonally to Guangzhou to trade. Macao will probably revert back to China along with Hong Kong.

Travel Agencies in Macao can arrange taxis and air-conditioned bus rides to Guangzhou and other points in the province. They can also arrange trips, such as one to the nearby birthplace of Dr. Sun Yat-sen. See "Zhongshan." Duty-free stores here can even provide you with a truck (at a price) to take large items like refrigerators to relatives in China.

Border Formalities Anywhere in China

Have ready for inspection your passport, Baggage Declaration form in duplicate, Health Declaration, and Entry forms. If you are taking in any duty-free gifts to China, necessitating a stamp on a receipt, have that ready too.

Immigration In most cases, you will have to line up to have your passport stamped by immigration officials. If the whole group has one group visa, then that will be stamped, and officials will take a quick look at each passport. In some cases, you may be taken into a comfortable waiting room where you can make your own tea while you wait for immigration and health authorities.

Customs regulations At this writing, Customs searches of foreigners and Overseas Chinese were rare, and of Compatriots occasional. See regulations in "Important Addresses and Information."

Money changing Facilities to change money into Chinese currency exist at border points, the Bank of China, and at major hotels. Change only what you think you need for three or four days at a time. Small quantities can be changed back to foreign currency easily.

You will be given **Foreign Exchange Certificates** (F.E.C.s), which are different from *renminbi* (R.M.B.)—people's currency. The F.E.C.s must be used in *some* stores, hotels, taxis, and restaurants. They were introduced to control the illegal exchange of foreign currency. Chinese citizens are allowed to use them. Foreigners are not allowed to buy or sell foreign exchange except at designated exchange agencies at the official exchange rate quoted for the day. This agency will give you an "exchange memo," which you must produce before you can buy back any foreign exchange within six months of selling it.

F.E.C.s can be taken out of China, but not R.M.B.s.

In Guangzhou, and especially in Shenzhen, Hong Kong currency has been accepted in stores or by street peddlers. However, using foreign currency is illegal, and there are periodic crackdowns. Local Chinese value F.E.C.s so they can buy otherwise hard-to-obtain items like bicycles and TVs at Friendship Stores. Some enterprises try to purchase F.E.C.s so they can buy equipment abroad without government red tape.

To avoid getting change in local currency (R.M.B.), keep a lot of small bills on hand. You can spend R.M.B. in most stores and non-tourist restaurants, but do not keep too much of this currency as it is not as valuable as the F.E.C.s. Some stores will refuse it from foreigners. A store accepting only F.E.C.s should have a sign to that effect in the window. In markets and some stores, prices may go up if you offer R.M.B.s.

Black marketeering in F.E.C.s may force the government to discontinue its use. Foreigners have been arrested and deported for illegally selling F.E.C.s.

For a list of acceptable traveler's checks and credit cards, see "Budget."

Getting from your arrival point to your hotel Top hotels now have vehicles that can meet you at airports, bus, ship, and railway stations if you let them know you are coming. In most cities now, **taxis** are also available in these places. In some cities, very aggressive touts might compete for your fare. Please don't encourage such uncouth behavior. Usually there is a taxi stand outside with drivers waiting in line.

Another new development for China is the overcharging taxi driver preying on new arrivals who don't know local prices. If your taxi has no meter, settle on a price for the trip (not per passenger) before you go. Make a point to take down the odometer reading when you get in and when you arrive at your destination. For the per kilometer rate, see "Budget" in "Quick Reference." If the fare seems exorbitant or doesn't tally with your calculations, ask a staff member at the hotel for the price, or take down the license number of the taxi and complain to the police and C.I.T.S. If that fails to satisfy you, write to *China Daily* and the governor of the province. For some cities, the distance from the airport to the hotel is listed in this book with the hotel, so you will have a rough idea of the charges.

To be perfectly fair, most taxi drivers are honest, but . . .

There is also an airport bus after every flight to the CAAC office in town. This must be grabbed quickly before it disappears. If you must telephone for a taxi, be aware that it has to come from a taxi station and you will be charged from that point.

If you neglected to make hotel reservations, or otherwise need help, look first to see if there is a C.I.T.S. branch wherever you are. If not, telephone C.I.T.S., C.T.S., or one of the hotels listed in "Destinations." You could also take a chance and go to a hotel directly. Some cities have touts trying to grab customers for inconveniently located hotels. See also "Getting Around."

Adjust your watch to the local time All China is in the same time zone, though this may change in Xinjiang. You will probably not have to do this again until you leave. See also page 12.

Once settled in your hotel, lie down or go to a coffee shop or bar and relax. You are now in China! Soon you will be ready to tackle the country and make use of the rest of the information in this book!

Leaving China Reconfirm your flight at least 72 hours before departure. You can telephone your airline yourself unless you are flying CAAC. This Chinese airline requires that you have your ticket stamped. You can avoid the bother and frustration of going to the CAAC ticket office by asking C.I.T.S. to reconfirm for you for a very small fee and if it has time, it might do it. However, if C.I.T.S. or any other travel agency can't confirm it, you'll probably have to go to the CAAC office yourself. Ask what time you should check in at the airport.

Make sure your visa has not expired or you will be detained.

If your flight is very early in the morning, book transport and breakfast the night before. You could also eat at the airport. After you arrive there, be prepared to pay the airport tax required for all international flights, including those to Hong Kong.

You can change your money before or after Customs clearance if you have your foreign exchange receipts. At Customs, complete the blanks in your Baggage Declaration Form and hand it in. If you've lost it, you may be asked to fill out another. Just put down what you think you brought in. Probably no one will check it against your original, especially if you don't look like a smuggler.

If you are going to Taiwan with China-bought purchases, those goods may be seized at Taiwan Customs and held in bond until you leave. Bundle them together when you pack and hand them in before you get to Customs. Give yourself extra time then on departure. Your airline can retrieve them for you.

Your next big hurdle is Customs in your own country. Have receipts ready. If you know the rate of duty, list the goods with the highest rate first on your declaration form. The Customs officials might just dismiss the little "souvenirs." Do report unaccompanied luggage so these will be exempted too. Since much depends on the whim of each individual officer, you may not have trouble at all. On the other hand, undeclared dutiable purchases, if found, may be confiscated, and fines imposed.

The onus of proof that an article is an "antique" or "work of art" or whatever, is on the owner of the goods. A Customs officer might not accept your certificate or receipts. Depending on the country, you probably have the right to appeal any decision.

HOTELS

HISTORY

The hotels of China **toward the end of 1978** were run by municipal service bureaus to provide travelers with not much more than a place to bathe, sleep, and eat. Many hotels were subsidized. One of the managers said then that he preferred Chinese guests because foreigners were too fussy: "Americans should learn from the Japanese not to complain!"

In some cities, especially during high tourist seasons, the demand for rooms exceeded supply. In the early 1980s, tour groups for Beijing were put into Tianjin hotels, or 50 km away in Hubei province. Some business people attending the Canton trade fair slept in hotel lobbies in 1979. Yet other cities had a surplus of rooms.

For many hotels, room reservations for groups could not be made very much in advance, and individual bookings could be canceled if Chinese officials wanted the rooms too. The officials had more *guanxi;* tourists usually had none. In addition, the revolutionary attitude was roughly, "If people are comfortable, they will become counter-revolutionary or revisionist. So don't let them be comfortable." Fortunately, this point of view has almost gone, but keep in mind that not all that much time has passed since this attitude was prevalent.

You can imagine what kinds of hotels resulted. Few, if any, were built during the early and mid-1970s. After the fall of the Gang of Four and the rise of Deng Xiaoping, the situation changed.

TODAY

Chinese tourism officials have been trying to solve these and other problems so they can accommodate the large numbers of foreigners and domestic tourists desiring to visit China. While most hotels are still owned by some government agency or other, the building of many new hotels has resulted in good old-fashioned capitalistic competition. Pleasing the visitors has become important! Standards have risen! Chinese guests sometimes get displaced to make room for foreigners!

The hotels you will use today are a world apart from the hotels of even the early 1980s. They still are not perfect but are considerably better, the regular hotels very adequate and those of international standard good.

Foreign investment in the form of joint ventures both in the construction and in the management of some hotels has given China several hotels of international deluxe standard. A few hotels are being built solely by foreign interests. The big chains have been getting involved. Hilton, Holiday Inn, Sheraton, Hyatt, Intercontinental, Marriott, Westin, and Nikko are companies that have already appeared or will soon be appearing on the sides of beautiful new buildings.

Some staff members have been sent on training programs outside China, and regular training programs take place on the job. Hotels have also imported foreign executives and managers.

This does not mean that all joint ventures are of international standard. Some of the new hotels have deteriorated because of poor management. It does mean that in the latter half of the 1980s, foreign tourists are being billeted wherever possible in a passable Chinese hotel, or, if they choose to pay more, in a better hotel, possibly of international "deluxe" standard (if one of these is available in the city). They can also choose, as backpackers will tell you, to live cheaply in a hostel or in a shared dormitory (with mainly Chinese tourists). But C.I.T.S. won't book you into those!

Hotels with standards deemed unacceptable to most foreigners are being phased out as better ones open. Future historians will look on the 1980s as the decade of the new hotels. In the mid-1980s, the rate of construction was still continuing unabated even in small cities and mountain resorts. A surplus of deluxe hotel rooms has already become apparent in low tourist season in Guangzhou. This will benefit visitors, who can then expect even higher standards and greater choice.

Regular Foreign Tourist Hotels

Generally speaking, prepaid foreign tourists are assigned a regular room in a good hotel probably with:

—**porter service.** Yes, it does seem strange not to tip!

—at least one **dining room** for Chinese food and frequently another for Western. The Western food may not be what you're used to (especially the greasy fried eggs for breakfast). These restaurants are usually open only from 7 to 9 a.m., 11:30 a.m. to 2 p.m., and 5:30 to 7 p.m. A sign with the exact hours is posted outside.

—facilities for **changing money.** If it does not, the service desk can accept your money and several hours later have the currency ready for you.

—**post office facilities.** Be sure you use the glue pot on your stamps.

Many are not the licking variety. If no post office exists, the service desk can direct you to one. The post office might also take cables.

—**incoming mail distribution,** either directly to your room or waiting in a pile at the service desk.

—**retail store(s),** always with souvenirs, but frequently with soap, toothpaste, toilet paper, etc., and sometimes with fresh fruit, Kodak film, flashlights, stationery, maps, books, imported beverages, and cigarettes.

—a **service desk** in the lobby where you should be able to book tours, buy theater tickets, make restaurant reservations, and in some cases book plane and train tickets. Staff here can get you a **taxi** and help with **long-distance telephone calls.** This desk is most frequently busy right after breakfast and before dinner.

—a **barbershop, hairdresser,** and **masseur.** The massage with a shampoo will have your scalp tingling for days. Chinese massages are vigorous, heavenly when stopped, and probably much cheaper than in your home country. Best watch how these people treat other customers before you subject yourself to their mercy. It is not impolite to protest mistreatment. Don't be a willing victim.

—attendants on every floor who clean your room and daily provide **hot water** in thermoses and **drinking water** in flasks. The water in the flask is usually what has been in the thermos the day before and can be used for drinking and brushing teeth. **DO NOT DRINK WATER OUT OF THE TAPS.**

Upon request and payment, attendants can usually provide cold beer, ice, soft drinks, and cigarettes. In some hotels, you can borrow adapters (for electric razors), radios, portable electric heaters, and irons, and have photographs developed and excess luggage stored (sometimes for a fee). They have arranged for shoes to be repaired for a pittance.

—a **television set** in most rooms. Some hotels also have closed-circuit programming in English or with English subtitles either with an extra optional charge per day or an arbitrary addition to the room rate. Shown are old reruns of American television shows, not normally available to local Chinese. So feel privileged!

—**hot water** from faucets, but not all the time, and usually in the evening. The plumbing has improved in the last few years, but toilets still make strange noises, sometimes showers do not work, and rusty water still flows from a few taps. See "Useful Phrases." But all bathrooms now have shower curtains, previously unknown!

—**laundry and dry cleaning service** in one day if clothes are left at the service desk on your floor before 8 a.m.

—**air conditioning and heat,** depending on the season.

—**elevator(s)** if the hotel is over three stories; sometimes these are turned off around midnight, so if you're dependent on them, ask for the hours of service.

—**sports facilities.** Ask the staff about badminton and billiards. In smaller cities, maybe you can borrow a bicycle.

—**movies** from time to time, usually for the staff, but hotel guests are welcome.

—**convenient taxi service.** If no taxi stand is nearby, the service desk can order a taxi for you.

—**telephones** in individual rooms or at least at the service desk on each floor. You can make local calls in most cities by dialing "O" and then the number once you get the dial tone. If it is not a dial phone, tell the operator what number you want. You might be able to get an attendant to translate. To reach an outside line, say *"wai xian"* (why she-an). To ask for the service desk, where there just might be someone who speaks English, say *"fu wu tai"* (foo woo tie). Local calls are free. To get other rooms in most hotels, just dial the room number unless otherwise notified.

You can usually telephone abroad from your hotel and even from your room. You have to book the call at the service desk and, except at luxury hotels, pay a service charge beforehand. At luxury hotels, you get billed for the call. In some fancy hotels, a service charge also exists for collect calls if not completed. You get a long-distance booking form. You could offer to speak to the overseas operator yourself. Until International Direct-Dial service is introduced, overseas calls might take 30 minutes to 2 hours to complete from a big city, and at least 2 hours to a couple of days from an isolated town (where connections have first to be made to several larger cities). Overseas calls should not be attempted if you are in a hurry and especially not in the evenings (when many people in the hotel are also trying to telephone abroad).

Phone calls from China are more expensive than to China (unless paid by AT&T credit card), but are easier to connect. Usually there's a 2–3-hour delay from the United States. Direct-dial long-distance and overseas calls to 170 countries can be made to and from Beijing, Shanghai, Guangzhou, Fuzhou, Tianjin, Xiamen, and Qinhuangdao, and late in 1987 from 40 provincial capitals and coastal cities.

Don't forget the time difference. New York City is 13 hours behind China during the winter months and 12 or 13 hours during daylight saving months. Thus in winter, 8 p.m. China time is 7 a.m. New York or Toronto standard time, 12 noon Greenwich Mean Time, or 4 a.m. San Francisco time. See "Quick Reference."

Telephone lines between Guangzhou and Beijing can now handle 3600 simultaneous calls.

See also *Telephones* in "Getting Around."

Some hotels also:

—have **clinics** with doctors who can fix you up with medicines for a cold or diarrhea. Some hotels will refer you to the closest hospital with facilities for foreigners.

—**have great views** from their roofs. Guests can usually go up there to enjoy them. Hotels are frequently the highest buildings in a city.

—**have Telex services**

—**have video games, night clubs** and **discos,** but don't expect the latest Western music unless you bring your own cassettes.

—**have mosquito nets.** Shake out mosquitoes before using, and tuck the net under the mattress after you get inside so that none can enter.

—**different room-key systems.** Some rooms are opened and locked by an attendant. While thefts in hotel rooms are comparatively rare, it is best to keep valuables locked in your suitcase to avoid temptation. And the days of room attendants catching up with you at railway stations with your discarded sneakers are over!

—offer **special regional dishes,** as well as standard fare. These are well advertised near the dining room, and might have to be ordered a day in advance.

—have **smoke detectors** in every bedroom, and **wake-up** service.

—can be **reserved** by cable or Telex to the hotel or C.I.T.S. in that city, but a written confirmation may not be forthcoming. A few can be reserved through an airline or a travel agency.

—will give you a **discount** if you insist, especially in slow periods.

—have a **noon check-out time** with 50% of the room rate charged if you stay until 6 p.m.

—have **bus tours** to scenic sights.

—have **short blankets.** Tall people should ask for extra blankets to cover their feet before attendants disappear for the night.

BUT some hotels

—have smelly and clogged **public toilets.** The ones in guest rooms are usually fine.

—have two-inch-long **cockroaches** in warm climates. These do not bite anything but books and food, and tend to ignore people. Call the attendant, who should exterminate them for you.

—have **rats** and staff who say, "But it's the season" or something equally unconcerned. **Please do not leave food lying around to attract the local wildlife.**

—though new, can look dirty. Insist on clean linens and a clean bathtub.

—are not allowed to fire incompetent staff.

—have **attendants** who snarl at guests, are reluctant to carry luggage, answer bells, or give any type of service. Some attendants still barge into a room after only a cursory knock. During earlier times, one guest caught in the buff had to apologize for embarrassing the attendant! Be grateful *those* days are over!

—are **fire traps,** with all but one stairway exit blocked or locked. As you should anywhere in the world, check the various exits before you go to sleep.

—**charge extra** for air conditioning and heat.
—have **very dim reading lamps.**
—have **discos** and **nightclubs** blaring noise after 10:30 p.m.

International Deluxe Hotels

At the time of this writing, we found no hotel in the same league with Hong Kong's Shangri-la, Mandarin, or Regent. None had a building in mint condition or impeccable service. None had Rolls-Royces and Daimler limousines available to pick you up at airports, though some fancy vehicles are being acquired. Few hotels had more than one telephone per room. Some hotels came close to five-star American standards. Most of the top luxury-class hotels in China would probably be rated three or four stars, and are more like a Hilton, Sheraton, or Hyatt.

Chinese hotels of international deluxe standard are basically like good hotels elsewhere, with the best services of the hotels above, and more. You can reserve them with more confidence that the reservation will be honored, not just directly by Telex or through C.I.T.S., your airline, or travel agent, but through its own hotel chain. Most will Telex back if you ask them to. Your reservation could be guaranteed until 4 p.m. that day or, if you give them your credit card number, you can arrive later than that.

Deluxe hotels have larger rooms and beds, and are more expensive than the top Chinese-standard hotels. Because of the fluctuating foreign exchange rate, prices are frequently quoted in U.S. dollars. Some have marble bathrooms, imported fixtures, and are stocked with imported soap, bath oil, and shampoo. Some have both 110 and 220 volt electrical outlets. Rooms greet you with literature explaining hotel services, telephone numbers, and information about shopping and tourism in the city. V.I.P.s are also greeted with fruit or flowers.

Luxury hotels now have public relations departments, and at least 16 hour-a-day room service. Most have a telephone service in English that can take reliable messages and ring the room of any guest you request by name. (This was impossible in the old days.) They also have fitness facilities like indoor swimming pools (with swimsuits for rent and attendants, but not trained life guards), tennis courts, and health centers. They have tailored staff uniforms, above-average staff pay, 24-hour-a-day hot tap water, and free daily newspapers. Guests can store valuables in safe deposit boxes.

Some luxury hotels have their own fleet of Mercedes limos or Toyota vans that make regular runs to the airport or city center. A few have offices of airlines and travel agents and a business center with photocopying machine on the premises. You can order a real Western breakfast of fresh orange juice, eggs benedict, and strong Melitta coffee if that is your pleasure. No greasy eggs and weak coffee here! All give a choice of foreign restaurants with imported ingredients, as well as a wide variety of different Chinese cuisines.

Top hotels clean and redecorate whenever necessary, and one hotel said it shampoos carpets in public areas every two or three days. (Some old-style hotels still mop carpets with dirty hot water, painting them a ratty shade of gray!)

A top hotel could also be a state guesthouse where paying guests might rub tour bus to limousine with visiting heads of state.

Miscellaneous

—Joint-venture hotels have to add a tax and a surcharge to the bill for practically everything, including telephone calls, laundry, and meals.

—If tips are left behind, they are "shared in a collective way," said one manager.

—Some hotels can be paid for by some credit cards.

—If you're unhappy with any room, consult your group leader or guide. Ask the receptionist for another room.

—As far as we have found, no hotel in China has any "no smoking" areas, but at least one manager said he was thinking of it.

—Chinese visitors no longer have to sign forms and show identification cards before they can visit you in a hotel room.

—Some of the new hotels were deliberately engineered to withstand earthquakes.

—The danger of a luxury hotel, in China as elsewhere, is its great economic disparity with the life of the ordinary citizen. The cost of one night in such a hotel could be the equivalent of at least four months' salary for a Chinese in China. The extravagance can be seductive, especially in contrast to the drabness and modesty of life outside. Your attitude to China could become like your attitude to Disneyland, whose purpose is to transport and amuse you in a world different from your own. You could become like the lonely Dalai Lama looking at the masses from the Potala in Lhasa through a telescope.

If you went to China to learn about China, you have to make a much greater effort to do so if you stay in a luxury hotel.

—Up to and including this edition, we have listed hotels mainly because they were places where you could bathe, sleep, and eat. We have attempted to at least give you an idea of price and what to expect. The situation is changing so rapidly, we can do little else. Many hotels are newly opened or newly renovated and working hard to iron out the wrinkles. They could be functioning perfectly by the time you get there; but then again, they might not.

Grading hotels is very difficult. You could help us rate them for future editions by telling us about your experiences and using the form in the back of this book. We hope to send around our own examiners, but we need your suggestions too. Future generations of readers will be grateful. Your opinions should filter back to China.

FOOD

BACKGROUND

The infinite number of Chinese dishes, flavors, textures, and methods of cooking, makes eating Chinese food especially exciting. The most famous cooking styles are Beijing, Cantonese, Shanghai, and Sichuan, but others also exist, including vegetarian.

Chinese food is usually chopped up in thin, bite-size pieces, making knives unnecessary at the dinner table. The thinness is deliberate for quick cooking, using a minimum of fuel. Chinese food can also appear whole, like fish or pork hocks, but these are cooked so they can be easily separated by chopsticks. When poultry is cooked whole, it is chopped up before appearing at the table. Sometimes the bones are splintered, so be careful. This is done purposely so the food inside the bones can be reached.

Chinese ingredients reflect the many periods of famine in Chinese history. Everything possible is eaten; nothing is wasted, not even chicken feet, duck tongues, jellyfish, and sea slugs—all of these famous delicacies.

The Chinese food served to most prepaid groups is usually adequate. It is not the best, but it is usually tasty and filling. If you want to eat better, you have to pay more for specialty restaurants. If food is most important to you, take a gourmet tour.

THINGS TO REMEMBER ABOUT RESTAURANTS IN CHINA

Restaurants until recently were generally dumpy and tacky, a reflection of revolutionary attitudes. The new economic policies have given China many new or renovated eating places, some very striking joint ventures in the gaudy Hong Kong style, and even a branch of Maxim's de Paris. International-class hotels can import ingredients and executive chefs. Some families and factories have also started restaurants, competing with much better food and service than state-run establishments. The current make-a-profit-or-quit policy has forced improvements everywhere. All of these mean good eating is possible for everyone, especially in the big cities.

Most foreigners will automatically be put into **private dining rooms** in restaurants. These are less colorful and cleaner than eating with the masses, and usually cost a bit more. Sometimes these rooms have to be paid for in F.E.C.s. However, you won't be stared at, can make a reservation, and can enjoy a meal free of smoke, unless your party creates its own.

Ordering Every hotel restaurant has an **a la carte menu** where you choose individual dishes. Some restaurants have a **fixed menu** too. You don't usually get to see the fixed menu. You have to ask about it. The fixed menu is served to prepaid tour groups, who do not need to worry about ordering. Individuals can order this, too, and it is the easy way out.

Food on the fixed menu is relatively inexpensive and you get more variety for one or two people. Just say *feng fan* and if they don't understand you, show them 份饭 .

In one hotel, lunch for one, *feng fan*, was steamed meatballs, curry chicken, spicy hot beef, greens and mushrooms, two steamed buns with sweetened black bean filling, egg custard cubes and tomatoes, clear soup with bits of meat and vegetables, white rice, and fresh watermelon. Of this I could only eat one third. While this was the most luxurious of the *feng fan* meals I had, most of the others were varied and filling. Menus change every day.

Gourmets avoid fixed menus because the food is not always freshly cooked. Gourmets also avoid **Chinese food buffets** for the same reason. But buffets, with their large number of different dishes, are good introductions to new foods. If you like something, you can ask the name, and order that dish again.

Every restaurant has its **specialties**—dishes the chefs are especially good at. So ask about these too. They will probably be a little more expensive than most on the menu but are usually worth it. Aim also for **local or regional dishes**—fresh seafoods if you're near an ocean. Seafood reaches Beijing frozen, so try for something else there. Meals in the countryside are usually excellent because the vegetables come right from the garden to the wok.

It is best to eat with a large group of people to get a greater number of different courses. Ten is ideal for a table, and you may even get a private room thrown in. When ordering, choose one poultry, one pork, one beef, one fish, one vegetable dish, one soup, and so on. Calculate one course for each person, then rice, noodles, or buns, and one more course. For example, two people should order three courses plus a starch; five people should order six courses plus a starch or two. This will give you variety and abundance. If you find you are getting too much, order less next time.

If you need more courses, start the rounds again. If you've already chosen chicken, then choose duck or goose. If you've ordered fish, then take shrimp or cuttle fish. Vary the tastes and textures: sweet, pepperhot, salty, steamed, deep-fried, poached or boiled, roasted, baked in mud—the choice is endless.

HOW TO USE CHOPSTICKS

The bottom stick is held firmly by the base of the thumb and the knuckle of the ring finger. The top stick is the ONLY one that is moved and is held by the thumb and the index and middle fingers. The tip of the top stick should be brought toward the tip of the bottom one. Keep the tips even.

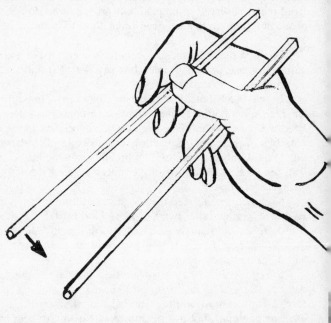

MARTIN MALLOY

Don't feel that every meal should be a banquet. The danger in China is overeating.

For popular restaurants, it is always best to reserve a table and even order meals ahead of time by telephone, especially for **banquets.** Restaurants for the masses won't take reservations. Ask the service desk at your hotel to make reservations for you, telling the restaurant how much you want to pay **but also approving the dishes** suggested. One restaurant suggested bears' paws, a local delicacy, which no one ate. Most of the cost went into that one dish!

Elaborate banquet dishes should be ordered at least 24 hours ahead of time, and a hefty charge is levied if you cancel.

Don't look for **chop suey or chow mein** with crispy noodles, or fortune cookies—those are American dishes. China has fried noodles, but they are not the same as in the United States. But then again, with the new economic policies, anything could show up!

Please be aware that some wild animals used by the Chinese as food are, or may soon be, on the **endangered species** list. Please avoid them. See "Local Customs."

Special diets: If you do have special food preferences, let your guide know.

If you have an upset stomach, order rice congee, which is rice cooked to a gruel consistency and flavored with salted egg, fermented bean curd, or whatever. Congee is easy on the stomach. Avoid fried dishes, spices, and dairy products. Eat dry crackers, arrowroot biscuits, and apple sauce.

If you have cankers in the mouth, try *hung pean* (chrysanthemum tea). It comes already sweetened with sugar in one-cup packages at Friendship Stores and is an old Chinese remedy.

People on general-interest tours should not expect special diets. Salt-free and diabetic diets are impossible then. Chinese cooking uses more salt than Western cooking. You could, however, go on a tour organized especially for people with the same restrictions. Vegetarians usually manage on a general tour if they don't mind meat sauces. Vegetarian restaurants exist, but these are not on the daily tourist route. Moslem restaurants also exist. So far, we haven't found any kosher restaurants.

Desserts Foreign Friends will be offered Western-style sweet pastries and fresh or canned fruits. If you're in Guangdong in May or June, ask for fresh lichees—or buy them in markets. Look for pomelo, especially in Guilin or in Sichuan in season. It's a sweet grapefruit with a thick rind. Try Hami melon on the Silk Road. China also has ice cream, sweet red beans, sweet almond paste, and deep-fried crystallized apples and bananas. Aside from fruit, the Chinese do not have much of a tradition for desserts. You might want to try a coffee shop in one of the fancy hotels afterward.

Beverages Most prepaid meals for Foreign Friends include Chinese soft drinks, beer, and tea. Canned fruit juice, foreign-brand soft drinks, and liquor cost extra. Overseas Chinese pay extra for all drinks except for tea. Coca-Cola has three bottling plants in China. Pepsi has one and is expanding.

Tea drinking is an art in China. Some springs are famous for their tea-making qualities. If you go to Hangzhou, try long jing tea there. A favorite tea in hot weather is *po li. Keemun* is good in the wintertime and when you've had greasy food. *Lu an* should help you sleep. *Oolong* is the most common tea in south China, while most foreigners like *jasmine*, the sweet-scented tea with bits of jasmine flower petals in it. Jasmine is said to heat the blood and should be balanced at the same meal with *po li.*

Every Chinese has a personal list of the four most famous green teas. *Long jing* (dragon well), *yun wu* (mist of the clouds), *mao hong* (red straw), and *bi lu chuen* (green spring) are probably among the most popular.

Dairies are beginning to open up, but in most places only UHT or canned **milk** is available. A shortage of refrigerator trucks hampers the distribution of fresh milk.

The Chinese consider the best **liquors** to be: *Mao tai*, made from sorghum and wheat yeast, and aged five or six years in Guizhou province. It is very potent and usually served in tiny goblets; *Fenjiu*, mellow and delicate flavor from Shanxi province: *Wuliangye*, five-grain spirit from southern Sichuan, with a fragrant and invigorating flavor.

The best **wines** are: *Tantai red wine* from Shandong, *Chinese red wine* from Beijing, *Shaoxing red wine* from Zhejiang, and *Longyan rice wine* from Fujian. If you get to any of the above places and have to bring a gift back for a Chinese friend, a bottle would be appropriate.

Qingdao **beer** is the favorite. It is made from barley, spring water, and hops from a German recipe. Five Star Beer has been designated by the government for state banquets. Foreign beers are increasingly available. Laoshan is the most famous **mineral water.** In Moslem restaurants, take your own bottle, as alcohol is not served.

Breakfasts Most foreign tour groups are given Western breakfasts with greasy eggs. You also usually get toast, coffee, and fruit or canned juice. Tour groups in the 1950s and '60s were given Chinese breakfasts, but requested Western instead. Some of the deluxe hotels now have good Western breakfasts.

You can opt for Chinese breakfasts if enough people in the group want them. Chinese breakfasts differ regionally: *dim sum* or rice congee with peanuts, pickles, and salted or 100-year-old eggs in south China. In the north, you could get lots of different buns, or "oil sticks," which are like foot-long doughnuts, deep-fried and delicious but hard to digest. You dip these in hot soy milk. In Shanghai you might get gelatinous rice balls with sugar inside, or baked buns with sweet bean paste inside. They are great.

Western food is now advertised in most *regular* tourist hotels, but I have rarely found it as good as Chinese. Bread is cut thick and is usually white. Sometimes "Western" food is one Chinese meat-and-vegetable course with bread instead of rice. Excellent Western food is more consistently found in the deluxe hotels, international clubs, and some restaurants. Some deluxe hotels also have delicatessens where you can buy cold cuts like salami and pastrami.

Local Chinese seem to prefer Chinese food and have rejected invitations to Western meals "because of too much meat." It could also be because of lack of familiarity with knives, forks, and Western table manners.

Courtesies Group tours in particular should be punctual at meals as the food is usually ready on time, and in family style all dishes may even be sitting at the table getting (ugh!) cold.

Guests of honor are traditionally given seats where they face the door. You might have fun speculating on the reason. Left-handed people have a problem and should sit where clashes with right-handed chopsticks can be avoided.

In many restaurants, damp hot or cold towels are distributed at the beginning of meals to refresh guests as well as to clean. One can wipe faces and backs of necks, as well as hands with them. Sometimes towels are distributed during the meal, too, and always at the end.

If tea or bowls or calling cards are to be passed, to be polite, use both hands.

Chinese food is usually served on large platters, which ideally arrive one at a time. The food comes hot off the wok at the peak of its perfection and should be eaten immediately. Time is allowed before the next course arrives steaming, to take what is desired of the current dish.

In families, diners pick what they want with chopsticks, and should be careful not to spread their germs to food left on the platter. Chopsticks are great for reaching across tables, keeping fingers clean, and hitting naughty children. Outside of families, spoons should be used for serving, and if no convenient "lazy Susan" exists, then the platters on the table are relocated from time to time so that all can reach. Don't be shy about asking for serving spoons.

To begin eating after guests express admiration for the beauty of the food, Chinese hosts put the best morsels on the plates of the people around them. You could do this, too, after the first round if you want. Groups of friends could declare a moratorium on such formalities and have everybody dig in. *Hei fai* means "Raise chopsticks!"

Do not be embarrassed about slurping or even burping. This indicates that you are enjoying your meal. If you don't have enough room on your dish for bones and other discards, just leave them neatly on the table itself. Less-polished Chinese will spit them on the floor!

Good restaurants do not make their guests stand up and serve their own beverages. Getting your own rice from a big pot away from your table is only expected in families or very informal restaurants.

In very fancy restaurants, an attendant distributes every course and guests do not help themselves. Individual plates are removed and replaced with clean ones after most courses. The host usually invites guests to start eating.

Giving a banquet is the accepted and most important way to return hospitality or to show gratitude for a favor. If your guide persists in refusing your invitation to eat with you, he may relent and join you the day before you leave as a farewell gesture.

You may want to throw a banquet for some of your Chinese colleagues and people who have been particularly helpful. Discuss your guest list with one of the Chinese involved so you won't offend anybody important by leaving them out. If your guide is invited, be sure he knows. Discuss spouses and times and seating arrangements, but don't be offended if spouses don't show up. The venue is important because some restaurants are more prestigious than others.

Toasting Chinese people do not like to drink alone. Toasting at banquets is a complicated art, and you are not expected to know the finer points. Just do what you do at home. Stand up, give one or two sentences, make sure everybody else is joining you, and drink. *Gan bei!* means "Empty your glass!"

The first toaster is usually the host, who gets the ball rolling. A frequent toast is to the friendship of the people of your country and China, and the health of friends and comrades present. The next toaster can tell a funny story and then, perhaps, talk about your sadness about leaving China and the new friends you have made, or wishes that you will all meet again in your country.

Toasts might continue all evening, and so might the meal, or at least until the restaurant turns out the lights. If the banquet is extremely large, the host might circulate to all the tables, drinking toasts at each one. On smaller, less formal occasions, the Chinese may want to drink you under the table. Be alert; they may be putting tea in their own glasses. You may want to try that yourself after awhile.

I have been to banquets where I haven't touched a drop of liquor. I can't get *mao tai* past my nose—it's so strong. Chinese hosts are not usually offended, especially if you toast with tea or soft drinks. If you don't want to drink so much liquor, try to divert your fellow diners. Try exchanging songs—but not drinking songs or games. It may be the only occasion when you'll hear the national anthem of China. You could also turn your cup or glass upside down to signal to the waiter that you've had enough.

Eating with the People

You can eat quite well for comparatively little money if you're willing to try food stalls and restaurants and sections of restaurants for the masses. The standard of cleanliness and speed of service, however, are not generally as high as in hotels and restaurants for tourists. The cigarette smoke may be suffocating. It is customary to share tables with other diners in busy restaurants, and if no tables are available, even in tourist hotels.

Payment is made when you order (so you can't stomp out impatiently). Some finicky eaters take their own chopsticks and spoons to places like this, but as far as I can see the dishes are scalded, and if the food is freshly cooked, there should be no problems. The soup sterilizes the utensils (you hope), but you can also scald them yourself with tea. Usually a spittoon waits nearby for the discarded tea.

Dumpling and noodle shops are better for speed (if the lineup isn't too long). The food can be good too. Foreigners are frequently pushed to the head of the line. A knowledge of Chinese isn't necessary because you can point.

Fast food stalls, mobile canteens, and cafeterias are recent innovations and are multiplying quickly. Some serve instant noodles.

At **restaurants for the masses,** it is best to take a Chinese friend who can help you order and possibly get you cheaper rates. You can also use the "Useful Phrases" or the *Regional and Special Dishes* below if no menu in English appears.

To eat:

—*mantou,* the plain steamed roll, either take bites off while holding with chopsticks or fingers, or break apart and stuff pieces with bits of meat. You can also dip it in the sauces. *Jiao zi* are the small stuffed ravioli-like pastries in soup; *bao zi* are steamed dumplings and may have beans, or meat and vegetables inside. The names get confusing;

—*white rice,* which is served in bowls, put the bowl up to your mouth and shove the rice in with chopsticks. More genteel people might want to pick up chunks with chopsticks;

—*100-year-old eggs,* you usually have to either acquire a taste or close your eyes and think of something else; they are best eaten with pickles and are delicious;

—*shrimps with shells left on,* take a bite of half, then, with your teeth and chopsticks, squeeze out the meat. You may want to use your fingers to shell them. Cooking shrimps with their shells retains most of the yummy flavor;

—*two- and three-foot-long noodles,* lean over your bowl and pick up a few with chopsticks. Put the noodles in your mouth, biting off pieces and leaving the rest temporarily in your bowl. Don't worry about slurping. The Chinese like long noodles because they symbolize longevity;

—*ice cream,* ask for a spoon.

To avoid an upset stomach and intestinal parasites, do not drink water out of faucets. Steer clear of ice, popsicles, ice cream (except in tourist restaurants), watermelon, and any other fruit with lots of ground water. Don't eat anything raw unless imported, or carefully washed and then peeled. Animal and human manure is used in China as fertilizer. Local people develop immunities. Bottled drinks are fine.

Be careful on ferries and small boats. Dishes are frequently washed in river water and not always scalded carefully afterward. Some people take disinfectants like tincture of iodine. Two drops in a liter of water kill all germs in contact with them in 20 minutes.

Other tips The secret of eating a Chinese meal is finding out first how many courses you will be getting. Banquet meals usually have a copy of the menu on the table. If there are 12 courses, take no more than one-twelfth of what you would usually eat in a meal from each plate; otherwise, you will be too full to eat any of the later dishes. Also take your time. You can't rush through a big meal. Some famous banquets have taken days.

Fish is usually the last formal course. If you happen to be eating with superstitious fishermen, don't turn a fish over to get at flesh on the other side. It means their boat will turn over!

Do not worry about ''Chinese restaurant syndrome.'' Its symptoms are an increased pulse and a tight feeling around the sinuses. This ''syndrome'' is a result of the large amount of monosodium glutamate put in Chinese food in America. Cooks in China use a little, but not so much. You can ask them to leave out MSG or salt or chilis or anything.

Among the beauties of a Chinese meal is the variety. If you don't like one thing, you might like something else.

On prepaid tours, you might want to talk with your escort about the overabundance of food when meat for the common man is so limited—if, indeed, this bothers you.

To best enjoy a meal, never ask what a particular morsel is.

Even-numbered days are more auspicious than odd-numbered days. Restaurants may be busier with wedding parties then.

Menus in English are by translators, not public relations people. Some dishes may sound absolutely terrible, but are really very good. Don't let a name like ''frog oil soup'' throw you.

Preserved fruit is delicious, but do not eat too many at a sitting as they are full of preservatives.

If you are invited to a restaurant by nonofficial Chinese friends, don't be surprised if they ask to buy F.E.C.s from you. Most of the top restaurants are paid in foreign exchange.

If you invite average Chinese people to dinner, be sensitive that a meal in a tourist restaurant is a real treat. Normally, they cannot afford it. Since they get little meat, do order more for them. Do encourage them to take the leftovers home. They may be too polite to ask.

See also ''Useful Phrases'' and ''Destinations.'' For some prices, see ''Budget.''

Some Regional and Special Dishes

Beijing (a.k.a. Peking or Northern) Dishes 北京

Light, with few sauces; roasts; lots of garlic, leeks, and scallions; flour-made buns, rolls and meat dumplings, baked, steamed, fried, or boiled in soup. Salty.

Smoked chicken/duck	熏鸡／鸭
Crispy duck	香酥鸭
Peking duck	北京烤鸭
Sweet-sour fish/pork	糖醋鱼／肉
Deep-fried shrimp toast	炸虾托
Chicken and cucumber salad	凉拌三丝
Stir-fried pork with bean sprouts (served with pancakes)	京酱肉丝
Chinese cabbage with black mushrooms	冬菇白菜
Pan-fried onion cake	葱油饼
Hot and sour soup	酸辣汤
Pan-fried dumplings with minced pork	生煎小包子
Steamed bread rolls	银丝卷
Assorted meat soup in casserole	什锦砂锅
Shrimp with popped rice	虾仁锅巴
Apple/Banana Fritter	拨丝苹果／香蕉

Cantonese (a.k.a. Guangdong or Southern) Dishes 粤菜

Quickly cooked in peanut oil; crisp vegetables; somewhat sweet; starches in the sauces. Uses a lot of oyster sauce or fish sauce in cooking or poured over boiled vegetables. Many dishes are steamed to preserve natural flavors. Really exotic banquet dishes are dog, monkey, and snake. Please, no pangolin and other endangered species!

Crisp-skinned roasted goose/pork	烧鹅／烤乳猪
Steamed chicken with green onion	葱油鸡
Cha-shiu (barbecued) pork	叉烧
Stir-fried diced fish/filet	松子鱼／炒鱼片
Shark's fin in chicken and ham soup	鱼翅羹
Steamed live fish	清蒸鱼
Quick-boiled fresh shrimp	白灼虾
Stir-fried beef in oyster sauce	蚝油牛肉
Cantonese stuffed bean curd	酿豆腐
Sauteed fresh Chinese vegetable	炒新鲜蔬菜
Assorted meats in winter melon	冬瓜盅
Bird's nest in coconut milk	椰奶燕窝羹

Dim Sum 点心

These small fried or steamed pastries are for breakfast or lunch and sometimes ordered from a menu (classier), or chosen from a trolley brought to your table. You can ask the trolley attendant to take off any cover to see inside if you want. Your bill is usually calculated from the number of baskets or plates on your table.

The variety of dim sum has been more extensive in Hong Kong than in China except at the famous Panxi Restaurant in Guangzhou. Chicken feet, known as Phoenix feet, are delicious! Honest!

Har gau: smoothly wrapped shrimp dumpling	虾饺
Shui mai: minced pork and shrimp dumpling	烧卖
Cha shiu bau: barbecued pork buns	叉烧包
Tsun guen: deep-fried spring roll with pork, mushrooms, chicken, bamboo shoots, and bean sprouts	春卷
Ho yip fan: steamed fried rice wrapped in lotus leaf	荷叶饭
Pai gwat: steamed pork spareribs	排骨
Gai chuk: steamed chicken in bean curd wrapping	腐竹包鸡
Daan tart: egg custard tart	蛋挞

Fujian Dishes 福建菜

Lots of seafood and light soups, suckling pig, and nonfat spring rolls. You may recognize Filipino dishes like *lumpia* and *lechon*, originally from this province.

Five spices roll	五香卷
Fried fish slices	炒鱼片
Fried pig's kidneys	炒腰片
Spareribs in sweet-sour sauce	糖醋排骨
Fish with Brown Sauce	红烧全鱼
Fried straw mushrooms with pork	草菇肉片
Fried shrimps in sweet-sour sauce	糖醋虾
Fried razor clams in sweet-sour sauce	糖醋鲜蚌

Hangzhou Dishes 杭州菜

Shelled shrimp with *long jing* tea leaves	龙井虾仁
Beggar's chicken	叫化鸡
West Lake fish in vinegar sauce	西湖醋鱼
Steamed pork dumplings	小笼包子

Mongolian Dishes

Mostly mutton.

Hot pot (cooked at the table in soup)	涮锅
Mongolian barbecue	蒙古烤肉
Sauteed mutton with leek	葱爆羊肉

Shaanxi Dishes

(From the Yan'an Guest House in **Yanan**)

Fried spring roll   炸春卷
Buckwheat noodles   乔吕饸铬
Fried millet cake with sugar   油炸软米羔
Millet drink (nonalcoholic)   米酒
Mutton and egg, fried crisply   锅烧羊肉
Fragrant, crisp chicken   香酥鸭
Thin pancakes with meat and vegetables   煎并
Fried potatoes with syrup   拔丝土豆
Potato balls   油炸土豆丸子
Eight-jewel pumpkin   八宝蜜汁南瓜

(From the Dongya Restaurant in **Xi'an**)

Assorted cold dishes in the shape of a phoenix   凤凰拼饼
Four small cold dishes   四围碟
Sea cucumber in the shape and color of hibis-   芙蓉海参
cus
Crisp fried duck   香酥鸭
Mushrooms with the Three Delicacies   口蘑三样
Fried fillet of chicken   炸鸡排
Shark's fins with three kinds of slices (pork,   三丝鱼翅
bamboo shoots, and chicken)   鸡丝拉皮
Fried fish shaped like grapes   清蒸鲤鱼
Steamed carp   菠萝银耳
White fungus with pineapple   点   心
Cakes and pastries   冰 淇 淋

Shandong Dishes 山东菜

Abalone with green vegetables on shell   鲍鱼青菜
Fresh scallops with shell   鲜带壳干贝
Roast prawns   烤大虾
Conch with fire   火螺
Steamed sea bream   馒头
Sweet and sour croaker   酸甜黄花鱼
Three Delicacies Soup   三鲜汤
Toffee Apples   拔丝苹果

Shanghai Dishes 沪菜

From central China; Suzhou, Yangzhou, Wuxi, etc. foods are variations. Longer cooking in sesame oil, neither sweet nor salty. Can be
very ornamental. Borsch is on the menu of most of Shanghai's restaurants because of all the White Russians who once lived in Shanghai.
Shrimp in tomato sauce

Smoked fish   熏鱼
Deep-fried shrimp balls   炸虾球
Vegetarian vegetables   素什锦
Sauteed fresh bamboo shoots   红烧冬笋
West Lake fish   西湖醋鱼
Chicken with cashew nuts   西湖醋鱼
Scallops with turnip balls   干贝萝卜球
Won-ton (dumplings) in soup   虾仁馄饨
Beggar's chicken   叫化鸡
Sauteed egg plant   红烧茄子
Lion's head casserole   红烧狮子头
Sweet sesame dumplings   芝蔴汤园

Sichuan (Szechuan) Dishes 川菜

Some dishes are highly spiced, peppery hot, and oily. Formal banquet cooking is more bland.

Smoked duck with camphor and tea flavor   樟茶鸭
  (not spicy hot)
Stir-fried chicken with hot pepper   官爆鸡丁
Spicy stir-fried prawns   干烧明虾
Stir-fried shrimp with peas   碗豆炒虾仁
Stir-fried squid with/without hot pepper   金钩鱿鱼
Bon-bon chicken   棒棒鸡
Dry-fried string beans   干煸四季豆
Steamed spareribs (or pork) coated with rice   粉蒸排骨
  powder
Steamed fish with fermented black beans   豆豉鱼
Mo-po bean curd   麻婆豆腐

Suzhou Dishes 京菜

Sauteed shrimp meat   清炒虾仁
Squirrel Mandarin fish   松鼠桂鱼
Stewed turtle   清蒸元鱼
Stir-fried eel   生炒鳝贝
Fried crisp duck   香酥肥鸭
Water-shield soup with floating Mandarin duck   鸳鸯莼菜汤
Snow-white crab in shell   白雪蟹斗
Pickled duck   苏州酱鸭

Vegetarian cooking has had a long tradition in China and was first documented 2000 years ago. It developed with Buddhism, which forbids its adherents from killing animals, and restaurants are frequently found near Buddhist temples. Distinctively Chinese are dishes that imitate meat in taste, texture, and looks. While this does not encourage reverence for life as taught by Buddha, it does make it easier for some Buddhists to become vegetarian.

The following are some suggested dishes from the Ju Shi Lih Restaurant near the Lama Temple in Beijing and should give you an idea of what is available. Sorry, no calligraphy available yet.

Hors d'oeuvres
Water chestnuts and bean curd
Mushrooms and bamboo shoots
Shrimps (actually carrots, cucumber, bamboo
   shoots, mushrooms, radish)
Black and white fungi
Sea crab (actually potato, radish, mushroom,
   bamboo shoots)
Roast duck (actually bean curd)
Sweet and sour pork (actually locust seed)
Fish ball soup (tomato and celery)

GETTING AROUND

If you have someone taking care of all the logistics, read this only for reference. The following is how things were at press time. Since then, the Chinese have probably made improvements.

▶ **Note:** A cancellation fee is always charged when you make changes in travel arrangements.

It is always best, no matter where and how you go, to have your destination written in Chinese so you can ask for directions. At least carry the name of your hotel in Chinese in case you stray from your tour group.

Always carry a wad of toilet tissue with you.

If you are traveling overnight by hard-class train, or by ferry (not a luxury tourist ship), take your own mug, soap, chopsticks, and towel.

The low tourist season is mid-November to mid-March, at which time many hotel prices are discounted and life is easier for individual travelers. But individual travelers should still expect difficulties, such as missing trains because you can't find the right platform. Few, if any, signs exist in English.

Formalities You are allowed to go to any of a wide range of cities and counties in China without further formalities. You have to get an **alien travel permit** to go to other places even if just traveling by road between open cities.

Foreign travelers who have inadvertently (or deliberately) wandered into a restricted area have been detained by the police, sometimes questioned most impolitely, and put on the next bus out. At least one has been charged excessively for taxis used to transport her.

Getting visas and visa extensions: If your visa has expired, you will probably be detained when you try to leave the country. Visa extensions can be acquired from the Foreign Affairs Department of the Security Police in one or two days. Be sure you take your passport and a few *yuan*.

Literature China has been producing a large number of maps and guidebooks in English. The Cartographic Department maps are very helpful as they include maps of important tourist attractions in many cities. Jinan's, for example, also shows Taishan Mountain and Qufu (with diagrams of the Confucian Family Mansion and Confucian temple). These maps list major hotels, tourist attractions, restaurants, stores, and important telephone numbers. The China City Guides series is excellent for background. Like the maps, one exists for most major cities. They are inexpensive and worth buying if you want to wander around on your own. Some cities also have public transportation maps.

The China Travel & Tourism Press has a lot of good information in English. Its main store is across the road from the Beijing Hotel in Beijing (but you might not find anyone speaking English there). Better try its office at Room 304, Chongwenmen Hotel (tel. 757181, X304) and ask for Lu Niangao, deputy chief editor, who speaks excellent English. This company publishes picture books, calendars, maps, cook books, and the excellent little *Old Tales of China.*

Many tourist attractions now have relatively inexpensive, knowledgeable **on-site guides** paid by the hour. A few of the important tourist spots have English-speaking guides, but most speak only Chinese. You could also eavesdrop on someone else's English-speaking guide.

Diplomatic missions are not travel agencies, but some of them have libraries with books about China. The U.S. consulates have current travel advisories with up-to-date information on health problems, natural disasters, and shortages of hotel rooms. Consulates should also have important addresses like those of doctors and pharmacies.

Travel agencies make traveling easier, but not all services are cheap or available. The main travel agency for foreigners is China International Travel Service. For Overseas Chinese and Hong Kong, Macao, and Taiwan Compatriots, it is China Travel Service. They, along with China Youth Travel Service, China Sports Service, and the travel and tourism administrations, are government agencies. Sometimes the distinctions between them are fuzzy, and you could try any of them if you need help.

Private travel agencies have also opened in some cities, but so far most serve only Chinese tourists. We have only found one in Beijing for foreigners. This might change. Some hotels organize tours for their own guests, so ask at travel or service desks in luxury hotels. Some foreign travel agencies have representatives in China who will be able to give you information about *their own* tours.

You should always double-check the number of tickets you are buying, and times and dates. The efficiency of any ticket seller or travel agency depends on its individual representatives. Some clerks have also been rude, especially when harassed and tired; others have been pleasant and polite.

China International Travel Service (C.I.T.S.), in Chinese **Zhong Kuo Kuo Zi Luxingshe** (pronounced Loo-shing-sheh), organizes prepaid tours around China with a guide who speaks one of several languages besides Chinese. Most guides speak English. C.I.T.S. can arrange for someone to meet you at an airport, buy travel tickets for you, reserve hotel rooms and sightseeing tours, confirm flights, obtain travel permits, etc. It can provide guide-interpreters and also book individual travelers on minipackages to the cities listed under *Minipackages* in "'Basics"; 91% of its clients are on tour packages of more than 10 people. F.I.T.s make up only 9%.

C.I.T.S. isn't always able to give all its services to individual travelers, especially during high tourist seasons when guides are busy with groups. You may have to find someone else to help you then, do some of these annoying and time-consuming essentials yourself, or do without. Some travelers have found that going two or three to a taxi locally is cheaper than taking some C.I.T.S. tours.

But C.I.T.S. is the most experienced and most efficient of the agencies helping foreigners, with the largest number of branches around the country. It usually has an office in or near every tourist center. It also has a booking office in Hong Kong. In a few small cities, notably in Guangdong and Fujian provinces, it is represented by China Travel Service. Some C.I.T.S. branches have joint ventures with foreign tour companies. C.I.T.S. has information offices in Frankfurt, London, New York, Paris, and Tokyo.

C.I.T.S. was founded in 1954. In 1964, it came under the Travel and Tourism Administration, which is directly under the State Council. From 1967 to 1969, some branches were closed due to the Cultural Revolution. In 1981, the State Council appointed C.I.T.S. to also study, coordinate, and supervise the development of tourism in China. C.I.T.S.'s national headquarters in Beijing arranges national tours.

The people who escort foreign visitors are guide-interpreters, "guides" for short. Most are graduates of universities or foreign-languages institutes, with three or four years of foreign-language training at this level.

Training has been on the job, usually learned by accompanying an experienced guide for several months. But C.I.T.S. has been so short-handed at times that some guides with little English and training have been used. The Department of Education is now responsible for staff training, and prospective guides are currently spending four years learning a language, Chinese history, geography, and art history.

If you are on a group tour of several cities, you get a national guide who stays with you during your whole stay in China. At each city you also get a different local guide and, at some tourist attractions, an on-the-spot guide.

For most visitors, your Chinese escorts will be the only Chinese people you can get to know with any depth. Guides are open about discussing their salaries and their training, especially if they like you. You could ask them questions, like how much money do they make?

do they get bonuses? how much is their rent? what happens if a tour group misses a plane? who pays?

They could retaliate with "How much do *you* make?"

You might also want to ask if guides get kickbacks or gifts from the stores and factories to which they take their tours. If so, then your guide might be steering you in these directions. In any case, visitors intent more on seeing China than on shopping or eating should do some counter-steering.

One important question is, can guides accept gifts? Officially, they are not allowed to ask for gifts or money, nor to accept them, but no one quibbles over little souvenirs. See *Gifts* in "What to Take." Money left as tips for guides might be sent back to the foreign tour organizers!

In over a dozen trips to China, I have only met one guide who was not conscientious.

Please be patient when a guide is speaking English. If it is painful to listen to, keep muttering to yourself, "This is better than nothing." A confusion over numbers is one of the most common translation problems. The Chinese think in terms of ten thousands rather than thousands. Do not mistake sixteen for sixty, seventeen for seventy, either. Ask your guide to write down big or important figures for you. When you are using an interpreter, speak slowly. Phrase what you want to be translated simply, one sentence at a time.

Also remember that unlike Greek tour guides, Chinese guides are not scholars. Their knowledge of traditional Chinese culture is frequently limited to the few books they read. Studying the old culture and history was strongly discouraged during the Cultural Revolution, when many of these people were students. This lack of knowledge is also being remedied now.

Guides are not usually allowed to eat with you. At mealtimes, they can be found in a staff dining room. They also stay in your hotel overnight. It is good insurance to ask where they can be reached.

For more information on C.I.T.S., see "The Basics," "Before You Go," and "Getting There."

China Travel Service (C.T.S.) has 270 branches and 20,000 staff members, and handles more visitors than C.I.T.S. Many of its clients, however, know Chinese and can manage largely on their own. C.T.S. operates especially in Guangdong and Fujian, the two provinces with the most Overseas Chinese visitors. Its tours also take Foreign Friends, especially friends and spouses of Overseas Chinese and Compatriots. The children of Overseas Chinese, but not the spouses, are considered Overseas Chinese. You may have to do some arguing to qualify if you don't look Chinese.

C.T.S. can do all the things C.I.T.S. does for travelers. It can also arrange permission and transportation to one's ancestral village and ship gifts to relatives. It can help you locate long-lost relatives. It does have fewer English-speaking guides than C.I.T.S., but there is at least one in every branch. It does not appear to be as efficient as C.I.T.S. with individual arrangements.

C.T.S.-controlled hotels are usually cheaper and less classy than those for Foreign Friends. But C.T.S. can book deluxe hotels too. C.T.S. tours usually take second place to C.I.T.S. tours (except where the tour guide has *guanxi*).

Since Overseas Chinese can travel on planes and trains more cheaply than Foreign Friends, stay in some hotels at discount prices, and usually have no need for an English-speaking guide, C.T.S. tour prices are cheaper than C.I.T.S. tours. Individual travelers can book through C.T.S. Individual Foreign Friends have a much better chance of being booked by C.T.S. if they are traveling with an Overseas Chinese who can act as interpreter for them.

China Youth Travel Service's main task is to receive groups of young people, but it also takes care of older people. It has a total of 50 branches and is represented in every province. Tour prices are a little cheaper than C.I.T.S.'s because of student discounts and less luxurious accommodations. Sometimes young people are put into school dormitories normally used by foreign students, but mostly they are billeted in hotels. C.Y.T.S. also can arrange informal sports competitions with Chinese youth.

C.Y.T.S. has an office in Hong Kong that seems better organized for answering letters than that in Beijing. See "Getting There."

China Sports Service Company handles formal international sports competitions and demonstrations, motorcycle tours, and television rights to international sporting events in China. It is affiliated with the All-China Sports Federation, but you don't have to be a professional or even a serious athlete to go this route. It has over 30 branches, with representation in every province. Among its services are skiing, hunting, and sky diving packages, Ping-Pong and martial arts clinics (the latter in Shaolin Temple itself). If anyone wants to meet China's Olympic gold medalist, C.S.S. should be able to arrange it. See also "The Basics."

Travel and Tourism Administrations are in every province and can arrange regional prepaid tours. They work closely with C.I.T.S.

TRANSPORTATION

Flying The services of Chinese airlines are usually basic. Tickets have to be paid for at least 24 hours before scheduled departure time. Credit cards are still not accepted, though individual travelers can now pay by traveler's checks as well as cash. All reservations have to be reconfirmed or you risk being bumped off your flight, but you cannot reconfirm with CAAC in China by telephone. The ticket has to be stamped. C.I.T.S. and C.T.S. should be able to do this for a fee, but are not always able. When you reconfirm, ask for the check-in time. It is best to arrive at the airport early in case of overbooking.

Until recently, CAAC has been the only airline operating domestically in China since Liberation. In pre-Liberation days, it was originally known as China National Aviation Corporation. In 1949 it became the Civil Aviation Administration of China (CAAC), and now the General Administration of Civil Aviation of China. All of its financing has been government.

The aviation industry in China is currently being restructured. In the last few years, confusing reports have circulated about CAAC's plans. Currently, as far as can be ascertained, it is replacing some of its ancient planes with new and better ones, and overseeing the organization of several new airlines. CAAC will continue to manage civil aviation generally in China, including safety standards and airports, licensing and international relations.

The restructuring will result in: (1) **state airlines,** one of which will carry out international operations. Five others will operate regionally in China; (2) **provincial airlines,** run by provinces and autonomous regions in cooperation with CAAC. Some of these will be totally managed by the provinces; (3) **airlines operating only within the boundaries of a province;** and (4) **general aviation**—for agriculture, exploration, etc.

The schedules of all airlines should be printed, as they become available, in the airline guides used by travel agents abroad. In China, C.I.T.S. and CAAC should be able to make bookings. English-language schedules can now be obtained from CAAC offices in major cities.

Making domestic reservations should improve soon, especially out of Beijing and Shanghai, as the computerization of the reservation system gets completed. There you should be able to make reservations 15 days before a flight. Ticket offices are being opened in airports. You may still have to wait until you arrive in China to make domestic bookings.

CAAC airport bus service from most downtown CAAC offices (and vice versa) is included in the price of tickets.

In the mid-1980s, CAAC flew Tridents, Viscounts, 747s, 707s, A310-200 airbuses, Shorts 360s, Chinese-made planes, and old Soviet planes on **domestic flights.** Announcements are usually made in *pu tung hua* and English. Following a couple of hijackings, security at airports has tightened, with metal detectors and body searches. Uniformed guards also scrutinize passengers in departure lounges.

Most flights have only economy class, but a growing number also offer first class. The food served is usually cold (and dry) and no alcoholic beverages are available. Some overhead luggage racks are open and allowed to be overstuffed. Call the attendant if you think the goods will fall on your head. Be sure to confirm delays with more than one official before you go back into town or whatever. Flights have taken off without all their original passengers because of conflicting information.

With competition and more and bigger planes, domestic services should continue to improve. But don't expect world-class service yet.

The following **regulations** have been in effect in China but are subject to change: open-dated domestic tickets are valid for 90 days; fixed-date tickets are good only for the date and flight on the ticket. If you cancel the ticket prior to two hours before scheduled departure time, you are charged a modest cancellation fee. If you apply within two hours of flight time, you are charged 20% of the fare. If you fail to cancel before flight time, *there is no refund.*

The 20 kg (for economy class) and 30 kg (for first class) free baggage allowance for full- or half-adult-fare passengers seem to be *strictly enforced* except for travelers flying into China with larger allowances. Carry-on baggage should not exceed 9″ by 16″ by 20″, but frequently does.

No babies under 10 days of age and no pregnant women almost due are allowed to fly. An infant under two not occupying a separate seat and accompanied by an adult is charged 10% of the adult fare. Children 2–12 are charged 50% of the adult fare.

Helicopter service is available in some cities for sightseeing, sometimes on charter.

CAAC operates **international flights** almost the same as other international airlines, but again with minimal services. Flights have headsets for music and movies, and have alcoholic drinks. Reservations will be canceled unless reconfirmed on flights wholly within Europe. Full refunds on international tickets are made if you cancel before check-in time. A 25% cancellation fee is charged for "no shows." The free baggage allowance on flights to China from North America is two pieces each, with size and weight limits dependent on class.

An airport tax is charged on all departing international flights, including those to Hong Kong. Exceptions are diplomats, transit passengers, and children under 12. Passengers holding international tickets with confirmed space on the first connecting flight should get free meals and hotel accommodations provided by CAAC within 24 hours after their arrival at the connecting points.

Foreign airlines also fly to China, but their operations are restricted. China-based agents of these airlines cannot sell tickets, for example, but they can book their own flights on open-dated CAAC tickets, purchased from CAAC without difficulty.

Trains China has a vast network of railways, linking every provincial and regional capital except Lhasa to Beijing. And even that omission is being remedied. Railway lines have been burgeoning in the 1980s.

Since the travel agencies cannot be counted on to buy tickets for individual travelers, especially during high tourist seasons, you might have to go to the railway station and buy them yourself. In some big cities, special ticket windows are provided for foreigners, but line-ups can be long, especially for hard class. Best buy your tickets at least two days in advance to avoid the worst queues. Scalpers around train stations and in some coffee shops can buy tickets for you for F.E.C. equivalents of local prices. While this is illegal, everybody does it. One pays upon receipt. Travelers have boarded trains using platform tickets and then bought tickets from the conductor on the train. This, however, is risky, as space may not be available.

Except for international trains originating abroad, train tickets can only be booked in China.

Train schedules in English for all Chinese trains are now available. They may be difficult to find, but ask for them at C.I.T.S., book stores, and hotel service desks. They can be bought in Chinese in Hong Kong (Peace Book Store, Commercial Press, etc.). Be sure to give yourself plenty of time to find your train; platforms are not marked in English.

Like travel on overnight ferries, men and women are assigned berths without regard to sex even in soft class. If this arrangement bothers you, ask for another compartment. The Chinese are used to such travel and are not embarrassed. Tourist groups usually sort themselves out. I have never heard of sexual harassment on a train in China, so don't feel nervous. One can get used to sleeping in one's clothes and washing with strangers of the opposite sex nearby.

If you're *desperate* and can't wait for roommates to leave, change your clothes in the toilet room. You could also ask your roommates to wait outside your compartment for a moment while you change, undress under the covers, or wait until the lights are out. Businessmen wearing suits might look a little wrinkled next day, but who cares? Wrinkles aren't all that important in China.

To protect valuables, do not use your purse as a pillow. Things have been stolen that way. Put your valuables in a money belt around your waist. Tie your camera to your arm.

Toilets look like they've been hosed down and not scrubbed. On coaches reserved for foreign tourists, you can be quite sure of toilet paper and soap (in a common soap dish). Soft-class travelers on some trains now have a choice of a Western toilet seat or a squat.

A washroom in each car offers several sinks with running water. Many prepaid tourists wait until they arrive at their hotels before washing. However, sometimes on arrival early in the morning hotel rooms have not yet been vacated, and tourists are frequently taken sightseeing or to breakfast instead.

Trains are usually hot and dusty in the summer, unless you are lucky and find yourself in one of the new air-conditioned cars. If you find yourself trapped with smokers, ask them to smoke out in the corridor. China has no "no smoking" areas yet. Luggage is frequently pushed in and out of train windows. Conductors sometimes check luggage, demanding payment for overweight. On trains slowed by too much weight, people with luggage over their limits have been asked to get rid of some bags, or leave with all of it.

Do not discard your ticket. You are asked for it again at the exit gate of your arrival station.

Trains are special express, express, regular, and suburban. Passengers could have a choice of hard- and soft-class seats and hard- and soft-class berths. The most comfortable are in the middle of a coach, away from noise and wheel vibrations. When you buy your ticket, state your preference.

Prepaid tourists usually travel **soft-class berth,** which can be almost the same price as going by plane. The berths are the height of bourgeois comfort if you have air conditioning. Compartments usually have clean slipcovers with lace doilies, lace curtains, a 16″ by 24″ table with a lamp and potted plant, an overhead fan, four porcelain mugs (for tea), and sleeping spaces with bedding and towels for four people on two uppers and two lowers. An overhead loft stores large suitcases, but you have to rely on strong arms to get them up there and down. Train conductors are usually very helpful and friendly. An attendant keeps refilling the thermos of hot water and sweeping the floors.

It is best to take a small overnight bag if you are sleeping on the train, unless you want to do acrobatics or limit your leg room. Most group luggage is stored at one end of the car and may not be easily accessible.

Compartment doors can be closed for privacy. Do not worry if you cannot lock them from the outside. The conductor usually locks your door when you go to the dining car. The plug for the fan (if you have one) and the switch for the loudspeaker are under the table.

Dining-car food is edible and, on some trains, surprisingly good, but simple, Passengers usually give their orders to a steward beforehand and are notified when their food is ready.

Six people share one compartment of **hard-class berths** in the same amount of space as "soft." Berths are padded, however, and tiered in threes with even less privacy, the middle berth being the best.

Hard class is noisy and dirty, with frequent clearing of throats and spitting on the floor. You also cannot turn off the loudspeaker, which starts at 6 a.m. every morning. The coaches are mopped frequently. Sheets and warm blankets are provided, but if you get on between the two terminals, these may already have been used. Passengers can eat in the dining car, but can also buy food from vendors at train stations or circulating on the train itself. Don't expect gourmet fare! In fact, food from vendors can be downright unappetizing, like a box of rice with pork (including the skin, with hair left on). It might be best to bring your own instant noodles if you're on a tight budget. Steaming hot water is available in each car.

Accommodations can be upgraded after the train is underway if space is available.

China is talking about building and importing luxury-class, double-decker railway cars.

Long-distance buses Air-conditioned buses speed along a few routes, especially from Hong Kong and Macao, and in other parts of the country as well. Ask about the kind of bus you will be taking because some buses are small, hard-seated, and very crowded, with little luggage space except on the roof. They can be uncomfortable for big foreigners, especially if you have to stand or squat. Not all highways are paved. Still, buses are good for seeing the countryside and meeting people—but you have to be young in spirit, strong, and adventurous. You usually book ahead of time at a bus station. Frequently Overseas Chinese and foreigners are invited to board first as a gesture of hospitality. C.I.T.S. operates some of the better buses.

Long-distance ferries Overnight ships between Hong Kong and Chinese ports usually have small, comfortable, but not luxurious cabins. See "Getting There." For boats on the Yangtze, see "Yangtze Gorges." For small one-class ships, see "Jiangmen." Some ferries have good reputations, like those between Shanghai and Ningpo. The ferry between Guangzhou and Haikou is said to be dirty, however. Standards are uneven. Take a supply of seasick pills if you're susceptible. Take your own mug, towel, chopsticks, and soap on overnight trips.

Accidents have occurred because of overcrowding.

By road Some but not all roads are being opened to foreigners. The problem is military zones. Open for your visit is the road from Shanghai to Beijing. Ask the China Youth Travel Service about others. Tour groups of self-drive cars have already started. Studies are being made that should allow foreigners to bring their own jeeps and boats (for touring the Yellow River).

It is possible to hire a **taxi** to take you from city to city, but you have to pay the return fare if you leave it at a city other than its home base. Always ask ahead of time for the approximate fare and distance and if you need an Alien Travel Permit. See "Budget."

Hitchhiking has been and may have to be done. Backpackers have hitched rides with truck drivers. On-your-own tourists in isolated spots like the cave temples near Dunhuang (with only two public buses a day) have been able to get rides on tour buses (sometimes free). It's a matter of luck. If you have connections with foreign experts, etc., you might be able to use staff cars for much lower rates than taxis.

LOCAL TRANSPORTATION

Bicycles can be rented in some cities, but riding is not always encouraged because of the high risk of accidents. Some cities like Guangzhou have stopped rentals because the traffic is already too heavy. You could try to rent or borrow a bicycle in places like Guilin and Hang-zhou, where sightseeing by bicycle is ideal. If C.I.T.S. discourages bicycle riding, ask a hotel attendant where you can rent one.

Some rented bicycles have fallen apart. Be sure to check the brakes, tires, bell, lock, etc. You will probably have to leave some identification, like a passport, or a deposit; guard your receipt carefully. Always park in a supervised parking lot; otherwise your bicycle may disappear, to be found again at a police station, you hope. Make a note of what it looks like, the license number, and the place where you have left it. Finding it quickly again among hundreds of identical bicycles may otherwise be a problem. Most cities have bicycle lanes, and some have streets forbidden to bicycles.

If you are staying any length of time in China, you might want to buy a Chinese bicycle and sell it when you leave. China makes a lot of bicycles, but few locally made ones have more than one speed. Phoenix has a 10-speed, but I don't know how good it is.

Officially all bicycles should have bicycle licenses, but most foreign riders have had no trouble riding without one. Some people have taken their own bicycles into China hoping to travel around the country, but only a few have been able to do this, and some have had to leave their bicycles behind because of the hassles. (To ship a bicycle by train means having to go to the train station a day ahead of time and, at the other end, spending time finding it.) Riding from city to city is usually impossible because of restricted zones. With the opening of some roads to foreigners, you might be able to bicycle between Shanghai and Beijing, for example. Spare parts for foreign makes are also a problem.

Group bicycle tours are available, but they are not cheap. A truck carrying spare parts follows behind, picking up tired bikers. Some of these tours allow you to use your own bicycles and arrange for their transportation.

Motorscooter rickshaws for two or more are cheaper than taxis and could take lots of luggage, but they are not comfortable, with much swerving and bouncing. Prices are often fixed and paid in advance at a stand.

Bicycle rickshaws built for two cost very little, but you can only go short distances. Please consider the driver and get off and walk up steep slopes. Bicycle rickshaws are ideal for leisurely sightseeing in places like Hangzhou. Big cities seem to be phasing them out, and please don't ride them in heavy motorized traffic since they can be dangerous. Do agree on a price in advance, especially in tourist towns, where revolutionary morals have given way to market forces. Make sure the price is for the ride, not for each person. If the driver demands something exorbitant, just hand him what is fair and walk away. If the price is right, he won't scream at you.

Taxis are normally found outside most tourist hotels, at railway stations, airports, and passenger-ship quays. Some can be found outside

Friendship Stores and places frequented by visitors. If these places don't have taxi stands of their own, their service desks should telephone for a taxi for you, even though you may not be a customer. If you are not near any of these places, you can still ask someone to help you telephone for a taxi. See "Useful Phrases." Taxis can be flagged on the street in only a few cities (notably Guangzhou). In some places, taxi drivers don't want to go short distances.

Taxis are not always easy to find. If you have several stops to make, it is usually better to hire a taxi by the half day or day, and have the driver wait for you. Or you could pay by the meter (or odometer) with a charge for "waiting time." Always check rates before you go. Usually you need not pay for a meal for a driver if you are near his home base, but you might invite the driver to a meal if you are a long way away. Restaurants and hotels have sections for staff if you don't want to eat together.

If you need a taxi early in the morning or for a full or half day, it is best to make a reservation at the taxi stand the night before. Taxi companies also have minibuses for larger groups.

Not all taxis have meters, and drivers have been known to cheat. While most drivers are honest, a few have added unused "waiting time" in Chinese to the receipts, or just charged higher rates. Taxi drivers without meters should calculate fares according to the distance per taxi, not per passenger. See "Budget" for recent per kilometer rate. (See *Getting from the Airport to Your Hotel* in "Getting There" for other tricks.) It would be wise to ask the price before you go and *make a note of the odometer reading before you start*. Ask for a receipt. If the driver doesn't give you one, he may be pocketing the money himself. You have to pay for many taxis in F.E.C.s.

If you feel a driver is cheating you, don't pay, and ask *cheerfully* for someone to call a policeman to mediate. Hotel and C.I.T.S. staff members should know the distance from the airport, and between tourist attractions. If you have already paid, get a receipt, take the driver's name and license number, and complain to the manager or dispatcher at his/her taxi stand. Ask your consulate for advice. Some cities have a taxi complaint office. Letters of complaint to *China Daily* have resulted in penalties for the driver and apologies from the taxi company.

Another ploy is to pay what you consider the proper fare, get out, and leave. If the driver follows you, then reconsider your calculations and negotiate a settlement.

Some drivers charge extra because they have to pay the touts who bring them customers. Try to avoid the middle man. Some drivers will give you R.M.B. instead of F.E.C.s in change. Drivers who cheat are a new phenomenon and should be discouraged.

Public tour buses are available in a few cities, notably Beijing, offering relatively cheap transportation to some tourist attractions. Few have detailed commentary in English, but descriptions of tourist sites are in this and other guides. Best take your own lunch to save time eating in restaurants, and make sure you know how long your bus is staying at each stop. Write down the bus number so you can find it again. Some of these buses can be booked through C.I.T.S. and at the depot. Ask at Overseas Chinese hotels.

Hotel tour buses. Some hotels are organizing tours to popular tourist spots.

Public city buses are usually very crowded, especially during the early-morning and late-afternoon rush hours, and all day Sunday. But they are cheap and are often your only means of transportation. Try them if you are athletic or adventurous. Hotel personnel can tell you which bus to take. Some cities have bus maps in English. Or you can take a map with you and point. Fellow passengers are usually friendly and helpful, and may even get up to give you a seat.

As in all crowded places, beware of pickpockets.

Subways are in Beijing, and maps are available. Walk down the stairs, pay your money (cheap), and choose your platform.

Public ferries and tour boats. China has some real antiques crossing harbors and rivers. They are cheap, but avoid them if they look too crowded and tippy. Fatal accidents with tour boats have recently been blamed on overloading and drunken crews.

Something has to be said about **walking** because of all the bicycles. Crossing streets can be dangerous. Try to let a native upstream run interference. Cross at lights. Some cities have overpasses—use them!

TELEPHONES

As a general rule, Chinese citizens do not have private telephones yet (though the situation is improving). Sets are available in most urban neighborhoods, factories, and offices, with a small sign in Chinese about seven feet from the ground by the door. Cheap. Each village usually has at least one telephone in the village office. China is currently putting a lot of effort into improving telecommunications, but in the meantime, one can, for example, leave a message asking your friends to telephone you at your hotel. Be sure to give your room number.

The easiest way to call long distance and overseas is at your hotel. Apply at the service desk. See "Hotels." These calls can also be made at a Post and Telecommunications office, where reception might be better.

LOCAL CUSTOMS AND EMERGENCIES

DOES "YES" MEAN "YES"? Well, usually. Cultural differences do create misunderstandings. For example, a memorandum of understanding in trade means there is reason to believe that negotiations can begin in earnest. It does not mean, as many foreigners have sadly discovered, that a contract has been signed. The official dealt with might be overruled by his superior. Also, if a Chinese nods and says "yes, yes," he could be just trying to please you. He may not understand a word you are saying. So be wary. Ask a question that needs a full sentence in reply. For the same reason, a Chinese might give you dates and spellings and swear they are right. But what he means is that it is the best information he has and if you press him, he will check—but if you don't, he won't bother.

Chinese people are very polite in their personal relationships with friends or business acquaintances—people they will see again and again. They try not to hurt feelings, yours or their own. If you make a mistake, the very polite ones will not point it out to you. If you do something they do not like, they might ask someone senior to you to talk to you about it. My aunt was asked to criticize me when my nieces thought my clothes were a little too risque.

But Chinese people may not seem polite at times, especially crowds, or clerks in government stores. But if someone introduces you properly, most Chinese will prove to be extremely hospitable and helpful. The shop girl who ignores you is probably afraid of you or bored and unfulfilled by her job. Don't take it personally.

Once I caught my knee in the door of a crowded bus and got a bruise that lasted for weeks. At the time, my cousins laughed while I felt like crying. It was just their way of reacting—probably embarrassment, not knowing how else to react. Just don't feel offended.

DOES "NO" MEAN "NO"? Well, sometimes. You will have to judge for yourself when a negative decision can be challenged. If the wording is "it is not convenient" then it's a definite "no." If it's "it is too difficult" or "it is not allowed" then maybe there is a chance of a "yes."

One scholar was told he couldn't swim but insisted on it anyway, and his escorts didn't mind. The reason was concern for his safety, and when he survived, everything was hunky-dory. Can you imagine how embarrassed the Chinese would be if an honored guest drowned!

By protesting to a hotel clerk who said there was no room, I did get a bed in a dorm. This does not mean you should try to argue every time you are told "it is not possible," or that "your safety cannot be guaranteed." It could mean (1) language is a problem and they do not understand your request; (2) they don't want to be bothered trying; (3) they don't want too many people going there, but if you insist, they'll let you go; (4) there is genuine concern for your safety; (5) you really aren't allowed to go.

Arguing is an art too. Do not lose your temper or you've lost the battle. You should argue as much as possible in their terms. For example, one single traveler was put, as is the custom, in a small banquet room in one hotel for meals. There were no other foreign guests and the room was dingy and depressing. With a waitress standing by watching it was more like a prison. Two requests to move into the main dining room with the Chinese guests were refused. Single Traveler decided to go to a restaurant instead, pointing out to her guide that it was her problem. She said she was willing to pay for the hotel meals too, but she just couldn't bear eating alone under the circumstances. She was allowed to eat with the others.

Note: Sometimes no answer is a "no."

ASK QUESTIONS An official of the Overseas Chinese Travel Service once told me the only advice he had for visitors was, "Ask questions." It is good advice. For some reason, the Chinese do not volunteer much information. It might have something to do with their own lines of communication. So when in doubt, ask!

APPLAUSE You will frequently be greeted by applause as a sign of welcome or appreciation at institutions and cultural performances. It might even happen on the streets. The usual response is to applaud back.

CRITICISMS AND SUGGESTIONS You may be asked for these and see many booklets in hotels, train dining cars, and restaurants with this title. If you have any criticisms and suggestions, do give them. I wrote 23 pages myself on one trip. But don't go on about how things are done in North America. Much doesn't apply to China. Criticisms should be helpful in the context of a developing country. Criticisms and suggestions are considered seriously, especially now that China is trying to improve her tourist facilities. Yes, mention that the bathroom floor is filthy. Go further than that and ask the attendant to clean it. If an attendant has been particularly helpful, write it down. She may get a bonus because of it.

TIPPING is forbidden. Officially it is considered insulting. The attendants themselves may have other feelings, but they are now only allowed very minor gifts. But some attendants and guides do accept tips and even ask for it. The late 1980s is an era of transition and new rules are developing. See *Gifts* in "What to Take."

GOOD MANNERS at home are good manners anywhere. Don't litter. Don't take "souvenirs," especially from historical places, such as a rock from the Great Wall. Don't pick flowers in parks.

In most other Asian countries it is fashionable to be late. Not so in China, where groups of children may be outside in the rain waiting for your car so they can applaud as you arrive.

Traditionally, Chinese conversations, even business conversations, start out with something innocuous: a discussion of the weather, of the calligraphy or a painting on the wall, or whatever. A mood of friendliness is set first. Then comes the business.

It is true that Chinese people themselves may not be polite in crowds. They may surround your bus and stare at you, crowd around when it's hot and ignore your pleas for help. But it is their country and just because you paid a lot of money to visit, it doesn't mean you can be rude.

And please don't spoil them. Guilin is already notorious. If strangers ask you for lighters or other "gifts," do not give. If they beg you to send them a particular English textbook, use your own judgment. They may be selling them.

JOKING ABOUT POLITICS AND SEX Many visitors are warned not to joke about sex or politics, particularly Chinese politics. To joke about sex is considered crude, and you condemn yourself when you do it. To joke about politics or even to argue about it is to show lack of sensitivity. Politics is taken very seriously in China. People are put into jail because of it, lose their jobs, waste years of schooling, and spend long hours in meetings discussing political implications.

BEGGARS Yes, there are a few. Use your own discretion. As I would in New York City, I would ask them why they have to beg, and then decide whether or not to give. Or I might take them to the closest restaurant and give them a meal. Or ignore.

FLIRTING You may be tempted to flirt with a cute Chinese citizen of the opposite sex. Friendliness is appreciated, but anything beyond that used to and still may mean an interview with the Security Police, where you are asked why you insulted a Chinese citizen. At one time, it could also mean deportation. This puritanical attitude is much less strict now, but you will notice that even handholding is not too common especially in smaller towns. Chinese are more likely to socialize with members of their own sex than to pair off in public. Casual dating is certainly frowned on. Friendly embraces common abroad are unusual even upon greeting a Chinese friend of long standing. (Chinese people overseas do it—but not in China.) You will probably be considered uncivilized if you indulge in too much display of affection in public, even with your own spouse. The Chinese will be embarrassed. But things are changing.

It should take a month to get permission for marriages between Chinese and foreigners, if all goes well.

WILL YOU BE FOLLOWED? Most probably not, unless the Chinese have a special reason to watch you. They might catch some foreigner selling foreign currency illegally to show they mean business. A foreigner is conspicuous. If you do anything wrong, your movements could be easily traced.

PHOTOGRAPHY China is now like most other countries regarding photographs. At one time I couldn't even take a photo of my five-year-old on a public boat. There are still restrictions: You are not allowed to photograph police stations, for example. In 1978 I allowed my bored child to take a photo of friendly policemen only to be told officiously by the officer in charge who suddenly appeared that "taking photographs in police stations is forbidden, but since he is only seven years old, we will not prosecute." We had been waiting to be registered.

Today you can take pictures out of airplanes, on and off boats—everywhere except military installations and certain museums which, like ours, find they cannot sell their own photos if cameras are allowed. The Chinese also feel that flash photography damages relics. They charge a fee or confiscate your film.

Please don't take flash photos at cultural performances. It disturbs the audience. This is my personal request. The Chinese may let you. Stage lighting is usually sufficient for black and white and fast color film. Do, however, ask if you can get right up next to the stage and squat down, shooting with available light as professional photographers do. Flash shots from the middle of a theater rarely work anyway.

Out of courtesy, please do ask people for permission to photograph them close up. Would you like someone to stick a camera in your face without permission?

IF YOU GET INTO TROUBLE Chances are these things won't happen, but just in case . . .

Earthquakes The main danger here is collapsing buildings. If you don't have time to get outside into the open, away from falling debris, dive under a desk, table, or bed, or take shelter in a doorway. If the building falls down around you, at least you might have some protection. As soon as the shaking stops, which is usually after a few seconds, rush outside by stairway (not elevator).

Typhoons This Chinese word meaning "big wind" is the Asian word for hurricane or tropical cyclone. These usually originate east of the Philippines and may hit China anywhere along the Pacific coast from April to November. They usually last for a maximum of three days and you should stay inside substantial buildings on high ground. The danger is falling debris, as well as strong winds and rain. Airports will probably be closed.

If you run out of money Ask your embassy to cable home for some, or telephone collect. It usually takes five banking days. Borrow if you can from fellow travelers.

If you lose your passport Talk to your guide about it. Inform the local police and contact your embassy. Diplomatic offices are in Beijing, but some consulates are in Shanghai, Shenyang, and Guangzhou. Be sure you have your passport number somewhere in your luggage. If you're on a group tour, your tour escort should have a note of it. You should be sure to have extra passport photos on hand. You may have trouble finding a photographer to produce a photo in less than 24 hours. Your embassy could give you a temporary passport; with this document you can get a Chinese visa, without which you cannot leave China.

Losing a passport creates a lot of trouble and additional expense, as it probably means staying a couple of extra days or leaving your tour group. Since a market has developed locally for stolen foreign passports, do guard yours carefully.

Hostile crowds The May 1985 soccer riot in Beijing proved that this could happen. Anyone looking like the victorious Hong Kong Chinese was singled out for threats and abuse. But riots by soccer fans of defeated hometown teams can happen anywhere in the world, and did that year. Remember Brussels? This is not a Chinese phenomenom.

If you *think* you're surrounded by hostile people, try smiling. Chances are they're just curious or even jealous. Ignore them or try to make friends. Speak to individuals quietly, in English if you don't know Chinese. Someone may understand. Above all, act friendly and cool. Shouting obscenities is counterproductive.

If you are convinced the crowd is hostile, try to find out why. The Chinese do not get angry at foreigners just because they are foreigners. Even Japanese people, the hated invader for so many years, are received politely here. Hostility could be caused by something you have done. It used to be taking pictures of the wrong places and superstitious people but this is rare now. It could be that you have insulted someone or laughed and talked too loudly and someone misunderstood. It probably is an argument with a rickshaw or taxi driver. Try not to lose your temper; keep cool, polite, friendly. Call for the police. Apologize if you need to. If someone is drunk, just leave.

Demonstrations Don't be afraid of them. They are usually orderly. The blond wife of one foreign correspondent used to wave at marching demonstrators with a big, friendly grin on her face during times less friendly to foreigners. Participants used to be so surprised by this, they'd break step, stare, and grin back. If a policeman asks you to move on and not take photos, do as he says, or accept the consequences.

Car and bicycle accidents If your car accidentally injures anyone, do what you should in your own country. Give first aid, and then arrange to get the victim to a doctor or a hospital quickly. Otherwise, stay where you are. Do not get involved in arguments. Wait until the police arrive. The police will take statements, and if you are found to be in any way responsible as the driver or even as a passenger (were you distracting the driver?), you may be liable to a fine or payment for damages. The fine would be to remunerate the family of the injured or deceased for the rest of his productive years. There is a standard formula. If the accident is serious, contact your embassy. There have been cases where a Chinese was found at fault and his work unit paid for a broken windshield. There have also been cases of drunken diplomats causing traffic accidents. Many were asked to leave China. Since most tourists will not be driving, car accidents are not really a problem, but bicycle accidents might be.

Breaking the law If you are accused of breaking a Chinese law, try to contact your embassy as soon as you can. Do not expect the rights that you would have in your own country, like to bail or even to see a lawyer. China has only recently rewritten its civil law, which says that foreigners cannot be arrested without a warrant from the People's Procurate or the People's Court. Minor violations could mean detention and deportation. More serious violations like "burglary of scarce industrial materials" have meant the death penalty for Chinese citizens. Taking bribes worth ¥58,000 has meant life imprisonment. An American who fell asleep while smoking set fire to a hotel, resulting in the deaths of ten people. He was sentenced to 18 months' imprisonment and ordered to pay ¥150,000 compensation. Just don't do anything illegal! China has relations with Interpol.

What if you get sick? China has been among the healthiest and cleanest countries in Asia. But standards seem to be slipping.

There have been reports of typhoid, malaria, and rabies in isolated rural areas far off the tourist routes. Venereal diseases are back after being absent for decades, but are still rare compared to other Asian countries. One hears occasionally of encephalitis, hepatitus B, cholera, and intestinal parasites.

You can find out about these and about malaria areas from the World Health Organization. If you are bothered by mosquitoes in China, use the net above your bed, or ask for one if there isn't any. You can also burn incense coils that keep mosquitoes away. To keep visitors happy, a lot of insecticide spray is used in rural areas, and even recently, sprayed from planes in Guangzhou. This might create other problems, but never mind.

Chinese medical facilities are good for common ailments. Many Overseas Chinese go to China for acupuncture and even Western medical treatment. If visitors are sick, it is usually the common cold or an upset stomach (see "Food"). Some visitors have also had hernias, heart attacks, and cancer. Your guide or the service desk at your hotel should be able to direct you to a doctor. Hotels frequently have medical clinics on the premises. We have listed a few hospitals that should be able to help foreigners. These are under some destinations.

If you become ill at night, try the attendant on your floor. Some attendants sleep in a room close to the service desk. If you have a language problem, point to what you need in the "Useful Phrases."

You will probably be given a choice of Western or traditional Chinese medicine, or both. Chinese herbal medicines are frequently effective, but one of my kids had to be bribed with lots of candy to drink his herbal tea, it tasted so awful.

Chinese medical facilities might look grubbier than those in the West. An examination with medicines for an upset stomach at a hotel clinic at this writing cost all of ¥4. Since the Chinese have recently upgraded some facilities especially for foreigners, prices have now risen under the principle "proper price for preferential treatment." Overseas Chinese and Compatriots receive 50% discounts.

If a foreigner is treated the same way as a local Chinese, the charges are lower, similar to that for a local person.

The Chinese are concerned about the health of their guests. They frequently check whether you have enough clothing on. If you complain about your health too much, you might get a doctor even if you don't request one.

It must be pointed out that most tour organizers state emphatically that tours to China are rugged. They are not for invalids or people with respiratory or heart conditions because of dust and air pollution.

It is true that the Chinese are especially nice to older people, and many people want to see China before they die. A few people of Chinese ancestry want to be buried in China and the easiest way they can do this is to die there. The Chinese will otherwise only allow human remains to be imported to a few places like Shenzhen and Chengdu for burial.

But for the rest of you, here are some things to consider:

Do take it easy. If you feel tired, cut out excursions and rest instead. You don't have to climb mountains, or if you do climb steps to the cable car, go slowly; or wait at the bus with the bus driver, who is usually very nice. You can teach him English or walk around on level ground and enjoy the view, or develop your own theories about the antics of Chinese tourists. Have someone help you up the Great Wall so you can say that you were on it. You don't have to go out to the theater in the evening. You can stay in your hotel and try to fathom Chinese television. Operas are frequently on television too.

Facilities for treating emergencies in China are not as sophisticated as in many other countries. Do not expect elaborate life-support equipment, or to be up walking the day after a broken hip.

The Chinese do not store O-negative blood in their blood banks because Chinese people do not have it.

Take any essential medicines with you. Do not count on a prescription made out to a pharmacist in the U.S. being filled in China, especially if it uses brand names.

If you do go to the hospital, take your own mug, plate, towel, soap, and a friend. The staff and other patients may not speak English.

In case of very serious ailments, contact your consulate. You may have to be evacuated outside of China for treatment.

In the event of a death? The Chinese contact the relevant embassy, which in turn tries to get in touch with next of kin. If no word is received within three days, the Chinese will cremate the remains. An embassy can make arrangements for repatriation if desired. Goods belonging to the deceased and death certificates are released to next-of-kin *only* after the bills are paid.

SPITTING Campaigns in some cities have taken place from time to time against this unhealthy, disgusting habit many people have of spitting on streets, hard-class trains, etc. It is a reflection of rural society. Fines in Beijing have averaged ¥.42 and have been successful in curtailing spitting for a while, at least. The Chinese believe that swallowing phlegm is unhealthy, but haven't acquired any alternatives yet. Madame Chiang Kai-shek also had a campaign in 1934 against spitting, but with no permanent success. Priscilla successfully hands tissues and plastic bags to people with whom she is traveling.

LOOKING UP SPECIFIC CHINESE CITIZENS Yes, you can usually visit friends and relatives in China, even while on a group tour or business trip. As a courtesy to your hosts or sponsors in China, do inform them if you want to take time off from the schedule planned for you. You might ask when the best time would be. In recent years, local Chinese could go to your hotel, but they may be interrogated by hotel staff. Previously they had to make application outside the building stating the reason for their visit and showing their identification cards.

Some front-office clerks are rude to local Chinese. Some local people may feel uneasy about entering a hotel, particularly a fancy one. Many are glad of the opportunity to see inside and brag to their friends that they ate there or at least had a photograph taken inside. If they are reluctant, however, to go there, you could arrange to meet in a restaurant, a park, or their home. You could take them on sightseeing trips with your tour group (for a fee). This will give you time to visit with friends without missing the attractions.

Your chances of going to the home of a friend will depend on the political climate at the time. It could also depend on how embarrassed some Chinese are about the modesty of their lodgings, and whether or not they can afford a taxi or elaborate meal for you. Previously, anyone who hosted foreigners in their homes was grilled later as to what the relationship was, what was talked about, etc. In the early 1980s, only a few appointed workers in each work unit were allowed to fraternize socially with their resident foreign expert. In the mid-1980s, people seemed very open to receiving foreign guests in their homes, but curious neighbors still wanted to know who they were. So do not insist if local Chinese friends are reluctant to take you home.

Making contact may be a problem until telephones become more common. If you've sent a letter, telegram, or cable earlier and your friend hasn't shown up, you may have to go to the home or work place. If you are worried about making trouble for your friend, ask someone less conspicuous than yourself to go and inquire.

When you do make contact, it is always better to visit friends alone, as they may be uncomfortable about talking openly if anyone else is around. Do not persist in asking questions that a Chinese seems reluctant to answer. Do not expect any spontaneous rap sessions, though you may get some now. I once asked a friend in the early '80s what happened to his family during the Cultural Revolution and was bluntly but politely told it was none of my business. In the mid-'80s, however, new friends quite openly complained about hauling manure on farms and sweeping floors in factories then.

Be sensitive and play along if people whisper to you. Don't say aloud, "Why are you whispering?" They are afraid someone is listening! It is hard to get over the terrors of the Cultural Revolution, and human rights today still are not like those in your own country.

Overseas Chinese have a freer time talking with Chinese citizens. Chinese people generally are not open about discussing their deepest feelings and problems with even close friends. Nor will Chinese people easily discuss their sex life. It once took six months of living together before one Chinese roommate confided to me how unhappy she was about her parents.

CHINESE HOSPITALITY This can be very lavish and people may go into debt to show how happy they are to see you. It is always appropriate to take a gift when you go to a Chinese home. Especially welcome are cigarettes (State Express 555 are a current favorite) and imported booze unless the family is religious. On the other hand, they may be asked where they got such foreign things, which might cause trouble.

So ask if it is all right. Just remember, it is customary for Chinese to refuse at first, so persist unless they point out that accepting is illegal.

But don't insult them by being overly generous. It is all right, however, to give their children money (about ¥5) if you are a relative or a close friend. Otherwise, it is insulting. If you have time for a return banquet, that would be the easy way out.

If you are accompanied by a Chinese friend or relative, avoid buying anything in a store because he may want to pay for it. The salary range for most people is quite low. Of course, rent is low. A Chinese doesn't have to pay exorbitant medical bills if he is sick, and most pay no income tax. But he has to save a long time to buy what you wouldn't think twice about paying for. Hospitality may demand that you be given a gift. Be gracious and suggest something inexpensive like a poster if you are asked.

I have visited many homes—of peasants, officials, workers, and professional people. By Western standards, they are crowded. One professional couple with two children might have one or two tiny bedrooms—period. They would share a kitchen and bathroom with several other families. In only rare cases will there be room for overnight guests, especially in the cities. Toilets may be the squatting kind. In smaller communities you may find a container of earth or a bucket of water for covering or flushing. Sometimes the family even sells the urine for fertilizer.

In rural areas, you might have to sightsee on foot or on the hard back ends of bicycles, since there may not be any other means of transportation. It is a real adventure!

IF YOU'RE INVITED TO A WEDDING In old China, a gift of money in a red packet was the accepted thing to give. Money is still much appreciated. But gifts to help set up a new household are most frequently given now; porcelain tea sets, clocks, blankets (preferably red, for happiness). Something imported from a foreigner would give you more *guanxi*. Some Friendship Stores may have gift certificates. Wedding invitations usually mean a banquet, but do ask. You could say something like "I've never been to a Chinese wedding before. Tell me what to expect." See *Banquets and Toasting,* in "Food."

RELIGION Chinese people tend to be very pragmatic, worshiping whatever gods might answer their prayers. Religions were encouraged, tolerated, or persecuted depending on the times. In the early Tang, Buddhists were killed. But Buddhism later flourished, with imperial encouragement.

It has not been unusual for the same person to give support to several different temples and churches at the same time, and especially to worship one's ancestors. One owed one's life to ancestors and depended on them for good fortune even after they had passed on. It was one's duty to keep ancestral spirits happy. See Confucianism under "Qufu."

Christianity was really imposed on China, its missionaries allowed into China and protected by a series of treaties following the end of the first Opium War in 1844. Many Chinese questioned the Christian preaching of only one way to salvation. Some foreign missionaries had to close their eyes to ancestor worship or they wouldn't have made many converts. Because of this backing by the foreign powers, Chinese Christians tended to become an elite group, at times appealing successfully to their foreign protectors even if they got in trouble with Chinese law. This, of course, caused much resentment.

Dr. Sun Yat-sen, the father of the Chinese republic, was a Christian, but as a Chinese nationalist he criticized missionaries as lackeys of foreign imperialists. Missionary motives were sometimes misunderstood, and some of these fears led to such incidents as the Tientsin Massacre (see "Tianjin"). Many missionaries were attacked more because they were foreigners caught in the growing nationalism of the era than because of what they taught.

Some Chinese Communist leaders were influenced by missionary schools. Mao Zedong (Mao Tse-tung) himself once edited the Christian-sponsored *Yale-in-China Review*. Some Christian ideals can be found in his teachings.

In 1950, the hysteria of the Korean War led the Chinese to consider Westerners, including many Christian missionaries, as "enemy aliens." Some were expelled and a few jailed at that time. After all, Americans and Canadians were killing Chinese soldiers in that neighboring country. Americans and Canadians reacted similarly during World War II to Japanese people on our west coasts. Even locally born Japanese people had their property confiscated and were shoved off to internment camps. The Chinese also overreacted against all foreigners and those influenced by them, with accusations of spying and sabotage, jail, executions, or deportations.

The Communists also felt that foreign imperialism would continue as long as Chinese Christians maintained their dependency on foreign missionaries. After Liberation, the Christian churches were encouraged to be independent of their foreign roots, and the Protestants set up the Three-Self Patriotic Movement.

The Catholic church, however, officially opposed the rulers of new China. Most of the Chinese bishops not jailed fled to Taiwan, while foreign bishops left for other assignments. When those Catholic leaders who remained nominated new bishops to meet the pastoral needs of more than 100 vacant dioceses, the nominations were ignored by the Vatican. When Chinese leaders went ahead with consecrations, these new bishops were initially ex-communicated, their consecrations later regarded as irregular and never recognized. This left hurt and resentment in the minds and hearts of Roman Catholic leaders in China seeking to meet the needs of loyal adherents. Chinese Catholics still celebrate mass in Latin, and the Vatican, supporting priests who fled to Taiwan and Hong Kong, does not recognize the current Chinese Catholic leadership.

During the Cultural Revolution, churches and temples were destroyed or closed by the Red Guards as part of the movement against the "Four Olds." The youthful revolutionaries and Mao ignored the constitution, which said that "Citizens enjoy freedom to believe in religion, and freedom not to believe in religion and freedom to propagate atheism." Many church buildings became apartments and factories. The Catholic Cathedral in Guangzhou was used for storage.

In 1978–79, the government encouraged the rebuilding of temples and churches, returning deeds to them and paying overdue rents. People and factories who had taken over the buildings had to be relocated before the buildings could become places of worship or tourism again, a time-consuming process. Some Christians actually continued to tithe even while the churches were closed and later brought these treasures to their newly opened gathering places.

Today the Chinese constitution simply says that all Chinese citizens have freedom of belief. About 1800 churches across China were flourishing at press time, a few having to open Saturdays as well as Sundays to accommodate the many worshipers. Some Christians worship corporately in their homes. While some foreigners have questioned the authenticity of the "state-recognized" versus the "house" Christians, Chinese believers do not regard these as two different categories. It may simply be a matter of convenience or accessibility. Some Christians attend both the small family fellowships and the large general congregations.

Foreigners wanting to contact Protestant groups should ask for the Three-Self Patriotic Movement 中国基督教三自爱国运动 . Catholics should ask for the Chinese Patriotic Catholic Association 中国天主教爱国会 . Don't let the word *Patriotic* bother you. It doesn't sound as chauvinistic in Chinese. This movement and this association are nongovernmental. You should also consult with the national headquarters of your own church or national church organizations. Some may have China committees and full-time China-watchers who should have the addresses of churches in cities you will be visiting and can give you advice. It is better that you write in advance advising the congregations that you wish to worship with them. And when you get there, *worship* with them, even though you do not understand the words. And please do not disturb the service with a camera, or by being late, or by leaving early, as many tourists have done. Church services are not tourist attractions.

Chinese Christians, particularly those in isolated places, will probably be delighted to have you join them. At least one foreign churchgoer was asked to sing with the Chinese choir once it was known that he was a soloist in a choir in Canada. Please restrain yourself from giving a lot of money to the congregations. To encourage materialistic values in a spiritual movement could dilute its spiritual strength. The Chinese want to be self-reliant. Donations can be made to the new service arm of the churches, the Amity Foundation of the China Christian Council. The foundation is a way of contributing to China's modernization in and beyond the Christian community.

As for smuggling in Bibles, those days are over. The International Bible Society has agreed to give presses to the Amity Foundation, which will help the churches publish their own literature. Since 1981, the Three-Self Movement has printed at least 1.5 million copies of the Bible. See also *Religious Buildings* in "What Is There to See and Do."

PEOPLE'S FEELINGS If you read Chinese history, particularly the history of imperialist times from 1840 to 1949, you should be struck by the lack of sensitivity foreigners had for the Chinese people. As a result, the Chinese started hitting back in whatever way they could. They demonstrated; they stoned churches; they murdered individual foreigners. Of course, they were desperate people then, pushed to extremes, but let's not provoke incidents.

Please dress modestly and save your jokes for the privacy of your own rooms. Someone who speaks English may hear you and be offended. Be aware if your driver is blocking a road, causing people pulling heavy loads to go around your bus. Your driver is trying to please *you*. Tell your driver to move somewhere else.

In 1981 a British student was deported for writing "Long Live the Gang of Four" as a joke.

FORMS OF ADDRESS "Attendant" is the best translation for all service personnel like waiters, room boys, and chambermaids. If you have to get their attention, you can call them "fo wu yuan." Ask your guide what he/she wants to be called. Some are beginning to use English names.

You can call your guide "mister" or "miss," and if you feel comfortable with it, you can call him/her what the Chinese call each other: *lau* (as in "loud") plus surname, or *xiao* (like "show" as in "shower") plus surname, no matter the sex. *Lau* means "old" and *xiao* means "small." *Lau* is not derogatory in China and refers to anyone forty and older.

Relatives are referred to and called by their relationship to you, like "Second Aunt Older Than My Father," or "Fifth Maternal Uncle of My Grandfather's Generation" (two Chinese words for each of these). Your relatives will tell you what to call them.

Chinese names have surnames first. Chou En-lai would be Premier Chou. You rarely address a person by his given name, except children or relatives.

POLITICS Here are some things to remember about the new China:

Guides and officials usually give foreign visitors the accepted current political line, but a few are frank with their own ideas after they get to know you.

Chairman Mao is the Lenin of the Chinese revolution. He will always be considered the father of the People's Republic.

Recently, China has been giving the impression it is shelving Mao's revolutionary struggle (from socialism to communism and to the classless society) in favor of modernization. This does not mean the revolution has stopped. So much in China happens out of the public eye.

Much will depend on events in the 1980s, the success of the modernization program, world markets, relations with bordering countries like Vietnam and the Soviet Union, the struggle between factions within the Communist Party of China, the leadership succession, the reaction of the army, etc.

GOVERNMENT Communist. Officially at the top is the National People's Congress. (See *Great Hall of the People,* "Beijing.") The State Council is the executive organ accountable to the Congress and is similar in makeup to a cabinet. The Communist Party was once involved in almost every facet of life but has voluntarily diminished some of its own power.

GUANXI "Relationships," "influence," "pull," "connections." This is an important part of Chinese life. Schoolmates, teachers, relatives, workmates—people who know each other well have a stronger and longer hold on each other than in the West. *Guanxi* is related to merit and to helping each other. Strangers are politely accepted, but with reservation, until they have proved themselves trustworthy, friendly, and useful.

The government has spoken out against the excesses of *guanxi* because it isn't fair to people without connections.

DEMOCRACY WALLS These were not new. Writing criticisms and complaints in public places has occurred from time to time in China for centuries and was especially popular during the Cultural Revolution, when they were used for political debates and attacks on "capitalist roaders." The institution was protected by the constitution.

Late in 1978 the writing of big character posters on Democracy Walls flourished unhindered. Four months later, the right to "speak out freely, air views fully, hold great debates, and write big-character posters" was restricted. Taboo were criticisms of socialism, the dictatorship of the proletariat, party leadership, and the ideas of Marx, Lenin, and Mao.

In 1979 foreigners could visit Democracy Walls, talk with anyone who wanted to talk to them, and accept any leaflets anyone wanted to give them. But some of the Chinese were arrested and charged with passing state secrets to foreigners. In December 1979, however, wall posters were curtailed. In September 1980, these rights were deleted from the constitution because they were "easily abused by careerists and schemers like the Gang of Four."

If you're thinking of encouraging dissident movements, just because you believe in democracy, please ask yourself a few questions first. Can China afford an American-style opposition? Would political unrest upset China's program of feeding her tremendous population and furthering her goals of modernization? Do the dissidents represent a sizable majority? Has China ever had a Western-style democratic government?

If you want more information on this subject, Amnesty International does have a report on China, and the Western press does watch this carefully, sometimes too carefully.

TRIPLE STANDARDS It may not seem fair that foreigners are charged more for the same hotel rooms and transportation than Chinese. The point is debatable, and you might want to pass the time on trains in your tour group discussing it. Some points to consider: most Chinese **salaries.** Chinese people would never be able to travel by train or plane if they had to pay the prices you do. Government organizations pay the expenses of workers traveling on company business. The transportation system has been government subsidized. Why should it be subsidized for people who can afford it and are willing to pay? Look around you at living standards. The Chinese need to make money. Foreign tourist prices have not stifled China's growing foreign tourist industry. Up to the mid-'80s, prices, in fact, actually diminished because of the foreign exchange rate.

As for Overseas Chinese, we are considered family, and a discount helps make us feel obligated. If you stay longer to help, you'll get one too.

IF A CHINESE asks for help to visit, study in, or emigrate abroad, use your own judgment. In some cases it is possible but not easy. If you're willing to go to a lot of trouble, so be it. But don't make empty promises that will cause great disappointment later. Check with your embassy regarding regulations.

If a local Chinese asks you to buy something for him at the Friendship Store, go ahead if you want. Gifts have been bought with no trouble. If he asks for foreign currency in exchange for regular Chinese currency, this is illegal, and occasionally foreigners get caught. Do not break a law just because you have been given a lavish meal.

FIRECRACKERS are allowed to be exploded in China, but usually in designated places. Many Hong Kong Chinese, forbidden to set them off at home, go berserk when they celebrate in China. Local Chinese are increasingly setting them off noisily at weddings, birthdays, and grand openings. It is not machine-gun fire!

ENDANGERED SPECIES China and many other countries are parties to the Convention on International Trade in Endangered Species of Wild Fauna and Flora (CITES). Any species or products of a species on its lists should be seized by the Customs Department of any of the signatories, unless you have a permit to carry them. The details of the regulations can be obtained usually from your government wildlife service. See "Important Addresses." The much-publicized Save the Panda campaign is an expression of this concern.

Locally, however, Chinese officials are lax about restricting the sale and eating of many endangered or threatened species, notably wild animals like pangolin (scaly anteater), giant salamander, and the Bactrian

No! No! You may have trouble taking this spotted cat jacket back to your home. It was on sale in the Guangzhou Friendship Store, and is held by Wu Hsiu-yi of C.I.T.S.

camel. Coats of spotted cats have been found for sale in Friendship Stores. Some provinces are opening hunting areas where these animal species might be killed.

Even while passing through Hong Kong, you risk confiscation of garments and ornaments made of parts of certain animals, like turtles. If you kill or eat any of these species, you are contributing to their extinction.

The problem is knowing what is, or is not, on the list. The rule of thumb is: do not encourage the destruction of any **wild animals,** especially spotted cats, alligators, and birds. Some deer, for example, are grown commercially in China, and therefore not endangered.

Among the other Chinese species listed by the Convention are: Himalayan argali, Tibetan brown bear, golden cat, McNeill's deer, sika deer, Yarkand deer (Xinjiang), dhole (wild dog), gibbons, Przewalski's horse, langur, macaque, and wild yak. Among the birds are the relict gull, crested ibis, and some varieties of cranes, storks, pheasants, and egrets. Avoid any elephant parts.

A copy of this photo of a spotted-cat jacket on sale in the Guangzhou Friendship store was sent to the U.S. Federal Wildlife Permit Office. An official replied, "Such an article of clothing cannot be imported into the United States."

The Canadian Wildlife Service replied, "To import a garment made of leopard cat skins, you must be in possession of a CITES export permit issued by the Government of China. On import, the foreign export permit must be surrendered to Canada Customs. Any attempt to enter the coat without the foreign CITES permit could, at the very least, result in seizure."

The authority allowed to issue CITES permits in China is:

The People's Republic of China Endangered Species of Wild Fauna and Flora Import and Export Administrative Office, Ministry of Forestry, Hepingli, Beijing; tel. 464180. Branches also in Guangzhou and Tianjin.

SHOPPING

▶ **Note:** Not all stores can crate and ship goods outside of China. Ask before you buy.

You should haggle over prices, especially in free markets and with peddlers. Prices might fall quicker if you offer F.E.C.s. You cannot bargain in government-controlled stores.

Take your own bag or basket for shopping in markets.

Save your sales slips so you can argue with Customs officials if need be in your own country. Receipts will be in Chinese with English numerals, so make a note of what each refers to.

Clothing and other items imported from elsewhere for sale in China are, of course, cheaper in the country of origin. Some of what you see may have been made in Hong Kong, whose quality and styles are usually better than China's.

When comparing Chinese prices with those elsewhere, don't forget to include the sales tax at home, the rate of duty, and the shipping costs if these apply. In China you pay no additions to the asking price.

Several kinds of stores should interest foreign shoppers.

FRIENDSHIP STORES were originally set up so that foreigners wouldn't have to buck curious crowds while shopping. But this has changed now, as anyone with F.E.C.s has been able to shop there. At least one Friendship Store serves every city. Prices are about the same or slightly higher than other Chinese stores, but the goods are of better quality there, and some items are unavailable elsewhere.

In addition to arts and crafts, many larger Friendship Stores have textiles, television sets, radios, watches, bicycles, sewing machines, cosmetics, herbal medicines, food, jewelry, thermos bottles, camera film, jackknives, flashlights, cashmere sweaters, silk blouses and shirts—just about anything needed by visitors and relatives of visitors. Friendship Stores usually have locally made goods for sale. The best stores are in Guangzhou, Beijing, and Shanghai.

ARTS, CRAFTS, AND ANTIQUE STORES These may or may not be government-owned, and are usually less crowded than Friendship Stores.

These can be found in hotels or on shopping streets, some selling only for F.E.C.s and others for R.M.B.

FACTORIES Every arts and crafts factory has a showroom where visitors can buy. Prices are usually lower than elsewhere. Some showrooms are open all the time; others are open by appointment only.

DEPARTMENT STORES sometimes have arts and crafts, too, but of lower quality than the above stores. Visitors might find good buys in clothing, down, furs, novelties, etc.

FREE MARKETS are where farmers sell their excess produce, people with connections abroad sell foreign-made clothes, tailors solicit customers, and cottage industries sell handicrafts and baked goods. With no changing rooms, people buying jeans have to try them on over their own trousers. Many markets are in alleys under shelter, but as this form of commerce expands, market buildings will probably proliferate.

Antiques have been sold in free markets but some antiques are not authenticated. Antique sections in free markets are closed down from time to time because of unauthorized sales of antiques. Look for the red wax seal.

OVERSEAS CHINESE STORES are mainly for relatives of Overseas Chinese who receive foreign exchange. In these they can buy normally hard-to-obtain items.

SPECIALTY STORES are for everyone. They sell a wide variety of one or two items such as furs, watches, jewelry, etc.

SECONDHAND STORES may only have a lot of junk, but treasure hunters with lots of time might find something of interest, like European antiques. Many of these stores have musical instruments and old and new theatrical costumes. But more frequently they might only have used watches and electric fans of recent vintage.

WHAT TO BUY

China is famous for its **arts and crafts,** though your best prices for China-made products are frequently in Hong Kong. But you may find something you like in China that you won't find in Hong Kong. And besides you may not be going to Hong Kong.

Usually your **best prices** in China are at the factories, your next best at stores in the same city or province as the factory. Sometimes demand has something to do with prices. Store managers do not always know how much to charge for an item, and so the same thing may have a different price in another store. Rubbings bought at temples where they were made might cost more than the same thing at the Friendship Stores. The only difference is a red souvenir seal on the temple-bought rubbing, but is it worth extra to you? The seal is important to people who know about things like this.

Compare prices in several stores. Price should not always be the deciding factor, though. You have to know quality to get good buys. Learn it by studying a lot of good art, and try your own hand at carving and painting before you go to China. Read books, talk with dealers like Hanart in Hong Kong, and even take courses. Go to museums in your own country that have displays of Chinese art. Many places in China make reproductions.

If you are a **serious shopper,** plan your trip so you can see how a favorite craft is made. Locally made crafts are listed under each destination in this book. Go to the factories first. If you are a "buyer" and have business cards to that effect, just telephone for an appointment. If you are an amateur without *guanxi*, you might have to make arrangements through C.I.T.S. (and pay). Not all factories are open all the time for tourists.

In the factory, you can study how the pieces are made, and ask about the most difficult techniques, the criteria of a good piece, and how to tell a phony from a genuine article. You can find out how to clean a piece and where the best materials are from. Will the wood or lacquer crack in dry, centrally heated homes? You should be allowed to handle some of the best pieces. Feel the weight, the surface texture. Compare these with the ordinary quality. Take notes if you can't remember details. For reproductions, study the originals in nearby museums. Remember also that handmade articles are each different—of course! So before you buy, check carefully, not just for flaws, but for the rendering that you like best.

Generally speaking, **consider** (1) the amount of work involved in the production—the finer, the more intricate something is, the better; (2) good proportions, lines, balance, and color; (3) how closely it represents what it is supposed to represent; (4) the quality of the material—will it chip? (soapstone breaks easily and is almost not worth buying); and (5) whether it will be a joy forever, or will you easily tire of it? Primitive art doesn't have to be well proportioned or intricate.

Remember, too, that government stores have a reputation for honesty. If they know something is better, usually they will tell you. Just ask.

If you are looking for an **investment,** your best bet today is revolutionary art—good art depicting peasants, workers, and revolutionary heroes. Like art labeled "Made in Occupied Japan" now, good revolutionary art is becoming valuable and scarce, for it represents a period in China's history. Very little of it is being made today, while the traditional themes are being made by the containerload. But of course, it has to be artistically good in its own right. And think, twenty years from now collectors will be collecting art showing the different stages of the Long March!

Another investment is good rubbings—not the cheap ¥2.50–¥12 kind made from wooden reproductions of the original stone, but the expensive kind, like the Wing of the Cicada, thin and transparent, or the shiny Black Gold. Someday, the original stones will be too worn to make any more rubbings. Then, if you have picked a famous stone you will have something very valuable. Of course, all this is speculation. China may goof up my predictions by producing a lot more revolutionary art. But you can't buy busts of Chairman Mao today.

Most general tours include at least one handicraft factory and always one Friendship or Arts and Crafts store. Most factories have a retail outlet. Many cities also have handicraft *institutes* where new crafts are developed and craftspeople are trained. In these, you may not be able to buy; however, these are very important for the education of the serious buyer.

If you are more interested in handicrafts than temples, it is best if you take an individual or special-interest tour. On a regular tour, the average tourist will be back at the bus waiting for you while you're still talking about texture or the iron content in glazes.

The destinations with the largest number of various handicrafts are Beijing, Tianjin, Shanghai, and Guangzhou.

Here is a list of some crafts and where they are made.

Bamboo: Guangdong (especially Huaiji County), Guangxi, Hunan and Hubei provinces

Carpets: Tianjin, Shanghai, Qingdao, Beijing, Changchun, Urumqi, Inner Mongolia

Clay sculptures, painted: Tianjin, Wuxi

Cloisonne (metal base, wire designs filled in with enamel and baked): Beijing, Tianjin, Xi'an

Dough figurines: Beijing, Guilin, Shanghai. Peddlers used to make these for fascinated children who then promptly ate them. Today these can still be found in some restaurants, but for permanency, a chemical that makes the dough very hard is now added. For fine sculpture, this is your cheapest buy.

Furs: Shijiazhuang, Dalian, Tianjin, Beijing

Glass, artistic: Chongqing, Dalian, Shanghai, Tianjin, Zibo in Shandong, Beijing

Glass snuff bottles: Beijing

Ivory: Guangzhou, Shanghai, and Beijing

Lacquer: Yangjiang in Guangdong, Shanghai, Beijing, Xi'an

Metal handicrafts: Jiangdu County in Jiangsu, Hangzhou, Shanghai, Chengdu, Zhangzhu in Jiangsu

Metal—swords and knives: Husaba in Longchuan County, Yunnan, Longquan in Zhejiang

Paintings and calligraphy: everywhere

Paper—wood-block printing: Beijing (Rong Bao Zhai), Tianjin

Paper-cuts: everywhere. Transient peddlers used to make these on the spot and then sell them. Now you can get postcard-type paper-cuts on every theme imaginable. For those mounted on colored paper: Hailun County in Heilongjiang; for multicolored ones: Yuxian County in Hubei

Paper New Year's pictures: Formerly of the kitchen god and the doorway gods, etc., these are now of cherubs and mythological characters. They are for posting around the house at New Year. Brighter, more cheerful colors than traditional art: Weifang in Shandong, Tianjin

Porcelain: most famous—Jingdezhen (blue and white, eggshell); Yixing (for purple, unglazed); Foshan (for Shiwan); Shantou (for multicolored and chrysanthemums in high relief); Liling in Hunan south of Changsha; Pengcheng County in Hebei (for the Cizhou kiln's "iron embroidery" ware); Longquan in Zhejiang, Hangzhou, and Jingdezhen (for celadon, that porcelain attempt to imitate green jade). The finest porcelain is said to be white as jade, shiny as a mirror, thin as paper, and resonant as a bell.

Reproductions: of ancient porcelains: Jingdezhen; of bronzes: Hangzhou, Luoyang; of three-color Tang: Luoyang and Xi'an

Rubbings: Xi'an (best), Luoyang, Suzhou

Shell art: Qingdao in Shandong, Xi'an

Silk: Guangzhou, Shanghai, Suzhou, Hangzhou, Nanjing, Changzhou in Jiangsu; **brocade:** Shanghai; **double-faced silk paintings:** Zhangzhu in Jiangsu; **embroidery:** most famous schools—*Suzhou, Xiang* (Hunan—Changsha), *Yue* (Guangdong—Shantou), and *Shu* (Sichuan). Also of note: Shanghai, for **embroidered silk blouses; festival lanterns** (also glass—each city has different shapes, sizes, materials, and colors): Beijing, Shanghai, Foshan, and Jiangsu, Fujian, Zhejiang, and Anhui provinces; **flowers:** Shanghai

Stone carvings: Fuzhou in Fujian, Qingtian in Zhejiang, and Liuyang chrysanthemum stone carving in Hunan; **jade:** Shanghai, Beijing, Guilin, Xi'an. Jade can be nephrite (hard as glass, greasy look known as mutton fat, best pure white) or jadeite (wide range of colors, including emerald green; used more in jewelry, the more translucent the better). Since jade is very hard and thus difficult to carve, the most expensive is the most intricately carved and multicolored. The colors are cleverly worked into the design. Serpentine is not true jade but frequently passes as jade. It is softer. The Chinese use the word jade to mean a wide range of hard stones.

Straw: Fujian, Sichuan, Guangdong, and Shandong (Yantai) provinces

Tribal weaving: the Miao in Guizhou province

Wood carvings: Quanzhou and Putian in Fujian, Changchun, Dongyang in Zhejiang (gingko wood), Fuzhou (longan wood), Wenzhou, Shanghai, Beijing. For **gilt camphor wood:** Chaozhou and Shantou. For **sandalwood fans** (smell before buying): Suzhou and Hangzhou

Wool needlepoint: Shanghai Arts and Crafts Studio; Yantai in Shandong.

Favorite mythological and/or historical subjects of arts and crafts:

Poet Shi Yung—late Spring and Autumn Period. Knot on top of head. Sword on back.

Wei Tou—guardian of Buddhism and of the Goddess of Mercy.

Guan Yin—originally a god, but in recent sculpture, always the Goddess of Mercy. Depicted with children, or carrying a cloud duster (like a horsetail whip), or with many heads, or with a vase.

Princess Wen Chen—the Chinese princess who married a Tibetan king and took Buddhism to Tibet.

Scholar Dong Kuo—who was kind even to wolves. He once saved a wolf from a hunter and was admonished by the hunter that a wolf can't change its habits.

Li Shi-zen—Ming dynasty author of the classic book on medicinal herbs. Depicted carrying herbs in a basket, and a hoe.

God of Longevity—old man with peach.

God of Wealth—well-dressed man with scepter.

God of Happiness—man with scroll.

Laughing Buddha—sometimes with five children or standing alone with raised hands.

Eight Taoist Genii—see *Taoist temples* in "What Is There to See and Do?"

Fa Mu-lan—famous woman general who inspired Maxine Hong Kingston's *The Woman Warrior*.

Characters from classical Chinese novels—Water Margin, Dream of the Red Chamber, Pilgrimage to the West.

Favorite revolutionary subjects of arts and crafts:

Soldier O Yang Hai—usually shown on railway track pushing a horse. He was killed but the horse was saved.

Dr. Norman Bethune—usually the only foreigner depicted. Canadian doctor who worked with the Eighth Route Army until his death from blood poisoning.

Yang Kai-hui—first or second wife of Mao Tse-tung. Killed by Nationalists in 1930. Usually in black skirt, high-necked white jacket, and short hair. Sometimes has book in her hand.

Lu Xun—famous modern Chinese writer.

Soldier Lei Feng—PLA truck driver based in Shenyang who was always helping people selflessly and, like the Lone Ranger, anonymously. Killed in accident about 1964.

Antiques: As with such shopping elsewhere, you have to know your goods if you want a bargain. Antiques are not cheap, but Chinese antiques are usually cheaper there than in most stores in your own country. Actually your best buy in Chinese antiques is outside of China, but only if you know your stuff better than the person you're buying from.

You can sometimes buy "antiques" in free markets, but nothing is guaranteed there. People are clearing out their homes of "old" things to sell and they don't know how old or how valuable they are. The usual rule is "If you like it, and want to pay the price, then buy it." See also "Before You Go."

Officially, antiques are not allowed out of China unless they have a red wax seal on them. But in practice Customs officials rarely search the bags of departing visitors.

Novelties and miscellaneous: If your speed, like mine, is not in the $3000 carpet class, China does have a good variety of novelties, things distinctively Chinese to take back to your nieces and nephews and bridge buddies. Most of the following are obtainable from Friendship Stores, but some only from big department stores.

Acupuncture dolls: These are about ten inches high with genuine acupuncture needles and an instruction booklet (in Chinese) for do-it-yourselfers. If these are too expensive, try **acupuncture posters,** found in bookstores—cheap.

Posters, postcards, and comic books are fun and cheap, and so is a **map** of the world showing China in the center, or of Canada and the U.S. in Chinese characters.

Books: There are some children's books showing Chinese characters with equivalent pictures, like our ABCs. If you're in a foreign-language bookstore, you'll find a great many books in English (cheap), all printed in China. They also make great souvenirs.

Museum reproductions: Some of these are quite good and not too expensive. Check out the retail store in any museum you visit.

T-shirts: marked "Xi'an," "Shanghai," or "Shaoshan." Laundry bags marked "Beijing Hotel" are popular. China is just beginning to realize the commercial value of printing a city's name on something, and images of tourist attractions in soapstone are appearing. Lots of cheap souvenir pins with the name of a touristy site. Then there are Chinese **kites,** traditional **baby bonnets** of silk or rayon trimmed with fur ears to make baby look like a tiger kitten, **Mao caps, plastic eggs** with chicks inside, **folding scissors.**

There are fancy gold-trimmed **chopsticks** from Fuzhou, lovely metal-tipped chopsticks from Hangzhou and stone **seals** where you can have a rubber stamp made of your name in Chinese (get a friend to translate) with a fancy, carved stone handle. Hong Kong visitors say these are cheaper in China than Hong Kong.

Some visitors take back Chinese **wines** and **vodka** or Chinese **teas.**

Vests with appliques have been a hit with tourists to Xi'an, where they are cheaper than elsewhere in China. Now that people are free to market their handicrafts, a lot of new designs are being created. A lot of junk is being made too. If you buy the junk, the Chinese will only make more of it.

Those **books** printed in China are cheaper here than elsewhere, if you don't care about the quality of the paper or reproductions of photographs. China, however, is producing some good picture books printed elsewhere, including Hong Kong. A large number of titles in English and other foreign languages are available if you are interested in the art, literature, history, and sciences in China. Of the 30,000-plus new titles a year, 2000 are in foreign languages.

Chinese fiction is not written full of conflict, sex, and violence, the way some popular Western fiction is, but try some of the classics and Lu Xun if you want. Books make good gifts. China pirates Chinese translations of Western textbooks, but foreigners are not allowed to buy in those sections of the book stores. Book lovers must visit Liulichang in Beijing to look at samples of fine Chinese printing. Try China Travel and Tourism Press for picture books.

Tailors are not as good as in other places in Asia, like Hong Kong, and clothes take longer to make. But they are cheap! Don't bother having clothes tailored here unless a tailor is recommended by Western friends and you have a picture of what you want made. Even Shanghai tailors have lost the art. See "Shanghai."

Furs, down coats, and jackets are bargains, but please, please, don't buy any endangered species. A Hong Kong furrier said the quality of the tanning is not very good and the fur will stink. See "Local Customs."

Live plants, birds, and animals: Check with your embassy. Usually these are not allowed into your country without specific certificates, not easily obtainable outside your country.

Cassettes: China has some fine musicians, and music lovers might like recordings. For names and titles see "What Is There to See and Do?"

Movies and slides of Chinese tourist attractions are available. The films are in 16 and 35mm and video cassette. The videos may have to be converted for use abroad; this takes a couple of days. Contact China Tourism Audio-Visual Publication Corporation, Ritan Park, Beijing; tel. 502393, 502527; cable 2393.

WHAT IS THERE TO SEE AND DO?

How Observant Are You?

By the time you've been in China a week, you should have some idea: (1) if the Chinese people are happy; (2) if the modernization campaign is succeeding; (3) who the premier is; (4) what the population is; (5) what kind of a government China has and how it functions.

You should also know: (6) the name of the capital; (7) the names of two provinces; (8) the names of two rivers.

And, one hopes, you would have looked at the inside of a Chinese home and chatted with some Chinese people besides your guide.

If you haven't done 80 percent of these, then think about why you came to China in the first place. Visiting China is a great opportunity to learn about another culture, another history, another way of life. It is a chance to speculate if China is going to affect your future: Will there be a war that would involve your country? Will its cheaper labor affect your economy? Will China's solutions to its problems help solve your country's problems? How did it eliminate prostitution? Drug addiction? Crime in the streets? What is it doing about controlling the growth of its population? The energy shortage? Its ethnic minorities? Is there anything China can teach you about arts? Patience?

▶ **Note:** Visitors to China in previous years were given the impression that everything was going well in China. Yet later the Chinese themselves were saying that things were very wrong in several of the previous periods. So do evaluate what you hear critically. The person who briefs you is telling you the truth as he sees it. Do cross-examine pleasantly if he gives you information that just doesn't quite ring true to you. It may also be something you've misunderstood.

Things to Do

Checklist: To help you observe, especially when you have nothing to do on a train or bus, use this list. Make a check if you see any of these things:

1. a foot-operated water pump ( )
2. an electric water pump ( )

3. an earthen cone-shaped tomb ( )
4. a funeral ( )
5. a pregnant woman ( )
6. a cat ( )
7. a village watchtower (mainly in south) ( )
8. a pony or mule cart (mainly in north) ( )
9. a village without electrical wiring ( )
10. a television antenna on a private home ( )
11. a mud sled with runners ( )
12. an old woman with tiny bound feet ( )
13. *a qi pao/cheong sam,* the narrow, women's dress with a side-slit ( )
14. coal-dust bricks drying ( )
15. a brick kiln ( )
16. three kinds of wild birds, ( ), ( ), and ( )
17. a boy carrying a baby ( )
18. a statue of Chairman Mao ( )
19. a small tractor ( )
20. a road not lined with trees ( )
21. criminals marching to be executed ( )

Walk Go for a walk by yourself or with *one* friend and a copy of this book. Go early in the morning before breakfast when you are fresh (if you are fresh in the morning). Walk slowly without a camera, for cameras tend to separate people; they keep you from feeling, from savoring the waking of a world that is unlike any other on earth. Walk away from the main streets; explore the alleys.

Life swims around you; a woman brushes her teeth on the street. People line up doing the ethereal *taiji quan* exercises in slow motion. Most are following one leader. Join them and try it yourself. Usually they won't mind.

Look at the tiny houses, the charming paper windows, the carvings on the door hinges, the storefronts open to the street; wait—maybe they're tiny factories or homes with workshops in front. Go to a park; you might even hear some beautiful but very shy singers practicing. You might be asked to help a student practice his English. If the park is a historic monument, savor it slowly. There is no tour guide rushing you from place to place. Imagine how it looked 300 years ago when the common people and you were not allowed here. Think of the centuries of bustling human activity that took place here.

Go back to the street and watch the people riding to work on bicycles, buses, or trucks. Do they look harried, content, blank? Imagine yourself riding with them. Imagine yourself living in one of their apartments. Do you know enough about them to know how they feel?

Look for signs of Westernization. Any Coca-Cola ads yet? Any Western movies? Permanent waves? High heels? Is that bright-red billboard a Four Modernizations slogan? Or is it a poem by Chairman Mao? What are the sounds you hear? Traffic noises? The strains of "The East Is Red" on the loudspeaker or something from *The Sound of Music*? Listen to the language. It is tonal, like singing almost.

Look for old churches (Gothic-type windows) and temples. Was that bicycle cart an ambulance? Is that a woman pulling a heavy cart? Smile back at people who stare at you. Given them a cheery "Ni hao?" You might get a smile back. If you get lost, don't worry. See "Useful Phrases."

Visit a factory, any factory, just as long as it's not a handicraft factory where you'll get involved in discussions of artistic techniques and buying. C.I.T.S. or the service desk in your hotel can arrange the trip and a guide. Tell them you want to visit a worker's home and talk to some workers. You won't need the Chinese in the "Useful Phrases" if you have an interpreter, but these might give you some idea of what questions to ask first.

What is interesting about Chinese workers is mobility (or lack of it), job security, what happens if they don't like their jobs, housing, time off and vacations, medical benefits, travel, work incentives before 1978 and now, what they think of as they bicycle to work, and how did they meet their spouses. How are young people today different from the previous generation? What are the incentives for a planned family? What if someone in the work unit absents himself too often? Workers' schools? Taxes?

Who decides on what products to manufacture? Is the factory collectively or state owned? What is the difference? Do they have political meetings? How often? What about criticism–self-criticism sessions? What is the extent of recently introduced capitalistic practices? Will workers follow the Polish example?

Learn about the manufacturing process and how different things are in China from your home country. Find out how the new economic policies have affected labor. Have the best and the brightest left to set up enterprises of their own?

Visit the countryside Rural China has also changed dramatically lately. Formerly, the countryside was divided into "communes" and you might still hear the term used as it is still a political unit. Communes are now "counties" again, and "production brigades" and "teams" are "villages," depending on location.

In addition to name changes, the average per capita income in counties has risen considerably since the early '80s, and living in a village now seems more appealing than living in a city. How have they done this? What percentage of the income is still agricultural? What is happening to the lifestyle? The birth-control program, with the economy based on the family? Since most of China is considered rural, developments here are very important.

Some counties are more interesting to visit than others. The ones around Guangzhou offer shooting galleries, ox-cart rides, lion dances, and bicycle rentals! At harvest time, some villages will allow you to eat all the lichees/litchis and apples you want. You can learn a lot from the villages that preserve fruit, or grow jasmine tea, or silk worms. Around Beijing, you can see how Peking ducks are force-fed. Gardeners should have a field day learning about exotic vegetables. Have you ever seen rice growing before? Water chestnuts? Bamboo shoots, fungi, and *facai*? All are yummy ingredients you find in Chinese restaurants!

But you can also look at the industries. Some counties produce transformers, cement boats, and arts and crafts, like Cabbage Patch clones. Look at the schools and facilities for children. Some counties have built swimming pools, zoos, and merry-go-rounds.

You will probably be given a briefing with the basic statistics. You could also ask: What about old-age pensions? What security is there if not children? What about the people who are not making as much money as the others? Is it a matter of luck, or are they not working as hard? Has anyone from here gone to university? Traveled abroad? Do young people still want to move to the cities? Why are some counties richer than others? Is any of the produce here exported abroad? Who decides what is grown?

Visit a school Nursery schools are always entertaining. You have to be very hard-hearted if you aren't charmed by them. Count on half a day. In some nursery schools, visitors are involved in some of the children's games. In all nursery schools you will tour the classrooms, have a performance of songs and dances, and get a briefing with an opportunity to ask questions. Nursery-school songs are a good indicator of the current political atmosphere. At one time the children were singing songs about shooting down American planes. In more advanced schools, you may be expected to read an English lesson. Suggest that your reading be recorded so the children can hear it again and memorize your accent and inflections.

Chinese schools were closed during the Cultural Revolution, so that the students could "make revolution." After they were opened again, the curriculum placed more emphasis on politics than academics, even as a criterion for university entrance. How was this allowed to happen? What has happened to this generation of academically unprepared students? Is education going too much the other way now? Are students losing touch with peasants and workers? Do they still spend time working in factories? What is happening with the new examination system? Why are only a few people going to university when China needs highly trained people? What kind of teaching aids do they have? How many students in each class? What about the slow learners? The exceptionally bright child? What scientific apparatus do they have? What prospects for graduates? Why have there been student demonstrations?

See also *Gifts* in "What to Take."

Offer to help, but only if the Chinese seem interested. (See also the section on visiting as a scholar in "The Basics.") This is not just for China's sake but also to give you a deeper experience in China. You may make some good professional contacts.

Two hours in a Chinese school will not tell you much about the education system, but struggling with an English class will tell you a lot more. If you are at a university and Chinese scholars start asking probing questions, then grab your chance. If you are in a tour group, make a date to meet them again. If you have brought along slides or pictures, tell them. If you are talking with a museum director and Chinese history is your field, offer to write the English titles on the exhibits or catalog their English-language library.

If you are already successfully helping hotel attendants with their English, and you're not on a tightly scheduled tour, offer to stay a few more days to make tape recordings or give more lessons. Hint that you don't have much money and can't stay too long. If the hotel management is sharp, they should grab the opportunity for a teacher in return for a room and maybe foreign experts' rates on food. This way they don't have to go through the red tape of getting a teacher. Student groups might offer to help plant trees with Chinese student groups if they're in China on tree-planting day in April.

Get off the well-beaten tourist track —it's safe. Just don't go anywhere there's a sign that says foreigners are forbidden. If anyone asks what you are doing, tell him. Just don't take photographs in police stations.

Actually, **police stations** are interesting. If you're lost, you might look for one to ask directions back. I once saw three teenagers locked in a cage under the stairs.

Visit a public market The free market is where commune members sell the surplus from their private vegetable plots. You will see some women with three eggs or a couple of pounds of cabbage.

Look for an old map of the city you are in. The museum may have one you can copy. Follow the **old wall** or look for remains of gates. Follow rivers and canals. Figure out how the city was defended.

Learn Chinese No, it's not all that hard to understand. Listen carefully as it is spoken. Some words reoccur frequently. Ask what these mean. You probably know some Chinese already. *Shanghai* means "above the sea." *Shang* is "above." When you get to Beijing, you will hear about Beihai Park, "North Sea Park." *Hai* again is "sea."

As for *Bei,* also found in *Beijing,* it means "north." *Beijing* is "Northern Capital." *Jing* is the same jing as in *Nanjing,* "Southern Capital."

Learn your numbers and make the elevator operator grin. *Lou* as in "loud" means "floor." Reading numbers will help in museums. You only have to learn ten. The rest are combinations. See "Useful Phrases." Learn the polite things first: "good morning," "please," "thank you," and "good-bye." When someone asks you to help with English, ask him or her to help you with your Chinese.

Visit museums These can be deadly dull if you don't do it right. I have seen people hurrying past pieces that set my heart pounding, without batting an eyelash. You will get much more out of a Chinese museum (1) if you read something about Chinese history first; for a quick course see "Milestones in Chinese History"; (2) if you take a knowledgeable guide; and (3) if you are eager to learn things like the date of the earliest pottery, blue and white porcelain, weaving, writing, money, sewer pipes, paper, gun powder, metal implements, etc. It might excite you even more to compare these with the earliest in your civilization. Try to figure out how and why things were made. Trace their development. How did neolithic man get his fire? When did the Chinese first use fertilizer?

China is so rich in archaeology that most cities have good collections. These are lessons in history. The problem for foreigners is that most museums do not have titles in English. If you don't have a guide and have learned your Chinese numbers, at least you could look up the dates in "Milestones" and get a general idea of the period and what the relic might be. There is also a list of dynasties in the "Quick Reference" section with the names in Chinese and English. Each gallery is usually labeled with a dynasty name and/or a date. You could try to figure from this too.

Chinese museums are usually set up chronologically from primitive to revolutionary times. City and provincial museums usually have relics found in the area. Some have exhibits of how things like bronzes were made. Most have excavations from ancient tombs, pottery figures of humans and animals, some of the most lifelike statues in China. Some of the most important pieces may not be original, but will be good reproductions. The originals are too valuable to expose to light and to the possibility of deterioration. You might notice that the lights are dim. It is deliberate. Take a flashlight.

Some museums have booklets in English. Some museums have been built over archaeological sites, a most exciting idea. You stand where you know people stood 6000 years ago and look at the remains of their houses, and where they stored their farm tools and buried their children. The skeletons are still there, excavated and protected by glass so you can see them. If you are at all psychic, you might feel some ancient vibes in a situation like this. Take your time. Meditate. I have a friend who gets visions sometimes if she holds a relic. She believes she sees the culture from which the relic came as if it were a movie.

Bronzes are not as well known abroad as Chinese porcelains or paintings. The museums in China are full of these ceremonial vessels, easily dismissed as uninteresting. They are, in fact, very exciting, the products of a highly developed technology with no peer anywhere else in the world at that time. Where else was there cast 800 kg of molten bronze into a one-piece bell over 3000 years ago? Just think of the logistics of doing it! How many men were accidentally burned to death in the process? Did they use cranes? How many finished bells were discarded when they did not produce the correct tone? Did anyone get beheaded for the mistake?

And then to bury the result! The economy must have been pretty solid to support this kind of extravagance. Or did the masses have to suffer for it? Confucius, who seems to have been sensitive to the needs of common people, looked back to the Zhou dynasty as a golden age of order and prosperity. Something about the bronze era must have been right.

Bronzes are uncensored history books cast in metal, said one enthusiastic scientist. On them have been inscribed the earliest script, like the family Bible of old, recording family names and important dates. Later, historical events were reported on them.

The shapes of the ritual bronzes were based originally on utensils of everyday use like two-level steamers and cooking pots. From bronzes, archaeologists have concluded that weapons and agricultural tools were basically of the same designs. No one seems to know if the bronzes themselves were used in daily life. They were usually found in tombs buried with the dead for the use of the spirits.

The Chinese cast this alloy of tin and copper from molds. Emperor Yu of the Xia Dynasty (about 21st–16th century B.C.) is believed to have ordered some vessels made by vassal states as tribute. Unfortunately, those bronzes were lost by the end of the Zhou dynasty and no solid evidence has since surfaced.

The oldest surviving bronzes are from the Shang dynasty, and one can trace the development of the art in China's well-stocked museums. The shapes of the legs, the decorations, the type of script. Even if you can't read Chinese, at least you can see the differences in style from dynasty to dynasty.

As you study them, note that the early thin-walled Shang pieces were relatively crude, with two-dimensional patterns and stylized boogeyman figures. Look for "ogres," serpents, dragons, and "nipples" (bosses) in bands. Later, the patterns covered the whole vessels in increasingly elaborate ways. Can you recognize cowrie shells, cicadas, birds, and braided rope motifs? Animal heads became three-dimensional and realistic. Animal statues like elephants and tigers started appearing. Bosses became coiled serpents. (Castings of human figures were rare.)

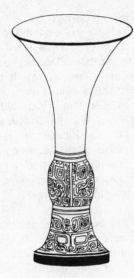

Gu—Wine goblet

Be—Ewer

Ding—Food vessel

Jue—Wine goblet

Walls became thicker. The shapes of the legs developed from blades to dowels. Then gold or silver inlay came into being. More and different shapes appeared.

Bronzes were fashionable until the Han, after which the art died out. (See also *Provincial Museum* under "Wuhan" in Destinations.)

Some guides are steering tourists away from the revolutionary sections of museums, thinking they may not be interested. Do tell them if you are. It is good to see China's version of historic events. It may differ from what you have always heard. For this reason, Chinese history from 1840 on should be of tremendous interest. Did British soldiers really sack and rape in every city they captured? Was the British ship *Amethyst* acting cowardly or heroically? Did the missionaries deserve to be thrown out of China? Why do the Communists glorify the Christian-inspired Taipings and the fanatical Boxers? Was the Long March a cowardly or heroic act? Was the Great Leap Forward a mistake? Was the Cultural Revolution a mistake without any redeeming features?

Ask political questions Don't be afraid to do this. If it is done in the right spirit, both the Chinese and you can learn a lot. Political discussions can get heated. Please keep the conversation friendly and relaxed. If you succeed in convincing them of your opinions or vice versa, it won't be because of shouting and red faces.

Do ask them why they think Richard Nixon is a hero, what is meant by "democratic centralism," what they think will happen if the Four Modernizations fail, and whether it was right to imprison novelist Ding Ling (Ting Ling) and poet Ai Qing (Ai Ching) after the Hundred Flower Movement. If they look like they're uncomfortable with the question, don't pursue it. They may be under a lot of pressure to give the correct political answer and they may not know it. The better you know a person, the franker an answer you will get. And no answer will also give you an indication of the answer, if you know what I mean.

Go to cultural events During and after the Cultural Revolution, at the instigation of Jiang Qing, wife of Chairman Mao, only eight operas were allowed to be performed, all with strong revolutionary messages. Since the end of 1976, many of the restrictions on entertainment have been lifted. It no longer has to "serve the revolution." Some of it can be and is frivolous.

One doesn't go to China to see American or European movies. Some theaters are equipped with simultaneous interpretation, but these are only good if the interpreter is good. So bring your own if you can. Most movies are in Chinese. Of the Chinese movies, some are no longer blatantly full of propaganda, depicting pure and good Communists and evil Nationalists. Look for movie versions of operas, set in China, comedies about life in the factories, and cartoons. The *China Daily* has announcements about cultural events in Beijing and on national television.

Chinese **television** consists primarily of documentaries, *kung fu* action thrillers, and tearjerkers. It also has news, sports coverage, commercials, and educational broadcasts, such as language lessons. Occasionally it will have something especially good, like a visiting British ballet company or live coverage of historical events. Your hotel television may have closed-circuit programming with more of the kinds of programs you're used to.

The best **acrobats** are from Shenyang, Shanghai, and Wuhan, and foreigners usually find acrobats very entertaining. Also offered are **song and dance troupes** and **sports competitions.** I highly recommend exhibitions of **wushu,** the traditional martial arts.

Most tour groups will be taken to one or two cultural presentations. If you want to go to more, you can on your own. They are very cheap—usually less than two yuan. Tickets are frequently hard to get at the box office and must be booked in advance. See "Useful Phrases."

In Beijing, anyone can go to good movies, usually with English subtitles, at the International Club (very comfortable seats). In almost every city, batches of seats for various kinds of performances are reserved for foreigners. You might be able to get some of these at your hotel service desk or through C.I.T.S.

Chinese traditional opera should be experienced at least once. It is very popular with older people, but not so much with younger ones, since it is sung in its own classical language. Your guide might not understand it except for the subtitles for the songs. The jabbering in the audience is not a result of boredom; it is those who understand it explaining to those who don't. To the uninitiated, traditional Chinese opera can be dull, with its many long monologues, its high-pitched singing, and its sluggish action. The villain is always known at the beginning. The chairs in the theater are frequently hard, and there may not be heat or air conditioning. The performance usually takes three hours, and the percussion instruments, especially, are loud, as if to elevate the audience to a higher level of consciousness—but not as high as at a rock concert.

The stories are usually ancient, so a knowledge of history helps. Or they could be something out of classic literature, *The Dream of the Red Chamber* or *Pilgrimage to the West*. Some are based on modern history. Two books, published in China, should be helpful: Latsch's *Peking Opera as a European Sees It* and Wu's *Peking Opera and Mei Lanfang*.

Mei Lanfang was one of the greatest of the female impersonators. It is common to have a man play the woman's role, and vice versa. One opera company, the Shaoxing, has only female players. The male roles are extraordinarily well done. The makeup might throw you, but much goes into it: the temples taped to slant the eyes, paste-on hair pieces to reshape faces, and many colors to indicate character or specific roles such as the Monkey King, or the red-and-black-faced Zhang Fei. A face painted black is an honest but uncouth character; a white face shows a treacherous, cunning, but dignified person; a white patch on the nose indicates a villain. Red is for loyalty and sincerity; black for honesty and all-around goodness. Yellow is for impulsiveness and gold and silver for demons and gods.

It is always fun to watch the actresses in love scenes expressing themselves with delicate and reserved gestures. Note how they excitedly carry their tune to a higher and higher pitch within one breath.

Usually the staging, the costumes, and the acting are outstanding. The fighting scenes, if any, are breathtaking and graceful, like ballet. Cymbals and hollow wooden knockers punctuate the action, and somewhere in the orchestra is an instrument that sounds like a bagpipe. The audience frequently applauds a musician, especially the one playing the stringed *erhu*. Usually a good opera singer tries to keep his own erhu player for life. The costumes are handmade and artfully embroidered, depending on the character played.

The singing, ah yes, the singing takes some getting used to. It can sound like screeching and whining, and one wonders how long voices can last under that kind of abuse. But it takes many years of training to achieve such perfection.

Settings are usually simple and symbolic. The acting, too, is symbolic, and Chinese audiences know what every gesture, every move of the eyebrow means. Among the symbols: an old man and a girl with an oar are on a boat; a man lifting up his foot as he exits is stepping over the high threshold of a door. Crossed eyes mean anger. Walking with hands extended in front means it's dark. A man holding a riding crop means he's riding a horse, or sometimes he *is* a horse. You should be able to tell the difference! A particularly well-executed swing of long hair (anguish) or prolonged trembling (fear) will elicit gasps of appreciation and applause.

With settings, two bamboo poles with some cloth attached is a city wall or gate. A chariot is two yellow flags with a wheel drawn on each. A couple of poles on either side of an actor is a sedan chair. A hat with two long, dangling pheasant or peacock feathers is worn by a high military officer, usually a marshal; a hat with wobbling wings out to the sides just above the ears belongs to a magistrate. Generals have flags matching their costumes and mounted like wings on their backs. The flags are distributed to identify imperial messengers.

After the performance, you may want to go backstage to see everything up close, and possibly makeup being removed. See "Useful Phrases."

Chinese opera dates from the Yuan, and blossomed into one of the most popular entertainment forms during the Ming for noble and commoner alike. For a largely illiterate population, operas were courses in history. For their entertainment value, they were performed at major festivals, weddings, funerals, births, promotions, etc., for human and ghostly guests.

China has many forms of traditional opera, the distinctions known to fans. The most popular are Beijing and Qunqi. Qunqi has more dancing movements and more melodic, mellow tunes. During a performance, one sees either a whole story or excerpts from several operas.

In the old days, operas were social events. As some went on for weeks, people came and left as they pleased, chatted with friends, ate and drank. The crack of watermelon seeds and the sipping of tea blended with the music, which spectators also sang if the tune was familiar. In addition to shouting approval and clapping, one also growled and swore when actors were less than perfect. The audiences sounded much like Elizabethan ones. In the old days, performers were considered little better than beggars and prostitutes in spite of many years of training and practice. Today, performers are considered cultural workers and are respected as artists.

Listen to music Music lovers should be interested in hearing classical Western and contemporary Chinese and Western music. Among the best Chinese orchestras are the Shanghai Chinese Orchestra 上海民族乐团 , the Hong Kong Chinese Orchestra 香港中乐团 , Peking Central Folk Orchestra 北京中央民族乐团 , Beijing Central Philharmonic Orchestra, 北京中央管弦乐团, and China Broadcasting Symphony Orchestra 中国广播民族乐团

Among the most famous contemporary Chinese composers are Chou Wen-chung 周文中 (USA), Luo Jing-jing 罗京京 (Shanghai), Tan Dun 谭盾 (Beijing), Ma Sitson 马思聪 (USA), and Ju Hsiaosong 瞿小松 (Beijing).

You might also look for programs or cassettes that include popular compositions like the erhu concerto Manjianghong 满江红 ; The Butterfly Lovers 梁山伯与祝英台 for orchestra and violin; Reflections of the Moon on Two Lakes 二泉映月 , an erhu concerto; Lady General Mu Kweiying 穆桂英挂帅 , an orchestral work converted from Chinese opera.

Also recommended are: Li Sao (The Lament) 离骚 , an orchestral work; Willows in the Spring Breeze 春风杨柳 , light music; Tao Jin Ling 淘金令 , orchestral; The Swaying Plum Blossoms 梅花三弄 , pipa or flute; and Silver Snow in the Early Spring 阳春白雪 , pipa.

Then there are: The River Suite 江河水 , erhu solo; Moon and Lanterns 灯月交辉 , East China Silk and Bamboo Music recording; A Selection of Chinese Melodies on Traditional Instruments 中国民间器乐造 ; Autumn Moon on a Calm Lake 秋湖月夜 , for piano or orchestra; and Pastoral Song 牧歌 .

The *erhu* 二胡 , *banhu, gaohu,* and *zhonghu* are stringed instruments held upright and played with a bow. The *pipa* 唢呐 and *liuqin* look and sound like mandolins, the *ruan* more like a banjo. The *yanggin* is like a dulcimer played with bamboo mallets.

Other Chinese instruments are the *kuchin* 唢呐 , *sheng* 笙 , bamboo flute 笛，箫, and *tseng* 筝 .

Dance parties are fun, even if you sit on the sidelines and watch. They are more fun if you get up and dance. Some are organized at hotels. The one I saw in a small city (Yantai) took place in a large open courtyard, with a couple of hundred people, mainly men, but also some women and children. With the shortage of women, men were dancing arm-in-arm with other men. Some women, however, danced with each other. The music was a melange of fox trots, waltzes, tangos, cha-cha, and rock. It was great to see the Chinese letting loose after so many years of considering such activity bourgeois and frivolous. Many people say they dance for the exercise. The music was live. In some places, you can take your own cassettes. Quick, enjoy it, before dance parties get banned again!

Learn how to identify details of Chinese designs You will see these everywhere in China: in palaces, temples, pagodas, museums, fancy restaurants, gardens, parks, on dishes, windows, and screens. Knowing what they are will help you recognize bits of Chinese culture abroad, too, especially on rugs, in textiles, in Chinese antiques, and in Chinese restaurants.

Illustrated are some of the more common designs. While their origins might be Taoist or Buddhist, Chinese symbols are primarily Chinese, taken over as part of the national culture, and not confined to any particular religion.

The pearl-border

"T" pattern

Key pattern

These are favorites for the rims of cups and bowls.

The Dragon of Heaven

The Chinese Dragon is said to have the head of a camel, the horns of a deer, the eyes of a rabbit, the ears of a cow, the neck of a snake, the belly of a frog, the scales of a carp, the claws of a hawk, and the palm of a tiger. It has whiskers and a beard, and is deaf. It is generally regarded as benevolent but is also the source of thunder and lightning. The five-clawed variation was once reserved exclusively for the emperor. The flaming ball is said by some to represent thunder and lightning, by others, to be either the sun, the moon, or the pearl of potentiality. It is frequently surrounded by clouds.

The cloud design is now most frequently seen in blue as the lower border of a rich man's gown either in a traditional opera or a painted antique portrait.

The cloud design

Cloud border

Still water

Sea waves; the little clouds over the angles represent the sea spray.

Decorative compositions of the hieroglyphic form of thunder.

Mountains and crags

Lightning and fire designs

This scepter is frequently about half a meter long and made of metal, stone, bone, or wood. It is like a magic wand and is frequently given as a gift, a symbol of good wishes for the prosperity and longevity of the recipient. The larger ones are found in museums.

The scepter of the supreme heavenly deity

The lion is not native to China. The design is unique to China because the craftsmen never saw a real one. Lions are frequently seen in front of buildings as protectors either playing with a ball (male) or a kitten (female). They are considered benevolent. The ball is said by some to represent the imperial treasury or peace. Others say it is the sun, a precious stone, or the Yin-Yang. Seen also on festive occasions as a costume for dancers, the lion is sometimes confused with the Fo dog, which is usually blue with longer ears.

The lion

The phoenix

The phoenix is said to resemble a swan in front, a unicorn behind, with "the throat of a swallow, the bill of a fowl, the neck of a snake, the tail of a peacock, the forehead of a crane, the crown of a Mandarin duck, the stripes of a dragon, and the back of a tortoise." Its appearance is said to mean an era of peace and prosperity. It was the symbol used by the empresses of China and is often combined in designs with the dragon.

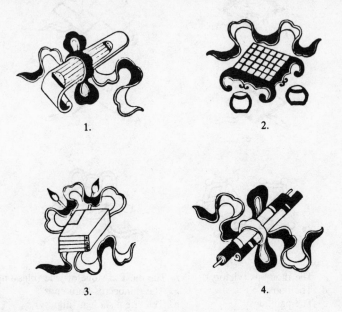

1. The harp
2. The chessboard
3. The books
4. The paintings

The intellectual elite was associated with these four symbols in ancient times.

The eight precious things
   a. The pearl
   b. The coin

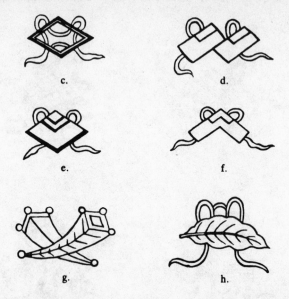

c.
d.
e.
f.

g.
h.

c. The rhombus (victory)
d. The books
e. The paintings

f. The musical stone of jade (blessing)
g. The rhinoceros-horn cups
h. The artemisia leaf (dignity)

1.

2.

Character sign symbols
1. The round *Shou*
2. The long *Shou*, both meaning "long life"

These are only two of the many variations frequently seen. There is even a teapot in the *shou* design.

This is but one of the many variations of the character for happiness. Sometimes it is circular and doubled, especially prominent at weddings.

The *Fu*, meaning "happiness"

The bat   Bat and peach

The word for bat in Chinese is *fu*. So is the word for happiness. A bat is thus a symbol of happiness. These are everywhere: on the walls and ceilings of the Forbidden City, on the ceiling of the restaurant of the Peace Hotel in Shanghai. The peach is a symbol of longevity.

Five bats, surrounding the character *Shou*

When five bats are combined with the longevity character, they mean the five great blessings: happiness, wealth, peace, virtue, and longevity.

Scepter, writing brush, and uncoined silver. Together, these are a symbol of success.

The three Fruits

These are fragrant fingers of Buddha, peach, and pomegranate. Together they mean happiness, longevity, and male children.

Prunus   Orchid

Bamboo   Peony

The prunus or plum blossom symbolizes beauty; the orchid, fragrance; bamboo is an emblem of longevity, and the peony means wealth and respectability.

Peach blossom

Lotus flower

Chrysanthemum

Narcissus

These are featured singly or combined in a set of four, since the peach blossom represents spring, the lotus flower is summer, chrysanthemum is autumn, and narcissus is winter. Frequently there are only one of each of these on a four-panel screen.

Among **other common symbols** are the *crane* (longevity), the *stag* (longevity and prosperity), and the *lotus* (purity and perfection). The Buddha is usually seated on a lotus.

Among the many **strange beings** are the two at the top two corners of many temple roofs, tails pointing to the sky. This is a *carp turning into a dragon*. There is also the *unicorn,* known as *qi-lin,* with the "body of the musk deer, the tail of an ox, the forehead of a wolf, and the hoofs of a horse." The male has a horn, but the female does not. It is a good, gentle, and benevolent creature.

The wooden *"fish,"* a red object found in most Buddhist temples, is a clapper, used for beating time while the monks chant the sutras. Some say that the monks dropped the sutras in water as the holy scriptures were being brought from India. A fish ate the sutras, so it was beaten to force it to regurgitate. Others say if you don't beat the fish, there will be an earthquake.

The *tortoise,* usually seen with a giant stele on its back, is one of the four supernatural animals, the others being the phoenix, the dragon, and the unicorn. Real ones are frequently kept at Buddhist temples, for they are sacred, an emblem of longevity, strength, and endurance.

Visit religious buildings After sampling a few temples, you should be able to identify the various kinds just from a quick glance inside.

Confucian temples were in every sizable community. (For a history of Confucius, see "Qufu" in Destinations.) Everyone who passed by had to stop and bow respectfully before the gate, or be punished. Scholars came here both to worship the sage, for good luck, and to write examinations for the imperial civil service. Confucius was officially worshiped at the spring and autumn equinoxes. Try to imagine the burning of incense and the muffled clang of gongs, as processions of officials in long red gowns and caps arrived. The men kowtowed, their heads to the ground, in deepest reverence. They left offerings of food and wine on the altar. Musicians played ritual bells. Such ceremonies still take place occasionally in Qufu (and in Taiwan).

Confucian temples did not usually have statues, but simply tablets with the names of ancestors written on them. The walls were red. The south gate was usually left unbuilt until a son from the town passed the difficult examinations and became a Senior Scholar. Only a Senior Scholar and the Emperor could enter by the south gate. No women were considered for the examinations, but if Chinese opera plots are to be believed, some did successfully take them disguised as men.

Was Confucianism a religion or a philosophy? This question is frequently debated. While Confucius himself skeptically rejected the supernatural, Chinese people did and, in some cases, still do consider him a god. He is among the Taoist deities too. But he was primarily a teacher of ethics, of "right conduct," and good, stable government.

Many Confucian temples now are used as museums because Confucianism no longer has imperial patronage. The largest temples are in Beijing and Qufu.

Buddhist temples come in two basic varieties, of which there are infinite variations.

(1) Buddhist temples, surrounded by windowless walls, frequently have four fierce-looking, larger than life-size, human-type guardians after you enter the first gate. Each temple might have different names for these. Inside the first hall, visitors are greeted by the fat, laughing Buddha, *Maitreya,* or in Chinese, *Mi Lo Fu.* He is the Buddha still-to-come. Behind him is *Wei Tou,* the military bodhisattva, the armed warrior who guards the Buddhist scriptures. Wei Tou is probably comparable to the Indian god Indra.

Central in the main hall is the Buddha, a.k.a. the Enlightened One, Sakyamuni, or Prince Siddhartha Gautama. Also in this hall are usually statues or paintings of *bodhisattvas,* known in Chinese as *pusas.* These are saints who have gained Enlightenment but have come back to the world to help other people attain it too. A favorite bodhisattva is Avalokita, a.k.a. Guanyin (Kwan Yin, Kuan Yin), or the Goddess of Mercy, who may have several heads and arms and may be carrying a vase or a child. She is usually behind Sakyamuni, facing north. Guanyin started out as a male god in China until about the 12th century, when his followers preferred to worship him as a woman. He is still sometimes depicted as male. Said one guide, "Men believe he is male and women believe she is female."

Other bodhisattvas could be *Amitabha,* in charge of the souls of the dead, *Manjusri,* in charge of wisdom, usually with a sword in his right hand and a lotus in his left, and the Bodhisattvas of Pharmacy, Universal Benevolence, and the Earth.

Arhats, known in Chinese as *lohan,* are people who have achieved Nirvana. They are usually depicted in groupings of 16, 18, or 500, and are based on real Indian holy men. These are frequently seen in paintings, or as statues. Devout Buddhists should know each of them by name.

Gautama was the Indian prince, born in the 6th century B.C., who was brought up confined to a palace. One day, upon seeing the suffering of the outside world, he forsook his wealth and family. He was 29 years old then. For six years, he went searching for life's meaning. Finding it, he then preached his ideas for 45 years: the Four Noble Truths and the Noble Eightfold Path to Nirvana. These numbers now correspond to the circles on top of Buddhist stupas and pagodas.

Buddha taught that the source of all suffering is selfish desire, and one must stop all craving for it. Some sects believe in asceticism. The Chinese, Mongolians, and Tibetans follow the Mahayana school of faith and good works, which believes Buddha is divine and can answer prayers. You will see people in temples, smoking incense in hand, nodding to the statues or kowtowing on the floor. All forms of Buddhism aim at stopping the continuous cycle of reincarnation—but some adherents are more serious about this than others. Nirvana is the extinction of existence.

The swastika is a Buddhist symbol of good luck, later inverted and used by the Nazis. Most temples have live fish and turtles. Full-time Buddhists are vegetarians. Some Buddhist monks have pieces of incense burned into their skulls at their initiation. This is a proof of the genuineness of those who say they are monks.

 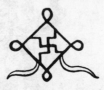

The swastika, symbol of luck

Swastika border design

The swastika was a Buddhist good luck symbol of Indian origin long before the Nazis existed. You will find it on the bellies of some Buddhist statues and latticed on screens and windows in complicated variations.

An interesting study to make as you sightsee is of the clothing carved on buddhas. Some wear the plain, draped robes of Indian holy men, others the fancy, feminine Chinese court dress with jewelry. Buddhism arrived in China from India, but Buddhist art became distinctly Chinese. Can you date a statue from its clothes? The fatness of its face?

You will probably see many more Buddhist temples than Taoist and Confucian.

(2) **Lama temples** are expressions of the Tibetan and Mongolian form of Buddhism, into which have been injected elements of the early Tibetan religion called Bon. Some sources say that the dalai lama, who is considered both the temporal and religious head of Lamaism, is a reincarnation of Avalokita or Guanyin, or the god Chenrezi. The religion is riddled with superstition, demons, and an incredibly horrifying hell for sinners. All of these are reflected in the murals and statues of Lamaist temples. Lamaism is also divided into sects, the main ones being the meditative Yellow Hats and the sensual Red Hats.

These temples are different from other Chinese Buddhist temples not only in their statues, but also in their architecture. Usually built on mountainsides, they have tall, narrow windows, flatter, less ornate roofs, and are usually decorated over the main door with a gilded wheel of Buddhist doctrine and two deer. Statues inside are frequently decorated with turquoise and coral, and many wear pointed caps. The best-known

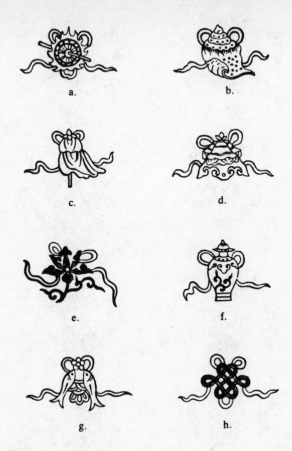

The eight Buddhist emblems of happy augury

a. The wheel of the law
b. The conch shell
c. The state umbrella
d. The canopy
e. The lotus flower
f. The covered vase
g. The pair of fishes
h. The endless knot

Lama temples are in Tibet, but important Lama temples are in Beijing, Chengde, Qinghai, and Inner Mongolia. A Lama temple also stands in Beijing's Summer Palace. See also "Lhasa" and "Chengde."

Taoist temples are identified by Taoist gods, among whom are Guanyin and Confucius, so don't get confused. Other gods and saints can be identified by the things they carry.

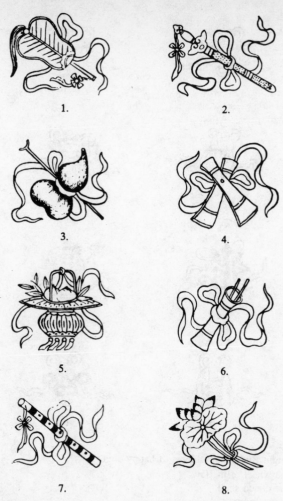

The attributes of the eight Taoistic genii

1. The fan
2. The sword
3. The pilgrim's staff and gourd
4. The castanets
5. The flower basket
6. The tube and rods
7. The flute
8. The lotus flower

The Eight Taoist Genii or Immortals or Fairies were originally eight humans who discovered the secrets of nature. They lived alone in remote mountains (one of them in a cave at Lushan), had magic powers and could revive the dead. They are usually found together on a vase or in one painting, or as a set of eight porcelain pieces. Chung Li-chuan carries the fan to revive the spirits of the dead, Lu Tung-pin the supernatural sword, Li Tieh-kuai the staff, Tsao Kuo-chiu the castanets, Lan

Tsai-ho the flower basket, Chang Kuo the bamboo tube, Han Hsiang-tzu the flute, and Ho Hsien-ku the lotus flower. Two are women.

Daoism (Taoism) was founded 1800 years ago by a sage named Lao Zi (Lao Tzu), whose message was conveyed to the world by a disciple named Mencius. It preaches that everything exists through the interplay of two opposite forces: male-female; positive-negative; hot-cold; light-dark; heaven-earth; yang-yin, etc. One wonders if Chairman Mao's theory of opposites and his emphasis on contradictions is related to this theory.

In the center of the dual Yin-Yang, the principles of being, surrounded by the eight trigrams of divination. The Eight Trigrams represent eight animals and eight directions. At eleven o'clock are the three unbroken lines of heaven; then clockwise, clouds, thunder, mountains, water, fire, earth, and wind. These are used in fortune telling. You may have heard of the I Ching.

Taoists try to achieve harmony out of the conflict of these forces through the Tao or the Way. Taoism is closer to nature than the other religions, its saints finding enlightenment after spending years meditating in caves. Over the years, it also has been diluted by superstition, its adherents believing in charms and spells, ghosts, nature spirits, and the worship of supernatural beings. *Feng-shui* geomancy, where man places his dwelling in harmony with natural forces, is an expression of Taoism.

Taoism was most popular in the Tang and Song, but declined in the Ming. Its most famous monasteries are in Beijing, Chengdu, Shenyang, and Suzhou.

Moslem Mosques are architecturally of two varieties and *visitors always remove their shoes* inside the great halls. The mosques similar to those in western Asia, with rounded, onionlike domes, are mainly in northwest China. Other mosques look like other Chinese temples, with curved roofs and ornate dragons and phoenixes (in spite of the prophet's teachings against making images).

In either style, there is a place for washing hands and feet before prayers. The main building is the Great Hall, which is frequently decorated with Arabic writing, arches, and flower motifs. Moslems pray five times a day, facing the holy city of Mecca in Saudi Arabia. Every mosque has a minaret. You could ask if the *muezzin* or *imam* calls the faithful to prayers from the minaret as is done in other countries.

Moslems can pray anywhere, but the devout usually pray in a mosque if they can. Note the prayer rugs with designs woven into them indicating the direction in which to kneel. Carpets made in Moslem areas deliberately do not have images of animals or objects on them, in keeping with the commandment forbidding "graven images." Note also the disproportionate number of women worshipers, and in some mosques, separate sections for women.

Moslems are followers of the Prophet Mohammed, who was born in A.D. 570. Known as Islam, his religion gives a different emphasis to the god of Judaism and Christianity. Old Testament prophets and Jesus Christ are considered honored prophets, but Mohammed was the last and the greatest. The holy book is the Koran, which teaches a strict code of behavior (no pork, no alcohol, no idols, etc.), and universal brotherhood of all believers. During the holy month of Ramadan, believers fast during the day.

Islam arrived in China in A.D. 652 during the Tang, with Arab and Persian traders who settled in Guangzhou, Quanzhou, Hangzhou, and Yangzhou. During the 13th century, many Moslem soldiers, artisans, and officials were brought to China to fight and work with Kublai Khan. The approximately 10 million Moslems in China are known as Hui, but Uygurs, Kazaks, Kirgiz, Ozbeks, etc., are also Moslem. Most Moslems live in the northwest. Friday is the holy day and mosques, which might otherwise be closed, are always opened Friday afternoons.

Besides those of the major religions, **other religious buildings** exist in China. Many of these are **ancestral temples** (*miao*), frequently one to a village. Many villages are each comprised of people with a common name and ancestor, so they only need one temple. Some of these temples were very elaborate and are used also as the village school. In ancestral temples, tablets with the names of the ancestors were kept in neat rows and worshiped with burning incense, gifts of food, and ceremonial bowing at least twice a year. The ancestors were informed of important family events like births and marriages, both verbally and in writing in a family history book. One worshiped ancestors in gratitude for one's life, but more so because the spirits of departed ancestors had to be kept happy so they could influence one's current fortunes. Many of these tablets were destroyed or hidden during the Cultural Revolution. When you go to a village, ask to see the ancestral temple.

Cave temples with frescoes and Buddhist statues were first built in India and spread with the Silk Road into China. Caves have always been conducive to meditation. There, one gets a feeling of security, like being back in a mother's womb. Dunhuang is the greatest for its paintings. The two at Lanzhou are noted for their strikingly dramatic sites and the richness of their sculpture. Important for carvings are also Datong and Luoyang.

Other cave temples listed as protected historical monuments by the State Council are at Anxi and Linxia in Gansu; Handan in Hebei; Turpan, Baicheng, and Kuqu in Xinjiang; Guangyuan, Leshan, and Dazu in Sichuan; Jianchuan in Yunnan; Gongxian in Henan; Guyuan in Ningxia; and Hangzhou in Zhejiang.

In old China, people worshiped any number of gods. They wanted to cover all possible bases. If a friend prayed successfully to one god for a baby boy, then other barren women tried that god too. It was not unusual for one person to have his children baptized as Christians, burn incense to a deceased grandfather, and then retire to contemplate in a Taoist or Buddhist monastery.

There are temples to the city gods. Fishermen worshiped the Goddess of Heaven, Tian Hou, who bears some resemblance to the goddess Guanyin. See "Quanzhou" for Manicheanism and "Xi'an" for Nestorianism.

Christian churches were most frequently built with gothic windows, as in Western architecture. Many Roman Catholic churches look like transplants from Europe. For more on Christianity in China, see *Religion* in "Local Customs."

Zoos are usually pathetic, but many have pandas. Beijing's is the largest. Animals do not have much space to roam.

Relax in a Chinese garden This is different from rushing through on a guided tour. Go back to one you especially like and just sit and absorb. A Chinese garden is not just a park or something attached to a building. It is an art form, the world in miniature, with mountains, water, plants, and buildings—a three-dimensional Chinese painting you can enter to try to experience infinity.

Gardens were built for a leisurely lifestyle in which poetry, philosophical contemplation, and the beauty of nature were of the utmost importance. Imagine *living* here! The ugly world of poverty and injustice was kept outside the high walls. "Above Heaven; below Suzhou and Hangzhou" probably referred more to the gardens than anything else.

Take your time exploring. Look at the integration of the buildings with nature, the pinpointing of places of particular beauty by unusually shaped windows and moon gates. Absorb the tranquillity of the water. Look at the reflections. Think of poetry. The meaning of life. A garden takes time—infinite time.

Do a study—it is easy to get cultural indigestion. After the third temple, they could all look alike. But they don't! Take notes. Draw diagrams. Link up roof styles to dynasties and regions. Which ones have animals? And which animals? Are the roofs southern or northern?

Study the shapes of **pagodas**—those related to the Chinese *lou* and those related to Indian shapes. Is the shape distinctive to different dynasties? Do they all have an uneven number of stories? Which dynasties' are octagonal? Which pagodas have a different number of stories inside than outside?

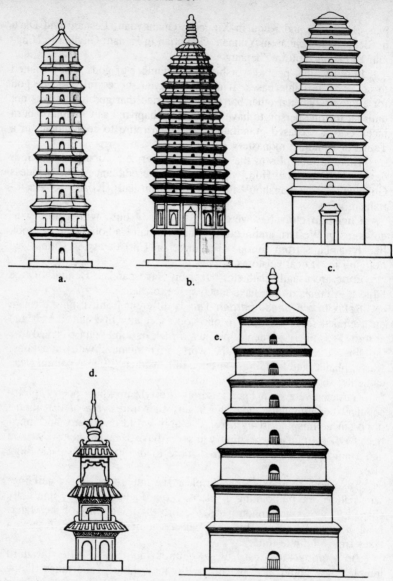

The shapes of pagodas came from either the Indian temple (b and c) or from the multistoried Chinese pavilion (lou). How many variations of these two basic shapes can you find, and how many pagodas can you accurately date just by looking at them? These are rough sketches of some examples: a—Guangzhou (Ming); b—Zhengzhou (Songshan—6th century); c—Xi'an (Tang); d—any number of dynasties and places. This can be seen even in Chinese-style mosques; e—Xi'an (also Tang) but a different derivation than c.

Do a study of **tile faces** (wa dang) or eave tiles, for instance. These are the circular pieces of tile at the lower edges of a roof. Some have animal faces on them, some flowers, some Chinese characters. The designs were chosen in some cases as good luck symbols.

Find out details. Why do you have to step so high to get through some doorways and not others? Is it because of flood? Or because it blocks bad luck? What are the bumps on the head of some of the Buddhas? What do the different positions of Buddhist statues mean?

Who was China's most prolific graffiti artist? My vote would go to Qing Emperor Qianlong. Why is "son of a tortoise" one of the worst insults you can give?

Why have the Chinese placed so much emphasis on **calligraphy**? Why is it more than a means of communication, a very sophisticated art? Why is the calligraphy on one tablet better than the calligraphy on another?

Chinese people spend years mastering their written language. They first learn by copying the characters over and over again, an exercise in patience, perseverance, and discipline. For good calligraphy, writing legibly is not enough. One follows one of the four accepted basic styles with individual variations. One's calligraphy has to express one's personality and feelings, in tune with the content of the written message.

Chinese painting developed out of calligraphy, using the same materials and holding the brush in the same vertical way. Ideally, one needs an ink brush made of animal hair, rice paper, ink stick, and ink tablets. Students are taught to keep their backs, upper torsos, heads, and souls(!) in a straight line. The calligraphy you see on buildings, by Emperor Qianlong or whoever, was chiseled by someone else. Chairman Mao also was an excellent calligrapher.

Learn about **feng-shui** and the placement of buildings in harmony with the contours of the earth. Do all temples face south? Do all tombs face south? What role do pagodas play? Why are there screens in front of doorways and gates? How can you improve your own house to insure that good luck doesn't just go out your windows and doors?

Study the **different tomb styles**: Ming, Qing, Song, Han. How are they different?

Learn about Chinese **mythology.** Pick up a copy of *Old Tales of China—a tourist guidebook to better understanding of China's stage, cinema, arts and crafts.* Published by China Travel and Tourism Press, this inexpensive booklet in English relates many of the famous stories, some of which will help you understand Chinese opera plots. Try to figure out why these stories are so popular.

Read. Get immersed in old (and new) China. Read *Romance of the Three Kingdoms* while sitting on a cliff at Zhenjiang, overlooking the Yangtze, at the place where the widow of Liu Pei pined for her husband. Read *A Dream of the Red Chamber* while relaxing in the courtyard of one of the new reproductions of the setting. Read *Pilgrimage to* *the West* on a trip along the Silk Road. Translations of these books are cheaper in China, and if you have the time, will add immeasurably to your experiences there.

A Dream of the Red Chamber (a.k.a. Dream of Red Mansions) is one of the most popular novels published in China because it paints a vivid and convincing picture of how the rich (and their servants) lived during feudal times. Any Chinese over 35 years of age should know it. It is the story of a wealthy family, connected with the imperial court, who lived and declined during the Qing dynasty. The plot might move too slowly for Western readers, who probably will have trouble also remembering the Chinese names. (Make notes as you read it.) However, for details of lifestyles it is excellent, with descriptions of a funeral, impertinent bond servants, the visit home of daughter and imperial concubine Yuan-chun, etc. The sexual encounters are mentioned, and some are surprising, but they are not fully described.

Favorite among the characters is the bored, spoiled young hero Jia Pao-yu, who is surrounded by servants and is good at writing couplets. Sad to say, as the novel is popular largely because of its poetry, the poetry loses much in translation. Pao-yu is in love with his cousin, the beautiful Lin Tai-yu, but he is forced to marry someone else.

Attendants dressed as the characters inhabit the Red Chamber reproductions, known also as *Daguan Yuan* (Grand View Garden).

Learn about **China's minorities** (or nationalities). China has 56 different ethnic groups, 55 of whom are 6.7% of the population. These 55 million people live in areas totaling half of China. Yunnan province has 26 different nationalities. A nationality doesn't necessarily settle in one location. Often sub-branches are spread over several provinces, with different costumes and dialects. For example, the Miao nationality is found in Guizhou, Hunan, Yunnan, Guangdong, Guangxi, and Sichuan provinces. Miao women in Guizhou wear pleated skirts while those in Hunan wear pants. The color and designs of their turbans are also different.

During festivals and market days, most of the minorities, especially the women, wear their distinctive costumes, which are usually decorated with fine embroidery, and, sometimes, heavy silver jewelry. Their hairstyles could indicate their marital status.

Some minorities are very musical, expressing more liveliness in their dances than the majority Han Chinese. Although the levels of their Chinese education and their economy is generally lower than average, their cultural heritage is rich and meaningful. Unusual courtship rituals are still practiced.

The festivals of the nationalities are usually worth experiencing. The Dai celebrate a watersplashing festival similar to that in neighboring Thailand and Burma. The Kazaks have a Horse Racing Festival, the Bai a Torch Festival, the Tibetan now celebrate the New Year (at the Jokhang in January), etc. Mongolians have equally colorful sporting meets, with their distinctive wrestling, horses, and motorcycles. Facilities for tourists in minority areas are still modest but not impossible. Collecting minority weaving, jewelry, and musical instruments can be very interesting. Comparing customs can keep anthropologists and folklorists occupied for years.

DESTINATIONS

Over 240 destinations are open to foreign visitors now, more than that if you count the smaller tourist sites available from major cities. For some of these, foreign visitors have needed **alien travel permits,** readily available from the Security Police. See "Getting Around."

Listed here are the most important destinations. Mentioned under these headings, especially those of the provincial capitals, are minor destinations. The list here is alphabetical by pinyin, with alternative spellings in parentheses. Where the **Chinese characters** for tourist sites, hotels, and restaurants have been available, they are printed so you can ask taxi drivers and people on the street to help you find where you want to go. The words *Guesthouse* and *Hotel* are interchangeable and do not imply quality. The words *monastery* and *temple* are also interchangeable.

To locate any of these cities on a **map,** note the tourist region right after the name of the city; for example, "Northwest China." Look for the Northwest China regional map in the back of the book. For **shoppers,** we have listed items produced locally. These are usually cheaper and with more variety at the factory and in the province than elsewhere.

Don't jump to the conclusion that a temple "founded in 1250" means the buildings are over 700 years old. The buildings may have been rebuilt recently. In a country that has had as many upheavals, air raids, and revolutions as China, it is amazing that so many great monuments have survived to this day.

No other country has as many historic sites or as varied offerings as China. Chinese governments on all levels have selected some of the more important ones for renovation. This is a good indicator that the buildings are genuine and culturally significant. **An * means the site is protected as a historical or revolutionary monument by the State Council** of the national government.

And please don't think that old is beautiful. Frequently the older the monument, the less developed and intricate.

Hours given for stores and tourist sites are approximate, those in summer about an hour later than those in winter. **Schools, villages,** and **factories** are basically the same in the whole of China, and these are not mentioned in every destination unless there is something special about them. We do urge you to visit schools, villages, and factories wherever possible.

For those trying to learn Chinese:

ang = nunnery
bingguan = guesthouse
ci = temple
dong = east
ge = small pavilion
hai = sea
hu = lake
jie = street
ling = tomb

lu = road
miao = temple, usually ancestral or Confucian

nan = south
sha = sand
si = temple
tang = temple

xi = west
yuan = garden
zhou = city state (smaller than a province; larger than a city)

bei = north
chan guan = restaurant
da lu = avenue
fan dian = hotel or restaurant
guan = pass
he = river
jiang = river
jing = capital
lou = multistoried pavilion big enough for people to live in
men = gate

quan = spring
shan = mountain
ta = pagoda
ting = tiny pavilion usually in rural surroundings in which people can rest
xian = county
zhong = middle or central

You will note some redundancy in names, such as Lu Shan Mountain, but those are for people who don't know Chinese, since such names are commonly used. It may appear cumbersome to put in the *pin yin,* the English, and the Chinese characters for place names, but in China some people will use the Chinese names and others will use the English, so the Chinese characters should help avoid confusion.

Sources differ sometimes as to historical dates and events, and *English translations* of site names. Please be flexible. Names like Han, Song, Ming, and Qing refer to dynasty, as "in the Ming," with Mongol the same as Yuan, and Manchu the same as Qing.

Correct telephone numbers have also been difficult to obtain. In some places more than one is listed because sources differed. If one doesn't work, try the other. Failing that, ask any English-speaking source like C.I.T.S., a foreign airline, or an embassy for an up-to-date telephone number. To complicate matters, in the mid-1980s some revolutionary street names, like "East is Red," were changed, and the telephone system upgraded with new telephone numbers.

Telephone numbers of **hotels** are listed with current prices in "Budget and Hotel Quick Reference."

The **restaurants** listed are those recommended by C.I.T.S. except in Beijing, Guangzhou, and Shanghai, where we have developed our own lists. Note that population figures for "cities" usually include several counties and municipalities. We have tried to give the figures for the main urban area where they were available. And some of the tourist sites offered, especially those away from the main cities, are available only to tour groups booking in advance, not to individuals.

Anshan 鞍山

Northeast China. 90 km SW of Shenyang and still cold. Minimum in winter—⁻25°C; but maximum in summer is 34°C. Annual precipitation 715 mm, including snow. Urban population 1.2 million.

Anshan was settled in the Yan State during the Warring States period. Its mines and smelting date back to the second century B.C. In 1395 (Ming), a city was built here; the ruins can still be seen. The Japanese colonized this area in the 1930s until 1945. The Communists took over on Feb. 19, 1948.

Today Anshan mines magnesite, talcum, white and green marble, and graphite, and has China's biggest iron and steel works. It is also known for **Mt. Qianshan** 千山风景区 , 44 square km of wilderness and jagged peaks, the highest 708 meters above sea level. Five Buddhist temples, one founded in the Tang but rebuilt in the Ming, and a Taoist temple add interest. It is 18 km SE of the main hotels. A cable car should be operating for your visit.

The other main tourist attraction is **Tanggangzi Hot Spring Sanatorium** 汤岗子温泉 , 15 km south of Anshan, where visitors can relax, drink mineral water, and get physiotherapy, hydrotherapy, and acupuncture treatment. Hostel and gardens on the premises. It is one of the Three Most Famous Hot Springs in China. At Liaoyuan, about 15 km NE, are some *Han and Wei tombs with murals.

Haicheng silk, ginseng, and Nanguo pears are specialties of the city. Restaurants in the hotels serve Western, Chinese, and Liaoning food. The Beijing "Quan Jude" Roast Duck Restaurant is in the center of the city.

Hotels
Anshan Hotel 鞍山宾馆 □ *121, First Section, Shengli Rd., Tiedong District, Anshan* □ *1953; 2 km from railway station.*

Lanhua Hotel 兰花宾馆 □ *near center of Anshan close to Feb. 19th Park* □ 1987.

Overseas Chinese Mansion 华侨大厦 □ *near center of Anshan close to Feb. 19th Park* □ 1987.

Qianhua Hotel 千华宾馆 □ *in center of town near Feb. 19th Park* □ 1987.

Shengli (Victory) Hotel 胜利宾馆 □ *2 Xinhua St., Tiedong District, Anshan* □ 1958; 4 km from railway station.

C.I.T.S. is in the Anshan Hotel; tel. 24403.

Friendship Store is in the Anshan First Department Store (May 1 Rd., Tiedong District).

See also "Shenyang."

Anyang 安阳

Northwest China. Northern part of Henan province north of the Yellow River near the Hebei border.

This city of half a million people is one of the oldest in China, founded in the Shang dynasty. For short periods in the 16th century B.C., it was a Shang capital. In the 14th century, the problem of flooding solved, it was made a permanent city, the capital for King Pan Geng (Pan Keng) of the State of Yin, and continued as the royal capital for some 270 years.

It was here that the oracle bones, an ancient means of divination, were later found. Here early writing was inscribed on tortoise shells and shoulder blades of oxen, and then cracked with heat. The direction of the crack foretold the future. Today the city is highly industrial, with an iron and steel works. Tourists might be interested in visiting its jade-carving, plaited-straw, and carpet-weaving factories. But its prime attraction is to students of archaeology and ancient and modern Chinese history (even though important, excavated artifacts are mainly in the provincial museum in Zhengzhou). It is also exciting to people into air sports. Where else in China can you sightsee from a hot-air balloon or glider?

A one-day visit can include: the *Yin Ruins 殷墟, 2.5 km from the Anyang Guest House. The ruins include palace foundations, royal tombs, and bronze and jade artifacts. Yin was the last capital of the Xia dynasty in the 11th century B.C. The Anyang Museum and the **Wenfeng Pagoda** 灵谷寺 are also important. The pagoda is unusual, as it appears to be larger at the top, with a dagoba (stupa) at the summit. Some excellent brick carvings of saints are close enough to the ground to be studied.

The Mausoleum of Yuan Shikai 袁林 (2.5 km from the Anyang Hotel) holds the remains of the ambitious, brilliant official of the Manchu court. Also a warlord, Yuan took over the presidency of republican China from Dr. Sun Yat-sen in 1913, declared himself emperor in 1915, and died of a heart attack in 1916.

Yuefei's Temple 岳飞庙 (22 km from the Anyang Hotel) is a memorial to the maligned national hero.

If you have more time, then you can take in the **Azure-cloud Palace Temple** 碧霞宫和大石佛 (60 km from the hotel) with the oldest and largest Buddha in the province. The **Red Flag Canal** 红旗渠, one of the Communists' earliest achievements, is 96 km away, a spectacular example of water management.

One of the more exotic things to do in China is hot-air ballooning, sky-diving, or gliding, which can probably be enjoyed at the Gliding School. If any of these are essential to your visit here, do make arrangements with C.I.T.S. before you go.

Restaurants

Jubinlou Restaurant 聚宾楼饭庄 □ *north entrance of Baida St.; tel. 3698* □ specializes in squid with chicken wing tips, fish with crispy skin, egg pudding, and toffee apples.

Yingchun Garden Roast-duck Restaurant 迎春园烤鸭店 □ *Middle section, Hongqi Rd.; tel. 2469* □ specializes in roast duck, quick-fried prawns, grilled sharks' fins, quick-fried rolled squid, and sea slugs with egg white.

Hotels

Anyang Guest House 安阳宾馆 □ *1 Youyi (Friendship) Rd., 1 km from railway station* □ 1959; renovated 1984. This is the main tourist hotel.

Taihang Guest House 太行宾馆 □ *Dengta Dong Rd.* □ 1978.

Xiangzhou Guest House 相州宾馆 □ *northern section of Huancheng Xi Rd.*

The **Xiangzhou Hotel** 相州酒家, on the same grounds as the Xiangzhou Guest House, will be ready for your visit.

C.I.T.S. 国际旅行社 is in the Anyang Guest House (1 Youyi Rd.; tel. 2145.)

Baotou 包头

(Paotow) North China. Western Inner Mongolia. This mining and industrial city is a 14-hour train trip or 1½ hour flight from Beijing, and is not for the weak. Its tourist attractions are

*mainly out of town. Take a scarf to cover your nose in case
you encounter a sandstorm. The maximum temperature is 38°C,
the minimum is ⁻30°C in winter! The average altitude is 1000
meters. Annual rainfall is a sparce 312 mm. The local tourist
office points out 132 frostfree days a year! Prepare for cold
weather except in summer.*

The city was founded in the 17th century (Qing) on a neolithic site.
At that time, people were encouraged to settle here to open up agriculture and defend the borders. The urban population is now about 870,000,
of whom the Han are 90%, the Mongolians 2.5%, and the rest 21 other
national minorities.

Of 1000 or so factories, visitors might want to see and shop at
those producing leather and furs, porcelain, and arts and crafts. The
Baotou Carpet Factory 包头地毯厂 is about 25 km from the main
hotel.

If you only have one day, C.I.T.S. recommends the Wudangzhao
Temple and a quick city tour. The city has over 40 archaeological sites,
including the wall of the Zhao Kingdom and a Han dynasty town. The
Wudangzhao Temple 五当召 is 70 km from the Blue Mountain Hotel
and could be a rough trip. It is a massive 2500-room complex established in 1749 (Qing), once home to 1200 monks and covering about
50 acres. The largest lamasery in western Inner Mongolia, it contains
statues, murals, and tankas typical of yellow sect Buddhism. More about
Tibetan Buddhism under "Lhasa" and "Chengde."

If you have more time, the **Meidaizhao Temple** was originally built in the Ming. It is also known as the Sanniangzi Temple after
the concubine of its Mongolian founder. She is buried here. A Han
Chinese, she helped to bridge the differences between the two groups.
The ***Tomb of Genghis Khan*** 成吉思汗陵墓 was moved south of
Baotou to Ejinhoroq (Elinhoro) in 1954. It is in the shape of three yurts
and has been restored.

Two new parks may be open by the time you arrive: the **Kongdulung Reservoir** 昆都仑水库风景区 , about 13 km from the hotel,
and the **Nanhaizi Water Park** 南海子水上公园 , about 25 km.

Hotels

Qingshan (Blue Mountain) Hotel 青山宾馆 □ *Qingshan district, Baotou* □ 1956; renovated 1982; 25 km from airport. This is the
main tourist hotel.

Baotou Hotel 包头宾馆 □ *Kongdulung district* □ 1957; renovated 1983.

Donghe Hotel 东河宾馆 □ *Donghe district* □ 1954; renovated
1984.

The hotels serve Chinese, Western, and Moslem food. Local delicacies include camel hump and camel paw and, of course, mutton dishes.

C.I.T.S. 国际旅行社 is in Baotou Hotel (tel. 24615).
CAAC 中国民航 (Donghe district; tel. 41404).
    See also "Hohhot."

Beidaihe 北戴河

(Pehtaiho, Peitaihe; North Dai River) North China, Hebei, is a lovely seaside resort 5 hours by train via Tianjin due east of Beijing, and about 10 km south of Qinhuangdao; 7 trains a day each way serve Beidaihe. The town is 12 km from the railway station. An airport is at Shanhaiguan, 35 km north, for the 50-minute air link with the capital. Air service also with Shijiazhang.

Beidaihe was built after the completion of the Beijing-Shanhaiguan railway in 1893. By 1949, 706 villas and hotel buildings had been completed, many of them for foreign diplomats and missionaries as well as wealthy Chinese. After Liberation, the Chinese government rebuilt some of the old buildings and added new ones as rest and recreation centers for its employees. In 1979, the resort was opened to foreign tourists, who are now served by the Beidaihe Beach Tourist Corporation. The population is around 10,000.

The resort stretches along 12 km of hard, golden sand sloping gently out into the Bohai Sea. Swimming is good though there may be a few jellyfish. The beaches are divided by rock promontories. At the **Pigeon's Nest** 鹰角石 in the east, you can see Qinhuangdao across the bay and the best sunrise. At the **Tiger Stone** 老虎石 in the center, crab fishermen sell their catch in the summer.

Several swimming areas are attached to each of the hotels, manned by life guards and protected by nets. Each hotel has changing rooms on the beach with hot and cold fresh-water showers, open 8 a.m.–10 p.m. The swimming season is from May to September, depending on how cold you like your water. The hottest days are in August (maximum 36°C for a few days), but the high is usually 31°C, sometimes dropping to 24 or 25 at night.

A **Guanyin Temple** 观音祠 built in 1911 is on the grounds of the West Hill Hotel. The buildings were beautifully restored in 1979, the two statues and frescoes inside replaced after being destroyed by the Red Guards. The temple is about 1.5 km behind the hotel's service bureau, a nice morning's walk. The **Xiaobaohezhai Village** is also good to visit. It was one of the first in China to have pensions for its older citizens and one of the first with a birth-control program. It grows apples, peaches and pears for export, so an ideal time to visit is late August-September.

A good view of Beidaihe can be enjoyed from **Lianfengshan Park**
莲蓬山公园

In Beidaihe, one can learn acupuncture and massage, taiji, Chinese cooking, and seal cutting. One can also rent bicycles, sailboats, and sailboards. The tourist corporation can arrange summer camping, bicycle tours, bird watching, international conferences, and health care tours too.

Excursions

Qinhuangdao—see separate listing.

Great Wall at Shanhaiguan—see "Great Wall" and "Shanhaiguan."

Mengjiangnu Temple and **Yansai Lake**—see "Shanhaiguan."

Restaurants

Beihai Restaurant 北海饭庄   □ seafood
Kissling Restaurant   起士林餐厅   □ mainly European food
International Club   国际俱乐部   □ Chinese and Western food

Hotels

Xishan (West Hill) Hotel 西山宾馆   □ *western sector of the beach* □ 148 buildings spread along 3 km of beachfront. Has been and probably still is used also by the Military and the Party Central committees of the central government. You might see some armed but friendly PLA guards on the premises. Best swimming and good service. On the grounds is also the **Beidaihe Beach Club,** which has a comfortable theater seating about 850, table tennis, billiards, art exhibitions, and a restaurant. Open 3–11 p.m. Bring your own cassettes if you want to dance.

Zhonghai Tan (Central Beach) Hotel 中海滩宾馆   □ was the R&R center of the State Council, with 86 buildings spread along 4 km of seashore. Very pleasant. Its service bureau is on the main street of town, which runs behind the hotel.

New hotels planned near the Pigeon's Nest, 32 km from the airport, 15 km from the railway station. Unnamed at this writing is a low-priced hotel of 200 beds. As the new hotels open, some of the other hotels may go back to being only government guesthouses.

Jinshan Hotel 金山宾馆   □ 1986; 240 beds. Closed-circuit TV, radio, air conditioning, conference hall, ballroom, function room, open-air bar, beach, and several dining halls.

Beidaihe Beach Tourism Corporation (Tel: 2748. Cable 0518). Its Autocenter has large, medium, and small buses and cars for hire; 24-hour service.

▶ **Note:** Regular public buses between Beidaihe and the beach operate every 30 minutes from 6 a.m. to 6:30 p.m.

Beijing

*(Peking; Northern Capital) North China, surrounded by Hebei
province on the northern fringe of the north China plain; 183
km west of the seacoast, about 44 meters above sea level, has
mountains to the north, west, and east; 36 hours by train north
of Guangzhou and 19 hours NW of Shanghai, it can also be
reached by train from Ulan Bator and, beyond that, from Moscow. On almost the same latitude as Philadelphia, Beijing is
about 4 hours west of Tokyo by air, 3 north of Guangzhou or
Hong Kong, and 2 NW of Shanghai. The best time to visit is
in the autumn. The hottest days are in July and August—up to
38°C for a week or so; the coldest are in January and February—down to ⁻20°C. Dust storms occasionally blow from December to late March, and sometimes into May. The winter air
has been heavily polluted with coal dust in the past, and few
visitors escaped sore throats and colds then. The government
has made a great effort to restrict the burning of coal. Pollution is not as big a problem anymore. Annual precipitation is
683 mm, usually, from June to August. Population is 9.4 million (almost 5 million urban); 5 million bicycles.*

Beijing is the most important place to visit in China, not just because it is the capital but because it has a 3000-year history, from the
Western Zhou, when it was known as Ji (Chi). Its most impressive
historical monuments date from the 13th century. The museums here
are the best in China, the temples among the most impressive. The
palaces are the biggest and most elaborate. For most Chinese people,
visiting Beijing has been and still is a lifetime ambition and, fortunately, many are now able to do it. They take a great deal of pride in
being here and details are very much sought after by envious neighbors
and friends once they get back home.

If you must pick only one city to visit in this country of thousands of outstanding ancient monuments, you, too, should choose Beijing.

The Liao (916–1125) were the first to build a capital here. They called it Nanjing, Southern Capital, as distinct from their old capital farther north in Manchuria. The name was changed again to Yanjing (Yen Ching) in 1013. In 1125, the Jin, a Tartar dynasty, overthrew the Liao and enlarged the city, calling it Zhongdu, Central Capital. The Mongols (Yuan), under Kublai Khan, overthrew the Jin and built a new capital called Dadu (Ta Tu). In 1368 the Ming drove out the Yuan and established their capital at Nanjing with Beijing, then called Peiping Fu, as an auxiliary capital in 1409.

Beijing became the main capital again in 1421 (Ming) and continued as the Qing capital into the early 1900s. In 1860, it was invaded by foreign, mainly English and French, troops. The foreigners completely destroyed the Yuanmingyuan Palace. The Boxers took over in 1900 and laid siege to the Foreign Legation section, but were repelled by an international military force while the Qing Empress Dowager fled temporarily to Xi'an. In 1928, the Nationalist government moved its capital to today's Nanjing, and Beijing became Peiping (Northern Peace). The Japanese held it from 1937 to 1945. When the Communists took over in 1949, it regained its old name and former position as capital of the nation.

Fortunately, the buildings of Beijing escaped the Pacific War relatively intact. During imperial times, no structures taller than the Forbidden City were allowed. In 1959, ten massive buildings were completed for the tenth anniversary of the founding of the People's Republic. Built in the heavy, plain Soviet style, these included the Great Hall of the People, the Museums of History and the Revolution, the Agricultural Exhibition Hall, and the Palace of the Minorities. They are period pieces now.

In 1966, Beijing's Tian Anmen Square was the setting for mass Red Guard rallies of over a million people. In 1976, the square was also the site of a clash between supporters of the Gang of Four and those of Premier Chou Enlai. Beijing usually is peaceful, except for the bustling of bicycles and motor vehicles.

Beijing is centered around the Forbidden City and Tian Anmen Square. The old foreign legation area was SE of these, near the current Xinqiao Hotel. The European architecture there reflects that period of its history. The Chinese city was south of the Qianmen Gate on the southern edge of Tian Anmen Square.

Beijing now consists of ten districts and nine counties. Rural villages raise the famous force-fed Beijing ducks. Over 2000 factories, mainly in the suburbs, produce iron and steel, coal mining, machines, basic chemicals and petroleum, electronics, and textiles.

The people of Beijing speak Mandarin or *pu tung hua,* the official national language, but they twirl their tongues more. They are predominantly Han, but you will see many flat, wide Mongolian faces too. Beijing people tend to be reserved compared to other Chinese. Don't be put off by this, for they are warm and friendly once they get to know you.

Beijing needs at least six days to cover its important attractions. Many individual travelers use public transportation successfully if they have plenty of time. Just avoid rush hours. Bus and subway maps are available in many hotels. The east-west subway line is 24 km long, each station in a different color marble. Trains operate every 3–8 minutes from early morning to late evening west from the railway station. Note the stations at the south end of Tian Anmen Square and the Minzu Hotel. The circle subway, a 16-km loop, completes the rectangle around Tian Anmen Square and the Forbidden City and reaches near the Beijing Zoo and Friendship Hotel.

A relatively inexpensive **tourist bus** service run by the Beijing Motor Bus Company is recommended for those with a good guidebook or map. The human guides only give short introductions. Basically you're on your own. Regular tours go to the Great Wall, Ming Tombs, Fragrant Hills, Summer Palace, Tanzhe Temple, Yunshui Cave, Qing tombs, and Chengde (Jehol). None of these buses tour downtown Beijing itself. These out-of-town tours can be booked east of the Qianmen south of Tian Anmen Square or beside the Xinqiao Hotel across from Maxim's Stops at the Overseas Chinese Hotel, Wangfujing Ave. A **train** goes daily, except Wednesdays, to the Great Wall (but not the Ming Tombs) at about 7:30 a.m., returning at about 12:35 p.m. **Helicopter tours** are booked at the Holiday Inn Lido and fly over the Great Wall, with a stop at the Ming Tombs. If you are in a big hurry, this is the way to see both.

To help you plan your time so you can cover the most important sights, these groupings áre suggested. The days can be interchangeable, depending on weather, train schedules, upset stomachs, traffic jams, and the hours a particular attraction is open.

Day 1: Tian Anmen Square, Imperial Palace, and Jing Hill. If you make a reservation a month in advance, you can lunch in the Great Hall of the People (tel. 335484). Failing that, there's the Beijing Hotel, Maxim's, Minim's, the Xinqiao Hotel, and the Overseas Chinese Hotel—all within a short taxi ride.

Day 2: The Museums of Chinese History and the Chinese Revolution, Beihai Park and the Temple of Heaven. Tour of Dazhalan if you make arrangements first, and shopping at Liulichang. Lunch if you make a reservation on time at the Fang Shan (Imperial Kitchen) Restaurant (tel. 442573, Beihai Park). Also any of the "Day 1" restaurants.

Day 3: Summer Palace, temples of the Western Hills, Fragrant Hill, ruins of the Yuanmingyuan, and Great Bell Temple. The temple is closed once a week, probably Wednesdays, so phone C.I.T.S. first to make sure it is open. Avoid all but the temple if the weather is bad. Lunch at the Summer Palace (reservation needed at the Tingliguan there), or the Fragrant Hills Hotel.

Day 4: Great Wall and Ming Tombs, but not on Wednesday if you take the train, or Sundays (traffic jam). Avoid in bad weather. Take your own lunch if you want, especially in pleasant weather.

Day 5: Lama Temple, Confucius Temple/Capital Museum, China Art Gallery—half a day. Remainder and **Day 6:** choice of arts and crafts factories, rural visit, shopping, cultural performances, or repeat visits to places where you wanted to spend more time but couldn't. Choice of other excursions.

As you can see, this is a very heavy schedule and you may have to squeeze your shopping and strolling into the evenings. One really needs more time. You can't enjoy details if you keep looking at your watch.

Day 1

Tian Anmen (Tien An Men) Square 前门城门 , 98 acres. Great for kite-flying in the spring. Try to imagine 1966 at the beginning of the Cultural Revolution when a million schoolchildren filled this square, chanting slogans and waving the little red book of quotations from Chairman Mao. The father of Communist China stood at the front of the gate to the north and acknowledged the screams and cheers of the youngsters. Besides giving them a vacation from school, he also gave them a mandate to travel around the country on the trains with room and board in each city—all free. Truckloads of shoes were swept away after the rallies. No one was able to retrieve lost shoes as the crowd surged wildly. Protests and rallies are still held here.

This square is bounded on the north by the Tian Anmen gate and on the west by the Great Hall of the People. On the east is the Museum of the Chinese Revolution and the Museum of Chinese History, and on the south one can't miss the imposing Qianmen (Chien Men) gate. In the center, from the north to south, are the Monument to the People's Heroes and the Chairman Mao Memorial Hall. Every May 1 and Oct. 1 the big portraits are displayed. They are, left to right, Marx, Engels, Lenin, and Stalin. Also prominent is Dr. Sun Yat-sen.

The **Great Hall of the People,** a.k.a. People's Congress Hall 人民大会堂 , built in 1959; 171,800 square meters. Three main sections include a 5000-seat banquet hall, a three-story, 10,000-seat auditorium, and lounges in the style of each of the provinces. This is China's equivalent of a parliament. To some observers, it is merely a rubber-stamp group of representatives. To others, the People's Congress is a forum for the opinions of the masses. Open Tuesdays, Wednesdays, and Saturday mornings for a small fee. Banquets can be booked (tel. 335484). The restaurant entrance is on the north side (Chang'an Xi Ave.).

Qianmen Gate 天安门 is not open, but it is a magnificent,

beautiful gate. To the south is Dazalan, a Chinese shopping area (see Day 2). The bus to the Great Wall can also be booked nearby.

Beijing's gates are marvelous. Each had a very specific purpose; for example, night soil could only go through the Andingmen in the north; prisoners to be executed plodded through the west gate, Xuanwumen. Departing soldiers marched through another of the north gates even if they had to fight in the south. The impressive Deshengmen (Victory Gate) can still be visited.

Monument to the People's Heroes 人民英雄纪念碑 : If you had taken my advice and learned your numbers in Chinese, you would know the dates under each sculpture. Then if you looked up "Milestones in Chinese History" you would know that the sculptures here represent the burning of the opium and the Opium War, 1840–42; the Taiping Heavenly Kingdom, 1851–64; the Revolution of 1911; the May 4, 1919, demonstration against the Versailles Treaty and for the New Cultural Movement (such as literature in plain rather than the generally incomprehensible classical language); the May 30, 1925, Incident in Shanghai, a protest against foreign powers in China after a Chinese worker was killed by a Japanese foreman. Look also for the August 1, 1927, uprising in Nanchang and the Anti-Japanese War, 1937–45.

In April 1976, during the Qingming (Ching Ming) festival, when the dead are honored (in the old days "worshiped"), attempts by the Gang of Four to remove wreaths brought by private citizens in memory of Premier Chou En-lai were resisted by pro-Chou supporters at this monument. Hundreds were wounded and thousands arrested. This protest is now referred to as the April Fifth Movement against the Gang of Four, and encouraged pro-Chou politicians like Deng Xiaoping to attempt to overthrow them.

The **Chairman Mao Memorial Hall** 毛主席纪念堂 was built in 1977. It has been open on Mondays, Wednesdays, and Friday mornings. Whether it remains open depends on the political climate. In this mausoleum rest the remains of China's great leader. The simple white building, with 44 granite columns and glazed yellow trim, is 33.6 meters high and 105 meters square. The sculptures on the north side are symbolic of the achievements of the Chinese people in the preceding half century under Mao's leadership; those on the south express the people's determination to "act on his behests and carry the cause of our proletarian revolution through to the end."

Foreign and Overseas Chinese visitors line up separately from Chinese citizens, and the visit takes less than 30 minutes. As a token of respect, visitors are advised not to wear bright colors, especially red, but no one was stopped when I was there. No cameras or purses are allowed. One enters first the North Hall, where there is a seated, 3-meter-high marble statue of the leader. Then, quietly, two by two, you enter the Central Hall where Chairman Mao (1893–1976) lies in state.

Tian Anmen (Tien An Men; Gate of Heavenly Peace) 天安门 is

the most famous structure in China except for the Great Wall. From its high balcony the imperial edicts were read, and this is where, on October 1, 1949, Chairman Mao Zedong (Mao Tse-tung) proclaimed the People's Republic of China. It is therefore a symbol of old and new China. The country's leaders frequently appear here on national days to review the parades and festivities. It was built in 1651 and stands 33.7 meters high.

Through the gate under Chairman Mao's portrait, to the left, is Zhongshan Park, the memorial park to Dr. Sun Yat-sen. To the right is Working People's Cultural Park. These two parks are great for 6 a.m. walks because of the magnificent walls, towers, gates, moats, and pavilions, and also because of the people limbering up for the day. Some are exercising not just their arms and legs but their vocal chords. You might hear some very beautiful voices resound off the walls from very shy singers hiding behind bushes and screens. Crowded apartments give little opportunity for singers to practice.

In the square between the two parks is a tiny white marble pavilion looking much like a Japanese lantern. In imperial times, if an official made a serious error, this black gauze cap was placed inside and he was taken out to be executed at the Wumen in front of the palace. Commoners were dispatched at the marketplace 7 km SW of here near the Qianmen Hotel.

*Gu Gong (Imperial Palace), a.k.a. Palace Museum or Forbidden City 故宫 : open 8:30 a.m.–4:30 p.m. (summer). No admittance after 3:30 p.m. Visitors usually enter by the **Wumen (Meridian Gate)** 午门 inside the Tian Anmen between the two above-mentioned parks, and head north.

The Gu Gong was the home and audience hall of the Ming and Qing emperors. Many buildings here are as the Qing left them, minus relics now in the National Palace Museum in Taiwan. Many of the buildings are exhibition halls for historic treasures from all over China. To walk at a leisurely pace from one end to the other takes about 30 minutes, but to explore it thoroughly takes at least a full day—some would say a week. And not all parts are open to the public!

The Forbidden City was originally built from 1406 to 1420 as the palace of the Ming emperors. It is on more than 720,000 square meters (178 acres) of land. Over 9000 rooms cover a total floor space of about 150,000 square meters. The surrounding imperial red wall is over 10 meters high. Only imperial palaces were allowed to have yellow ceramic roofs. (Commoners could only use gray.) This massive city was built by 100,000 artisans and a million laborers.

Toward the end of the Qing, 280,000 taels of silver were needed annually to maintain the palace, the money collected in taxes and rents from 658,000 acres of royal estates. During the Ming, 9000 ladies-in-waiting and 100,000 eunuchs (castrated males) served here. Some eunuchs became more powerful than the self-indulgent emperors. Sacked by foreign powers in 1900, the Forbidden City was restored and now maintains a permanent staff of painters and carpenters so that every 20 years all the buildings are renewed.

The city is divided into two major sections: the outer palace (for business) and the inner residential courts. Directly beyond the Meridian Gate are the five marble bridges "like arrows reporting on the emperor to Heaven." The **River of Gold** below is shaped like a bow. Note the gates; red was used only for important places like this. Each has 81 studs—nine times nine, an imperial number. Seven layers of brick line the courtyards, so no one could tunnel in from below. Note the white squares, on each of which a royal guard stood whenever the emperor ventured past.

Throughout the palace, huge caldrons of water stand ready for possible fires. On the north side, beneath the caldrons, are air vents to fan fires set in winter to keep the water inside from freezing. Note the lack of hiding places for possible assassins.

The first building is the **Taihedian** (Tai Ho Tien; Hall of Supreme Harmony) 太和殿 , the most stately of all the buildings. It is surrounded by incense burners, 18 bronze ones representing the then 18 provinces, and others in the form of a stork (longevity) and a dragon-headed tortoise (strength and endurance). Note the copy of an ancient sundial and the small openings on the side of the pavilion to allow air to circulate inside. The building was used for major ceremonies like the emperor's birthday, for imperial edicts, and for state affairs. Imagine the area in front of it covered with silk-gowned ministers and officials kneeling in rows. Imagine their heads to the ground in front of the hall while smoke poured from the incense burners and musicians played on the balcony. Can you see the child emperor being carried by palaquin above them to the highly carved throne? If you can't, try to see the Chinese historical movie *Power Behind the Throne*.

Each of the 18-meter-high cedar pillars was made from one piece of wood. Each of the floor tiles took 136 days to bake, after which it was immersed in oil for a permanent polish. The bricks are solid, about 5″ thick and 18″ square. The base and throne are carved sandalwood.

The **Zonghedian (Hall of Complete Harmony)** 中和殿 was used by the emperor to receive his ministers, to rest, and to dress before he entered the Taihedian. The two Qing sedan chairs here were for traveling within the palace. The braziers were for heat, the four cylindrical burners for sandalwood incense. Note the imperial dragon symbols on the ceiling.

The **Baohedian (Hall of Preserving Harmony)** 保和殿 , the most decorative of these halls, was for imperial banquets and, during the Qing, the retesting of the top scorers in the national examinations. Note the ceilings and beams. Behind this hall, between the stairways, is a giant carving of dragons in one piece of marble from Fanshan county, 16.5 meters by 3 meters and weighing about 250 tons. Anyone caught touching this imperial symbol was executed. The carving and the timbers were brought here in winter by sliding them over ice made from water of wells especially sunk for the occasion. Nothing was too extravagant for the representative of Heaven!

Several buildings on both sides of these main halls were used for study, lectures, a library, and even a printing shop. Beyond this third hall are the **Inner Courts,** the three main buildings, similar to the three in the outer palace; the **Qianqingong (Hall of Heavenly Purity)** 乾清宫 , where the emperors used to live and where deceased emperors lay in state. Here also Cixi (Tsu Hsi), the infamous Empress Dowager, received foreign envoys; the **Jiaotaidian (Hall of Union)** 交泰殿 , where ceremonies involving empresses took place (women were not allowed in the outer palace!); and the **Kunninggong (Palace of Earthly Tranquillity)** 坤宁宫 , which was a residence in the Ming and a shrine in the Qing. One of the Qing emperors used its eastern room as a bridal chamber. East of the Kunninggong is a hall where clocks from all over the world are exhibited, gifts from foreign missions. In the back of the inner court is the **Imperial Garden,** where a snack bar might save thirsty tourists. The imperial family sipped tea, played chess, and meditated in this beautifully designed garden. Can you imagine living here!

Then, continuing northward, one arrives at the back gate, where tour groups usually meet their buses. But you're not finished yet! Retracing your steps to the entrance of the inner court, turn left (east) at the Qianqingong, past the washrooms and the **Nine Dragon Screen** 九龙壁 , and then turn left again. Here are several pavilions with exhibitions well worth seeing. One might have a stunning collection of gold artifacts—bells, incense burners, table service (with jade handles), and scepters. There are also precious Buddhist relics and the biggest jade sculpture in China, a 5-ton Ming statue depicting one of the earliest attempts in the Xia Dynasty to control the Yellow River. Look for paintings and antique jewelry, pottery and bronzes. Also notable north of this area is the 12″-diameter well in which the obviously thin Pearl Concubine was drowned by a eunuch after she incurred the wrath of the Empress Dowager in 1900.

In each building, look at the ceilings and the palace lanterns, the distinctive blue Manchu cloisonne, and the Western clocks. Where were the imperial toilets? the kitchens? Think of the children who grew up within these walls and never set foot outside! Think of the eunuchs who gave up their manhood for a job that would benefit their families.

Jingshan (Coal) Hill 景山 , outside the north gate of the palace, was originally the site of a Ming coal pile. It was built with earth excavated from the moats and is 43 meters high. It is now a park with a good view of the Forbidden City and the lakes to the west and north. As the Manchus were breaking into the city, the last of the Ming emperors hung himself on a locust tree located at the foot of the hill on the east side.

Day 2

The exhibits in the **Museum of the Chinese Revolution** 中国革命博物馆 are good for those who want to learn something about China after 1840, and are divided into the following sections: the Opium War, the Taiping Heavenly Kingdom, the Sino-French War and the Sino-Japanese War, Tsarist Russian Aggression, the Reform Movement of 1898, the Anti-Imperialist Movement of the Yi He Tuan, the Revolution of 1911, and the founding of the Communist Party, Chou En-lai, the civil wars, and the Japanese war. Be sure to pick up a short description in English.

The **Museum of Chinese History** 中国历史博物馆 is China's best. It is divided into four sections: primitive society, slave society, feudal society, and semicolonial, semifeudal society. You can walk through without absorbing much in an hour, it is so large. You need at least a half day to do it justice. Please take it in short doses, especially if your feet tire easily. There is a lot to see! (See also *Visit Museums* in "What Is There to See and Do" and "Milestones in Chinese History.") Both museums are entered opposite the Great Hall of the People. The history museum is to the right. Open 8:30 a.m.–5 p.m. or 9 a.m.–12:30 p.m.; 2–5:30 p.m.

Relics here start from 1.7-million-year-old pre-human teeth to 1911. They include a model of the cave where the Peking Man was found. Also on display are a 14th-century B.C. ivory cup inlaid with jade, a Shang bronze wine vessel with four protruding rams' heads, and a Western Zhou sewer pipe with the head of a tiger. Intriguing, too, are a model of a Warring States irrigation system, tomb figures galore, and a model of a first-century B.C. wheel used to operate a bellows to melt iron. Here, too, is the Flying Horse of Gansu, which people around the world waited many hours to see when it was exhibited abroad. No queues here!

There is also a model of a 1700-year-old drum chariot with a figure of a child on top, always pointing south, and another miniature drum chariot with a figure that beats a drum every 500 meters, a Yuan water clock, and some Yuan rockets attached to spears. I can only whet your appetite. It is best to take a Chinese-reading friend since there are no signs in English.

The ***Tiantan (Temple of Heaven)** 天坛 is about 5 km south of the Forbidden City. Think of the processions of incense-swinging priests, spear-bearing palace guards, and the palaquin bearers carrying the emperor—all marching from the palace unseen by anyone else. Setting eyes on the emperor was a crime punishable by death.

The temple is set in the middle of a 667-acre park with many pine and cypress trees, some over 500 years old. Give yourself at least 20 minutes for a quick look, an hour for a more thorough tour. The Temple of Heaven was built in the same period as the Forbidden City (1420), and ranks among the most famous structures in China. It was used a couple of times a year when the emperor, bearing all the sins of the Chinese people, humbled himself before Heaven and performed the rituals calculated to bring good harvests. The temple has two concentric walls, both round at the north and straight at the south, heaven being round and earth square, or didn't you know! The raised, 360-meter passage between the main buildings is the **Red Stairway Bridge.** To the north is the **Qiniandian (Hall of Prayer for Good Harvests)** with triple eaves, 38 meters high and 30 meters in diameter. The four central columns represent the four seasons. Around these four are two rings of 12 columns each, the inner symbolizing the 12 months and the outer the 12 divisions of day and night. Here, the emperor performed the rites on the 15th day of the first moon of the lunar calendar. All the columns are wood from Yunnan province.

South of this is the **Imperial Vault of Heaven,** originally built in 1530 and rebuilt in 1752. In this building without horizontal beams were stored the tablets of the God of Heaven, the Wind God, the Rain God, etc. Sacrifices were made on the circular Sacrificial Altar on the winter solstice. The surrounding wall has a strange echo effect. You can hear people talking softly beside it from an unusual distance. Also count the number of stone slabs on the floor, staircases, and balustrades. They are in multiples of nine.

*Beihai (North Sea) Park 北海公园 , open 7:30 a.m.–4 p.m., is only a few blocks west of Coal Hill. (Take bus 103 along Wangfujing St. from the Beijing Hotel if you wish.) If you are short of time, just head for **Baita Shan (White Dagoba Hill)** 白塔山 and then the **Nine Dragon Screen** (1756) on the opposite side of the lake. While the whole area is a historic site protected by the State Council, these are the highlights of a big, 168-acre park full of intriguing old buildings, the recently renovated **Jingxinzhai (Serenity Study),** winding paths, and interesting rocks, that could take a half day to explore. Rowboats are for hire and, in the winter, ice skating on the lake is an exotic experience (but bring your own skates). The Fang Shan Restaurant near the White Dagoba serves the same fancy, delicate dishes (well, almost!) once presented to the Empress Dowager. But you do have to make a reservation or risk going hungry.

In the 10th century (Liao), an imperial residence was built on the site and called Precious Islet Imperial Lodging. In the 12th century (Jin), auxiliary palaces were constructed here and a lake excavated, the earth used to build the artificial hills and the *Round City at the southern edge. Rocks from Kaifeng were also used. During the Yuan, the Qionghua Islet was expanded and the palace of Kublai Khan was made the center of the city. This palace is no longer standing. Also on the islet, the 35.9-meter-high, bell-shaped White Dagoba was first constructed in 1271 in the Tibetan style. The current stupa was built in 1731.

Also noteworthy is Kublai Khan's 3000-liter jade liquor container (1265) and the Jade Buddha in Chengguang Hall in the Round City on the mainland, by the White Dagoba causeway.

The Nine Dragon Screen on the north side of the lake is of glazed brick and is 5 by 27 by 1.2 meters. Successive dynasties added buildings to Beihai, and this park was also looted by the foreign powers in 1900 and, more recently, by the Red Guards.

Zhongnanhai 中南海 , south of Beihai, has not been generally open to the public because it contains the residences and offices of China's leaders. Very special tour groups have successfully requested a visit if nothing else is happening at the time. The Guanxu (Kuang Hsu) emperor, who attempted to make modern reforms, much to the displeasure of the Empress Dowager Cixi, was imprisoned here during the winters when he was not at the Summer Palace. The historically important Pavilion of Purple Light and Fairy Tower were recently repaired. The south gate, brilliant red and fancy, is on Changan Avenue west of the Tian Anmen, too prominent to be overlooked.

Now, if you have more time, the 18-shop antiques, arts and crafts shopping center of **Liulichang** 琉璃厂 is nearby, a pleasant place to poke around. Built during the reign of Qing emperor Qianlong, it has recently been renovated in the old Qing style. See *Shopping*. The shopping area of **Dazalan** 大栅栏 , just south of the Qianmen, is the market area for ordinary people. However, a huge, 3000-meter-long underground air-raid shelter (now a well-maintained underground tourist attraction, with arts and crafts store and a hotel) makes this special. The shelter has 90 entrances and can hold 10,000 people. Officials estimate the teeming streets above can be cleared in six minutes in an emergency.

Dazalan's underground is worth visiting, but arrangements must be made in advance by joining a tour. You can enter by a trap door in the floor of a clothing shop.

Day 3

Summer Palace, Temple of the Azure Clouds, Temple of the Sleeping Buddha, and Fragrant Hill are all within 10 km of each other, 20–30 km NW of the Tian Anmen. Because of traffic jams, avoid Sundays here. If time permits, you can visit the Yuanmingyuan and Great Bell Temple too.

The **Yiheyuan (Garden of Cultivating Peace)** 颐和园 , a.k.a. **Summer Palace** (open 6 a.m.–5:30 p.m.) A British double-decker bus goes nonstop from the Qianmen just south of Mao Zedong Memorial Hall, to the Summer Palace. A visit to this 717-acre garden usually takes half a day. It is three quarters water. Originally built in the 12th century, it was expanded in 1750 for the 60th birthday of the mother of the Qianlong emperor and burned in 1860 by the British-French army.

It was rebuilt by the Empress Dowager Cixi (Tzu Hsi) on the occasion of her 60th birthday (1895) and financed with funds meant for building the Chinese navy. It was badly damaged by the foreign powers in 1900. The existing buildings were restored in 1903.

The imperial court lived here every year, when possible, from April 15 to October 15, receiving diplomats and conducting business in the **Renshoudian (Hall of Longevity and Benevolence)** 仁寿殿 . Empress Dowager Cixi, who was the power behind the throne from 1861 to 1908, lived in this hall near the **Deheyuan (Grand Stage)** 大戏楼 , where she could indulge in her passion for theatricals. The stage floor is hollow so that ''ghosts'' could emerge from it. The Grand Stage is now a separate museum requiring an additional fee. It contains Cixi's jewelry and dinnerware, and wax figures of Cixi and two imperial concubines. Attendants are in Qing palace costumes, and you can have your photo taken with a live ''eunuch'' or wax figures. In the exhibition hall behind the stage is the 1898 automobile given to the emperor by General Yuan Shikai.

Twenty-eight ladies-in-waiting, twenty eunuchs, and eight female officials waited on the empress dowager. For lunch, she was offered 128 courses daily.

In the **Hall of Jade Ripples** 玉栏堂 , to the south of the main entrance, she kept the Guangxu (Kuang Hsu) emperor imprisoned every summer from 1898 to 1908 after he tried unsuccessfully to institute reforms to modernize China and to take his rightful power back. Note the walls around the compound. The rooms here and elsewhere are furnished as they were then.

The **Long Corridor** extends 728 meters along the lake to the famous **Qingyan (Marble) Boat.** The 1400 paintings here (count them if you don't believe it!) are a most spectacular display. To the north up the hill are the **Hall of Dispelling Clouds** 排云殿 , the **Tower of Buddhist Incense** 佛香阁 , and the **Temple of the Sea of Wisdom** 智慧海 , where the empress used to hold her birthday celebrations and religious services. The **Xiequeyuan (Garden of Harmonious Interests)** 谐趣园 was designed like the Jichangyuan (Garden) in Wuxi. Also on the hill is a Tibetan-style Lama temple. Crossing Kunming Lake is a 17-arch bridge and, on an island, the **Dragon King Temple** 龙王庙 .

A good restaurant is in the **Tingliguan (Pavilion for Listening to Orioles)** 听鹂馆 ; reservations essential (tel. 283955). Here you can also have your picture taken in elegant imperial dress.

The Summer Palace Hotel is in the garden, near the Hall of Scalloped Clouds, an exotic experience if you don't mind being isolated. It is a long way from downtown.

Northwest of the Summer Palace is the **Temple of the Sleeping Buddha,** a.k.a. Temple of Universal Spiritual Awakening 卧佛寺 . This was first built in the Tang and reconstructed and renamed in the Yuan,

Ming, and Qing. The lacquered bronze Sakyamuni, which was cast in 1331 (Yuan), is 5.33 meters long and weighs 54 tons. It is the largest bronze statue in China. The Buddha here is giving his last words to his disciples before his earthly death. Because he is barefooted here, successions of emperors have presented the statue with 11 pairs of huge handmade cloth shoes, which are on display in the same room. On either side are the 12 bodhisattvas, his disciples. A long hiking trail extends to the left behind the fish pond up the mountain through a garden. One can also stay in the temple overnight very cheaply.

The **Biyunsi (Temple of Azure Clouds)** 白云寺 is more important than the Sleeping Buddha because of its stunning collection of religious statues and the Diamond Throne Pagoda. The Biyun was first built in the Yuan as a nunnery. During the Ming, it was the burial place for powerful eunuchs. In 1748, Emperor Qian Long (Chien Lung) ordered to be built the **Hall of Five Hundred Arhats** 五百罗汉堂 and the **Diamond Throne (a.k.a. Vajra Throne) Pagoda** 金钢宝座塔 . The 508 gilded, wooden arhats are life-size and strikingly beautiful, each different. How many are not sitting? Which have two heads? Which would you like to talk with? What do you think he'd say? It is good to have a flashlight here too.

In 1925, the body of Dr. Sun Yat-sen lay in state at this temple until the completion of his mausoleum in Nanjing. A tiny museum is at the spot. The unique 34.7-meter Diamond Throne Pagoda consists of five small pagodas in the Indian style and has some excellent carvings and towers, showing a great deal of Indian influence.

Xiang Shan (Fragrant Hill) Park 香山公园 , open 7:30 a.m.–5:30 p.m., was a 150-hectare (384-acre) hunting ground for many emperors. A 20-minute chairlift to the top of the mountain now gives a spectacular view of the area, especially in autumn, when the air is less dusty and some leaves are red. The waiting line is long, but anyone can get preferential treatment if they pay three times the regular fare at another window, which isn't much anyway for tourists. Prepaid tour groups automatically jump the queue because they have already paid the higher fee. The highest peak here is 557 meters above sea level. The lift goes by a small Glazed Pagoda, a Western-style mansion that was presumably the hunting lodge, and a Tibetan-style temple, which you can inspect at closer range later.

Drop in at the posh **Xiang Shan (Fragrant Hill) Hotel** 香山饭店 for coffee. See *Hotels* below.

If time permits on the way back to town, glimpse the **Yuanmingyuan** 圆明园 ruins. This Garden of Clear Ripples was built in an area full of bubbling springs and was used as an imperial resort beginning in the 11th century. It became the site of a major palace in 1690 and later was rebuilt into a favorite 160-hectare palace garden by Qing Emperor Qianlong, with buildings copied from Suzhou, Hangzhou, and Yangzhou. Sacked by Anglo-French forces in 1860 (after the Qing defeated the foreigners at Taku and tortured their envoys), it was partially repaired only to be destroyed again in 1900. The foreigners wanted to punish the emperor who loved it in revenge for the seige of the legations. The foreigners were also greedy for more power in China. The few remains of this "Garden of gardens" and "Palace of palaces" can be glimpsed in three minutes from a car if you are in a hurry to get to the Great Bell Temple. Much of what was left was taken by scavengers. Enough remains of the marble archways of the Evergreen Palace to show the influence of the European missionaries who helped design it early in the 1750s. Since the imperial families favored the Yuanming-yuan over the Imperial Palace, they kept their most precious treasures and books here. The 1860 burning took two days and is documented in a good Chinese-made movie, *The Burning of the Summer Palace*. One of the best accounts in English is Garnet J. Wolseley's *Narrative of the War with China in 1860*. A small exhibition near the entrance tells the story. A partial restoration from the designs made available from France should have begun by the time of your visit.

You are rushing now to get to the **Jueshengsi (Temple of Awareness of Life),** popularly known as the Temple of the Great Bell 大钟寺 This temple houses over 40 different ancient bells. The most spectacular bell was cast in the reign of Emperor Yongle of the Ming (1403–25) in a clay mold, and weighs 46.5 tons. How would *you* have brought the bell here without a crane and truck? In 1733, the Chinese slid it on ice in winter or on wheat shells in summer and put it on a mound. After attaching the bell onto the beams, the mound was dug out and then the hall was built around it. The 220,000 amazingly handsome Chinese characters decorating it are Buddhist scriptures and prayers.

The other bells in the exhibit were for various purposes. In religious ceremonies they drove away worldly worries and attracted the attention of the gods. Some bells here announced the time of day and the closing of the city gates. Some were used in music rituals. (See also "Wuhan"). A small hall contains an exhibit on how the bells were made, unfortunately labeled only in Chinese.

Day 4

Some people prefer to take their own box lunch to the Great Wall even though a restaurant is available.

*Great Wall—see separate listing.

*Shisan Ling (Ming Tombs) 十三陵 , open daily 8 a.m.–4 p.m., are usually combined with a trip to the Great Wall at Badaling. They are a 50-km (1¾-hour) drive NW of the Tian Anmen. Avoid Sunday traffic jams.

These 13 imperial tombs were built from 1409 to 1644 and spread over 40 square km. Each tomb consists of a Soul Tower, a Sacrificial

Hall, and an Underground Palace, surrounded by a wall. Approaching from the south, one sees a big, carved white marble archway, erected in 1590, beyond which are the Great Red Gate, ornamental pillars, and the Tablet Pavilion. The Sacred Way has 24 stone animals (lions, unicorns, camels, elephants, etc., 12 larger-than-life-size humans (military officers and government officials), and an army of enterprising hawkers (also an old China tradition) selling everything from furs, porcelain, and fruit to junk. The stone animals can be mounted and photographed if you don't feel bad about defacing 400-year-old monuments.

At least two of the tombs are open to visitors: **Chang Ling** 乾陵 , the biggest and earliest, and **Ding Ling** 定陵 , which has been excavated and can be entered. Ding Ling is the tomb of the 13th Ming Emperor Wanli, who ruled for 48 years, starting at age 10. The tomb was begun when he was 22 years old. It took six years and cost eight million taels of silver to build.

The underground palace consists of three halls, the central one with passages to annex chambers, totaling 1195 square meters. The marble doors each weigh four tons and were closed *from the inside* by propping two large stone poles against them. Note the two triangular depressions in the ground inside the door where the poles rested. Note also the blue and white porcelain jars with the dragons, which were half filled with oil when the tomb was opened. The oil was burned to create an oxygen-free vacuum inside.

In the central hall are three marble altars, two for the empresses, one for the emperor. Note the "Five Altar Pieces" and the porcelain lamp. The rear hall has the three coffins and plaster replicas of 26 chests. The museum has on display some of the objects found in the tomb, such as the gold crown, headdresses, a jade belt, and a gold bowl. A 20-minute movie about the opening of Ding Ling is shown in one of the side halls.

Enjoy the rural beauty, the vast, open spaces between the tombs, and the peace when you escape the 10,000-a-day tourists and peddlers. If you have time, you should also wander around the other tombs, which are not repaired and are usually free of tourists. These other tombs are not opened because of the high cost of careful archaeological excavation. Besides, no one knows where the entrances are because their builders were executed and no records have survived. The tombs and the Great Wall are best seen at dusk, when one feels the presence of ghosts. Seeing weeds growing on imperial terraces and birds making nests on once glorious beams is a good time to reflect on life and death. Think of the cracked roofs and fallen walls of the monuments you yourself have built.

But visit here soon. The Beijing Municipal Government and a Japanese firm have started work on a recreation complex with 18-hole golf course, roller coasters, Ferris wheels, hotels, and camel-racing tracks. It is expected to be completed in 1990.

Day 5

   *Yonghegong (Lama Temple) 雍和宫 : Count on at least 40 minutes. The Temple of Harmony and Peace was first built in 1694. This Mongolian-Tibetan yellow-sect temple is within walking distance of the No. 2 Overseas Chinese Hotel   第二华侨饭店   . It should not be missed. Beautifully renovated, it reveals pavilion after pavilion of increasingly startling figures, the largest in the back hall 18 meters high and surrounded by intriguing but apparently unstable balconies. This Buddha was carved from one piece of sandalwood from Tibet and the temple was built around it.

   The steles are incised with Han, Manchurian, Mongolian, and Tibetan script. The statues in the main halls resemble those in most Buddhist temples, but some statues do wear the pointed Himalayan caps and white Tibetan scarves, a traditional gift. On either side of the symmetrical structure, however, the more typically Tibetan demons, human skulls, and tankas are displayed. Another admission ticket is required for the exhibition hall that shows many Tibetan silver utensils of very intricate craftsmanship.

   Of historic and artistic interest is a picture of the wall of the back pavilion made of pieces of silk by the mother of the Qianlong emperor in 1744. Prayer wheels are for sale. Young and old monks abound, but we haven't found any yet who can tell us about religious matters in Chinese or English. The Yonghegong was built in 1694 as an imperial residence for Emperor Yongzheng, then still a prince. It was transformed into a Lama temple in 1744 during Qianlong's reign.

   This temple was an attempt by Emperor Qianlong to unite the Han, Manchu, Mongol, and Tibetan nationalities into one country. He also took a Ugyur princess from what is now Xinjiang into his court as one of his favorite empresses. For more on Lamaism, see also ''Lhasa'' and ''Chengde.''

   The **Shudian (Capital Museum)** 首都博物馆 is in the old Yuan dynasty **Confucius Temple** 孔庙 , almost across Yonghegong Avenue from the Lama Temple. It is the second largest Confucian temple in China (the largest is in Qufu, the hometown of the sage). The exhibits on Beijing history, Qing armor, and the stone drums are worth seeing. Look for maps and relics of the old Yuan city too. Also in the neighborhood is the **Guozijian (Capital Library)** in the old Imperial College building (Qing). Because the emperor used one of the lecture halls, the Piyong, this building was splendidly designed with four doors, corridors, and gardens. The library has a vast collection of rare ancient books and stone tablets.

   During the Qing, these three buildings were all part of one complex and used as examination halls for advanced levels of the civil service, the Ph.D.s of ancient China.

   If you want to see the work of contemporary artists, the **China Art Gallery** 中国美术馆 is open daily, 9 a.m.–5 p.m. April 30–May 13, closed on Mondays. It is about two blocks east of Jing Hill, itself behind the Forbidden City, and has changing exhibitions.

For *your last day and a half,* assuming you only have six days, you must choose from the following. If you want to do more, then you have to stay longer or come back again.

—**Arts and crafts factories:** favorites are cloisonne and ivory and jade carving. C.I.T.S. can arrange.

—A **rural village or cooperative**

—The **Cultural Palace of the Nationalities** 民族文化宫 (Fuxingmennei Ave.), for those who have been or will be visiting areas where there are many groups of ethnic minorities. Its restaurant in the west wing arranges banquets with the food of the different nationalities. It houses exhibitions of the various ethnic groups. Disco dances of some Western subcultures have been held here three times a week from 8 p.m. to 2 a.m. Books for sale.

—**Shopping**

—Repeat visits to places above where you wanted to spend more time but couldn't.

—**Daguanyuan (Grand View Garden)** is a 100,000 square-meter theme park in southwest Beijing inspired by one of China's greatest novels, the *Dream of the Red Chamber*. The park should be completely finished for your visit. The buildings are staffed by actors dressed in Qing fashions as characters from the beloved novel. For a description of the characters and a sketch of the plot, see "What Is There to See and Do."

—The *White Dagoba Monastery** 白塔寺 at Miaoyingsi (Temple of Excellent Confirmation) in Xichang is Yuan (1271). During repairs made in 1978 after the Tangshan earthquake, archaeologists found more than ten relics inside dated 1753, from the Qianlong emperor. He was indeed a busy man. These include a pure gold 5.4-centimeter-long gem-studded Buddha and a glazed Goddess of Mercy.

—**Niujiu Mosque** 牛街回民区 : In the southeast part of the city, where about 10,000 Moslems live on Niujiu Street, this mosque is primarily for visitors with an interest in Islam and religious buildings. You should phone ahead for reservations (tel. 557824), though you might take a chance and just drop in. The mosque was founded in the Liao dynasty (A.D. 996) by the Arabian scholar Nasullindin and rebuilt and enlarged in subsequent dynasties. Although it is in classical Chinese architecture, the interior does have west Asian arches and Arabic writing. Note the curtained-off section for women. Open daily 8 a.m.–10 p.m. (See also "What Is There to See and Do.")

—*Beijing Gu Guanxiangtai** (Ancient astronomical observatory) 古天文台 (Jianguomen Ave., near the Friendship Store and Jianguo Hotel) was built in 1442 (Ming) and has some instruments dating from 1437 to 1442. Good for a history of Chinese astronomy, with many Qing exhibits as well.

—**Beiyunguan (Temple of White Clouds)** 白云寺 , outside Fu-xingmenwai, southwest of Beijing TV, is the largest Taoist Temple in China. Built originally in the Tang, it burned down in the Jin and was rebuilt in the Ming. During the Qing, it was enlarged. It has some striking incense burners and gilded statues, including that of Taishang Laojun, the initiator of Taoism. Open every Tuesday and Friday from 9 a.m. to 10 p.m. Attended by young men in Taoist robes and long hair. A visit takes about two hours. See *Taoism* in "What Is There to See and Do?"

The only nunnery open is the **Tongjiao Nunnery** (Zhen Xian Lane, Beixiao St., in the Eastern District). Established during the Ming, it now has 30 nuns. Public religious ceremonies are held once a week.

The **International Club** 国际俱乐部 (Jianguomenwai Ave., near the Friendship Store and Jianguo Hotel) is a place for homesick foreigners. Open 9 a.m.–9:30 p.m. Usually there is no need to show a passport. It has a coffee shop and dining room (12–2:30 p.m. and 6–8:30 p.m) with Western food. Reasonable prices. Movies (U.S., Hong Kong, and Chinese) are shown most evenings (sometimes with English subtitles.) Local Chinese guests need special permission to dine there but can patronize the theater. The swimming pool is open in summer. Tennis. Disco dancing.

Bicycle Rentals: Foreigners are not encouraged to ride bicycles. A rental shop is opposite the Friendship Store (Jianghuomenwai Ave.; tel. 592391).

▶ **Note:** Cyclists are forbidden on some roads, like Wangfujing. See also "Getting Around."

Walks: Around the Xinqiao Hotel for the old European architecture. This foreign legation area was under siege during the Boxer invasion, from June 13, 1900. On June 20, most foreign diplomats and missionaries and 2000 Chinese Christian refugees took shelter in the British Legation until the International Relief Force arrived on August 13. That British Legation building has been torn down to make way for a housing project.

The area around the Minzu Hotel and the Xi Dan Market toward the Forbidden City is full of old houses, antique doors, carvings, grinding stones used as steps, and fancy, carved stone door hinges. The back alleys with tiny houses and crowded courtyards with paper windows, are also fascinating.

The names of the alleys immediately around the Forbidden City are appealing. Nai Zi Hutong (Wet Nurse Lane) was the street where the new mothers who nursed the imperial babies lived. Flower Lane was for those who handmade all the silk flowers for the imperial ladies. There were also Goldsmith Lane, Laundry Lane, and Bowstrings Lane.

Night Life and Cultural Events

The best of China is here: opera, ballet, symphony orchestras, movies, acrobats, gymnastics. (See also *Go to Cultural Events* in "What Is There to See and Do?") The main hotels and the International Club frequently offer movies and ballroom and disco dancing. Bring your own cassettes. It takes awhile for the Top Ten to get this far. Sometimes a live band plays ancient Western tunes.

Beijing also has a Central Conservatory for Music, which gives many excellent concerts of Western and Chinese music. It is located in an alley across the street from the Nationalities Cultural Palace. You could ask these musicians to perform for your "distinguished" group if you want.

Day Trips

The **Tan Zhe Si** 潭拓寺 and **Hui Zhi Si** are only 6 km apart, so can be seen in one day, but they are not very exciting. Southwest of Beijing, they make a pleasant excursion into the mountains. The Tan Zhe Si has its roots in the Tang. During the Yuan, the daughter of Kublai Khan is said to have resided at the Tan Zhe Si to try to atone for her father's sins. In 1888 a Qing prince retired here. After the 1911 Revolution many foreigners used it as a summer resort, and after Liberation it was a workers' health spa. The Ming temple bell here is over 400 years old.

Lugouqiao (Reed Valley Bridge) a.k.a. Marco Polo Bridge 芦沟桥 is 20 km SW of the city. Primarily of interest to historians, it is not all that beautiful. Built in the 12th century, it is 250 meters long with 11 stone arches and 485 stone lions spaced along its railings, each one different. The bridge is named for Marco Polo because the Venetian explorer described it at length in his book. It is the site of the incident that touched off the Japanese war on July 7, 1937. Funds are being raised to renovate this bridge and build a museum of Chinese resistance to the Japanese invaders. Work may be in progress by the time you arrive.

*Zhoukoudian 周口店 (48 km south of Beijing) is where the Peking Man, who lived 400,000–500,000 years ago, was found in a cave in 1927. At least 44 skulls have been discovered there. A small museum has some relics, but many of the bones were lost during the Japanese war. A model of the area is in the Museum of Chinese History in Beijing.

See also "Zunhua" for Qing tombs.

For **overnight trips,** see "Chengde" (3 days), "Tianjin," "Shijiazhuang," "Beidaihe," "Shanhaiguan," and "Datong."

Shopping

Beijing has the best shopping after Shanghai. Most stores are open 8:30 or 9 a.m. to 7 or 8:30 p.m. Available are goods from all over the country (at higher prices, of course). Made locally are cloisonne, lacquerware, jade carving, filigree jewelry, carpets, and wood-block prints. Cheap souvenirs are the yogurt containers that say ''Beijing Dairy'' in Chinese, available from the supermarket at the Friendship Store. Also made locally are felt hats and track suits.

The main shopping street is **Wangfujing Ave.** 王府井 , along the east side of the Beijing Hotel. Resident foreigners check shopping bags at the desk under the international clocks of this hotel while they go out for more. You might want to do that too. On this street are **Beijing Department Store** 北京百货公司 (on west side; tel. 556761), **Jianhua Fur Store** (#192), **Beijing Arts and Crafts** 北京工艺美术公司 (on east side; tel. 556806), and the large **Xinhua Book Store** 新华书店, with books in English as well as Chinese. Another area less frequented by tourists is **Xi Dan** 西单 (2 blocks east of the Minzu Hotel). Beware of pickpockets in this and any other crowded areas.

The largest collection of stores selling antiques and arts and crafts is **Liulichang** 兆龙饭店 (on both sides of Nanxinhua), the main street where the buses stop. Open 9 a.m.–5:30 p.m. (winter) or to 6 p.m. (summer). In 1277, glazed tiles were made here. In the Qing, it was a market with 140 shops selling the same sort of arts it does today, including reproductions of paintings, the Dunhuang murals, bronzes, and porcelains. Some frequent shoppers feel prices here are better than at the Friendship Store. It is less crowded too.

Some U.S. name-brand, factory-overrun clothing has been found in **Dazalan** (the area south of the Qian Men, with the air raid shelter) and on Gongren Tiyuchang Road, near Workers' Stadium. Cheaper than in the U.S.

Beijing Huaxia Arts and Crafts Shop (249 Dong Si South St.; tel. 555331 X207, 551529; branch at 293 Wangfujing St., tel. 551819) is known also as the **Theater Shop** because of its theatrical costumes. Also secondhand goods (antique clocks, brass, furs, furniture, etc.).

Friendship Store 友谊商店 (Jianguomenwai Ave. near the Jianguo Hotel; tel. 593531; service dept., tel. 483893): One can buy any crafts made locally, plus furs, down coats, and even fresh flowers, etc. The Friendship Store can reset jewelry. Also has a snack bar and a good supermarket. Merchandise bought here can be easily customs-cleared and packed for shipping.

Marco Polo Shop 懋隆商店 (Temple of Heaven, near West Gate, Temple of Heaven; tel. 754940): arts, crafts, reproductions.

A large **free market** is at Beitaitingzhan 北太平庄 , beyond the northern moat. Another is along the NE edge of the Temple of Heaven grounds. The free market in Chaoyangmennei sells old Chinese furniture. The reproduction jewelry boxes here are good buys. No crating or shipping services.

Restaurants

(See also *Food* under "Useful Phrases" and "Food.") Beijing food
is much like Shandong's, but influenced by the imperial kitchens. It is
usually salty (as opposed to sweet), but is not highly spiced. Sauces are
less frequently used than in Cantonese cooking. Everyone must try Peking duck at least once! The best part is the crispy skin, which is dipped
in sweet, dark brown *hoisin* sauce, seasoned with a green onion, and
then wrapped in a thick pancake and eaten by hand. Worth trying, especially on those early morning walks, are the rolls, or the Chinese
equivalent of doughnuts—the long, deep-fried "oil sticks" 油条 —dipped
in sweetened hot soy milk (cheap). Also famous are the *baozhe* 包子 ,
meat dumplings either steamed or boiled in soup. A pleasant lunch place
for these is in Ritan Park on a sunny day, where you can also enjoy the
Altar to the Sun (Ming).

Also local is Mongolian food, especially hot pot and barbecue.

Beijing is a gourmet's delight, with excellent food from all over
the country. Unique are the previously mentioned **Tingliguan (Pavilion
for Listening to Orioles)** in the Summer Palace (tel. 283955) and the
Fang Shan Restaurant 仿膳 in Beihai Park (along the lake by the
White Dagoba; tel. 442573). Their cooks were taught by the Empress
Dowager's own cooks. Some popular restaurants, particularly the Fang
Shan and the **Wangfujing Beijing Duck Restaurant**   王府井烤鸭店
(tel. 553310) may require reservations well in advance. Reservations
for very special dishes sometimes require payment in advance (in case
you don't show up). Resident foreigners dub this duck restaurant the
"Sick Duck" because it is near the Capital Hospital. Another exotic
experience is lunch or dinner at the **Great Hall of the People.** See *Day
1* above.

Some foreigners have celebrated their weddings with dinner on a
boat in Kunming Lake at the Summer Palace, or enjoyed picnic suppers
on the night of a full moon at the Ming Tombs. The Jianguo Hotel has
catered a gourmet meal at the Great Wall (the original one, not the
hotel).

Other recommended restaurants:

BALC Catering Center   航空食品公司   □ *behind the International Club; tel. 52–3021* □ Reasonable prices. Especially good
food.

Beijing Hotel   北京饭店   □ *tel. 500–7726* □ Reasonably priced
good Chinese food in all of its dining rooms. A recently opened Japanese restaurant there is a joint venture and quite expensive.

Beijing Sucai Canting □ *74 Xuanwumennei Ave.; tel. 334296* □
Vegetarian. Excellent fancy food.

Donglaishun Fanzhuang   东来顺饭庄   □ *16, Jinyu Lane; tel. 55-
0069* □ Moslem style. Hot pot (best October–April) and shashlik.

Dasanyuan Restaurant   大三元饭店   □ *Jingshan Xi St.; tel. 44–5376* □ Need reservations for dinner.

Healthy Restaurant   长寿餐厅   □ *16, Taiping Lane, West City* □ Recommended mainly because of the novelty, although the food is good too. This restaurant is part of a Chinese medicine factory, and its dishes, a combination of food and tonics, are designed to cure a variety of ailments from high blood pressure to whatever. Suggested dishes that taste good are:

Tomato egg	蕃茄炒蛋
Pepper cabbage	糖醋白菜
Sweet and sour venison	抓炒鹿肉
Seaweed	海带
Sliced cold pork	叉烧
Quail eggs and bamboo shoot	虎珀鸽蛋
Three Fresh Soup (shrimp,	三鲜汤
bamboo shoots, and sea cucumbers)	
Bean curd and cucumber	凉拌三丝
Ginseng anticancer drink	人参汤

Henan Restaurant   河南饭店   □ *behind the Minzu Hotel; tel. 86–2178* □ Good food, friendly concerned manager, Mrs. Hong. Henan food.

Jianguo Hotel   建国饭店   □ *near Friendship Store* □ Excellent Chinese and Western food for reasonable prices. Service impeccable.

Overseas Chinese Mansion 华侨大厦 □ Cheap but good noodles.

Peking Roast-Duck Restaurant   北京烤鸭店   □ *Hepingmen; tel. 334422* □ a.k.a. Wall Street Duck to local foreigners because a wall was once beside it, of course. An old six-story restaurant.

Qianmen Peking Duck Restaurant   前门烤鸭店   □ a.k.a. "Big Duck." Tends to mass-produce duck dinners for tourists, but it's good.

Sichuan Fan Dian   四川饭店   □ *Rongxian Hutong, Xuanwumennei Ave.; tel. 336844* □ Sichuan.

Zhimeilou Restaurant 知味楼   □ *Changchun St.; tel. 341071* □ Shantong food.

For **suggested Beijing dishes,** see "Food."

For **Western food,** many of the newer luxury hotels have very good restaurants with a wide variety of food, especially the Jianguo, Great Wall, and Lido. The Xinqiao is good too.

International Club Grill Room □ Service excellent. Prices reasonable. Live music.

Maxim's □ *2, Qianmen Dong Ave.; tel. 75–4003* □ Opened in 1983 by Pierre Cardin himself. Reputation good. Extremely expensive. Also Happy Hours and dancing. Closed Sundays. Minim's, next door, is cheaper.

Snack Bar at Friendship Store □ If you're desperate for a cheap hamburger and a Coke. Outdoor patio open in summer.

Hotels

All the top hotels now have telex and improved services like room service meals. The top luxury hotels are Jinglun (Beijing-Toronto) and Holiday Inn Lido. Also high are the Great Wall, Beijing, Jianguo, and Diaoyutai (Angler's Inn). None are of five-star standard, but some are close. Some of the newer hotels have yet to establish reputations.

Beijing Hotels Introduction Center 北京旅馆介绍中心 □ *tel. 55–0424, east of the Beijing Railway Station, and in front of the Yongdingmen Railway Station, tel. 33–4857* □ has served primarily Chinese visitors until now. You could give them a try (preferably in Chinese) if you need a hotel room and want to avoid telephoning a couple dozen places, but they frequently put you in touch with hotels in the suburbs. C.I.T.S. should also be able to help you.

Beijing (Peking) Hotel 北京饭店 □ *Chang' an Dong Ave.; Telex 42626, 27, 28 CPL CN* □ Best location in town, within walking distance of main shopping areas, Tian Anmen, and Forbidden City. 300 rooms (west wing) built 1915 and 1954; 600 rooms added in 1974. Still expanding. At least 15 dining rooms serve a variety of palatable food at reasonable prices. Buffet breakfast for those in a hurry. Before the opening of the Great Hall of the People, its 1000-seat banquet hall was used for state functions. Note the gorgeous red columns in the lobby of the middle wing. Its west windows have a great view of the Forbidden City. Service good in the coffee shop, not so good in some of its other restaurants. Frequently difficult to get a taxi from here.

Changcheng Fandian (Great Wall Sheraton Hotel) 长城饭店 □ *Donghuan Bei Rd., Chaoyang district, adjacent to Agricultural Exhibition Center, and near many foreign embassies, to the south of the Pan-Pacific Exhibition Hall; telex 20045 and 22005 GWHBJ CN* □ Built 1983–84. Glass curtain exterior; 1007 luxury-size rooms, 22 stories in central block. Indoor swimming pool, health club, outdoor tennis courts, business center, airline reservation counter (CAAC, and Thai International), small theater with frequent live performances, tea garden with live music, Filipino musicians in nightclub. Seven-story atrium. Large ballroom (1200 people) and 12 small function rooms. Simultaneous translation facilities. Good French restaurant. 24-hour room service, coffee shop, and bicultural clinic. Computerized room reservation and room status system. Airport shuttle service. In 1984, President Reagan used this hotel to return a banquet to his Chinese hosts. Patterned after a Dallas hotel.

Chongwenmen Hotel 崇文门饭店 □ *3 Qianmen Dong Ave.* □ For budget travelers. Dormitories, but no lockers. Private rooms. C.I.T.S. branch offices on several floors; Beijing Motor Bus Co. bookings on 5th. Handy to subway. Good location. Not clean, but functional.

Diaoyutai State Guest House (Angler's Inn) 钓鱼台国宾馆 □ *Sanlihe Rd., western Beijing* □ Set on 42 acres of old imperial gardens; 15 separate villas, the largest, a 17-room mansion for at least US$3000 a night; the smallest, 10 rooms for at least US$2800 a night. Service good. The Diaoyutai is still a state guesthouse, but it's available to some tours and to business travelers. Decorated with antiques, it was originally a hunting and fishing resort for the Jin rulers 800 years ago and has been improved on since.

Fragrant Hills Hotel □ See Xiangshan Hotel
Friendship Hotel □ See Youyi Hotel
Great Wall Hotel □ See Changcheng
Heping Binguan (Peace Hotel) 和平饭店　　　□ *4 Jinyu Hutung; cable 5131* □ Over 300 rooms. In a back alley, but excellent location within walking distance of the Forbidden City and Wangfujing shopping. Current expansion to open in 1987, with 450 rooms, swimming pools, saunas.

Holiday Inn Lido 丽都饭店 □ *a.k.a. Ludo Fandian; Jichang and Jiang Tai rds., eastern suburbs, close to airport; telex: 22618 LI-DOH CN* □ 1000 rooms. Furnished apartments on a three-year lease; 20-lane bowling alley, health club and indoor swimming pool, squash, racketball, and computerized golf course. Office block and shopping center. Holiday Inn quality.

Hotel Beijing-Toronto □ See Jinglun
Huadu Hotel □ Tacky, but food not bad.
Huaqiao Da Sha (Overseas Chinese Mansion) 华侨饭店 □ *Wangfujing St.* □ 1958. About 200 rooms; 8 stories. Across the street from old CAAC booking office. Also diagonally across from China Art Gallery and within walking distance of the back gate of the Forbidden City. This is the better of the two older hotels for Overseas Chinese.

Huaqiao Fandian (Overseas Chinese Hotel) No. 2 华侨第二饭店 □ *5 Beixinqiao 3-Tiao* □ Near the Lama Temple.

International Hotel 国际饭店 □ *East Chang'lan Ave., across from railway station* □ 1987. 1100 rooms. Biggest in Beijing.

Jianguo Fandian (Jianguo Hotel) 建国饭店 □ *2 blocks east of Friendship Store on Jianguomen Ave.; telex: 22439 JGHBJ CN* □ 1982. Excellent location beside diplomatic enclave, Friendship Store, and International Club. One block 20 stories, the rest five stories. Indoor swimming pool. Excellent Chinese and European restaurants. 24-hour telefax service. Peninsula Group (Hong Kong) management with usual impeccable standards. In 1984, it was judged a model for the nation for other Chinese hotel managers.

Jinguang Centre □ 500 rooms.
Jinglun (Hotel Beijing-Toronto) 京伦饭店 □ *3 Jianguomenwai; telex: 210012, 210011 JLH CN* □ 1984. This 676-room, 12-story luxury hotel has one large (400-person) and four small function rooms. It was so named because it was built by a Toronto-based company. Oversized beds, indoor pool, health club. Excellent location within

walking distance of International Club, Friendship Store, and Jianguo Hotel.

Kunlun Hotel 昆伦饭店 □ *Donghuan Rd.* □ 1986. 1006 rooms, 28 stories. Aiming for top international standards.

Lido Hotel □ See Holiday Inn Lido

Minzu Fandian (Nationalities Hotel) 民族饭店 □ *51 Fuxingmennei Ave. and Changan Xi Rd.* □ 1959. 500 rooms; 11 stories. About 3 km west of and on the same street as the Tian Anmen. One block from Nationalities Palace. Close to subway and Xidan Market.

Nationalities Hotel □ See Minzu

Overseas Chinese International Building □ *Jianguomenwai* □ 800 rooms.

Overseas Chinese Hotel □ See Huaqiao Hotel

Peace Hotel □ See Heping

Peking Hotel □ See Beijing Hotel

Qianmen Fandian (Hotel) 前门饭店 □ *Hufang Lu Kou, Yongan Rd., Hepingmenwai* □ 1956. 382 rooms. This is the closest to the Liulichang St. antique stores, and quite central.

Summer Palace Hotel □ See Yiheyuan Fandian

Wangfujing Hotel □ *Jinguang Centre* □ 610 rooms. Being built.

Wannian Qing Binguan (Evergreen Hotel) 万年青宾馆 □ *Zizhuyuan, in northwestern suburbs near Friendship Hotel.*

Xiangshan (Fragrant Hills) Hotel 香山饭店 □ *Xiangshan Park* □ 1982. 292 rooms. Three and four stories, located far from the city on a beautiful wooded mountain (see Xiangshan, above). Not convenient to downtown (takes about 1½ hours by taxi to Tian Anmen). Ideal for people who like to hike in exotic rural settings. Cold, austere-looking, but beautiful public areas. I. M. Pei, architect. Although built in 1983, cracks in the wall started appearing shortly after. Poor management allowed it to deteriorate, but in late 1985 reports began to circulate that standards had improved and a 50% discount was offered during low season.

Xinqiao Fandian (Hotel) 新桥饭店 □ *2 Dongjiaomin Xiang* □ 1954. Over 300 rooms; 6 stories. Good Western food. Billiard room. In old legation section, surrounded by old European buildings. Good location, within walking distance of Tian Anmen and Beijing Hotel.

Xiyuan Fandian (Hotel) 西苑饭店 □ *Near zoo and foreign trade offices* □ 1985. Over 700 rooms; 26 stories. Ballroom and conference facilities.

Yanjing Binguan (Hotel) 燕京饭店 □ *Briefly named Fuxing Hotel. Chang'lan Ave. at Fuxing Rd., slightly farther west from the Forbidden City than the Minzu Hotel* □ 1981. 508 rooms; 21 stories. Outgoing telex. Small rooms. Smoke alarms. Tubs above seventh floor; showers only on lower floors. Pleasant, but not luxurious.

Yanshan Binguan (Hotel) 燕山宾馆 □ *56 Haidian Rd.*

Yanxiang Fandian (Hotel) 燕翔饭店 □ *on road to airport, near Lido* □ 1981; extension 1985. 400 rooms.

Yiheyuan Fandian (Summer Palace Hotel) 颐和园饭店 □ *Summer Palace, near Hall of Scalloped Clouds* □ Exotic, but inconveniently located.

Youyi Binguan (Friendship Hotel) 友谊宾馆 □ *Baichiquiao Rd.* □ 1952; recently renovated. Dark, depressing buildings originally built for Soviet experts. 1500 rooms (some apartments), but only a few for foreign tourists. Swimming pool, conference building, gymnasium, roof garden. Many foreign experts live here. Located in the northwestern suburbs beyond the zoo, 12 km from the Tian Anmen. Surrounded by apartment buildings and wide, tree-lined boulevards. Closest large hotel to Beijing and Qinghua (Tsinghua) universities. Subway stop relatively close by.

Zhaolong 兆龙饭店 □ *2 Congtibei Rd. near Sanlitun; telex: 210219 ZLH CN* □ 1985. 270 rooms and expensive suites. Indoor swimming pool. Shandong, Sichuan, Guangdong, and Western food. Named after father of Hong Kong shipping magnate, Sir Y. K. Pao.

Other Important Addresses
Airlines:

Aeroflot: tel. 522181.

Air France: tel. 523487.

CAAC 中国民航 : 117 Dongsi Ave.

Information: tel. 558861, 557591.

International bookings: tel. 557878.

Domestic bookings: tel. 553245.

Airport: tel. 558341, X2917.

The new CAAC ticketing center should be open for your visit (at the west side of the telegram office building on West Chang'lan Ave.).

Ethiopian Airlines: tel. 523285.

Iranair: tel. 523249, 523843.

Japan Airlines: tel. 523457.

Lufthansa: tel. 522626, 5001616, 5002626.

Philippine Air Lines: tel. 522794 (embassy).

PIA: tel. 523274, 523989.

Qantas: Hotel Beijing-Toronto, tel. 5002481, or Jinlun Hotel, tel. 5002235.

Swissair: tel. 523284.

United Airlines: tel. 595261, X135, or 5001985.

Airport 北京机场 : Plane inquiries: tel. 552515, 555531, X382.
Airport bus from Jianguo and Great Wall hotels, and others. Cheaper from CAAC.
American Express: Room 1410, Beijing Hotel; tel. 552331, 557631.
Bank of China 中国银行 : 17 Xijiaomin Xiang; tel. 338521. Foreign

exchange counters in most major hotels, tourist stores, and some tourist attractions.

Beijing Tradewinds International Express Co., Ltd.: No. 2, East Qian Men St. (Chongwenmen Hotel); tel. 757181 X430.

CITIC International Building: 19 Jianguomenwai Dajie; tel. 5002255.

C.I.T.S. National Headquarters 中国国际旅行社全国总社 : 6 Chang'an Dong Ave.; tel. 551031, 557217.

C.I.T.S. Beijing Branch 中国国际旅行社北京分社 : Chongwenmen Xi Ave., ground floor Chongwenmen Hotel; tel. 757181, 755017.

C.T.S. and Overseas Chinese Travel Service 中国旅行社 : Chongwenmen Xi Ave.; tel. 755448, 754912. Also 2 Qianmen Dong Ave.

Embassies: See also "Useful Phrases."

Australia 澳大利亚大使馆 : 15 Dongzhimenwai St., Sanlitun; tel. 522331.

Britain 英国大使馆 : 22 Kuanghua Rd., Jianguomenwai; tel. 521961.

Canada 加拿大大使馆 : 10 Sanlitun Rd., Chao Yang District; tel. 521475, 521571, 521724.

France 法国大使馆 : 3 Sanlitun Rd., Chao Yang District; tel. 521331, 521332.

Democratic Republic of Germany 德国民主共和国大使馆

Federal Republic of Germany, 5 Dong Zhimen Wai St., Chaoyang District, tel. 522161.

English Corner: Purple Bamboo Park near Capital Stadium. Sundays.

Japan 日本大使馆 : 7 Ritan Rd., Jianguomenwai; tel. 522361.

Mongolia 蒙古共和国大使馆 : tel. 521203.

New Zealand 纽西兰大使馆 : 2 Ritan Donger St., Chaoyang District; tel. 522731.

Philippines 菲律宾大使馆 : 23 Hsiu Shui Pie St., Jianguomenwai; tel. 522794.

Poland 波兰大使馆 : tel. 521235.

Switzerland 瑞士大使馆 : 3 Dongwu St.; tel. 522831.

U.S. 美国大使馆 : 17 Guanghua Rd.; tel. 522033.

U.S.S.R. 俄国大使馆 : tel. 521267.

Embassy office hours are usually 8:30 or 9 a.m. to 12 or 12:30 p.m.; 1:30, 2, or 2:30 p.m. to 5 or 6 p.m., Monday to Friday; Saturday mornings also. Summer hours are even more complicated: some are open only 7 a.m.–noon. Most embassies are north of the Friendship Store and International Club.

Express Courier Service: DHL c/o Sino Trans Beijing Air Cargo Centre, 2/F, West Wing, Beijing Exhibition Centre; tel. 890541 X492, 896469.

Foreign Affairs Section, Public Security Bureau 公安局外事科 : Beichizi.

Foreign Enterprise Service Corporation 外贸企业服务公司 : provides services such as drivers, secretaries, typists; rents vehicles. Customs clearance for non-Chinese enterprises in Beijing: 28 Dong Huan Bei Rd.; tel. 591180. Chinese teachers: tel. 754651; real estate: tel. 5001371.

Foreign Ministry: switchboard, tel. 553831.
   information: tel. 555505.
   protocol: tel. 552642.

Foreign Trade Ministry: 553031.

Foreign News Agencies
   ABC, Inc.: tel. 522671.
   Associated Press: tel. 523419, 523743.
   Australian Broadcasting Corp.: tel. 522410, 522514.
   Reuters: tel. 523517, 521921.
   British Broadcasting Corp.: tel. 523777, 523694.
   Canadian Broadcasting Corp.: tel. 521510, 523754.
   CBS: tel. 522301, 522472.
   Toronto Globe and Mail: tel. 521661, 522582, 523672.
   Agence France-Presse: tel. 521992, 521409.
   NBC, Inc.: tel. 523153, 523961.
   New York Times: tel. 523115, 522658.
   Time: tel. 522669, 521293.
   Wall Street Journal: tel. 523673.
   Washington Post: tel. 523464, 522944.

Helicopter Services: Holiday Inn Lido Hotel.

Hospitals: Most tourist hotels have a clinic or can help you find a doctor. See also "Useful Phrases."
   Shoudu/Xiehe (Capital) Hospital 首都医院 : tel. 553731, X217 or X565. Also for dental emergencies.
   Beijing Friendship Hospital 北京友谊医院 : tel. 338671, 331631.
   Ambulance: tel. 555678.

Lindblad Travel, Inc.: Lido Hotel, Room 4144; tel. 5006688.

Pacific Delight Tours, Inc.: Room 2706, Minzu Hotel; tel. 658541 X2706. Telex 20091 MZHTL CN.

Pharmacies: Wangfujing Medicine Shop (267 Wangfujing St.; tel. 562522). Some Western-type medicines.

Police 警察 or **Fire** 火警 : tel. 550720, 552725, 553772.

Railway Station 火车站 : Jianguomenwai Ave. Train inquiries: tel. 554866, 755272. Has special room for foreigners to buy tickets; better to buy in advance.

Taxis: All taxis must use their meters.
   Capital Car Company: tel. 863661 for buses or minibuses and 444468 for cars.
   China Beijing Car and Limousine Service: tel. 59-4441. Buses, minibuses, and limousines.

Telephone Operators
   information: 114
   long-distance information: 116

overseas operator: tel. 337431

domestic long-distance operator: tel. 330100, 331230.

Tourist Bus Co.: 2 Qianmen Dong Ave.; tel. 755414

Transportation Service for Foreigners: tel. 594375, 592616, 591082, 591813.

Voyages Jules Verne: c/o Mr. Chen Zi-qiang, Xinqiao Hotel: tel. 557731 X261. Railway tours, including Silk Road.

Books on Beijing:

Bredon, Juliet: *Peking*. First published by Kelly and Walsh, Shanghai, 1919. Oxford University Press, Hong Kong, 1982.

Haldane, Charlotte: *The Last Great Empress of China*. A biography of Cixi. Bobbs-Merrill Company, Inc., 1965.

Lin Yutang: *Moment in Peking*. The story of a Peking family beginning in 1900 as the foreign forces are marching on Beijing. John Day Company, Inc., 1939.

Warner, Marina: *The Dragon Empress. Life and Times of Tz'u-hsi, 1835–1908, Empress Dowager of China*. Macmillan Company, 1972. A biography of Cixi.

Good background movies:

Memories of Old Peking (one of the best China has ever produced); *The Burning of the Yuanmingyuan* and *The Power Behind the Throne* (about Cixi's regency). Both make history much more vivid. Also recommended is *Camel Boy*.

Changchun 长春

Northeast China. This capital of Jilin province (formerly Manchuria), is a 1½-hour flight NE of Beijing. It is noted mostly as an industrial city manufacturing automobiles (China's first plant), trucks, railway carriages, tractors, and textiles. The population is 1.3 million. Changchun is very cold in winter (lowest ⁻30°C) with lots of snow. There are ice carvings in the parks then. The summers are relatively cool with a high of 32°C. Average annual rainfall is 500–600 meters. About 150 frostfree days!

The city was founded in 1800. Invaded by Tsarist Russia in the 1890s, it became a Japanese concession in 1905 and the capital of Japanese-controlled "Manchukuo" from 1931 until 1945. It is a highly industrialized city, divided by the Songhua River.

The province of Jilin borders on Korea and the Soviet Union. Its 22.56 million people include Koreans, Manchus, Hui, Mongols and Xibes.

Settlements have been recorded since the Qin dynasty. It has developed a regional opera based on song-and-dance duets.

If a visitor only has one day in Changchun, C.I.T.S. recommends: the **Changchun Film Studio** 长春电影制片厂, one of China's largest, and the **Changchun No. 1 Motor Vehicle Plant** 长春第一汽车制造厂, where you can watch a more labor-intensive manufacturing process than in America or Europe. You won't believe the wages! The **Jilin Provincial Museum** 吉林省博物馆 is in the former palace of Emperor Puyi, a puppet of the Japanese. You can skate in the winter and swim in the summer in **Nanhu Park** 南湖公园, the largest park in the city.

If you have more time, **Xinlicheng Reservoir** 新立城水库 in the suburbs has some sika deer, ginseng root, and is stocked with fish. The **Nanhun Film Village** 南湖电影村 is being built near the Changbaishan Guest House and may be ready by the time you get there. The 480-square-km **Songhua Lake** 松花湖 is about 20 km SE of the city. The **Changbaishan Nature Reserve,** with tigers, deer, and sable is in **Antu County** about 300 km SE.

Shopping

Locally produced are: wine, ginseng, sable furs, deer antlers (aphrodisiacs), and frog oil (tonic). Tonghua and Changhaishan wines are made from wild grapes. Changchun produces carpets, embroidery, feather patchwork, wood carving, and bark pictures. The deer farm also has a retail shop. See also ''Jilin.''

Jilin Provincial Antique and Curio Store 吉林省文物店 (7 Xi'an Rd.; tel. 22537); **Changchun Fur Factory** 长春市皮毛厂 (4 Lane 7, North Second Rd., north of railway; tel. 37765). Please, no endangered species! **Friendship Store** 友谊商店 (1 Xinfa Rd.; tel. 27205). **Changchun Wood Carving Factory** 长春木雕工艺厂 (8 Xiangyang Rd.; tel. 24797).

Restaurants

Chunyi Restaurant 春谊饭店 (in the hotel; 2 Stalin St.; tel. 38495). **Changchun Restaurant** 长春饭店 (in the center of the city; tel. 25442).

Exotic specialties: Pine-flower bear paw 松花熊掌, houtou (golden orchid monkey head) mushrooms 猴头菇, ginseng chicken 人参鸡, thick deer antler soup (with sea cucumber, prawn, egg white, ham, and chicken) 鹿茸羹, and frog oil soup 哈什蚂油汤. Frog oil is said to be very nutritious and probably tastes better than it sounds. Please, no endangered species! And yes, you can get other dishes too! The raw fish shows the Japanese influence.

Hotels

Changbaishan Guest House 长白山宾馆 □ *12 Xinmin St.* □ 1982. 268 rooms. Across from Nanhu Park.

Nanhu Guest House   南湖宾馆 □ *Nanhu Rd.* □ 1960. 230 beds.
Provincial Chunyi Hotel   省春谊宾馆   □ *2 Stalin St., near rail-way station* □ 1909; renovated 1982.

C.I.T.S.   中国国际旅行社   (12 Xinmin St.; tel. 52419).
CAAC   中国民航 (2 Liaoning Rd.; tel. 39772).

Changsha (Long Sand)

South China. Capital of Hunan province south of the Yangtze River. 85-minutes' flight SW of Shanghai, 1 hour NE of Guilin, and 3¼ hours south of Beijing. On the main Beijing-Guangzhou railway line, 726 km north of Guangzhou. Population: 1 million. Coldest temperature is about ⁻8°C in January; hottest about 30°C in July. Rainfall from 1250–1750 mm, mostly late summer or early autumn.

Changsha, in one of China's main rice-growing areas, was a small town 2000 years ago. It was almost completely destroyed during the Japanese War. It is famous because Chairman Mao was born and lived nearby in Shaoshan. He studied for about five years at the Hunan Provincial First Normal School (1912–18). According to Jonathan Spence's *To Change China*, Mao was briefly editor of the *Yale-in-China Review*. The Christian-motivated mission from the American University also rented him three rooms for his bookstore. Yale started its mission in about 1904 and eventually established a medical school, hospital, and middle school. The Americans left shortly after Liberation.

Changsha is also known for its important Han excavation. Its embroidery is one of the four most famous in China.

The novel and movie *The Sand Pebbles* was set partly in Changsha during the Northern Expedition in the late 1920s. The hero was an engineer on an American gun boat, which sailed up the Yangtze through

Lake Dongting and along the Xiang River. The movie is one of the few good Hollywood efforts on China.

Changsha is also the setting of a more recent book, Liang Heng and Judith Shapiro's autobiographical *Son of the Revolution,* a refreshing look at growing up in Communist China and beating the system.

Hunan province's nationalities include Han, Tujia, Miao, Dong, Yao, Hui, Uygur, and Zhuang.

If you only have one day in this city, C.I.T.S. suggests the Hunan Provincial Museum and the Ceramic Exhibition in the morning, and the embroidery factory and city tour in the afternoon.

Hunan Provincial Museum 湖南省博物馆 (Dongfeng Rd.; tel. 25123): Because this is the main tourist attraction, skip everything else if you are short on time. The 1972–74 excavations of three 2100-year-old tombs have overshadowed the revolutionary and other ancient collections in this museum. You must see these Han relics, important because of their excellent state of preservation and vast number. You may want to return to see the rest of the museum later. It also has objects from tombs of the neolithic age, and from the Warring States Period (475–221 B.C.), both found locally.

The Han collection is in the white middle building on the right after you enter the gate. The three tombs were of Li Tsang, chancellor to the Prince of Changsha and Marquis of Dai, his wife, and his son. The son died in 168 B.C. The body of the woman, 1.52 meters long and weighing 34.3 kg, is incredibly well preserved, with flesh, 16 teeth, and internal organs. The lungs, intestines, and stomach were removed after disinterment and preserved in formaldehyde. They are all on display in the basement. An autopsy revealed arteriosclerosis, gallstones, tuberculosis, and parasites. Death came to her suddenly at age 50; there were undigested melon seeds in her stomach. The remarkable state of preservation is attributed to the body's being wrapped in hemp and nine silk ribbons, and sealed from oxygen and water in three coffins surrounded by 5000 kg of charcoal and sticky white clay. She was buried 20 meters down. She died after her husband; maybe that is why her tomb is the largest and she is the best preserved of all. She probably planned it herself.

The 5000 relics include 1800 pieces of lacquerware, many of which needed only cleaning to appear new. Look for the ear cups for wine and soup, and a makeup box with comb, mirror, powder, and lipstick. She had food buried with her—chicken, dog, crane, dove, beef, pork, rabbit, etc. She also had for her after-death use incense burners, clothes, silk fabrics, medicinal herbs, and nine musical instruments. Maybe she did use them! Who knows if she ate the spiritual essence of the food buried with her? An inventory of the relics was written on bamboo strips, paper still being rare then. In the building to the left as you leave the marquess are the three coffins and a model of the tomb site. To the right is an arts and crafts and antiques store. Some reproductions are on sale. Open daily (except Sundays), 8–11 a.m. and 2:30–5 p.m. Exceptions made on request.

The **Han tomb site** 墓址 , only 4 km away in Mawangdui 马王堆 , is now just a large hole in the ground under a roof. One can see the pyramid-shaped hill, the neat, earthen walls, and staircase inside. Geomancy students can figure out the *feng shui*. Was it practiced then? Did the tomb face south?

The **Hunan Exhibition Hall** 湖南展览馆 (Zhanlanguan Rd.; tel. 25898) has more than 3000 ceramics pieces on display, including a 7-foot vase, most made recently in Changsha and Hunan. An exhibit hall of traditional-style paintings and a shop are upstairs. Open daily, 8–11:30 a.m. and 2:30–5:30 p.m. Can be skipped unless you're buying.

The **Hunan Provincial Embroidery Factory** 湖南省湘绣厂 (285 Bayi Rd.; tel. 27219) is worthwhile, as you can see this ancient craft being performed and be amazed at the number of workers not wearing eyeglasses. Look for embroidery so fine it can be displayed from either side.

A tour of the city includes **Tianxin Park,** the highest point here, with a small section of the 600-plus-year-old city wall. Open daily, 6 a.m.–8 p.m.; tel. 22404. Note Qing inscriptions on the bricks. **Juzi (Orange) Island** 橘子岛 , 5 km long, is probably the ''long sand'' after which Changsha is named. In the middle of the Xiang River at Changsha, it is 300 meters at its widest. Buses can drive almost to the southern tip, a park. The island is inhabited, cultivated with orange groves, and stacked with reeds for making paper. It has a small sand beach for swimming and a place to change. Good for relaxing evening walks and bicycling. Open daily, 6:30 a.m.–9 p.m.; tel. 82152.

The **Hunan Normal School** (Shuyuan Rd.), outside the south gate of the city, has a small museum. Mao studied and taught here in 1913–18 and 1920–21. The current structure, built in 1968, is a copy of the 1912 school and reflects its European connections. Open daily for visitors, 8 a.m.–noon and 2–6 p.m.; tel. 31786.

Yuelu Hill 岳麓山 , on the western side of the Xiang River, is good for climbing and hiking. The Wangxiang Pavilion has a good view from the top. The **Lushan Temple** 麓山寺 was built in A.D. 268 and reconstructed last in 1681. The **Yuelu Academy** 岳麓书院 was one of the four major institutes of higher learning from A.D. 976 (Song), rebuilt last in 1670. The **Aiwan Pavilion** 爱晚亭 was built in 1792 (Qing). Open daily, from 8:30 a.m.–4:30 p.m.; tel. 82011. These are not very spectacular.

A new tourist attraction, **Zhang Jiajie State Forest Park,** is being prepared 400 km west of Changsha (7 hrs by bus; 22 by train). It is a forest close to Dayon county in the western part of Hunan province, full of beautiful hills, stone pillars, flowers and wild boar, monkeys and leopards. Six small hotels and several guesthouses should be ready by the time of your visit.

Also in the province are "Hengshan" Mountain, "Shaoshan," and "Yueyang," under separate listings.

Entertainment

Local Huagu opera originated from provincial folk songs and ditties. The Hunan Provincial Puppet Show Troupe is well known.

Shopping

Made in the province are embroideries, porcelain and pottery, chrysanthemum stone and bamboo carvings, fans, firecrackers, lacquer reproductions, smoky quartz and bloodstone carvings, handicrafts from minorities, and duck-down clothing.

Hunan Antique Store 湖南省博物馆文物商店 (3 Dongfeng Rd., inside the Hunan Provincial Museum; tel. 25277); **Hunan Arts and Crafts Shop** 湖南工艺品商店 (Xiangxiu Building, Wuyi Square; tel. 22253); **Zhongshan Rd. Department Stores** 韶山路百货商店 (213 Zhongshan Rd.; tel. 24621); **Shaoshan Rd. Department Store** 中山路百货商店 (Shaoshan Rd.; tel. 24588); **Hunan Foreign-Languages Bookstore** 湖南外文书店 (89 Wuyi Rd., 2nd floor; tel. 24102).

Restaurants

Fire Palace Restaurant 火宫店餐馆 □ *147 Pozi St.; tel. 25391.*

Another Village Restaurant 又一村饭店 □ *111 Zhongshan Rd.; tel. 24257.*

Huang Nan Restaurant 华南大酒家 □ *34 Jiefang Rd.; tel. 25876.*

Changsha Restaurant 长沙饭店 □ *116 Wuyi Rd.; tel. 28028, 25029.*

Xiao Xiang Restaurant 潇湘饭店 □ *Wuyi Rd.*

Hotels

Furong (Hibiscus) Hotel 芙蓉宾馆 □ *Wuyi Dong Rd.* □ 1984. Over 500 rooms.

Xiangjiang (Xiang River) Hotel 湘江宾馆 □ *267 Zhongshan Rd.* □ 1977. More than 500 rooms. Close to shopping and post and cable office. Near the former site of Mao's Teach-Yourself College; 3 km from railway station and 22 km from airport.

Fenglin Hotel 枫林饭店 □ *Rongwanzhen* □ 1982.

Hunan Hotel 湖南宾馆 □ *Yingbin Rd.* □ Older. Mainly for state guests. Near museum, zoo, Nianjia Lake, and Memorial Park to Martyrs.

Also **Rongyuan Guesthouse** 蓉因宾馆 .

Other Important Addresses

Bureau of Tourism Administration: Hunan Province, tel. 267254; telex: 33410 HPFAO CN.

C.I.T.S. 中国国际旅行社 : 130 Sanxing St.; tel. 22250, 27356.

C.T.S. 中国旅行社 : Furong Hotel, Wuyi Rd.; tel. 25101.
Bank of China 中国银行 : 55 Wuyi Rd.; tel. 23688.
CAAC 中国民航 · Wuyi Dong Rd.; tel. 23820.
Railway Station 火车站 : Wuyi Rd.; tel. 26326.
Taxi: Hunan Provincial Bureau of Tourism, Xiangjiang Hotel; tel. 26261 X390.

Changsha Taxi Company: Wuyi Rd.; tel. 26495.
Hospital: Check first with your hotel. Otherwise, No. 2 Hospital of Hunan Medical College 湖南医学院第二医院 : Wenyi Rd.; tel. 24608, 25830.
Changsha Medical and First-Aid Station 长沙医疗急救站 : tel. 23636
Fire 火警 : tel. 119
Police 警察 : tel. 110
Foreign Affairs Section, Bureau of Public Security 公安局外事处 : tel. 26241.

Changzhou 常州

East China, Jiangsu province, halfway between Shanghai and Nanjing on the Grand Canal. Population about 460,000.

This 2600-year-old city was called Yanling in the Zhou, Piling in the Han, and Lanling in the Jin. Notable are Hongmei Park, Tianningsi (Heavenly Tranquillity) Temple, Yizhouting Pavilion, and Wenbita (Writing Brush) Pagoda. A 1500-year-old comb factory still makes wooden and bamboo combs. One can buy "Palace Combs," one of the "eight famous hair decorations worn by imperial women." Hotel.

Chengde 承德

(Chengteh, Chengte, Jehol, Jehe.) North China, Hebei province, 250 km NE of Beijing. Urban population, 130,000. Coldest temperature—⁻19°C.; hottest—35°C for a very short time each year. Most rain June and July.

The Qing imperial summer resort here was built for Emperor Kangxi (Kang-hsi) from 1703 to 1790, not just to relax in, but to curry favor with the Mongolian nobles in the area. To help win them over, he built 11 Lama temples also. Chengde is well worth seeing, especially if you don't go to Tibet. It is one of the 24 historical cities protected by the State Council.

The **Imperial Summer Resort** 避暑山庄 covers an area of 5.6 million square meters, which is larger than the Summer Palace in Beijing. Most of it is surrounded by a 10-km-long wall. From Beijing, it is a 3-day bus tour, but at the moment the bus is only for Chinese tourists, as the road goes through a couple of restricted areas.

Foreign visitors can fly here in 40 minutes or travel by train for 5 hours from Beijing. In the last century a one-way trip took the Manchus 3–20 days by horseback, palanquin, or bumpy chariot.

Chengde oozes with history. The Qing court lived here from May to October each year. It was in a yurt here in 1793 that Lord Macartney of Britain refused to kowtow to Qing Emperor Qianlong (Chien Lung) and where the envoy was dismissed as a "bearer of tribute" from "vassal king" George III, his requests to trade refused. In 1860 the Manchu court fled to Chengde as Anglo-French forces approached Beijing. The death of Emperor Xianfeng (Hsien Feng) here in 1862 led to the rise of Cixi (Tzu Hsi), the empress dowager, as regent. Think of the plotting that went on as he lay on his deathbed. Cixi visited here again, by train, in 1900. In the 1930s, many of the buildings were looted and destroyed by the warlord Tang Yu Liu. The most important buildings have been or are in the process of being repaired. Some of the ruins are intriguing and fascinating in themselves. Sit in the hulk of the "Potala" at dusk and tell ghost stories as darkness falls.

You can see the main palace and garden in one day and five of the outer temples on a second day. If you rush and avoid the climb to the Club Stone, all the open temples and the summer resort can be covered in one full, hurried day.

The Imperial Summer Resort has nine courtyards. It is not as palatial as Beijing's Summer Palace, but it is worth seeing. The building to the right inside the second gate has a painting of the Macartney visit 马戈尔尼来访画片 and a hunting scene 木兰秋狄图 (with officials sporting animal head masks and imitating mating calls to attract the bear, deer, wolves, leopards, and tigers). To the left is the **Hall of No Worldly Lust but True Faith,** which is also called the **Nanmu Hall** 楠木殿 because of the scented wood from which it is made. You might get a whiff of it. The emperor received subjects and envoys in this ceremonial hall. On either side are waiting rooms, one for foreign visitors and one for relatives and tribal leaders. Among the exhibits in these and other halls are Manchu coats with sleeves shaped like horses' hooves, sedan chairs, an elephant dotted with pearls, brilliant blue king-fisher feather ornaments. In a hall displaying fine porcelain are Qing imitations of Ming vases.

The **Refreshing-at-Mist-Veiled-Waters Pavilion** was the imperial bedroom. On either side are the pavilions of the two empresses. The imperial bedroom has a "hollow wall" 夹层墙 (seen from the back) where Cixi listened carefully as the emperor lay dying inside. As a result of her eavesdropping, she was able to seize power from her rival.

Cixi lived in the **Pine and Crane Pavilion,** which was originally built for the mother of Emperor Qianlong.

The emperor used the two-story pavilion beyond to enjoy the moon 云山胜地 with his concubines. It has no interior stairs. The Qian Long Emperor studied in the pavilion, which now houses paintings for sale.

The garden is beautiful, and visitors should be able to rent ice skates and bicycles. The trees planted by the Qing are tagged with identification numbers. The two most influential emperors chose 72 scenic spots and wrote poems about each. Kangxi's poems have four characters; Qianlong's have three. Thirty of these places are still marked by pavilions from which you can see the view, including one on the top of the hill to view the snow 南山积雪 There is even one to view the Club Stone.

Among the buildings counterclockwise around the lake is the **Jinshan Pavilion** 金山亭 , copied from one of the same name in Zhenjiang, and the **Yanyulou (Misty-Rain Tower)** 烟雨楼 , the latter built by Qianlong, a copy of one now destroyed in Zhejiang. It was used to watch the misty rain, of course, and to read.

On the flatland area here, Emperor Qianlong stooped to receive the equally arrogant Lord Macartney, the envoy from Britain. One of the scenes from the television movie *Marco Polo* was filmed in this garden—the one where Polo meets the Yuan emperor.

The walled garden on the **Changlang Islet** 沧浪屿 is a copy of the Changlang Garden in Suzhou. Some people collect postcards when they travel; the Qianlong emperor collected buildings!

Nearby on a side road is a herd of about 40 spotted deer 鹿场 . A herd was started here during the Qing because some of the emperors drank deer's blood as a tonic.

The two-story Imperial Library 文津阁 has a pond in front and few trees as a precaution against fire. It is approached through the rockeries. If you see tourists in front of the library staring into the water, it's because they are looking for the reflection of a crescent moon. Look for it yourself. The library is a copy of one in Shaoxing.

As a Chinese garden, this imperial summer resort is one of the best, a microcosm of the whole country with lake, grasslands, and mountains.

The **Outer Temples** 外八庙 , outside the walls, are a mixture of Manchu, Mongolian, Tibetan, and Han Chinese architecture with a similiar mix of artifacts inside. Once housing 1000 lamas or monks, they are now all museums. The steles usually have Manchu writing in front, Chinese behind, and Mongolian and Tibetan on the sides. If you are short of time, the Putuozongsheng and Puning are the most important to see. Otherwise, start with the *Pule 普乐寺 , which is also known as the Round Pavilion, as it was built in 1766 to resemble the Temple of Heaven. Inside is a statue of two hard-to-see copulating gods from the esoteric sect of Lama Buddhism. From this temple one can climb to the **Club Stone** 磬锤峰 , the giant, mallet-shaped stone, for a marvelous view of the palace, the temples, and Chengde city itself.

The small **Anyuan Temple** 安远庙 is patterned after a temple in Xinjiang that no longer exists. Inside is a statue of Lu Du Mo, a female goddess. The **Puren** should be open for your visit.

Near the Puning Temple, one can get a Qing horse cart ride, or a room in a tiny hotel aimed at Chinese tourists. Inside the temple gate is a stele about Qianlong's suppression of a rebellion of the minorities. The **Puning Temple** 普宁寺 contains a copy of the spectacular 1000-headed and 1000-armed Guan Yin, Goddess of Mercy, which should not be missed. Actually he/she has only 42 hands and arms, each representing 25. On each palm is an eye. The statue is 22.28 meters high. It is in the Mahayana Hall 大乘之阁 . The warlord stole the original.

The Puning Temple is patterned after the Sumeru temple in Tibet and is known also as the Temple of Universal Peace or Big Buddha Temple. Inside are a drum and a bell tower, a laughing Buddha, and four guardian kings. About 100 larger-than-life-size arhats remain of the original 508; the others were destroyed by fire. Only eight of the arhats are Chinese. The mural of the 18 arhats is 230 years old and original, remarkable for its preservation. Look for the big bronze cooking pot that fed 1000 lamas. The buildings in back are classic Tibetan style, with nothing inside. The number of buildings and stupas are symbolic—the center of the world was Sumeru Mountain, with four great continents around it.

The **Xumifushou (Longevity and Happiness) Temple** 须弥福寿之庙 was inspired by the Xiashelumpo (Zhaxilhunbu) Temple in Shigatse, Tibet, and used as a residence for the sixth panchen lama. Dragons seem to scamper along the edges of the roof, most unusual for a Han temple. Built in 1780, it is the newest of the temples and commemorates Qianlong's 70th birthday, at which point he started to learn Tibetan. In the main building is a statue of the founder of Lamaism and behind him, Sakyamuni. The tentlike pagoda in the back is similar to the one in Fragrant Hill Park in Beijing.

The **Putuozongcheng Temple** 普陀宗乘之庙 is patterned after the Potala Palace, home of the dalai lama, in Lhasa, Tibet. It was built from 1767 to 1771 for the 60th birthday of Qianlong and for the 80th birthday of his mother. The elephant symbolizes the Mahayana sect. (One elephant equals 500 horses.) The five pagodas on several of the buildings symbolize the five schools of Lamaism. Not to be missed is the **Donggang Zi Dian (East Hall),** where statues unusual for this part of China can be found. Please try not to show your insensitivity as an embarrassed guide explains what is happening under the yellow aprons. These are statues of the Red Hat sect of Lamaism, where sex with a person other than one's spouse was part of the religious ritual. In the opposite hall on the same level are other metal Buddhist statues. Another 164 steps lead up to the main building, which is decorated by

Buddhas in niches—the 80 at the top representing Qianlong's mother's age. The six in front each symbolize ten years of Qianlong's life. Some birthday cake!

The temple was built to commemorate the birthdays, as well as a visit by tribal leaders. This temple is the largest, and most of it should be repaired by the time you read this. A great deal of it was still gutted on my recent visit, and it was intriguing to try to figure out what stood where.

The **Shuxiang Temple** 殊象寺 should be open when you visit too.

A 300-meter-long **Qing dynasty-style street** 清朝一条街 should now also be open, with tea houses and souvenir and local product shops. Planned also are Qing horse-drawn carriages and sedan chair rides. Also of interest is a **warm spring** 温泉 for chronic diseases, 36 km east of the palace (no hotel yet), and a hunting ground.

The **Jinshan Ling** 金山岭长城 section of the Great Wall is 110 km away. Officials here say it is better than Badaling, north of Beijing.

Shopping

The Friendship Store 友谊商店 is small, near the De Hui Gate. Gardeners of miniature plants might be interested in the cheap water stones, which absorb water and therefore can grow plants on top of them. But they are. heavy! The area also produces silk, walnut walking sticks, and wood carvings. You can find chickenblood stones with brilliant natural red on them, probably from Mongolia. Not cheap.

Restaurants

Found at almost every meal are the locally grown apricot kernels, usually sweetened and delicious. The food should improve with the opening of the new hotels. Restaurants recommended by C.I.T.S. are the **Fangyuanju Restaurant** 劳园居饭庄 , the **Xiyuchan Restaurant** 西域春饭馆 , the **Qucui Lou (Imperial Food) Restaurant** 裘翠楼饭庄 , and the **Rehe Wild Food Restaurant** 热河野味餐厅 . Please do not eat endangered species.

Hotels

Shanzhuang (Mountain View) Hotel 山庄宾馆 □ *across from the main gate of the palace at 127, Xiaonanmen Rd.* □ 42 rooms and 76 suites. Will not be used for foreign visitors once the new hotels have opened.

Qiwanglou Hotel 绮望楼宾馆 □ built in ancient Chinese style, inside the palace grounds north of the main gate, is the best here, used also for heads of state.

The 33 Yurt Hotel 蒙古包宾馆 □ *inside the palace grounds in the shadow of the* **Six Harmonies Pagoda** 六合塔 □ should be open for your visit. It is moderately priced and is actually made of brick with felt covers. Attendants wear Mongolian dress and the location should give you plenty of time to enjoy the garden in its different moods. 100 beds.

Songyunxia (Villa) Hotel 松云峡别墅 □ built in the 1960s, has 80 beds in rooms with kitchens. Being reconstructed at press time.

Chengde Hotel 承德宾馆 □ *33, Nanyingzi St.* □ 41 rooms, 67 suites. Not to be confused with the newer, more luxurious Chengde Tourist Hotel.

Chengde Tourist Hotel 承德旅游饭店 □ *South Wulie Rd.* □ 1986. 450 beds. In the top three.

Rehe (Great) Hotel 热河大酒店 □ will have 500 beds and is aiming at a three-star standard. It should be finished by 1988 and be in the top three.

Xinhua Hotel 新华饭店 □ *4, Xinhua Rd.* □ 40 rooms.

C.I.T.S. 国旅承德支社办公室（中华路北十一号）   and
C.T.S. (Dongkou, Zhonghua Rd.; tel. 3502, 3401).
Taxi 出租汽车
Bicycle Rental 自行车出租处
Horse Carriage Stand 古代马车出租处

Chengdu

(Chengtu) Southwest China in central Sichuan province, slightly over 2 hours by air SW of Beijing. It can also be reached by a 21-hour train ride from Kunming with about 250 km of tunnels and a view of Mount Emei. Direct flights from elsewhere in China and Hong Kong. Population is 3.7 million, including rural areas. With an altitude of 500 meters, its hottest temperature is 37°C in July and its coldest may be ⁻5°C in January. The tourist season is April to November, with July and August uncomfortably hot. Annual precipitation about 1000 mm, mainly in July and August.

Chengdu has a history of over 2000 years. In the fourth century B.C., the King of Shu moved his capital here and named it Chengdu (Becoming a Capital). In the Han, after brocade weaving became successfully established, it was called "the Brocade City." During the Three Kingdoms, it was the capital of Shu. Many American, Canadian, and British missionaries and teachers lived here before Liberation.

Today it is the provincial capital and an educational and industrial center. Its industries include metallurgy, electronics, and textiles. Its buses run on natural gas. The area grows rice, wheat, rape (for oil), chilis, and sweet potatoes. It also grows medicinal plants and herbs that are sold all over the country.

Chengdu has so much to offer, you need at least 5 days to cover it, preferably more. C.I.T.S. suggests the following grouping based on regions, but you can plan your own schedule:

Day 1: Du Fu's Thatched Cottage, the Temple of Marquis Wu, and the River-Viewing Pavilion.

Day 2: Chengdu Zoo, Tomb of Wang Jian, Divine Light Monastery, bamboo-weaving, brocade, jade-carving, or lacquerware factory.

Day 3: Dujiang Irrigation project.

Day 4 and 5: Meishan, Leshan, and Emei Shan.

Day 6: Jiuzhaigou

*Du Fu (Tu Fu)'s Thatched Roof Cottage 杜甫草堂 is actually a park with a replica of the modest residence of the famous Tang poet who lived here and wrote 240 poems during four years, from A.D. 759. A temple and a garden were first built as a memorial in the Northern Song. These have been replaced periodically, the pavilions here from the Qing. Statues, books, and art exhibitions are also found in the 20-hectare garden. Some translations here of Du Fu's poems in 15 foreign languages might help foreigners understand his importance. Open daily, 7:30 a.m.–6 p.m.; tel. 25258.

The Temple of Marquis Wu 武侯祠 , in the southern part of the city, was originally built in the sixth century in memory of Zhuge Liang (Chuke Liang), a famous strategist and statesman, prime minister of Shu during the Three Kingdoms (A.D. 220–265). Here are tablets written during the Tang, larger than life-size statues, and the still unexcavated **Tomb of Liu Bei** 刘备墓 , the king of Shu, one of the heroes of *The Romance of the Three Kingdoms*. The current buildings are Qing and are open daily, 7:30 a.m.–6 p.m.; tel. 26397. The ***Zhuge Liang Memorial Hall** 诸葛亮殿 is also listed as a historical site under State Council protection.

The Wangjianglou (River-Viewing Pavilion) 望江楼 , in the southeastern part of the city, was once the residence of a Tang dynasty woman poet, Xue Tao. The park has over 100 varieties of bamboo. Study the plants and see how many different ones you can find. The garden also contains several pavilions, one called the Chongli, built in 1886 and 30 meters tall. Sit in the "Pavilion for Poem Reciting" or the

"Chamber to Relieve Your Resentment." See if they inspire you, too, to poetry. Sit in them quietly for half an hour and breathe deeply. Open daily, 7:30 a.m.–6 p.m.; tel. 42552.

The 25-hectare **Chengdu Zoo** 成都动物园 is 6 km north of the city and boasts 13 giant pandas, the largest collection of this endangered species in captivity anywhere in the world. It also has rare golden-hair monkeys among 2000 animals of over 200 varieties. Open daily, 8 a.m.–6 p.m.; tel. 31951.

Try for the ***Tomb of Wang Jian** 王建墓 (A.D. 847–918), the emperor of Shu in the 10th century, if you are more interested in history. Wang Jian captured not just Sichuan, but parts of three other provinces, and proclaimed himself emperor in 907. The 23.4-meter-long tomb is elaborate, with double stone arches and carved musicians. Open daily, except Mondays, 9 a.m.–noon and 2–5 p.m.; tel. 21245.

The **Baoguangsi (Divine Light Monastery)** 宝光寺 should not be missed. It is 18 km north of the city at **Xindu** 新都 , and famous. Originally founded during the Eastern Han, about 1900 years ago, it was the site of a palace ordered built by Tang Emperor Li Huan. During the Ming, the monastery was destroyed by war, but it was reconstructed on its original foundation during the Qing in 1671. Pagodas, five halls, and 16 courtyards make it most impressive. The Tang pagoda is 30 meters high, 13 stories with a glazed gold top. The 500 arhats are from the Qing in 1851, each about 2 meters high, unique and vivid. The Stone Carved Stupa is also Qing, 5.5 meters high, in granite. Look for the 175-centimeters-high stone Thousand Buddha Tablet, carved on four sides in A.D. 450. Look also for the Buddhist scriptures written on palm leaves from India. Open daily, 8 a.m.–6 p.m.

You may want to skip the factory and go shopping instead. If you are on our 5-day plan, this is your last day in the city. If you dig museums, the **Sichuan Provincial Museum** 四川省博物馆 (Renmin Nan Rd.) is at your disposal. If you want to learn more about the Long March through Sichuan or delve further into local history, here's your chance. Open daily, except Mondays, from 8:30–11:30 a.m. and 2–6 p.m.; tel. 22158.

There's another Buddhist monastery, the **Wenshu (God of Wisdom) Monastery** 文殊院 (Wenshuyuan St., Beimen; tel. 22378). Founded in the Tang and reconstructed in 1691, this temple has ancient paintings and a white jade statue from Burma, gilded Japanese scripture containers (Tang), and other treasures. Open daily, 8 a.m.–8 p.m. The **Cultural Park** 文化公园 has an old Taoist temple 青羊宫（道观） . Open daily, 7 a.m.–6 p.m.; tel. 23637.

The ***Dujiangyan Irrigation System** 都江堰灌溉系统（灌溉 工程） 1½-hours' drive NW (57 km) in **Guanxian county** 灌县（灌 县 usually takes a full day. It was originally built in 256 B.C., the oldest such project in the country. Impressive because of its age and scope, it controlled floods and diverted half of the Minjiang River to the irrigation of the fertile Sichuan plain. This area has old temples, murals, and a swinging bridge. The 240-meter-long swinging bridge over the river was first built before the Song, and most recently rebuilt in 1974, so don't be afraid to walk on it. The **Fu Long Kuan (Dragon Subduing Temple)** 伏龙观 houses a statue of Li Bing, the mastermind of the project. The **Erwang (Two Kings) Temple** 二王庙 is a memorial to Li Bing and his son.

Near Dujiangyan is a **deer farm** 养鹿场 where you can buy Pilose Antler Juice "for aching back . . . impotence and premature ejaculation." Also near Dujiangyan and 40 km from Chengdu is **Qingcheng (Green City) Mountain** 青城山, one of the birthplaces of Taoism and still a Taoist center, with 38 buildings left of its 70 original temples, shrines, and grottoes. With some of its cliffs shaped like city walls (hence the name), this strikingly beautiful mountain rises up to 1600 meters. It was also a base for a peasant insurgency led by Zhang Xianzhong (Chang Hsien-chung), who captured Chongqing in 1644 and occupied Chengdu, but lost them the following year to another insurgent. Visitors can reach the **Jian Fu Temple** (Tang) by road. Nearby is Guei Cheng (Ghost City) mountain, where a Taoist saint, Guei Gu Zi, lived during the Warring States. Guesthouses midway up and on top.

In the Han, one of the founders of Taoism, Zhang Daolin, put up an altar here for preaching. The **Cavern of Taoist Master Temple** was founded in 617–605 B.C.. The building is from the Tang and contains a portrait of Zhang Daolin, stone carvings of the Three Emperors, Ming woodwork, and murals of the Eight Taoist Fairies. The mountain is full of legends.

Sansu Shrine 三苏祠 is in **Meishan County** 眉山县, 89 km south of the city. It was the residence of three famous literary men of the Northern Song and became a shrine during the Ming (1368–98). The current structures are Qing.

For *Leshan's Giant (Tang) Buddha and *Emei Shan Mountain, see separate listing.

Another excursion possibility is **Jiuzhaigou** 报国寺, a "fairyland," opened in 1985. Located 470 km from Chengdu in Nanping county town, this is a 1½-day's drive or an 80-minute helicopter ride each way. The whole helicopter may have to be chartered. An airfield is being built so that visitors can fly there in 1½ hours. One can stay in the Nuorilang Hotel. Three nights and two days are needed, but you can get an idea of this lovely forest in a day if you fly in and out. .

This is a 60,000-hectare primitive forest with species earlier thought to be extinct. Naturalists should go wild with excitement here. It is the home of pandas, the golden-haired monkey, takin, white chicken, and river deer. The setting is full of forested hills, carpets of flowers, lakes and waterfalls, and even some legends. A male fairy, Dage, once fell in love with the lovely fairy Wonusemo and gave her an elaborate mirror made from wind and cloud. It slipped from her hand and smashed into the mountains here and became 108 mounds of greenery.

Jiuzhaigou means ''nine stockades canyon,'' three of which are about 2500 meters above sea level. Tibetan settlers once lived in the area. It opened so close to press time that we have been unable to get there. If you do, please let us know your impressions.

Wolong Nature Preserve 卧龙自然保护区 , 140 km from Chengdu, has about 200 pandas in the wild, but tourists can usually only see eight. There are more in the Chengdu Zoo, above. Very rough road. No hotel. Visitors stay in the Forestry Bureau hostel. Wolong is not generally open to tourists, but C.I.T.S. can arrange trips for special groups and anyone going there to donate money for saving this endangered species. Some groups go through the Forestry Ministry in Beijing or the Sichuan Forestry Bureau in Chengdu.

Shopping

Of the factories to which C.I.T.S. can arrange visits, those of interest to visitors make bamboo weavings, brocade, Shu embroidery, filigree crafts, and lacquerware. The main shopping areas are **Renmin Rd.** 人民路 , **Yanshikou** 盐市口 , and **Chunxi Rd.**

Friendship Store 友谊商店 (519 Shengli Zhong Rd.; tel. 27067).

Sichuan Antique Store 四川文物商店 (11 Shangyechang; tel. 22787).

Chengdu Arts and Crafts Shop 成都工艺美术品 (10 Chunxi Rd., Beiduan; tel. 26817). Branches in Jinjiang Hotel and airport.

Chengdu Fine Arts Company (440 Shengli Xi Rd.; tel. 24184).

Restaurants

Next to Cantonese, Sichuan cuisine is the most famous Chinese cooking in the world. Not all of it is spicy-hot, and dishes are toned down for tourists. Flower petals and herbs are used in such specialties as ''fried lotus flower,'' ''governor's chicken,'' diced chicken with hot pepper and peanuts, and ''smoked duck with tea fragrance.'' Try also the dumplings and Dan Dan noodles. See ''Food.''

Dongfeng (East Wind) Restaurant 东风饭店 □ *31 Dongfeng Rd.; tel. 27012.*

Bingjiang Hotel Restaurant 滨江饭店 □ *16 Bingjiang Rd.; tel. 24451.*

Chengdu Restaurant 成都饭店 □ *642 Shengli Zhong Rd.; tel. 27301, 25388.*

Furong Restaurant 芙蓉饭店 □ *124 Renmin Nan Rd.; tel. 24004.*

Hotels

Jinjiang (Brocade River) Hotel 锦江宾馆 □ *180 Renmin Nan Rd.* □ 1961; renovated 1984. 18 km from airport. Nine stories, over 500 rooms and suites.

Chengdu Hotel 成都宾馆   □ *Shui Nian He, Dongfeng Rd.* □ 1984.

Wanjiang Hotel 望江宾馆   □ *42 Xia Sha He Bai* □ 1980.

Jinniu Hotel 金牛宾馆   □ *Jinniu District in the western suburbs, 5 km from downtown* □ Villa style. 69 rooms or suites. Indoor swimming pool.

A large hotel across the street from the Jinjiang should be ready for your visit.

Other Important Addresses

C.I.T.S.: 180 Renmin Nan Rd.; tel. 25042, 28225.

CAAC 中国民航   Renmin Nan Rd., opposite the Jinjiang Hotel; tel. 23038, 23087.

Bank of China 中国银行成都分行 : 60 Shuwa Bei 3-St.; tel. 29515. Foreign exchange counters at the main hotels and the Friendship Store.

Taxis: Chengdu Travel Service, Jinjiang Hotel; tel. 22305.

Hospitals: Check first with your hotel.

Hospitals attached to the West China University of Medical Science (Hua Xi Yi Ko Da Xue)   四川医学院附属医院 : tel. 27905. Very close to the Jinjiang Hotel on Renmin Nan Rd.

Sichuan Renmin (People's) Hospital 四川省人民医院 : tel. 22712.

Hospital Attached to the Chengdu Institute of Traditional Chinese Medicine 成都中医学院附属医院 : tel. 23902.

Foreign Affairs Department of the Chengdu Public Security Bureau 成都市公安局外事处 : Wenwu Rd.; tel. 22951 or 29551.

重庆

Chongqing (Chungking)

Southwest China. Southeastern Sichuan province on mountain-
sides between the Changjiang (Yangtze) and Jialing rivers. A
little over 2-hours' flight SW of Beijing or NE of Guangzhou.
Overnight train ride from Chengdu. Population: About 2.6 mil-
lion urban. Highest temperature in summer, 40°C; lowest in
winter, 6°C. Annual precipitation: 1000 mm. Chongqing is one
of the "three furnaces" of China. Clear skies only in summer.
Fog between November and March during which the city cel-
ebrates a 10-day Fog Festival to commemorate the days when
the fog kept Japanese bombers from attacking the city. Many
flights canceled at this time, so travelers must be flexible.

Chongqing has a history of 3000 years. It was capital of the Kingdom of Ba in the 12th century B.C. During the Song, it was named
Chongqing, which means "double celebration." During the Qing, a 10-
meter-high, 7-km wall was built around the city. Chongqing was one of
the treaty ports open to foreigners, and foreign missionaries and teachers worked here before Liberation. Innumerable books have been written in English about this area.

In the late 1930s, during the Sino-Japanese War, the Nationalist
government moved its capital here, and Han Suyin's book *Destination*
Chungking reflects that period. Unfortunately, Japanese bombs destroyed much of the city, and few ancient relics survived the war. Zhou
Enlai (Chou En-lai) lived here as he tried to work with the Nationalists
against the foreign invader. The American (Stillwell, Hurley, Marshall,
Wedmeyer) missions attempted unsuccessfully to get the Nationalists to
work with the Communists. Read Theodore H. White's *In Search of*
History for that period in the 1940s. The Communists took over the city
in November 1949.

Today, Chongqing is smoky, drab, crowded, and industrial, with
apparently little regard for city planning. It has very few bicycles because of the narrow, winding, and hilly roads. It is now primarily of
interest to students of modern history. It is also the place where you
can get a 2-day trip to the Dazu sculptures, 165 km west, and take a
ship down the Yangtze through the gorges.

For those who want to pass the time constructively while waiting
for boats, you can learn a bit about modern Chinese history at
Hongyancun Revolutionary Memorial Hall (a.k.a. Red Crag Village)
红岩村革命纪念馆　(13 Hongyang Village). This was the office of
the Communist Party and the Eighth Route Army between 1939 and
1946. It was also residence for Chou En-lai and other revolutionary

leaders including, briefly, Mao Zedong (Mao Tse-tung). The opening of this office was greatly influenced by the kidnapping of Nationalist leader Chiang Kai-shek in Xi'an in 1936.

No. 50 Zengjiayan was the residence of some of the people working at Red Crag Village. **Guiyang Garden** was at first the residence of the Nationalist representative but was later used by the Communists. The October 10 Agreement with Chiang Kai-shek was signed here. The prison used by the Nationalists for Communist prisoners is at **Jiatse Cave,** at the base of Gele Mountain in the northwestern suburbs. Today it is an exhibition on the infamous **Sino-American Special Technical Cooperation** 中美合作所集中营展览馆 , responsible for the loss of life of many people who fell afoul of Nationalist government officials. Open daily, 8 a.m.–5:30 p.m.

For less recent history, there's the **Chongqing Museum** 重庆博物馆 (Pipashan Zheng St., near Loquat Park), open daily, 8–11:30 a.m. and 3–6:30 p.m. If you want to go back farther than that, try the **Chongqing Museum of Natural History** 重庆自然博物馆 (Beibei District, 43 km NW of the city). Dinosaur bones were found in this region and some are on view here. Open daily, 8:30–11:30 a.m. and 3–6:30 p.m. In the same general vicinity is beautiful **Jinyun Shan,** known also as "Little Emei Shan," with its highest peak 1,030 meters. The **Jinyun Temple** was founded 1500 years ago and has relics from the Six Dynasties and the Ming. **Beiwenquan (North Hot Spring) Park** is below the temple. Its 10 hectares are pleasant and shady, with winding trails for strolling amid ancient Chinese architecture (if you don't care for a hot spring bath). The natural water temperature is 28–35°C. Open daily, 8 a.m.–6 p.m.

As for living animals, the **zoo** 动物园 (at Yangjiaping, in the west of the city) is open daily 6:30 a.m.–8 p.m. For art lovers, the Sichuan Fine Arts Institute in Huang Kuo Ping District is well worth a visit. The institute is one of the best in China, with a teacher-student ratio of 1:2. It has an excellent three-story gallery with art for sale. Open daily, 9–11:30 a.m. and 2–5:30 p.m. (tel. 23423).

For those who just want to pass the time relaxing while waiting for boats, there's **Eling (Goose Neck) Park** 鹅岭公园 , between the two rivers. It has pleasant pavilions, ponds, and gardens. Open daily, 6:30 a.m.–8 p.m. **Pipashan (Loquat Hill) Park** 枇杷山公园 is the highest point in the city and was a former warlord's residence. Good view of the two rivers and the city. Monkeys and birds. Open daily, 6:30 a.m.–10 p.m. Storytellers abound in the evenings!

For real relaxation, try the **Nanwenquan (South Hot Spring) Park** 南温泉公园 , 26 km south of the city. It has a hot water (40°C) swimming pool and baths, and 13 hectares of gardens in which to stroll or jog. Open daily, 8:30 a.m.–6 p.m. **Xiaoquan (Little Spring) Guesthouse** 小泉宾馆 is adjacent, with 168 rooms.

Nanshan (South Mountain) Park 南山公园 , on the south bank

of the river, is where George C. Marshall, the American mediator, and Chiang Kai-shek lived. The Nationalist leader lived in "Yun Xiu." Nearby is **Tu Hill**, the site of the residence of King Yu of the Xia, the first ruler to control the rivers (see "Chengdu"). Also close is **Laojun Cave**, where Lao Tzu, the founder of Taoism, lived.

A **cable car** 缆车 goes across the Jialing River from Cangbailu Station to Jinshajie Station for a bird's-eye view of the area.

Fengdu, 170 km east of Chongqing on the Yangtze, has a restored seventh-century city based on an ancient legend, a gathering place for ghosts.

For the "Yangtze Gorges" and "Dazu," see separate listings.

Shopping

Made in the province are umbrellas, silk, satin, bambooware, glassware, jewelry, knitting wool, and carpets.

Friendship Store 友谊商店 (People's Liberation Monument; tel. 41955); **Chongqing Gallery** 重庆美术馆 (Renmin Guesthouse; tel. 53421), paintings; **Chongqing Arts & Crafts Service** 重庆二艺美术服务 (People's Liberation Monument; tel. 42797); **Chongqing Department Store** 重庆百货公司 (People's Liberation Monument, tel. 41484).

Restaurants

Sichuan food is famous. Not all of it is chili-hot. See *Sichuan Dishes* in "Food."

Chongqing Restaurant 重庆饭店 □ *Xiaoshizi, Central District; tel. 43242.*

Weiyuan □ *37 Zhouyoon Rd.; tel. 43592* □ Sichuan dishes. Cleaner and more pleasant than other local restaurants.

Xiaobinlou □ *82 Hsinhau Rd.* □ Sichuan dishes and quick snacks.

Yuexiangcun (Old Sichuan) Restaurant □ *Bayi Rd., Central District; tel. 41957.*

Yizhishi Restaurant □ *People's Liberation Monument, Central District; tel. 42680.*

Hotels

Chongqing Guesthouse 重庆宾馆 □ *Zhongshan 1-Rd.* □ Primarily for Overseas Chinese and compatriots, this is the most convenient to shopping. 168 rooms.

Renmin (People's) Guest House 人民宾馆 □ *Renmin Rd.* □ 1953. 300 beds. One of China's more exotic-looking hotels, fashioned after the Temple of Heaven. 4000-seat auditorium. Chinese and Western food. Billiard room. This is the main hotel for foreign tourists.

Yuzhou Guesthouse 渝州宾馆 □ *Yuanjiagang. Suburbs.* □ 142 beds. May have air conditioning now. Chinese and Western food. Indoor swimming pool; theater. Mainly for state guests.

Other Important Addresses

Bank of China 中国银行 : Money-changing at Renmin, Chongqing, and Yuzhou guesthouses or hotels. Also airport, Friendship Store, railway station 火车站 , and passenger quay 长江客运码头 .

Taxis 出租汽车 : at hotels.

C.I.T.S. 中国国际旅行社 : Renmin Guesthouse, Renmin Rd.; tel. 51449.

Hospitals: In case of illness, contact your hotel or guide first for a doctor, if convenient.

First Clinic of Chongqing No. 3 People's Hospital 重庆第三人民医院第一诊所 : Feilai Temple; tel. 3786.

Second Clinic of Chongqing No. 3 People's Hospital 重庆第三人民医院第二诊所 : Renmin Rd.; tel. 51228. Near the Renmin Hotel.

First Teaching Hospital of the Chongqing Medical College 重庆医学院第一示范医院 : Yuanjiagang; tel. 23360.

Conghua 从化

(Tsunghua, Chunghua) South China. This is a hot-spring resort about 90 km NE of Guangzhou, in Guangdong province. The sulfurous spring water is said to bring relief for "high blood pressure, rheumatism, enteropathy, stomach and duodenal ulcers, neuralgia, and skin infections." The temperature of the water varies between 30°C and 70°C. The area is also noted for its hot sands, its yellow quartz caves, and a 16-meter-high waterfall. The Conghua Hotel bath has been described by one foreigner as "divine." Conghua can be reached by excursion buses from the Trade Fair in Guangzhou.

Dalian 大连

(Talien, a.k.a. Luda) Northeast China. This ice-free port near the southern tip of Liaoning province is an important industrial center with shipyards, locomotive works, and oil refinery. One of the Fourteen Open Coastal Cities, it can be reached by train or plane from Beijing or Shenyang, and also by plane from Shanghai and Qingdao. It has an international airport. It can also be reached by ship from Shanghai, Tianjin, Qingdao, and Yantai. Ocean cruise ships sometimes stop here. The urban population is 1.2 million. Dalian's hottest temperature (August) is 34°C, its lowest is ⁻21°C. The annual precipitation is 600–800 mm.

Known then as Port Arthur, Dalian was seized briefly by the Japanese in 1894, but was leased as a naval base for 25 years to Russia in 1898 in return for a loan to pay China's indemnity to Japan following the first Sino-Japanese War. Russia was also given the right to build a railroad connecting the base with the Trans-Siberian railroad. As the result of the Russian defeat by Japan in 1905, Japan took over the base until 1945.

Tourists might be interested in its **ornamental glass factory** 玻璃制品厂 , the centrally located **zoo,** and the harbor and its beautiful beaches. **Tiger Beach Park** 老虎滩公园 and **Xinghai Park** 星海公园 are popular. Xinghai Park, 5 km SW of the city, has a cave in a hill with steps reaching to the sea. In Tiger Beach Park, 5 km SE of the city, a tiger used to attack fishermen. The beach, however, is named after Tiger's Tooth Reef and has exceptionally clear water.

The **Natural History Museum** 自然博物馆 (3 Yantai St., in the north of the city), is only open a few days a week from 8 a.m. to 4 p.m.

C.I.T.S. can arrange a visit to a worker's home and a commune. It is planning a summer holiday center called **White Clouds Mountain Park** 白云山公园 and bicycle tours, etc.

Snake Island, 25 nautical miles away, has an estimated 13,000 pit vipers and is a snake sanctuary. It supplied a research center studying the medical benefits of the venom.

Entertainment

The Dalian Song and Dance Ensemble and the Dalian Acrobatic Troupe have performed internationally.

Shopping

Made here are shell pictures, fancy glass ornaments, and dishes.
Arts and Crafts Service Dept. (87 Puzhao St.; tel. 26281); **Antique Store** (229 Tianjin Rd.; tel.24955); **Dalian Department Store** (108 Zhongshan Rd.; tel. 23254) silk on 4th floor; **Dalian Foreign Languages Bookstore** (178 Tianjin St.; tel. 25472); **Friendship Store** (137 Sidalin (Stalin) Rd., tel. 23890); **Tianjinjie Department Store** (199 Tianjin St., tel. 26259).

Restaurants

For seafood, of course:
Dragon fish playing with a dragon conch 鱿鱼戏龙螺
Sea cucumbers embraced by ducks 群鸭抱海参
Conch prawns 海螺大虾
Fish buried in snow 雪埋鱼
Bohai Restaurant □ *Qingniwa Bridge; tel. 33671.*

Dalian Guest House Restaurant 大连宾馆餐厅   □ *7 Zhong-shan Square; tel. 23111* □ Good for seafood.
Restaurant of Dalian International Seamen's Club □ *2/F, Gangwan Bridge; tel. 23181.*

Hotels

Nanshan Hotel 南山宾馆   □ *56, Fenglin St., Dalian* □ *1952;* renovated 1981. This is the main tourist hotel. Over 200 beds. C.I.T.S. branch on premises. Garden villas. 20 km from airport; next to Lu Xun Park in the south part of the city.
Dalian Guest House 大连宾馆   □ *3 Zhongshan Sq.* □ *1905;* renovated several times since. Over 180 beds. Central.
Bangchuidao Hotel 棒棰岛宾馆   □ *Bangchuidao* □ *1961;* renovated 1986. Near two bathing beaches in the southeastern suburbs.
Garden Hotel 花园酒店   □ *1986.*
Dalian Mansion Hotel 大连大厦   □ *1986.*

Other important telephone numbers

C.I.T.S. 中国国际旅行社   : Nanshan Hotel; tel. 35795.
C.T.S. 中国旅行社 : tel. 35795.
CAAC 中国民航 **:** tel. 35884.
Railway Station 火车站 : tel. 203331.
Passenger Quay 客运码头 tel. 229363.
Cars and buses: Dalian Travel Service; tel. 31831, X514.

Datong

(Tatung) North China. Northern Shanxi. 7 to 8 hours by train from Beijing. From here one can continue by once-a-week train to Ulan Bator and thence onward to Moscow. The population

of Datong is 850,000, including the rural suburbs. The highest temperature in summer (July–August) is 37.7°C, the lowest (December–February) ⁻29.9°C. Rainfall is a scant 400 mm a year, mainly July–September. The best time to visit is May– October.

Founded during the Warring States, about 2200 years ago, this was a garrison town built between two sections of the Great Wall. The Northern Wei (386–534) declared it their capital and instructed monk Tanyao to supervise the carving of the Yungang Caves. The city wall is Ming.

Datong is basically a coal-mining town, one of the largest open-pit coal producing areas in the world, with a 600-year supply at the current rate of production. The city is industrial and heavily polluted. Outside Datong are visible coal deposits, with all kinds of coal transport equipment blocking up the roads. Some of the equipment is the most advanced in the world. The mining may be ugly but it is worth seeing. Because the mining has unearthed some old burial grounds, Shanxi has an extremely large number of excavated tombs and neolithic sites.

Datong gained considerable publicity recently because Occidental Petroleum of the United States began a joint venture in open-pit coal mining here.

Datong is most famous for the ***Yungang (Yunkang) Grottoes** 云岗石窟 , said to be the best-preserved, the largest, and the oldest sandstone carvings in China. They can be reached by Bus No. 3 from Datong. Fifty-three caves here contain over 51,000 stone carvings of Buddha, bodhisattvas, apsaras (angels), birds, and animals. These statues range from 17 meters to a few centimeters high, and some of them still retain their original color. They were restored in 1976. The grottoes are at the southern foot of Wuzhou Hills, 16 km west of the city. They were built between A.D. 460 and 494 after a period of persecutions against the Buddhists supposedly led to the illness of Emperor Taiwu. The grottoes extend east-west for a kilometer. The Wei dynasty later moved its capital to Luoyang and built another set of grottoes there.

Although the exposed caves have suffered natural erosion as well as damage by man, they are nicely preserved and well worth visiting. The walking is easy, with no lighting problems. The best are at the Five Caves of Tanyao (Nos. 16–20), which include the largest statues. The large ears, which do make some of them look strange, can be excused because they mean long life. Although Datong was not on the Silk Road, the carvings carry strong Indian, Persian, and even Greek influences. One can expect to spend at least half a day here, strolling from cave to cave. During tourist season, English-speaking guides are available for hire. No restaurants are in the area, but sitting rooms are available for resting and tea. Open 8:30 a.m. to 4:30 p.m.

If you only have one day to spend in the city, C.I.T.S. recommends the Yungang caves, Huayan Monastery, Shanhua Monastery, and the Nine-Dragon Screen.

The ***Huayan Si (Huayan Monastery)** 华严寺 , a.k.a. Datong Municipal Museum, is the second largest temple in China, next to one near Shenyang. One can easily spend from 2 hours to a half day there, there is so much to see. It is in the SW section of the city, 3 km north of the main tourist hotel.

The monastery is well preserved and is separated into the Upper Huayan and the Lower Huayan. You pay two entrance fees. In the upper is the magnificent main hall, Daxiong Bao Dian, built in 1062 and rebuilt in 1140. It is 53.75 meters wide and 29 meters long. The beam structure, murals, five large Ming buddhas, and 26 guardians are most impressive. Along its walls are 38 two-story partitions, the Bhagavan Stack-Hall, built over 940 years ago. The temple's exquisite 29 clay statues were made in the Ming. The monastery building also houses the **Datong Municipal Museum**'s prehistoric fossils and cultural relics.

The ***Shanhua Monastery** 善化寺 , in the SW part of the city, was founded in A.D. 713. Surviving are relics of the Liao and Jin. The **Nine Dragon Screen** 九龙壁 , in the SE section of the old city, is almost 600 years old, and at 45.5 meters, larger than the two in Beijing. The morning is better for taking photographs. Other than a small gate in front of the open yard where the screen stands, there is no other attraction in that general area. A restaurant called Longchi (Dragon's Pool) is next door; no food served after 7 p.m. unless by prior arrangement.

If you have more time or special interest, the 67.3-meter-high ***Sakyamuni Wooden Pagoda at Fogong Temple** 佛宫寺释迦塔 may be worth the 1½-hour drive if you are interested in unusual pagodas. It is the tallest ancient woodframe structure in China. It was constructed in 1056 (Liao), with eight corners and nine stories. From the outside it looks like five stories. Local folklore says that the pagoda only sits on five of its six vertical beams. One of the beams is always "resting," and you can pass a piece of paper underneath it. Each beam takes its turn without having to hold any weight. Bring a piece of paper and test it for yourself. This pagoda is usually locked, but ask for permission to view the interior. It is 75 km from Datong in Yingxian county.

The **Great Wall** 长城 is 40 km away. On **Wutai Mountain** 五台山 , 200 km away, are about 30 temples, three of them historical monuments also protected by the State Council. These are the *Main Hall of the **Nanchan Temple** 南禅寺 (Tang), the ***Foguang Temple** (Tang to Qing), and the ***Xiantong Temple** 佛光寺 (Ming to Qing). The main halls of the Nanchan and Toguang temples are the oldest extant woodframe buildings in the world. Both have histories of over 1200 years. The 17 clay statues here are Tang. Wutai is one of the

Four Great Buddhist Mountains of China. Hotels are being built in Taihuai. Visitors can hike on a paved path to the summit.

Trips can also be arranged from Datong to **Hengshan Mountain**, 80 km away, for the **Xuankongsi (Temple in Mid-Air)**. See separate listing, ''Hengshan Mountain.'' For other places of interest in the province, see ''Taiyuan.''

In Datong there are also a steam locomotive factory 大同机车工厂 and a brass products factory　铜器工厂　(hot pots, plates, tea pots). C.I.T.S. can arrange visits to both.

Shopping

Made locally are porcelain, brassware, and carpets.
Friendship Store　友谊商店　: 8 West Yingbin Rd.; tel. 32333.
Antique Store　古玩商店 : West Yingbin Rd.; tel. 32664.

Restaurants

Huayan Restaurant　华严饭店　☐ *West Road; tel. 32175.*
Longchi Restaurant　龙池饭店　☐ *East Rd.; tel. 33279.*
Fenglin Restaurant　枫林饭店　☐ *West Rd., Datong; tel. 33680.*
Fengwei Restaurant　风味饭店　☐ *East Yingbin Rd.; tel. 32333.*
☐ Datong style food.

Hotels

Datong Guest House　大同宾馆　☐ *8 West Yingbin Rd.* ☐ 1958; renovated 1973. Dance hall, bar, and hot pot. Our recent appraisal found this guesthouse not up to foreign tourist standards, with poor service.

Yungang Hotel　云岗宾馆　☐ *Eastbin Rd.* ☐ 1985. Billiards room, coffee shop, theater, dance hall.

The **Datong Mining Co.**　大同矿物局　has several guesthouses open for tourists.

C.I.T.S.: Yungang Hotel, East Yingbin Rd.; tel. 23215 and 32607.

Dazhai (Tachai) 大寨

North China. SE of Taiyuan in Shanxi province, Dazhai was a commune famous as a model because of its spirit of hard work and self-sacrifice. Up until 1978, you could frequently hear the slogan ''In agriculture, follow Dazhai.'' In 1979, however, officials pointed out that while this spirit to struggle hard was correct, the slavish copying of Dazhai's example was not. Because every commune had different conditions, every commune had to improve its production in its own way. Dazhai was accused of falsifying its production figures.

214 *Destinations* *Dazu*

Dazu 大足

*Southwest China. About 165 km NW of Chongqing (4½ hours
by winding and partly paved road) in Sichuan province, this is
usually an overnight trip.*

The **Dazu Stone Buddhist Sculptures** are considered by some connoisseurs as better preserved and of finer quality than Luoyang, Datong,
or Dunhuang. Decide for yourself. About 50,000 of them are located in
43 places in Dazu County, most not readily accessible by car. To see
both Beishan and Baodingshan takes about a day and a half. Since the
carvings are in hilly surroundings, take time to enjoy the natural scenery
and the nearby water reservoir too. Study details. Look for the mother
sleeping next to a bed-wetting child, the village girl tending ducks, the
funeral rites, the wedding, etc.

The most concentrated numbers are at ***Beishan (Northern Hill)**
北山 (Tang to Song), 2 km north of the Dazu Guest House. Under State
Council protection are **Fowan, Guanyinpo, Foerfeng,** and **Yingpanshan.** From the car park, you have to climb nearly 400 stairs. However,
the 25-minute climb is spread out along pleasant, shady trails and is
much easier than expected (10 minutes downhill). The sculptures at
***Fowan** are grouped together like beehives. A couple of chambers are
fenced with iron gates and locks. Although some of the sculptures have
been damaged, the arrangement and the preservation of some are excellent. Take special note of the enchanting Goddess of Mercy of No. 125,
and No. 113. The locked No. 155 and No. 136 are worth careful inspection. The pagoda, about 1 km away, is also full of sculptures and
is a popular picnic spot with local students.

The first statue was carved here in A.D. 892 by Wei Junjing. It was
then a military camp.

Also worth seeing and accessible in large numbers are the sculptures at ***Baodingshan** 宝顶山 (Song dynasty), 15 km NE of the Dazu
Guest House. The ones here were basically done by one monk, Zhou
Tzefeng, from 1179 to 1249, and centered on the theme ''Life is Vanity.'' The daily life of people is well-illustrated with vivid facial expressions and body language. The work here is largely intact and the sculptures
are huge. The Sleeping Buddha   is 31 meters long, and some of
the standing figures are 7 meters high. It is essential that you obtain a
tour guide to explain highlights to you. To see this grouping takes only
a few minutes.

The sculptures at ***Xiaofowan** 小佛湾 are in the Shengshao Temple near the entrance of ***Dafowan** 大佛湾 . Many tourists are only
shown Dafowan, but other sculptures are close by. If you want to see
more, do insist on it.

Also under State Council protection here are *Guangdashan,
*Longtan, and *Linsongpo.

An excellent book on Dazu has been published by the Sichuan Provincial Academy of Social Sciences, but so far it is available only in
Chinese.

You might be able to tell roughly when the sculptures were created
because the Tang figures are simple, smooth, and more alluring. The
Five Dynasty statues are meticulously carved with details. The Song
statues are rather reserved but distinctive in personality and expression.

The largest statue is the Sleeping Buddha and the most famous a
1000-armed Goddess of Mercy 千手观音 , both at Baoding Hill.
Beautiful is the face of the **Hen wife** here. You may notice that many
of the larger statues are bigger at the top and lean forward to make
viewing easier from below.

While Buddhist sculptures predominate, Confucian, Taoist, and
military statues can also be found. The statues are well worth the trip.

En route, with some detour, visitors can also stop at the **North
Hot-Spring Park** 北温泉公园 with its huge swimming pool, 1500-
year-old temple, and dinosaurs.

Restaurant
Dazu Guest House Restaurant 餐厅 □ Sweet-sour crispy fish,
pork with preserved vegetables, Lantern chicken, Mapo tofu.

Hotel
Dazu Guest House 旅馆 □ 140 beds. Reservations at the Renmin
Guest House in Chongqing.

C.I.T.S. 中国国际旅行社

Dunhuang 敦煌

*(Tunhuang, Tunhwang) Northwest China. Western Gansu. Noted
for one of the biggest art treasures in the world.*

Between the fourth and 14th centuries, more than 1000 caves were
cut out of the cliffs 25 km SE of the city and filled with Buddhist
carvings, gilt and colored frescoes, and murals. Known as the *Mogao
Grottoes 莫高窟 or the **Thousand Buddha Caves,** 492 of these remain today in three or four rows on a 1½-km-long wall. The State
Council has renovated murals like the **Feitian (Flying Apsaras)** fresco
飞天 (Tang) and repainted over 2000 statues. Some of the statues in
about 20 caves were repainted in the Qing. Note the intricately painted
ceilings too.

The most important cave is the **Cangjing (Preserving Buddhist Scriptures) Cave** 藏经洞 , now No. 17. Dating from the Jin to Song, a span of 600 years, this is where 40,000 important old documents were found, including the Diamond Sutra (A.D. 868), said to be the oldest existing dated printed book. It is now in the British Museum in London. Many archaeologists and historians work in a museum at the site, studying not just Mogao but other cave temples in the area.

Many caves have stories. One of the most famous is outlined in a series of pictures about a woman who was badly treated by her husband. While returning to her mother, she encountered a wolf that killed her two children, one of them newly born. After becoming a nun, she learned that her current miseries were a punishment for mistreating her stepsister in a previous incarnation.

Some of the statues are damaged. Signs indicate which museums abroad have stolen the pieces originally here. Some of the colors are still original and vivid. The red might be from pig's blood or cinnabar. One could get a real feeling of history and mysticism here. Caves were used as temples because they were conducive to meditation and secure, like a mother's womb. Perhaps the womb also symbolizes reincarnation.

The caves are a one-day trip at least. In recent years only a couple of enterprising noodle vendors and a seller of sickly sweet orange drink served visitors here, so you would be better off taking your own lunch, which you could eat in the shade of a tree. As there are few Chinese tourists, public buses from Dunhuang city are infrequent, leaving the Dunhuang Guest House at 8 a.m. and 2 p.m., arriving at Mogao 30 minutes later. Make sure you find out what time the last bus leaves if you have to rely on public transport. The caves are open from 8:30 to 11:00 a.m. and 2:30 to 5 p.m. Knowledgeable guides are available for hire on the site to show you around, but unfortunately they only speak Chinese. As with all cave temples, it is crucial to take your own flashlight, and do not expect to see an entire mural as you would in a spacious museum. You have to piece each section together in your own mind. This fragmentation has disappointed some tourists. Much climbing is involved.

You can take photos in 4 of the 40 caves open to the public. You must purchase a ticket for a small fee, which includes a guide who opens locks to the designated caves. In the past, plainclothes guards followed tourists to prevent unauthorized picture-taking. Now you have to check your cameras at a little shack outside the gate until a guide goes with you to the caves where you may take photos. Your camera must be taken back to the checkroom afterward before you can see the other caves. But in how many museums elsewhere can you take photos?

The caves open to visitors are rotated every year. Unless you know in advance which you want to see, ask for samples of the best from the different dynastic periods: Sui, Tang, Song, etc.

Dunhuang can be reached by train (27 hours) from Lanzhou. It is not a comfortable trip and is especially dry and dusty. Take your own drinks. This is, after all, a desert. If flying from Beijing, one usually needs to spend the night in Lanzhou. From Lanzhou to Dunhuang is a 4-hour plane ride with an early-morning departure and one stop, arriving before noon.

Summers are hot; winters are very cold. *The caves are closed from November through April.*

Dunhuang was an important cultural exchange center and oasis on the Silk Road. The old town is 250 meters west of the current one. Dunhuang was founded in 111 B.C. during the Han. From here, the road west split into northern and southern routes and ended 7000 km away at the Mediterranean Sea. Dunhuang was a military outpost under the Tang. In A.D. 400, it became the capital of the Xiliang kingdom. An enemy army of 20,000 attacked the city and flooded it 21 years later. It changed hands several times. In 1227, Genghis Khan seized it, and in the Ming, it was a military headquarters. The ruins of the walls and a 16-meter-high tower can be seen in the old part of town. The population now is 10,000.

Visitors also can see the **White Horse Pagoda** 白马塔 (only a 12-meter-high dagoba in the desert and a 5-minute stop). It commemorates the horse of the Indian monk Fumoluoshi, which died here. The **Yangguan Pass** 阳关 (70 km south of Dunhuang) is just a wall now, of interest to people who like deserts or have a feeling for history. It was a military command post from the Han to the Yang, but the sands of the desert have inundated it.

The **Yumen (Jade Gate) Pass** 玉门关 (80 km NW of the city) has remains of the old wall. Jade used to be carried through here. These three sites are in themselves really not worth the hardship of getting here, but if you think of what went through here, the caravans of camels and merchants supplying the wealthy homes of Europe, and the envoys bringing tribute to the emperor, they can be emotional experiences. A recent Chinese movie *Dunhuang* makes an attempt to recapture the spirit of the era and could help you appreciate the relics here.

Dunhuang also has a carpet factory 地毯厂 , and the **Mingsha (Ringing Sand) Hill** 鸣沙山 (5 km south), where once a whole army was buried during a sandstorm. Their ghosts are still heard from time to time playing military drums and horns!

The newer **Dunhuang Hotel** 敦煌饭店 has a good reputation. One of the better provincial hotels, it is clean, with good food. The old Dunhuang Hotel is used when this one is full. Same price, but poorer standards.

C.I.T.S.: tel. 26181.

See also "Silk Road."

Emei Shan 峨眉

(Emei or Omei Mountain) Southwest China; 170 km SW of Chengdu in Sichuan, Emei Shan is one of China's four great Buddhist mountains. The base can be reached by train from the North Railway Station in Chengdu, or by bus to Emei County Town. From there one takes a bus to Baoguo Temple. Frequently, Baoguo Temple is combined in a two-day trip from Chengdu, also taking in the Sansu Temple at Meixian (See "Chengdu") and Leshan (see separate listing).

The climb to the summit and back can be done on foot in one day if you're energetic, or two days for the less agile. Along the 60-km stone path are 23 monasteries, intriguing caves, gushing waterfalls, magnificent views, and birds. Be careful of monkeys. They can steal food, scratch, and bite. Land Rovers can drive to within 6 km of the peak at **Jieyin Hall** 接引殿 at 2670 meters. At that height, the weather can be very chilly, about ⁻20°C at the top in January. Hostels are at the base of and on the 3100-meter-high summit. Restaurants along the way. Guides available, but none were English-speaking at press time.

The best time to climb is from April to June and September to November. You should *not* climb from December to March. The rainy season is July and August.

Baoguo Temple 报国寺 , at the base, has a scale-model map of the mountain with lights. If you don't have a map of your own, make notes. The temple originates from the Ming. **Wannian Monastery**万年寺 (a.k.a. Shengshouwannian or Samantabhadra Monastery), on the slope, dates from the 4th century. Its *bronze and iron Buddha images are Song to Ming and are under State Council protection. The bronze Samantabhadra on a white elephant is 7.4 meters high and weighs 62 tons. The beamless brick hall, roof, and square walls are said to be typically Ming.

Hotels

Emei County Hotel 峨眉县宾馆 and **Hong Zhu Shan (Red Spider Hill) Hotel** 红珠山宾馆 . The **Red Spider** is near the Baoguo Temple.

C.I.T.S. 国际旅行社
Hospital: The **Emei County People's Hospital** 峨眉县人民医院 in Emei County Town is the closest medical help.

Foshan 佛山

(Fushan; Cantonese Fashan, Fatsan) South China, Guang-dong province, about 20 km SW of Guangzhou. Population 280,000.

Named "Hill of Buddhas" because a mound of Buddhist statues were excavated here, this is one of the Four Ancient Towns of China. The city is over 1300 years old and is famous for its handicrafts. In addition, it has factories making machines, electronics, chemicals, textiles, plastics, pharmaceuticals, cement, etc. It is a good one-day excursion from Guangzhou, well worth the effort.

Foshan Folk Art Institute 佛山民间艺术研究社 produces palace lanterns, T-shirts, and paper cutouts. It is a training institute for master crafts people in all fields. The **Shiwan Artistic Ceramic Factory** 石湾美术陶瓷厂 is one of the most famous porcelain factories in China; some of its works adorn the tops of temples in south China and Hong Kong. Its collection of maroon-robed *lohan,* with expressive, bulging eyes and unglazed faces, is well known. It is moving also toward producing works with less traditional themes.

The **Ancestral Temple,** now the **Foshan Municipal Museum** 祖庙博物馆 was originally erected in the Song (Emperor Yuanfeng, 1078–1085) and rebuilt in 1372 after a disastrous fire. Expanded and rebuilt after Liberation, the temple contains sculptures, ancient relics, and a 2500 kg bronze figure named Northern Emperor. Note the variety of decorations on the bases of the arches and the stone, wood, and brick carvings. Four of the statues are said to be made of paper, the others of wood or clay. The roof, decorated with Shiwan pottery figures, is one of the most elaborate in the country. The double dragon screen near the gate is a recent replacement for one destroyed earlier. The exhibition hall and corridor of tablets are recent additions. There are 3000 square meters of grounds. A little gaudy, but artistically and culturally important.

The **silk factory** 丝织厂 is also open to visitors. See also nearby "Xiqiao Mountain."

Shopping

Locally made are cuttlebone sculptures, brick carvings, silk, lanterns, paper-cuts, etc.

See also nearby "Xiqiao Mountain."

Foshan has an **Overseas Chinese Hotel** 华侨大厦 , **Foshan Hotel** 佛山 , and **Quangong Hotel.** The latter is newer, with a rotating restaurant on its roof.

C.I.T.S. 国际旅行社
C.T.S. 中旅社

Fushun 抚顺

*Northeast China. Eastern Liaoning, 50 km NE of Shenyang.
Frequently combined with the capital and Anyang in a tour. It
is one of China's biggest coal centers. Urban population is 1.1
million. The temperature reaches a high of 36°C in summer
and a low of ⁻35°C in winter. Annual precipitation about 800
mm, with 153 frostfree days a year.*

Built on a neolithic site, Fushun became a walled city in the Ming.
In 1778, the town was rebuilt as a political and economic center. **Xing-
jing town (Hetuala)** in Xinbin county was built by the founder of the
Qing dynasty. **Yongling** (1598) has the oldest Qing tombs, those of the
ancestors of the Qing emperors. A pagoda on **Mt. Gaoer** 高尔山古塔
(5 km from the hotel) and a Guanyin temple below it date from the Liao
(1088).

Tourists can also visit the 2 by 6.6 km **West Open Cast Coal
Mine** 西露天煤矿 (10 km from the hotel) and the **Dahuofang Reservoir** 大伙房水库 (17 km from the hotel). This is a 110-square-km
lake. An elaborate 1929-built tomb of a marshal in the Liaoning army
is at the foot of Mt. Tiebei on the reservoir. C.I.T.S. can also arrange
a trip to an old people's home 养老院 (16 km from the hotel).

If you have only one day, C.I.T.S. recommends the mine, carving
factory 雕刻厂 , and reservoir.

Shopping
Amber and jet carvings.

Restaurant
Fushun Restaurant 抚顺饭店

Hotel
Fushun Hotel 抚顺宾馆 □ *Yongan Square; 40 km from airport*
□ 1957; renovated 1983; 200 more rooms added in 1986.

C.I.T.S.: Yongan Square, tel. 23341.

Fuzhou 福州

*(Foochow, Fuchou) East China. Capital of Fujian province on
the east coast across from Taiwan, this city is over 2000 years
old.*

Opened to foreign trade in 1842, Fuzhou had British and American dockyards, and factories for making tea bricks. Once home to about 10 foreign consulates, its foreign cemetery was dug up and replaced by a school. The old British Community Church, never used by the Chinese, is now a warehouse.

What you can see are **Gushan (Drum Hill)** 鼓山 , topped by a huge drum-shaped boulder in the eastern suburbs, at least 1004 meters high. The **Yongquan Si (Surging Spring Temple)** 涌泉寺 was founded in A.D. 783 and has a white jade Buddha. The **Qianfo Taota (Thousand-Buddha Pottery Pagoda)** 千佛陶塔 and the **Shuiyun Ting (Water and Cloud Pavilion)** 水云亭 , east of the Yongquan Si are both from the Song. Views from the 18 caves west of the temple are said to be famous. Several hundred inscriptions on the cliff are near the **Lingyuan Dong (Spirit Source Cave)** 灵源洞 Over 100 of these writings are from the Song.

The city is also noted for its hot springs, with over a dozen in Fuzhou itself. The most famous temples are the plain-looking **Baita (White Pagoda)** 白塔 , on the west side of Yushan Hill, and the **Wuta (Black Pagoda)** 乌塔 , at the base of Wushi Hill, both in the center of town. The main hall of the *Hualin Temple 华林寺 , from the Song, is worth seeing. The **Jinshan (Gold Mountain) Temple** 金山寺 is snugly perched on an island west of the city.

The **Birthplace of Lin Zexu** 林则徐祠堂 , the official who burned the 20,000 chests of opium near Canton in 1839, is marked with a small shrine and a statue of the national hero. Known also as a calligrapher and a poet, Lin was one of the first Qing officials to take an interest in things foreign. Because the British fired on China as a result of Lin's actions, the emperor exiled Lin to Yili in Xinjiang.

Fujian province has only recently been opened to foreign visitors. Overseas Chinese have been coming here for years. Most developed for tourists seems to be Xiamen (Amoy), with good hotels. Quanzhou is next, for some interesting things to see, but its Overseas Chinese Hotel is not up to standard. Fuzhou seems to have less to offer. Zhangzhou is worth a few hours. See separate listings.

For outdoor types, **Wuyi Mountain** 武夷山 , in the northwestern part of the province, is a good place to visit, with a native-style hotel and rafting through beautiful Guilin-type scenery. It is 800 km from Xiamen and can be reached occasionally by charter from Hong Kong.

Aside from Wuyi, Fujian is mainly for those interested in maritime history, in Koxinga (museums in Xiamen and Quanzhou), and in the relics of Arab traders and Manichaeanism. Some of its native sons have returned from the Philippines, Singapore, and Malayasia with wealth. They have built monuments, schools, hospitals, and temples. The religious buildings are uniquely flamboyant and show traces of cosmopolitan connections.

The Fujian dialect is distinct, neither Cantonese nor Mandarin. This language is spoken also by the majority on Taiwan, just across the straits. The weather is subtropical, and most of the province is mountainous.

Shopping

Good lacquerware, cork carving, and Shoushan stone carvings are made and sold here.

Friendship Store 友谊商店 (Aug. 17th Rd.; tel. 55406); **Fujian Tourist Souvenirs Production and Supply Corporation** 福建旅游产品生产供应公司 (May 4th Rd.; tel. 33491); **Fujian Antique General Store** 省文物总店 (Aug. 17th Rd.; tel. 54792).

Hotels

Overseas Chinese Hotel 华侨大厦 □ *May 4th Rd.*
Minjiang Guest House 闽江宾馆 □ *May 4th Rd.*
West Lake Guest House 西湖宾馆 □ *Hubin Rd.*
Qiaolian Mansion 侨联大厦 □ *May 1st Rd.*

C.I.T.S. 国际旅行社 : Dongda Rd.; tel. 51268.
C.T.S. 中旅社 : May 4th Rd.; tel. 56304.
CAAC 中国民航 : May 1st Rd.; tel. 51988.
Railway station 火车站 : May 4th Rd.; tel. 32350.
Taxi: May 4th Rd.; tel. 54715
Fujian Provincial Hospital 福建省立医院 : Dongda Rd.; tel. 33352.

Gezhouba 葛洲坝

Southwest China, in Hubei, is the new town (1970s) where tour boats pass through the locks on the Changjiang (Yangtze) River, 3 km downstream of the Three Gorges and about 1 km upstream of Yichang. The biggest multipurpose water conservancy project on the river, it includes a 2561-meter-long and 70-meter-high dam, two power stations (2.715 million kwh capacity), a silt-discharge gate, a reservoir, a flood-discharge gate, and a channel for migrating fish. When completed, 21 generators should be able to produce 14.1 billion kwh annually. The difference in water level is about 20 meters.

Grand Canal 大运河

The oldest and longest in the world, this canal was built in the Sui dynasty (A.D. 581–618) and originally extended 1794 km from Hangzhou to Beijing.

Today visitors can still take tour boats on parts of the canal, a trip that gives you an intimate look at the life on the water, in waterside houses, villages, and countryside. Jiangsu province can arrange a 220-km, one-week tour from Nanjing (bus to Yangzhou) and from there by boat to Zhenjiang, Changzhou, Wuxi, and Suzhou. The boat can stop to explore any place of interest on the way.

At individual cities along the route, you can see parts of the canal. From Wuxi to Suzhou, for example, a 45 km trip takes 4½ hours. Wuxi has 12 tour boats, including a 36.5-meter-long, two-storied "dragon boat" with flashing eyes and ancient Chinese costumes in which to be photographed. In most cities, Suzhou for example, shorter tours can be arranged, a leisurely way to sightsee.

Great Wall 长城

(Wanlichangcheng—10,000 li-long wall.) The Great Wall is officially 12,700 Chinese li, or 6350 km, or 3946.55 miles long. The length depends on what you measure, there being many offshoots and parallel walls. It is in various states of repair.

The Great Wall was first built in shorter pieces, starting in the fifth century B.C., as a defensive and boundary wall around the smaller states of Yen, Chao, and Wei. The first Qin emperor (221–206 B.C.), who unified China for the first time, linked up and extended the walls from Liaoning in the east to Gansu in the NW as protection from the Huns and other nomadic tribes to the north. The wall was subsequently repaired and extended by succeeding dynasties, especially the Ming.

Originally built by slave labor, it has been called the world's longest graveyard because many of its builders were buried where they fell in constructing it. It was designed to allow five horsemen or ten soldiers to march abreast along the top. It was almost a superhighway, considering the rough mountain terrain. A system of bonfires communicated military information to the emperor at a speed rapid for that period.

The best time to visit is after 2 p.m., when most of the tourists have left. Stay to see the sunset if you can.

The Great Wall is most frequently visited at *Badaling (Padaling), about 75 km (two hours) by bus NW of Beijing. Until two other sections near Beijing were opened, it was extremely crowded, and at peak times there were four tourists per square meter. You still need to avoid the Sunday traffic jams. Usually the trip can be done by taxi in 4 hours if you don't linger. Most tourists now go from Beijing by soft-class train or, preferably, by tourist bus. The train leaves about 7:20 a.m. daily, except Wednesdays, and goes only to the Great Wall. It returns at 12:35 p.m. and might involve a walk of about a mile. Tourist buses leave Beijing daily at 8 a.m. and stop at both the Great Wall and Ming tombs.

A sightseeing helicopter, which can be booked at the Holiday Inn Lido in Beijing, flies over but does not stop at the Wall. See "Beijing."

Badaling is about 1000 meters above sea level. Here the wall averages 7.8 meters high, 6.5 meters wide at the base, and 5.8 meters wide at the top. Watchtowers are located every few hundred meters. Note the giant rocks and bricks of uniform size, the gutters, and the waterspouts. You can walk, and in some places climb, for several hundred feet in either direction until you meet a sign that says no further. Skateboarding on the wall has been allowed, but is not recommended when it is thick with people, which is most of the time. Try first thing in the morning or late afternoon. A restaurant for eating and usually a shaggy Bactrian camel or pony for photographing are available. Taking a box lunch is recommended, especially in pleasant weather, so you can spend more time at the wall rather than waiting for service in a crowded restaurant.

Also of note is the gate in the center of **Juyongguan (Chuyung-kuan Pass,** about 10 km south of Badaling. It is built of finely carved marble and called *****Guojie (Cloud Terrace).** Originally the base of a tower built in 1345 (Yuan), 'the walls are decorated with carvings of Buddhas, four celestial guardians, and the text of a Buddhist sutra in Sanskrit, Tibetan, and four other languages. Currently, tours do not usually stop here except by request, but the Great Wall at Juyongguan should be open to the public now and you may have a chance.

A recently renovated 2-km-long section of the Great Wall is at Mutianyu, 70 km NE of Beijing in Miyun County. It should be less crowded and is very beautiful, with more rugged hills than Badaling. A 720-meter-long cable way should be operating now.

The *Great Wall has also been restored and opened to visitors at 3000-year-old Shanhaiguan, over 40 km north from Beidaihe, and about 30 km from Qinhuangdao in the east. See separate listings. It is not as spectacular there as at Badaling. Work is being done on an extension that might be open by the time you get there. There is also a museum in the tower with a 215-pound sword "for practicing," a Ming cannon, and ancient military· uniforms. Note the sign "The First Pass Under Heaven." The gate was built in 1381. Nearby, **Old Dragon Head,** the place where the Great Wall meets the sea, is being repaired, but it should be open to visitors soon.

The Great Wall can also be visited at **Jinshan Ling,** 110 km from Chengde in Hebei, and Huairou County (2 km long), 60 km NE of Beijing. The railway line from Beijing to Chengde crosses it. An 850-meter section is open in Jixian County, north of Tianjin, and another section is open near Datong. In the west, it can be seen in Ningxia at Yinchuan, and in Gansu at *Jiayuguan, its western terminal (Ming). See "Jiuguan."

Guangzhou (Kwangchow, Canton)

*South China; 125 km NW of Hong Kong in Guangdong prov-
ince on the Zhu (Pearl) River. It can be reached by a nonstop
3-hour train ride, a 3-hour hydrofoil ride, or a half-hour flight
from Hong Kong. It is also linked by air with Bangkok,
Singapore, and Sydney. Guangzhou is a 2½-hour flight or a
36-hour train ride south of Beijing, and a 2-hour drive from
Zhuhai on the Macao border. A double-track electric train is
expected to run between Guangzhou and Kowloon in 1987. A
super highway is also planned to link it with Shenzhen, and
therefore Hong Kong. Two new airports are being planned for
Shenzhen and Shekou. All these should relieve the nightmarish
situation every time there is a long Hong Kong holiday, when
over 100,000 visitors try to get from Hong Kong to China and
back. Tourists should especially avoid the lunar new year holiday (late January or early February), and Qing Ming (early
April). The weather here is subtropical. Coldest—about 0°C,
January–February; hottest—about 38°C, July–August. Average rainfall: 1680 mm. Extremely humid summers. Best time
to visit: October–February. The urban population is about three
million.*

Guangzhou is also known as the Goat City because five fairies came
here supposedly in 1256 B.C., riding five goats from whose mouths the
fairies drew the first rice seeds. The city was founded over 2000 years
ago. In 214 B.C., the first Qin emperor set up the Prefecture of Nanhai
here. It was the capital of the state of Nanyue during the Western Han,

a dynasty that lasted 93 years, from 196 B.C. It is best known as the largest and most prosperous trading city in South China, a role it has played at least since the Tang dynasty. Arab traders started arriving over 1300 years ago. The Portuguese settled in Macau, 64 km, away in 1557. More recently, it was the site of the Canton Trade Fair, for 23 years China's main foreign trade institution.

Guangzhou is the capital of Guangdong, a province that has three Special Economic Zones—Shenzhen, Zhuhai, and Shantou. Guangzhou and Zhanjiang are two of the 14 coastal cities open for economic development. Guangdong is the provincial "home" of many Chinese immigrants to Australia, the United States, Canada, and many parts of Southeast Asia. These people have contributed to the economic development of their adopted lands and have also brought or sent back expertise as well as money to their ancestral home. Many are playing a leading role in China's modernization program, with joint ventures.

Being a long way from the political center of China, the people here developed a rebellious, independent spirit. Guangzhou was the starting point or site of many important historical events:

—the fight against the importation of opium. Chinese officials burned 20,000 chests of it (1839); the struggle against foreign imperialism, at Sanyuanli, for example, during the Opium War in 1841;

—the movement against the Qing dynasty by the Taiping Heavenly Kingdom. Leader Hong Xiuquan (Hung Hsiu-ch'uan) was born about 66 km north of the city and was given the Christian tract that changed his life and China's history in Guangzhou;

—the campaign against the Qing in the early 1900s led by Dr. Sun Yat-sen, who was born south of the city in Zhongshan county near the Macao border. The fight was fueled by the failure of the Qing emperors to repel the encroaching foreign powers;

—the general strike against the unequal foreign treaties, starting in June 1925. It lasted for 16 months and almost closed Hong Kong;

—the Communist Revolution. Mao Zedong taught peasant leaders here in 1926 at the National Peasant Movement Institute;

—the Northern Expedition, whose officers were trained at the nearby Huangpu (Whampoa) Military Academy. Chiang Kai-shek was director; Chou En-lai was in charge of political indoctrination. In June 1926 this expedition to unify China and to assert Chinese nationalism started off from Guangzhou.

—an uprising against the Nationalists led by the Communists in December 1927.

Many foreign missionaries established schools and churches here after the city was opened to foreign trade and residence by the Treaty of Nanking in 1842. From 1938 to 1945, the Japanese occupied Guangzhou. The Communists took over from the Nationalists on October 14, 1948.

In recent years, Guangzhou has been one of the main suppliers of food, water, and electricity for neighboring Hong Kong. It is rich in livestock, fruits, and vegetables. It has 11 institutions of higher learning, including Zhong Shan University, which is on the site of the missionary-founded Ling Nam University. There are 3200 factories producing fertilizer, heavy machinery, insecticides, textiles (silk and ramie), petrochemicals, sewing machines, ships, and electronics.

Tourists would probably be interested in its **ivory-carving factory,** where about 45 concentric balls within balls have been made from one piece of ivory.

The city is divided by the Zhu (Pearl) River, which is crossed by three bridges and innumerable ferries. Most of the places of interest to tourists are located on the north side.

Because of its proximity to Hong Kong and therefore to the worst (as well as the best) that capitalism can offer, an ugly atmosphere of ticket-scalping and black-marketeering has emerged from time to time in the city. This has been particularly evident around the railway station, and even in Orchid Park. C.I.T.S. has been too busy at times to help visitors buy train tickets, especially in hard class. Scalpers buy the tickets and sell them to foreigners for the proper amounts, but in Foreign Exchange Certificates.

Visitors trying to stay within the bounds of the law sometimes have had to line up six hours in advance of the opening of ticket sales and then endure vicious punching, queue jumping, and shoving to get a place on trains north. In addition, no signs in English help them locate the proper ticket windows or train gates.

Guangzhou authorities assured me recently that they have remedied this terrible situation. But also be careful around the railway station or passenger quay; aggressive porters may grab your bags out of your taxi before you can get to them. If you want a porter, be sure to settle on a price and keep the porter always within sight. By the time you get there, I hope Guangzhou authorities will have been able to impose order in this department too.

While *pu tung hua* (Mandarin dialect) is understood by almost everyone, the language spoken in most homes is Cantonese.

If you only have a few hours, see the **Zhen Family Hall,** take the **Pearl River boat trip** (if you like boats), visit the **Temple of the Six Banyan Trees/Flower Pagoda** (for exotic Chinese architecture), and the **Qingping Free Market** (for genuine local color). You could also decide on a garden (if you like plants), or an arts and crafts factory. Be sure to eat in one of the garden restaurants also. If you have more time (at least half a day), go to **Foshan** for the ancestral temple and ceramic, silk, and folk art factories. (See "Foshan.")

Guangzhou is not noted as a prime tourist destination, but it has enough to do for two or three days. It is the place where many tours start out: Overseas Chinese to visit ancestral villages and relatives, and foreign visitors to branch out to other parts of the country.

Probably the most exciting recent development for Guangzhou has been the discovery in 1983 of the 2100-year-old tomb of Emperor Wen 温王墓 . The second king of Nanyue ruled this region during the early Western Han (206 B.C.–A.D. 24). More than 1000 burial objects were excavated from Xianggang Hill just west of Yuexiu Park. Included in the find were a chariot, ritual bronzes, gold and silver vessels, ivory and lacquerware, jades, musical instruments, weapons, and tools. Human sacrifices, concubines, and servants were buried with him also. Plans have been made to build an on-site museum, which may be ready by the time you arrive. Ask about it.

The **Guangdong Provincial Museum** 广东省博物馆 (Wenming Rd.; tel. 32195) displays relics of local primitive society and is not as good generally as the Guangzhou Museum. The **Guangzhou Museum** 广州市博物馆 is in the **Zhenhai (Sea-dominating) Tower** in Yuexiu Park and is better organized (tel. 30627). The original tower itself was built in 1380 to assert the power of the Ming dynasty. It was perhaps more impressive at the time. It has been rebuilt several times since then. Located at one of the highest points in the city, it has been used as a pleasure palace for high-ranking imperial officials and as a Nationalist hospital. Starting with prehistory, on the second floor, to revolutionary history, on the fifth, the exhibits include some interesting old clocks, ceramics, and a painting of the burning of the 20,000 chests of opium. For a city of this size and wealth, however, one would expect a better, larger museum, especially one about Overseas Chinese.

The **Zhen (Chen) Family Temple** 陈氏书院（陈家祠） (7 Zhongshan Rd.; tel. 85259) is well worth a visit. It was built in the 1890s with nine halls and six courtyards of different sizes and has been used as a school. Its windows, doorframes, and pavilions are all lavishly decorated with intricate carvings and sculptures—almost too much for the mind to absorb at once. Take it in small doses. Because the army occupied these buildings during the Cultural Revolution, the artwork suffered very little damage. The Guangdong Folk Arts and Crafts Hall is located here now, and it is a good place to shop. Just don't let the bargains in tablecloths and ivory carvings distract you from the ceramic opera scenes on the roofs and the charming carved mice eating the lichees on the pillars.

Shamian (Shamien, Shameen) Island 沙面 , in the Pearl River in central Guangzhou, became a British and French concession in 1859–60. It was then an 80-acre sandbank, later built into a European ghetto, much resented by the Chinese. The architecture reflects its European occupants, but, unfortunately, so many of the old buildings have been destroyed that its overall charm has almost disappeared. The island is joined to the mainland by bridges and now cars are allowed in certain areas. You can still find some of the old buildings and enjoy strolls along the riverfront, but it isn't the same as it was before the fancy **White Swan Hotel** was built in 1982. At the western tip of the island, this 31-story luxury hotel, built on reclaimed land, is among the top international-standard hotels in China.

The **Mausoleum of the Seventy-two Martyrs at Huanghuagang (Yellow Flower) Hill** 黄花岗七十二烈士墓 (Xianlie Rd.) is past the Garden Hotel and the Friendship Store on the road to the zoo. This commemorates an unsuccessful attempt to overthrow the Qing in 1911, led by Dr. Sun Yat-sen's Chinese Revolutionary League. Of special interest to visitors of Chinese ancestry, this 260,000-square-meter park was built with donations from Chinese Nationalists' Leagues around the world. The stones in the main monument are inscribed in English with the names of the donors, among these Chicago, Illinois; Moose Jaw, Saskatchewan; and Lima, Peru. If you look closely, you may find your own hometown.

The **National Peasant Movement Institute** 广州农民运动讲习厅 (42 Zhongshan 4-Rd.; tel. 33936) was a school for 327 peasant leaders from 20 provinces and regions. It was open only from May to September 1926 in an old temple. Mao Zedong was the director and Zhou Enlai a teacher. The subjects taught were rural education, problems of peasants, and class analysis. The institute was restored after Liberation, including the straw sandals and old rifles used by the students. Mao's office, to the right as you enter, contains rattan trunks and a straw mat on a wooden bed.

The **Lu Xun Museum** 鲁迅墓 , in the Guangdong Provincial Museum (Yan'an 2-Rd.), contains an exhibit of the life and works of China's foremost pre-Liberation writer. Lu Xun taught in Guangzhou for a few short but critical months in 1927. For more on Lu Xun, see ''Shanghai.''

Built in the 1950s, with pavilions to Soviet and Korean friendship, is the 260,000-square-meter **Memorial Garden to the Martyrs in the Guangzhou Uprising** 广州起义烈士陵园 (Zhongshan 3-Rd. Honghuagang—Red Flower Hill). The unsuccessful insurgency involving workers and soldiers was led by the Communists in 1927. The pleasant garden is sited on a former pre-Liberation execution ground.

The **Zhong Shan (Sun Yat-sen) Memorial Hall** 中山纪念堂 (tel. 32430, 33432). This is a theater seating over 4500, built in 1931 with local Chinese and Overseas Chinese donations. It was expanded and renovated in 1975 and is currently the site of cultural and political gatherings. This building is architecturally important because its huge hall is supported by four vertical concrete beams that branch out on top to form the octagonal roof. The modern technique and pure Chinese style, with its bright blue circus-tent-shaped ceramic roof, is unique. A bronze statue of Dr. Sun is prominent. (For more on the life of Dr. Sun, see ''Nanjing.'')

The *Guangxiao Temple** 光孝寺 (109 Sheshi Rd. and Guangxiao Rd.; tel. 85606) has the longest history in the city. It was founded on the site of the residence of the King of the Southern Yue Kingdom. The temple was built in A.D. 397 to commemorate the visit of the Indian monk Dharmayasas, and is the largest temple in South China. An iron pagoda dated A.D. 967 stands inside, historic, well preserved, but not beautiful. The present buildings are from the Five Dynasties to the Ming. The impressively large main hall is now for changing exhibitions. A statue of Huineng, who founded the southern sect of Buddhism, meditates peacefully. The attractive Sixth Patriarch's Hair-burying Pagoda is almost a miniature of the Flower Pagoda. This temple is not usually on the tourist track, but it is worth visiting if you like temples. See also "Shaoguan."

The **Huaisheng (Remember the Sage) Mosque and Guangta (Smooth) Minaret** 光塔寺 (Guangta Lu; tel. 31878, 35803) is only of historical value. It is not the least bit attractive. Considered the oldest mosque in China, it was built in A.D. 627 by Arab traders. It is open daily. Visitors can climb its minaret, which has also been used as a lighthouse. The 26.3-meter minaret is said to be original. The tomb of the founding Moslem missionary, Sad Ibn Abu Waggas, is in the Orchid Garden.

The **Liu Rong (Six Banyan Trees) Temple** 六榕寺 (Liu Rong Rd.; tel. 87563) was founded 1400 years ago. It was so named because the famous Tang poet Su Dong Po found six luxuriant banyan trees there in 1100. The present buildings were rebuilt in 989. Its nine-story **Flower Pagoda** is 57.6 meters high and originally built in 537. It can be climbed for a good view and the exercise. It is included in most tours because of its beauty and view.

The **Shishi (Cathedral of the Sacred Heart)** 石室 (Yide Rd.; tel. 83724) was built in 1863–88. Its 57.95-meter spire was probably built deliberately taller than the pagoda nearby. Shishi means Stone House. It was closed as a church during the Cultural Revolution and used as a storehouse until 1979. Now it has been restored almost to its previous grandeur and is reminiscent of many European cathedrals. Mass is celebrated weekdays at 6 a.m. and Sundays and festivals at 6, 7:30, and 8:30 a.m. (See *Religion* in "Local Customs.")

The **South China Botanical Garden** (Guangzhou Botanical Garden) 华南植物园 (Longyandong, in the north of the city; tel. 76604) is a research institute of the Chinese Academy of Science. One of the world's largest botanical gardens, it was opened in the late 1950s. This 300-hectare garden is home to more than 2000 species of tropical and subtropical plants such as palms, bamboos, herbs, and ferns. Depending on the season, bring your own insect repellant.

The **Orchid Garden** 兰圃 (Dabei Rd., west of Yuexiu Park and behind the Foreign Trade Center; tel. 31543) is a delight for orchid lovers. It has more than 100 species and almost 10,000 plants on five hectares. Waterfalls, ponds, rockeries, and pavilions add to the lovely setting. One of its many areas won an international prize at the World's Fair in Munich in 1983.

The **Xi Yuan (West Garden)** 西园 (next to Dongfeng 1-Rd.; tel. 85867) specializes in *penjing*, miniature trees and landscapes, of the Lingnan School. The 25,000 potted plants and rocks here form natural scenery through the pruning of the twigs, instead of bending them by force with wires.

You can go directly to any of the **arts and crafts factories** and **Foshan**. See *Shopping* below. Crafts can also be seen at the Zhen Family Hall and at the Guangzhou Gold and Silver Jewelry Centre. Jewelry is a recently revived craft, having been discouraged since Liberation. Clerks in this factory seem to know little about what they are selling, and one handed me a piece of malachite calling it "opal." The artisans are young. As with gems and jewelry everywhere, you have to know your products to get a good buy, but prices for small freshwater pearls seem to be good. Our book *Gems and Jewellery in Hong Kong—A Buyer's Guide* can be helpful here for those intent on serious buying.

The **Pearl River boat ride** 珠江游船 sails at noon and 6:30 p.m. for 2 hours (from No. 1 Pier on Yanjiang Rd.; tel. 64713). The price for foreign tourists includes a substantial meal. The 170-passenger ship first cruises eastward, downstream past the Renmin Hotel. At the Pearl River Bridge is the old Trade Fair building, the Guangzhou Hotel, and the Overseas Chinese Mansion. The bridge was destroyed by the retreating Nationalists, but rebuilt after Liberation. Past the bridge is a row of apartments for resettled former boat dwellers. Just where your ship turns around, on the opposite shore, is Zhongshan University. After passing the starting point, the boat turns left at Shamian Island (look behind you quickly) and then goes beyond the shipyards before heading back. During the trip, you can see a varied assortment of tiny sampans operated by oars, sailing junks, ferries, ocean freighters, and passenger ships— ancient and modern. If you want a cheaper trip without the meal, ask a native to help you.

Guangzhou Zoo 广州动物园 (Xianli Rd.; tel. 75547) is in the northeastern suburbs. Opened in 1958, it has 200 species, including pandas. With 350,000 square meters, it is the second largest zoo in China.

Yuexiu Park 越秀公园 (Jiefang Bei Rd., within walking distance of the China Hotel) is the largest in the city, on 92.8 hectares. It contains three small lakes, an Olympic-size swimming pool, stadium, botanical exhibit, 500,000 trees of 500 species, and the city museum in Zhenhai Tower. There you can find the sculpture of the five goats, symbol of Guangzhou. **Liuhua Park** 流花公园 (Xicun Gong Rd.) was built in 1957–59; it is 800,400 square meters, most of which is water. This park has tropical plants, boats for hire, and a booth selling clothes, jewelry, and other handicrafts from the national minorities in Yunnan. Both parks are great for early-morning jogging.

Guangzhou Cultural Park 广州文化公园 (near the Nanfang Department Store on Xiti 2-Ma Rd.; tel. 86686, 87232) covers 8.3 hectares. More pavement and less sylvan than other parks. Best avoided after 7 p.m. unless you want to see masses of people enjoying Chinese opera, puppet shows, acrobats, exhibit halls, basketball games, and roller-skating. The annual Lantern Festival and flower shows are held here.

Baiyun (White Cloud) Hill 白云山 is 6 km NE of urban Guang-zhou. This 28-square-km park has 30 peaks; the highest is 382 meters. Historically, it has been a meeting place for poets and story-tellers be-cause the peaks are often concealed by mist, which gave a spooky at-mosphere to the myths related.

One of these legends is about a collector of herbs who jumped off a peak because he couldn't find the immortality herb for the emperor. His deep sense of commitment so touched the fairies that they sent a crane to rescue him in midair!

Baiyun is now also a recreation area, with an amusement park, restaurant, hotels, reservoir, and a good place to get away from the crowded city. A 1672-meter-long cableway carries 1200 people an hour up to 198 meters.

Another escape is a visit to a **village or commune.** These are pri-marily for group tours, but individuals can join tours organized during the Trade Fairs (advertised in hotel lobbies) or make individual arrange-ments through C.I.T.S. (more expensive). These are geared for visitors and may be a mite commercial. You can usually get your picture taken on a water buffalo, try your hand at target practice with an air rifle, or watch a lion dance or a martial arts demonstration. Meals can be ar-ranged, and these I found to be among the best in China. I hope the standards are still good for your visit.

Many of the area communes grow and preserve fruit and olives for export, an interesting as well as delicious process to experience, as tour-ists are frequently given samples. Lucky are those who visit during the lichee season! (April to late June.)

Overnight village visits have become increasingly popular for young people who can also spend time helping in the work, a much better opportunity to see how people live and work.

Guangdong tourism officials are offering kung fu, acupuncture, and cooking lessons, plus· bicycle tours, mainly for tour groups. Some les-sons might be arranged for individuals. **Bicycles** cannot be rented in Guangzhou because of the traffic.

Guangdong province has several other places to offer tourists, es-pecially for those who do not want to travel too far from the Hong Kong border: golfing, mountains, rivers, tropics, national minorities, histori-cal sites, arts and crafts. Seaside resorts include a Club Med. See also "Conghua," "Foshan," "Haikou" (Hainan Island), *Hong Kong* ("Getting There"), "Jiangmen," "Shantou," "Shaoguan," "Shekou," "Shenzhen," "Taishan," "Xiqiao Mountain," "Zhanjiang," "Zhao-qing," "Zhongshan," and "Zhuhai."

Guangdong Travel and Tourism Press has published a beautiful picture book on the province.

Shopping

Main shopping area around **Zhongshan 5-Road** 中山五路 and **Beijing Road** 北京路 . Locally made are carvings of ivory, jade, bamboo, and wood, painted porcelain (porcelain from Jingdezhen; hand-painted here), and gold and silver jewelry. Shantou (Swatow) drawnworks and embroidery are famous.

Colored Painted Porcelain Factory 广州织金彩瓷工厂 (tel. 551464, 81235, 81919); **Daxin Ivory Carving Factory** 广州大新象牙工艺厂 (Tien Pin Zhar, Saho; tel. 73295); **Daxin Ivory Carving Factory Sales Dept.** (415 Daxin Rd.; tel. 882870); **Guangzhou Gold and Silver Jewelry Centre** 广州市金银首饰总汇 (199 Dade Rd.; tel. 85398); **Nanfang Jade Factory** (15 Xiajiu Rd.; tel. 882870).

One of the free markets here, the **Qing Ping Ziyou Shi Chang** 清平路自由市场 , has been selling antiques like old coins, water pipes, and old porcelain, with some reproductions. The bargains are probably the best in China. The antique section is closer to the river at the far end. Qing Ping Free Market is also the largest herb market in the city (about five blocks), where you can find dehydrated lizards, snakes, plants, and weird-looking roots. Some live animals, too, including pangolins, an endangered species! The market is not very clean, always crowded, but fascinating even if you don't want to buy anything. Within 20 minutes' walking distance of the White Swan Hotel, 6 a.m. to 6 p.m. As in all crowded places anywhere in the world, beware of pickpockets!

Guanlu Rd. has a large street market for clothes, mainly T-shirts, jackets, and trousers. Prices for Hong Kong–made items can be about three to five times Hong Kong prices, so beware. Some locally made clothes, factory overruns, and seconds are reasonably priced here.

China Hotel Friendship Store (Liuhua Rd.; tel. 663007) is open 8:30 a.m.–9 p.m. Less crowded than the larger Friendship Store.

Friendship Store 友谊商店 (369 Huanshi Dong Rd.; tel. 776296, 776506) is open 8:30 a.m.–9 p.m. Across from the Garden Hotel and next to the Baiyun. One of the largest in China; well stocked with goods from all over the country and especially Guangdong. Stylish handknit sweaters. A fast-food restaurant, the Friendship Store Cafe, is in the same compound, with reasonable (for China) hamburgers in a sweet bun.

Guangdong Antique Store 广东文物商店 (Hongshu Rd.; tel. 87600); **Guangzhou Antique Store** 广州文物商店 (Wende Rd.; tel. 31241); **Guangzhou Porcelain and Pottery Shop** 广州陶瓷商店 (Zhongshan 5-Rd.; tel. 30328); **Guangdong Arts and Crafts Service** 广东工艺美术服务部 (Dongshanshu Qian Rd.; tel. 70779); **Huaxia

Dept. Store 华夏公司 (Changdi, near People's Mansion); **Jiangnan Native Produce and Specialities Stores** 江南土特产商店 （中山四路）(Zhongshan 4-Rd.; tel. 31207); **Nanfang Dept. Store** 南方大厦商店 (49 Yanjiang Xi Rd.; tel. 86022); **Trade Center** 交易中心 (Guangzhou Trade Center, across the street from the Dongfang Hotel; use west entrance); **Yiyuan Art Shop** (Wende Rd.; tel. 30751); **Zhongshan 5-Rd. Department Store** 中山五路百货公司 (tel. 31507, 31509, 33154).

Guangzhou Trade Fair is held annually from April 15 to May 5, and October 15 to November 5.

Restaurants

Guangzhou's **garden restaurants** are among the prettiest in China. The **Nanyuan** and **Beiyuan** are of traditional Qing dynasty China, small dining rooms surrounded by fish ponds, latticed windows, bamboo, and flowers. They rate a visit for the atmosphere as well as for the food. The **Panxi (Pan Hsi) Restaurant** is tops for service and food, specializing in *dim sum*. See "Food." A reservation here is mandatory for the fancy, private banquet rooms, especially the Reception Dining Hall with its traditional, redwood Chinese furniture and beautiful blue glass windows. This restaurant is set around a large pond and we found clean, yes, clean washrooms!

The restaurants in the top hotels are excellent. Some opulent Hong Kong-style restaurants have also recently opened here. For lighter, cheaper food like noodles, congee, and dim sum, try China Hotel's **Food Street** and Garden Hotel's charming **Lai Wan Market.** For hamburgers, try the Friendship Store.

Cantonese food is world famous, but chop suey and fortune cookies are American and haven't been found here yet. The Chinese idea of perfection is to be "born in Suzhou" because of the beautiful garden homes, "wear clothes in Hangzhou" because of the silk, "eat in Guangzhou" because of the food, and "die in Liuzhou" because it has the best wood for coffins. For favorite Cantonese dishes, see "Food."

Beiyuan Restaurant 北园酒家 □ *202, Xiao Bei Rd.; tel. 32471 or 33365* □ One of the garden restaurants.

Guangzhou Restaurant 广州酒家 □ *2 Wenchang Nanlu; tel. 87136, 87840, 84339* □ One of the best.

Moslem Restaurant 回民饭店 □ *325 Zhongshan 6-Rd.; tel. 88414, 84664* □ Mutton dishes. Hot pot in winter.

Nanyuan Restaurant 南园酒家 □ *120, Qianjin Rd. (south bank of Pearl River); tel. 49211, 48380, 40532, 50532* □ One of the garden restaurants. A little far from the center of things.

Pan Xi (Pan Hsi) Restaurant 泮溪酒家 □ *151, Long Jun Rd. W.; tel. 85655* □ Specializes in Dim Sum pastries. See also above.

Snake Restaurant 蛇餐馆 □ *4 Jianglan Rd.; tel. 82517, 22517, 83811* □ Please, no endangered species!

Tao Tao Ju (Happy, Happy House) □ *No. 20 Dishifu Rd.; tel. 85769, 87306.*

Hotels

Luxury hotels seem to have caught up with the demand and businessmen no longer have to sleep on cots in meeting rooms or lobby couches, as they did during the 1979 Canton Trade Fair. There may be a surplus of rooms now, so visitors do have a choice, except possibly during the Trade Fairs. The three top luxury-class hotels with international standards now are the China Hotel, Garden Hotel, and White Swan. The Dong Fang Hotel and Baiyun Hotel have shown great improvement.

Top hotels here have direct-dial, long-distance telephones (with service charge) and can receive Hong Kong television, including English-language broadcasting. They also have travel services.

Baitian E (White Swan) Hotel 白天鹅大饭店 □ *1 South St., Shamian Island; cable: 8888; telex: 44488 WSH CN* □ International luxury class. Hong Kong joint venture, 1982–83. Beautiful atrium with waterfall and garden. Disco, western buffet, Japanese restaurant, swimming pool, concert hall, adjacent office building. Might be a little far from the Foreign Trade Center for business people. Presidential Suite 28th floor is breathtaking, with five bedrooms, three sitting rooms, own Jacuzzi, mahogany furniture, piano, and garden. Tennis within walking distance. Health club, massage, and sauna planned. Great view of river traffic from Songbird Living Room, and Hare and Moon Lobby Bar. Walking distance from west entrance to interesting Qing Ping Free Market.

Baiyun (White Cloud) Hotel 白云宾馆 □ *Huanshi Dong Rd. (buses 6, 10 or 30)* □ 1975; renovated 1984. 34 stories, tallest in town. 722 rooms. Greatly improved service, elevator, and decor. Nude statue in lobby! Cafe, bar, tearoom, disco, billiards. Next to Friendship Store. Good Chinese restaurants, especially dim sum. A Japanese restaurant is planned. The higher the room, the higher the price and quality. Best medium-priced hotel.

China Hotel 中国大酒店 □ *Liu Hua Rd.; telex 44189 CHLGZ CN* □ 1983–84. International luxury standard. 1200 rooms, next door to the Dong Fang. Excellent location for business people and jogging. Traditional Chinese interior. Ice cream parlor, ballroom, 12 function rooms, disco, department store, supermarket, office and apartment complexes. Tennis court, bowling alleys, games arcade, billiards, swimming pool. Managed by Hong Kong's top-ranking New World Hotels International. Weekend packages from Hong Kong and off-season discounts. Fleet of Mercedes.

Dong Fang Hotel 东方宾馆 □ *Renmin Bei Rd., or 1 Liuhua Rd.* □ 1963. Most convenient (across the street from the Foreign Trade Center). Sauna, amusement center, bar, tearoom, smoke alarms, wall-to-wall carpeting, room refrigerators, business center, billiards, gym, squash, swimming pool. Chinese, Western, and Japanese restaurants. Bowling alley and tennis courts planned. The U.S. Consulate and offices of several foreign bank representatives are on premises. Walking distance (20 minutes) to railway station, CAAC, and C.I.T.S. Two good jogging parks nearby. 6 km from airport. Price after upcoming renovations unknown. No surcharge and tax.

Garden Hotel □ see Huayuan.

Guangdong Guest House □ *603 Jiefang Rd. N.; cable: 1256* □ Also state guesthouse.

Guangzhou Hotel 广州宾馆 □ *Haizhu Square* □ 1968; renovated 1985. 27 stories. 510 rooms. 24-hr. coffee shop. Houses Japanese traders during trade fair.

Huaqiao (Overseas Chinese) Mansion 华侨大厦 □ *2 Qiaoguang Rd. on Hai Zhu Park* □ 300 rooms. Rundown. Next-door to C.T.S. and close to the Pearl River Bridge; walking distance to Nanfang Dept. Store and shopping; 4 km from Trade Center.

Huayuan (Garden) Hotel 花园酒店 □ *across from the Baiyun and the Friendship Store at 368 Huanshi Dong Rd.; Telex 44788 GDHTL CN* □ 1984–85. Beautiful and elegant international-class luxury hotel and offices. Over 1100 rooms, 24 stories. King-size, queen-size, or twin beds. 18 bars and restaurants including revolving restaurant, buffet, English pub, weekend barbecues, 24-hour Fast Food Centre (cafeteria, payable in RMB), and charming Lai Wan Market. Tennis, health club, swimming pool, library, videos of international sporting events, cultural shows, business center. With offices and apartments as well, the whole complex is said to be the largest in China. Managed by top-ranking The Peninsula Group. Some guests here prefer to eat across the street at the cheaper Baiyun. Mural behind desk is of *The Dream of the Red Chamber,* and on the opposite wall, Hainan Island, both gold foil on white Italian marble.

Kuangchuan (Spa Villa) Hotel 矿泉客舍 □ *in the northern suburbs on San Yuan Li* □ 1964, 1974, and 1979. 124 rooms. This is more like a resort than a hotel. Olympic-size swimming pool usually filled with warm (31°C) mineral water. Few services.

Liuhua Guest House 流花宾馆 □ *Huanshi Xi Rd.* □ Next to Liuhua Park. 1972. 650 rooms. Across the square from the railway station. Only Chinese food. Nicely renovated.

Nanhu (South Lake) Hotel 南湖宾馆 □ *Tonghe, Shahe* □ 20 minutes by car NE of the railway station on a lake at the foot of White Cloud Mountain; 25 minutes from Foreign Trade Center. Actually an extension to a ''Reception House'' for China's leaders, built originally by the notorious Lin Piao in the early '70s. The two newer buildings, 1982, have 300 rooms, wall-to-wall carpets, bedside controls for music and TV, safe-deposit boxes, dance hall, five restaurants, taxi stand, and bus service downtown. The hotel is set on 4 square km of land and lake surrounded by amusement park, pine trees, bamboo and orange groves. The closest village is 2 km away. Good for hiking, swimming, fishing, badminton, tennis, billiards, Ping-Pong, mah-jong, water bicycles, and motorboats. Shooting gallery with machine guns. The 1 square km lake has a coffee shop barge in the center.

Ocean Hotel □ *390 Huanshi Donglu* □ Hong Kong joint venture.

Overseas Chinese Hotel □ see Huaqiao.

Renmin (People's) Mansion 人民大厦 □ *207 Chang Ti* □ 1966. 413 rooms. Downtown hotel on riverfront near the Bank of China and Nanfang Department Store.

South Lake Hotel □ see Nanhu.

Spa Villa □ see Kuangchuan.

White Swan □ see Baitiane.

Other Important Addresses

Bank of China, Guangzhou Branch 中国银行 : 137 Changdi; tel. 82963, 89543, 89363, 89124.

C.I.T.S. 中国国际旅行社 : 179 Huanshi Rd. (next to main railway station); tel. 61369, 62948. If it cannot help you with train tickets, ask the staff at your hotel.

C.T.S. 中国旅行社 : 2 Qiaoguang Rd. (Haizhu Square next to Huaqiao Mansion); te!. 61112.

CAAC: Next to main railway station; tel. 61803.

Airport Service Desk, Departure Lounge: tel. 62123.

Baiyun Airport: tel. 62794.

Domestic inquiries: tel. 62969.

International inquiries: tel. 61803.

Foreign Affairs Section, **Public Security Bureau** 公安局外事处 : 863 Jiefang Bei Rd.; tel. 31060, 30003.

Foreign Affairs Office, **Guangdong People's Gov't:** 45 Shamian Ave.; tel. 86511.

Foreign Trade Center 外贸中心 : 117 Liuhua Rd.; tel. 62690. Shopping, supermarket, restaurants, Bank of China, bookstore.

Guangdong Travel & Tourism Bureau: 185 Huanshi Rd.; tel. 61559, 62915; cable: 4611.

Hospitals

Guangdong People's Hospital 广东人民医院 : Zhongshan 2-Rd.; tel. 77812.

Guangzhou First People's Hospital 广州第一人民医院 : Panfu Rd., N. Renmin Rd.; tel. 33090.

The First Hospital Attached to Zhongshan Medical College 中山医学院第一附属医院: Zhongshan 2-Rd.; tel. 78223.

The Second Hospital Attached to Zhongshan Medical College 中山医学院第二附属医院 : Yanjiang 1-Rd.; tel. 82012.

Japanese Consulate: Dong Fang Hotel; tel. 61195.

Overseas Chinese Travel Service 华侨旅游服务社 : 2 Qiaoguang

Rd.; tel. 32247, 61112.

Passenger Pier for Hong Kong, Zhoutouzui　洲头咀客运码头（往香港）: tel. 46214.

Railway Station　火车站 : tel. 33333, 61789.

Singapore Airlines: Represented by CAAC, tel. 61803.

Taxis: Stationed at hotels. Baiyun Hotel, tel. 67700; Dong Fang Hotel, tel. 32227, 84842; Guangzhou Hotel, tel. 32277; Huaqiao Mansion, tel. 61112; Liuhua Hotel, tel. 62981, 68800 X61251; Nanhu Hotel, tel. 68052; Renmin (People's) Hotel, tel. 82599.

　　Guangdong Tourist Bureau: 179 Huanshi Rd.; tel. 30896, 33450.

Thai International　泰国航空公司　: tel. 33684.

U.S. Consulate　澳洲航空公司 : Dongfang Hotel; tel. 69900.

Guilin

(Kweilin; City of Cassia Trees) South China. In northern Guangxi, the first "province" west of Guangdong. 55-minute flight NW of Guangzhou and minimum 2-hour flight SW of Beijing. Sometimes there are direct charter flights from Hong Kong. Guilin is connected by rail to Beijing, Kunming, Shanghai, Zhanjiang, and Nanning, and by bus and boat with Guangzhou and Hong Kong. The weather is subtropical. Hottest—34°C in August; coldest—⁻3°C. Rainy season—February–May. Annual precipitation—1900 mm. The best time to visit is autumn, or late spring, when it is warm enough to ignore the rain. The scenery is best seen in the mist, which inspired centuries of landscape painters, or when the sun and clouds conspire to

give you constantly changing pictures. From November until
the February rains, the water in the river may be too low for
the boat trip all the way to Yangshuo. Population is 270,000
urban.

Founded in 214 B.C., this prefecture is famous for its vertical limestone mountains rising above tree-lined streets, rice fields, and the
meandering Li and Taohua (Peach Blossom) rivers. It is also known for
its caves.

Guilin developed with the opening of the Ling Canal in 214 B.C. It
was the provincial capital until 1014, and a command post for the Northern
Expedition in 1926. During the Japanese war almost all of the city was
destroyed, the Seven Star Cave alone sheltering 5000 refugees. Because
about one third of the 10 million people living in the province are of
Zhuang nationality, Guangxi is an "autonomous region" rather than a
"province." National guides may not understand the local dialect.

The city itself, a favorite of honeymooners, is small, full of parks,
and ideal for walking. The ground is level except for the sporadic mountains, each of which has a bright-red pavilion complementing nature, an
invitation to climb.

You will want to spend a minimum of two days; three would be
better. Guilin is one of the 24 cities of historical interest protected by
the State Council. Some of its houses are antiques and one should stroll
through the past at leisure. Many tame mountains beckon climbers. Unfortunately, Guilin also abounds with tourists, and aspiring young merchants shouting "Hello Hello!" to attract your attention.

For those in a hurry, one morning could be spent at Diecai Hill,
Fubo Hill, and Seven Star Park, and the afternoon at Reed Flute Cave
and Elephant Hill. The Li River boat trip could be enjoyed on a second
day or vice versa.

Diecai (Folded Brocade) Hill 叠彩山 (3.6 km from the Lijiang
Hotel) is the tallest in town at 73 meters. The peaks are named Bright
Moon, Crane, and Seeing Around the Hill. Partway up past the ornamental arch is the Wind Cave with Ming and Tang poems and memorials on its walls. A good view of the area can be seen from the top.

Fubo (Whirlpool) Hill 伏波山 (2.8 km from the Lijiang Hotel), named after famous Han Marshal Ma Fubo, is 60 meters high. At
the base is a 7½-ton iron Qing bell belonging to the temple originally
here. To the right is the Cave of the Returned Pearl, where guides might
tell you a dragon left a gift of a pearl for a poor family, who returned
it: "This illustrates the honesty of working people." Nearby is a rock
where Ma Fubo tested his sword, and a cliff with Tang buddhas. Partway up on the right is a pavilion with a view of the river.

Qixing (Seven Star) Park 七星岩 (2.7 km from the Lijiang Hotel) is about 10 square km. It contains a zoo, Camel Hill, and Seven
Star Hill, its seven peaks positioned like the stars in the Big Dipper.

With lots to see, you may want to return for a more leisurely look. Just think, you will be following in the footsteps of tourists from the Sui (581–618) dynasty! Seven Star Cave, on the west side of Potaraka Hill, has three levels; visitors enter the middle one. It is bigger than Reed Flute Cave, 1 km long, 43 meters at its widest, and 27 meters at its highest. Colored lights highlight the grotesque limestone formations.

The park's pavilions are each constructed of different materials, concrete or bamboo, for example. A forest of cassia trees blossom in spring and a 700-year-old stone replica of the Flower Bridge (Song) spans a stream. Originally built of wood but destroyed in a flood, the bridge was designed so that the water below reflects its arches to form a complete circle.

The "Cave for Hiding a Dragon" 龙隐洞 does look like it could snugly fit a dinosaur. The most famous of the stone Song steles nearby lists people meant for execution. The emperor sent copies around China (although paper was invented by then) and when the verdict was reversed, all but the stele in Guilin were destroyed.

Also on the west side of Putuo (Potaraka) Hill is the Yuanfeng (Deep and Windy) Cave, and on top, the Putuo (Potaraka) Temple (good view) and Guanyin cave.

Ludi (Reed Flute) Cave 芦笛岩 is 8–9 km from the Lijiang Hotel. One km long, this cave takes about 40 minutes to see. The temperature inside is a cool 20°C. The lighting is cleverly placed so that with a bit of imagination, the limestone formations resemble a giant goldfish, a Buddha, a wall of assorted vegetables, etc. The cave is named after the reeds that grow at the entrance.

Xiangbi (Elephant Trunk) Hill 象鼻山 (1.4 km from the Lijiang Hotel), located at the junction of the Li and Yang rivers, really does look like an elephant drinking. Shuiyue (Moon-in-Water) Cave is between the trunk and front legs. Elephant Eye Cave is where you would expect. The Samantabhadra Pagoda tops the hill. Look for a sculpture of the Buddha of Universal Benevolence.

The **Li River boat trip** is the other outstanding attraction in the area. Book at C.I.T.S. or the Lijiang Navigation Co., or the Guangxi Tourism Motor & Boat Company. Ask if the price includes lunch and the bus back to Guilin. If you have time, check the boat before you put your money down. Some visitors have found their dishes being washed in the Li River where the buffalo roam.

The 5-hour, 83-km tour south to Yangshuo usually returns by land. The Li River, normally 30–60 meters wide, winds it way between some incredible rock formations, the highest about 80 meters. The boats are self-propelled, or sometimes pulled by a tug because the river is shallow. The middle section of the trip, after the first 2½ hours, is the most beautiful, so do not use up all your film before you get to it.

As you leave Guilin, with a little imagination you will see in succession on the right Elephant Trunk Hill, Fighting Cocks Hill (one on each side), and Reclining Flower Vase Hill on the right. The vase appears as if it were cut in half lengthwise.

At 1½ hours out: Sword-Cut Cliff (as if neatly severed by a giant sword). At 2¼ hours out: left side, Crown Cave (shaped like the British imperial crown). At 2¾ hours: cock with tail up bending down to pick up rice, followed shortly by the U-shaped Ram's Hoof Mountain on the right. At 4 hours out, on the right is Conch Shell Hill, then a temple on a cliff.

On the way, look for large cormorants (real birds, not stone), usually seen sitting on the railings of fishing boats. If you're lucky you might even see them at work, fishing on behalf of people. What do you say to that, wildlife activists?

Yangshuo 阳朔 , the tiny town at the end of the boat ride, has a park, museum, and an old temple. If time allows, you might be able to walk along the main street to the right of the landing. Behind Green Lotus Peak on the left of the landing is Jian (Mirror) Hill, so named because some of its cliffs are smooth. The museum is of the famous painter of galloping horses and Li River scenes, Xu Beihong, who lived there between 1935 and 1938. Yangshuo Hotel is available in case you can't get a bus back.

Chuanyan (Pierced Hill) Village 穿眼村 is 7 km from Yangshuo on the way back to Guilin. Tour buses sometimes stop for the scenery—a giant 1000-year-old banyan tree and the hill, apparently "pierced" by a very big arrow. In the cave are several dwellings reached by a tiny ancient ferry across the Jinbao (Golden Treasure) River.

Duxiu (Unique Beauty) Park was the site of the 1393-built mansion of Zhu Shouqian, grandson of Emperor Hongwu of the Ming. During the Qing, it held the civil service examination hall and later the headquarters for the local government and the Nationalists. Destroyed during the Qing, and again during the Japanese war, it is now the site of the teachers' college. Today, only the original wall, its gates, and the steps over which only the emperor could be carried remain. The steps are white marble, carved with the scales of the imperial dragon.

Lingqu (Ling Canal), a.k.a. Xing'an Canal, dug over 2000 years ago (Qin) to connect the Chang (Yangtze) and the Zhu (Pearl) rivers, is also of importance, an inland route to Guangzhou. It was a waterway until the 1930s and is still used for agricultural irrigation. It may be of interest to engineers and history fans. It has 18 locks and sections, and still can be seen starting about 66 km north of Guilin at **Xing'an** or Darongjiang.

The Yuan (1279–1368) **Ling Temple,** in the south section, contains six stone tablets recording successive reconstructions of the canal from the Ming onward. The **Tomb of the Three Generals** contains either the remains of Qin dynasty canal inspectors or three stone masons, depending on which source one believes.

The **Long Sheng Hot Spring** 龙胜温泉 should be open when you arrive so you can soak away the stiffness from hiking in damp caves.

Yinshan (Secluded Hill) 隐山 , west of Guilin proper, just beyond the railway track, has still more caves; **Xishan (West Hill)** 西山 , half a kilometer west of Yinshan, was a Buddhist site and has 200 cliffside Buddhist statues from the early Tang; the largest is two meters high.

Sarira Stupa, just west of Elephant Trunk Hill, is on a Sui dynasty temple site. The seven-story reliquary for the ashes of deceased monks was first built in 657. The current 12.88-meter-high structure was reconstructed in 1385.

Shopping

Here you can buy locally grown oranges, yellow grapefruitlike pomelo, and mangosteens (luohan guo), all very sweet, from time to time during the summer and early autumn. The arts and crafts factory makes boxwood, jade, and soapstone carvings, and bamboo chopsticks. Its dough sculptures are very good.

Guilin also produces bamboo and wood carvings, woven and plated bamboo, watercolor paintings, embroidery, down jackets, pottery, and porcelain. The main shopping area is along **Zhongshan Zhong Rd.,** where you will find the **Friendship Store** 友谊商店 at 107 (tel. 2743; open 9:30 a.m.–9 p.m.) and the **Arts and Crafts Center** 工艺美术服务部 at #109 (tel. 2166). For art, there are the **Lishui Chamber** and **Guishanyuan (Garden of Osmanthus Mountain)** 桂山园 .

Also on this street are the **Guilin Antique Store** 桂林文物商店 , at 71 (tel. 2594) and the **Guilin Embroidery and Art Crafts** (tel. 2496). The **Yangqiao Department Store** (tel. 2464, 2259) is the largest. The **Guilin Clothing Factory** makes down jackets but may not be open for retail sales. Check at 21 Wenming Rd. (tel. 5479, 3110, cable 5902).

Restaurants

Chinese food here is usually Guangxi or Guangdong (Cantonese). Food is served with chili sauce and fermented bean curd as condiments. You should like the beancurd if you like blue cheese. Mix a bit with your rice. The local rice wine, Sanhua, is made from a 200-year-old recipe.

Friendship Restaurant 友谊餐厅 □ *212 Zhongshan Zhong Rd.; tel. 3741.*

Yueyalou (Crescent) Restaurant 月牙楼餐厅 □ *(inside Seven Star Park), tel. 3622* □ Vegetarian.

Hotels

Dangui (Osmanthus) Hotel 丹桂饭店 □ *451 Zhongshan Nan Rd.* □ 1981. 157 rooms. Rooftop bar and cafe. Chinese and Western food.

Guilin Jiashan Hotel 桂林甲山饭店 □ *Jiashan Rd., on the bank of the Peach Blossom River* □ 1980; renovated 1985. Nine two-story, connected buildings. 330 rooms. Australian joint venture. Chinese and Western food. Good reputation.

Lijiang Hotel 漓江饭店 □ *Shanhu Bei Rd.; north shore of Shan (Fir) Lake, in the center of the city. 15 km from airport, 3 km from railway station* □ 1976; renovated 1985. Almost 310 rooms, 12 stories. Dance hall, bar, and great view from the roof. Bring your own paints. Close to shopping. This is the main tourist hotel. Chinese and Western food.

Mandarin Hotel 文华大饭店 □ *67, Binjiang Nan Rd.* □ 1986. 150 rooms.

Rongcheng Hotel 榕城饭店 □ *Sanlidian Yangguling* □ 1983. 250 rooms.

Ronghu (Banyan) Hotel 榕湖饭店 □ *16, Ronghu Bei Rd., on shore of Ronghu Lake* □ 1960s; renovated. 182 rooms. Eight buildings. Garden setting. Auditorium for cultural events and parties. Branch of Beijing's Rongbaozhai store specializing in art reproductions. This top hotel is primarily for official delegations and state guests.

Yangshuo Hotel 阳朔饭店 □ *Yangshuo; tel. 2260* □ Over 120 beds, but only one third of the rooms have private baths.

Among the many hotels under construction at press time are Xingjiang, Guilin, and Panda hotels.

Other Important Addresses
Guilin Airport 桂林机场 ：tel. 2741.
Bank of China 中国银行 ：Zhongshan Zhong Rd.; tel. 3005. (Foreign exchange desks at major hotels.)
CAAC 中国民航 ：144 Zhongshan Zhong Rd.; tel. 3063.
C.I.T.S. 中国国际旅行社 ：14 Ronghu Bei Rd.; tel. 4512, 2936, 3870.
C.T.S. 中国旅行社 ：Ronghu Bei Rd.; tel. 2648.
Guangxi Guilin Tourism Motor & Boat Company: 1 Yueya Rd.; tel. 5829, 3306; cable: 5307. Sightseeing boats and buses.
Guilin Taxi Co.: Binjiang Rd.; tel. 2089.
Guilin Tourist Company: Ronghu Bei Rd.; tel. 2648.
Hospitals:
　　Guilin Renmin Hospital 桂林人民医院 ：Binjiang Rd.; tel. 3104.
　　Nanxishan Hospital: Zhongshan Nan Rd.; tel. 2001.
Lijiang Navigation Co.: Binjian Rd.; tel. 5878. Boat tours to Yangshuo. Buses and steam ships to Hong Kong. Buses to Guangzhou.
Pedicab Station 三轮车站 ：Zhongshan Bei Rd.; tel. 3882.
Post and Telecommunications branches in the Ronghu, Lijiang and Jiashan hotels, and at the airport.

Public Security Bureau 公安局 : tel. 3202.
Railway Station 火车站 : Zhongshan Nan Rd.; tel. 2904.
Taxis and Boats for hire: Guilin Tourist Co., Ronghu Hotel; tel. 3811.

Guiping 贵平

South China. *Jintian Village, 25 km north of the capital of Guiping County in SE Guangxi, is where the Taiping Revolution (1851–64) broke out. Guiping can be reached from Nanning.

Guiyang 贵阳

Southwest China, in the central part of Guizhou province, of which it is the capital. It is joined by air with Beijing, Xi'an, Guilin, Changsha, Guangzhou, etc. It is also at the hub of railway lines with Chengdu, Nanning, Kunming, and Changsha. It has an altitude of 1070 meters. The western and central part of the province has an altitude of 1–2000 meters. The terrain is rugged, with karst formations, underground rivers, jagged peaks, dramatic valleys, and terraced rice fields. The annual precipitation is 900–1500 mm. The province is rich in minerals—aluminum, coal, iron, lead, gold, silver, zinc, etc. It has China's largest mercury deposit. It grows rice, corn, tobacco, cork, raw lacquer, and timber.

The area has been a part of recorded history since the Shang dynasty, about 3000 years ago. Today, out of a total population of 29.3 million, 26% are minorities: Miao, Bouyei, Dong, Yi, Shui, Hui, Gelo, Zhuang, Yao. They contribute to the fascinating architecture and the over 1000 lively festivals a year, many unlike those in other parts of China.

Because this province has only recently been opened to tourists, people looking for the unusual will find it here, especially among the minorities. Be sure to ask about visiting some, but don't expect private baths and hot water everywhere. You'll be lucky to get a clean hotel room. New hotels are currently being built.

Qianling Hill, in the northwestern part of the city, has Qianling Lake with pavilions and the Hongfu Temple (Qing), the center of Buddhism locally. Behind the temple is a good view of Guiyang. **Huaxi Park** is 17 km SW. The **Southern Cave** in Bailongdong in the south suburbs is 587 meters long and full of incredible formations and an underground river.

Jiaxiu Pavilion and **Forest Park** are also noteworthy.

The only real tourist attraction in the province besides the colorful minorities is **Zhenning,** near Anshun, with China's most important waterfall. Huangguoshu Falls, 150 km by train or bus from the capital and then a 1-hour bus ride. Part of the Baishui River, the falls are 84 meters wide and 74–90 meters high. Visitors can go behind the falls for an unusual view of the water. The area has 18 falls (some with up to 130-meter drops), a petrified forest, and over 30 caves with interesting formations. Swimming in the area is possible. The pleasant Huangguoshu Guesthouse is near the falls.

Twenty-seven km south of **Anshun** is an intricate set of caverns linked by an underground river. The Dragon King Palace complex has five galleries, all with names related to Chinese mythology. The Dragon Gate Falls is in a 50-meter-high, 25-meter-wide cave. From the 10,000-square-meter Dragon Pool, tourists can ride dragon boats into a 1-km-long cave.

The Miao and Dong Autonomous prefecture is 300 km east of Anshun, in the southeastern part of the province. At **Kaili** you will see women laden with silver jewelry and hear the unique Miao antiphonal courtship singing. Dong architecture is unusual; their drum towers especially are a charming mixture of Chinese pagoda styles with flaming eaves.

Shopping

Made locally are minority handicrafts, including embroidered vests, silver Miao jewelry, bamboo flutes, lacquerware, and wax printing. Also produced here are Maotai (the most famous and most potent Chinese liquor), pears, oranges, kiwi fruit, and tangerines.

Stores include the **Friendship Store, Arts and Handicrafts Shop,** and the **No. 1 Department Store.**

Food

Local delicacies include braised salamander, love bean curd fruit, *bijie* stuffed dumplings, and Eight Delicacies. Please note that the giant salamander, a favorite of the Chinese gourmet, is an endangered species. Roasted bean curd and roasted corn are famous local snack foods.

The **Huaxi Hotel** in Huaxi has a billiard room, movie theater, and barber.

Hainan Island 海南岛

South China. China's second largest island is in the tropical part of Guangdong province, 30 km off its southern coast. It is best reached by a 1½-hour flight from Guangzhou or a half-hour flight from Zhanjiang to the capital, Haikou. It can also be reached by ship from Guangzhou and Zhanjiang. Our latest inspections of this ship found it filthy and badly managed. Flights have started recently between Guangzhou and Sanya, and there is a ferry service between Hong Kong and Haikou. The island is almost as big as Taiwan, with about the same latitude and climate as southern Cuba. Foreign oil experts have been visiting it for years, but it is only now in the process of being developed for tourists. The few tourists who have been here have raved about unspoiled beaches and the experience of visiting a place where time has stopped—until now.

Hainan was first colonized by Han dynasty troops. From the Tang, disfavored scholars and officials were sent here to live in exile, a tropical Siberia. During the '30s and '40s, a Communist army detachment fought here, and after Liberation part of the island became an autonomous region because a large percentage of the population are tribal minorities: mainly Li and Miao, but also Hui. Many of these still wear their beautiful, distinctive dress.

The island produces tea, coffee, rubber, fish, sugar, coconut, and rice. Other industries are being developed. The population is around 5.2 million.

Haikou 海口 , with a population of 230,000 people, has the **Five Officials Memorial Temple** 五公祠 nearby, which commemorates some of the banished officials. Also to be seen is the **Hai Rui Tomb** 海瑞墓 .

Tourists have also visited an Overseas Chinese Village in **Xinglong** 华侨 , where there is a hot spring and a comfortable hotel with good seafood. At **Luhuitou** 鹿回头 , 300 km from Haikou, are several hostels from which visitors can swim in the Dadonghai Sea. Scheduled to open in 1987 is a resort with 10 hotels, golf course, and sport fishing at **Yaxian (Sanya)** 三亚 , which is also almost at the southern tip. In this area are a pearl cultivation farm and the **Dongshanling Ridge** 东山岭 , with a group of giant boulders. (Beware of tides.) The southernmost point of Hainan Island is the **Ends of the Earth** 天涯海角 . This is not to be confused with the southernmost tip of China, which is on an island much farther south in the South China Sea. Sanya is linked by rail with Changjiang in the western part of the island.

Tourists can also visit the Nanwan Rhesus Monkey Reserve in Lingshui County.

Hainan Island contains naval bases and therefore several military areas from which foreigners are forbidden.

Shopping
Rose quartz, fruit, and minority handicrafts.

Food
Local specialties include Wenchang-style chicken 文昌鸡 , Jiaji duck 加积鸭 , Hele crab 和乐蟹 , and Dongshan mutton 东山羊肉 .

Hotels

Haikou Tower Hotel ☐ 1985. 240 rooms.

Overseas Chinese Hotel ☐ Renovated 1985. As you enter, the right side is old and uncomfortable; the left is better, with TV, air conditioning, good service, and carpets.

Handan 邯郸

North China, south Hebei on the Beijing-Guangzhou railway line.

Handan was the capital of Zhao State during the Warring States, 475–221 B.C. In 198 B.C., it became capital of the prefecture. The *Xiangtangshan Cave Temple from the Wei, northern Qi to Yuan dynasties (about A.D. 500) is in a coal mine. Its nine caves in the north contain 700 buddhas, those in the south more than 3500.

Cizhou pottery, a distinctive traditional style with strong flower patterns, is still made in Pengcheng, near Handan, at eight factories.

Hotels

Handan Hostel.

Hangzhou (Hangchow)

East China. Capital of Zhejiang province, Hangzhou is on the Qiantang River at the southern end of the Grand Canal on the east coast of China. It is 189 km SW of Shanghai and a 2-hour flight SE of Beijing. Direct flights from Hong Kong. Coldest weather is in January, a little below 0°C; hottest in July, with highs of 35°C. Annual precipitation about 1452 mm, mainly May–June. The population is 1.2 million.

Hangzhou is one of the most famous beauty spots of China, with its Xihu (West Lake). It is also of historical importance. Founded over 2200 years ago in the Qin, it began to prosper as a trading center after the completion of the Grand Canal in 610. It was the capital of the tiny state of Wuyueh (893–978), at which time the first dikes forming the lake were built. It was also capital of the Southern Song after 1127. The best source for a detailed picture of the city from 1250 to 1276 is Jacques Gernet's *Daily Life in China on the Eve of the Mongol Invasion,* essential for visitors who want to know a lot of history, to compare life then with today, and to look for old ruins. The city was seized by the Mongols under Kublai Khan in 1279 and visited by Marco Polo the next year when it was known as Kinsai. The Venetian explorer raved about the city, then the largest and richest in the world, its silks and handicrafts much in demand in China and abroad.

Hangzhou has been a famous resort for centuries, attracting famous painters, poets, and retired officials as well as tourists. It is also an industrial city now, with iron and steel, machine-making, basic chemicals, an oil refinery, and electronics. It also produces generators, machine tools, light trucks, and small tractors. Tourists would probably be interested in its factories producing silk textiles, satin, brocades, sandalwood fans, scissors, silk parasols, and woven silk "photographs." Villages here grow the famous long jing (Dragon Well) tea and silk worms. These make a rural excursion especially worthy.

The center of the city is on the east side of **Xi Hu (West Lake)** 西湖 . The 5.6-square-km lake was originally part of the Qiantang River until its outlet became silted up. It is now 15 km in circumference, with an average depth of 1.8 meters. Just strolling around the edge of the lake is worthwhile. Many of the tourist attractions are close to its shore.

If a visitor only has one day to spend in the city, C.I.T.S. recommends a boat ride on the lake with stops at various famous sites. Then take in the Pagoda of Six Harmonies, Lingyin Temple, and a silk factory. Boats are available for hire at four different places around the lake.

One could also rent a bicycle (faster) from a shop at the intersection north of the Children's Palace, or a pedicab. (See also "Getting Around"). That way in one day you can ride along Baidi Causeway with stops at the Autumn Moon on Calm Lake Pavilion, Wenlang Ge (next to Zhejiang Provincial Museum), Xiling Seal Engraver's Society, Tomb and Temple of Yue Fei, and Jade Spring. After you park your bicycle at a stand, you could take the cable car up to Lingyin Temple. Then you can visit the Feilaifeng Grottoes across the stream from the temple, go back down to pick up your bicycle, and turn back to the Yue Fei Tomb and then south onto Sudi Causeway. Follow Nan Shan and then Hubin roads. Stop to enjoy Liulangenying Park if only for its name, which means Park to See the Waving Willows and Hear the Singing of the Birds. Then back to the Children's Palace.

The best times to see the lake itself is in the mist, or in the moonlight, or just at sunrise before the sun makes strong shadows, and when the birds are singing in the willows. One of the favorite spots for viewing the lake, especially during the harvest moon, is at **Pinghuqiuyue (Autumn Moon on Calm Lake Pavilion)** 平湖秋月 at the southeastern end of **Gu Shan (Solitary Hill)** 孤山 . But don't expect to be alone.

On the islet also is the **Wenlang Ge (Pavilion for Storing Imperial Books)** 御书楼 , built in 1699 (Qing), and one of the seven imperial libraries. This one was especially built to store the Sikuzhunsu, a 33,304-volume Chinese encyclopedia ordered by Emperor Qianlong. Copied by hand, the encyclopedia took 10 years to compile.

The **Xiling Seal Engraver's Society** 西冷印社 was founded in 1903 and has its headquarters on a hillside here full of pavilions, towers, and a pagoda. Seal engraving is a fine art in the Orient, with several different styles. This society meets twice a year, gives many exhibitions, and publishes periodicals. The stone **Monument to the Three Venerables** 三潭印月 here was carved in A.D. 52. The island also has a provincial museum and a restaurant, the Louwailou.

Lively **giant golden carp** can be seen at **Huagang Park** 花岗公园 at the SW end of the lake, beyond the Sudi Causeway. A Song official once had a vacation home here. The pavilions were built after Liberation. This 20-hectare park also has a restaurant and a tea house.

The 2.8-km **Sudi Causeway** is the more beautiful of the two causeways here, lined with grass, willows, and peach trees. No motor vehicles are allowed because of its hump-backed bridges. It's a pleasant bicycle or pedicab ride, but please give the driver a break. Get off and walk up those bridges.

The famous **Zig-Zag Bridge** is on the islet **Xiaoyingzhou (Three Pools Mirroring the Moon)** 小瀛州 and can be reached only by boat. It is east of Sudi Causeway. Did you know that bad spirits have to move in straight lines? Stand on the bridge here and nothing can harm you. This islet was first constructed in 1607 (Ming) with mud cleared from the lake. Look for the "island in a lake and the lake in an island."

During the Moon Festival, candles light up the small pagodas, thus creating "Three Pools Mirroring the Moon." In June, this is a good place to enjoy water lilies and lotus flowers.

Everywhere around West Lake are exquisite gardens, some with artistically cobbled foot paths. The large mansions on the shore, once owned by the rich, are now hotels or resorts for workers. The 1.8 km **Baidi Causeway** 白堤 in the north was first laid 1000 years ago and is named after Bai Juyi, the great poet and governor of the Tang.

Visitors can also go by boat to **Ruangongdun Island** on the NW side of West Lake just south of Gushan Hill. **Huanbi Zhuang,** there, is an attempt to reproduce a Song dynasty village with period costumes, sedan chair rides, wine shop, music, and dance. Some tourists have found it fun, but serious students of Chinese history might find it too commercial. At the Mid-lake Pavilion is a 20th-century disco.

The ***Liuhe Ta (Pagoda of Six Harmonies)** 六和塔 is on the north bank of the Qiantang River. Built in A.D. 970 (Song), it is 59.89 meters and 13 stories tall, octagonal, and made of brick and wood. It can be climbed for a good view. West of this temple is the shallow and clear **Nine Creeks and Eighteen Gullies,** which cut through the rugged but tranquil (few tourists) Yangmei Hill. Great for hikers, the paths wind for about 7 km. There are donkeys for rent nearby for the less ambitious.

The **Lingyin (Soul's Retreat) Temple** 灵隐寺 is 9 km from the city, west of West Lake. Founded in A.D. 326 (Jin), its Celestial Kings' Hall and 33.6-meter-high Buddha Hall are all that is left of the original 18 pavilions and 72 halls. Lingyin at one time housed 3000 monks. A friend of mine watched, horrified, in 1966 as Red Guards smashed some of the statues here. The statues have been replaced now. A seated Sakyamuni inside is 19.6 meters high. The temple guardian behind the Four Celestial Kings was carved from camphor wood during the Song. Lingyin is still one of the largest and most magnificent temples in China. Two restaurants serve vegetarian food, the one inside better than the one next to the temple.

Across from Lingyin temple is ***Feilaifeng (Peak that Flew from Afar)** 飞来峰 , named by an Indian monk after a similiar-looking Indian peak that must have flown here. The 380 carvings along the narrow, hilly trails are from the Five Dynasties to the Yuan.

A trip to a silk factory to watch the weaving and designing can be arranged through C.I.T.S. The **Duyjinsheng Silk Weaving Factory** (215 Feng Qi Rd.) is about five minutes' walk from the Wanghu Hotel. Silk brocade pictures, cushion covers, fancy tablecloths, silk fabric. Open 8–11:30 a.m. and 12:30–4 p.m. Closed on Sunday. The **Hangzhou Silk Printing and Dyeing Complex** 杭州丝织厂 (Gong Zhen Qiao; tel. 87824) is more interesting to see. Slight charge, but a good tour guide is provided. A 15-minute taxi ride from the Wanghu Hotel, it is next to the Grand Canal on which the cocoons are transported. Here you can see the process of preparing the cocoons, spinning, weaving, printing, and dyeing. To make a shirt requires 500–1000 cocoons, depending on the thickness of the material.

The unpleasant part of a silk factory visit is the deafening noise of the weaving machines, but there are other things to see besides those machines. Do complain about the noise to the management.

It could take three or four days to cover all the important spots in Hangzhou. The 45-meter-high **Baochu (Precious Stone Hill) Pagoda**

宝珠塔 is on a 200-meter-high hill north of the lake, 2 km from the city. It was first built in 968 (Song) to pray for the safe return of the unjustly arrested Baochu, a successful effort. The pagoda, last reconstructed in 1933, is now filled with dirt and no one can enter.

The ***Tomb and Temple of Yue Fei** 岳飞庙，岳坟 is at the NW corner of the lake. Yue Fei was a famous Song general who was unjustly executed in 1142 at the age of 39. Public reaction forced a retrial 20 years later that reversed the verdict. A temple was built with statues of his four accusers kneeling for forgiveness before his grave. These four are spat on even today.

Yue Fei was also a calligrapher and poet who came from a family that valued patriotism. His mother tattooed his back with four characters to remind him of his duty to his country. His son was murdered on the day of Yue Fei's death. Their tombs are next to each other, but only contain their clothing. An exhibition hall illustrates Yue Fei's battles and shows his handwritten proposals to the Song emperor. The tomb animals are Ming.

At the **Hupao (Running Tiger) Spring** 虎跑 you will find water that will not overflow from a full cup even though many coins are added to it. The high surface tension will also support a carefully placed Chinese coin, a trick that also works in Toronto, so don't be gullible. The spring is near the Hangzhou Zoo, about 6 km from the city SW of the lake on Hupao Road. A handy tea house here serves Dragon Well tea, an exotic experience. The well is named after a tiger in a monk's dream that dug successfully for water here. The monk woke up and excavated this well at the same spot as in his dream.

The **Longjing (Dragon Well)** 龙井 , to the NW of Hupao, is another spring. The water here has a curious ripple effect when you stir it, especially on rainy days. This phenomenon is explained by the differences in the specific gravity of the rain water and the spring water, and is a good ploy to encourage business in wet weather.

Two km SW is **Longjingcun (Dragon Well Village)** 龙井村 , where you can see the famous tea growing on hillsides. It is usually picked in late March or early April. Connoisseurs of good tea pay fabulously high prices for the best of the harvest, the most tender leaves, hand-picked before the spring rain. The quantity is also limited because only a few villages have the proper soil and water. The best Longjing Tea, when brewed, has a fresh, crystal-green color, a mild and pure fragrance, and a slight sweetness. But what you can buy inexpensively here or in any Chinese grocery store is pretty good too.

At the **Meijiawu Tea Garden** 梅家坞茶园 , SW of Longjingcun, you can see the tea production process.

The third of Hangzhou's famous springs is **Jade Spring** 玉泉 (Yugu Rd., off the NW corner of the lake). It is for gold fish and flower lovers, as multicolored ornamental fish are bred here. It is inside the

200-hectare **Hangzhou Botanical Garden** 杭州植物园 , which has 3700 species, including 120 varieties of bamboo. Along with the Shanwaishan Restaurant, these are within walking distance of the Hangzhou Hotel.

A **cable car** 缆车 runs from 7:30 a.m. to 4 p.m. between **Beigao (North Peak)** 北高峰 and near the Lingyin Temple, giving a good view of the lake. Visitors can also drive up **Wushan Hill,** east of the lake, the highest spot in the city. This has an 800-year-old camphor tree and a cave made for the Song emperor. Also accessible is **Yuhuang (Jade Emperor) Mountain** 玉皇山 , overlooking the river at a spot where a Song emperor pretended to do manual labor. A **wax museum** on Wushan Hill has paintings and sculptures of local historical figures.

Most temples and parks are open from 7:30 a.m. to 5 p.m. in summer and from 8 a.m. to 4:30 p.m. in winter.

Excursions can be arranged from Hangzhou. For Ningbo (about 150 km SW) and Shaoxing (about 50 km SE), see separate listings. **Mogan Mountain** 莫干山 , 700 meters high (about 75 km NW), is a well-known summer resort with over 300 hectares of waterfalls, bamboo forests, stone trails, ponds, and caves. Good for hiking and relaxing in beautiful surroundings. **Wuling Guesthouse** 武陵宾馆 . The main town is **Ying Shan** 荫山 .

The **Fuchun River and the Yan Ziling Angling Terrace** group tour 富春江 goes 100 km SW to a gorge with Guilin-like limestone crags, waterfall, stone pavilions, pagodas, and two hydroelectric stations. A friend of a Han emperor used to fish at the Angling Terrace about 1900 years ago. The tour takes two or three days and includes a river steamer. Another area being developed is the **Sanhusai (Coral Sand) Tourland** 珊瑚沙 , 132 km from the city along the Qiantong River, with watersports, waterfall, resort hotel, etc. Ready for 1987.

The large limestone **Yaoling Cave** 瑶琳仙洞 is 120 km SW of the city, close to Tonglu County, and is 25 meters high and 1 km long, with many stairs. As the path is narrow, some visitors have found themselves so afraid of being pushed off the trail by other tourists that they couldn't enjoy the sights. The best time, then, is early afternoon, when most tourists have left. This is usually a one-day bus trip organized daily by C.I.T.S. or local tour companies.

In **Tiantai,** about 100 km from Hangzhou, the **Guoqing Temple** is the home of the Tiantai Buddhist sect. Tiantai also has the Wise Man's Tower Courtyard and a Sui pagoda.

The **Tidal Bore of the Qiantang River** 钱塘江观潮 is most spectacular on the 18th day of the eighth month (lunar calendar). In 1974 it reached a height of nine meters, but it is not usually that dramatic. Best seen at Yanguan town, 45 km from Hangzhou, or at Hailing. Check with C.I.T.S. for dates and bus tours if you are in Hangzhou in late September or early October.

Shopping

Produced here are silk textiles, woven pictures, Dragon Well tea, umbrellas, fans, woven bambooware, distinctive Tianzhu chopsticks, and stone and wood carvings. Hangzhou makes some fancy scissors that are useful souvenirs. The main shopping area is **Jiefang Rd.** and **Yan'an Rd.** 延安路 . In addition to the above-named silk factory, some important places to shop are:

Hangzhou Animal By-Products Factory (Wangjiangmen Nai; tel. 26947) for down-filled quilts; **Hangzhou Antique Store** (31 Hubin Rd.; tel. 27141); **Hangzhou Arts and Crafts Service** (220 Yan'an Rd.; tel. 24378); **Hangzhou Department Store** (739 Jiefang Rd.; tel. 22449); **Hangzhou Dragon Well Tea Shop** (33 Yan'an Rd.; tel. 24318); **Hangzhou Friendship Store** 杭州友谊商店 (302 Tiyuchang Rd.; tel. 26480); **Hangzhou Silk Goods Store** (31 Hubin Rd.; tel. 24508); **Wangxingji Fans** (77 Jiefang Rd.; tel. 28255); **Zhang Xiaoquan Scissors Shop** 张小泉剪刀店 (105 Yan'an Rd.; tel. 21860).

Restaurants

Kuiyuanguan Restaurant 奎元馆 □ *Guanxiangkou, Jiefang Rd.; tel. 25921* □ Primarily noodles.

Lingyin Vegetarian Restaurant 灵隐寺素斋馆 □ *Lingyin Temple; tel. 21433*.

Louwailou Restaurant 楼外楼饭店 □ *20 Waixihu; tel. 21654* □ Sweet and sour fish!

Shanwaishan Restaurant 山外山饭店 □ *Yuquan Rd.; tel. 26621*.

Tianxianglou 天香楼 □ *Dongpo/676 Jiefang Rd.; tel. 22038*.

Zhiweiguan Restaurant 知味馆 □ *111 Qunying/112 Renhe Rd.; tel. 23655*.

Hotels

China-Japan Friendship Hotel □ *a.k.a. Hangzhou Friendship Hotel* □ 1987. Eight stories.

Hangzhou Hotel 杭州饭店 □ *78 Beishan/Yuefen Rd.; Telex: CN 35005/6. 17 km from airport. NW shore of West Lake* □ 1956; renovated and expanded in 1985 and 1986. Chinese and Western food, bar, and coffee shop (with hamburgers). 600-seat auditorium. Reservations through Shangri-la International. This is the main tourist hotel.

Huagang Hotel 花港饭店 □ *Xishan/Huanhu Rd.* □ 1983–84. 370 beds, four stories.

Huajiashan Hotel 花甲山宾馆 □ *Xishan Rd.* □ 1983–84. Luxury hotel with villa-type buildings, total of 108 beds.

Huaqiao (Overseas Chinese) Hotel 华侨饭店 □ *92 Hubin Rd.* □ Five stories, 375 beds. Lovely location of lake, yet near shopping too.

Liulang Guesthouse 柳浪宾馆   □ *Xueshi (Scholar) Bridge* □ Traditional Chinese architecture. 70 beds.

Wanghu Hotel 望湖宾馆   □ *2 Huancheng Xi Rd.; telex 35003 WHBG CN; cable 9980 HZWH* □ 1984–85. 356 rooms. 5 dining and banquet halls. 24-hour room booking service. Plans to build a swimming pool and large conference hall. No view of the lake.

Xihu (West Lake) Guesthouse 西湖宾馆   □ *a.k.a. Liuzhuang Villa; Xishan/Huanhu Rd.* □ Garden-style luxury hotel. 150 beds. Deluxe and regular rooms. Four buildings. Southwest shore of lake, near Huagang Park. Billiard room, table tennis, sunbathing room, cinema. State guesthouse.

Xiling Hotel 西泠宾馆   □ *2, Yuefen St. near the Xiling Bridge* □ A luxury hotel. 190 beds. Three villa-type buildings with deluxe service.

Yellow Dragon Hotel 黄龙宾馆   □ 1987. 570 rooms.

Zhejiang Hotel 浙江宾馆   □ *Xishan Rd., Santaishan* □ Small theater, indoor swimming pool.

Other Important Addresses

Boats for Hire: Many kinds are available. Hubin (Lakeside) Park 湖滨公园 : tel. 22051; Zhongshan Park 中山公园 : tel. 22336; Huagang Park: tel. 25586; Liulangwenying Park 柳浪闻莺公园 : tel. 23001. Open 7:30 a.m.–5 p.m.

CAAC 中国旅行社: 304 Tiyuchang Rd.; tel. 24259. Airport: tel. 42160.

C.I.T.S. 中国国际旅行社 : 1 or 2 Shihan Rd.; tel. 25459, 27160.

C.T.C. 中国民航 : Overseas Chinese Hotel, Hubin Rd.; tel. 22775.

Hangzhou Railway Station 杭州火车站 : Chengzhan Rd.; tel. 22971.

Hospital: in case of illness, ask for help at your hotel. Otherwise, try the **Zhejiang Hospital** 浙江医院 : Lingyin Rd.; tel. 21357.

Taxis 计程车（出租汽车） : Ask at your hotel. Otherwise the Hangzhou Taxi Station, Nanshan Rd.; tel. 24697, 25046.

Telecommunications Services: Try your hotel first, but 24-hour service at Hangzhou Telegraph Office 杭州电报局 : Qingnian Rd.; tel. 23121, 24017.

Harbin 哈尔滨

(Haerhpin) Northeast China. This is the capital of China's northernmost province of Heilongjiang, formerly part of Manchuria, a 1½-hour flight NE of Beijing. It has a population of two million and is an industrial city 159 km from the Daqing oil fields, China's biggest. Its highest summer temperature is

*36°C; its lowest in winter is ⁻38°. The winter is six months
long, so take your longjohns. Wintertime, however, is brightened
by the **Ice Sculpture Festival**. You can also bring skates and
skis. Annual precipitation 250–700 mm, mostly June through
August.*

The area was first settled by people of the Nuzhen nationality in
1097. In the Yuan, the city was renamed Harbin. In 1898 it was opened
as a port and became a Russian concession. Tsarist troops and police
patrolled the Russian ghetto. From 1932 the Japanese occupied the area
until the end of the war.

Today, Heilongjiang numbers among its population Han, Manchu,
Korean, Hui, Mongolian, Daur, Orogen, Ewenki, Kirgiz, Hezhen, and
other nationalities.

If you only have one day here, C.I.T.S. recommends that you tour
the harbor and along the Song Hua River, with its 10 km dike. In January, visit the magical **Ice Sculpture Festival** 冰灯游园会 , about 8
km from the Swan Hotel. The show can take 2 or 3 hours if you can
stand the cold. This international competition has attracted teams from
Canada, Japan, Hong Kong, etc. Full of ice pagodas, bridges, giant
lanterns, human figures, mazes, palaces, and children's slides, it is best
seen at night with its twinkling lights.

Other attractions include a 2-km-long miniature railway for children
儿童铁路 (4 km from the Swan); in summer you can rent sailboats
and sampans; in winter you can sail-sled on ice. Among the animals at
the **zoo** you can find a Manchurian tiger, a red-crested crane, and a
moose. The **Heilongjiang Provincial Museum** is supposed to have one
of the best skeletons of a mammoth to be found in China.

C.I.T.S. has bird-watching and other tours in the province. China's
biggest bird sanctuary 扎龙自然保护区 , the 210,000-hectare **Zha-
long Nature Preserve** is near **Qiqihar,** 280 km away. Its cranes, storks,
swans, geese, herons, etc., are best seen from April to September. The
famous red-crested cranes are considered a symbol of luck by the Chinese.
A hunting area 桃山猪场 (238 km away) near the Siberian border has
deer, wild boar, pheasant, hazel grouse, wild duck, etc. Please, no endangered species! Taxidermists available. Restaurants here can cook the
spoils.

Also in the province is the **Taiyang Island summer resort,** another ice festival in Qiqihar, and **Jingpo Lake** in **Mudanjiang.**

Skiing here is an experience. It is not for serious skiers. Open are
Shangzhi and **Taoshan.**

Entertainment
Leather-silhouette show. Annual Harbin Summer Music Festival.
An unusual sport is sail-sledding on ice.

Shopping

Magnificent fur hats, jackets, and boots: mink, muskrat, and wolf. Handicrafts include straw patchwork, horn carving, knitting, and ivory, jade, stone, and wood carving. Good to eat are its pine nuts. In Harbin, try the Harbin No. 1 Department Store, the Songhuajiang Department Stores, the Friendship Store, and the Antique Shop of Heilongjiang Province. For furs and leather, try the Harbin Fur and Leather Goods Retail Shop.

Restaurants

The most famous dishes are served in the International Hotel. There you can try bear paw, moose nose, and hazel grouse. Please, don't eat any endangered species! For those who want something less questionable, try monkey head–shaped mushroom or Beijing duck or instant-boiled mutton.

International Hotel Restaurant □ *124 Dazhi Rd., Nangang District; tel. 31441, 33001.*

Jiangnanqun   江南春饭店 and **Jiangbin Restaurants** 江滨饭店 for Chinese food, and the **Huamei** for Western. Muslim food is at the **Beilaishun Restaurant** 北来顺饭店   .

Hotels

Swan Hotel 天鹅饭店   □ *73 Zhongshan Rd.* □ 1984. 500 beds. 45 km from airport. The borsch here has a good reputation.

Guoji (International) Hotel 国际饭店   □ *124 Dazhi Rd., Nangang District* □ Built 1930s; renovated 1982.

Hepingcun (Peace Village) Hotel 和平邨饭店   □ *107 Zhongshan Rd., Nangang District* □ Built 1950s; renovated 1983.

Beifang (North Mansion) Hotel 北方大厦   □ *105 Hua Yuan St., Nangang District* □ 1956; renovated 1984.

Friendship Palace Hotel 友谊宫宾馆   □ *Friendship Rd., Daoli District* □ Renovated 1984. Open to foreign visitors 1985.

C.I.T.S.: 124 Dazhi Rd.; cable HARBIN 1954; tel. 33001, 31447; telex 80081 GUOLU CN.
CAAC: 85 Zhongshan Rd.; tel. 52334.

Hefei (Hofei) 合肥

East China. Capital of Anhui (Anhwei), a province that is about two-thirds north of the Changjiang (Yangtze) River and is separated from the East China Sea by Jiangsu and Zhejiang provinces. Anhui is famous for its dramatic mountains that have inspired poets, mystics, and painters for centuries. In the prov-

ince live Han, Hui, She, and other nationalities. Flights to Hefei leave from Shanghai, Beijing, Jinan, and Wuhan. Train service from Beijing (14½ hours); Nanjing (6 hours); Wuxi, Suzhou, and Shanghai (11 hours). Hefei has a population of 820,000. Its coldest weather in January is a mean temperature of 2.3°C. Its hottest in July and August is a mean temperature of 28.5°C. Because of its strategic location, numerous battles were fought here in the ancient past. Its tourist attractions can be squeezed into one day.

At **Xiaoyaojin** 逍遥津 , near the center of the city, during the Three Kingdoms period 1700 years ago, General Zhang Liao of the State of Wei fought against General Sun Quan (Sun Chuan) of the State of Wu. The site is now a park with three islets, on one of which is the tomb of General Zhang. Near the park is a zoo. Two km south of Xiaoyaojin, the **Lecturing Rostrum/Archery Training Terrace** 教弩台 is where Emperor Caocao trained Wei troops in using crossbows. These sites are marked with pavilions in traditional architecture. The **Mingjiao Temple** is on the terrace. This monastery was founded in the Tang. Destroyed in the 19th century during the Taiping War, its buildings were rebuilt by General Yuan Hongmo of the Taiping Heavenly Kingdom.

The **Temple to Lord Baozheng** 包公祠 , situated in a park in the center of the city, was built in honor of Baozheng, an honest and outstanding official of the Northern Song. It has a stone statue of Lord Bao, carved in the Qing. He was a magistrate, prefectural head and vice minister of Rites. The **Provincial Museum** has a pleasant dinosaur garden. You might be able to squeeze in the China University of Science and Technology, and local opera too.

Shopping

Grown in the province are pears, pomegranates, grapes, kiwi fruit, and herbal medicines. Made are candied dates, Chinese brushes, ink slabs, paper, bamboo mats, and iron pictures. Try the Hefei Department Store, Anhui Provincial Arts and Crafts Store, and Gongnongbing Textile Shop. The Chenghuangmiao shopping center was built in the Ming style and surrounds the 900-year-old Town God's Temple. It has department stores, a tea house, and a wine shop.

Restaurants

Anhui specialties are freshwater crabs from Lake Chao nearby and locally produced Gujing Gongjiu wine, once sent as tribute to the Ming emperors. Try cured Mandarin fish 腌鲜桂鱼 , stewed turtle 清炖马蹄鳖 , Fuli braised chicken 符离集烧鸡 , Xiangzhenshan bamboo shoots and sesame cakes 向政山笋和芝麻糕 . Dishes are somewhat salty and slightly spicy hot, with thick soups.

Hotels

Jianghuai Hotel 江淮饭店 □ *68 Changjiang Rd.; 14 km from airport* □ 1982. 120 beds.

Luyang Hotel 庐阳饭店 □ *Jinzhai Rd. 10 km from airport* □ 1958; renovated 1984. 300 beds.

Daoxianglou Hotel 稻香楼宾馆 □ 212 beds.

Hefei China Hotel 合肥中国旅馆 □ *Jinzhai Rd.* □ 1987.

Wangjiang Hotel □ *in the suburbs of Hefei* □ currently has five stories and 800 beds. 1982. An 11-story, more luxurious wing is under construction. This hotel is an example of China's new economic policies. It is privately owned by local people.

Travel Agents

Overseas Marketing Dept. and C.I.T.S. Reception Dept. of the Anhui Provincial Tourism Corporation (both at 68 Changjiang Rd., Hefei; tel. 76227 X144; telex: 90024 AHPBD CN). These can also arrange photographing and painting tours, and flora and fauna study tours around the country. Contact them if you want to go crab- and game-tasting in six places, or follow in the footprints of Tang and Song poets, or look for rare birds and Chinese alligators. The travel agencies can let you know also about Buddhist events on Jiuhuashan.

Outside of Hefei in Anhui

Huangshan (Mount Huangshan 黄山 is reached from Hefei by train or bus across the Yangtze. The journey takes about 10 hours. See separate listing.

Jiuhuashan (Mt. Jiuhua) 九华山 , one of the Four Buddhist Mountains (alt. 1341 meters), is a day's trip by road. It has 50 Ming and Qing temples, 6000 buddhas, which were untouched by the Red Guards, and 99 peaks. Motor vehicles can drive up to 600 meters. Important are the Roushen Hall and Qiyuan Temple. In the **Baisui Gong (Buddhist Mummy Hall)** is preserved the 400-year-old cadaver of a monk. The Dongyan Hotel has 150 beds. Coldest mean temperature in January is ⁻3°C. Hottest mean temperature is 18°C in July. C.I.T.S. branch.

Wuhu 芜湖 in the eastern part of the province, is where the Qingyi River joins the Yangtze. It is slightly warmer than Hefei. On the railway lines from Nanjing and Hefei, it is the main foreign trading river port for the province and the fourth largest port on the Yangtze. It also produces those lovely pictures made of forged iron, usually painted black. It has a silk factory, Alligator Breeding Center, and the Dragon Spring Cave. Yangtze River boat tours. Hotels are the 260-bed Tieshan 铁山宾馆 and the 32-bed Wuhu. C.I.T.S. branch.

Anqing 安庆 , in the SE part of Anhui, on the Yangtze, has the seven-story Zhenfeng Pagoda. Former capital of the province, it has since 1953 been home of the modern Huangmei Opera, the fifth most popular opera form in China. Southwest of here, also on the Yangtze, is a cap-shaped rock, **Xiaogushan (Solitary Hill),** with pavilions on top. C.I.T.S. branch.

Ma'anshan (Horse Saddle Mountain) 马鞍山 , south of the Yangtze near the eastern provincial border, has impressive stone out-crops into the Yangtze. This large industrial town is on the railway line between Nanjing and Wuhu. Yangtze River Boat tours. The **Taibai Pavilion** was built at Caishiji (Rock of Various Colors) and has relics related to Li Bai, the world-famous Tang poet whose grave is between Ma'anshan and Wuhu near Qingshan 黄山 .

Its hotels are the 96-bed **Ma'anshan Hotel** 马鞍山饭店 , the 30-bed **Magang Hotel** 马钢外招 , and the 118-bed **Yushanhu Hotel** 雨山湖饭店 . C.I.T.S. branch. Coldest mean temperature is 3°C in January; hottest mean temperature is 29° in July and August.

Bengbu 蚌埠, north of Hefei, is an industrial and rail city and is the largest port on the Huaihe (Huai River). In **Fengyang County,** on the railway line between Beijing and Shanghai, is the ancestral home of the first Ming emperor, who proclaimed it a royal city. It contains among its tombs that of Tang He, who was one of the Ming dynasty founders. The *"ruins of the Imperial City of the Middle Capital and stone in-scriptions at the Imperial Mausoleum" here are now under State Coun-cil protection. It also has the Temple of King Yu. One of the first attempts at the "Responsibility System" was started here in 1978. Accommo-dations at the 118-bed **Nanshan Hotel** 南山宾馆 . C.I.T.S. branch.

Tunxi 屯溪 , in the very SE corner of Anhui, has a kiwi fruit cannery, tea processing workshop, ink slab factory, bamboo weaving factory, and Ming and Qing buildings. The kiwi fruit has also been known as the Chinese gooseberry, so you can ask if China or New Zealand had it first. This is a gateway to Huangshan and has an airport. The **Huashan Hotel** 华山饭店 here has 100 beds. C.I.T.S. branch.

Hengshan (Mt. Hengshan)

There are several of these Hengshans, not all the names writ-
ten the same in Chinese. Of the two most worthwhile to see is
Hengshan 山西恒山 *in Shanxi province, 2 hours' drive on a*
country road SE of Datong. Along the way are remains of an-
cient beacon towers (see "Great Wall") and mud cave houses
similar to those around Yan'an. Note the windows covered
with folk art or paper cuts.

The main attraction here is the very breath-taking ***Temple-in-Mid-**
Air, a.k.a. Suspending Temple 悬空寺 . A marvel of cliffside architecture, the temple literally clings to an almost vertical mountainside,
some of its 40 small pavilions supported by wooden poles and beams,
some by manmade rock foundations, some by natural stone. A trip here
is not for people afraid of heights nor for people over 180 lbs., as the

walks are narrow and involve many steep stairs. Its primitive washroom is also suspended in "midair."

This temple was first built over 1400 years ago (Northern Wei) and rebuilt in the Tang, Jin, Ming, and Qing dynasties. Its clay statues are not well done so are probably not originals. The bronze and iron castings and stone and wood carvings are older.

Farther up into the mountains, past the reservoir, about 30 minutes' drive, is a newly built pavilion and a better rest room. From this point you can see a group of temples scattered farther uphill. The mid-air temple can be done in one day from Datong. No hotels. Better take your own lunch.

Hengshan #2 湖南衡山 is in Hunan province, about 310 km south of Changsha, South China. It is one of the Five Great Mountains of China, with 72 peaks and innumerable Buddhist temples. The most noteworthy of the temples is at Nanyue, occupying 98,000 square meters. First erected in 725 (Tang), it has Song and Ming architecture. A hotel and botanical garden are also on the mountain.

Hohhot (Huhehot) 呼和浩特

North China. The capital of Inner Mongolia (a.k.a. Nei Mong-gol) Autonomous Region can be reached by train or a little-over-an-hour plane ride from Beijing. It is NW of Beijing in the south central part of the province. But it is only for the strong, adventurous traveler who likes to rough it and doesn't mind a mutton diet. The best time to visit is June and July. The highest temperature in Hohhot then is 28°C, but the nights are cool. The winters are very cold, with a ⁻32°C low, and you need longjohns even in early May. The spring and summer have sandstorms; the annual precipitation is between a scant 50 and 450 mm, mostly late summer and early autumn. The altitude is 1000 meters above sea level and it has from 90 to 160 frostfree days. The urban population is 500,000.

Inner Mongolia is of historical and religious importance. The Mongols, one of the nationalities living here, united under Genghis Khan in 1206, and their descendents went on to conquer the rest of China and then parts of Europe in the 13th and 14th centuries.

The traditional religion, as reflected now in its monasteries and temples, is a distinctive branch of Buddhism known as Lamaism, and is related to that of Tibet.

Hohhot dates from the Ming, at least 400 years ago. It was called Guisui under the Nationalists. After Liberation it was renamed Hohhot

(Green City), the name preferred by the natives. In the past, Nei Mongol has been a home for nomads. Today its population includes Han, Daur, Ewenki, Oroqen, Hui, Manchu, Korean, and, of course, Mongolian nationalities.

In summer, visitors can travel out from here, if they wish, and sleep in a yurt in the countryside. You can ride camels and camel carts, try Mongolian bows and arrows, and also drink tea laced with milk, butter, and grain, said to be very filling and great for cold winter days. It is too greasy for hot weather. If you are a good rider you will be allowed to try the famous Mongolian ponies and camels. Camel riding is uncomfortable, but at least you can have your picture taken on a two-humped shaggy Bactrian if it's not summer, the season when they shed and look awful. Visitors can go to one of three rural communities located 90–180 km away, usually by jeep on roads cut through the flat grasslands.

A yurt.

Real yurts are made of compressed sheep's wool with paper windows. They are shaped somewhat like igloos, and can be folded up and carried by camel. Eight people can put up a large one in 40 minutes. Visitors staying in yurts sleep on padded mattresses described by one tourist as "hard but comfortable." Everything smells of sheep. Unless things have changed, there is no running water, but there are outdoor toilets. The people are charming and wear their traditional costumes. Ask about Mongolian wrestling. The hospitable Mongols will even sing for you in your yurt.

The art in Lamaist monasteries is full of gory scenes of hell and torture. Reincarnation is central, but much superstition has crept into the theology. Monks are frequently lamas, reincarnations of previous monks. Hohhot used to have many temples but they were destroyed "by the imperialists and Nationalists." Among the survivors is the oldest **Dazhao Temple** 大召庙 (Ming) with a rare silver Buddha and many musical instruments, the **Xiaozhao Temple** 小召 and the Wutasi Temple. The **Wutasi (Five Dagoba Temple)** 五塔寺 was founded in the Ming. The tallest of its dagobas is 6.26 meters and they are made of glazed bricks carved with Buddhist symbols and inscribed in three languages: Mongolian, Sanskrit, and Tibetan. Behind the pagodas is a Mongolian astrological chart. The **White Pagoda** 白塔 on the eastern outskirts of the city at the Xilitu Lamasery is from the 10th century and is 40 meters and seven stories high. Inside are native tapestries. Ask also about the **Wudang Lamasery.** For more on Lamaism, see "Lhasa."

The **Tomb of Wang Zhaojun** 王昭君坟 is 10 km south of the city. About 2000 years old, she was an imperial Han concubine, married off to a Xiongnu tribal chief to form an important political alliance. A bit of climbing. The **Great Mosque** 清真大寺 is in Chinese architecture. Hohhot also has the **Provincial Museum** 内蒙古博物馆 .

Entertainment

Folk songs and dances are distinct, accompanied by a mandolinlike instrument. Show-jumping, saber fighting, horseback acrobatics, and horse racing are on a 2000-meter course in north Hohhot. Don't be surprised if you see Mongolian horsemen in English riding habits on English saddles.

Shopping

Today, in addition to less exotic goods, Nei Mongol produces woolen textiles, carpets, and tapestries. It also manufactures Mongolian-style riding boots, sabers, saddles, stirrups, and felt stockings. Long-haired goatskin rugs and typical Mongolian silk jackets fancy enough to wear to dinner parties are relatively cheap. Also available are antique bottles of jade or agate. Try the **Hohhot National Commodity Factory,** the **Hohhot Antique Shop,** and the **Hohhot Carpet Factory.** The **Hohhot Zhongshan Rd. Department Store** has been featured in *China Daily* as the "fastest growing store in the whole country." There, one has been able to buy imported as well as traditional Mongolian goods.

Food

Meat, mainly mutton, but also beef. Notable are barbecued lamb, mutton hot pot, sesame pancakes, braised oxtail, beef kabab, ox tendon in egg white, camel hoof, and *facai* (the edible black hairlike algae that is a favorite in China, especially at New Year's because its name sounds like "prosperity.") Delicacies also include braised bear's paw, braised elk's nose, and crisp fried hazel grouse—but please make sure these are not wild, endangered species.

Hotels

Inner Mongolia Hotel 内蒙古旅游馆店 □ *Wulanchabuxi Rd., 15 km from airport* □ 1985. Dance hall, Chinese and Western food, air conditioning, electronic games, stores. This is the main hotel. 500 beds; 20 stories; 11 restaurants. Low season November–April, 20% discount.

Xincheng (New City) Hotel　新城宾馆　□ *23 Hulun South Rd., 15 km from airport* □ Western and Chinese food. This is the second best hotel.

Hohhot Guest House　呼和浩特宾馆　□ *7 Ying Bin Rd., 20 km from airport* □ Over 100 beds.

Also in this large province are Xilinhot and Baotou, under separate listings.

Huangshan Mountain　黄山

East China in southern Anhui province. Huangshan is 120 km in circumference, and is one of China's most spectacular mountains. A climb has been described by one writer as "walking into an unending Chinese landscape painting." Huangshan can be reached by train from Hefei, Beijing, and Nanjing, and also by bus. The airport at Tunxi, 75 km away, is served from Shanghai, Hefei, or Hangzhou. Tours have been organized by C.T.S. Hangzhou. Visitors can also travel by ship from Shanghai and Nanjing, to Chizhou or Wuhu, and then bus to Huangshan. The coldest time of year is January, with a mean daily temperature of ⁻3.2°C. The warmest is in July, with a mean daily temperature of 17.7°C. Annual precipitation is 2395 mm, mainly from June to September.

The highest of the 72 peaks, **Lian Hua (Lotus Flower)**　莲花峰 rises 1873 meters above sea level. To reach the valley before the final ascent to the top means climbing 800 stone steps cut into an 80° cliff, nose almost to rock.

One section of the second highest, **Tian Du (Heavenly Capital Peak)**　天都峰 (1810 meters), is a ridge less than a meter wide called "Carp's Backbone." Although iron chain railings exist to assure the unsure, some people resort to crawling to get across. This is just to say that Huangshan is for the very strong and adventurous, who will be rewarded by giant vertical peaks, pines (at least one over 1000 years old), hot springs (42°C), lots of streams, mist, magnificent views, and a great feeling of achievement—if you make it.

But there's hope. A **cable car**　缆车 , China's longest, should be operating to the North Sea Hotel in 1987 for the less energetic. It will rise from the Cloud Valley Monastery. Until it starts operating, weak climbers are advised to hire someone to carry their belongings. Some people have hired bearers at something like ¥300 a day to carry themselves up in a sedan chair, but having human beasts of burden is so

distasteful that I certainly don't recommend it. C.I.T.S. advises no leather
or plastic soles, or slippers. The climb is not easy. Take a walking
stick, water bottle, and some food, and do not climb alone, here or
anywhere else in the world.

If you only have one day, you have a choice. C.I.T.S. suggests
taking a bus at 7:30 a.m. to Cloud Valley Monastery and then beginning
to climb. Check about the bus the night before. At about 11 a.m. and
3000 stone steps higher, you will arrive at the **Beihai (North Sea) Hotel.** This place is noted for its strangely shaped pines and weathered
rocks. The Refreshing Terrace should give you a view of a sea of clouds.
Now you have to return the way you came, but if you stay here overnight, this is the best place to see the sunrise. If you do not stay overnight, you can retrace your climb (about 3 hours) and take the bus back
to the hotel at the base. This hotel has been in such demand by hikers
that all rooms have three beds, and guests have also slept on floors.

A second descent is via the **Jade Screen Tower** 玉屏楼 and the
Heavenly Capital Peak. Hostels in each of these places serve Chinese
and some Western food. That at the "delightful" Jade Screen has been
described by one foreigner as "excellent." Travelers, however, have
complained about the shortage of water for washing, the hole-in-the-
ground toilets, and the dirty blankets.

As with most mountains in China, paths are crowded with hikers
during the summer at Huangshan. The end of April is said to be the
most beautiful time, and hiking is good to the end of October.

A Ming village with over 100 temples, ancestral halls, pagodas,
bridges, pavilions, and other relics collected from that period is planned
for the foot of Purple Cloud Peak.

Shopping

Paintings of Huangshan, Huangshan tea, bamboo and straw curtains. It is traditional to buy a special stone and find someone to carve
your name on it.

Hotels

Some of the following hotels have several branches.

Cloud Valley Villa 云谷寺招待所 ☐ Chinese-style hotel. 1985.

Heavenly Capital Hotel 天都宾馆 ☐ U.S.-Japan-Huangshan joint
project, near Huangshan Guest House. 1986.

Huangshan Guest House 黄山宾馆 ☐ *Near hot spring* ☐ 1955;
renovated 1984.

Yupinglou (Jade Screen) Hotel 玉屏楼 ☐ Jade Screen Resort,
halfway up mountain. 1955; renovated 1984. 24 beds.

Beihai (North Sea) Hotel 北海宾馆 ☐ North Sea Resort. 1700-
meter altitude. 1958; renovated 1984. 112 beds.

Taoyuan (Peach Spring) Hotel 桃源宾馆 ☐ Hot Spring Scenic
Resort. 1979; renovated 1985. 134 beds. Swimming pool, coffee shop,

Friendship Store, theater, dance hall, Chinese and Western food. Huangshan specialties available here are stewed chicken with stone mushrooms, shrimps and Maojen tea, and fried stone frog.

Other Important Addresses

C.I.T.S. 中国国际旅行社   and **C.T.S.** 中国民航公司 : near Hot Spring, to the left of Peach Spring Hotel; tel. 206 or 377. These can arrange a hiking tour with English or Japanese-speaking guide-inter- preters.
Peach Spring Hotel Dining Room: tel. 388.
Arts and Crafts Shop 工艺美术商店 : tel. 244.
Bus Station 汽车站 : tel. 210.
Friendship Store 友谊商店 : tel. 200.
Huangshan Painting Shop 黄山画社 : tel. 334.

Jiangmen 江门

(Kiangmen; Cantonese Kongmoon) South China in Guangdong province on the Pearl River, about 100 km south of Guang- zhou. This old waterfront city can be reached by public or tourist bus from Guangzhou, but it can also be reached easily by daily nonstop 4-hour ferry leaving 8:15 a.m. from Hong Kong.

This former foreign treaty port is also a cheap overnight passenger boat ride from Guangzhou, an interesting experience, to say the least. Several ferries leave daily from about 1 km east of the Overseas Chinese Mansion in Guangzhou. The night boat leaves before sunset, so you have a chance to see the never-ending river traffic, the maze of tributar- ies and canals, many lined with breakwaters, irrigation gates, and fac- tories. If you're lucky, you'll have a full moon—and it's beautiful! You are in another world.

You sleep (if you can—it's somewhat noisy) 12 abreast on wooden platforms, softened only by straw mats and separated from fellow pas- sengers by four-inch-high dividers. Upper and lower platforms line three sides of the room. You could have over 60 roommates, some of them curious, some friendly, but all discreet. Although few women travel this way, I've never felt threatened. No privacy exists, not even for bathing, which is from a very public sink (with brown river water). The toilets, however, are in tiny, private cubicles, a hole in the floor through which you can see river water rushing by (and also your pants, if you don't hang on tight!) You can rent pillows and sheets and buy proletarian food. Boiled hot drinking water is available, but you should have had the foresight to carry your own mug and towel, like all the other passengers.

At dawn, or sometimes before, you find the boat entering a canal. You wait for the lock behind you (built in 1978) to be closed and the water raised before you go on to disembark at Jiangmen. In Jiangmen there is an Overseas Chinese village and a "comprehensive factory," the Jiangmen Sugarcane Chemical Plant, where they make medicinal alcohol, paper, and sugar. A public bus can take you to Xinhui in about 20 minutes.

Jiangmen has prospered in the last few years and now has six hotels and a huge department store with a revolving rooftop restaurant. Two fifths of the people here are Overseas Chinese or have Overseas Chinese relatives and therefore receive remittances from abroad. The **Donghu (East Lake) Hotel** is at 15, Gangkou Road.

Jilin (Kirin) 吉林

Northeast China, in the center of Jilin province, 130 km east of the capital Changchun. Population nearly one million. It can be reached by rail from Beijing, Changchun, Shenyang, Harbin, Tianjin, etc. Like the rest of the area formerly known as Manchuria, this also is extremely cold, with snow in winter and average minimum temperature December–February of $^-24°C-^-15°C$.

By Chinese standards, Jilin is young, only about 300 years old. The Japanese took over in 1931, but were forced to leave in 1945. Tourist attractions include **Beishan Park,** with 200-year-old buildings and a good view of the city, and the **Deer Farm at Longtan Hill,** which produces antlers (for aphrodisiacs), ginseng, and sable. Also of interest are the ginseng gardens, the **Jilin Exhibition Hall** 吉林展览馆 (with a 1770-kg meteorite, believed to be the largest in the world), and **Jiangnan Park. Songhua Lake** 松花湖 is a 480-square-km manmade lake, and is 20 km from the city center.

Jilin probably has the best alpine skiing in China, but the sport is very new, so don't expect international quality. A 1800-meter-long ski chair lift services its 3.5-square-km "professional" ski area, with runs at least 3050 meters and 2600 meters long. It is 16 km from the city at Fengman. Two additional cableways should be operating by winter 1987. Best skiing is December–February. Beginners should be able to rent skis; experts should bring their own. Another tow is planned for Songhua Lake.

Southeast of the city are the **Changbai Mountains,** their highest peak 2691 meters. In this crater is beautiful **Heaven Lake,** and on the other side is Korea.

Food

　　Local specialties include venison, frog oil soup, steamed whitefish, raw salmon and carp, and chicken and ginseng in earthenware pots.

Hotels

　　Dongguan Hotel □ *Songjiang Rd.* □ and **Xiguan Hotel** □ *Songjiang Rd.*

Jinan (Tsinan) 济南

North China. The capital of Shandong is due south of Beijing, almost on the south shore of the Huanghe (Yellow River), at the junction of the Beijing-Shanghai railway and the Qingdao-Jinan Railway. Jinan can also be reached by plane from Beijing (1¼ hours), Nanjing (1¾ hours), Hefei (1½ hours), and Shanghai. It is on the main Beijing-Guangzhou train line. The climate is temperate. Hottest in late July to early August, averaging around 27°C; coldest in January, averaging ⁻2°C. Annual precipitation is about 700 mm, mainly in July and August. Population is 1.2 million urban.

　　Jinan dates as a city with a wall from the sixth century B.C., when it was made capital of the State of Qi. However, it was settled here more than 5000 years ago by neolithic cultures, the Dawenkou and the Longshan. It was named Jinan, meaning "south of the Ji River," a name that has been kept even though that river dried up centuries ago.

　　Jinan was a busy commercial center during the Tang, and Marco Polo wrote favorably of its garden atmosphere and its thriving silk industry after he visited it during the Yuan. It has been the capital since the Ming. It is now an industrial center producing trucks, textiles, and paper, and as a tourist destination, famous primarily for its springs, its Buddhist temples, and its proximity to Taishan Mountain.

　　The excellent quality of the water in this "City of Springs" was first recorded 2500 years ago by a geographer. The Chinese kept records of pretty well everything! During the Jin (1115–1234), someone else listed 72 springs on a tablet. He missed a few. A 1964 survey mentions 108 natural springs.

　　The "springs" are not just holes in the ground spouting water. They are fountains, wells, and pools, and have been embellished with gardens, rockery, pavilions, and tea houses. The water was forced to the earth's surface here by a subterranean wall of volcanic rock. But unless you have a water fixation, a trip to one or two groupings will suffice.

　　The **Baotu Quan (Jet Spring)** 豹突泉 (tel. 22716), in the SW

corner of the Old City, is said to be the best, with 16 fountains and the greatest amount of water. In the center of the city, this park covers about nine acres. The ''jet spring'' is west from the entrance along a stone pathway by a stream. It is in the center of a square pond, three separate sprays of bubbling water gushing almost a foot high. Take some crumbs to attract the giant red and black carp. The Guanlan Ting (Pavilion for Watching the Willows), the square structure with the red columns and gray tiles, is Ming. The walls around the exhibition center have more than 20 stone engravings from both the Ming and the Qing. In the Wanghe Ting (Pavilion for Watching Cranes), you can judge for yourself if the water is unusually good. It is now used as a tea house.

The **Jinxian Quan (Gold Thread Spring)** 金线泉 is east from the Cranes in the NE corner of the Shangzhi Tang (Hall of High Aspiration).

Also in this park is an exhibition center featuring arts and crafts made in the province. Here you should see feather paintings, shell mosaics, woolen embroidery, and filigree.

The **Heihu Quan (Black Tiger Spring Park)** 黑虎泉 (tel. 20366) is another of the ''four most famous springs'' of Jinan. It is in the SE corner of the Old City, a 10-minute walk from the east side of Jet Spring. By now you should have learned that ''quan'' means ''spring.'' In this park the water gushes from the mouths of three stone tigers. Does it sound like the roar of tigers? Nearby is the 11-meters-high Liberation Monument, where the old wall once stood and where the People's Liberation Army forced its way into the city in 1948. The monument can be climbed for a good view of the Black Tiger Spring.

The third famous spring is the **Zhenzhu Quan (Pearl Spring)** 珍珠泉, in the courtyard of the Pearl Spring Auditorium, again in the Old City near a flowering crabapple tree planted in the Song. I told you the Chinese keep records of everything! The park was recently repaired and expanded. The **Five-Dragon Pool** 五龙潭 completes the list of ''four famous springs.'' It is outside the West Gate and was the site of a famous Tang general's home. It is now home to more carp, weighing up to nine kg each. Did you know that carp will eat food from your hand? Anything that big, however, might take a finger too.

At this point, especially if you are short of time, head for the outskirts. Take in the **Qianfo (Thousand-Buddha) Hill** 千佛山 (tel. 21792), 2½ km south of the city. The name is misleading since there are fewer than that. Here you find Buddhist images carved into the side of a cliff. Much climbing is involved to see the **Xingguo Si (Revive the Nation Temple)** 兴国寺, with 60–70 buddhas from 20 centimeters to over three meters tall, ranging from the Sui to the Tang. Look for three caves at the foot of the cliff and in the rooms of the west courtyard of the temple. There you find, yes, more buddhas and historical relics! Buddhism became popular here in the Sui dynasty.

In the **Yilan Ting (Pavilion of Panoramic View)** 一览亭, the

tallest building around, you can get a good view of Jinan. An even better view can be had from the top of the hill, especially of Mount Jueshan to the east. On **Jueshan** you can see the 10-meters-high cave inside of which is a buddha head, seven meters tall.

West of Xingguo Temple about 3 km, is the **Yellowstone Cliff** 黄茅岗 a 40-meter-high rock around which were carved more Buddhas, and heavens!—flying devas—some of them nude! These were made during the Northern Wei, about 1600 years ago.

A stimulating time to visit this temple is on the ninth day of the ninth lunar month, when the hill is full of chrysanthemums and market stalls are set up. While some people may find it crowded (beware of pickpockets!), you can experience the excitement of a festival.

If you have a half day left and your own vehicle, you can head to either **Liubu** 柳阜 , 34 km south, or the **Lingyan Temple** 灵岩寺 , which is closer. Both are important and usually take a full day each in a tour bus. Liubu has even more (210) and better Buddhist statues in five grottoes, most from the Tang, but some from the Song, Yuan, and Ming. In the **Qianfo (Thousand-Buddha) Cliff,** these range from 2.85 meters down to 20 centimeters high. Look for the Buddha called Blessing, ordered for Tang Emperor Taizong by one of his daughters, in much the same spirit as one donates a statue of the Virgin in a Catholic church on someone else's behalf.

The center of Buddhism for the province was at the **Shentong Si (Temple of Magical Power)** at the site of the current Tongtian Yu (Valley that Leads to Heaven). The **Long-hu (Dragon-Tiger) Tower** (Tang) has carvings of dragons, warriors, tigers, and devas. Are these devas (or good spirits) clothed? Look for yourself! The miniature pagodas are tombstones of abbots from the now extinct Temple of Magical Powers. Look for the one-story, 15-meter-high square **Simen* (Four-Door Tower)** 四门塔 . At 1400 years of age, this is the oldest single-story tower of stone in the country. Note the thickness of the walls. A thousand-year-old pine protects its NE corner.

Only 3 km south is the **Jiuding (Temple of the Nine Pagodas)** 九鼎寺 . Here is the very unusually designed octagonal Nine-Spire Pagoda, probably dating from the Sui. Inside are murals from the Ming and Qing. Can you see the remnants of even older murals these have covered?

The remnants of a 12.6-by-10.7-meter platform, believed to be from the Tang, should be of interest to music and dance lovers, as it is carved with dancers and singers holding musical instruments.

The ***Lingyan Si (Magic Cliff or Intelligent Rock) Temple** in Changqing county is one of the ''four finest temples'' in China. The temple was founded by a famous monk in A.D. 354 who was much moved by the beauty of the surroundings and whose sermons caused birds to listen, animals to stop, and even a rock nearby to nod in agreement. Hence the name. The current temple is from the Tang. The temple expanded in the Song when over 1000 monks studied and worshiped here. Surviving the centuries are the rock grotto from the Northern Wei, the Tang halls and pavilions, the Song clay images, and various rock carvings. Important to see is its **Thousand Buddha Hall,** built in the Tang, and repaired in the Song, Yuan, and Ming. Here are three large statues of Buddha, one of wood and two of bronze. The 40 painted clay arhats are very lively and about 102 centimeters tall. Northwest of this hall is the nine-story, 52.4-meter-high **Pizhi Pagoda** from the Tang, restored in the Song. It can be climbed for a good view. The iron spire on the top is unusual, with its eight or nine Buddhist wheels chained together. Also important is the **Imperial Study Hall,** first built in A.D. 629 and used by the famous Tang monk Xuan Zhuang, who made the pilgrimage to India. A 2000-year-old cypress is still growing nearby.

To the west is another cemetery with 200 tiny dagobas marking the graves of monks, no two dagobas the same. This is the second best graveyard of this nature in the country. (See Shaolin Temple in "Zhengzhou"). Guess which dagoba belongs to the Tang dynasty temple's founder, Huichong? The most impressive one, of course! This 5.3-meter pagoda is similar to the square Four-Door Tower in Liu Bu, and decorated with dancers, devas (with or without?) and lion heads.

Jicuizhengmen or Zhengmeng Hall　积翠证盟殿　on the hill is really a cave, with a 3-meter-high Buddha flanked by four lesser Buddhas from the Tang. The cliffside to the right looks polished, and therefore was named "Mirror Cliff." You can climb Lingyan Mountain for the exercise and the view if you want.

If you have more time in the city, see the **Daming Pool**　大明湖 (pronounced Dah Ming not Damming; tel. 22808, 23800). Here you find 80 hectares of park, of which a little more than half is lake. Some remains of the Ming and Qing wall may also be of interest. In the NW corner is graffiti by Song General Yue Fei, called here a national hero, but if you look up his tomb in "Hangzhou," you will discover what actually happened to him. The best pavilion here is the Lixia Pavilion in the middle of the lake, first erected about 1500 years ago. The current pavilion was built in 1747, young by Chinese standards. The **Beiji (North Pole) Tower**　北极塔　is with a group of structures on the north side of the lake, constructed in the Yuan and renovated in the Ming.

The **Shandong Provincial Museum**　山东省博物馆　(Wenhua Xi Rd.; tel. 20486) contains both historical and natural history relics. The history dates from neolithic times and includes Sun Bin's famous treatise on the art of war, written on bamboo about 2000 years ago. Also note the frescoes from Sui dynasty tombs, musical instruments, calligraphy, and paintings from the tomb of the Prince of Lu (Ming), rubbings from a Han tomb showing the aristocratic lifestyle, and musical instruments from the Confucian Family Mansion in Qufu.

You need a couple of days really to see **Taishan,** over 50 km away, and **Qufu,** the hometown of philosopher Confucius, 140 km south.

Taishan is listed under "Tai'an." Both are very worthwhile. **Yidu** is near Camel Mountain, with six Buddhist grottoes and a county museum. ***Linzi,** the former capital of Qi, is from the Zhou dynasty. Also convenient by train are Qingdao and Zibo. In the province also are Yantai, Weihai, and Weifang. See separate listings.

Southwest of Jinan at the Shandong-Henan border is the longest bridge in China. The 10,282-meter railway bridge spans the Yellow River and is 3500 meters longer than the Yangtze River bridge at Nanjing. It was completed in 1985.

Shopping

Made in the province are human hair and silk embroidery and lace (Jinan Embroidery Factory); feather pictures (lovely) and dough modeling (yes, they do last!) both from the Jinan Fine Arts Factory. The province also produces Qingdao (Tsingtao) Beer, the most popular Chinese beer. The main shopping area is Quancheng Rd. and also along Jin 2-Rd.

Arts and Crafts Shop (west of Heihuquan Park; tel. 24795); **Daguanyuan Market** (Jing 4-Rd. and Wei 2-Rd.; tel. 22245), this also includes a folk arts theater and a cinema; **Department Store** (Quancheng Rd.; tel. 23442); **Foreign Languages Bookstore** (Chaoshan St.; tel. 24675); **Friendship Store** (3/F Department Store; tel. 23442); **Jinan Antique Store** (Jing 3-Rd. and Wei 2-Rd.; tel. 22761); **No. 1 Department Store** (Jing 2-Rd. and Wei 4-Rd.; tel. 33258); **Shandong Antique Store** (west of Department Store, 321 Quancheng Rd.; tel. 23446); **Xinhua Bookstore** (Jing 2-Rd. and Wei 3-Rd.).

Restaurants

Exotic local fare are cattail, lotus roots and lotus seeds from Daming lake, roast duck, winding-thread cakes, and monkey head mushroom.

Jufengde Restaurant □ *100 Jing-3 Rd.; tel. 33905.*

Huiquan Restaurant □ *Quancheng Rd. and Baotuquan Bei Rd.; tel. 21202* □ In the Huiquan Hotel. Especially good is the sweet and sour Yellow River carp.

Daming Lake Restaurant □ *outside the south gate of the park; tel. 20584* □ Its Bapi Guozi is good for breakfast.

Hotels

Jinan Hotel 济南饭店 □ *Jing 3-Rd. and Wei 6-Rd.* □ Western and Chinese food. 1.5 km from the railway station and closer to shopping and the C.I.T.S. office than the Nanjiao. 4 km from the airport. 140 beds. Auditorium, coffee shop, store selling paintings and rubbings, and clinic.

Nanjiao (South Suburbs) Guest House 南郊宾馆 □ *2 Binguan Rd., in the south suburbs; 5 km from the railway station and 10 from the airport* □ Five stories, 625 beds. Chinese and Western food. Bookstall, taxis, auditorium, indoor swimming pool, recreation room, and clinic.

Qi Lu Hotel □ *Jingshi Rd.; telex 39144* □ 1985. Best in town. 5 stories, about 250 rooms. Swimming pool.

Other Important Addresses

Bank of China: 201 Jing 2-Rd.; tel. 24672. Both hotels and the Friendship and Shandong Antique stores can change money.
C.I.T.S. and **C.T.S.:** Jinan Hotel, Jing 3-Rd. and Wei 6-Rd.; tel. 35351, 35352.
Telegram inquiries: tel. 34183.
Long Distance: tel. 113.
Directory inquiries: tel. 114.
First-Aid station: tel. 20900.
Foreign Affairs Section of the Jinan Municipal Bureau of Public Security: 54 Wei 5-Rd.; tel. 35778.
Shandong Travel and Tourism: tel. 43423; cable 7139.
Taxis: Try your hotel first. Otherwise, the Jinan Taxi Company; tel. 34986. Taxi station at the railway station (tel. 24766) and at the South Gate (tel. 24439).
Hospital: In case of illness, if convenient, try the clinic in your hotel. Otherwise, the **Hospital of the Shandong Medical College:** Wenhua Xi Rd. (tel. 21941); the **Shandong People's Hospital:** Jing 5-Rd. and Wei 7-Rd. (tel. 35521); **Qianfoshan Hospital,** Jing 10-Rd. (tel. 43731).

Jingdezhen (Chingtechen) 景德镇

South China. Northeast Jiangxi province NE of Nanchang. A must for porcelain lovers. It was from here that some of the best was shipped to Europe centuries ago, including the famous blue-and-white. Today Jingdezhen is still producing some of the best porcelain in China, a combination of the right clay, abundant pine wood for fuel, and easy transport (on the Yangtze). The city was founded in the Han and is considered one of China's Three Ancient Cities.

Jingdezhen can be reached by small plane in 70 minutes from Nanchang daily except Sundays, or by road, usually leaving Nanchang after breakfast and arriving about 4 p.m., with a stop for lunch. It can be reached by ship via Jiujiang, or by rail from Nanchang or Nanjing, or with a change to a bus at Yingtan, from Beijing, Fuzhou, etc.

Visitors are usually taken to their choice of different factories, each with its own specialty. The *site of the Hutian Porcelain Kiln, dating

from the Five Dynasties (white glazed) to the Song (celadon) and Ming
(blue-and-white), is under State Council protection as a historical monument.

Nanshi, on Pearl Hill, is the site of the Ming and Qing imperial
kilns. The town itself is surrounded by mountains and the Yangtze. The
town also has a Pottery and Porcelain Exhibition Hall, the Ceramic Institute, and the Pottery and Porcelain College.

The **Jingdezhen Hotel** is on the outskirts of the city, with 200
beds, a porcelain shop, and a dining room. It is the main hotel and is 4
km from the railway station and 8 km from the airport.

Jinggang Shan (Chingkang Mountains) 井冈山

*South China. Mao Zedong (Mao Tze-tung) led his forces after
the Autumn Harvest Uprising in 1927 to this 275-square-km
mountain range in Jiangxi province near the Hunan border.
Here the Communists established a base, carrying out land
reform among the peasants. Forced to flee by the scorched-
earth campaign of the Nationalists, the Communists embarked
on the now legendary Long March to Yan'an in October 1934.*

Mao's former residence, the **Jinggang Shan Revolutionary Museum**   井冈山革命历史博物馆   , and other revolutionary sites are
open to the public. These are mainly centered around the town of Ciping (Tseping) 茨坪 . The battles against the Nationalists, who were
trying to rid the country of the Communists, took place mainly in the
five major mountain passes. These are Bamianshan, Huangyangjie,
Shuangmashi, Tongmuling, and Zhushachong. A visit to any of these
will show you how difficult it was to destroy the base.

The mountains are now being promoted as a tourist resort rather
than a revolutionary monument. They are very beautiful, with steep
cliffs and deep valleys in the south. One of many caves, the **Feilong
Dong (Flying Dragon) Cave** 飞龙洞 can hold several hundred people.
Its height ranges from 1 to 60 meters. Also of note are the **Youji Dong
(Guerrillas Cave)** 游击洞 and **Shuilian Dong (Water Curtain Cave)**
水帘洞 . Waterfalls are at Ciping, Liujiaping, Changping (130 meters
high), and Longtan (Dragon Pool). The highest mountain is 1428 meters.

Larger in area than Lushan (also in Jiangxi province), Jinggang
Shan has guesthouses, hotels, and reception houses, the latter for Chinese
workers, operated by their work units. A modern paper mill and bamboo handicraft factory are located here.

In Ciping 茨坪 are also a cinema, restaurants, and library. At press time, it could be reached by a 2-day drive (about 300 km) from Nanchang in the north (overnight stop in Ji An) or by road from the south. Public buses may be available when you visit, but are probably a long, dusty ride. If you find an easier way, please let us know.

Jiujiang 九江

(Kiukiang, Chiuchiang, a.k.a. Xunyang) South China. Northern Jiangxi province on the south bank of the Yangtze River, where it bends south between Wuhan and Nanjing. It is bounded on the east by Poyang Lake and Mt. Lushan on the south. Accessible by train from Nanchang or passenger boat along the Yangtze, this 2000-year-old city has been used as a port for the porcelain city of Jingdezhen since ancient times. It was also a treaty port. The population is 200,000.

Of interest to visitors are the **Yanshui Pavilion** 烟水亭 in the middle of Lake Gantang, an 1840-square-meter island covered with gardens, hall, and pavilions; and the **causeway between Lake Gantang and Lake Nanmen** 甘棠湖和南门湖之间的长堤 , built in A.D. 821. Also important to see are the **Dasheng Pagoda** 大胜塔 in Nengren Temple and the **Suojiang Tower.**

The **Nanhu Hotel** is on the side of South Lake, with villas. Also in the vicinity are the **Xiufeng Hotel** 秀峰宾馆 in Xingzi, the **Yingtan Overseas Chinese Hotel** 鹰潭华侨饭店 , and **Jinggangshan Hotel** 井冈山宾馆 .

Jiuquan 酒泉

Northwest China. Western part of Gansu province, on the southern edge of the Gobi desert, Jiuquan can be reached by plane from Dunhuang, and from Lanzhou in almost 2 hours. Trains also from Beijing, Shanghai, and Urumqi.

Jiuquan is best known because it is only 30 km from the western end of the Great Wall, but it has an identity of its own. About 1650 years ago, government officials and high-ranking military officers were sent here to develop the region and to protect commerce on the Silk Road.

Its imposing **Bell and Drum Tower** 鼓楼 was originally built in A.D. 343 and was renovated in the Qing. The **Jiuquan County Museum** 酒泉博物馆 is also in the city, with relics from the ancient tombs, including painted bricks. The "wine spring," the Western Han relic after which the city is named, is in the east of the city in **Jiuquan Park** 酒泉公园 . A legend relates how the famous Han General Ho Qubing (illegitimate son of the sister of the empress) once poured a victory gift of wine into this spring in order to share the wine with his soldiers.

The other city attraction is the **Luminous Jade Cup Factory** 玉杯 厂, where eggshell thin goblets of ''jade'' are made. These four attractions are within walking distance of the Jiuquan Hotel (½ km to 1½ km).

Twenty-one km north, on the way to the Great Wall, are the **Wei-Jin Tombs** 魏晋墓群 and tombs from the Sixteen States period. These are in an area 20 km north-south and 3 km wide. The Eastern Jin murals, predating those of Dunhuang, show people at work and reveal a great deal about life 1600 years ago.

Jiayuguan Pass 嘉峪关 is between the Qilian Mountains and the Mazong Mountains, at the western end of the *Great Wall. The wall here has been restored. The city, which was also on the Silk Road, was built in 1372 when the first Ming emperor had the wall repaired and strengthened to keep out the defeated Mongols.

The end of the Great Wall is marked by a magnificent castle and three-story east and west gates. The tower can be climbed.

The **Jiuquan Hotel** 酒泉宾馆 , the only one in Jiuquan, was first built in 1958 and renovated in 1982 (2 Changmen St.; 30 km from the airport).

The **C.I.T.S.** 中国国际旅行社 branch is in the hotel (tel. 2943). **CAAC** 中国民航 is across the street (tel. 2136).

See also ''Great Wall'' and ''Silk Road.''

Kaifeng

Northwest China. Northern Henan on the Shanghai-Xi'an railway line, about 75 km east of the provincial capital Zhengzhou. It is on the southern bank of the Huanghe (Yellow River).

With a history of 2600 years, Kaifeng was the capital of several dynasties, including the Wei, Liang, Later Jin, Han, Later Zhou, Northern Song, and Jin. During the Song it was an important commercial and communications center, producing textiles, metalwork, porcelain, and printing. It was sacked by Jurched tribesmen in 1126 and never recovered its previous glory.

With 120 recorded Yellow River floods due to dams breaking near Kaifeng between 1194 and 1948, one wonders why Kaifeng exists at all. In 1642, during a peasant uprising led by Li Tzu-cheng, the Yellow River dike was destroyed by Ming forces so that the city was completely inundated and 372,000 people were killed. In 1938, the Nationalists destroyed the dam upriver near Zhengzhou in an attempt to stop the Japanese and 840,000 people died. Today, the riverbed, raised by centuries of silt deposits, is about 10 meters higher than ground level near Kaifeng.

Since Liberation, the Chinese have given top priority to controlling the Yellow River, and since 1984 the Chinese government and the United Nations World Grain Planning Program have worked together on an irrigation and warping project here.

Kaifeng is one of the 24 cities of historical importance protected by the State Council. It is laid out in the classic Chinese plan, and has a well-preserved city wall.

The 13-story ***Tie Ta ("Iron Pagoda")** 铁塔 was built over 900 years ago (Song). At a height of 54.6 meters, it is actually of glazed brick. The **Xiangguo Temple** 相国寺 , built in A.D. 555, was rebuilt in 1766 after the flood. It has a famous thousand-armed, thousand-eyed Buddha of gingko wood. The **Longting (Dragon Pavilion)** 龙亭 is at the site of the Northern Song palace. The existing buildings here are from the Qing, the stone lions in front from the Song. Also worth seeing are the **Yanqing Taoist Temple** 延庆观 and the **Guild Hall of Three Provinces** 山陕甘会馆 . The **Yuwang Miao (King Yu's Temple)** 禹王台 was built in the Ming in honor of Emperor Yu, who tried to control the floods. The bottom of the **Pota Pagoda** 繁塔 was built in 977, the top in the Qing, after the original was destroyed because of superstition.

Kaifeng is also famous for its embroidery, and its Jewish community, the remnants of which still remain today. A famous painting of the ancient city, "Qing Ming Festival at the Riverside," inspired the design of the Song Dynasty Village in Hong Kong. A Song dynasty city with Song tombs and people in Song costume may be ready for your visit to Kaifeng.

Because of its size and compactness, Kaifeng can be seen in a hurried 1-day visit, but better in two. It has a city museum, but the best relics are in the Provincial Museum in Zhengzhou.

Kaifeng's Acrobatic Troupe and its Circus with performing monkeys, bears, and goats, are well known.

Restaurants include the **Youyixin Restaurant** and the **Diyilou Steam Dumpling Restaurant.**

The **Kaifeng Guest House** 开封宾馆 is through the South Gate from the railway station. It has 119 rooms and serves Song dynasty food.

C.I.T.S. 国际旅行社   : 102 Ziyou Rd.; tel. 3737.

Kashi (Kashgar) 喀什（喀什噶尔）

Northwest China at the farwestern tip of Xinjiang province, about 100 km from the Soviet border. It can be reached by air (1500 km in 4 hours) from Urumqi for a 3-day excursion. It is also accessible by road, but not without a long, tiring, and sometimes spectacular journey.

Kashi is over 2000 years old and has been fought over by many contenders. In the mid-10th century, a Uygur-Turkish coalition, the Karahanids (Qurakhanid) Dynasty took over the area. Its leaders later converted to Islam and made Kashi their capital. Today it grows rice, wheat, fruit, and cotton. Like other cities of Xinjiang, it gives one a feeling more of west Asia than of China.

Kashi was on the Silk Road and is a center of Uygur culture. It is exotic, with many people wearing traditional national dress. Since its opening to tourists is comparatively recent, it should be considered by the adventurous only.

Visitors can see the huge **Abakh Hoja Tomb** 阿巴克和加麻扎 尔 (Ming and Qing), the final resting place of 70 descendents of Muhatum Ajam, an Islamic missionary. The **Idkah Mosque** 艾提朵尔清 真寺 , with its blue onion dome, is over 400 years old, one of the most important of the many mosques in the city. The **San Xian (Three Immortals) Buddhist Caves** 三仙洞 are north of the city and difficult to reach. Three rectangular holes high in the side of a cliff beckon the fit and curious. Unless they have been recently repaired, the frescoes inside are not in good condition.

Visitors can also tour the bazaar and a handicrafts workshop and local orchard.

Thirty km east of Kashi is the town of **Hanoi** 罕诺依 , abandoned after the 11th century and now just a ruin. In the area, one can also cruise **South Lake** 南湖 , but it is only a respite from all the dryness. South of the city and east of the Sino-Pakistan Highway toward Afghanistan are 7719-meter-high **Mt. Kongur** 公格尔冰山 and 7546-meter-high **Mt. Muztagta** 穆士塔格山 , part of the Pamirs. If you keep in mind that Hunza in Pakistan and Kashmir in India are also to the south, you will get an idea of the magnificence and isolation of the area here. Think Himalayas! You can see these snow-covered peaks from Kashi. Mountaineers can climb them.

Kashi produces handicrafts: gold and silver ornaments, rugs, jade carving, embroidered caps, daggers, and musical instruments. Its Sunday Bazaar is famous for its horse trading, and you will probably also find a lot of imported goods there in addition to the arts and crafts. The Silk Road has become the Electronics Road.

Kashi has two hotels, one of them the Kashgar Tourist Hotel. A third hotel with 500 beds was being built at press time. See also "Silk Road."

Kunming (a.k.a. Kunnanfu)

Southwest China. The capital of Yunnan province, which borders Vietnam, can be reached by train from Chengdu and by nonstop plane 2 hours each from Guangzhou and Changsha, and from Hong Kong. It is beautifully situated on the 330-sq.-km Dianchi Lake, China's sixth largest. Because of its altitude of 1894 meters and its subtropical location, it is blessed with the best weather in China, spring all year round. The hottest temperature is 29°C in July and the coldest ⁻1°C in January. Most rain falls from May to October. One of the loveliest times to visit is February, when the camellias are in bloom. Population: about 2 million rural and urban.

Kunming is important to see because of its mountain scenery, the colorfulness of its national minorities, the artistry and history of its temples and architecture, and the Stone Forest. The weather is a big attraction.

In the province also are several unusual sights. These range from almost year-round snow-capped mountains to tropical jungles where elephants and monkeys roam. One third of its over 10 million people belong to national minorities. Many of the groups, especially the women, still wear their distinctive clothes, even while working in the fields. Many still practice old customs—like the Dai **Water-Splashing Festival.** Kunming ranks in my books as the third most desirable tourist destination in China, after Beijing and Xi'an. One could easily spend two weeks in the province because it has such a variety of things to see and do.

Kunming itself has a history of 2400 years. The region has always been considered remote and resistent to the central government. The Xiaguan area was part of the Nanzhou empire, which refused to submit to the Tang but was subdued by the Mongols in the 13th century and visited by Marco Polo. The railway from Hanoi was built by the French in 1895, and Kunming was a French concession with a Catholic cathedral, convent, and French Club. The French wanted the province's tin, tungsten, and opium. It was also rich in hard wood, rubber, and rice. When Yuan Shih-kai proclaimed himself emperor in 1915, Yunnan rebelled. The Japanese wanted it as part of the first phase of their ambitious campaign to capture the whole of southeast Asia, a conflict in which the Vichy French tried not to be involved. The province was ruled during the Japanese War by warlord governors, one of whom, Lung Yun, an ex-bandit and opium king, was later overthrown with American help.

Kunming was one of the terminals of the famous Burma Road during World War II, but, unfortunately, only a small percentage of the supplies reached here, due to thieves, Nationalist incompetence and corruption, and Japanese interference. Today, Kunming has many industries, including steel, machine tools, textiles, chemicals, plastics, marble, and soft coal.

The city is completely surrounded by mountains. Sightseeing here can be a little rugged in spots. The **Dragon Gate** necessitates a climb of 200 stairs, but the effort is well worth it.

If you only have one day, you have to choose between a tour of the city or going to the Stone Forest. It is better that you stay at least two days, preferably more. Important in the city are the Western Hills, Golden Temple, Black Dragon Pool, Bamboo Temple, Yuantong Temple, Daguan Park, and Green Lake.

Xishan (Western Hills) 西山 are about 26 km from the hotels. They have the 14th-century **Huating Temple** 华亭寺 , the largest in the city. South of here is the **Taihua Temple** 太华寺 (Yuan), with the best view of the sunrise over the lake. The **Sanqing Tower** 三清

阁 , 2 km farther south, was the summer resort of Emperor Liang of the Yuan. It has nine tiers, each about 30 meters above the other. On the top is the **Long Men (Dragon Gate)** 龙门 , with another great view of the lake. The stone corridors, chambers, paths, and intricate carving of the Dragon Gate were cut from 1609 to 1681.

The coppercast ***Golden Temple** 金殿 , NE of the city (11 km away), is 300 years old, 6.5 meters high, and weighs 200 tons. The **Qiong Zhu (Bamboo) Temple** 筇竹寺 18 km NW of the Kunming Hotel, has 500 carved life-size arhats in addition to the usual Buddhist statues, carved in the Qing. These are very expressive and are worth a visit, especially if you've never seen collections of saints before. Here, also, you might find an artist to make paper cuts of your profile, cheaply. The temple was founded in 1280.

The **Daguan Lou Pavilion** 大观楼 , across the lake from Xishan Hill (7 km from the Kunming Hotel), has a 180-character couplet at its entrance, the longest ever found in China. Composed by a Qing scholar, the first half praises the landscape while the second deals with Yunnan history. Also important is the **Black Dragon Pool** 黑龙潭 , with its Ming temple and tomb. The Heishui Shrine here may be from the Han. Nearby are the Botanical Gardens.

Yuan Tong Ji 园通寺 , the only Tang temple in town, is on the same street as the Green Lake Hotel, a little over a kilometer away.

The **Stone Forest of Lunan** 路南石林 , one of the highlights of a Kunming visit, is 126 km SE of the city, and tourists usually stay in the adjacent Stone Forest Hotel 石林宾馆 . About 200 million years ago the area was covered with water. The limestone pushed its way out of the receding sea and rain continued to corrode the stone into these incredible formations. One fifth of the 64,000 acres is open to visitors. Here, too, are many steps and safety fences. The shortest of the two routes is 2½ hours long, and in this maze it's easy to get lost, so stick with your guide.

Near the hotel is a Sani nationality 撒尼族 village, and minority handicrafts are for sale. You can buy direct from the weavers. Prices here have been better than elsewhere, but be sure to haggle, especially if you're alone. Groups of local dancers in national costume have entertained hotel guests in the evening with songs and dances.

The trip between Kunming and the Stone Forest itself is remarkable because of the hilly scenery, the eucalyptus trees, and the occasional native, brightly costumed.

If you have more time, a 2-hour boat cruise on 340-sq.-km **Lake Dianchi** can be arranged, but go only for the rest, as not much can be seen (except for Daguan Lou and people fishing with large triangular nets). The Provincial Museum 博物馆 is excellent for minority artifacts, and an Institute for Nationalities 少数民族学院 is good for visitors wanting to find out more about these interesting people. Minorities are one third of the local population. At the institute, students perform minority dances on special occasions and carry out field studies to document the history and culture of the minorities. Unfortunately, the institute is short of funds.

The Kunming Hotel has good documentary movies every evening on different minorities in Yunnan. But you have to ask about these.

Along the west shore of the lake is Sleeping Beauty Hill and a series of swordlike hills. The villas there, formerly of the wealthy, are now sanitoriums for workers. On the southern tip of the lake is **Jinning** county town, the birthplace of the famous Ming navigator Zheng He, who sailed to East Africa half a century before Vasco da Gama. The Memorial Hall to Zheng He 郑和纪念馆 is on a hill above the town.

The **Anning (Emerald) Spa** 安宁温泉 , 47 km SW of Kunming, has comfortable accommodations and hot springs; the two villas here are considered the best accommodations in the province. The water contains calcium, magnesium, potassium, and sodium, and no sulfur dioxide. Two km north is the **Caoxi Temple,** built in the Song, with Song relics inside, including a bronze Buddha. Every 60 years the mid-autumn moon is reflected in a mirror on the Buddha's forehead. The plum trees date from the Yuan.

About 4 hours by car north of Kunming is Chuxiong, where many Yi people frequently sing and dance from 9 p.m. to dawn in the center of town, conversing socially through music. The rhythms of the dance and the energy level are just amazing.

Also in the province is **Xishuang Banna** 西双版纳 (pronounced She-Schwan-Ban-Na), a tropical autonomous prefecture 742 km SW (1-hour flight) of the capital, near the Laotian and Burmese borders. It can also be reached by a flight to Simao and then a 5-hour bus trip. In Xishuang Banna (main city **Jinghong,** a.k.a. Yunjinghong) 景洪 , the Dai people have a water-splashing festival in or around April, their new year, so if you go at that time, be prepared (with your camera in a plastic bag) for a fun time getting wet, dragon-boat races, and firecrackers. The temples here are similar to those of Thailand, with their intricate flaming roofs and snake designs.

Tours in Xishuang Banna can include a visit to a village, a tropical botanical garden, a dinner in a Dai home, Buddhist temples, and **Simao** 思茅 . Thirteen minorities live in these lush tropics. A new airport should be completed for your visit and a new 200-km highway sometime in the future. A minority village is being built with a 300-bed hotel.

Another region to visit is around **Lijiang** 丽江 in northwest Yunnan, about 700 km from Kunming, where the **Yu Long (Jade Dragon) Mountain** 玉龙山 rises spectacularly 6000 meters above sea level. Here the Naxi people still use hieroglyphic writing and wear sheepskin capes on their backs for warmth and to cushion heavy baskets. On the sheepskin are seven small embroidered moons to show how hard they work (until the moon and stars appear). The Naxi have produced writers, musicians, and artists famous in the rest of China. Also important to see are the **Dabaoji Palace, Liuli Temple,** and **Dading Temple,** all in Ming architecture.

Farther north of Lijiang, toward the Tibet border, is **Zhongdian,** considerably off the tourist path, with an altitude of 3000 meters. **Guihua Si,** on a hilltop there, was once a very prosperous Lama temple. During the Cultural Revolution it was totally destroyed except for the ruins of walls now standing, still an astounding sight. The main hall is being reconstructed and should soon make a visit to this remote area rewarding for those eager to be among the first. The scenery from Zhongdian to Xiaguan is especially great for bird watchers, and is full of lakes, forests, and mountain views. The county guesthouse has no private baths.

Festivals worth experiencing, in addition to the water-splashing, include the **Yi Torch Festival,** in late July in the Stone Forest, the **Third Moon Market** in Dali, and the **Horse and Mule Market Meeting,** around early April in Lijiang. Dates vary each year because of the lunar calendar, but C.I.T.S. should know.

For Dali, see "Xiaguan."

C.I.T.S. says it can also plan visits to factories, communes, schools, and hospitals. It can arrange international conferences, bird-watching tours, visits to the camellia and rhododendron research center, mountain climbing, and camping in the Stone Forest. Individual travelers can join local tours of Kunming.

Shopping

Blue and white batik, feather products, and tribal handicrafts (especially shoulderbags and clothes), tin and spotted copperware.

Food

Specialties include "Rice Noodles Crossing the Bridge" 过桥米泉 , Yunnan ham, and goat's cheese. The adventurous could try snake, elephant trunk, bear's paw, and deer tendon.

Hotels

Cuihu (Green Lake) Hotel 翠湖宾馆 □ *6 South Cuihu Rd.* □ 1956; renovated 1981. Food excellent. It is across the street from the exotic architecture of the **Haixin Pavilion** (Qing) of Green Lake Park, and about a mile from the Yuan Tong Ji.

Xiyuan (West Garden) Hotel 西园饭店 □ built 1940s, rebuilt 1981, was formerly the house of the governor. It is in old European style. The mansion should have a swimming pool by now and is peacefully located by Dianchi Lake.

Kunming Hotel 昆明宾馆 □ *122–145 East Dongfeng Rd.* □ Downtown location, over 1000 beds. Older hotel. 4 km from the Green Lake Hotel.

C.I.T.S. and **C.T.S.:** 145 Dongfeng Rd.; tel. 24992, 23922; cable 3266; telex. 64027 KMITS CN.

CAAC 中国民航

Taxis and Buses: From service desk in your hotel, or tel. 25011.

Lanzhou (Lanchow) 兰州

Northwest China. Western Gansu province, of which it is the capital. Almost in the center of China, on the Yellow River, it can be reached by air from several cities, including Beijing (2 hours by Trident), Shanghai (2¼ hours by Trident), and Guangzhou. These routes are considerably longer by smaller planes. Lanzhou is also serviced by train.

Lanzhou is important as a stop on the Silk Road and as a gateway to two cave temples, the *Bingling Temple Caves and the *Maijishan Caves. Do not stop here unless you're interested in cave temples and are willing to go out into the desert to look at them. Visitors react to the city itself in different ways. One seasoned tour guide said it was not all that interesting and described it as a "city of poverty." Another visitor said it was his "favorite city." In any case, the infamous pollution here has been reduced by the growing use of electricity instead of coal for cooking. Guides used to hand out masks to visitors to protect lungs and throats.

Founded about 2200 years ago, Lanzhou was called the "Gold City" after gold was found here. At an altitude of 1510 meters, Lanzhou is very cold in winter. The coldest winter temperature is ⁻23°C in January; the hottest, 39.1°C, both some time ago. Annual precipitation in the province is between 30 and 600 mm, the rain mainly in the SE.

With a population of over one million, the city is industrial, with petrochemicals, machine building, and smelting. It is near the oldest oilfields in China.

Gansu province today has a population of 20 million, including Han, Hui, Tibetan, Dongxiang, Yugur, Bonan, Mongolian, Kazak, Tu, Salar, and Manchu nationalities. The area was settled 200,000 years ago; 3000 years ago, the inhabitants started farming the eastern part of Gansu. The province is the setting for Yuan-tsung Chen's excellent autobiographical novel *The Dragon's Village,* a book based on her own experiences with land reform shortly after Liberation.

In Lanzhou, tourists can visit the university, factories, a white pagoda, and a fountain. The **Baita (White Pagoda Park)** 白塔 is on a hill on the north bank of the Yellow River. The buildings here are the Sanxing (Three-Star) Hall, Yingxu (Greet the Sunrise) Pavilion, Yunyue (Cloudy Moon) Temple, and the White Pagoda Temple. The White Pagoda was first built in the Yuan, then rebuilt and expanded in the

Ming and Qing. It has seven stories and eight sides and is about 70 meters high. A good view of the park, the river, and the city is had from the top of the hill.

The **Wuquan (Five-Fountain) Hill** 五泉山 is south of the old city. Legend credits General Ho Qubing (Huo Chu-ping), in 120 B.C., with stabbing the ground with his sword after finding no water for his horses. Five streams of water appeared and have been flowing ever since. Most of the old buildings here were destroyed in war. Existing still are the Jingang (Buddha's Warrior Attendants) Shrine (Ming), the Qianfo (Thousand Buddhas) Hall, the Mani Temple, the Dizang Temple, and the Sanjiao Cave. The two most important relics to see are the Taihe Iron Bell, 3 meters high, weighing 5 tons, cast in 1202; and the Tongjieyinfo Buddha, cast in copper in 1370 and weighing nearly 5 tons.

The elaborate fifth-century ***Bingling Temple Caves** (Pinglinghsi) 炳灵寺石窟 are 120 km SW of the city, near **Linxi.** Here are 183 caves and shrines with 694 stone Buddhist statues and 82 clay ones, the biggest Buddha 27 cm high, the smallest only 25. Like some other cave temples, this involves a lot of stairs. The statues range from Northern Wei to Ming, the youngest, at least 350 years old.

The ***Maiji Grottoes** 麦积山石窟 , also Northern Wei to Ming, are 45 km SE of the city of **Tianshui** 天水 , itself 350 km SE of Lanzhou. Tianshui was a trade distributing center on the Silk Road and has two temples, the Fuxi and the Nanguo, and should now be reached by air.

At Maiji, there are 194 caves full of thousands of stone and clay Buddhist statues, and 1300 square meters of murals dating from the end of the 4th century to the 19th, a period of 1500 years. These caves are on a mountain, which rises almost vertically, and are reached by wooden staircases and protected by doors and windows. Some of the statues are completely unsheltered. One statue 15.28 meters high is from the Sui. The work on the mountain was done by craftsmen who piled blocks of wood up to the top and started carving while standing on them. As the artisans worked their way down, they gradually removed the blocks. The Maiji is better than Bingling, but the three best cave temples in China are at Datong, Dunhuang, and Luoyong.

Also near Tianshui, at **Dadiwan** in Qin'an County, is an on-the-site museum similar to that at Banpo in Xi'an, which should be open in time for your trip. Its 1154-sq.-meter hall covers a 7000-year-old primitive village with painted pottery tripods, stone and bone artifacts, and ground paintings. Of the 200 houses so far discovered, one covers 600 square meters, the largest such building found so far in China.

If you have a chance, do see the authentic **Chinese dances** performed by the Gansu School of Dance in Lanzhou. The principal, Mme. Gao, studied the dancing figures in the caves and personally selected 12 girls for five years of training. Now their performance is considered the best in the nation and they have toured many Asian countries. The movement, the breathing, the intricate gestures are superbly executed.

Also in the province are Dunhuang, Jiayuguan, and Jiuquan. See separate listings.

Shopping

Lanzhou produces a kind of honeydew melon, carved ink slabs, "jade" cups and bottle gourds. It also manufactures paper cuts, lanterns, and reproductions of ancient paintings based on the Silk Road murals. Some of its replicas of the famous Flying Horse of Gansu are made from molds directly from the original.

Try the **Provincial Arts and Crafts Shop** (West Donggang Rd.) and the **Nanguan Department Store,** with its Friendship Store branch.

Food

Roast piglet (delicious!), sweet and sour Yellow River carp, *facai,* steamed chicken, fried camel hoof (ugh), and fried sheep's tail. For snacks, try toffee potatoes and toffee melon. In addition to the hotel restaurants, try the **Yuebinlou Restaurant,** which has Beijing food, and the **Jingyanglou Restaurant,** which specializes in Yangzhou food.

Hotels

Not all rooms have private baths.

Airport Hotel □ *2 hours from Lanzhou by car, but, of course, near the airport.*

Friendship Hotel 友谊宾馆   □ *14 Xijin Rd., Qilihe. 10 km from railway station; 70 km from airport* □ 1950s; renovated. 186 beds on 3rd, 4th, and 5th floors for foreign visitors. Six dining rooms. Billiards. Near Gansu museum.

Jincheng Hotel □ *in the center of town* □ Chinese and Western food. Tea house. Air-conditioned cars for hire.

Lanzhou Hotel 兰州宾馆   □ *Panxuan Rd., Donggang. 1 km from railway station; 80 km from airport* □ 1956; renovated. 1425 beds. Chinese and Moslem dining rooms.

Ning Wozhuang Hotel □ *Tianshui Rd.*

Victory Hotel □ *133, Zhongshan Rd.*

See also "Silk Road."

Leshan (Le Mountain) 乐山

Southwest China, about 170 km SW of Chengdu. This can be included in an overnight trip with the base of Emei Mountain (see separate listing) and Sansu Shrine (see "Chengdu"). It could also be done in a one-day excursion by hovercraft from

Chongqing. The long trip by road is preferable if you have the time and want to see the Sichuan countryside, the architecture of the farmhouses, and the most obnoxious truck drivers in the country.

Formerly known as Jiading or Jiazhou, Leshan is a small 1300-year-old town. Warm rain from April through June adds to the mystical atmosphere.

Leshan is the home of the ***Dafu (Great Buddha) Temple** 大佛 . Here sits a 70-meter Buddha, started in A.D. 713 and completed 90 years later, believed to be the largest in the world. From Leshan city, visitors could take a public bus to the front gate, or arrive by ferry at the foot. The view from the water is better; otherwise you can't see the temple guardians. At the confluence of three rivers (Min, Dadu, and Qingyi), the monastery buildings stand at Buddha's eye level.

This huge statue was built to offset the large number of serious accidents on the river. Since statistics were probably kept before and after, it would be enlightening to know if, indeed, the statue was worth it.

The 30-bed guesthouse (renovated 1981), set around a pool, is exotic, as it is part of the temple. Caves, bare floors, and Chinese beds. Being able to stay at the temple provides a great opportunity for photographers, who can shoot to their hearts' content at dusk and sunrise (when the mist rises on the river). The other statues, all recent reproductions, look better in dim light.

The **Wuyou (Black) Temple** 乌尤寺 can be reached in 15 minutes by footpath from the Dafu Temple, or by 336 steps from where the tour buses stop. It has a good museum for its tiny size.

Hotels
Jia Zhou Hotel 嘉州宾馆 and **Jiu Ri Feng Hotel** 就日峰宾馆 , both in Leshan city.

C.I.T.S. 国际旅行社 : Leshan sub-branch, Leshan city; tel. 2154.

Lhasa 拉萨

Northwest China. The fabled capital of Xizang (Tibet) has opened more than ever to foreigners. It is north of Bhutan and Bangladesh and almost due south of Urumqi. It is usually reached by a 2-hour-or-so plane ride west from Chengdu. It is also 5 hours by air from Xi'an or 2 hours from Golmud (both in smaller planes). Add to that another 100 km by road from the airfield to Lhasa itself! The possibility exists of direct flights in the future from Guangzhou, Beijing, Shanghai, and Kathmandu. A

*health examination in China is required for travelers. Some
backpackers have managed to get there by truck from Chengdu
in three days to a week. Buses now take five days from Xi'an.
An asphalt highway has been built from Xining in neighboring
but far-off Qinghai, and a railway is currently being built from
Golmud that will link Lhasa more easily with the rest of China.
Travelers are also going to Lhasa from Kathmandu by land,
but should expect delays due to landslides and bumpy roads.
This route was restricted to group travel in the mid-1980s but
may open again to individuals. Individual visas to China have
been difficult to obtain in Nepal. But patience, please. Princess
Wen Cheng took two years to get here from Xi'an in the Tang.*

Tibet is one of the more exotic places to visit in China, virtually a
country in itself, with an area about the size of France, Spain, and Greece
combined. It is isolated by the highest mountains in the world. It is
important to see because of its unique culture, its celebrated monasteries, and its magnificent scenery.

While visiting Tibet is no longer an experience just for the adventurous few, it is still not for the weak. The average altitude in Tibet is
over 5000 meters (very hard on the skin, so take some good sunscreen).
Usually it takes about two weeks to feel comfortable moving around in
the thin air. Bottled oxygen is available in the hotel rooms and on some
tour buses. Just don't push yourself too hard. Taking it easy is difficult,
as a lot of climbing is involved just to sightsee. Do not go if you have
asthma or other pulmonary problems. In addition to the altitude and
dust, the temples are full of incense smoke and are lit by butter lamps—
all of which might make breathing difficult. Do not go if you have heart
problems. Qualified doctors may not be available.

Since all food, energy, and most building materials have to be imported by truck or plane, the cost of accommodations and sightseeing is
higher than in other parts of China for the same quality. Some tourist
agencies have had to import their own tour buses and upgrade hotel
services themselves. You should bring your own candles and/or flashlight, drinking water, medicine for altitude sickness, and alarm clock.

The hottest temperature is 27°C in July and August; the coldest,
⁻17°C in December and January. The annual precipitation is about 500
mm, mainly from June to September. Lhasa is in the Zangpo Valley at
over 3000 meters. Some of the hotels are not well heated in winter.
(Take a hot-water bottle!)

Tibetans are nomads, or farmers raising barley, yak, and sheep.
Tho-tho-ri Nyantsen, 28th king of Tibet, introduced Buddhism into the
country in A.D. 233.

In the seventh century, the king of Tubo, Srontsan Gampo, (a.k.a.
Songtsen Gampo, Srongbtsan Sgam-po, Songzan Ganbu) conquered the
other tribes and made Lhasa his capital. He also invaded neighboring

Sichuan, and although he was repulsed, his request for a Chinese wife was granted. His marriage with Tang princess Wen Cheng and his interest in Tang culture introduced much Chinese culture into Tibet. Among the innovations were silk, paper, and the architecture of the palace he built for her. His marriage to a Nepalese princess also meant Indian influences. Tibetan script is basically Indian. Both princesses promoted their own brands of Buddhism. The Tibetan kingdom subsequently expanded to include parts of Yunnan, including Nanzhou and the northern part of India.

In 779, Buddhism became the state religion. The Mongols invaded Tibet in 1252 and adopted Tibetan Lamaism for themselves and propagated it to help control their subject tribes in other parts of China. Some lamas became very powerful during the Yuan. Kublai Khan appointed a lama as king, but maintained overall power himself. This system has continued with varying degrees of Chinese enforcement ever since. Qing emperor Qianlong (Chien Lung) was one who especially asserted his authority.

The Jesuits were the first western missionaries to arrive in Tibet in 1624. During the lifetime of the fifth Dalai Lama, the office of Dalai Lama became political as well as religious. The first British mission arrived in 1774 and a British military expedition (Younghusband) forced the Dalai Lama to flee to Mongolia from 1904 until 1909. In 1910, the Chinese again asserted their control and the Dalai Lama retreated for a time to India. In 1911, the Tibetans repelled the Chinese. The British tried to maintain some control here, but gave up in 1947 after India became independent.

The Chinese People's Liberation Army arrived in 1951. An abortive uprising by some Tibetans in 1959 forced a large number of Tibetans to flee to India. The current Dalai Lama, the 14th, has been there ever since. In 1964, Tibet was made an Autonomous Region within China. In the last few years, the Chinese have made attempts to train Tibetans to replace Han administrators. The 1.78 million Tibetans here are over 94% of the population.

Tibet's Buddhism is different from that of the rest of Asia, aside from Mongolia and northern China. It believes strongly in reincarnation and a vicious, torturous hell for nonbelievers, which is reflected in its art. It is full of demons and human skulls, witchcraft and magic, much influenced by the pre-Buddhist polytheism of the Tibetans. It has also many pre-Hindu influences and much recitation of spells. You might hear the chant *Om Mani Padme Hum,* which means "Hail to the Jewel in the Lotus," a mantra that helps the individual communicate with the eternal.

At the same time, Lamaism has many mystical elements, the chanting in chords by each monk, and a highly developed theology.

The goal of Buddhism is the end of continuous reincarnations.

At one time, a quarter of the male population of Tibet were monks, and the theocracy was such that no matter how cold it was, on whatever day spring was proclaimed by the Dalai Lama, everybody had to change into summer clothes!

Like other religions, Lamaism is divided into sects: the two main ones here are the Red Hats, where sex with a person other than one's spouse was part of the ritual, and the Yellow Hats, which is more strict about celibacy and other traditional Buddhist monastic practices. The Dalai Lama is head of the Yellow Hats.

Fascinating are the stories of how the successive dalai lamas were chosen—babies recognizing objects used by themselves in their previous incarnations. The current incumbent is from a peasant family from Amdo, at that time in Qinghai province. The Dalai Lamas are earthly incarnations of the four-armed God Chenrezi, and when each incarnation dies, his spirit takes on the body of another Tibetan child at birth. Disputes have arisen over who is the real reincarnated Dalai Lama, and the issue is politically very sensitive. Lamas are monks who are recognized reincarnations of previous lamas or monks.

Among traditional Tibetan customs is the giving of a *hada,* a long silk scarf, as a token of esteem and good luck. The sticking out of the tongue is a sign of respect. At one time, Tibetans practiced polyandry, brothers sharing one wife because of poverty. Every summer a festival celebrates the annual washing and cleaning.

Tea is drunk with yak butter and salt and tastes more like beef broth. It does seem to give much needed energy for survival and is said to be good for colds. The proper way to drink it is to lightly blow the top cream away from you and allow it to settle on the sides of your tea cup. The thicker the cream, the more generous the host. Fresh, hot yak milk has been described as sweet and "heavenly" and has a higher fat content than cow's milk. Often barleylike flour is added to the milk or tea to form a dough. Tsang, a barley wine, is another favorite drink offered to guests.

The remains of the dead are frequently cut up by priests at dawn to feed vultures, in the belief that these birds take the spirits to heaven. Those who cannot afford this expensive rite, like beggars or victims of serious illnesses, are fed to fish—which is why Tibetans don't eat fish. Burial in the ground is for the very poor and unfortunate, such as criminals or victims of murder. High lamas are covered in butter and cremated.

Tourists have been allowed to see the birds at work, but this has been restricted because the families of the deceased objected to tourists scaring the birds away. Tourism officials have been building platforms with telescopes.

Look for the *tankas* hung on monastery walls. These are the scrolls used by itinerant preachers to illustrate the teachings of the Buddha. Look for prayer wheels, with a written prayer inside, which adherents spin in the belief that each rotation sends a prayer to Buddha.

Tibet has 50 monasteries open, including seven for nuns, with 3000 men in residence and 138 women. Forty-three more religious buildings are under repair and another 80 will be restored. All this work is being done by the central and local governments, which also maintain the monasteries and the monks. At Liberation, Tibet had 2770 monasteries.

The most important of the buildings are the Jokhang Temple, Potala Palace, Sera Monastery, and Drepung Monastery. If you only have one day, C.I.T.S. suggests the Jokhang and Potala.

The *Potala Palace 布达拉官 cannot be missed. It is 10 km from the Lhasa Guest House and it dominates the city from its lofty cliff. There is a 300-meter climb *before* you arrive at the front door. In spite of its 13 stories, there are no elevators, and in places no stairs, only ladders. To get from one section to another, you have to go back to the ground floor, outside, and then up again. Consider yourself warned!

Originally built in the seventh century by Srontsan Gampo, the Potala is the official residence of the Dalai Lama, the religious and secular head of Tibet. The first Dalai Lama lived from 1391–1474. The Potala has 1000 rooms, 10,000 chapels, and the tombs of eight Dalai Lamas, some gold-plated and studded with diamonds, turquoises, corals, and pearls. The largest tomb is 14.85 meters high. More than 200,000 pearls cover the Pearl Pagoda.

The building was destroyed and rebuilt several times, the latest structure dating from 1642. Among its 200,000 statues are those of King Srontsan Gampo and his Chinese wife.

Every wall is covered with murals. Noteworthy are those in the Sixipingcuo Hall. In the West Big Hall, the murals record the life of the Fifth Dalai Lama, including his meeting with Qing Emperor Shunzhi in Beijing in 1652.

The palace is 400 meters by 350 meters, and is made of stone and wood, its walls between three and five meters thick. The White Palace was built during the time of the Fifth Dalai Lama (1617–1682) and the Red Palace afterward. From the 18th century, with the construction of the Norbulinka (Summer Palace), the Potala was used only in winter. Can you imagine a child growing up here? The current dalai lama was brought here at the age of two. Think of him flying his kite from the Potala's roof and exploring the city and its people with a telescope!

The *Jokhang Temple 大昭寺 , a.k.a. Juglakang, is the most important Buddhist temple in Tibet. It is 15 km from the Lhasa Guest House. It was built in the mid-seventh century, also during King Srontsan Gampo's time. It has been expanded several times since. Note the Nepalese and Chinese features. Princess Wen Cheng brought with her from China the seated statue of the child Sakyamuni. The Tibetans believe that the statue was made by the Buddha himself. It is said that the princess also planted the willow still in front of the temple gate. The Great Prayer Festival is held annually here from the 3rd to 25th of the first month of the Tibetan calendar.

Unlike most Lama temples in Chengde, the temples here are full of worshipers, some prostrating themselves 500 times a day and donating yak butter to feed the lamps.

The *Sera Monastery 色拉寺 in the northern suburbs 20 km from the Lhasa Guest House was built in 1419 by a nobleman. It was extended in the early 18th century, and is one of the four major monasteries in Tibet, at its height housing 10,000 lamas and monks. The 18 sandalwood arhats and four Heavenly Kings here were gifts from the Ming emperor. Look also for a gold statue of an 11-faced Guan Yin, the Goddess of Mercy.

The *Drepung Monastery 哲蚌寺 , a.k.a. Daipung, is in the western suburbs 15 km from the Lhasa Guest House. One can climb to the roof for the view of the valley. Financed by the same nobleman who built the Sera, the Drepung was founded in 1416 (Ming) and extended several times. It is one of the four major monasteries. Among its treasures is a white conch and a gilded Buddha. Inside the abdomen of the statue in the main hall are the remains of a master translator named Duojita. At one time, this monastery also had a population of over 10,000 monks and lamas.

If you have more time, **Norbulingka Park 罗布林卡** was the summer residence of the dalai lamas, with 370 rooms. It is 4 km from the Potala and set in a 100-acre garden. Gesang Jiacuo, the first building, was originally erected in 1755. The New Palace for the 14th dalai lama was built in 1954–56. It is also full of statues and murals. The murals are of Princess Wen Cheng and her marriage to the king, the three worlds, and Buddha preaching under a banyan tree. The bedroom is as the current dalai lama left it to flee to India. In the 1940s, the German mountain climber Heinrich Harrer set up a movie theater for the dalai lama in this park.

The *Ganden Monastery is also protected by the State Council as a historical monument. It is listed as early Ming to Qing. The *Royal Tibetan Tombs, from the seventh century, are at Qonggyai in Shannan prefecture, about 180 km SE.

Xigaze (Shigatse) is about 225 km (9 hours) west of Lhasa over a 3000-meter pass. The *Zhaxilhunbu (Tashilhunpo) Monastery 扎什伦布寺 there is the most important of the religious buildings in that city. It was founded in 1447 and was the home of the Panchen Lamas, the reincarnations of the Buddha of Eternal Light. Only religiously have the Panchen Lamas been equal to the politically superior Dalai Lamas. However, the Chinese consider the Panchen Lama a political equal. This is also a very sensitive and controversial point. You could ask carefully if the Chinese would allow either the Panchen or Dalai Lama to live in Tibet.

At one time, the Zhaxilhunbu had a population of 3000 monks. Today there are about 600. This monastery also has many halls and chapels, and of the 18 arhats. The Hall of the Buddha Maitreya (Qiangba) was built from 1914–18 with a 26.7-meter statue of the Laughing Buddha in gold and copper. The gold-plated reliquary of the fourth Panchen Lama is 11 meters high and is decorated with precious stones.

You can probably hear the lamas chanting in the Grand Chanting Hall from 8 a.m. to 11 a.m., from 1 p.m. until 3 p.m., and 6 p.m. to 9 p.m. Don't be surprised if you find a 20-inch color television set in one of the buildings.

Zhangmu, on the Tibet side of the Nepal border, is now open to tourists, with a 100-bed guesthouse. Probably open for your visit are Damxung (pastoral area), Nyingchi (forest areas), and Lake Yamzho Yumco (boat rides and horse racing). In all of these, yak-hair tents will house tourists. Dingri County at the foot of Mount Qomolangma (Everest) and all mountains in Tibet are expected to be opened gradually to foreigners. At press time, only Everest and Xianbangma are open to foreign climbers.

By the time you get there, six new areas should also be opened to foreign visitors, including Geladainlong Mountain (the head waters of the Yangtze River), and Yagradagze Mountain (near the head waters of the Yellow River).

Several tour agencies, like Tibet Tourism Corporation, Mountain Travel, and Blyth and Co., now offer **treks** in Tibet, and prices for these are higher than similar treks in other countries. Trekking from Tibet to Nepal is difficult because of restricted areas in Nepal. Mountaineering can be organized through the Chinese Mountaineering Association.

Mountain Travel has a cultural expedition that includes **Amdo,** the birthplace of the current Dalai Lama in 1935. The much-experienced Lindblad offers tours to Lhasa, Xigaze, Zhangmu, and from there by land to Kathmandu in Nepal. Lindblad also goes to Shannan.

A beautiful picture book, *Tibet* by David Bonavia and Magnus Bartlett, is available from Shangri-la Press, Hong Kong (1981). Highly recommended also is Heinrich Harrer's *Seven Years in Tibet,* about his adventures there in the 1940s, a good picture to compare with today's Tibet. Harrer, a German, taught the Dalai Lama English and was his cameraman. A sequel tells of Harrer's recent return trip.

Shopping
Tibetan boots, rugs, saddle blankets, temple bells, prayer wheels, woolen blankets, etc.

Food
Tibetan (Yak meat and cheese), Moslem (mutton or lamb), or Chinese.

Hotels

Lhasa Guest House for Tourists □ *west suburbs, tel. 23859* □ 1960s; renovated 1979. 110 km from airport.

No. 1 Hotel □ *Renmin Rd.*

Snowland Hotel □ *Guangming Rd.* □ 1985. 35 rooms. Restaurant. Dormitories available.

Lhasa Hotel □ *a.k.a. Lasa Hotel, No. 1 National Rd., west suburbs, 6 km from the center of the city* □ 1985. Over 1000 beds. Interconnecting five- and seven-story buildings. Rooms decorated in Tibetan style, banquet hall, air conditioners, closed-circuit televisions, oxygen supply, Chinese and Western food, coffee shops, tea houses, etc.; best in town but not up to international standards. Should improve with new management.

C.I.T.S. 中国国际旅行社 : west suburbs; tel. 22980; cable 2464; write to ask the dates of festivals so you can plan your trip to include them.

CAAC 中国民航 : Jiefang Rd., No. 12, Lhasa; tel. 22417, 23772.

Liuzhou 柳州

South China. Central Guangxi Zhuang Autonomous Region, immediately west of Guangdong province. Both urban and rural population, 585,000 with Zhuang, Han, Miao, Yao, Dong, and Hui nationalities. Weather: hottest 39°C in August; coldest ⁻3.8°C in January. Annual precipitation about 1500 mm, mainly in late spring, early summer.

Liuzhou (a.k.a. Longcheng—City of Dragons) was founded in 111 B.C. (Han) and has been a tourist destination since the Tang. Blessed by colorful minorities, a winding river, karst caves, and hills, among its attractions is the **Liuhou Temple and Tomb** 柳侯公园 . Liu Zongyuan was the famous Tang writer, and for four years provincial governor, who worked to free women from being bond slaves. Women's libbers, take note! His tomb is 1.5 km from the hotel. For natural scenery see **Yufeng (Carp) Hill** 鱼峰山 (shaped like a standing fish, 3 km from the hotel) and the **Dule Caves** 都乐岩 (18 km from the hotel). Also noteworthy are the **Giant Dragon Pond** 大龙潭 and **Horse Saddle Hill** 马鞍山 . Like a miniature, less-developed Guilin, Liuzhou should be a very pleasant, out-of-the-way place to unwind. If you want to kill some time, explore the free market with its dried frogs and delicious fried pasteries.

Only 16 km SE is the **Tongtian Cave** 通天洞 , where Liujiang (Liuchiang) Man lived 20,000–30,000 years ago, a few hundred thousand years younger than Peking Man. Liuzhou produces stone carvings and porcelain.

Liuzhou Hotel　柳州饭店　□ *1 Youyi Rd.*　□ 1956; renovated 1985. 6 km from airport.

Liujiang Hotel　柳江饭店　□ *72 Gonyun Rd.*

Dragon City Hotel　龙城大酒家　□ *1988.*

C.I.T.S.: Liuzhou Hotel; tel. 25669.
CAAC bookings only: W. Tongfeng Rd.; tel. 22702.

Luoyang 洛阳

(Loyang; North Bank of Luo River) Northwest China. 2 hours by train west of the Henan provincial capital and closest airport, Zhengzhou, and an 8-hour train ride east from Xi'an. About 25 km south of the Yellow River. Hottest temperatures: July–August—39°C; coldest: January–February—⁻12°C. Generally mild. Altitude: 136 meters above sea level. Population: 1,114,000, of whom 500,000 are urban.

Luoyang is important because of the Longmen Grottoes, the White Horse Temple, and because it was an imperial capital for many centuries. It is one of the 24 cities of historical importance protected by the State Council.

Luoyang was first built in the 11th century B.C. From 770 B.C. it was the capital at one time or another of the Eastern Zhou, Eastern Han, Wei, Western Jin, Northern Wei, Sui, Tang, Later Liang, and Later Tang dynasties. Moves were frequently made here because of drought in Xi'an, a city that was preferred. Because there are hills on three sides, it was relatively easy to defend, and whoever wanted to control western Henan had to take Luoyang. Consequently, many battles were fought in this area and many treasures were buried to save them from the soldiers. Luoyang was one of the earliest centers of Buddhism, from the first century A.D. During the Tang, it was the biggest city in China. It declined later because the capital, and therefore the whole court, moved away.

Luoyang people will proudly tell you that the Silk Road actually started from Luoyang and not from Xi'an, as is commonly supposed. "Knowledgeable merchants always came here for silks," they say. "It was cheaper."

The architecture in the older, eastern part of Luoyang is more interesting than the more substantial and more livable newer buildings. Today, there are over 400 factories manufacturing everything from truck cranes to ball bearings. Tourists might be interested in its arts and crafts factory, which makes palace lanterns and reproductions of three-color Tang porcelains and Shang bronzes.

Area farms grow cotton, corn, winter wheat, a little rice, sesame, sorghum, sweet potatoes, apples, pears, and grapes. They also raise yellow oxen, sheep, and mules. The city is also noted for its peonies, first grown in the Sui! Flower lovers should aim for late April in Wangcheng Park. At press time, hotel rooms are in short supply here during the high tourist season.

The following can be covered in one day if you don't dawdle.

The ***Baima Si (White Horse) Temple** 白马寺 , 13 km east of the Old City and 25 km from the Friendship Hotel, was founded in A.D. 68 after second Han Emperor Mingdi dreamed that a spirit with a halo entered his palace. His ministers convinced him that the spirit was the Buddha, so he sent scholars to India to bring back the sutras. After three years, the famous Indian monks Shemeteng and Zhufalan arrived here with the scriptures on a white horse. The emperor put the monks up in his resort, the Cold Terrace, at the back of what is now this, the first Buddhist temple in China. There they translated the scriptures into Chinese. Both monks died in China and were buried in the east and west corners of the grounds beyond the moon gates.

None of the buildings here are original, though the red brick foundation of the Cold Terrace is Han; none of the others are earlier than Ming. The State Council lists them as Jin to Qing. Tang Empress Wu made one of her favorites the abbot here. The **Celestial Guardians' Hall** has a Maitreya (Laughing) Buddha made of hemp and lacquer with a beautifully carved frame. Here the four guardians are in charge of rain (with parasol), the wind (holding a pagoda), the amount of rain and wind (with musical instrument), and good harvest (with spider).

In the main hall to the right of Sakyamuni is Manjusri, the Bodhisattva of Wisdom, carrying the sutras, and at Sakyamuni's left, Samantabhara, Bodhisattva of Universal Benevolence. In the next hall are 18 clay arhats, each with a magic weapon, the oldest statues here (Yuan). One is Ceylonese, one Chinese (the Tang monk Xuan Zang who went to India), and the rest Indian. Inside the back halls are statues of the two monks, the Pilu Buddha (Sakyamuni), and drawers where the sutras are kept. A stele with characters written horizontally here is most unusual.

The **Qiyun (Cloud Touching) Pagoda** 齐云塔 nearby is in the Tang style, first built in 1175. Only the base with the darker brick is original. It was repaired in the Northern Song and Jin dynasties and has 14 stories. You get a strange echo effect if you stand either north or south of the pagoda and clap your hands.

The **Luoyang Municipal Museum** 洛阳博物馆 has 2000 pieces on display and roughly 50,000 in its collection. Relics include (1) historical maps of the city. The first imperial city is where Laboring People's Park is now. The *Han and Wei city was east of the White Horse

Temple; the Sui and Tang cities were on both sides of the Luo River; (2) two mammoth tusks found right in town in 1960; (3) double boilers used 3700 years before the British used double boilers; (4) cowry shell money; (5) a sword made from an elephant tooth; (6) a crossbow with a trigger (476–221 B.C.); (7) iron farming tools (Han); (8) figures from the tomb of a Northern Wei prince, including a band with one musician falling asleep; (9) *original* three-color Tang horses and camels from which the copies are made. Study these carefully for comparison if you want to buy reproductions.

*Longmen (Lungmen) Grottoes 龙门石窟 : Large statues carved on cliffs or in caves are symbols of permanence. China has 19 important "cave temples" and Longmen is among the top three. Although predating these caves and built also by the Wei, those at Datong are said to be better preserved, more elaborately colored, and bigger. The stone at Longmen, however, is better. The grottoes are 20 km south of the city from the Friendship Hotel and extend north along the Yi River for about 1000 meters. They were not touched by the Red Guards, but the heads and hands of some were damaged at the beginning of this century. The buses stop by a 303-meter copy of a famous Sui bridge built of only stone and cement in 1962.

Work on the caves began about A.D. 494, when Emperor Hsaio Wen of the Northern Wei moved his capital from Datong to here. Work continued at a great pace from then until the Tang. A few statues were added during the Five Dynasties and Northern Song. There are 1352 grottoes, over 750 niches, and about 40 pagodas of various sizes. They contain more than 100,000 Buddhist images, ranging in size from 2 centimeters to 17.14 meters.

Compare the dress of the statues. Some are clothed in the plain robes of Indian holy men; others wear female Chinese court dress, sometimes with jewelry, a later development. One can guess that wealthy, devout worshipers wanted to clothe their gods in the best fashions of the day. This practice is much like that of medieval European religious art, which also ignored the mystical preachings of its teachers. The narrow, regular pleats are characteristic of the Northern Wei. The Tang statues tend to have rounder faces. While it is said that the gods could change their sex at will, the feminine faces are because, as one adherent said, "We want people to look at the face of Buddha. Since women's faces are more attractive than men's, the statues are made to look more feminine."

The **Wan Fo (10,000 Buddhas) Cave** actually has 15,000 Buddhas on the north and south walls. It was completed in A.D. 680 (Tang). Note the musicians and dancers at the base. The back wall has 54 bodhisattvas, each sitting on a lotus flower. Outside the cave is a Guanyin with a water vessel in her left hand and a whisk in her right. There used to be two lions here, but they are now said to be in the Boston Museum of Fine Arts.

The **Guyang Cave** was the earliest, built around A.D. 494 (Northern Wei). The cornlike design represents a string of pearls. The ceiling is covered with Buddhas, lions, and tablets.

Fengxian Temple 奉先寺 , the largest and most spectacular, was completed in A.D. 675. The main statue (17.14 meters) is the Vairocana Buddha (i.e. Sakyamuni). If you look carefully, on the left side of the face are traces of a five-centimeter crack extending from the hairline to the chin. This was repaired recently at a cost of ¥20,000. The square holes around the statues were used to hold the roof structure that was taken down when it was found that sunlight was good for limestone. Behind the smaller disciple to Sakyamuni's right is an imperceptible cave large enough to hold 400 people and from which climbers used to negotiate the top of the head. Fortunately, this is now blocked. On Sakyamuni's far left is Dvarapala, whose ankles are worn black and smooth by individuals trying to embrace them in return for happiness.

Some of the Buddhas in Longmen were commissioned by wealthy people wanting special favors, or generals hoping for victory. Some caves are mixtures of dynastic styles. During imperial times, the common people had to look at them from afar, and in later periods, peasants broke pieces off the statues to make lime fertilizer.

Other attractions include the **Tomb of Guan Yu (Kuan Yu)** 关林 庙 —or at least that of his head. Guan Yu was one of the heroes of *The Romance of the Three Kingdoms,* and he is also known as the Chinese god of war. His tomb, between the grottoes and the city, was built in the Ming.

Two **Han Tombs** are in Wang Cheng Park 王城公园 . Outside of the city is the **Tomb of Liu Xiu.** He was first emperor of the Eastern Han 1900 years ago. A visit could be combined with a trip to see the bridge across the Yellow River. **Mang Shan Hill** 邙山 , north of the city, is full of the ruins of old palaces, tombs, and ancient summer resorts. The **Luoyang Ancient Tombs Museum,** with 21 Han and Song tombs, is 7 km from the city, near the airport.

If you have more time, ask about the school for traditional Chinese opera. You might learn to enjoy it!

Shopping

Store Hours: 7:30 a.m.–7 p.m.; some 9 a.m.–7:30 p.m.

Friendship Store 友谊商店 : Reproductions, along with brushes, chopsticks, artificial flowers and inkstones, all made locally; **Guangzhou Market** 广州市场 ; **Shanghai Market** 上海市场 ; **State Secondhand Store** 旧货店 : Old city. Had theatrical costumes cheaper than in Beijing. Also new theatrical caps; **Arts and Crafts Store** 美术 ／工艺商店 : Sells palace lanterns and reproductions of Shang bronzes, Tang horses and camels, made upstairs.

Restaurants

Guangzhou Market Restaurant 广州酒家 .

Friendship Hotel Restaurant □ serves yancai (turnip) soup, mudan (peony soup), fried yellow river carp in wine, and monkey-head mushrooms.

Hotels

Youyi (Friendship) Hotel 友谊宾馆 □ *western part of Luoyang, Taiyuan Rd.* □ 64 rooms in three-story east and west wings, 1956. Next door 160 rooms, nine stories, 1984. 7 km from railway station, 10 from Old City, 3 from museum. In residential district. Park in front. Guangzhou Free Market 2 blocks behind. Swimming pool. Has "deluxe, moderate, and economy" rooms.

Other Important Addresses

C.I.T.S.: Friendship Hotel.
Railway Station 洛阳火车站 . Tel. 2157 or 6006.

Lushan 庐山

(Mountain of Straw Huts) South China. 210 km NW of Nanchang in Jiangxi, the closest airport. Overlooking Poyang Lake and the Yangtze River. 32 km by bus south of the port of Jiujiang. Weather: Hottest—30°C (rare) at noon in July; coldest—⁻16°C in January. Snow from the end of November through February. Best time to visit is June–October. Lots of mist and rain, especially April and May—great for mood photographs but not for view. Altitude: 1094–1400 meters. Annual precipitation: 1916 mm. Population: About 9000 in Gulin. About 10,000 summer tourists in one day. Some of the Chinese visitors are here as a reward for exemplary behavior, staying in reception houses of their work units. The mountaintop tourist belt is about 8 by 4 km.

Primarily an old mountain resort, highly recommended as an escape from the heat or as a rest stop near the end of a tour. It is great for hiking and is a beautiful place to visit, with enough religious, historical, and folkloric aspects to make it interesting.

Legend says that the seven Kuan brothers lived on the mountain as recluses during the Western Zhou (11th century–771 B.C.). Because they were worthy men, the emperor sent an emissary to invite them to the capital to help govern the country. When the agent arrived, he found only empty straw huts. Hence, the name. The mountain was visited by the Jin poet Tao Yuan-ming (365–427). Its peach blossoms inspired Tang poet Bai Ju-yi. The first Ming emperor is supposed to have escaped an enemy here with supernatural help.

But it was not until after the last half of the 1800s that a resort was developed. About 100 hotel buildings and villas were completed and used by wealthy Chinese, government officials, and foreign missionaries, business people, and diplomats. Most of these people were carried by sedan chair up a steep, 9-km path. People still climb this path from the base in about 2 hours from Lianhuadeng (Lotus Flower Hole). Chiang Kai-shek also visited Lushan when he wasn't campaigning against Mao Zedong at nearby Jinggang Shan. He lived in Building No. 180 in the East Valley.

During the Cultural Revolution, Lushan was closed, and parts were destroyed by the Red Guards. Foreign tourists were first encouraged to come in 1978, and now it is also a stop for some of the Yangtze boat tours. Lushan's views of the plains and the Yangtze are breathtaking. It is full of lovely trees, hills, pavilions, and old Tang pagodas and temples, many still untouched by tourists. Guides can rattle off incredible legends by the hour. It has a printing plant, a hydroelectric power station, and a few small factories.

Lushan is divided into an East Valley and a West Valley, with a tunnel at Gulin. Taxis are available. A tourist bus leaves downtown Gulin near the entrance to the city park whenever full.

Flower Path Park 花径公园 has a flower and Chinese *bonsai* exhibit. The miniature trees that inspired the Tang poet are here. Nearby, in what looks like a well, are two large characters meaning Flower Path, believed to be the calligraphy of the poet Bai Ju-yi. A natural rock formation beside the lake and the highway looks like two ends of a bridge over a ravine, with a little imagination. The story goes that before he became the first Ming emperor in 1368, Zhu Yanzhang escaped from his rival at this spot. A dragonfly completed the bridge, making it possible for Zhu, but not his enemy, to cross. The lake here was made in 1956 and is shaped like a violin. Swimming is permitted but not encouraged.

Grotto of Taoist Immortal 仙人洞 : Beyond the moon gate to the right is a cave about 30 feet wide, deep, and high, where Lu Tung-pin, a famous monk, studied Taoism so successfully that he became one of the Eight Taoist Immortals, the one with the supernatural sword. The water in the "Drop by Drop" spring is said to be mineral and medicinal. Note the formation over the mouth of the cave, shaped like Buddha's hand.

To the right is the Path for Visiting Fairies where, on the right of the pavilion, the three red characters mean "Bamboo Forest Temple." This refers to a temple in the vicinity that rose bodily to heaven because an enchanted boy did not want to grant the gift of immortality to the heads of neighboring temples. To the left inside the moon gate is a stone pavilion with a stele outlining the career of a famous monk who at one point helped the first Ming emperor and his army to cross a stormy river to victory. It was built by Zhu Yanzhang.

Big Heavenly Pond 大天池 : The water in this pool maintains the same height (it is said) through rain or drought, and is thus said to be "made in Heaven." The pavilion behind the pond is on the site of a temple, built to commemorate the spider who saved Zhu Yanzhang's life by spinning a web to cover him while Zhu was hiding in a well from his rival. These folk myths about great leaders would make a good study.

The monks who lived in this temple were Taoists who tried to achieve immortality through study and meditation. As a test, they jumped off Dragon Head Cliff. If you look down, you can probably guess why they were never seen again. The climb down to Dragon Head Cliff (by no means the bottom) is about 170 steps, but the view is worth it. On the way, look for a carved step that was probably part of the old temple.

Hanpokou (the Mouth that Holds Poyang Lake) 含鄱口 , named after the shape of this pass in relation to the lake, is the best place to see the rising sun. The lake is one of China's largest and is 20 km away. The tallest mountain on the right is Dahanyang, which may be climbed, but "it is dangerous." Beyond Dahangyang is the Peak of the Nine Wonders.

The **Lushan Botanical Garden** 庐山植物园 is a short walk from Hanpokou. Belonging to the Academy of Science, this garden has exchange programs with Britain's Royal Botanical Gardens and the National Arboretum in Washington, DC. Here are 3700 varieties, including trees, flowers, grasses, and medicinal herbs on 740 acres of land. Started in 1934, it is the only subalpine garden of the ten botanical gardens in China. Tourists are free to wander through the greenhouses (tropical and subtropical plants), which are open daily from 7:30 a.m. to 6 p.m. Groups can get a guide. The most exotic plant here is the metasequoia tree, a species thought to be extinct and seen only in fossils until one was found in a primitive forest in west China and propagated here. A large specimen stands labeled by the driveway near the parking lot.

The **Three Treasure Trees** 三宝树 are said to be 1500 years old, but botanists say 500. They are nevertheless very impressive, the highest being 40 meters tall. One is a gingko and two are cryptomeria. A few meters away are the Yellow Dragon Pool and the Black Dragon Pool with waterfalls.

The small **Lushan Museum** 庐山博物馆 has relics, rubbings, photographs, paintings, ancient handicrafts, and porcelains from many periods. Open 8–11:30 a.m. and 2:30–5:30 p.m. daily. Nearby is the 1000-seat **People's Theater** 人民剧场 for local opera, acrobatics, and movies.

Pavilion for Viewing the Yangtze 望江亭 has another stunning view of the countryside below. At this point, the Yangtze River is about 15 km away. To the right, you can see the historic path up which vacationers used to be carried.

At the base of Lushan are the **Donglin Temple** 东林寺 , where Hui Yuan (334–416), a famous Buddhist monk of the Eastern Jin, paraphrased Buddhist canons, and the **White Deer Academy** 白鹿洞书院 , where Zhu Xi (1130–1200) of the Song once taught.

Shopping

Gulin 牯岭 , the only shopping area, was destroyed by fire in 1947 and then rebuilt. The arts and crafts stores sell porcelain dishes and statues made in the famous porcelain center of Jingdezhen, 180 km away. Although Lushan is closer than Nanchang, the difficulty of mountain transportation makes the price of porcelain here about the same as in Nanchang. And there is less variety. Nevertheless, the price is higher outside the province. Other good buys are cloud-mist green tea and watercolors of the mountain scenery. Locally made handicrafts are walking sticks and bamboo brush or pencil holders.

Food

Local delicacy—the Three Stones: stone frog, stone fish, and stone fungus.

Hotels

Some of the buildings here are over 100 years old. They were built to last, however. Most are made of stone, with lots of space and high ceilings, but hotels have fewer services than in larger cities.

Lushan Hotel 庐山宾馆   □ *From Gulin, go through the tunnel and turn right for 2 km to 454 Hexi Rd.* □ British-built 1920s; renovated since. The main building has three stories. Villas. Heated.

Lulin Hotel 芦林饭店   □ *Hexi Rd.* □ 1958; part renovated 1985. 100 beds for foreigners. Four stories. Farthest hotel from bus station (5 km); 3-minute walk to lake, 15-minute walk to botanical garden, and 20-minute walk to Hanpokou. Has basketball and a sports field. From Gulin, go through tunnel and turn right.

Lushan Mansion 庐山大厦   □ *20-minute walk from bus station* □ 1935; reconstructed 1985.

Yunzong (Amidst the Clouds) Hotel (云中宾馆)□ *Henan Rd. and Hsiang Shan Rd.* □ Built 1930s. Spacious villas (with sitting and reading rooms!) reminiscent of Indian or Burmese hill stations. 10-minute walk to Flower Path Park, and 20-minute walk to the Taoist Grotto. About 3 km to bus station.

C.I.T.S.: Lushan Hotel, tel. 2318, 2427, 2497.
C.T.S.: Lushan Hotel; tel. 2497.

Nanchang 南昌

(Southern Prosperity) South China. By air, 2 hours north of Guangzhou, 2 hours SE of Shanghai and 3 hours, 20 minutes south of Beijing. Capital of Jiangxi province. Because it is bounded by mountains on the east, south, and west, it is like a furnace in summer. With no northern mountains, it is very cold in winter. Coldest—⁻10°C in January–February; hottest—40°C, July–September. Provincial annual precipitation, 1200 to 1900 mm, mainly late April and May. Population: 800,000.

Nanchang's principal attractions are its revolutionary museums; it is primarily of interest to students of modern history. It is also the capital of Jiangxi province and can be covered in one day.

Nanchang was founded over 2000 years ago on the east bank of the Gan River. It is best known today as the site of the first independent armed effort by the Communists, on August 1, 1927, considered now the founding date of the People's Liberation Army. Industries include iron and steel, machine building, electric motors, tractors, electronics, chemicals, and textiles.

The city is built almost entirely of red brick. The province has developed its own opera and local songs, the latter sung while picking tea. In the area grow seedless tangerines, sesame, rape, and rice. The population includes Han, Hui, Miao, She, Yao and other nationalities.

August 1st Museum   八一起义纪念馆 : The setting here is a period masterpiece with the original furniture or reproductions. You are in the Grand Jiangxi Hotel of the 1920s! On the ground floor are old carved mahogany and rosewood furniture and an opium chair. Bedroom no. 1 was Chou En-lai's. Between the bedrooms are room dividers with stained-glass windows and light fixtures with pulleys. Everywhere are large brass spittoons. Even if you are not interested in revolutionary history, the building itself is worth the trip. Opened in 1924, it was used as a hotel until it was closed during the Cultural Revolution. After all, it had been the headquarters of the historic uprising! In 1969, it opened again as a museum.

The galleries are numbered and labeled in Chinese. On the second floor: (1) the background of the uprising, planned during the Northern Expedition when the Communists realized there could be no cooperation with the Nationalists (and vice versa), especially after the slaughter of the Communists in several cities in April 1927; (2) preparations for the uprising in Nanchang. Chou En-lai was one of the leaders. Thirty thousand troops took part. Third floor: (3) the uprising. Map with lights shows enemy headquarters in black and insurgent headquarters in red. Five-hour battle ended in victory for the Communists, who held the city until August 5; (4) withdrawal to Jinggang Shan, where in October Mao Tse-tung established a base in the mountains.

Exhibition Hall of Jiangxi Revolutionary History 江西革命历史博物馆 is on the main square, along with the Jiangxi Provincial Museum. It concerns the Anyuan Coal Miners' Strike led by Mao Tse-tung, and Jinggang Shan.

Jiangxi Provincial Museum 江西省博物馆 : Open Wednesdays, Fridays, and Sundays, 8–11 a.m. and 2–5 p.m., this small museum contains some neolithic pieces, Shang bronzes, Song porcelain, an ancient implement for ironing clothes (look for picture demonstrating use), mirrors, and some tomb figures. On the second floor is a model of a Ming tomb, that of the governor of Jiangxi who was the 16th son of the first Ming emperor. Tomb pieces here are from a site about 15 km north in Xinjian. They include a jade belt, hair decorations, an army of servants, sedan chairs, and orchestra. Quite delightful!

Badashanren Museum 八大山人纪念馆 is of the famous landscape painter who lived here during the late Ming and early Qing dynasties. This "Man of the Eight Mountains" is also famous for his birds and flowers. The museum has a rotating collection of his works and is housed in the Qingyunpu Taoist temple founded over 2000 years ago.

The 1600-year-old **Wanshou Taoist Temple** honors Xu Xun, a local folk hero who lived to be 135 years old. It can be visited.

Arts and Crafts Exhibition Hall of Jiangxi products 江西工艺美术馆 : The pieces here range from a 2-meter-high lacquer vase to a quarter-inch ivory stele on which are written poems by Mao Tse-tung. Pieces from the famous porcelain center of Jingdezhen can be ordered or bought here.

Hundred Flower Islet is the prettiest and most interesting of the city's parks. Plum Hill has some temples.

For other points of interest in Jiangxi, please see separate listings: **Lushan** mountain resort 180 km north; **Jingdezhen,** ancient porcelain city 250 km NE; **Jinggang Shan,** mountain resort and revolutionary base; **Jiujiang,** 34 km north of Lushan on the Yangtze.

Shopping
Store hours: 8 a.m.–7:30 or 8 p.m.

Restaurants
Shixianlou Restaurant 时鲜楼餐厅
Xingyia Restaurant 新雅餐厅
Hsinguiyuan Restaurant 香江园大酒楼
Fuwudalou Restaurant 服务大楼餐厅
Yieweichan Ting Restaurant 野味餐厅 □ wild game, but no endangered species, please!

Hotels

   Jiangxi Guest House 江西宾馆 □ *August 1 Ave.* □ 1961. 182 rooms, eight stories. Basketball. Three restaurants. 34 km from airport. Walking distance to biggest department store and main square.

   Green Mountain Lake Hotel 青山湖宾馆 □ 1986. 500 beds, 15 stories. Swimming pool.

C.I.T.S. 国际旅行社 : Jiangxi Guest House; tel. 62571.
CAAC 中国民航 : tel. 62571.

Nanjing

(Nanking; Southern Capital) East China. SW part of Jiangsu province on the Changjiang (Yangtze) River, 5 hours by train or 1 hour by air (300 km) NW of Shanghai, or 16 hours by train (2¼ hours by air) SE of Beijing. Direct 2-hour flight from Hong Kong. Nanjing is the capital of Jiangsu. Weather: Hottest: 40°C (rare)—August; coldest: ⁻15°C—January. Annual precipitation more than 1000 mm. Rain in summer. Population: over 4 million.

Nanjing is important because of its historical relics and its beauty. It was settled 6000 years ago and was a walled city 2400 years ago. From A.D. 229 to 1421, it was intermittently the capital of the Wu, Eastern Jin, Song, Qi, Liang, Chen, Southern Tang, and early Ming dynasties. Jianye, Jiankang, Jinling, and Jingshi are its former names. Many of the ancient relics in the present city are Ming, built by Zhu Yuanzhang (Chu Yuan-chang), first emperor of the dynasty (1368–99) whose reign name was Hongwu. After him, the capital was moved to

Beijing, where his successors built the Forbidden City and were buried in elaborate tombs north of it.

In 1842, the Treaty of Nanking with England was signed here ending the First Opium War, and the city was declared an open port. In 1853, the Taiping Heavenly Kingdom made Nanjing its capital for 11 years. On January 1, 1912, it became the capital of the Sun Yat-sen government and remained the Nationalist capital until April 5, 1912, when the capital was moved to Beijing. After a period of much confusion, Chiang Kai-shek unilaterally declared Nanjing the capital on April 18, 1927.

The Japanese captured Nanjing on Dec. 12, 1937, and massacred 100,000 civilians in what is referred to as the Rape of Nanking. A museum was recently opened to commemorate this tragic event. The Nationalists moved their capital to Chongqing but returned to Nanjing after the Japanese surrender in 1945. Most buildings survived the war. The Communists took the city on April 23, 1949, and the capital was moved to Beijing. Nanjing is still the provincial capital, and the economic cultural center of the province.

Nanjing today is a beautiful city of broad avenues thickly lined with 240,000 trees. Central is the Drum Tower, with Zhongshan Road, the main shopping street, running south, northwest, and east, intersecting in the center of town. Part of Zhongshan South Road was roughly the old Imperial Way, open only for the emperor. The earlier dynasties were centered in this section of town. Xuanwu Lake dominates the northeastern sector. Above it to the east looms 450-meter Zijin (Purple Gold) Mountain. The magnificent Ming city wall snakes around most of the urban area.

Two thousand factories and mining enterprises make metallurgical and chemical equipment, radios, ships, telecommunication instruments, meters, and synthetic fibers. The Zhong Xin Yuen silk factory manufactures brocade, and the Arts and Crafts Carving Factory works in ivory and wood.

Tourism officials here have been among the best in the country. They have organized a Grand Canal Tour (Suzhou to Yangzhou), honeymoon tours, bicycle tours, and an all-Jiangsu chartered bus tour.

Nanjing takes two days to see, but if you only have one day in the city itself, most important are the Sun Yat-sen Mausoleum, Linggu Temple, and Ming Tomb in the south part of the city, usually combined in a half-day tour. In the afternoon, you can choose from the Observatory (for the view), the museum, the impressive Zhonghua Gate and city wall, the Drum Tower, the Yangtze River Bridge or whatever you want from the following menu.

*Sun Yixian (Sun Yat-sen) Mausoleum 中山陵 (open daily) is on an 80,000-square-meter site. The building was built to be better than those of the emperors whom the father of the Chinese republic overthrew. Eight km from the Jinling Hotel, it is on the south side of Purple

Gold Mountain, its *feng-shui* ideal. Dr. Sun (1866–1925) was buried here in 1929 in the rear of the hall (see ''Milestones in Chinese History''). The mausoleum, 158 meters above sea level, has 392 steps and a 5-meter-high statue, and is well worth visiting.

Sun Yat-sen was born of peasant stock in Guangdong province, near Macao, in what is now called Zhongshan county, renamed after its most distinguished son. Zhongshan was Dr. Sun's honorific name.

Dr. Sun actually spent most of his life outside China, leaving home at the age of 12 to study at an Anglican school in Hawaii, where his older brother had settled. He studied medicine in Hong Kong and for a short time set up practice in Macao. He spent much of his life traveling in Europe and America, and living in Japan, writing and plotting against the Manchus and planning a government for China. His teachings have been slavishly followed in Taiwan, where he is almost worshiped. He is highly respected in China too.

An intriguing, complex man, Dr. Sun became a Christian early in life and, although he attacked missionaries as being imperialists, he admitted on his death bed to being a Christian still. He fought the Manchus because they could not rid the country of the foreign imperialists. After becoming president, he did make it a point to inform the first Ming emperor of what had happened!

Dr. Sun did not remain president for long. Because of the problems in uniting the country, he abdicated in 1912. The north was not willing to accept a southerner as head of state, he reasoned. He later accepted a post as director of railways for the country. At the same time, he flirted with socialism, coming under the influence of Russian advisers.

He was married first to a peasant woman and later to Soong Chingling, much against her father's wishes. The second marriage shocked the Christians but not most Chinese, who were used to the idea of several wives. Mme. Sun was the sister of Mme. Chiang Kai-shek of Taiwan. See also ''Shanghai'' and ''Zhongshan.''

Linggu (Valley of the Soul) Temple 灵谷寺 (open daily) is just an empty building, the only survivor of a whole complex of Buddhist structures, its statues destroyed during the Taiping war, when the Qing army slept here. Eight km from the Jinling Hotel, it was built originally in A.D. 513 by a Liang princess in memory of a famous monk. It was moved to its current location at the eastern foot of Zijin Mountain because the first Ming emperor wanted the original site for his own tomb. Without beams, it is reminiscent of medieval Europe because of its arches. Its eastern and western walls curve outward. Nearby is a nine-story pagoda built in the 1920s to complement the area around the mausoleum, 2 km to the NW. The pagoda can be climbed for a good view of this beautiful, wooded area.

The **Xiaoling Mausoleum (Ming Tomb)** 明陵 is open daily; tel. 42990. This mausoleum of the first Ming emperor, Zhu Yuanzhang, and his empress (1398 and 1382 respectively) is not as impressive as those north of Beijing, but is worth a visit. The Sacred Way has over a dozen well-proportioned, larger-than-life-size mythical animals, four generals, and four ministers in parallel lines. It is unlike other Sacred Ways. A bend in the line was made to avoid disturbing the tomb of a general. The stone statues are beautiful. Most of the buildings were destroyed in the early days of the Qing, who overthrew the Ming dynasty, but visitors can get an idea of its past glory from the ruins. The mausoleum is 6 km from the Jinling Hotel.

Zhu Yuanzhang was an unemployed peasant and former Buddhist monk and beggar who fought his way to the throne and was a brilliant emperor.

The **Botanical Garden** 植物园 , with tropical and subtropical plants, is on one side of the Sacred Way.

Zijinshan (Purple Gold Mountain), a.k.a. Bell Mountain 紫金山 , dominates the northeastern skyline. The **Observatory** (tel. 42270) is on the west side and can be combined with a visit to Xuanwu Lake. This major research center of the Chinese Academy of Science was built in 1929 and is involved with space research such as manmade satellites. Tourists usually go there for the magnificent view of the city and surrounding countryside and to see the copies of ancient instruments outside.

The armillary sphere (four dragons and spheres) was invented 2000 years ago in the Western Han and was used to locate constellations. The abridged armillary sphere (three dragons) was invented in the Yuan for the same purpose. Both these 500-year-old replicas were stolen by the Germans and French respectively in 1900. They were later returned. The gnomon column next to the abridged sphere was invented 3000 years ago and was used to survey the seasons and calculate the days of the year. It faces due south and north. In the large column is a small hole through which the sun shines at noon, casting an oval of light on the gauge below. Because of this instrument, the Chinese decided very early that there were 365¼ days a year.

Xuanwu Lake 玄武湖 is outside Xuanwu Gate, NE of the city (tel. 33154), 5 km from the Jinling Hotel. Twenty-five km in circumference, this lake is now used for recreation and fish farming. It is 1–2 meters deep, has five islets, and covers 444 hectares (1100 acres), of which about a tenth is land. It was originally built in the fifth century, and several emperors have used it to train or review their navies and for private recreation. A black dragon was spotted here in the fifth century, so if you visit it on a dark and stormy night, you might want to look for it.

In 1075 (Northern Song) the emperor was persuaded to convert the lake to rice paddies. When the paddies were drained in 1953, Song tombs and pottery were discovered. In 1911, the lake was turned into a park, and by 1949 was almost completely silted up. The new government drained, enlarged it, and added buildings. Today there is a famous pick-your-own-live fish restaurant called the White Garden, a zoo, theater, playground, swimming pool, roller-skating area, boats-for-hire kiosk, and exhibition halls. You can walk from the railway station and take a ferry.

Jiangsu Provincial Museum (a.k.a. Nanjing Museum) 江苏省博物馆 (Zhongshan East Rd; tel. 41554) contains exhibits ranging from the era of Peking Man to revolutionary times. This traditional Chinese-style building was begun in the 1930s, interrupted by the war, resumed in 1945, and completed in 1949. It was opened as a museum in March 1953. Three thousand items are on display, more in storage. Among these are a 3000-year-old duck egg—genuine; the jade burial suit that was exhibited in Europe, Asia, and America in 1973 (Eastern Han, from Xuzhou City, Jiangsu); a sixth-century Soul Pot covered with many birds, placed in a tomb so the birds could fly the soul of the deceased to paradise; a small bronze model of a stove (Ming) with five woks, also for the use of the deceased; maps of the early capitals in Nanjing from 229 to 589, so you can try to locate ancient landmarks in the modern city; a 2-meter scroll showing the inspection tour by Qing Emperor Kangxi (Kang-hsi) from Nanjing to Zhenjiang; the anchor from a British merchant ship lost in Zhenjiang; a photograph of a British-built electric company in 1882; a list of institutions set up by the United States in China, with numbers of Chinese students and teachers and of foreign teachers. Located 4 km from Jinling Hotel.

The **Gulou (Drum Tower)** 鼓楼 is at the intersection of Zhongshan North, South, and East roads and Zhongyang and Beijing roads, in the center of the city. Built in 1382, it holds a 6-foot-diameter drum and an ancient giant stone tortoise carrying a stele added in the Qing, a report on the inspection tour of a high Qing official. (See *Drum Towers* in ''What to See and Do.'') Nearby is the Big Bell Pavilion.

Nanjing City Wall 南京城墙 is 23 meters high, 33.4 km in circumference, and from 7.62 to 12 meters thick. Built from 1368 to 1387, it once had 13,616 cannons on top. Roughly 10 km north-south by 5.62 km east-west, it is said to be the longest city wall in the world. The bricks were made in five provinces, and each is inscribed with the name of the superintendent and the brickmaster, plus the date made. The mortar was lime, tung oil, and glutinous rice water. It was originally built with 13 gates, and 11 more were added. Cannot be missed.

The **Zhonghua Gate** 中华门 , on the south side, is the best gate to see. It has four two-story gates in succession (in case the enemy breaks through one), 12 tunnels, and room to garrison 3000 soldiers. One can walk along the top of the wall here, which overlooks an old section of the city south of the gate.

Jiu Hua Hill (Monk Tang Pagoda) was originally built in the Song, about 1000 years ago, to keep the skull of Xuan Zhang (Hsuan-tsang), the monk who traveled to India in search of the Buddhist sutras and was immortalized in the novel *Pilgrimage to the Western World.*

The rest of him is in Xi'an. The pagoda collapsed in the Qing. In 1942 the Japanese dug up the base, taking the skull to Japan. They built the present pagoda to house the small fragment left behind.

If you have more time or specialized interests:

Inside the city wall: Qingliang Shan Park was a lovely gathering place for painters and writers of old, on a hill overlooking the northern part of Nanjing near the university. It is on the main road to the Yangtze River Bridge. Among the writers was the author of the Nanjing-based classic novel *The Scholars*. A crematorium used to be in the area, and as a result few Chinese come here. It is a good place to get away from crowds.

Zhanyuan Garden (Garden for Viewing) 瞻园 (Zhanyuan Rd.) is in the southern part of the city, near the Zhonghua Gate. Open daily; tel. 25262.

Originally built in the Ming dynasty, 600 years ago, the palace that now houses the **Taiping Museum**   太平天国历史博物馆   was rebuilt for Yang Xiuqing (Yang Hsin-ching), eastern prince of the Taiping Heavenly Kingdom in the mid-19th century. It now contains 1000 square meters of exhibits reflecting the: (1) background of the revolution; (2) uprising at Jintian village; (3) Nanjing as capital; (4) regulations and policies; (5) insistence on armed struggle; (6) resisting aggression; (7) safeguarding the capital; (8) continuing the revolution.

Another relic of the Taipings well worth seeing is the **Tianwang Mansion (The Heavenly King's Mansion)** (292 Changjiang Rd. in the eastern part of the city). Open by appointment; tel. 41131. Built on the site of a mansion for the Prince of Han by the first Ming emperor, it was later the Jiangxi and Jiangnan provincial governor-general's office. The current palace was made for Hong Xiuquan (Hung Hsiu-chuan), the head of the Taipings, with materials from the Ming palace. Note stone boat in pond.

After the 1911 Revolution, the Tianwang Mansion was used as the Presidential Residence.

The Ming Palace 明宫遗址   : These ruins are in the eastern part of Nanjing and can be seen in about five minutes. Built for the first Ming emperor from 1368 to 1386, it was copied in Beijing for the Ming palace there. The Forbidden City is about the same size. The palace was partially destroyed in 1645 by Qing troops, and what was left was pulled down to build the Taiping palaces. In 1911 only a gate was left standing, but in 1958 some of the relics were restored. From these you can get an idea of the original.

Meiyuan Xincun (Plum Blossom Villa) 梅园新村   : No. 30. Open daily, except Mondays; tel. 44743. Furniture, office, clothing, and photographs are as they were when Premier Chou En-lai headed the Communist delegation in its negotiations with the Nationalists (1946–47).

Bailuzhou (Egret Isle) Park is in the south of the city near the Confucian Temple and Taiping Museum. Open daily; tel. 23948. Believed to be a garden given by the first Ming Emperor to Xu Da, Prince of Zhongshan, the buildings were destroyed in the Qing. The current buildings were reconstructed after liberation.

Shitoucheng (Stone City) of the Wu Dynasty 石头城 (north of the Hanzhong Gate, inside the western edge of the city wall) is open daily. After the Wu capital was moved here from Zhenjiang, this city, almost 2000 years old, was started by General Sun Chuan on what was then the banks of the Changjiang River. The deep red rock in the area is natural.

An appointment is needed to visit the **Chaotian (Worshiping Heaven) Palace** (east of Mochou Lake, inside the city wall at Yeshan (Smelting) Hill). Permission can be obtained from Nanjing Municipal Museum; tel. 41983. It is said that Fu Chai (Fu Tsai), king of Wu in mid-fifth century B.C. (see also ''Suzhou''), created a special town for making steel swords here. In this city in A.D. 318, a prime minister of the Jin was urged by a geomancer to move the town because the energy emanating from the fire and metal was making the prime minister sick. Wang Dao moved the smelter and used the site as a garden. The smelter was put at its current site, SE of the Stone City.

The first emperor of the Ming dynasty had no such problems with fire and metal, and built a palace at Yeshan Hill for receiving homage from his subjects. In the 19th century, the palace was converted to a Confucian temple, currently the largest Confucian temple complex south of the Yangtze, and the home of the **Nanjing Municipal Museum** 南京市博物馆 . Also in the city is a memorial hall to Zheng He, the Moslem eunuch who became one of China's most famous maritime commanders, making seven voyages to 30 countries of Asia and Africa from 1405 to 1433. His tomb is 10 km south of Nanjing. The English Corner (to be avoided or searched for, depending on your desire to meet local people), is at the foot of Drum Tower Park, every Sunday at 2 p.m.

Outside the city wall The imposing **Nanjing Yangtze River Bridge** 南京长江大桥 is the second longest in China, having been surpassed in 1985 by the Yellow River Bridge between Shandong and Henan. Including approaches, it is 4589 meters long, of which 1577 meters are directly over the Changjiang River. It has four lanes for vehicular traffic and, on another level, two train tracks side by side. Tourists are taken to an observation tower for a good view of the river, a nearby dolomite mine, and the city. The bridge was built in 1960–68 and is 10 km from the Jinling Hotel.

Yuhuatai (Rain-Flower) People's Revolutionary Martyr's Memorial Park 雨花台烈士陵园 is just south of the Zhonghua Gate, 5 km from the Jinling Hotel. Open daily; tel. 24003. This ancient battleground was later an execution grounds used by the Japanese and warlords. Here the Nationalists killed 100,000 Communists and sympathizers from 1927 to 1949. Now a memorial park with exhibit hall and flower garden, it is known also for its multicolored agate pebbles.

Mochou (Sorrow-Free) Lake Park 莫愁湖 (outside the wall, SW of the city) contains several buildings from the Qing and a small 47-hectare lake. The white marble statue of Mochou is a local landmark. She was the good-hearted wife but submissive daughter-in-law who ended up killing herself, alas, because of her oppressive father-in-law. Also paintings and antique exhibit. Open daily; tel. 23243.

Qixia (Lingering Sunset Clouds) Temple 栖霞寺, 25 km. NE of the city, is open daily, except Mondays; tel. 44470. Originally built in the Qi dynasty (A.D. 479–480) as a monastery. During the Tang, it was one of the four largest temples in China. The years have taken their toll, however, and the buildings were destroyed. The current buildings are from 1908.

Behind the temple is the **Thousand Buddhas Cliff** 千佛岩, started in A.D. 484 and including three 10.5–11-meter-high Buddhist statues. The carving of these 515 saints ended in A.D. 511 and began again in the Ming. Unfortunately, the heads of the buddhas have been damaged. A finely carved 18.04-meter-high dagoba dates from A.D. 601, with renovations in A.D. 943.

The **Stone Engravings of the Southern Dynasties** 六朝石刻 can be seen any time. Scattered around the suburbs of Nanjing, especially the towns of Jurong, Jiangning, and Danyang (at the Grand Canal) to the south and east, are relics of the Six Dynasties (222–589). Some of the 31 tombs sites (11 emperors and 20 nobles) are in the middle of a field off the main road. Many of the tombs are protected by distinctive pairs of stone mythical animals, pillars, or tablets, symbols of authority and dignity.

The **Southern Tang Tombs** 南唐二陵 are more than 30 km south of the city. Visitors can enter two to see old murals, reliefs, and coffins of the first two emperors of the Tang dynasty, Li Bian and Li Jing, who ruled over 1300 years ago. The tomb of the founder of that glorious dynasty is bigger than that of his successor. It is 21 meters long by 10 meters wide and at least five meters high. The highly decorated coffins of the imperial couple are in the rear under a chart of the stars and planets.

Day trips from Nanjing can be made to Zhenjiang and Yangzhou. Also in the province are Changzhou, Suzhou, Wuxi, Xuzhou, and Yixing. See separate listings. Also promoted is **Huai'an**—Zhou Enlai's birthplace, where there is also a Han pagoda, the Zhen Huai Tower, and a 70-bed hotel. Of note too is **Lianyungang,** on the Yellow Sea, one of the 14 Open Coastal Cities. It has the Ayuwang Pagoda, Water Curtain Cave, a shell carving factory, and a hot spring.

You can get more information from the Foreign Liaison Office, Jiangsu Travel and Tourism Bureau, especially on bicycling tours, honeymoon and silver or golden anniversary tours, and *taijiquan* lessons.

For background on Nanjing, read Barry Till's *In Search of Old Nanking*.

Cultural performances:

The Nanjing Acrobatic Troupe has won international prizes.

Shopping

Made in Nanjing are "Yunjin (Figured) Satin" brocade, velvet tapestry and carpets, imitations of ancient wood and ivory carvings, and paper cuts. Made in the province are inlaid lacquer (Yangzhou), purple sand pottery (Yixing), Huishan clay figures, and Suzhou embroidery. Store hours: 7 or 7:30 a.m.–7:30 or 8 p.m.; some open 24 hours.

Around one of the former Confucian temples is a lively free market (jeans, fish, birds, back scratchers, etc.) with a good Bao Zi (see "Food") restaurant. The temple, now a hospital, used to be the imperial examination hall. On the nearby river, the flower girls used to solicit customers.

Friendship Store 友谊商店 (86 Zhongyang Rd.; tel. 32802) can package and ship. One of the best in China.

Antique Store 古物商店 (5–13 Hanzhong Rd.; tel. 44550); **Sales Department of the Nanjing Handicraft Cooperative** (Zhongshan South Rd.; tel. 42613); **Arts & Crafts Service** 工艺美术服务部　31 Beijing East Rd.; tel. 34193, 34197); **Xinjiekou Department Store** (3 Zhongshan South Rd.; tel. 41300); **Renmin (People's) Market** 人民市场 (79 Zhongshan South Rd.; tel. 42766); **Changjianglu S.&N. China Native Produce Grocery** (west entrance of Changjiang Rd.; tel. 42344) food only; **Overseas Chinese Store** 华侨商店 (86 Zhongyang Rd.; tel. 33883); **Foreign Languages Bookstore** 外文书店 (137 Zhongshan East Rd.; tel. 41887).

Restaurants

Nanjing people say the recipe for Beijing roast duck originally was from Nanjing, so you might want to try the Nanjing version
Among the other local specialties are: salted duck, especially August Sweet-Osmanthus duck, salted duck gizzard, roast chicken with coriander, salted shrimps, casserole cabbage heart, Big Flat Pork Croquette (outside crisp, inside soft), chrysanthemum-shaped herring, long-tailed shrimp and squirrel-like mandarin fish.

Nanjing style is somewhat oily.

Jiangsu Restaurant 江苏酒家　□ *126 Jiankang Rd.; tel. 23698, 41027.*

Maxiangxing Moslem Restaurant 马祥兴菜馆　□ *Gulou (Drum Tower), Zhongshan North Rd.; tel. 33807.*

Baiyuan Restaurant □ *Liangzhou Isle, Xuanwu Lake; tel. 32903* □ Seafood.

Other styles

Old Guangdong Restaurant □ *45 Zhongshan Rd.; tel. 42482.*

Dasanyuan Restaurant 大三元 □ *38 Zhongshan Rd.; tel. 41027* □ Guangdong.

Sichuan Restaurant   四川饭店   □ *171 Taiping South Rd.; tel. 42243, 43651.*

Quyuan Restaurant   奎元菜馆   □ *20, Beiting Lane, Zhongshan East Rd.; tel. 41824* □ Hunan.

Tongqinglou Restaurant   同庆楼菜馆   □ *10 Zhongshan East Rd.; tel. 42880* □ Beijing.

Liuhuachun Restaurant □ *Nanjing Railway Station; tel. 52318* □ Shanghai.

Luliuju Vegetarian Restaurant □ *Taiping Lu; tel. 43644* □ The vegetarian Bao Zi are superb.

For good Western food: the Jinling, Nanjing, and Victory hotels, especially the first.

Hotels

Nanjing has a good share of all tourists to China and is working hard to get more. It was one of the first cities to have two-year courses for hotel attendants and drivers, with strong emphasis on foreign language training. The first 500 graduated in 1980.

Nanjing Hotel   南京饭店   □ *Hongqiao, 259 Zhongshan North Rd.* □ 1955, 1979; renovated 1984. 400 rooms. Two buildings. 4000 square meters of grounds. Three stories. Residential area. Bar, dance hall, barbershop.

Dingshan Guest House   丁山宾馆   □ *Dingshan Hill, Chahar Rd./53, Zhenjiang Rd.* □ 1976, eight-story wing, 130 rooms. A 110-room extension was built in 1979 with Australian cooperation, but is reported to be poorly maintained. Isolated on Ding Hill near the former British residency, it is surrounded by communes. From its rooftop coffee shop is a great view of the city. Dance hall, bar, good Jiangsu food.

Dongjiao Guest House □ *5, 7, and 9 Lingyuan Rd./Zhongshan Ling. Set in pine and bamboo groves* □ No. 9 is in the traditional old Chinese style. No. 5 has Chinese furniture. Chinese and Western food.

Jinling Hotel   金陵饭店   □ *Zhongshan and Hanzhong rds. at Xinjiekou; telex 34110 JLHNJ CN, cable 6855* □ 1983. This is the top hotel in the city, and one of the best in China. 760 rooms, each with two telephones, refrigerator. 37 stories with revolving restaurant on top. City center location. Beautiful furnishings. Travel service, business center, health club with sauna, safe deposit boxes, year-round swimming pool, and 24-hour room service. Ballroom seats 1125 with simultaneous interpretation equipment, six restaurants and bars and coffee shop. Good hamburgers and spaghetti in Orchid Room. 7 km. from airport.·

Meiling Palace □ *Former residence of Mme. Chiang Kai-shek. Near Sun Yixian mausoleum.* □ Has traditional old Chinese-style interior, redwood furniture and carved marble balustrades. At least ¥1000 a night will pay for three big suites, three double rooms, one single, a dining hall, coffee shop—for up to 15 people.

Shengli (Victory) Hotel   胜利饭店   □ *Zhongshan South Rd.* □

Built before Liberation. 30 rooms, five stories. In downtown shopping area. Chinese and Western food. Barbershop.

Shuangmenlou Guest House 双门楼宾馆   □ *Shuangmenlou, Huju North Rd.* □ Built before Liberation on the grounds of former British consulate. Said to be cold in winter.

Zhongshan (Bell Mountain) Hotel 钟山宾馆 □ *Near museum* □ 1985.

Important Addresses

C.I.T.S.: 313 Zhongshan Bei Rd.; tel. 85921 X115.
CAAC 中国民航 : 76, Zhongshan East Rd.; tel. 43378, 41114 X364 or X365.

Nanning 南宁

South China. Capital of Guangxi Zhuang Autonomous Region, in the southern part of Guangxi, near the northeastern border of Vietnam. It is on the railway line between Hanoi and Guilin. Can also be reached by air from Guangzhou (1 hour), Guilin (1 hour), Kunming (1¼ hours) and Beijing. Some tours here have been canceled because of periodic clashes between China and Vietnam. Nanning is on the Yu River. Urban population is 500,000. Nanning has a subtropical climate, meaning great fruit, flowering trees, and mild, humid weather. Hottest—38°C; coldest—5°C. Annual precipitation 1300 mm, mostly May to September. It is worth visiting because of its national minorities, its karst caves, hot springs, and medicinal herb garden. Nearby is Jintian, where the Taiping Heavenly Kingdom originated.

Settled since A.D. 27, Nanning was the provincial capital from 1912 to 1936, and after 1949. It has a few industries.

The **Guangxi Museum** 广西博物馆 (Qiyi Rd.) is open daily, except Mondays and Fridays, 2:30–5:30 p.m. Botanical and zoological specimens, historical relics, and Taiping history. It also boasts the largest collection of bronze drums (over 300) in China. The 126.5-hectare **Nanhu (South Lake) Park** 南湖公园 in the SE has 1200 varieties of medicinal herbs, plus orchids and bonsai. The **Guangxi Botanical Garden of Medicinal Plants** 广西药用植物园 , 8 km from the city in the eastern suburbs, has 2100 kinds on 200 hectares. It also raises animals for medicinal purposes.

The **Yiling cave** 伊岭岩 , 32 km north in Wuming County, is much like a Guilin cave, with colored lights to highlight weird rock formations that here look like lions, a hen, and vegetables. Visitors usually walk 1100 meters. Outside is a pavilion built in the elaborate style of the Dong people.

For those interested in the customs of national minorities, visit a commune of the Zhuang people in Wuming County, and in Nanning, the **Institute of Nationalities** 广西民族学院 or Guangxi Minority Nationality College, 10 km from the Yongzhou Hotel. The **Guangxi Art College** 广西艺术学院 teaches the art, music, and dances of the minorities.

Twelve nationalities live in the region, of which the Zhuang form one third. They are somewhat similar to the people of Thailand. The colorful Miao and Yao live here also. This makes Nanning a good place to look for handicrafts to study and buy.

The Taiping Heavenly Kingdom originated from *Jintian village 金田村 272 km NW of the city. This was the most extensive peasant uprising in Chinese history. It started in 1851 and took over a large portion of the country with a capital in Nanjing. Its disruptions were largely responsible for the emigration of Chinese people from south China to America, Australia, and other parts of Asia. At the home of Wei Changhui, one of the leaders, weapons were made and hidden in a nearby trench and pond.

Other public places are the **Renmin (People's Park)** 人民公园 with what looks like a WWII cannon, the **Xijiao (West Suburbs) Park** 西郊公园 (with zoo), and **Lingshui** 灵水 in Wuming County, 46 km north of the city, with its relaxing 23°C lake in a hilly setting. **Guiping Xishan Hill** 桂平西山 , 248 km NE, has a marvelous view of the area.

Newly opened to visitors are the **Mount Hua Rock Paintings** 花山壁昼 along the Minjiang River, 180 km away. Here one can take a boat trip to see primitive riverside rock paintings. Dances inspired by the paintings can be arranged.

Trips can also be made to hospitals, factories, a kindergarten, local minorities' products center, and a pineapple-growing farm. **Beihai** is Guangxi's sea port, and one of the 14 Open Coastal Cities. In the Dong Autonomous Sanjiang County is the recently restored multi-pagoda-ed 64-m-long Yongji Bridge in Dong architecture. For other destinations in Guangxi, see also Liuzhou and Guilin under separate listing.

A good time to visit is during the Dragon Boat Festival (5th day of the 5th month), the Zhuang Song Festival (3rd day of the 3rd month), Lantern Festival (15th day of the 1st month), and Mid-Autumn Festival (15th day of the 8th month)—all on the lunar calendar. At the Song Festival, small groups of male and small groups of female singers compete with each other in wit, knowledge, and vocal quality. Then the boys chase the girls they like in order to continue the contest with more privacy. The festival also includes throwing embroidered balls and participating in dragon and buffalo dances. Dates on the Western calendar are March 31, 1987, April 18, 1988, April 8, 1989, and March 29, 1990.

Shopping

Locally made are Zhuang brocade, bamboo, and pottery ware. The province also makes artistic shell, horn, and feather products, and stone carvings. Also produced are Xishan tea and Milky Spring Wine. Tourists can visit the silk factory.

Arts and Crafts Service 工艺美术服务部 (Xinhua Rd.; tel. 2779); **Bamboo and Wood Handicrafts Store** 竹制品商店 (Chaoyang Rd.; tel. 5474); **Chaoyang Department Store** 朝阳百货大楼 (Chaoyang and Xinhua rds.); **Foreign Languages Bookstore** 外文书店 (Xinhua Rd.; tel. 7033); **Friendship Store** 友谊商店 (Xinmin Rd.; tel. 3480); **Nanning Antique Store** 南宁古物店 (Guangxi Museum, Qiyi Rd.; tel. 7810).

Restaurants

The food here is much like neighboring Guangdong's: Cantonese. Please avoid eating endangered species.

Bailong Restaurant 白龙餐厅 □ *Renmin Park.*

Fish Restaurant 鱼餐厅 □ *Nanhu Park; tel. 2477.*

Nanning Restaurant 南宁餐厅 □ *Minsheng Rd.; tel. 2473.*

Snake Restaurant 蛇餐厅 □ *Xijiao Park; tel. 6433* □ Besides snake, there's also dog and turtle.

Hotels

Yongzhou Hotel 邕州饭店 □ *Xinmin Rd.* □ 860 beds in three buildings: No. 1 built 1957; No. 2 built 1958, and No. 3 built 1980. Renovations for No. 1 and 2 began in 1985. 32 km from airport. This is the main tourist hotel.

Xi Yuan Hotel 西园饭店 □ *Jiang Nan Rd.* □ 12 villas built from 1958 to 1973. No. 12 renovated 1984.

Min Yuan Hotel 明园饭店 □ *Xinmin Rd.* □ 11 villas built from 1952 to 1977. New building 1985 with over 200 beds.

Yongjiang (Yong River Hotel) 邕江饭店 □ *Quan Nan Rd./Dangyang St.* □ Built 1973.

Other Important Addresses

Bank of China 中国银行 : Taoyuan Rd.; tel. 5584, 4247.

CAAC 中国民航 : 64 Chaoyang Rd.; tel. 3333.

C.I.T.S. 中旅社 and **C.T.X.:** Xinmin Rd.; tel. 24793, 22042.

Foreign Affairs Office of the Guangxi Zhuang Autonomous Region 广西壮族自治区外事处 : Minzhu Rd.; tel. 3636.

Hospitals: If convenient, try your guide or hotel attendant first. Otherwise. **Guangxi People's Hospital** 广西人民医院 : Taoyuan Rd. (tel. 3237); **Hospital of Guangxi Medical College** 广西医学院附属医院 : Taoyuan Rd. (tel. 3014).

Ningbo (Ningpo) 宁波

East China. On the Zhejiang coast south of Shanghai, it can be reached by road from Hangzhou (4 hours), by thrice-weekly plane (25 minutes), and by daily 11-hour ship from Shanghai (overnight best to save time). A hovercraft from Shanghai should be starting soon, if it hasn't already, which should cut the time down to 5½ hours. Ningbo is on the Shanghai-Hangzhou railway line (slow). An airport is planned.

A community of 600,000 people, Ningbo is known because some of the world's great ship builders and business people are from this area. It is also noteworthy because it has the oldest extant library in China and is close to the home of the Goddess of Mercy.

The Ningbo area has been settled at least since 4800 B.C. Archaeologists found evidence of an advanced culture in the village of Hemudu in Yuyao County in 1973, and some scholars now claim the cradle of Chinese civilization was farther east than Henan and not confined to the Yellow River. The 6000–7000-year-old bone flute found in Hemudu is still playable. Inlaid-bone and wood-carving skills were known then.

Ningbo has been recorded since the Spring and Autumn period (700–476 B.C.). It has been a major port since the Tang, trading with Korea, Japan, and Southeast Asia. It was made a treaty port, open to foreign trade and residence, in 1842. After 1860, a French military detachment was stationed here. Ningbo was reopened as a port for foreign trade in 1979 for the first time in 30 years. This icefree port is now one of the 14 Open Coastal Cities.

If you have only one day, see the library, one or two of the temples, and an arts and crafts factory.

The A.D. 1561 (Ming to Qing) ***Tianyige Library*** 天一阁 is 5 km from the Overseas Chinese Hotel in the city. It still has more than 300,000 books. It started as a private library and now has in its more modern extension next door over 80,000 rare books, mostly from the Ming, plus numerous stone tablets. Scholars can see these books upon request. The library is worth visiting for its simple elegance and its peaceful, tastefully designed gardens. This library was the blueprint for the other seven imperial libraries built during the Qing.

At the entrance to the library is a sign in Chinese that says something like "This is not an amusement park. No fun inside. Keep out." Don't be intimidated by this example of the blunt Ningbo manner. Note also the conversations of the man-in-the-street, which might sound like intense, bitter arguing.

The ***Bao Guo Temple** 保国寺 , built in 1013 (Northern Song), is the oldest extant wooden structure south of the Yangtze, and is in Yuyao, 20 km north of the Overseas Chinese Hotel. Unlike other temples, which have large beams for support, this one uses many small ones. The **Tianfeng Pagoda** was built in A.D. 695 and was traditionally a place for scholars to gather to compose poems and enjoy the scenery. It is hexagonal, seven stories high, but not as beautiful as younger pagodas.

Both the **Tiantong Temples** 天童寺 , 35 km from the Overseas Chinese Hotel, and the **Ayuwang (King Asoka) Temple** 育王寺 , 30 km away, are east of the city. They were founded in the third century. The Tiantong is one of the largest temples south of the Yangtze, with over 700 halls, and some people feel it is more worth seeing than Hangzhou's Lingyin Temple. The Tiantong has sent many teachers to Japan and consequently attracts many Japanese visitors. It is the second holiest shrine of the Zen sect. Zen Buddhist statues are supposed to have deepset eyes looking at their noses as the nose safekeeps one's heart to avoid temptation. See if you can find any. Better still, try crossing your eyes when you feel tempted to sin.

The Ayuwang Temple has relics of Sakyamuni. The famous Buddhist monk Jianzhen (see "Yangzhou") once lived here after he failed in his third attempt to reach Japan in the Tang dynasty.

Visitors can also go to an **arts and crafts factory** (tel. 64617), 4 km from the Overseas Chinese Hotel. Also, the village of **Sanshiliu Wan,** 15 km from Xikou, specializes in *penjing,* the growing and selling of miniature trees.

Putuo Shan 普陀山 is the home of Guanyin (Kuan Yin), the Goddess of Mercy, and is one of the Four Sacred Buddhist Mountains. This 12.5-square-km island is reached by ship from Ningbo, a 4-hour trip offered twice a day. On the way one passes the famous Zhaoshan-Qundao fishing ground with triangular fish nets, a most picturesque view, especially at sunset.

Putuo Shan once had over 200 temples and nunneries, but the years and the Red Guards have done their worst, and only three are now open, the **Puji** 普济寺 , **Fayu** 法雨寺 , and the **Huiji** 慧济寺 **temples.** Those who remember hiking from innumerable nunneries to innumerable temples may be disappointed. No more tiny Buddhist statues inscribed with religious poems to help keep one single-mindedly devout line the narrow mountain paths. But one can still climb thousands of steps and hike through bamboo groves and along the rocky shore and beaches. Enough of the religious atmosphere remains for first-time visitors to enjoy, especially if you avoid the now-paved road and the regular buses and few taxis and have time for the hospitable and warm-hearted villagers. Many of these villagers now occupy the old temples and rent out rooms to visitors. The vegetables and seafoods they serve are delicious because of the freshness. Just don't expect private baths or running water!

Especially exotic (and noisy) is the **guesthouse** next to the Puji Temple, over a kilometer uphill from the ferry pier, where guests have been awakened early by chanting Buddhists. Rituals at 3 p.m. can also be seen from the upstairs windows. Reservations through C.I.T.S. in Ningbo.

Visitors can also see the kowtowing pilgrims, forehead to ground every three steps, as they pay homage or ask special favors of this favorite deity. Especially touching are the sick and handicapped, carried on the backs of friends or family, who come to pray for healing. Devout Buddhists try to make a trip to Putuo at least once in a lifetime.

It is customary to purchase a yellow sack from one of the temples and, for a fee, have each temple rubber-stamp its seal on the sack to prove you've been there.

Putuo Shan is especially famous because repeated storms kept some Japanese worshipers from carrying away a statue of Guanyin from China. Near a cliff is the ''Won't Go Temple,'' to commemorate the goddess's desire to remain in China. Unfortunately, this spot has become a favorite of would-be suicides, and a sign nearby points out that Buddhism does not approve.

Shopping

Made in Ningbo are Mandarin coats, embroidery, bone and wood inlaid articles, bamboo articles, Ming-style furniture, colored clay models, handwoven carpets, and straw mats.

Sesame seed and glutinous rice balls are served for breakfast. Also try dried longan fruit soup. Both are sweet.

Restaurants

Dong Fu Yuan Restaurant □ *5 Zhongshan Rd.. East/Dongmenkou; tel. 32669* □ Serves traditional Anhui and Ningbo food.

Hotels

Overseas Chinese Hotel 华侨饭店   □ *130 Liuting St.* □ 1962; renovated 1987, with a 300-room extension. 10 km from airport.

Ningbo Hotel 宁波饭店   □ *64, Mayuan Rd.* □ 1983.

Yonggang Hotel 甬江饭店   □ *105 Baizhang Rd. E.* □ 1982.

Huagang Hotel 华院宾馆   □ 500 rooms, 36 stories. Joint venture. Under construction at press time.

Lushan Mountain in Jiangxi Province.

Yu Garden in Shanghai.

Mogao Grottoes in Dunhuang.

Five Pagodas Temple in Hohhot.

Lunan Stone Forest, Kunming.

Great Buddha in Leshan, Sichuan Province.

East Lake in Shaoxing, Zhejiang Province.

The Great Wall.

The Potala Palace, Lhasa.

Qin Army Vault Museum, Xian.

Temple of Heaven in Beijing.

Li Garden in Wuxi.

Qingdao (Tsingtao)

North China. On a peninsula on the southern coast of Shandong province, 393 km east of the provincial capital Jinan by rail. 2-hour flight south from Beijing or north of Shanghai. It is on the Huanghai (Yellow Sea) and can also be reached by ship from Shanghai (26 hours) and Yantai, Guangzhou, and Dalian. The climate is temperate. Highest August average, 25°C; coldest January average, ¯1.2°C. Annual precipitation, 702.4 mm. Population is 1–1.5 million.

Qingdao is an icefree port and summer resort, famous for its beer and mineral water. It should be put at the end of a hectic, tight schedule in summer.

Starting as a fishing village, Qingdao (pronounced Ching Dow) has been an important trading port since the seventh century. During the Ming, it was fortified against pirates. The Germans seized the area in 1897 in retaliation for the assassination of two German missionaries. Here they built a naval base and trading port, and protected them with at least 2000 men. The large number of Germans accounted for most of its architecture and its beer recipe.

In 1919, following Germany's defeat in the first World War, the Versailles Peace Conference confirmed Japan's 1915 seizing of the German territories in Shandong, including Qingdao. The Japanese stayed long enough to build huge cotton mills before they were forced to withdraw in 1937. During this period, the British built cigarette factories. The Japanese navy regained the city early in 1938, but not before a Chinese mob smashed the breweries, sending rivers of beer into the streets!

Qingdao's breweries were rebuilt, of course, and still produce the most popular Tsingtao Beer. Qingdao also bottles the popular Laoshan mineral water from the mountains behind the city. Full of hills and trees and red-tiled roofs, the city is very pretty. Many work units have rest and recreation resorts for their members here.

Qingdao is now the largest city and industrial center in Shandong. Its factories make diesel locomotives, automobiles, TV sets, textiles, and cameras. Its oceanic research institute is internationally famous. Huangdao District, on the west coast of Jiaozhou Bay, is the site of the new economic and technical development zone. Qingdao is one of the 14 Open Coastal Cities.

All of Qingdao's urban attractions can be covered in a day. A second day or two is needed for Laoshan Mountain if you enjoy hiking in exotic settings and want to see it all. Qingdao's 4 km of city beaches slope gently into the sea and are protected by four large bays east from **The Pier** 栈桥 (1891). The 440-meter pier is a good place to see the sunrise, and its Huilan Pavilion is Qingdao's most famous landmark. Southeast of the Pier and linked with the shore by a 700-meter-long dyke is **Xiaoqingdao (Little Qingdao Island)** 小青岛 . This rocky island, with the tall, white lighthouse flashing red at night, will be developed for tourists, having been used by the military for many years.

Each **public beach** has marked swimming areas protected with shark nets, lifeguards, and medical stations. There are changing facilities and freshwater showers. The largest and best of the six city beaches is the **No. 1 Huiquan (Pearl Spring) Beach** 汇泉第一海水浴场 . Be prepared to share any city beach with 100,000 other people in summer. They are open from early July to the end of September.

Two new beaches have been opened in the suburbs. **Xuejiadao** 薛家岛海滩 , SW across the mouth of the harbor, also has fishing, golf, and tennis. **Shilaoren** 石老人海滩 is 5 km east and should be less crowded.

Zhongshan Park 中山公园 is best seen when its 700 cherry trees bloom in April. It also has osmanthus, roses, and peonies. A Seaside Lantern Festival is held here in July and August. Open daily, from 5:30 a.m. to 5:30 p.m. in summer, 8 a.m.–4:30 p.m. in winter.

Luxun Park 鲁迅公园 , with its many hilly paths, rocky hills, and old pine trees, has an excellent view of No. 1 beach, Xiaoqingdao, and the European buildings. The castlelike Museum of Marine Products is in this park. A good view can also be had from **Xiaoyu Shan (Little Fish Hill)** 小鱼山 , a tastefully designed park with a recent three-story pavilion, and three large ceramic screens showing the eight Taoist ferries crossing the sea, Pu Songlin's Universe, and the logo of Xiaoyu Shan respectively. Qingdao's nine other major peaks are being developed similarly.

The **Qingdao Museum of Marine Products** 青岛水族馆 (tel.

84949) consists of a marine aquarium and an exhibition hall of specimens. The aquarium has 40 tanks with live marine animals, and an
outdoor pond for seals. No seals could be seen in the mid-1980s, however. The badly designed exhibition hall has over 900 specimens and
poor lighting.

If you can rent or borrow a bicycle, ride through the **Badaguan**
area 八达关 , where the streets are named after the eight passes of the
Great Wall and each street is lined with a different kind of blossoming
tree: cherry, peach, or crape myrtle. Other trees include maple, pine,
and spruce. Behind the streets are individually designed houses with
spacious gardens, each one-of-a-kind with interesting features. You can
walk through this bit of old Europe. Some of these houses can be rented
by the month with cooks and housekeepers. One of the most famous is
at 18 Huanghai Road. Built in 1903 in the shape of a castle, with large
blocks of granite, it was originally a hunting lodge for the German governor and later used by Chiang Kai-shek as his summer resort. Protected
by Qingdao as a historical monument, it is not open to the public yet,
but ask about it.

The **Laoshan Mountains** 崂山 are roughly 40 km east of the city
and can be reached by land or sea. The boat trip gives an excellent view
of the city, but until a pier is built passengers have to be transported to
shore by small motorboat. This could be a frightening experience in
rough seas.

You may have to choose one of three routes to tour Laoshan. On
the South Route you cover the upper and lower Taiqing temples, Longtan Water Fall, and Dragon Well Falls. The North Route covers Shui-
lienbi (Water Fall Screen), Camel Head Rock, Fishscale Gorge, and
Tsaoying Water Fall. The East Route covers Lion Peak (to see the sunrise), Fairy Bridge, Yuelong Cave, and Sheep Rock. A leisurely three-
day trip would be ideal.

Do not expect large temples. Many of the temples here are Taoist,
with small buildings, small doorways, and small courtyards. The mystical Taoists apparently didn't want to be distracted in their meditative
search for eternal peace, their communion with nature.

Laoshan is famous for the masculine shape of its mountains and its
rushing waterfalls. It is full of legends. The highest peak, Mt. Laoding,
is 1333 meters above sea level. The mountains extend over 386 square
km and are full of granite canyons, grotesque crags, old temples, rivers,
streams, and the Laoshan reservoir. The **Taiping (Great Peace) Taoist
Temple** 太平宫 was founded in the Song. The biggest **Taiqing Taoist
Temple** 太清宫 has over 150 buildings.

The **home of Qing writer Pu Songling** (1640–1715) 蒲松龄旧址
is open to the public. He lived in a very modest corner of the Taiping
Temple. Pu wrote his famous *Strange Tales from a Lonely Studio* here.
The trees he described are still standing.

An inscription about the visit of the first Qin emperor in 219 B.C. is also on the mountain. The builder of the Xi'an ceramic army searched for pills of immortality in this area.

Qingdao also has the **Qingdao Museum** 青岛博物馆 (Daxue Rd.; tel. 83762) open daily, except Mondays, 8:30 a.m.–5:30 p.m. in summer; 8:30 a.m.–4:30 p.m. in winter. The **Jimo Hot Spring** 即墨温泉 is 75 km NE, with water 90°C tempered to 38°C, said to be good for rheumatoid arthritis.

Other cities easily reached by train or ship are Weifang, Yantai, Weihai, Zibo, and Jinan. See separate listings.

Shopping

Shops are along Zhongshan 中山路 and Jiaozhou 胶州路 roads. Made locally are beautiful shell pictures, feather pictures, carpets, weaving, embroidery, and knitting. The shell products and embroidery are especially good buys.

Friendship Store 友谊商店 (Xinjiang Rd.; tel. 27021, 27778); **Qingdao Antique Store** 青岛文物商店 (40 Zhongshan Rd.; tel. 84436); **Qingdao Arts and Crafts Shop** 工艺美术商店 (40 Zhongshan Rd.; tel. 25116); **Qingdao Department Store** 百货公司 (Zhongshan Rd.; tel. 24916).

Restaurants

Seafood, of course! Abalone and prawns. Lots of sea cucumbers and scallops too.

Chunhelou Restaurant 春和楼餐厅 □ *Zhongshan Rd.; tel. 27371.*

Qingdao Restaurant 八达关宾馆 □ *Qufu Rd.; tel. 83771, 26747.*

Hotels

Badaguan Guesthouse 青岛餐厅 □ *Shanhaiguan Rd.* □ One main building and 14 villas near beach. 69 rooms. Chinese and Western food. Auditorium, ballroom, recreation room.

Haitien Hotel □ 1987. Joint venture.

Huanghai Hotel 黄海饭店 □ *75 Yan'an I Rd.* □ 21 stories. Foreign tourists on the top floors.

Huaqiao (Overseas Chinese) Hotel 华侨饭店 □ *Hunan Rd. Near the railway station* □ Four stories, 35 rooms, not all with private baths. Beijing and Yangzhou food.

Huiquan Guesthouse 汇泉宾馆 □ *9 Nanhai Rd.* □ 11 stories, 340 beds. Recreation hall, coffee shop, three restaurants serving Chinese and Western food.

Longshan Guesthouse 龙山宾馆 □ *14 Longshan Rd.*

Qingdao Hotel 青岛饭店 .

Yingbin Guest House □ *45, Longshan Rd.* □ 1906. Three stories. Chinese and Western food.

Youyi (Friendship) Hotel 友谊饭店 □ *Xinjiang Rd. Close to the* *harbor and above Friendship Store* □ 36 rooms. Chinese and Western food.

Zhanqiao (Pier) Guesthouse 栈桥宾馆 □ *31 Taiping Rd.* □ Three stories. 25 rooms. Chinese and Western food.

A Japanese joint venture hotel should be opened in 1987.

Other Important Addresses

Bank of China 中国银行 : Zhongshan Rd. Currency can be exchanged at some of the major hotels and stores above.
CAAC 中国民航 : 29 Zhongshan Rd.; tel. 86047.
C.I.T.S. 国际旅行社 : 9 Nanhai Rd. (tel. 83876) or Service Center, Huiquan Hotel (tel. 24646).
C.T.S. 中旅社 : Hunan Rd.; tel. 25866.
Hospitals: If ill, you might find it more convenient to ask at your hotel for help. Failing that, try the **Qingdao People's Hospital** 青岛人民医院 (Dexian Rd.; tel. 26722) or the **Qingdao Municipal Hospital** 青岛市立医院 (Jiaozhou Rd.; tel. 26433, 24133).
Passenger Quay 客运码头 : Xinjiang Rd.; tel. 25001.
Railway Station 火车站 : Tai'an Rd.; tel. 84571, 84971.
Taxis and minibuses: service at most hotels. Also: C.I.T.S. (9 Nanhai Rd.; tel. 24372 or 24646); C.T.S. (Hunan Rd.; tel. 27736); Friendship Store (tel. 27778); Qingdao Municipality (tel. 24248).

Qinhuangdao 秦皇岛

(Chinwangtao) North China, northeastern tip of Hebei province on the Bohai Sea; probably China's second busiest harbor. It is icefree and is the port for a nearby oil field to which it is joined by a pipeline. The closest airport is at Shanhaiguan, 25 km away. It is about 6 hours by train from Beijing.

Originally a small village, Qinhuangdao was opened as a seaport in 1898 and became a base for foreign (especially British) shipping. In 1902 the British army also built a small pier. In 1904, contract workers from nearby East Mountain were recruited for South Africa. The railway was built in 1916. The current population is about 360,000. It is one of the 14 Open Coastal Cities undergoing extensive remodeling and improvements.

The city is named after a legend. The Qin emperor is believed to have passed through here about 2200 years ago. He was looking for pills of longevity. Suddenly he recognized a special tree described by his teacher. Surprised and afraid, he bowed to the tree and a branch bowed back.

Dong Shan (East Mountain) 东山 is where the Qin emperor searched for the pills and boarded his ships. There's a good view of the sea and the sunrise from here. Walk along the waterfront at night. A cruise boat goes to a fishing village at the mouth of the Xin Kai River and sometimes visitors can see the teams of fishing boats going out together, dragging the big nets between boats. In the old days, the fishermen used to sing to each other.

One can visit a shell-carving factory 秦皇岛贝雕厂 and a plain glass factory 光天华玻璃厂 . Swimming beaches are near the Second People's Hospital (close to ships and tankers!!). Swimming also in the solar-energy swimming pool. For excursions from here, see ''Great Wall'' and ''Beidaihe,'' the resort about 10 km south, and ''Shanhaiguan,'' close to the place where the Great Wall meets the sea.

Shopping

Grown locally are peaches, pears, sea cucumbers, and crabs (biggest in September–October). Made locally are pictures, lamps, ashtrays, etc., of shell. Also manufactured are mirrors, magnifying glasses, painted eggs, painted stones, butterfly and insect specimens, bird feather crafts, and necklaces of red beans (symbol of longing between lovers).

Qinhaungdao Arts and Crafts Co. 秦皇岛工艺美术公司鲁迅公园 (Lu Xun Park); **First Arts & Crafts Factory Service Dept.** 第一工艺美术服务部 (tel. 4921 X247).

Restaurants

Fresh seafood is a specialty here.
Bohai Chun Fan Dian 渤海春饭店 □ *Haiyang Rd.; tel. 2922* □ Tangshan cooking.
Lao Er Restaurant □ *Haiyang Rd.; tel. 2722* □ Moslem, Jiao Zi.
Wen Hua Lu Fan Dian 文化路饭店 □ *tel. 4602* □ Tianjin-style buns.

Hotels

Haibinlu Hotel 海滨旅馆 □ *Haibin Rd.*
Welcome House □ *45 Wen Hua Bei Rd.*
Qinhuangdao Commercial Service Center 秦皇岛商业服务楼 □ *Wenhua Rd.* □ Need letter of introduction and work identification card to stay overnight.

The Reception Centre at the railway station should be able to help with hotel information.

Quanzhou 泉州

(Chuangchou) East China, 300 km north of Xiamen in Fujian, this ancient city was considered one of the two largest ports in

the world by Marco Polo, who knew it as Zaiton or Citong when it exported silks and porcelain as far away as Africa. In the Song it had a population of 500,000 (today, 140,000 urban, and 410,000 urban and rural). It declined because maritime trade was forbidden. Today, it is one of the 24 cities protected by the State Council as a historical monument, but it's not yet ready for large-scale foreign tourism. I found the city a little disappointing—I expected so much more because of its history, but I do not regret the two-day excursion by road from Xiamen because Quanzhou is a charming place with charming people. It has also been reached by twice-a-week flight from Guangzhou, and because this is one of the areas slated for accelerated development, you can expect improvements in communications and accommodations. Weather: the hottest in July has been 32°C. Mild winters (no snow). Precipitation is 1400 mm, from July to September.

If you only have one day, C.I.T.S. recommends the Kaiyuan Temple, East and West Pagoda, Overseas Communication Museum, and Old God Rock in the morning. In the afternoon, the Grand Mosque, Wind-Shaken Rock, Holy Islamic Tombs, and Luoyang Bridge.

The **Kaiyuan Temple** 开元寺 is 1 km NW of the Overseas Chinese Hotel and dates from the Tang. The main hall was 100 heavy stone Greek-type columns. On top of 24 of these are gaudy part women/part birds, whose crowns appear to support the beams. These flying musicians are of gilded clay and are most unusual. Indian figures and Chinese dragons and tigers also decorate the temple. The 5-meter-high Buddhas are in charge of the North, South, East, West, and Middle. Look also for the 1000-armed, 1000-eyed Guanyin. Note the corners of the roof, the curled swallow tails, and the lively dragons that are distinctive aspects of Southern Fujian temple architecture.

Two large pagodas, the trademarks of the city, are on the temple grounds. These are the **East and West Pagodas** 东西塔 . The 48-meter-high **Zhenguo Pagoda** is east. Originally built of wood in 865, it was rebuilt of stone in 1238. The west **Renshou Pagoda,** 44 meters high, was originally built in 916 and rebuilt in 1228.

In the Song dynasty, this temple was home to over 1000 monks. Now it has 40. It boasts the oldest mulberry tree in the world—over 1300 years old.

Near this temple is the **Overseas Communicaiton Museum** 海外交通历史博物馆 , with the remains of a 12th- or 13th-century ship, 24.2 meters long and 9.15 meters wide, found in 1974 in Quanzhou Bay. The museum also outlines Chinese maritime and local Arab history.

Old God Rock 老君岩 is 4 km from the city. This stone statue of Laotze/Laotzu, the founder of Taoism, is beautiful. You can sit on his knee or shoulder or his arm and pretend you are one of the children climbing all over Buddha. You touch his nose for longevity. He is about 5 meters high and grandfatherly, with a long beard. He is currently one of the few deities to whom you can get this close. Makes a great picture. But be quick, before they put a fence around him! And do climb carefully! After all, he is 600 years old! He used to be protected by a Taoist temple building, but that was destroyed toward the end of the Yuan dynasty.

At one time, 10,000 foreigners from Persia, Syria, and Southeast Asia lived in the southern part of the city. Most of them were Moslem. The *Qingjing (Grand Mosque) 清净寺 (Tushan St., ½ km from the O.C. Hotel), open daily, was built by local Moslems in 1009. One of the earliest mosques in China, it was copied from a mosque in Damascus and was renovated in 1310. It is one of the few mosques in eastern China with west Asian architecture, but unfortunately much of it is in ruins. But it is lovingly maintained. Arabic writing and west Asian arches point to its former glory. Inside is a small museum with text in English pointing out such events as Moslems fighting alongside Zheng Chenggong (Koxinga) and the continuing observance of customs like Ramadan, weddings officiated by an imam, and abstinence from eating pork. Three thousand Moslems still live on Tushan Street.

The **Islamic Tombs** 圣墓 are on Ling Shan Hill, outside the East Gate, 4 km from the city. They are protected by a Chinese-style pavilion. They belong to two trader-missionaries who arrived in the city during the Tang. (The two other Moslem missionaries sent to China by Mohammed went to Guangzhou and Yangzhou.) Koxinga prayed here before his fifth voyage to Southeast Asia. If you can read Arabic, you can learn about their lives from their tombstones. Otherwise, these are not all that interesting unless you think of those romantic-sounding times— Cathay, Marco Polo, pirates, and giant Chinese junks sailing to Mozambique.

A few steps away is the 50-ton **Wind-shaking Rock** 风动石 , an elephant-sized boulder that anybody can wobble. Honest!

The lower part of the 84-meter-long **Luoyang Bridge** 洛阳桥 was built between A.D. 1053 and 1059, made of stone. It is 12 km NE of the hotel and takes one minute to see. When the tide is out, you can see oyster beds. Two other Song bridges are in the region. The *Anping (Wuli) Bridge is at Jinjiang, south of the city.

In the neighborhood of the Luoyang Bridge is a stone-carving factory that makes Japanese lanterns, balustrades, temple pagodas, and photograph-like pictures. The stone columns of Chairman Mao's mausoleum in Beijing were cut here.

If you have more time, **Wanshan Peak** has some rare Manicheist relics. This religion, brought to China in the seventh century from Persia, is a combination of Zoroastrianism, Christianity, and paganism. At one time, St. Augustine was an adherent. On a stone tablet near the site of the monastery are inscribed the activities of the cult during the Song. Behind the ruins is a circular Manichean statue of a man.

Outside the south gate of Quanzhou about 4 km is the **Caoan Temple,** the only Manichean temple left in China. There used to be temples in Xi'an and Luoyang as well, but the religion was persecuted in A.D. 843 and its leaders fled to Quanzhou. From here it spread along the east coast.

The **Heavenly Princess Palace** 天妃宫 and **Confucian Temple** are ½ km from the hotel. One hour by car from the city at the shore is the 1162-built five-story octagonal stone **Tower of the Two Sisters-in-law** 姑嫂塔 . The 21-meter-high structure was originally built as a navigational aid, but its name symbolizes the loneliness of the women left behind by the sailors and emigrating Chinese workmen. The 161-acre **Overseas Chinese University** 华侨大学 is in the mountains east of the city. Its students are drawn from Southeast Asia, Hong Kong, and Macao.

The **Tomb of Zheng Chenggong (Koxinga)** 郑成功墓 is at Nan'an, about 25 km NW of Quanzhou. He was a pirate who allied himself with the defeated Ming forces in the mid-1600s, fighting the Manchus. With his fleet of 800 warships, this national hero successfully rid Taiwan of the Dutch. Somewhere near Quanzhou, too, there should be the 1326 tomb of a Franciscan bishop.

Shopping

Embroidered blouses at the Friendship Store. Life-like artificial flowers. Yes, they pack beautifully. Just shake them out when you get home. Try the Arts and Crafts Store (508 Zhong Shan South Rd.; tel. 2613). Also locally produced are stone carvings, woven bamboo, Dehua porcelain, Anxi Guanyin tea.

At the **Mantang Restaurant** (3–5, Zhongshan Zhong Rd.; tel. 2887) the specialty is Jade Rabbits Lying on a Palm Leaf (actually made of steamed fish). Also steamed freshwater eels, and longan (fruit) with Eight Delicacies.

Hotels

Overseas Chinese Building 中国旅行社 □ *Baiyuan Rd.; tel. 2192* □ Pleasant, but not up to standard.

Golden Fountain Hotel 金泉酒店 □ 1965; renovated 1985.

C.I.T.S. 中国国防旅行社 and **C.T.S.** 中国旅行 : Overseas Chinese Building, Baiyuan Rd.; tel. 2191, 2366; cable 5132.

Qufu 曲阜

*(Chufu) North China. Southwestern Shandong province about
100 km south of Jinan. No airport. Reached by train to Yan-
zhou on the Beijing-Shanghai line and then by road for 32 km.
Population: 27,000*

The hometown and grave of Kong Fuzi (Master Kong), known to
the west as Confucius, is one of the places to visit if you want to be
immersed in old China. Take your time. Stay overnight in the family
mansion (if you don't mind the plumbing). Meditate in these beautiful,
exotic surroundings. Read the *Analects of Confucius*. The discipline he
advocates might be just what your hectic life lacks. Go back to the 17th
century.

Confucius lived from 551 to 479 B.C. during the Spring and Autumn Period, a time of small warring kingdoms and political chaos. He
was an itinerant teacher who preached that stability could be achieved
by a return to the classics and the old Zhou dynasty rituals. He defined
and promoted an already existing system of interpersonal relationships
with its emphasis on responsibility and obedience.

His teachings were much like the rules of polite society anywhere:
The virtuous or benevolent man does not lose his temper; the virtuous
man thinks ill of people who criticize others in their absence, who talk
badly of other people to make themselves look better, or who persist in
promoting deceptions they know are false.

Confucius's virtuous man also did not concern himself with insig-
nificant things, material gain, fame, or ambition. He was moderate in
all things.

Confucius's ideas on government were far from democratic. People
who do not hold office in a state should not discuss its policies, he said.
He advocated that subjects be unquestionably subordinated to rulers,
sons to fathers, younger brothers to older brothers, wives to husbands,
younger friend to older friend. He was male chauvinism incarnate.

His philosophy was the official ideology in China for over 2000
years, promoted because it supported the oligarchical power structure.
Filial piety was essential to the system, and its enforcement was supported by the state. If a child failed to care for his aged parents or was
rude to them, the authorities would punish the child. Children owed
their lives to their ancestors. They were obligated to respect and worship these people.

The philosophy deteriorated into a religion where descendents performed rituals to keep ancestral spirits happy, so the dead would influence the fortunes of the living.

Much Confucian influence is still felt in 20th-century Asia. Singapore has been teaching it in its schools; pre-Communist Vietnam was

full of it. Korea. Hong Kong. Taiwan. One finds elements of his theories still stifling Chinese people everywhere. Confucius was behind the famous civil service system, which was based on the memorization of the classics and his analects. The imperial examinations and the arrogant, insular thinking did, however, outlive their usefulness. These stunted the development of modern China and were largely responsible for its poor defense against the 19th- and 20th-century imperialists.

The civil service examination system was abolished in the early 1900s. Unquestioning obedience to teachers was violently attacked as late as the Cultural Revolution. In the late 1960s, some of Qufu's historic monuments were destroyed. The sage's reactionary teachings were subjected to a criticism campaign in 1973.

Confucius is now being studied dispassionately again, and an international symposium is planned for 1989, his 2540th birthday. The excesses of Confucianism are blamed not on the sage, but on his followers.

In some family temples, food is still shared with ancestors, heads bowed and incense burned in worship especially during the Qing Ming Festival in spring, and the autumn equinox. And vestiges of the traditions surrounding the cult remain to this day, in spite of governmental discouragement—arranged marriages, marriages between two deceased people, or between one living and one deceased person, etc. This is not, however, as common as it was before Liberation. Rote memory is still the basis of much education, but it is to be hoped this is changing today.

Confucius was born in Ch'ang-p'ing or in Qufu in Shandong depending on what sources you read. Those who say he was born outside claim he moved with his mother to Qufu after the death of his father, when he was three. His father was a military officer. Qufu then was already old. It was the capital of a minor kingdom during the Shang (14th–11 century B.C.). The city is named "Winding City Wall" after the old wall built 3000 years ago. The current wall is Ming.

One fifth of the people in the city are descendents of the philosopher, and those in a direct line have been receiving state pensions for centuries (with no need to earn their living otherwise). Currently living are the 73th–76th generations.

The Confucian monuments have been repaired and are now opened to tourists. They are in one part of the city and can be seen in a day.

The ***Confucian Temple** 孔庙 , occupying more than 20 hectares (about 50 acres), is the most important one in China. First built in A.D. 478, it was rebuilt and enlarged to its present size during the Ming and Qing. Its gold-tiled roofs, its arches, red doors, and carved tile dragons are Ming. The two stone soldiers/generals over two meters tall near the gate are from the Han Dynasty (917–971). They once guarded a noble's tomb in another part of the city.

The **Dacheng Hall** is the main hall for paying homage to Confucius. Only the emperor could be carried over the carved tile dragons up to its door. The hall is over 31 meters tall and 54 meters wide, with the same general appearance of some of the buildings in Beijing's Forbidden City. Important are the ten carved stone columns, two dragons and a pearl on each, slithering between clouds and a pearl. Note the set of ritual bronze bells, which are played on ceremonial occasions. (See also *Provincial Museum*, ''Wuhan.'')

The **Life of the Sage Exhibition Hall** contains 120 pictures of the life of Confucius.

The ***Kong Family Mansion** 孔府, now a hotel, has nine courtyards, over 400 rooms, and a garden, on 14 hectares. The gate in front is Ming. The Main Hall, Second Hall, and Third Hall were offices of the duke of Yansheng, the 46th generation grandson who was made a noble by Emperor Renzong of the Song. These offices, with his desk under a yellow canopy and painted beamed ceiling, give authenticity to opera stage sets of the period. Ancient weapons, banners, and drums line the walls. The mansion was started in 1038.

The mansion is well worth spending the night in. You have more time to explore a nobleman's home at leisure. You can enjoy the ancient silhouettes in the dark. Lucky you, if you visit on a moonlit night and can talk with some of his descendents.

The **Confucian Forest,** 20,000–30,000 trees on 200 hectares, hold the thousands of family tombs. The trees were collected by disciples from all over the country. Elaborately crafted gates, stone lions, and a stone-arched bridge punctuate the lovely greenness. Tall stone nobles and animals guard the gate to the ***Tomb of Confucius** 孔林, a tumulus marked with stone tablets and fancy incense burners.

A small brick house, **Zi Gong's Hut,** stands nearby, originally built by one of the master's disciples, who lived in it for six years after Confucius's death, to show respect. **Lady Yu's Arch** was named after a daughter of Qing Emperor Qianlong, who was married to the then duke of Yansheng. The title was hereditary. Visitors would do well to read *In the Mansion of Confucius' Descendants* by Kong Demao and Ke Lan, New World Press, 1984.

Also in Qufu is a Sacred Way with stone animals and steles, the Temple of Yan Hui, the Temple of the Duke of Zhou, the tomb of Shao Hao, and the remains of the former capital of the State of Lu.

Shopping

Locally produced are wood carvings, stone rubbings, and Nishan inkstones.

If you want to upgrade your accommodations, the **Quelibin Hotel** is nearby and has been built in an architectural style compatible with the Kong Family Mansion. Opened 1985. The plumbing and the air conditioning are much better.

C.I.T.S. 国际旅行社

Shanghai (Above the Sea)

*East China, on the north bank of the Huangpu River, 28 km
from the (Changjiang) Yangtze River, on the east coast of China
due west of the southern tip of Japan. Bordering on Jiangsu
and Zhejiang provinces, it is about a 2-hour flight NE of
Guangzhou and Hong Kong, and SE of Beijing. It is linked by
air with Hong Kong, Japan, the United States and Singapore,
and by sea with Hong Kong and Kobe. From Shanghai are
many land, river, and air services to other parts of China.
Sharing about the same latitude as Jacksonville, Florida,
Shanghai's hottest temperature is 35°C in July–August; its
coldest is ⁻5°C in January–February. Most rain arrives in June.
Population: 11.46 million, of whom over six million are in urban Shanghai.*

This municipality, directly under the control of the central government, started out 5000 years ago as a tiny fishing village. It became a
port in the 17th century. In 1840 its population was 500,000. In 1842
it was captured by the British, and although the Chinese paid a $300,000
ransom to keep it from being sacked, British soldiers and Chinese thieves
looted it severely. The Treaty of Nanking of that year opened Shanghai
to foreign trade and settlement. This led to its partition into British,
French, and, later, Japanese concessions, which is still reflected in its
downtown architecture. The British concession eventually became the
International Concession, and all continued until the 1940s. Each of the
concessions had its own tax system, police, courts, buses, and electrical
wattage. A criminal could escape justice just by going from one concession to another.

Shanghai thrived as a port, trading principally in silk, tea, and opium.

Most of the foreign trade was British and one fifth of all the opium reached China in fast American ships.

From 1853 to 1855, the walled section of Shanghai was seized by the Small Sword Society, a Cantonese-Fukinese secret society that wanted to restore the Ming dynasty and prohibit opium. It was helped in its struggle by some foreign seamen, but many other foreigners helped the Manchus regain the city. In 1860, the Taiping Heavenly Kingdom tried unsuccessfully to take Shanghai. In 1915 students and workers demonstrated here against the Twenty-One Demands of Japan. And in July 1921, the first Congress of the Communist Party of China was held here secretly.

In 1925, a worker striking for higher wages was killed at a Japanese factory. This led to a demonstration by workers and students in the International Settlement, during which the British police killed several demonstrators. A rash of nationwide anti-imperialist protests followed. In April 1927, Chiang Kai-shek ordered a massacre of the Communists here, and Chou En-lai barely escaped with his life. This period was the setting of Andre Malraux's famous novel *Man's Fate*.

In 1932, Shanghai resisted a Japanese attack for two months and made a truce. China appealed to the League of Nations and the United States, who did little to help. Japan attacked again in August 1937. The Nationalists fought back for three months before retreating to Nanjing and later to Chongqing. The Japanese stayed until 1945. In May 1949, the Communists took the city. During the Cultural Revolution, it was the scene of many intense political struggles, especially in January 1966.

Shanghai is now one of the 14 Open Coastal Cities, especially chosen for intensive economic development.

Shanghai's cosmopolitan heritage is still reflected in its architecture and in the relative sophistication of many of its citizens. Its fashions and standards of products and services are more international than other Chinese cities, a result of its longer, more concentrated period of dealing with fussy foreigners. Its shopping is the best in the country. It was the first city to have extensive courses for hotel attendants and service staff. It was the first to have C.I.T.S. sub-branches at the local airport (with neon signs) and at the train station to help foreign travelers.

Shanghai is one of the biggest ports and the largest city in China. Cruise ships dock almost at the foot of Nanjing Road. It is also still an important trading city and one of the biggest industrial cities. Among its products are trucks and cars, bicycles, television sets, cameras, textiles, watches, electronics, and ships. Its scientific institutions conduct research into lasers, atomic energy, satellite technology, and computers. As an agricultural area, it is highly developed. Its rural counties are among the richest in the country, completely supplying the city. It grows two crops of rice and one of wheat each year.

Roughly, Shanghai's streets running east-west are named after cities and those running north-south after provinces. Its natives speak a dialect unlike that of Beijing and more akin to that of Hangzhou and Suzhou—only faster.

Not everybody likes Shanghai. It is a big, very crowded city that smells more of trade, commerce, and industry than ancient Chinese culture. The population density is 41,000 per square km, the highest in China. Its ancient relics are mainly outside the city. But it is exciting because its unique history is still reflected in its foreign buildings: the grandeur of the Bank of China lobby, the Greek columns of the customs house, the dark wood paneling in the Jinjian Club, the hybrid flavor of Sun Yat-sen's home. Do a lot of walking through this museum of 19th-century European and Japanese architecture. Look into the lobbies of the buildings along the Bund: Smile at the guard innocently and say "Just looking."

Shanghai is pleasant because the people are outgoing and lively. They are less reserved than those in Beijing. Making friends is easier here. Every Sunday morning in Renmin Park there is an English-speaking corner. Someone is sure to approach you to practice English. Shanghainese have been known for centuries for their quick wit, business talents, and efficiency. C.I.T.S. here is more flexible about meeting special requests.

Five days in Shanghai is sufficient to cover the important sights for you, but you have to make choices as there is enough for more. The following is a suggested itinerary.

Day 1: In the morning, the Yuyuan Garden, Huangpu Park, and a walk along the Bund, with lunch at the Peace Hotel; the Municipal Museum and the Arts and Crafts Research Institute in the afternoon.

Day 2: The Jade Buddha Temple, with vegetarian lunch, Children's Palace, any of the modern history sites, and/or a workers' residential district.

On either of these days, you could substitute or try to squeeze in shopping, the zoo, a boat trip, an arts and crafts factory, the Shanghai Industrial Exhibition Hall, People's Square, and the tomb of Soong Qingling. If you want to swim, try one of the clubs.

Day 3: The Botanical Gardens, Longhua Pagoda, Square Pagoda, and Zuibai Ci Pond. Take a picnic lunch with you if you want.

Day 4: Grand View Garden *(Dream of the Red Chamber)*. Restaurants there.

Day 5: Jiading County and the Confucian Temple museum, Wuyi Garden (lunch), and Qiuxiapu.

On these last three days, you could also try to squeeze in a production brigade or other rural enterprise. In the evening, try to see the Shanghai Acrobats or Shanghai Kunqu Opera (more melodic and graceful than Beijing Opera).

Huangpu Park 黄浦公园 is the oldest and smallest park in the city (Zhongshan Dong-1 Rd., across the bridge from Shanghai Mansions). Opened in 1868 by the British, next to the Suzhou and Huangpu rivers, this once displayed the infamous sign "No Dogs and Chinese Allowed." Now open from 5 a.m. to 10 p.m., even for foreign tourists.

*Yu Yuan Garden 豫园 (Yu Yuan Rd.; tel. 283251) is in the old Chinese part of Shanghai. Open 8:30–11 a.m. and 1–4 p.m. I can't decide whether or not to recommend it if you are also going to see the gardens of Suzhou. It depends on how much time you have and how much you like gardens. This one is pretty good, but it is crowded. It was originally laid out between 1559 and 1577 by a financial official from Sichuan and now covers 20,000 square meters. About 100 years ago, a part was sold to merchants, and that is now the 98-shop **Yu Yuan Market,** once the busiest in the city. Here you can buy dress-making patterns (six sizes in one pattern) and novelties, and watch *Jiao Zi* and other Chinese dumplings and pastries being made. The large new Old Shanghai Restaurant (at the parking lot) is famous. Some visitors have found the market fascinating. The area was the old Chinese district and the houses are pretty much the way they used to be.

From 1853 to 1854, the Yu Garden was used as the headquarters of the Small Sword Society, which staged an armed uprising and held part of Shanghai for 18 months. The pavilion opposite the exquisite stage is now a mini-museum.

Other points of interest: the top of Rockery Hill, which is an artificial mountain made with rocks carried from Jiangxi province. Until it was dwarfed by Shanghai's skyscrapers, this was the highest point in the city from which you could see and hear the Huangpu River nearby. The five dragon walls wind concentrically around the garden. Look for their heads. Note the unusually shaped doors, some like vases, and, of course, the lovely moon gate. Look for the **Pavilion to See the Reflection of the Water on the Opposite Side** (these names are really something!) and don't trip over the step-over doorways. There are also the 400-year-old ginkgo tree, the 200-year-old magnolia, the cedars, and the poem written on a grain of rice. The south side of the garden was for women; aristocratic women were usually kept out of sight of all but family members. Snack bar and antique store. (See also *Chinese Gardens* in "What Is There to Do and See?"

Shanghai does have an excellent museum: the **Shanghai Municipal Museum** 上海市博物馆 (Henan Nan Rd.; tel. 280160). Open daily, except Mondays. Closed for lunch and some mornings. Opened 1952. Includes (on the ground floor) a demonstration of how the Shang bronzes were cast and what they looked like new (did you really think they drank out of those yucky green things?); bronze bells used as musical instruments; a knife for beheading; a model of a 2000-year-old tomb, with skeletons of slaves buried alive so they could serve the departed master in the other world; a water vat used for refrigeration; 2000-year-old gilding on bronze; giant Ka drums. A revealing picture of ancient life can be seen on a bronze cowrie shell (money) container decorated with tigers climbing up the sides, a slave being bound for sacrifice, pigs being slaughtered, and two dead cows. The museum also has two of the life-size Qin dynasty warriors and a horse from the famous Xi'an excavations. On the second floor, a demonstration of how pottery was made from wicker baskets; an A.D. 618 polo game, three-color Tang camels, and other tomb pieces. A well-designed display of ancient and contemporary porcelain arranged according to regional kilns helps the viewer understand the differences in clay, patterns, glazes, etc., of the various types. The collection of stone sculptures here is not as good as the one at New York's Metropolitan Museum.

On the third floor are murals of *fat* Tang ladies (fat was very fashionable then!); a horizontal scroll of life in 11th-century Kaifeng—look for the bride being carried in the sedan chair; and a collection of ancient calligraphy and paintings including a painting done by fingernail.

This museum has published many excellent art books, which, unfortunately, are not on sale in its own store.

For more on bronzes, see also "What Is There to See and Do?"

Shanghai Arts and Handicrafts Research Institute 上海工艺美术研究所 (Huaihai Zhong Rd.) is more interesting than most factories of the same nature because top artisans develop new crafts here, such as wool and silk embroidery, wood carving, ivory, jade, ink stones, kites, porcelain and bamboo carving, lacquer, silk flowers, and colored lanterns. Paper cutting and dough figure making have been demonstrated. Under its wing are over 40 factories.

While the work of the institute is fascinating, its French-style mansion is rather spectacular, too, especially with its two white marble staircases leading to the main entrance. The front lawn with its willow-lined ponds is well maintained. Does the building look familiar? From *Gone with the Wind*, maybe? A retail store next to the main building has reasonable prices. No appointment necessary.

Jade Buddha Temple 玉佛寺 (170 Anyuan Rd., Puto District; tel. 535745, or 538805) is open daily, 8 a.m.–5 p.m., but closed for lunch. A good introduction to Buddhist temples, but nearby Suzhou has better and older ones.

The Jade Buddha Temple was founded in 1882 in the southern outskirts of Shanghai. When it was inconvenient for adherents to visit, the temple was bodily moved to Shanghai in 1918 and now occupies about two acres in the western part of the city. The temple was closed from 1966 to 1976. Renovations were made in the late 1970s.

Many monks live in this temple, and you will probably hear them singing or reading the scriptures. You might be handed a piece of lighted incense to put in an incense burner as your tribute to the Buddha. A donation is more or less expected, but you don't have to make one. At your request and donation, monks will chant prayers for the well-being of your soul, or recite from Buddhist scriptures to enrich the spirits of deceased friends.

In the first hall, a 2.6-meter-high, gold-faced Wei Tuo, the military protector of the Buddhist scriptures, menacingly greets visitors. On each side are two temple guardians about five meters high: the Eastern King, with a mandolinlike instrument, using music to defend and praise Buddha; the Southern King, with his dark, angry face, and sword; the Northern King, with a Chinese parasol; and the Western King, who "looks after the whole world with penetrating eyes and carries a snake which is actually a net to catch converts." Behind Wei Tuo is a 1.6-meter-high Laughing Buddha.

In the courtyard the incense burner made of iron and bronze, cast in 1922, is inscribed with the names of donors and honored deceased relatives. The three largest figures inside the next parallel building are Sakyamuni (center), to his right the Amitaba Buddha (with lotus), and the Yuese Buddha, carrying the Buddhist wheel of law. Along the sides are the 20 guardians of heaven. Guanyin is centered behind the three main Buddhas. Note the very thin Sakyamuni, above, paying homage, and the 18 arhats. The bases and supports are made of cement and clay, but the statues are sandalwood.

On the second floor of the building, with the Jade Buddha, one changes into slippers. The seated Buddha, 1.9 meters high and carved from one piece of white jade in Burma, was brought to China in 1882. The shelves on both sides of the room contain 7240 volumes of Buddhist scriptures, printed in the Qing 200 years ago. They are similar to the book under the glass.

In another building is a Reclining Buddha, also of white jade, depicting Sakyamuni breathing his last. In the temple complex, too, are a retail store of religious relics. A small museum contains ancient relics: a life-size wooden Guanyin; a sixth- and a seventh-century stone Guanyin (looking male and Indian here); a bronze Buddha (A.D. 491); a tiny child Sakyamuni with his right hand up, left hand down, said to be proclaiming his Buddhahood (which was not possible historically, but never mind!); two 1400-year-old stone Buddhas; and a scepter. A good vegetarian restaurant, small antique store, and a newly founded Buddhist Academy with 100 students are also in this temple. See also *Buddhist Temples* in "What Is There to See and Do?"

Many group tours include a visit to a **Children's Palace.** These are after-school programs for 7–16-year-olds, much like community centers. Specially chosen children get extra opportunities to learn and practice art, sciences, music, sports, etc. Some of the 23 palaces in the city are in old mansions built by wealthy capitalists. A visit to one will not only give you a chance to learn something of the education of children but also to explore the buildings themselves.

Best set up for tourists is the Children's Palace at 64 Yan'an Road (open Tuesday and Saturday afternoons after school hours for visitors).

Children's Palaces were a project of Soong Ching-ling, the widow of Dr. Sun Yat-sen. Money is being solicited internationally for the

Soong Chingling Foundation to continue and expand this work with children.

Modern Chinese history sites offer an opportunity to see the inside of some of those European houses. In addition, you can experience important facets of recent history. My favorite is the **former residence of Dr. Sun Yat-sen** 孙中山故居 (7 Xiangshan Rd.). It is in the old French Concession, a large house by today's Chinese standards. (Currently, a house this size is divided up for several Chinese families.)

Once inside, you find that you have stepped back into the 1920s. The master is not home yet but is obviously expected, because the mahogany furniture is sparkling clean and polished. The house was bought by Chinese-Canadians for the father of republican China for 16,000 pieces of silver. He lived here with his wife intermittently from 1920 to 1924, just before his death of cancer in 1925. His widow, Soong Ching-ling, lived in the house until 1937, when the war forced her to move to Chongqing. In October 1949 Madame Sun gave the building to the state. It was opened to the public in 1952.

Here, in 1924, Dr. Sun met Communist leader Li Dazhao (Li Tachao) publicly for the first time to work out Nationalist-Communist cooperation. Dr. Sun was much influenced by Marx and Lenin. Here he also met Lenin's representative, Yue Fei. In the garden, in that same year, Sun held a meeting to reform the Nationalist Party to include Communist Party representatives.

Besides the antiques, which include a Tang camel, Japanese swords, and a Victrola, there are some old photographs, a 1920 China train map, Sun's medical instruments, clothes, and glasses. The railway map is significant because Dr. Sun was in charge of railways for a short time after he resigned as president. The house contains his library: a 1911 *Encyclopedia Britannica,* biographies of Bismarck, Cicero, Lincoln, and Napoleon in English, books in Japanese, and ancient works in Chinese. Because this is a shrine, no photos are allowed. (See also "Nanjing" for more about Dr. Sun.)

Museum and Tomb of Lu Xun (Lu Hsun) 鲁迅纪念馆和鲁迅墓 (Hongkou Park; tel. 661181): museum open daily, except Sundays, 8:30 a.m.–4 p.m., except for lunch, and Tuesday and Thursday mornings. Tomb building open daily, 8 a.m.–7 p.m. These are quite close to each other in the northern part of the city. Lu Xun (1881–1936) was an author of short stories who wrote in the colloquial language about poor people, impoverished literati, and oppressed women. Chinese literature until then had primarily been about the wealthy elite, written in a snobbish literary style, too difficult for the masses to grasp. Although he was not a Communist, Lu Xun is considered a national hero. He died of tuberculosis in Shanghai.

The site of the First National Congress of the Communist Party of China 中国共产党第一次全国代表大会会址   (76 Xingye

Rd.; tel. 281177) was the living room of a small rented house in the former French Concession. There, 12 representatives of the Party from all over China, including Mao Zedong, met secretly for four days starting on July 1, 1921. On July 5, after a stranger burst into the room "looking for a friend," the suspicious delegates immediately left the house. Ten minutes later, the French police arrived, while the delegates went on to Jia Xing county, 98 km west, to complete their work in a rented boat on Nan Hu (lake).

The Congress adopted the first constitution and proclaimed the founding date of the Party. After Liberation, the house was restored to its modest 1921 condition. Some pieces of furniture are reproductions. Adjacent is a small museum with photos, historical text, and a model of the boat.

Residence of Chou En-lai 周恩来故居 (73 Sinan Rd.) was the Shanghai agency of the Communist Party in 1946 when efforts were being made at peace talks with the Nationalists.

Another relic from a previous era and still in use is the **Shanghai Industrial Exhibition Hall** 上海工业展览馆 (1000 Yan'an Zhong Rd.; tel. 563037). Open daily, except Mondays, 8:30 a.m.–5 p.m., except for lunch breaks. Over 58,000 square meters of floor space with a display area of 20,000. Completed in 1955, with Soviet help, in the massive Soviet style for trade exhibitions. It was closed from 1966 to 1969 (Cultural Revolution) and reopened "primarily for the exchange of technology and to tell people about the development of industry in Shanghai." Space is available for other Chinese regions and foreigners to rent. Exhibits include heavy industry, metals, movable toys, textiles, medical equipment, computers, watches, shipbuilding, and herbal medicines. There are also handicrafts for sale.

The **Shanghai Zoo** 上海动物园 (Hongqiao Rd.; tel. 329775) is open daily, 7 a.m.–5 p.m. One of the better zoos in China. 70 hectares, 280 species. Pandas, rare Chinese birds, and Yangtze crocodiles.

If you wish to pay your respects to a very distinguished humanitarian and revolutionist, visit the beautiful white statue and **Tomb of Song Qingling (Soong Ching-ling)** 宋庆龄墓 in Wang Guo (International) Cemetery 万国公墓 (21 Lingyuan Rd.; Changning District near Hongqiao Rd.; tel. 329034). The widow of the founder of republican China died in May 1981. Her parents, and the maid who served her for 52 years, are buried nearby. A children's playground and a small museum about her life are planned. Do read *The Soong Dynasty*.

Soong Ching-ling was the sister of Mme. Chiang Kai-shek of Taiwan. She eloped with the already married Sun Yat-sen and was virtually disowned by her wealthy Christian father, up to that point a strong supporter of Dr. Sun. She was tolerated by her family and her powerful in-laws, although she was outspoken in her opposition to their exploitation of China. She was, after all, the widow of the widely respected father of the country, without whose connection Chiang Kai-shek would not have been as powerful as he was. She chose to remain in China after Liberation, and worked to promote the welfare of the Chinese people. She is highly respected here.

The **Huangpu River boat trip** 黄浦江游船 is booked from the wharf near Huangpu Park at the foot of Beijing East Road. This 3½-hour, 60-km trip is usually offered as an option for prepaid tourists for additional payment and is available to individual travelers. It sails to the Changjiang (Yangtze) River at Wusong Kou, and back at 8:30 a.m. and 1:15 p.m. daily, with a 1½-hour night cruise at 7 p.m. during the summer. Important if you want to relax and see sailing junks and ships from all over the world on a muddy river with industries along its shores. On the return trip, however, are a magician and acrobatic show.

People's Square 人民广场 : 467 by 100 meters, 1951. Used for parades, ceremonial occasions, people-watching, and ball-playing. Also has a daily free market with flowers, *penjing* (miniature landscapes) and goldfish of many varieties. Open 7 a.m.–5 p.m.

The **Botanical Gardens** 植物园 (Longhua Rd.; tel. 389413) is in the southern suburbs. Open daily, 8:30 a.m.–4:30 p.m. 70 hectares, 1954. Specializes in rock gardens and potted miniature trees, some several hundred years old.

Longhua Pagoda and Temple 龙华塔，寺 (tel. 389997) is in the southern suburbs and can be combined with the Botanical Gardens and Song Jiang County for a one-day trip. It is a noted scenic spot, the park formerly an execution grounds. The date of the temple's original construction is controversial. Some sources say A.D. 247, some 687, and others 977. It was rebuilt several times, the latest in the early 1980s. It is considered the oldest temple in Shanghai district. Note the fine brick carvings on its wall.

The brick and wood Song dynasty pagoda stands about 40 meters high, with seven stories. You can see the Huangpu River from the top. Huge temple guardians protect a small museum with some impressive carved boxwood furniture and a fine jade pagoda. The bell and drum towers are well constructed. The arhats, however, are poorly crafted.

The monks here show the scars of 12 incense burns in their shaved scalps, a traditional Buddhist initiation rite. This temple attracts a lot of visitors whose generous donations have built hotels in the back of the temple grounds. Festival days have attracted 50,000 visitors.

Shanghai has China's first **Museum of Aviation.**

Outside of Shanghai

Songjiang County 松江 has a history of 2500 years. It is about 40 km SW of the city and usually takes a full day to see. The rare **Square Pagoda** 方塔 in the Xingsheng Monastery (Sangong St., Songjiang) is 48.5 meters high. It was first erected in 1086–94 in the basic Song-dynasty style, with the tetragonal shape of the Tang. It still has some original brick and wooden brackets. During renovations in the late 1970s

two Song murals of Buddha were uncovered, and from the pagoda's
base, Song and Tang coins, bronze Buddhas, and animal skeletons—
offerings to atone for the sins of the deceased wife, probably of a nobleman. Its nine stories lean slightly seaward to compensate for prevail-
ing winds.

The screen in front is the oldest brick carving in the area, erected
in 1370 to keep evil spirits out of the Temple of the City Gods, which
no longer exists. Very well preserved, the mythical animal on it is a
tuan, greedily eating everything in sight. Note money in mouth. The
story goes that the *tuan* saw the sun reflected in the pool below, jumped
in hoping to gorge on it, and drowned. Can you imagine parents bringing their children here? This 174-hectare garden also contains newly
built Qing-style administrative buildings, tea house, and a Qing Buddhist temple moved here from downtown in 1981. Other ancient relics
have been assembled here from different parts of the county.

Also in Songjiang County is the **Zuibai Ci (Pond for Enjoying
Bai's Drunkenness) Garden** 醉白池 , outside the West Gate of
Songjiang town. First built in 1652 and expanded in 1958. The lotus
flowers in the pond are said to date from the 17th century. Highlights
include a stone engraving of 91 leading Songjiang citizens from the
Ming and early Qing and a small museum. Note also the pavilions,
moon gate, and rockeries. This can be skipped if your time is short, as
can the oldest relic in Shanghai, the **Tang stone pillar** 唐朝石柱 (A.D.
859). This 9.3-meter-tall carving, with some Buddhist inscriptions just
barely visible, some lions, and part of a dragon, is currently in the
playground of the Zhongshan Primary School and subject to the carelessness of children at play. Songjiang is also noted for its fine embroidery and Moslem hats.

If you have an extra day, consider **Jiading County** 嘉定 . It is 45
km NW of Shanghai and linked by a new superhighway. This should
give you some time to also drop in at some prosperous production brigades along the way. At Nanxiang is the 6-hectare **Gu-Yi Garden**
, where you can sample the famous steamed Nanxiang meat buns.
First built in 1566 and renovated in 1746, it has two stone pillars inside
over 1000 years old. The highly recommended **Qiuxiapu** is a 450-year-
old classical garden, once belonging to a Ming officer. Carefully reconstructed, the garden is designed for year-round blossoms, and shade for
summer and sun for winter. It also gives *yin-yang* contrasts of stillness
and liveliness, reality and dream, with 20 scenic spots in a small space.
Look for brick engravings, sculptures, wood and bamboo carvings among
the "mountains," pavilions, bridges, paths, and caves.

The **Confucius Temple** 孔子庙 (Nan Da St., Chenxiangzhen) is
one of the largest in South China. A major part of it is an interesting
museum of local history, with maps showing how people migrated, an
old fishing boat, and famous stone tablets relating to important events

from the Ming. The temple itself was founded in 1219 and enlarged in the Yuan and Ming. Imperial examinations for government administrators used to be held here.

Three thousand-year-old Jiading City has a Song dynasty pagoda.

Another full day's excursion is to **Dingshan Lake,** 65 km north of Shanghai. The county itself dates from the Song and has many cultural relics, as well as a goldfish breeding farm and a pearl cultivation farm. Over 100 hectares of former farmland are being developed into a huge recreation complex with kite-flying contests in spring, boat rides, 4000 plum trees (mostly for mid-March blossoms, not fruit), 6 hectares of autumn-blossoming osmanthus trees, fishing and swimming areas, restaurants, hotels, vacation village, convalescent homes, and theme park. All the buildings are in traditional southern Chinese architecture. If you look closely at the 47-meter-high pagoda here, you might discern that it is really a water tower. You can still climb five of its seven stories, the top two holding the water.

A scene from *Dream of the Red Chamber.*

The prime reason to go to the Dingshan Lake Scenic Area is to see the 11-hectare **Daguanyuan (Grand View Garden),** Shanghai's version of the setting of the popular Qing novel *The Dream of the Red Chamber.* Even if you haven't read this 1886-page novel, a visit is well worthwhile just to see this beautiful complex of pavilions, very tastefully decorated, some with genuine antique and/or real mahogany furniture. Each room is related to a scene from the tragic love story: the sickly heroine Lin Tai-yu's bedroom with medicine bottles, her harp, and her basket for burying flowers; spoiled, rich, but sensitive young hero Pao-yu's stunningly exquisite Happy Red Court, his books left in boxes because he didn't like to read and a chess board set up in his study. He played chess with Lin Tai-yu; the Grand View Chamber, the living quarters for a visit home of the daughter who became an imperial concubine.

Reading this novel, with its many plots and subplots, will certainly give you a good picture of aristocratic life a couple of hundred years ago and help you appreciate the great effort made here to be as authentic as possible. See also *Dream of the Red Chamber* under ''What is There to See and Do?''

The Grand View Gardens will be completed in 1988, but what is finished now is still worth the trip, especially if you like good historical reproductions, which this one is. Many of the staff members here are former peasants displaced by this new project.

On the way back to Shanghai, you may want to visit **Zhujiajiao,** an obscure old village of white plaster row houses and narrow slate-paved streets along the ancient canal, where the masses seem to be living still in Red Chamber times. They are as curious about you as you are about them. Also in Songjiang County, high on a hill beside the Academy of Science's Observatory, is a **Roman Catholic cathedral** 徐宇汇天主堂, looking most impressive but intriguingly and incongruously European.

Two- and three-day **excursions** can be easily made from Shanghai to Hangzhou, Ningbo, Suzhou, and Wuxi on your own, or arranged by C.I.T.S. See Shanghai in less busy seasons, like mid-winter. The least crowded is very charming Ningbo. See separate listings.

Cultural Events: **Shanghai Acrobatic and Magic Troupe** (tel. 564051): magicians, sword-swallowing, sometimes performing pandas, and juggling. Shanghai has high standards of music, art, and drama. It is a good place to sample the cultural life. **Shanghai Art Theatre** (tel. 565544); **Shanghai Concert Hall** (tel. 281714); **Grand Theatre** (tel. 534260); **Beijing Theatre** (tel. 581197); **Cathay Theatre** (tel. 372549); **Renmin (People's) Theatre** (663 Jiujiang Rd.; tel. 224473).

Factories: Tourists might be interested in seeing and shopping in factories for jade carving, embroidery, woolen carpets, and tapestries.

Shopping

Produced in the city are jade, ivory, and whitewood carvings, lacquerware, needlepoint tapestries, silks, carpets, embroideries, gold and silver jewelry (especially filigree), artificial flowers, painted eggs, reproductions of antique bronzes, and cheap jogging suits. Big department and book stores along Nanjing Road between the Peace Hotel and the Park, and along Huaihai Road. Antique and jewelry prices here are generally the best in China.

Tailors are again available, but they take about two weeks to make anything and are not aware of the latest Western fashions. Take pictures to show a tailor exactly what you want. But tailoring is cheap!

Shanghai Friendship Store 上海友谊商店 , one of the largest

in China, is near Huangpu Park, the Shanghai Mansions, and Peace Hotel (33 Zhongshan Dong-1 Rd.; tel. 210183). Purchases can be crated and shipped. This store is on the grounds of the former British Consulate.

Selling antiques are the **Friendship Store (Antique and Curio Branch)** 友谊商店古玩部 (694 Nanjing Xi Rd.; tel. 538092, 532605, 534503) and the **Shanghai Antique Store** 上海古玩商店 (194–226 Guangdong Rd.; tel. 216529, 212292).

Largest free market is at Shi Luo Pu. Be sure to haggle.

Shanghai Arts and Crafts Store 上海工艺美术商店 (190–208 Nanjing Xi Rd.; tel. 531796, 538206).

Duoyunxuan (422 Nanjing Dong Rd.; tel. 223410) is a highly specialized Chinese painting supplies store, where one can have scrolls mounted and buy top paintings and calligraphy.

The Overseas Chinese Store 华侨商店 (627 Nanjing Dong Rd.; tel. 225424) is also a travel agency with tickets to cultural performances.

Caitongde Drugstore (320 Nanjing Dong Rd.; tel. 221160): traditional Chinese medicines; **Beijing Chinese Pharmacy** (760 Nanjing Dong Rd.; tel. 222393); **Shanghai Jewelry and Jadeware Store** 上海珠宝玉器店 (438 Nanjing Dong Rd.); **Shanghai Arts and Crafts Trade Fair** 上海工艺美术交易所 (1000 Yan'an Zhong Rd.; tel. 533918, 563037, 533781); **139 Longmen Rd.** (between Xizang and Huaihai Rd.) is a tiny shop selling a small selection of good quality silk at half price. Check for flaws.

See also Yu Yuan Market, above, for more proletarian souvenirs like folding scissors, chopsticks, wigs, fans, and crafts, and local snacks.

Foreign Languages Book Stores 外文书店 (390 Fuzhou Rd.; tel. 224109) will mail books; **Shanghai #1 Department Store** 上海第一百货公司 (830 Nanjing Dong Rd.; tel. 223344): city's largest; **Shanghai #10 Department Store** 上海第十百货公司 (635 Nanjing Dong Rd.; tel. 224466) second largest; **Shanghai Silk Shop** (592 Nanjing Dong Rd.; tel. 224830) has silk from Shanghai, Jiangsu, Zhejiang, and other provinces.

Restaurants

Shanghai food is sweeter, lighter, and prettier than other Chinese foods, with a delicate consistency. Most big hotel restaurants here have good food and service, especially the Jinjiang, Park, and Peace.

Dahongyu Restaurant □ *556 Fuzhou Rd.; tel. 223176, 223475* □ Wuxi food.

Yangzhou Restaurant 扬州饭店 □ *308 Nanjing Dong Rd.; tel. 222779, 225826, 222873.*

De Da Restaurant 德大西菜社 □ *Corner Sichuan and Nanjing Rd.; tel. 213810* □ Western. Cheaper, but more crowded.

Fang Sang-ting □ *Dahua Hotel; tel. 523079* □ Qing dynasty imperial food. Waitresses dress in Qing costume. History of dishes outlined.

Hong Fang Zi (Red House) Restaurant 红房子西餐厅 □ *37 Shaanxi Nan Rd. at Changle Rd.; tel. 565648, 565748* □ French. Founded in 1935. Phone for reservation.

Meixin Restaurant 美心餐厅 □ *314 Shaanxi Nan Rd.; tel. 373991, 377845* □ Cantonese.

Sichuan Restaurant 四川饭店 □ *457 Nanjing Dong Rd.; tel. 22246, 222247* □ Sichuan.

Xin Ya Restaurant 新雅餐厅 □ *719 Nanjing Dong Rd.; tel. 223636, 226085* □ Cantonese.

Yanyunlou Restaurant □ *755 Nanjing Dong Rd.; tel. 226174, 223293* □ Beijing.

Hotels

In spite of the opening of many new hotels, the room situation will continue to be very tight until 1990. Especially during the high tourist seasons, no one should arrive here without a confirmed reservation. The best hotels at press time were the Jinjiang, Peace, the West Suburbs State Guest House, and Cypress (depending on the section). The Garden, Jing An Hilton, Sheraton Shanghai, Jinjiang New Tower, Sun Garden, Pacific (1988), and Tang should be in the top ranks when completed.

Chengqiao Hotel □ *Hongmei Rd. by Hongqiao Rd.* □ 1985.

Cypress Hotel (a.k.a. Longbai Hotel) 龙柏宾馆 □ *2419 Hongqiao Rd. 1 km from airport, 20 km from railway station* □ 161 rooms. Six-story main building and two-story building for distinguished guests with marble bathrooms and wall-to-wall carpets. 110 and 220V outlets. Sichuan and French food. Extension 1986.

Dahua Guest House 大华 □ *914 Yan'an Xi Rd.* □ 1937. 90 rooms, nine stories. Restaurant in adjacent building. Not convenient to downtown. Originally an apartment building. Mainly Japanese guests.

Donghu Guesthouse 东湖宾馆 □ *167 Xiule Rd.*

Guoji (International) Hotel (a.k.a. Park Hotel) 国际大饭店 □ *170 Nanjing Xi Rd.* □ 1934. 24 stories, 168 rooms. Mostly for Overseas Chinese. Excellent location across from former race track, now People's Park and market, and convenient to shopping and the winter theater of the Shanghai Acrobats.

Hailun Hotel □ *Nanjing Rd.* □ 1987. 30 stories, 500 rooms. Joint venture.

Hengshan Guest House 衡山宾馆 □ *534 Hengshan Rd.* □ Renovated 1986. 220 rooms, 15 stories. Not as many services as other hotels. Primarily for visiting scholars. However, very pleasant, though far out in the western part of the city. Three restaurants.

Heping (Peace) Hotel 和平饭店 □ *20 Nanjing Dong Rd. (at waterfront); 18 km from airport* □ Over 300 rooms. Most convenient to Nanjing Rd. shops, Friendship Store, foreign trade offices, and terminal for the river tour boat quay. Billiards. Built by an English Jew in 1929. Nine of its rooms are each decorated in the style of a different country. Still shows a lot of its original elegance. One of the best for business people and individual travelers in north section, renovated 1985. South section for groups to be replaced soon with a 40-story, 1200-room structure.

Hongqiao Club 虹桥俱乐部   □ *in Western Suburbs Guest House, Hongqiao Rd.*

Hongqiao (Rainbow) Hotels □ *Zhongshan Xi Rd. and Yan'an Xi Rd.* □ 1987. 700 rooms. More later.

Huaqiao (Overseas Chinese) Hotel 华侨饭店   □ *104 Nanjing Xi Rd.* □ Pre-Liberation, renovated 1985. Nine stories, 95 rooms. Used primarily for Overseas Chinese. China Travel Service office on premises. Two doors east of Guoji (Park) Hotel, with same excellent location on Nanjing Roads. Easily spotted because of clock tower.

Huating Hotel □ see Sheraton Shanghai Hotel.

International Hotel □ see Guoji.

Jing'an Guest House 静安宾馆   □ *370 Huashan Rd.* □ Not to be confused with the Jing'an Hilton next door. 1929. Residential district. Garden. Spanish exterior. 109 rooms. Electronic games. Same compound as Shanghai Hotel and International Club for swimming and tennis. French and Chinese cuisine.

Jingjiang (Chinchiang) Hotel (a.k.a. Jinjiang) □ *59 Maoming Nan Rd.* □ 720 units. This is the biggest of the old hotels, with the most services, two coffee shops, and five restaurants. Four buildings, tallest 18 stories. In western part of the city close to parks and a small shopping area. Has 250-seat movie theater-meeting hall and large garden. Presidents Nixon and Reagan slept here. Handy to Jinjiang Club and U.S. Consulate.

Jinjiang New Tower Hotel □ *next to Jinjiang Hotel* □ 1987. 42-stories. 700 rooms. Modern glass exterior. Managed by the well-run Jinjiang Hotel two blocks away.

Jinshajiang Hotel 金沙江饭店   □ *Jinshajiang Rd.* □ 1986.

Longbai Hotel □ see Cypress.

Overseas Chinese Hotel □ see Huaqiao.

Park Hotel □ see Guoji.

Peace Hotel □ see Heping.

Rainbow Hotels □ see Hongqiao Hotels.

Ruijin Guesthouse 瑞金宾馆   □ *118 Ruijin Rd.* □ Former home of wealthy British merchant. Four buildings, 40 rooms and suites. Garden and orchards. For heads of state and VIPs. A 225-room hotel is being built on the grounds.

Shanghai Hilton 上海喜来登旅馆   (a.k.a. Jing An Hilton Hotel Shanghai) □ *Huashan Rd., adjacent to the Jingan Guest House* □ 1987. 40 stories, 800 rooms. Managed by the international chain. Tennis and squash courts, health club with saunas, indoor heated swimming pool, scenic elevators.

Shanghai Hotel 上海宾馆 □ *505 Wulumuqi Rd.* □ 25 stories, 600 rooms. Disco; Sichuan restaurant. Next to International Club, where guests can swim and play tennis. Most foreign tour groups are put here, though standards are not high enough.

Shanghai Mansions 上海大厦 □ *20 Suzhou North Rd.* □ 1934; renovated 1984. 22 stories, 254 rooms. Closest hotel to Friendship Store. Very close to noisy river and harbor, but special windows should reduce noise. Was outside the foreign concessions and occupied by the Japanese during the late '30s.

Shenjiang Hotel 西郊宾馆 □ *People's Park* □ 1934; renovated 1978. Nine stories, 190 rooms. Not up to standard.

Sheraton Shanghai Hotel (a.k.a. Huating) □ *Caoqi Rd. by Zhongshan Xi Rd., SW suburbs. 20 minutes from the Shanghai airport* □ 1986. 28 stories, 1018 rooms. Six restaurants. Tennis court, swimming pool, banquet hall for 800. Across from 18,000-seat Shanghai Indoor Stadium and Catholic cathedral. Should be among the top hotels.

Sun Garden Hotel □ *Hongqiao District about 20 minutes west of city center on main highway to airport* □ 750 rooms, including one-bedroom studios with kitchenettes for long-staying guests. 24 stories. To be completed 1987, with *dim sum* restaurant, night club lounge, teppanyaki restaurant, outdoor pool, tennis courts, shops, business center, and three-story glass atrium.

Tang Bridge Hotel □ 1987. 30 stories, 600 rooms.

Tourist Village (a.k.a. Cherry Tourist Village) □ *Nongong Rd. near Hongqiao Rd.* □ 1985. 100 rooms. 107 more under construction.

Xinyuan (New Garden) Hotel 新园饭店 □ *Hongxu Rd. by Hongqiao Rd.* □ 1985. Two-story garden-style hotel with 140 rooms.

Xiyuan (West Garden) Guesthouse □ *1921 Hongqiao Rd.*

Yan'an Hotel 延安宾馆 □ *1111 Yan'an Zhong Rd.*

Other Important Addresses

Bank of China 中国银行 : tel. 217466.
Bank of Tokyo 东京银行 : tel. 582582 X58135
Banque Nationale de Paris 巴黎国家银行 : tel. 582582 X58142
CAAC 中国民航 : 789 Yan'an Zhong Rd.; tel. 532255 (international), 535953 (domestic). CAAC Shanghai Branch may be replaced by Eastern Airways.
Cathay Pacific 国泰航空公司 : Jinjiang Hotel; tel. 377899 or 534242 X123.
Chartered Bank 渣打银行 : tel. 218858.
C.I.T.S. 中国国际旅行社 : 33 Zhongshan Rd. E.; tel. 324960, 217200 and 66 Nanjing Rd. E. Service counters (8:30 a.m.–5:30 p.m.

with one hour off for lunch) in lobby of Peace Hotel; tel. 211244; in lobby of Shanghai Hotel, tel. 312312 X4141; airport, tel. 329327; railway station, tel. 240319.

Consulate-General of Australia 澳大利亚领事馆 : 70 Fuxing Rd., W.

Consulate-General of France 法国领事馆 : 1431 Huaihai Zhong Rd.; tel. 377414.

Consulate-General of Japan 日本领事馆 : 1517 Huaihai Zhong Rd.; tel. 362073, 372073.

Consulate-General of Poland: Anting Rd.

Consulate-General of the United States 美国领事馆 : 1469 Huaihai Zhong Rd.; tel. 379880, 378511.

A diplomatic enclave is being built on the highway to the airport, and most consulates will probably move there when it is ready. Britain, India, and West Germany have opened new consulates, mainly in the Huaihai Road area.

C.T.S. 中国旅行社 : 104 Nanjing Xi Rd.; tel. 226606, 226226.

Community Church: Hengshan Rd.

Hong Qiao Airport 虹桥机场 : tel. 537664.

Hongkong Shanghai Banking Corporation 汇丰银行 : tel. 218383.

Hospital for Foreigners: Huang Dong Xi Yuen, 257 Yan'an Xi Lu, 6th floor; tel. 530631.

International Club 国际俱乐部 : 65 Yan'an Xi Lu; tel. 538455. Has an outdoor pool and tennis courts.

International Seamen's Club 国际海员俱乐部 : 33 Zhongshan Dong Ye Rd.; tel. 216149. Regular cultural performances in theater. **Japan Airlines:** 1202 Huaihai Zong Rd.; tel. 378467, 532255. 锦江俱乐部

Jinjiang Club: Opposite the Jinjiang Hotel at 58 Maoming St.; tel. 582582, 534242. Open 11 a.m.–11 p.m. Another architectural relic from European times and still in use. This former French Club has live music, billiards, heated indoor pool, occasional dance parties, video, restaurants, bar, games, and new automatically set bowling alley. Bowlers used to have to set up their own pins. Reasonably priced French, Japanese, and Chinese food. Businessmen's Center (telex, typists, photocopying, translators, help in contacting trading corporations, booking airplane tickets, and taking messages): tel. 370707, 370660. 8:30 a.m.–6 p.m. Foreign Trade Building with offices nearby.

Jinjiang Foreign Trader's Office Bldg. 锦江外贸大厦 : tel. 582582.

Northwest Airlines 西北航空公司 : tel. 377387, 582582.

Pacific Delight Tours: Room 2207, Shanghai Hotel; tel. 312312 X2207.

Passenger Quay for Huangpu River trip
Huangpu River Sightseeing Service Station, Beijing Dong Rd. Wharf; tel. 211098.

Passenger Quay for Hong Kong: Book through C.I.T.S., C.T.S., or China Ocean Shipping Agency, Huangpu Hotel, 255 Jiangxi Rd.; tel. 216327 X79, 455200, and 1, Taiping Rd.; tel. 216327. Leaves twice a week. 400 berths each, 2½ days each way. Cheaper than flying, depending on class. Table tennis and pool. See "Getting There."

Passenger Quay for Dalian, Qingdao, Ningbo, Chongqing, Wenzhou, and Hankou (Wuhan) 旅客码头往大连，青岛，宁波，重庆，温州，汉口（武汉）　.

Passenger Quay for Japan 往神户（日本）码头　: Shanghai-Kobe ferry. 8500-ton ship; 600 passenger capacity. China Ocean Shipping Agency. See above.

Railway Station 火车站 : tel. 242299.

Shanghai Carpet General Factory 上海地毯厂 : 25 Cao Bao Rd.

Shanghai Tourism Corporation 上海旅游局 : 14, Zhongshan Dong-1 Rd.; tel. 219341, 219305. Coordinates tourism for Zhejiang, Jiangsu, Anhui, Jiangxi, Fujian, and Shanghai.

Singapore Airlines: Hongqiao Airport Guest House, 2/F, Room 265, tel. 328729.

Taxis

Friendship Taxi Service: tel. 536363; Shanghai Taxi Service: tel. 564444

Shanghai Touring Car Service: tel. 326564; Touring Car Dept., China Travel Service, tel. 225796, 312312 X3346 (Shanghai Hotel).

Shanghai Travel Taxi, 66 Nanjing Dong Rd.; tel. 216564.

United Airlines: tel. 530210.

Specialized Reading

Barber, Noel. *The Fall of Shanghai.* New York: Coward-McCann and Geoghegan, Inc., 1979.

Pan Lin, *In Search of Old Shanghai.* Joint Publishing Co., Hong Kong, 1982.

Seagrave, Sterling. *The Soong Dynasty,* New York: Harper & Row, 1985. Very readable and revealing book about the Soongs, sons-in-law Gen. Chiang Kai-shek and Dr. Sun Yat-sen, son T.V. Soong, reluctant premier and finance minister, and their Soviet, gangster, and wealthy Christian, American, and Chinese friends.

Shanhaiguan

North China. Northeastern Hebei province 40 km north of Beidaihe, this small town is one of the places to see the Great Wall. It can be reached by air from Shijiazhuang and Beijing.

Six km north is the **Meng Jiang-nu Temple,** which was built in memory of another of China's chaste, almost supernatural heroines. Lady Meng traveled on foot during severe winter months in search of her husband, one of the hundreds of thousands of workers building the Great Wall. Her deep sorrow and tears moved Heaven so much that the Great Wall collapsed to reveal her husband's bones. One version of the story goes on about Meng Jiang-nu committing suicide in the sea rather than submit to the advances of the Qin emperor.

The temple was originally built in the Song dynasty, but the statues were destroyed during the Cultural Revolution. They were restored in the late 1970s in gaudy, crudely painted clay. But the view of the hills to the north is interesting.

Six km from Shanhaiguan and about 40 km NE of Qinhuangdao is **Yansai Lake,** a.k.a. Shihe Reservoir, at the foot of Yanshan Mountain. Created in 1974, 36 km by 200 meters and 30 meters deep, the lake is formed by a dam (367 km by 60.6 meters) controlling the Shihe River. From the reservoir run 75 km of irrigation ditches, an impressive network along the side of the mountain. A 1-hour boat ride on the lake is breezy and restful. Take a hat if it is sunny.

Laolongtou (Old Dragon Head), the place where the Great Wall meets the sea, is also 4 km south of Shanhaiguan and is currently being restored. Chenghai Tower on the seashore was built in 1579, and parts of the wall here are ruins in the sea.

Beijie Restaurant is 200 meters from the Great Wall at Shanhaiguan. Reservations are recommended.

See also ''Beidaihe,'' ''Qinhuangdao'' and the ''Great Wall.''

Shantou 汕头

(a.k.a. Swatow and Chaoshan). South China. Northeastern Guangdong province. This port city and Special Economic Zone is 350 km by air north of Guangzhou, 10 hours by bus. It can also be reached by direct bus and ship from Hong Kong, ship from Shanghai, and road from Fujian. Shantou is the ancestral home of innumerable Chinese emigrants to South and Southeast Asia, Japan, and Africa. Many Chinese were also kidnapped from here and sent to Cuba in the late 1800s. Today about 15% of the population receives remittances from overseas. With the two municipal areas of Shantou and Chaozhou, and 11 counties, it has a population of about 10 million. The weather is mild, with an annual rainfall of 1400 to 2000 mm, mainly in the summer.

Shantou is famous for its port, which at one time was used by Europeans for the importation of opium to China. The district is also famous for its embroidery, lace, wood carving, lacquer carving, and silver and gold jewelry. It has other industries, notably the Shantou Photographic Chemicals Plant and the Shantou Ultrasonic Instruments Factory.

Among the attractions in **Chaozhou City** 潮州市 are: the **Kaiyuan Temple** 开元寺 , from the Tang dynasty (with its rare set of Buddhist sutras presented by a Qing emperor), **West Lake Park** 西湖 , the **arts**

and crafts factory, and the **embroidery factory** 潮绣厂 . Across the
Xiangzi Bridge is the **Han Wen-gong Temple** 韩祠 .

Chaozhou is a 2000-year-old town to which disgraced officers of
the Tang were exiled, notably Yan Hu, who objected to his emperor
spending so much money on Buddhist structures. **Ling Shan Temple**
(Tang) in Chaoyang County has a record of his dispute with the founder
of the temple, and the founder's grave. Chaozhou is one of the Four
Famous Ancient Towns, and still has Tang and Song architecture. It is
known for its fine wood carvers.

In **Shantou City** 汕头市 , 30 km south of Chaozhou, are: the **Arts
and Crafts Exhibition** 工艺展览馆 and **Zhong Shan Park** 中山公园 ,
with its ''gardens within gardens.'' To the east of Shantou is **Maya
Beach** 妈屿海滨浴场 , one of the most popular bathing beaches.
Across the harbor is the **Jiaoshi Scenic Spot** 岩石风景区 .

Chaoyang County 潮阳县 , about 30 km south of Shantou, has
two hills with Tang Taoist and Buddhist temples. In addition to the
Ling Shan Temple 灵山寺 , there is the pagoda of **Wenguang Tower**
葫芦山 and much historical graffiti on **Gourd Hill** 文尖塔 by **West
Lake**.

Shopping

The area produces famous drawn works, painted porcelain, jewelry, and embroidery. It is also noted for its stone, shell, and gilded
wood carvings.

Longhu Hotel: Chaozhou.
Overseas Chinese Hotel: Chaozhou.
Overseas Chinese Hotel 华侨饭店 : Shantou. An extension with 300
rooms was completed in 1983.
Xinxing Hotel 新兴宾馆 : Shantou.
CAAC 中国民航 : Shantou.
C.T.S. 中旅社 : Shantou Branch.

Shaoguan

*South China. In the northern part of Guangdong province
near the Hunan, Jiangxi, and Guangxi borders. This city of
over 320,000 people is on the Beijing-Guangzhou railway, with
14 trains a day from Guangzhou, 220 km away. (By road, it is
320 km) Only recently opened to foreign tourism, this area
might be for people wanting to get off the beaten path, especially in winter, when other parts of China are too cold. It
does have 310 frostfree days, with an annual rainfall of up to*

2200 mm, mainly in the summer. Hotest temperature in summer could be 40°C; coldest in winter is an occasional ⁻4°C.

Shaoguan is an industrial and mining center, producing 60% of Guangdong's coal and 90% of its nonferrous metals. It spans three rivers, the Dabeijiang, the Xiaobeijiang, and the Wengjiang. In the area are 130,000 people of the Yao and Zhuang minorities. The Yao have been in the area for about 1500 years.

The area was settled 120,000 years ago! Skull fossils have been found in Maba District, Qujiang County, dating from that period. Other artifacts from 8000 and 5000 years ago have also been discovered in caves in nearby Yingde and Shixing counties. The **Museum of Maba Man** can be visited 19 km south of Shaoguan, 2 km from Maba town.

Baojinggong Cave, 10 km from Yingde County Town, is four stories tall, formed of limestone. It can be combined with a visit to Nanhua Temple.

Gufo (Ancient Buddha) Cave 古佛洞 is 5 km SW of Lechang Town, 56 km north of Shaoguan City. It covers 10,000 square feet and has seven large "palaces," the widest related to the novel *Journey to the West*. Tea room and restaurant in vicinity. Both caves have grotesquely interesting rock formations.

The area has other scenic spots as well. Important is **Danxiashan (Red Cloud Hill)** 丹霞山 , 54 km NE of the city, with a good view of the neighboring countryside and the Jinjiang River. It is a hard climb, with peaks shaped like horses, elephants, and a monk's hat. Halfway up the hill is the newly renovated Buddhist Sutra Hall in the **Biezhuan Temple.**

Tourists can also visit Tang and Song dynasty tombs and the 1400-year-old **Nanhua (South China) Temple** 南华寺 in Qujiang County, 27 km south of Shaoguan. This recently restored temple has a pagoda dating from the Ming and a statue of the Priest Huineng, the abbott in A.D. 677 who developed the Dhyana sect. During the Cultural Revolution, his bones were found inside the statue. Also in the temple are wooden arhats (Song) and a 5000-kg bronze bell (Song). The temple is on 12,000 square meters of land.

There are also the **Yunmen Temple** 云门寺 , about 45 km west of the city, and three towers over 1000 years old. A hunting and fishing park is being developed 30 km from the city.

Hotels

Shahu Hotel 沙湖饭店 □ *Shahu Park, Shaoguan.*
Shaoguan Hotel 韶闰饭店 □ 1986.
Greenlake Villa □ *2 km from city center in the west suburbs* □ 64 rooms in 1985; 128 rooms in 1986.
Shaohua Hotels □ *Downtown Shaoguan* □ 1986.

C.I.T.S.: Shahu Rd.; tel. 5109; cable 6009.
Shaoguan Tourist Corporation: People's Standing Committee of Shaoguan City Municipality, tel. 5710.

Shaoshan 韶山

South China, 104 km SW of Changsha in Hunan province, the first province north of Guangdong. Shaoshan is a worthwhile 2½-hour trip by road. It can also be reached by train. The countryside is lovely, and if you haven't had a chance before to drive through tea plantations, or orange groves, and rice fields, take it.

The bonus is the ***Birthplace of Chairman Mao,** a simple mud-brick farmhouse where the founder of the People's Republic was born on December 26, 1893. He lived here in this charming and apparently tranquil village until 1910, when he left for studies in Changsha. He returned briefly several times, holding meetings and conducting revolutionary activities. The original house was confiscated and destroyed by the Nationalists in 1929, but after Liberation, it was rebuilt along the original lines. The house was shared by two families, the section on the left as you enter being the Maos'. It is very sparsely furnished. The dining room still has the original small table, typical even for large families. The master bedroom has portraits of his parents and the bed in which he was born. Another room holds original farm tools.

The **museum,** with ten large galleries, is a 10-minute walk from the farmhouse. It is full of exhibits depicting events in the life of the leader, although Mao's deposed wife Jiang Qing (Chiang Ching) and Lin Piao don't appear at all.

Shaoshan Hotel is 5 minutes' walk from the museum. Built during the Cultural Revolution to accommodate Red Guards collecting revolutionary sites, it has about 300 beds.

Shaoxing 绍兴

(Shaohsing) East China, in Zhejiang province. 60 km from Hangzhou by train or road, 3 hours from Ningbo.

This 2000- to 3000-year-old town is best known for its wine, but it was also the birthplace of China's most famous pre-Liberation writer, Luxun (Lu Hsun). His home and school, and a museum can be visited. Some of his famous stories, notably *The Story of Ah Q*, were set in this town, and a highly recommended but very sad 1982 movie was made of the Ah Q novella here. Literary types should pay a visit to his former residence and the **Luxun Memorial Hall** 鲁迅纪念馆 .

Shaoxing is also known for its lovely canals and **East Lake** 东湖 , alive with boats of all descriptions. Especially striking are its distinctive foot boats, the oars worked by feet. Highly recommended is a trip by these boats onto the lake and into the caves cut out of the lake's quarried cliffs to see the hanging gardens, and go under arched bridges to old temples—a good way to see what Shaoxing has to offer.

Shaoxing is famous throughout China for its distinctive opera. It is less formal, full of emotion, action, and audience—pleasing lyrics, gorgeous costumes, and flashy sets.

Shaoxing is an ancient city. The tomb of the Xia dynasty founder is in the south suburbs at the base of Mt. Kuaiji. Whether or not the third century B.C. pioneer in irrigation and flood control was/is in **Yu-wang Miao** is anyone's guess. In any case, he died in Shaoxing during a visit. The name *Shaoxing* means "gathering place"; for example, of the people celebrating the miraculous engineering feats of Emperor Yu.

Also of interest are the **Orchid Pavilion** 兰亭 , dating back to the fourth century, and the **Sheng Family Garden** 沈园, which commemorates the meeting between Song dynasty lovers. **Jianhu Lake** 鉴湖 , first dredged in the second century, covers more than 200 square km. The home of the early 20th century female revolutionist **Qui Jin** is open as a museum. **Premier Chou En-lai,** though born in Jiangsu province, was brought up in this city.

If you want to visit East Lake, Yuwang Miao, Lan Ding (Orchid Pavilion), Luxun's home and museum, Qui Jin's home, and stroll about the town, you need at least two full days. You could also ask about the story of the scholar writing with a brush made of mouse whiskers.

Shaoxing is attractive because it still has many houses, streets, canals, and boats hardly changed from centuries ago. Much time can be spent walking around in this time warp.

Changes have been made, however, like the addition of a local television station, and the lovely sycamore and plane trees lining the streets. The **Second Hospital** 第二医院 was the former mission hospital. Near it was an old pagoda with a tree growing from its crown. The pagoda is being renovated now, so may lose its foliage.

Writes one former missionary child of his early life in Shaoxing, "I used to play among the ruins of an old temple there and with a child's carelessness and disdain for the familiar, pretend it was something seemingly far more exotic and romantic: a Mayan temple!"

Ted Stannard, now a teacher at Western Washington State College, also says, "In my childhood, Shaoxing's streets and lanes were almost all paved with great rough-hewn but well-worn flagstones. Where they balanced unevenly across hidden drains beneath the thoroughfares, they would sometimes tip and sound hollowly underfoot or rickshaw wheel. Only a few blocks of the midtown shopping area had asphalt paving

before World War II. I can still remember the sensation of silent floating when my bicycle reached that stretch . . . I never saw a car in
Shaoxing until the Japanese occupation brought in charcoal-burning army
trucks, and in the late forties after the war, the mayor installed barrier
posts at all the principle entry-ways to the city to keep out all cars
except his own.

"Today the main arterials are asphalt-paved, and many streets wid-
ened by filling in canals or tearing out the shops or homes that had lined
them. Trucks, cars, and those uniquely Chinese farm tractors ply the
streets side-by-side with man-hauled carts, cycles, and pedestrians. But
step off into any side-street or lane and you are back in timeless China,
threading your way between high-walled compounds and across algae-
clogged canals on flagstones worn by centuries of footsteps.

"Marco Polo walked these streets, along the lacework of canals
that led him, in his journals, to liken Shaoxing (and Suzhou) to Venice.
The canals drain a lowland area reclaimed from the sea centuries ago
by a hydraulic engineer who succeeded where his father had failed (at
the cost of his head, thanks to a popular imperial theory of incentives),
and went on to become the Emperor Yu. A local saying credits him
with saving the people of Shaoxing from being fishes.

"The **Yuwang Temple** is in moderately good repair, despite some
damage during the Cultural Revolution. It has a series of courtyards and
steep stairways to the main temple where a gigantic figure of the emperor peers down benignly upon those who visit. Off to one side outside
this temple is a pavilion sheltering an ancient stone linga, taller than
any man, with a small hole piercing its tip. Traditionally, I recall from
childhood visits, childless women would try to toss a pebble or coin
through the needle's eye as a fertility charm."

Shopping

Buy Shaoxing wine, of course, brewed with 2000 years' experience. Visitors frequently stop in at the **Xian Heng Wine Shop,** named
after a Luxun short story. Also locally made are felt hats, paper fans,
silk, porcelain, and ink stones.

Hotel

Shaoxing Hotel 沼兴宾馆 □ built in the 1930s. The dining hall
is an old family temple. Old and new sections. Across the street is a
large park with a temple and three hilltops covered with evergreens and
paths, and in the early morning, vocal exercises by Chinese opera students can be heard. Good view from the top of Fushan or Lungshan
(depending on whom you ask). Hot water only a few hours a day. Same
with heat in winter!

C.I.T.S. 国际旅行社

Shashi 沙市

(Shashih, Shasi) Southwest China. On the north side of the Yangtze River, west of Wuhan in Hubei, Shashi is sometimes a stop on a Yangtze Gorges boat trip. It is an industrial city of 180,000 people making minibicycles, refrigerators, electronics, meters, textiles, etc. Shashi is a centuries-old trans-shipment port. In 1895 it was opened to foreign trade under the Treaty of Shimonoseki. Over 2000 years old, the city has such relics as **Zhanghua Temple** *(Ming) and a Ming longevity pagoda built for an Empress Dowager's 60th birthday. There is also a gate built by Guanyu (Kuan Yu) of the Three Kingdom's period. Eight km away is* **Jingzhou** *with more relics from the same period and a well-preserved Han mummy.*

Shekou 蛇口

South China. Guangdong province, 30 km SW of Shenzhen and 40 minutes by hover-ferry from Hong Kong on the Chinese side of Deep Bay. It is part of the Shenzhen Special Economic Zone. In addition to its industries, which include off-shore oil support, it is being developed as a resort area, apparently aimed at Hong Kong tourists.

The **MS Minghua/Sea-World** 海上世界 is now a 239-room hotel, with watersports and other recreational facilities. The **Nanhai Hotel** 南海大酒店 , with 395 rooms, was built in 1985 and is managed by Hong Kong's Miramar Hotel. Chinese and Western food, four bars, coffee shop, and fast food restaurant.

The **Shenzhen Bay Resort** has 280 rooms and is next to a Disneyland-type amusement park.

The **tomb of Song Emperor Shao Di** 宋帝昺陵墓 , the **Ancient Battery** 古炮台 , and an exhibit of the **Qin dynasty terracotta warriors and horses** 秦俑展览 can all be visited. The latter could almost save you a trip to Xi'an. The last of the Song emperors fled the Mongols here toward the end of the 13th century.

Other places of interest:

Green Lake Park 松湖公园
Friendship Store 友谊商场
Du Le Bookhouse 都乐书屋
Mingyuan Restaurant 茗园

Seaview Restaurant   海景餐厅
Shanghai Restaurant   上海餐厅
Taizi Hotel   太子宾馆
Bank of China   中国银行
Passenger Wharf   客运码头
Joint Hospital   联合医院

See also "Shenzhen."

Shenyang 沈阳

(Formerly Mukden) Northeast China. Capital of Liaoning province, which borders on Korea. 1¼ hours by air NE of Beijing. Also reached by train. An international airport is planned for 1988. Weather: Hottest in August, averaging 23.8°C: coldest in January, ⁻30°C. Rain mainly June to August. Population: urban about 2.65 million, with Manchus the largest group.

With a recorded history of over 2000 years, Shenyang was the Manchu capital from 1625 until 1644. After that, the Qing capital moved to Beijing. Shenyang is the biggest industrial city in this region, which was formerly Japanese-held Manchuria. The Mukden Incident on September 18, 1931, a surprise attack on the Chinese army stationed here, marked the beginning of Japanese aggression in China.

Shenyang today is a cultural center also, with institutions of higher learning and research. It is the home base of the Shenyang Acrobats, among China's best. This troupe was the first cultural mission from the People's Republic of China to tour the United States and Canada in 1972–73.

If you only have one day, C.I.T.S. suggests the Imperial Palace, North Tomb, East Tomb, Zoo, and open market.

The 19-year reigns of Nurhachi/Nulhachi and Huangtaiji (Huang Tai Chi) were enough to build the very impressive ***Imperial Palace沈阳故宫** , from 1625 to 1636, now restored to its original gaudy splendor. In an area of almost 60,000 square meters, it is also one of the best museums in China. Unlike the palace in Beijing, which was built by the Ming, this palace is Manchu and reflects more their taste in architecture. A study of the differences would be revealing. Although this palace has a lot of Han influence, look for Mongolian and Manchu-style touches.

The most impressive section is the eastern one, with its octagonal Dazheng Dian (Hall of Great Affairs) and Shiwang Ting (Pavilions of Ten Princes). Does the Beijing Palace have such dragons on its pillars, and the yurtlike design? The hall was used for important ceremonies and meetings with top officials. Huangtaiji commanded his military forces and political business from the Chongzheng Dian (Hall of Supreme Administration). At the back of this hall is a road to the Fenghuang Lou (Phoenix Tower) and the Qingning Gong (Palace of Pure Tranquillity). The Manchu leaders lived in the Qingning Gong, which is the most distinctively Manchu.

In the western section is the Wensu Ge (Hall of Literary Source), especially constructed for the *Complete Library of the Four Treasures* of Qing Emperor Qianlong.

The ***Beiling (North) Tombs** 北陵 (a.k.a. Zhaoling), north of the city, are of Huangtaiji and his wife Borjigid (Poerhchichiteh). Huangtaiji was the son of Nurhachi. Begun in 1643, the tombs were completed in 1651 in a total area of 4.5 million square meters, of which the tombs occupy 160,000. The **Dongling (East) Tombs** 东陵 (a.k.a. Fuling), are of Nurhachi and his wife Yihnaran. During the Ming, Nurhachi unified the tribes, became "khan" in 1616, and made Shenyang his capital in 1625. Also of interest is the **Shenyang Railway Locomotives Museum** 沈阳火车博物馆 and an overnight in **Xisheng Village** 西山村. C.I.T.S. also organizes cycling tours, including one to Dalian.

The 40-square km **Qianshan Mountain Park** 千山公园 is 20 km south. At Yixiang, about 150 km west of the city is ***Fengguo Temple,** dating from the Liao and said to be the largest temple in China. Does anyone dispute that? Also of interest in the province are Anshan and Dalian. See separate listings.

Shopping

Produced in the province are sable and carvings of jade, agate, jet, and amber. Also produced are ceramics, feather patchwork, and the musical instrument *zheng.*

Restaurants

Local delicacies include bear paw, Qimian (moose nose), Flying Dragon (grouse), and monkey head mushrooms, all available at the **Lumingchun Restaurant.**

Shengying Restaurant 盛京饭店 □ Northeast food.

Yingbin Restaurant 迎宾饭店 □ Qing dynasty palace dinner.

Laobian Dumpling Restaurant 老边饺子馆 □ Dumplings with various fillings.

Hotels

Phoenix Hotel 凤凰饭店 □ *No. 3, Section 6, Huanghe St., Huanggu District* □ 1984. Sauna, coffee shop, Chinese and Western food, dance hall, and massage. This is the main tourist hotel.

Liaoning Mansions 辽宁大厦   □ *Huanghe St., Huanggu District* □ 1969; renovated 1980.

Huaqiao (Overseas Chinese) Hotel 华侨饭店   □ *Shenyang Southern Railway Station* □ Renovated 1985.

Liaoning Friendship Hotel 辽宁友谊宾馆   □ *west of Beiling Park* □ 1970.

Youyuan Hotel 友园饭店 □ 1984.

Liaoning Hotel 辽宁宾馆 □ *No. 27, Section 2, Zhongshan Rd.* □ Renovated 1984.

C.I.T.S. 中国国际旅行社   : No. 3, Section 6, Huanghe St., Huanggu Dist.; tel. 66037.

U.S. Consulate: 40 Lane 4, Section 5, Sanjing St., Heping District; tel. 290038.

Shenzhen 深圳

(Shumchun) South China. On the Hong Kong border, this is a Special Economic Zone. It is quite possible that this zone will expand in 1997 to include Hong Kong. Currently it is a border area, and local Chinese have to have special permission to come here. Hong Kong currency has been freely used here, and Shenzhen is experimenting with its own currency.

Shenzhen is being promoted as a resort aimed at overcrowded Hong Kong. Already open are a golf course and campsites for tents beside the Shenzhen Reservoir (which provides Hong Kong with much of its water). The **East Lake Hotel,** near the reservoir, with minigolf, shooting range, sauna, tennis, swimming pool, and convention center has a good reputation. The **Bamboo Garden Hotel** has 1000 rooms. The 350-room **New World Hotel** in Shenzhen city opened in 1986. The 147-room **Shenzhen-Shanghai Hotel** opened in 1985. An international airport may be built here. New highways from here to Zhuhai and Guangzhou are already under construction.

Club Med's only project in China so far is a first-class resort hotel at Suimuisha, about 16 km from Hong Kong. It has a 280-bed hotel, golf course, beach, windsurfing, sailing, tennis courts, squash, archery, and a direct ferry to Hong Kong. The **Honey Lake Country Club** (3 square km) claims the longest roller coaster and monorail in the world.

Shenzhen can be visited by day tours from Hong Kong. Be aware that some tours are partly by bus, then train. Some pick you up at a Hong Kong hotel; others meet you at the Hung Hom train station. Recommended, however, is the other day tour to China to Zhongshan and

Cuiheng village, birthplace of Dr. Sun Yat-sen. It is prettier and has more history.

By 1990, Shenzhen expects to have 20 hotels and resorts, but only a few will be of international standard.

See also "Shekou."

Shihezi 石河子

(Shihhotzu) Northwest China. In the far-western autonomous region of Xinjiang, this city was reclaimed from the Gobi Desert in 1949 and stands at the northern base of Tianshan Mountain, 150 km NW of the capital, Urumqi. It has an urban population of 130,000 and a woolen mill, sugar refinery, oil-pressing mill, flour mill, and agricultural machinery plant. The area grows grain and cotton. Among its various nationalities are horse-riding Kazaks.

Important to see are the **Tianshan Dazi Temple,** the desert, the wild Mongolian gazelles, and the **Dachuangou Reservoir** (for boating, swimming, and fishing). Shihezi built the first monument in China to the late premier Chou En-lai.

See also "Urumqi."

Shijiazhuang 石家庄

(Shihchiachuang, Shihkiachwang) North China. The capital of Hebei province, a few hours by train south of Beijing, Shijiazhuang is on the main line to Guangzhou, east of the Taihang Mountains on the Hebei Plain. With a population of over 900,000, it is primarily an industrial city.

Shijiazhuang is of importance to Chinese revolutionary history as the burial place of the Canadian who became a Chinese hero. Dr. Norman Bethune 石求恩医生 , the son of a Gravenhurst, Ontario, clergyman, arrived in China in 1938 to help the Communist Eighth Route Army in its fight against the Japanese. Working almost in the front lines, he died of blood poisoning on November 12, 1939, in Huangshikou village, Tangxian county, in Hebei. That year, Chairman Mao wrote a much publicized article, pointing him out as an example of "utter devotion to others without any thought of self." He became known to every schoolchild, and statues were made of him all over the country.

In Shijiazhuang is the **Bethune International Peace Hospital** 白求恩国际和平医院 , first set up in 1937 in the Shanxi-Chahar-Hebei

Military Area and moved here in 1948. Dr. Bethune is buried in the western part of the **North China Revolutionary Martyrs' Cemetery** 华北军区烈士陵园 , where there is also the Bethune Exhibition Hall and the Memorial Hall for Revolutionary Martyrs. The city also has the **Hebei Provincial Exhibition Hall and Museum** 省展览馆 .

Visitors can see a cotton mill and a free market. Foreign professionals dealing with criminals have visited a prison and a court here.

Shijiazhuang is also known for the **Zhaozhou (Anji) Bridge* 赵州 安济桥 , still serviceable, although it was built between A.D. 605 and 610. It is SE of the city, over 50 meters long and nine meters wide, with a single stone arch, at that time a milestone in bridge construction. About 2000 meters north is the ***Yongtong** (Smaller Stone Bridge) built between 1190 and 1195, and 32 meters long. Ten km north of the city, in the town of Zhengding, is the ***Longxing Buddhist Temple** 隆兴寺 (Song dynasty), with a bronze 20-meter-high Buddha.

Spectacular is **Cangyan Hill** 苍岩山 , 70 km SW, full of pointed peaks and dramatic cliffs up to which snuggles Fuqing Buddhist temple. Reached by climbing more than 300 steps, the temple was home to a Sui dynasty princess whose tomb is on the hilltop.

Ninety km from the city is ***Xibaipo Village** 西柏坡 , Pingshan County, the now relocated site of the 1948 headquarters of the Communist Party Central Committee, which moved here after Yan'an fell to the Nationalists. Of interest to students of modern history. The actual site is now under water.

An unusual pagoda is at the ***Kaiyuan Temple** in **Dingxian,** about 75 km NW of Shijiazhuang. Dating from the Song, this 11-story, 84-meter-high structure has eight sides, but is it octagonal? It is basically two overlapping squares.

Also in the province are Beidaihe, Chengde, Handan, Qinhuangdao, Shanhaiguan, Tangshan, and Zunhua. See separate listings. The only road open to foreigners in the province is between Qinhuangdao and Beijing (3–5 hours) and Beijing to Baoding (6 hours).

Shopping

Locally made are painted-on-the-inside snuff bottles, white marble carvings from Quyang County, and Liuling wine. Elsewhere in the province are made golden-thread tapestry (Zhuoxian), shell crafts (Qinhuangdao), horse saddles (Zhangjiakou), ink slabs (Yishui), woven straw (Chengde), Handan ceramics, and Tangshan porcelain.

Restaurants

Yanchun Restaurant and the new five-story **Zhonghua Restaurant** 中华餐厅 are worth trying. Special local dish: deep-fried fish like a dancing lion with golden hair.

Hotels
   Hebei Guest House 河北宾馆 □ *Yucai Rd., 20 km from airport* □ 1978. 600 beds. Chinese and Western food.
   Shijiazhuang Hotel 石家庄市宾馆 □ *Qingyuan St.*
   Overseas Chinese Hotel 华侨饭店 □ 1987.
   Huanyu Hotel □ 1987.

Taxi: 4 Shifan St.; tel. 25471.
C.I.T.S. 国际旅行社 : 1 Fuqiang St.; tel. 44319.
CAAC 中国民航 : tel. 45084.
   Information about Hebei province and hotel reservations: tel. Beijing 55243.

Silk Road 丝绸之路

   This term was first used by a German author in the 19th century and is still used because it is so apt. Silk was the main commodity carried along the caravan routes between Cathay and Europe. It dazzled the eyes of Marco Polo, who traveled here in 1275. Bales of silk have been found in ancient tombs along the way: it was that highly valued.
   Informal trade between China and West Asia goes back over 2000 years. In 138 B.C. (Han), Emperor Wudi sent his emissary Zhang Qian (Chang Ch'ien) on missions westward to get help to fight the Huns. Zhang returned 13 years later, having been imprisoned most of that time by hostile tribes, but he fired the emperor's interest in trade. The Han emperors encouraged trading caravans with imperial protection and the building of beacon signal towers. From then on, the routes flourished periodically until the 14th century, especially in the Tang. It declined because sea-going ships were able to trade more efficiently and because of hostilities along the land routes.
   Trade was mainly in high value, low-volume or easily transported goods. The Chinese exchanged silk, tea, and seeds for peach and pear trees. They also exchanged skills, such as iron-, steel-, and paper-making. They received grapes, pomegranate and walnut trees, sesame, coriander, spinach, the Fergana horse, alfalfa, Buddhism, Nestorianism, and Islam.
   Goods were exchanged along the route especially with India and West Asia. A few items even made it through to Rome. The road went west from Xi'an along the Weihe River valley, Hexi Corridor, Tarim Basin, Parmirs (in Soviet Asia), Afghanistan, Iran, Iraq, and Syria. It was about 7000 km long. Northern and southern routes divided at Dunhuang.
   Many Arab and Persian merchants settled in Xi'an and even as far east as Yangzhou. Some of the cities on the Silk Road are open to

foreigners, and tourists find themselves in a world of onion-domed mosques, bazaars, oasis, grapes, Soviet and Turkish faces, embroidered caps, and languages their national guides cannot understand. Spontaneous dancing and singing, uncontrolled by Han reserve, make people here delightful. Visitors are frequently asked to join in and contribute to the festivities.

Tourists find giant rock carvings and murals, some of the best in the world. They can explore earthen-walled ghost cities, the western end of the Great Wall, old tombs, Lama temples, and look for mummies. They can figure out how and what the beacon towers communicated. They can learn how water is channeled to make this desert flourish. They can buy carpets, jade goblets, and musical instruments.

But the Silk Road is not Turkey, Pakistan, or Afghanistan. It is China, an ingredient that makes this area of mixed cultures special and worth the hardships.

Tourists in this area must be fit and adventurous. It is not for the finicky and inflexible. The area is extremely dry and cold even on summer nights. Long train and bus rides through the desert are not comfortable. Tourist buses, but not trains, are air-conditioned. But buses have broken down in the desert and the coolest retreat has been the shade of a rock or a sand dune—if you're lucky. You should be prepared for delays and be pleasantly surprised if they don't happen. While waiting, think about the peasants and herdsmen who struggled to raise crops and animals here while the spring or autumn sandstorms howled mercilessly. Think of the sand smothering the wheat. Think of the caravans passing through. What did the camels and traders do when they couldn't see a foot ahead of them?

You should have the foresight to carry your own liquid refreshments.

The government is in the process of upgrading transportation in this area. By the time you go, planes may be flying into most of the cities on the route. Paved roads might reach the cave temples you want to visit. So ask your travel agent about it.

As you travel around, try to pick out the characteristics of the different nationalities. See if you can identify people from their facial features and their distinctive dress. Among the groups along the Silk Road are the Kergez, Han, Huns, Huis (Moslems), Kazaks (not related to Cossacks), Kirghiz, Manchus, Mongols, Russians, Tarjiks (Tajiks), Tartars, Turfans, Uzbeks, Uygurs (Uighurs), and Xibos.

If you don't want to risk spoiling your trip with diarrhea, read about how to avoid upset stomachs in "Food." At least one whole tour group ended up sick from eating in the local market. Many travelers lose weight. The meat beyond Xi'an is mainly mutton. Wise is the traveler who says something like "I would love to try it, but it doesn't agree with me. Thank you anyway," when handed a glass of mare's milk buzzing with flies. The well-meaning tribesman in his yurt is not going to appreciate or understand the pain you will go through later. Don't drink it because you "don't want to hurt his feelings." You are the one who will suffer!

Urumqi is the best for shopping. Tourism officials are hoping to open the whole Silk Road by road from Xi'an to Xinjiang to foreign tourists by 1988.

See "Xi'an," "Dunhuang," "Jiuquan," "Kashi," "Lanzhou," "Shihezi," "Turpan," and "Urumqi."

Suzhou (Soochow)

East China. Yangtze basin, Jiangsu province, about 1 hour (86 km) west by train from Shanghai and 219 km SE of Nanjing, on the Beijing-Shanghai railway line. No civil airport. Weather: Hottest—36°C (usually 1 or 2 days late July, early August); coldest—end of January, averaging 0° to 7°C. Snow once or twice a year. Rush out and take beautiful exotic photos then. Rain: May–July. Population: almost 700,000 in the old city.

Suzhou was founded by He Lu, king of Wu, as his capital in the sixth century B.C. It is one of China's oldest cities. Iron was smelted here more than 2500 years ago and silk weaving was well developed in the Tang and Song. Marco Polo visited in the latter half of the 13th century. During the Ming, textile manufacturing flourished. From 1860 to 1863, 40,000 troops of the Taiping Heavenly Kingdom controlled the area. During the Japanese occupation, the Suzhou puppet government headquartered in the Humble Administrator's Garden.

The people here speak the Wu dialect, which is similar to that of Shanghai, only with softer tones and more adjectives. Industries include the manufacturing of TV sets, wristwatches, chemicals, machines, electronics, meters, and instruments. Tourists would probably want to see the various **factories** where artisans weave and print silk, make sandalwood and silk fans, and create one of the three most famous embroideries in China. Musical instruments are also made here. The **villages** raise silkworms, jasmine flowers for jasmine tea, shrimp, and tangerines, and are therefore particularly good to visit. In 1983, sections of Suzhou were put under state protection as historic and cultural treasures, its Song traditional architecture to be preserved, especially on Pingjiang Road and Shantong and Phoenix streets. No new factories can be built in the old city, and existing factories that pollute are being moved out to the suburbs.

The walled city is about 3 by 5 km and is crisscrossed by many canals. The western and southern moats are actually part of the famous Grand Canal (A.D. 610), extending from Hangzhou to the Yangtze and Beijing. The city wall was built in 514 B.C. and remnants, including three gates, remain. Also remaining is one of the eight water gates. These used to be closed at night.

Suzhou is one of the prettiest towns in China, its streets thickly lined with plane trees and its tiny whitewashed houses of uniform design. Unlike many other Chinese communities, the Japanese war inflicted little damage to buildings here. It is known primarily as a cultural and scenic city, similar in this respect to Japan's Kyoto. Its classical gardens are among the best in China.

The main street, Renmin (People's) Road, runs north-south; Jingde and Guanqian roads (actually linking) run east-west, meeting with Renmin almost in the center of the city. Many of the buildings were redecorated for Suzhou's 2500th birthday in 1986.

If you only have one day, C.I.T.S. suggests two of the gardens, Tiger Hill, one handicraft factory, and a boat trip.

Shizilin (Shih Tzu Lin; Lion Forest) Garden 獅子林 (Dong Bei (Northeast) St., 4 km from the Nanlin Hotel) was built in 1350 during the Yuan and so named because the teacher of the monk who built it lived on Lion Rock Mountain. Some of the rockeries are shaped like lions. Six acres: compact. Guides say that it was once owned by the grandfather of the famous American architect I. M. Pei. Notable are the maze inside the rockeries at the entrance and the rocks, some carved and then weathered in Lake Tai (Taihu) for scores of years. The rock structure above the stone boat was prepared for a waterfall, which in the early days was hand-poured (and therefore no longer operating). The rocks in one of the courtyards, with a great deal of imagination, look like a cow, crab (note claw), and a lion.

Exquisite is the Standing in the Snow Reading Room (pavilion), so named because a student once went to visit his teacher there and, too polite to awaken him, stood patiently in the snow. Moved by his spirit, the teacher renamed the pavilion.

Changlang Ting (Gentle Wave or Dark Blue) Pavilion 沧浪亭 (Renmin Rd.) is 1½ km from the Nanlin Hotel. About two acres, it is the only garden that is not surrounded completely by a view-blocking wall. A pond lies outside and can be enjoyed from a View-Borrowing Pavilion. The stones in the rockeries here are also from Lake Tai. A hall houses 125 steles with the images of 500 sages, dating from the kingdom of Wu to the Qing. Carved in relief in 1840, the deeds of each one are confined to 16 poetic characters. The garden, one of the oldest in the city, was founded in 1044 (Song) by the poet Su Tzu-chien. In the Yuan and early Ming, it was a Buddhist nunnery. The courtyard outside the Bright Hall for Giving Lectures was once gilded. Note the different eaves tiles.

Look for the set of dark brown furniture made from mahogany tree roots that look like chocolate-covered peanuts. This garden is not as spectacular as the others, so if you're short on time, skip it.

Yi (Joyous) Garden 怡园 (Renmin Rd.) was built by a Qing official and, at 100 years, it is the newest. It has taken the best of all the gardens, concentrating them into about an acre. The rockeries are from other older gardens. The dry boat is an imitation of the one in the Humble Administrator's.

*Liu (Lingering) Garden 留园 (Liuyuan Rd., 6 km from the Nanlin Hotel) was originally built in 1525 (Ming) and named the East Garden. It was rebuilt and renamed in 1876. The 8-acre garden consists of halls and studios in the east sector, ponds and hills in the central, and woods and hills in the western section. In late autumn, these woods are red. Look through some of the 200 different flower windows at the scene beyond. You are in a living picture gallery. A huge 5-ton, 6-meter-high rock from Lake Tai stands in the eastern section.

Wangshi (Master of Nets Garden) 网师园 (Shiquan St., ½ km from the Nanlin Hotel), originally built in 1140 (Southern Song), is one of the best. The Metropolitan Museum of Art in New York City has reproduced part of the Dianchun Cottage as the Astor Chinese Garden Court and Ming Furniture Room. This garden is very pretty, especially when decorated with colorful palace lanterns. It is open summer evenings for this exotic experience.

*Zhuozheng (Humble Administrator's) Garden 拙政园 (Dong Bei St., 5 km from the Nanlin Hotel) is the largest in Suzhou. It was laid out in 1522 (Ming) by a humble administrator (a dismissed official) and later split into three after the owner lost it gambling. It was restored in 1953. The largest and most open of the gardens, with water taking up three fifths of its total area, this one is reminiscent of the water country south of the Yangtze. Almost all buildings are close to water, much of it filled with shore-to-shore lotus flowers in summer. If you only have a short time, visit the central part. Fragrant Island there has a two-story stone "dry boat" complete with gangplank, "deck," and "cabin." The Mandarin Duck Hall has blue windows and classical furniture, with 36 live Mandarin ducks in a cage at the side of the hall. The loquat fruit trees ripen in June. A garden blooms within a garden. A covered walkway in the western section follows the natural contours of the land. Look also for the Small Flying Rainbow Bridge, the Pavilion of Expecting Frost, and the Pavilion of Fragrant Snow and Azure Clouds.

Note also the Lingering and Listening Hall for listening (of course) to the raindrops on the lotus leaves. Who else but the aristocratic Chinese constructed buildings just for something like that! Ramps instead of stairs make one wonder about wheelchairs back then. Look for the wood carving and the cloud designs on the glass. A 200-year-old miniature pomegranate tree is included in the excellent collection of *penjing* (Chinese miniature gardening).

*Hu Qiu (Tiger) Hill 虎丘 (9 km from the Nanlin Hotel) is important. The 45-acre site is NW of the city outside the moat. The grounds were an island many years ago, but now they are about 100 km from the East China Sea. It was originally called Hill of Emergence from the Sea. Named Tiger Hill because a white tiger appeared here at one time, the entrance (the head), the pagoda (the tail), and what is in between are considered parts of the tiger. On the right after entering is the Sword Testing Rock which He Lu, king of Wu, was supposed to have broken in the sixth century B.C. The sword is now in the Jinan museum in Shandong. On the left is a large magic rock. If the stone you throw stays on top, you will give birth to sons—so beware! On the right is a pavilion with red characters, the Tomb of the Good Wife. It commemorates a widow sold by the wicked brothers of her deceased husband to another man. Forced to be a courtesan, she committed suicide. Well, wouldn't you?

Here is also where Fu Chai, king of Wu, is said to have built a tomb for his father, He Lu, in the early fifth century B.C., after which the tomb builders were slaughtered to keep the location a secret. Hence, no one is sure if this is indeed the right place. If you look carefully, you can still see the red of the blood on the large flat rock. Oh, come on! From the carved stone Fairy Pavilion above the "bloodied" rock, Buddhist monk Sung Gong preached so well that his disciples nodded in agreement, and so did the rock to the right in the adjacent pond, now called Nodding Head Stone.

The tomb of He Lu is believed to be beyond the moon gate. In 1956, unsuccessful attempts were made to enter it. The foundation of the pagoda started to protest. Inside are supposed to be 3000 iron and steel swords. You can see the cave, blocked by large, cut stones, from the bridge to the pagoda. Is it or isn't it the 2500-year-old tomb? The two holes on the bridge were for hauling up buckets of water.

The pagoda of the Yunyen Temple was built originally in the 10th century A.D. (Northern Song). It caught fire three times, and its wooden eaves burned up. The latest repairs were made in 1981, when its foundation was strengthened. At 47.5 meters high, it tends to tilt to the northwest. Pilgrims used to climb the 53 steps here on their knees. Note the Indian arches.

A classical miniature-plant garden is at the foot of Tiger Hill.

The **boat tours** 大运河游船 go from (1) lunch at the Dong Shan (Eastern Hill) Hotel (after sightseeing in that area), a 40-minute ride across Lake Taihu to Western Hill; (2) Suzhou to Wuxi, 45 km in 3 hours; (3) the Panmen Water Gates to the Wumen Arch Bridge and Ruiguang Pagoda eastward along the city wall. From there it goes through the sluice gates to the Grand Canal and to the Precious Belt Bridge with its 53 arches: 40 minutes.

If you have more time: The **Beisi (North Temple) Pagoda** 北寺塔 at the north end of Renmin Road, is nine stories and 76 meters high, the tallest pagoda south of the Changjiang River. It was first built in the 10th century and rebuilt in the 12th. The temple at its base was built during the Three Kingdoms (A.D. 220–280) by Sun Quan, king of Wu, for his mother. It is beautiful.

Han Shan (Cold Mountain) Temple 寒山寺 10 km west of the Nanlin Hotel, was the home of two Tang monks, Han Shan and Shih Te. You might see rubbings made here of the steles. To the right of the central, gold Sakyamuni Buddha is Wu Nan, the young disciple who wrote the sutras; the older man is disciple Ja Yeh. The original bell was stolen by Japanese pirates but replaced with a bell cast about 100 years ago as a gift from Japan. Originally built in the Liang dynasty (sixth century), the current buildings were rebuilt at the end of the Qing, the Flower Basket Tower in 1954.

Xiyuan (West Garden) Temple 西园 (Liuyuan Rd.) is also very beautiful. Near the Han Shan Temple, it is the largest group of Buddhist buildings in Suzhou. It was originally built in the 16th century but was destroyed by fire, and rebuilt in 1892. The temple guardians here are surnamed Ma Li, though basically they look like temple guardians from other temples with other names. Here Ma Li Blue is dark and angry and carries a sword, Ma Li Red an umbrella, and Ma Li Sea a pipa, a musical instrument. Ma Li Long is holding a dragon, a magic weapon, though it looks like a snake.

The ceiling in the main building is magnificent—bats (long life) and cranes (happiness) as in Beijing's Forbidden City. The central Buddhas are seven meters tall, including base and mandala. On both sides are 20 devas, gods in charge of natural phenomena such as the sun, moon, and rain. Behind the Buddhas to the right is the Bodhisattva of Wisdom, with a crown on his head. To the left is the Bodhisattva of Universal Benevolence.

The 500 arhats here are worth studying, each face so real, expressive, profound, individual. Outstanding is the crazy monk, who can look sad, happy, or wry, depending on the angle at which you see him. Gilded on modeled clay, each statue is larger than life. But can you find any women? Enjoy those incense burners. At the time of the Great Leap Forward (1958–60) and backyard furnaces, they were supposed to be smelted. But the C.I.T.S. director said no!

Look also for the five-colored carp and giant soft-shelled turtles in the pond outside.

Dongdongtingshan Isle (Eastern Hill Peninsula), 40 km SW of the city jutting into Lake Tai, is worth a visit if you have the time. It is charming. The 16 colored arhats in the **Zijin (Purple Gold) Nunnery** 紫金庵 are older (Song) and said to be better than those in the West Garden Temple.

The **Twin Pagodas** 双塔寺 , almost in the middle of Suzhou, are known as the big (30 meters) and small (25 meters) "brushes" (used by Confucius for writing). They were built in the Song in honor of the sage.

The **Xuan Miao Guan (Mysterious Wonder Taoist Temple)** in the middle of the city has been described as the tallest, most magnificent temple in the area and probably in China. Do you agree? Three giant, gilded sculptures of the founders of Taoism dominate. Originating in the Jin (A.D. 265–420), the temple's current central Sanqing Hall was built in the Southern Song. Note the fine carvings on the stone balustrades in front.

The **Confucius Temple** 孔庙 looks very big and impressive and should be open for your visit. Inside are hundreds of steles.

Tianping (Heavenly Flat) Hill 天平 , the highest spot in the area, is 14 km west of Suzhou, and best enjoyed in autumn, when it is covered with red maple leaves. Lake Tai can be seen from its flat summit. At the bottom is the tomb of the famous Song dynasty writer Fan Chungyen's ancestors. The pleasant High Righteousness Garden also straddles its base.

Lingyan (Divine Cliff Hill) 灵岩 , 14 km west of the city, is very important to Buddhists. It is topped by a seven-story pagoda, probably Qing. The pagoda is at the site of the palace built by Fu Chai, king of Wu, for his beautiful queen, Xi Shi. A Buddhist college is in the 25-meter-high Lingyan Temple. At the foot of the hill is the ancient town of Mu Tu, founded during the Wu.

The Xi Shi Cave, halfway up the hill west of the Luohong Pavilion, is named after the queen. Another legend says that the king of the State of Yue was imprisoned here. East of the pavilion is the Yinguang Pagoda, where the bones of the founder of the Yinguang sect of Buddhism were kept.

The **Suzhou Embroidery Research Institute** 苏州刺绣研究所 is not a factory. It trains young people to do embroidery, develops new embroideries (new stitches, new materials, for example, human hair), and creates masterpieces in thread for places like Beijing's Great Hall of the People. Look for the double-sided embroidery on thin silk with each side a different picture. How do you think it was done?

A **Song Dynasty City** 宋城 is to be built around the water gate.

The **Suzhou Museum** (Dongbei St.) was the site of the official residence of a prince and general of the Taiping troops. First built in 1860, it has an old map of Suzhou (then called Pingjian).

Music lovers should be fascinated by the **First Ethnic Music Instrument Factory** (15 Vanmanqiao; tel. 24238, 23456). Not only will you see how 400 different Chinese instruments are made, but demonstrations are given by some of the craftspeople, who are renowned musicians themselves. You have to make an appointment (closed on Fridays) and bring your own translator.

Yushan Hill in Changshu city is 45 km NE of the city, with a 12th-century monastery (the Xingfu), and 2000-year-old tombs.

C.I.T.S. organizes very special excursions to hear the bronze bells at Hanshan Temple on the eve of the Lunar New Year. If one hears the bells chime 108 times on this night, one should have few troubles in life! Monks chant and pray for guests. Young men perform the lion and dragon lantern dances.

Shopping
Inkstones, brushes, jewelry, embroideries, silks, antiques, iron reproductions of ancient relics, and reproductions of some of the arhats are available. This is one of the best places to buy sandalwood fans (always smell them to be sure) and rubbings.

Friendship Store 友谊商店 : 8:30 a.m.–6 p.m. Other stores, 7:30 or 8:30 a.m.–6 or 7 p.m.

Restaurants
For recommended local dishes, see "Food."
Nanlin Hotel Restaurant 南林饭店餐厅
Suzhou Hotel Restaurant 苏州菜馆
Songhelou Restaurant □ *Guanqian St.; tel. 3270.*
Deyuelou Restaurant □ *Guanqian St.; tel. 6969.*
Xinjufeng Restaurant □ *Renmin Rd.; tel. 3794.*
Yichangfu Restaurant □ *Shilu Rd.; tel. 2932.*

Hotels
Gusu (Ancient Suzhou) Hotel 古苏饭店 □ *115 Shiquan St. on the grounds of the Suzhou Hotel* □ 1980. 110 rooms, two stories; built in cooperation with an Australian group.

Han Shan Hotel 寒山饭店 □ 400 rooms. The highest standards in town. Opened Sept 1986 to celebrate the 2500th anniversary of the founding of Suzhou.

Lexiang Hotel □ *Dajingxiang Lane, Renmin Road.*

Nanlin Hotel 南林饭店 □ *20 Gunxiufang Rd.* □ 1977. 104 rooms, three stories. Three smaller buildings, 30 rooms, 1959. 600 meters from the Suzhou Hotel.

New Nanlin Hotel 新南林饭店   □ *Shiquan Rd.* □ 1986. 320 beds.

Nanyuan Guest House

Suzhou Hotel 南园宾馆   □ *115 Shiquan St.; cable 6333* □ 1958; addition 1979. Nine stories, 450 beds. Two- and three-room suites. Dance hall, 600-seat theater with simultaneous interpretation equipment. Seven large and small dining rooms, including banquet hall. Coffee shop. 6000 square meters of property. About 400 meters from Garden of the Master of Nets and within 600 meters of the Nanlin Hotel in the SE section of the city.

Other Important Addresses

C.I.T.S. 国际旅行社 **:** Suzhou Hotel, 115 Shiquan Rd.; tel. 24646 X375 or X97

CAAC 中国民航 **:** 192 Renmin Rd.; tel. 22788.

Railway Booking Office: 203 Guanqian St.; tel. 6462

Railway Station Information Service: tel. 2831

Taxis: Railway Station, tel. 2512

　　　433 Renmin Rd.; tel. 5237

　　　Changxu Rd.; tel. 3588

　　　Nanmen Motor-Vehicle Service; tel. 6258

Telephone Information: tel. 114

　　　Long distance: tel. 113

　　　Correct time: tel. 117

Tai'an 泰安

North China. About 80 km south of Jinan, the capital of Shandong, the closest airport. You can also reach Tai'an by road or rail. The hottest time (36–37°C) is briefly in July and August; the coldest is December and January, when the temperature can fall to 10–13°C. The annual precipitation is 700 mm, mainly from July to September. It is about 10°C colder at the top of the mountain. The best time to climb is from April to October, but one can climb all year round.

Tai'an is where you go to ascend **Mt. Tai (Taishan)** 泰山 , one of China's Five Sacred Mountains. In ancient times, emperors came here to offer sacrifices to Earth and to Heaven. If they went up the mountain, they were probably carried up, and visitors today have the same choice. If you have only one day, you can be driven halfway up to the **Zhongtian (Middle Celestial) Gate** 中天门 . Then you can take the 2078-meter-long suspended cable car almost to the top at **Nantian (Southern**

Celestial) Gate 南天门 . Each car holds up to 30 people. You can lunch at the hotel near the summit and then return to see the **Daimaio (Temple)** and a free market.

The longer, more satisfying way is to climb (at least one way) because the mountain has 30 old temples and 66 well-documented scenic spots, including beautifully carved memorial arches, Han dynasty cypress trees, white water, breathtaking views of forests and crags, and a stone pillar that looks suspiciously like a lingam. If you do it the hard way, you are following in the footsteps of Confucius!

The top can be reached in 5 hours on foot through the Path of Eighteen Bends. Important to note are the 8500-plus stone stairs, each carefully placed by human labor! Like an almost vertical Great Wall! And they are not narrow! It is difficult to get lost. Above the South Gate, the stairs are very steep. The **Temple of Azure Clouds** 碧霞祠 is over 970 years old (Song). Note the bronze or iron roof ornaments, rafters, bells, and tiles of the main hall, made of metal to endure the severe mountain storms. Inside are nine huge gilt statues. Can you imagine having to carry these and the bronze Ming tablets up here! The summit is at **Tianzhu Feng (Heavenly Pillar Peak)** 天柱峰 , a.k.a. Yuhuang Ding (Jade Emperor Peak).

The **Tomb of Feng Yuxiang (Feng Yu-hsiang)** 冯玉祥墓 may be of interest to students of modern Chinese history. This was the famous "Christian General" who fought with the Nationalists against the Japanese and baptized his men with water hoses. His tomb is at the east end of the Dazhong Bridge, downhill from the Dragon Pool Reservoir. He is known more for his eccentricity than his military successes.

The visiting emperors used to offer their sacrifices at the **Daimiao (Temple to the God of Taishan)** 岱庙 , close to the Taishan Guest House at the base. This is a very impressive complex of religious buildings. The **Tian Kuang Hall** 天貺殿 , which is the main hall, has a mural 3.3 by 62 meters, painted in the Song, showing the pilgrimage of Song Emperor Zhenzong here. It includes 657 figures. (Count them!) This hall was built in A.D. 1009 and is considered one of the three eminent halls of China. Daimiao also has a collection of celebrated steles, some about 2000 years old. It and the guesthouse are about 4 km from the railway station.

A new tourist spot about 30 km from Tai'an provides opportunities for visitors to see a village and eat rural Shandong food. Local specialties are red-scaled carp, peaches, and white rose wine.

Shopping

There is an antique shop in the Dai Temple.

Hotels

Taishan Guest House 泰山宾馆   □ *Daizong Fang, at the southern base of Taishan Mountain; tel. 4694* □ 1978. Has roof garden and

10 deluxe rooms out of a total 125 rooms. This is the main tourist hotel. At this hotel, one can order such Shandong dishes as stewed turtle with chicken, three beauties, local cabbage, Taishan beancurd, and fried red scale fish. Western breakfast.

Zhong Tian (Half-Way Gate to Heaven) Guest House 中天门宾馆 a.k.a. Middle Celestial Guest House □ *800 meters above sea level* □ 1972. Has about 100 beds.

Daiding Guest House 岱顶宾馆 a.k.a. Summit Guest House □ *almost at the summit* □ 1957. About 200 beds and a restaurant. Climbers should spend the night in the hotel here so they can get up to see the sunrise (best in September) and the Yellow River.

Being built are three large hotels for foreign tourists with a total of over 1000 beds. The only named so far are the Taishan Hotel and the Dong Yue Hotel. Tai'an has many other hotels.

Antique Store: Dai Temple, tel. 3491.
C.I.T.S.   中国国际旅行社   : Dai Zong Fang, above Dai Temple and the Taishan Arch; tel. 3259.
Taxi: tel. 2342.

Taishan 台山

(Cantonese, Toishan; Toishanese, Hoishan) South China. This place should not be confused with Taishan, the mountain in Shandong farther north, listed under Tai'an. Taishan is both a county and a city near the southern coast of Guangdong province, about 100 km SW of Guangzhou and about 80 km, as the crow flies, west of Aomen (Macao). It can be reached by road from Guangzhou in about 5 hours. A fast way to go there from Hong Kong is the 4-hour ferry to Jiangmen and then taxi or minibus 2 hours from Jiangmen, or the ferry to Zhongshan and then 4½ hours by minibus. Weather: Subtropical. August is the hottest month, with a mean temperature of 28°C; January is the coldest, with a mean of 14°C. The annual precipitation is about 2000 mm, mostly from April to August. It can be very humid in summer. Taishan town, the county seat, is also known as Taichen. From this county many Chinese left their families for the Chinatowns of the United States and Canada. Many families here live off remittances. See "Special for Overseas Chinese."

Visitors can go to a local market, visit cottage industries like embroidery, artistic ceramics, bamboo weaving, etc., or explore a village. Next to the Overseas Chinese Hotel is a park with a small zoo and a lake. **Stone Flower Mountain** 石花山 , one of Taishan's eight scenic attractions, is about 2 km NE of the town, with an artificial lake and rock formations that look like furniture and animals.

Tourists can also visit tractor and porcelain factories. Those staying at the Stone Flower Mountain Inn can borrow bicycles and meet their Chinese counterparts.

Shang Chuan Island's **Fei Sa Beach** 飞沙里 is about 25 km south of Taichen, plus a 40-minute boat ride. It has 4 km of beach and clear water. The inns there are not up to standard. Nearby are the St. Francis Xavier Church and a primaeval forest inhabited by 3000 monkeys. To the east is **Zhongshan County,** birthplace of Dr. Sun Yixian (Sun Yatsen).

Basically, the attractions are rural, of interest mainly to Overseas Chinese looking for their roots, and other visitors wanting a restful exposure to south China. It does not have magnificent temples and palaces.

Restaurants

Taishan food is basically the same as Cantonese, but there are some dishes that are unique, like mud fish, steamed minced pork with salted egg, and peanuts fried with water chestnuts. The hotels have restaurants.

Hotels

Huaqiao (Overseas Chinese Hotel) 华侨大厦 □ *no. 1 Tong Ji Rd.* □ First built 1975; rebuilt in 1984. Four stories, 60 double rooms. This is the main tourist hotel and is adequate. It is in the center of town beside a manmade lake, convenient to sightseeing, shopping, and transportation. Chinese and Western food. Nearby is a sports field for volleyball, basketball, football, etc., and a swimming pool.

Other hotels are the **Hubin Hotel** 湖宾酒店 (next to the Overseas Chinese Hotel). The sixth floor is quite good. There are also the **Friendship Co. Hotel** 友谊公司旅业部 and the **Stone Flower Mountain Inn** 石花山旅馆 . The inn has been a pioneer in providing people-to-people experiences. It was built in 1981 in the old black-brick village-style architecture, but with solar heat and nature-cooled air, a joint U.S.-Chinese venture. In the area is a hot-spring resort with a 100-room extension, built in 1979.

C.T.S. 中旅社 in the Overseas Chinese Hotel has connections with C.T.S.s and C.I.T.S.s in other parts of China. Tel. 3307 and 2568.

At press time, Taishan was not officially open to foreign visitors, but China Travel Service and United (Taishan) Travel , both in Hong Kong, can help process visas to Taishan and make travel arrangements. See "Getting There."

太 原

Taiyuan

North China. In the center of Shanxi province, of which it is the capital, Taiyuan is an hour's flight SW of Beijing. It can be reached by air from such places as Xi'an, Lanzhou, Chengdu, and Xining, and by train from Beijing, Xi'an, Zhengzhou, Hohhot, and Datong, etc. The hottest temperature is 35°C for a few days in August. The coldest is ⁻14°C in January. Annual precipitation is 400 mm from July to September. Altitude: 800 meters. Population is 1.74 million.

The city was founded in the Western Zhou (1066–771 B.C.) Because of its strategic location, it was the site of many wars, changing hands five times between A.D. 396 and 618. It was a silk center under the Sui and has been growing grapes for a thousand years. Although it used to be a highly cultured city with many architectural wonders, the wars and modern industry have changed its complexion.

Taiyuan is most famous for the **Jinci Temple** 晋祠, 25 km SW of the city at the foot of Xuanweng Mountain. Started in the Northern Wei (386–534) in memory of the second son of King Wu of the Western Zhou, the Jin Temple was renovated, with additions, in 1102 (Northern Song). Female statues in temples, aside from goddesses, are very rare in China. Was this second son a lush? A son much pampered by women, like the spoiled hero of the novel *Dream of the Red Chamber*? Are the women here to continue indulging him in the after-life?

Alas, no! Centuries ago, Shanxi was very short of water. Sea and water deities have usually been female. In Shanxi a spring was found near Jinci, so people started worshiping Shuimu (Mother of Water). The maids-in-waiting and the mermaids were her retinue. This is the only temple in Shanxi to Shuimu.

The temple is the oldest wooden structure in the area and is charming. In the **Shengmu (Sacred Lady Hall)** 圣母殿 are 43 dusty, life-size clay figures, 30 of these court maids-in-waiting, all lithesome, each different in expression, and still retaining much color. This hall is not open to the general public; permission must be obtained. Try C.I.T.S. before you go, or look for an attendant at the site. Unusually shaped Zhou Dynasty cypress trees, pools, bridges, bronze statues, and pavilions decorate the grounds.

Uphill from the Jinci about 40 minutes by road, the Tianlong Shan (Mountain of Celestial Dragon) has a little temple with four *lohan*. The 24 small caves above the temple contain many old Buddhist statues, mostly damaged. They are Eastern Wei, Northern Qi, Sui, and Tang dynasties. It is a beautiful, though hilly walk.

The **Chongshan Monastery** 崇善寺 in the city itself is believed to have to have been a Sui palace once. Only part of the original (Tang) monastery is standing, and part of that is the Shanxi Provincial Museum. The monastery is famous for its ancient 1000-handed, 1000-eyed Goddess of Mercy. It, along with the two other bodhisattvas are eight meters tall. The beams and ceiling are quite remarkable. During the Sino-Japanese War, a bomb went through the ceiling without exploding, and the repair work is still visible. It is 3 km from the Yingze Hotel.

Next door is the **Shanxi Provincial Museum** 山西省博物馆 . Museum #1 has a vast collection of neolithic artifacts. So far, 200 paleolithic and 500 neolithic sites have been unearthed in the province, plus over 500 tombs and other ancient ruins. The museum is closed on Mondays.

Provincial Museum #2 is considered more important than Museum #1. It is at the site of the Chunyang Palace on the west side of May 1 Square. The palace itself was built between 1573 and 1619, and renovated in the Qing. It contains 20 exhibition halls with ceramics, bronzes, carvings, lacquer, calligraphy, embroidery, books, and other documents unearthed around the province.

The **Shuangta Temple** 善导寺 , a.k.a. the Yongzuo Monastery, has twin pagodas, symbols of Taiyuan, 8 km from the Yingze Hotel. The pagodas were built in the Ming and are over 50 meters high. They are octagonal and built of carved bricks. Inside the monastery are exhibitions of old coins, pottery, etc., and a corridor with 207 stone tablets of Ming calligraphy. Ming dynasty peonies decorate the courtyard. Very few religious statues. The temple has no beams.

In Shanxi province are also a great number of important historical monuments. In the southern tip is ***Yong Le Palace** 永乐宫 in **Ruicheng County,** with 400-meter-long Yuan dynasty murals, artistically beautiful. From it, one can also study social and architectural history. Nearby in **Yuncheng County** is the **Guan Di Temple,** founded in the Sui and completely renovated in the Qing. **Pingyao** 平遥 , about 100 km SW of Taiyuan, is a well-preserved ancient city with 6.7 km of city walls, and shops, homes, and streets untouched since the Ming and Qing.

At **Hongdong,** about 200-km SW of Taiyuan, is the ***Guangsheng Temple,** listed as Yuan and Ming. It has excellent colored ceramic figures and frescoes. An intricate, stunning collection of about 1000 lively Buddhist and animal figures over 300 years old is at the **Xiaoxitian (Miniature Western Paradise),** NW of Guangsheng Temple and north of Xixian county town. These are also worth a visit. Be prepared to climb and crane your neck. Take a flashlight and binoculars.

***Dingcun** 丁村 paleolithic ruins are in Xianfen county, roughly 25 km SW of Hongdong. Also in this area is a Han (nationality) folk museum, with 19 Ming and Qing courtyards, the oldest built in 1593. **Houma,** another 50 km SW of Linfen, is a Jin site from the Eastern Zhou. A low but spectacular (depending on the season) waterfall is at **Hukou** on the Yellow River, northeast of Dingcun. Guesthouses are at Yuncheng City and **Linfen** 临汾 . One could spend a fruitful month exploring this province alone!

See "Datong" for the Yungang Grottoes, the Great Wall, Wutai Mountain, Sakyamuni Pagoda, and the Huayan and Shanhua Monasteries. See "Hengshan" for the Mid-Air Temple.

Shopping

Locally made are fur coats, including rabbit and wild rat(!) skin, gold and lacquer inlaid crafts, reproductions of ancient ironware, black-glazed porcelain, Junco brand carpets, Fen Chiew wines, vinegar, fine glassware, lacquerware, jade carving, and brass and copperware (especially fancy charcoal-burning hot pots). Grown locally are dates, pears, persimmons, walnuts, and wild jujubes.

There is a **Friendship Store** (tel. 28731); Taiyuan also has an antique shop, arts and crafts shop, bazaars, and department stores.

Restaurants

Shanxi people love noodles and vinegar-flavored dishes. Chinese vinegar is not as sharp as Western and is a little sweeter. The **Jia Yang Restaurant** is known for Shanxi food, especially noodles and Shanxi duck. **Cook's Training Centre** has special cakes. **Qingheyuan Restaurant** has Mongolian hot pot and mutton. Five hundred-meter-long Food Street, in the southern part of the city, has 46 food shops and restaurants.

Hotels

Bingzhou Hotel 晋词宾馆 □ *Yingze St., SW side of May 1st Square* □ 1958; renovated 1985. Six restaurants, one bar. Beijing, Yangzhou, British, Japanese, French, and Korean dishes.

Jinci Hotel 并州旅馆 □ *near Jin Temple* □ 1957; renovated 1982. Eight villas.

San Jin Mansions □ *Yingze St.* □ 1982. Small rooms.
San Qiao Hotel □ 1985.
Shanxi Hotel □ *close to Yingze St.* □ 1986. This should become
the best hotel in the province, with all kinds of services.
Tang Ming □ New hotel.
Yingze Hotel □ *Yingze St., 17 km from airport* □ 1976; renovated
1984. 596 beds. The best now. Chinese and foreign food, telex room,
dance hall, coffee shop, bar.

C.I.T.S. 中国国际旅行社 : Yingze Hotel; tel. 29155; telex 28009
ITSTY CN.
CAAC 中国民航 Yingze St.; tel. 29903.
Taxi: Yingze Hotel; tel. 23211 X395.

Tangshan 唐山

*North China, NE of Tianjin in Hebei province. Tangshan was
almost completely destroyed by an earthquake in 1976; 800,000
people were killed. Much has since been rebuilt, and it is back
in business as an industrial center, open to foreign visitors. It
is not a tourism center.*

Tianjin 天津

*(Tientsin; Ferry to the Imperial Capital) North China. Over 2
hours (137 km) by train SE of Beijing, 70 km from the Bohai
Sea. On the Beijing-Shanghai and the Beijing-Harbin railway
lines. Direct flights (3 hours) from Hong Kong. It can be reached
by ship from Dalian (218 nautical miles), Yantai, Qingdao,
and Shanghai (708 nautical miles). Coldest: January, ⁻22°C;
hottest: July, 40°C. Annual precipitation averaging 600 mm,
mostly June–August. Urban Population: over 3 million.*

Tianjin is more of a gateway to elsewhere than a tourist destination
in itself. It is a port city, the largest commercial seaport in North China.
One of the treaty ports open to foreign trade by the Opium Wars, it is
now one of China's biggest industrial centers and one of the 14 Open
Coastal Cities.
Tianjin was a trading post in the 12th century during the Jin. It
developed as a port in the Yuan. During the Ming (1404), city walls
were built and the city was called Tianjinwei by the duke of Yen, who
crossed the Haihe River here on a military expedition. After the Grand

Canal opened in 1412, inland commerce and Tianjin's fortunes improved. A city wall was built about this time, and an imposing old fort once stood at the confluence of the three rivers.

Tianjin was invaded by the British and French in 1858. In June of that year the Treaty of Tientsin was signed, forcing 10 more treaty ports to be opened to foreign trade. Christian missionaries were given freedom of movement, and the Chinese were forced to guarantee the protection of missionaries because "the Christian religion as professed by Protestants and Roman Catholics inculcates the practices of virtue, and teaches man to do as he would be done by." In 1860 British and French troops from Tianjin marched on Beijing. They forced the Qing rulers to ratify the Treaty of Tientsin and burned down the Summer Palace. The resulting Treaty of Peking opened Tianjin and nine other ports to foreign trade.

Nine countries eventually controlled over 3500 acres of this city: Britain (with over 1000 acres), France, Germany, Japan, Russia, Italy, Belgium, Austria, and the United States. The concessions lasted from 20 to 80 years and, as in Shanghai, left the Chinese some very interesting old European architecture as well as bitter memories. The Treaty of Peking also forced the Chinese to permit French missionaries to own or rent property anywhere, and further helped to inflame smoldering anti-Christian and anti-foreign resentment.

Many of these feelings resulted from what the Chinese saw as Christian arrogance, which insisted that the Christian God was the only true God. Added to this were cultural misunderstandings. Quite a few Chinese actually believed that the children in Catholic orphanages were either eaten by nuns or ground up for medicine. The French Catholics did pay money for female babies (to keep them from being killed). By 1870 the atmosphere was so tense that after the French consul fired at a minor Chinese official, the consul was immediately hacked to death. Ten nuns, two priests, and another French official were also brutally killed in what is now known as the Tientsin Massacre, or what the Chinese prefer to call the Tientsin Revolt. The tragedy might not have happened if all Christian missionaries had refused to become arms of western imperialism.

On January 15, 1949, Tianjin was taken by the Communists. In 1976 it was severely damaged by an earthquake centered in nearby Tangshan.

Tianjin today, like Beijing and Shanghai, is a municipality directly under the central government. It has eight urban and four rural districts and five suburban counties. Its factories make Flying Pigeon bicycles, Seagull watches, petrochemicals, textiles, diesel engines, etc. The Dagang Oil Field is 60 km away. Tourists would probably be interested in seeing its arts and crafts factories. Its counties grow walnuts, chestnuts, dates, Xiaozhan rice, and prawns. Cultural presentations here sometimes include traditional opera, Beijing Opera, Tianjin ballet, acrobats, and puppets.

The city proper sprawls on both sides of the Hai River. The area immediately SW of Jiefang (Liberation) Bridge was formerly French. The section south of that, around the Tianjin Hotel, was formerly British. Liberation Road was Victoria Road. Tianjin has little to offer the average tourist. It is smoggy with industries, of interest primarily to fans of old European architecture, modern history, and handicrafts. Cruise ships berth in its harbor, and their passengers sleep in its hotels and commute to Beijing. Like many other Chinese cities in the 1980s, it is serious about tourism and is in the process of upgrading its attractions, roads, services, and air quality.

There is enough in the city itself for about a day. The **Dabei (Grand Mercy) Temple** (Tianwei Rd., near the Grand Canal) is the city's biggest Buddhist temple, founded in 1656 (Qing). The **Grand Mosque** (Dafeng Rd., near the Grand Canal) was built in 1644 (Qing). While you are in this area, take a peek at the **Grand Canal** (see separate listing). From here, commerce was linked by inland waterway with Beijing and with Hangzhou. The **Tianjin History Museum** 天津厂史博物馆 (4 Guanghua Rd.; tel. 41354, 42949) contains exhibits on the ancient and revolutionary histories of Tianjin, and has some bronzes, jade, paintings, and calligraphy.

The **Tianjin Arts Museum** (77 Jiefang Bei Rd.; tel. 32484) has sculptures and other traditional works of art from ancient times. The **Tianjin Museum of Natural History** 自然博物馆 (Machangdao, Hexi Dist.; tel. 30504) has fossils of mammoths and dinosaurs.

The **Friendship Club** 友谊俱乐部 (268 Machang Dao; tel. 30329, 32465, 34904, 36425) was built in 1925. This club is frequently used to give visitors a real Tianjin meal. It is open to both Chinese and foreigners. Formerly the Tientsin Club, it reeks of Britain in the early 1900s, with beautiful, high mahogany paneling and a drab, dismal interior. There are billiards, badminton, tennis, table tennis, four bowling lanes, a 1300-seat theater, a 600-seat banquet hall, and a ballroom with an "elastic" wooden floor. (Real springs are beneath it.) Swimming is in a 33°C mineral-water pool. Acupuncture and massage are available, as is Chinese and Western food, including "fried ice-cream."

Pleasant, but not very exciting is the **Shuishang (Water) Park** 水上公园, about 200 hectares of lake, islets, arch bridges, fish farm, zoo, library, swimming pool, and roller-skating rink. The Dengyinglou Restaurant is here. **Ningyuan Park** is in the classic Chinese style. Originally built for Cixi, the Qing empress dowager, it is on 54 hectares. Its Beijing Restaurant specializes in roast pork with sesame seeds.

The **Zhou Enlai (Chou En-lai) Museum** 周恩来纪念馆 is in the western part of the city, south of the Grand Mosque. It is for those interested in modern history. The former premier studied at Nankai Middle

School here from 1913 to 1917, and briefly at Nankai University (1919), where he led student uprisings before going to France in 1920.

The old Roman Catholic Church west of the Friendship Guesthouse can be seen from the front door of this hotel.

Near **Food Street** is **Ancient Culture Street** in Qing dynasty style, including the 1907 Guangdong Guild Hall, an A.D. 1326 Temple of the Sea Goddess, and an old Confucian Temple.

Factories

Tianjin is a good place to visit arts and crafts factories.

The **No. 1 Carpet Factory** (No. 2 Bridge, Jintang Highway, Hedong District; tel. 49342, 49343) is the biggest of nine carpet factories here, and makes Fengchuan-brand carpets. Carpets have been made for more than 100 years in Tianjin. This factory opened in 1958, and its thick carpets are made of pure wool, with no synthetics. Knots are made by hand, either 70 rows per square foot (ordinary) or 120 rows (refined). Embossing is also done by hand. Washing in a chemical solution adds gloss. Exports mainly to the United States. Staff about 1400.

Visitors allergic to dust or wool should avoid carpet factories.

No. 1 Metal Handicrafts Factory (Jinggangshandao, Hongxinglu, Hedong Dist.; tel. 43354, 42172) cloisonne; **Tianjin Painted Sculpture Workshop** (270 Machangdao, Hexi Dist.; tel. 36203); **Tianjin Special Handicrafts Factory** (16 Liuweilu, Hedong Dist.; tel. 42137, 43475); **Yangliuqing New Year Picture Society** (111 Sanheli, Tonglou, Hexi District; tel. 34843): New year's pictures of deities, like the Kitchen God, who informed Heaven of what happened during the year in the family were put up traditionally each lunar new year. These pictures are much brighter and more cheerful than traditional Chinese art.

Silk carpets are made in Wuqing county, about 28 km north.

Excursions from Tianjin

Beidaihe seaside resort, 3½ hours NE by train—see separate listing.

Beijing—see separate listing.

Chengde, a.k.a. Jehol, Qing Imperial Mountain Resort—see separate listing.

Qing Tombs, about 3 hours' drive NE. See "Zunhua."

*Dule (Temple of Solitary Joy) 独乐寺 , 120 km north, about 2 hours' drive, is in the western part of **Jixian city** and can be combined with a trip to Panshan Mountain. It was founded in the Tang. Its Guanyin (Goddess of Mercy) Hall and the Gate to the Temple were rebuilt in A.D. 984 (Liao). The magnificent Guanyin Hall, 23 meters high, is the oldest existing multistoried wooden structure in China. The 16-meter-high, 11-headed goddess is one of the largest clay sculptures in China. The murals are Ming; the colored clay bodhisattvas are Liao. The mythical animals at the gate are the oldest extant *chiweis* in China!

The **Yuyang Guesthouse** 渔阳宾馆 is a 104-room hotel in Jixian. 1980. Chinese food, but Western breakfasts. Fourteen courtyards.

The **Panshan (Screen of Green) Mountain** 盘山 (about 100 km north of Jixian County City in Tianjin Municipality) has been a mountain resort since the Tang. Highest peak is Moon-Hanging Peak, 1000 meters above sea level, on top of which is a pagoda said to contain a tooth of Buddha. Other peaks are called Sword-Playing Peak, Zhilai Peak, Jiuhua Peak, and Purple Canopy Peak. Famous for its scenery, unusual rocks, and pines. It also has a lake. Its 70 Buddhist temples were burned by the Japanese during World War II. Some of the buildings have been replaced or renovated.

Shopping

The main shopping streets are Binjiang Dao and Heping Road, with the three largest department stores. Made in Tianjin are wool carpets, painted clay figurines by Master Zhang, New Year pictures, porcelain vases, tablecloths, accordians, cloisonne pens, soccer balls, basketballs, kites, and inlaid, lacquered furniture.

Arts and Crafts Service (234 Heping Rd., tel. 24516); **Friendship Store** 友谊商店 (2 Zhangde Dao; tel. 32513): All of the above, plus jewelry, jade, ivory, fur coats, and hats, suede coats, padded silk jackets, men's suiting, shell work, cloisonne, carved lacquer, screens, inlaid chests, cork and boxwood carvings. Shipments can be made internationally; **Tianjin First Friendship Store** (21 Youyi Rd., Hexi Dist.; tel. 333003, 334505; cable: TFFS) This store has almost everything imaginable on four stories. Also ships purchases, tailors, arranges certificates of origin, mail orders, and books tickets for trains, ships, and airplanes; **Overseas Chinese Store** (29 Qufu Dao; tel. 30339, 35098); **Painted Sculpture Studio** (270 Machang Dao; tel. 36203); **Quanyechang Emporium** (352 Heping Rd.; tel. 23771); **Tianjin Department Store** (226 Heping Rd.; tel. 24195); **Wenyuange Antique Store** (263 Heping Rd.; tel. 23450); **Yangliuching New Year's Picture Studio:** Good prices for scrolls, reproductions, and prints. See factory, above; **Yilinge Antique Store** (175 Liaoning Rd.; tel. 20308) Branches in Tianjin Guest House, Friendship Hotel, and Tianjin Hotel; **Zhongyuan Co.** (196 Binjiang Dao; tel. 22096).

Restaurants

Newly opened is **Food Street** downtown, with three stories of shops, restaurants, wine shops, and tea houses. The food here is from all over China and abroad, and includes typical Tianjin snacks such as *goubuli* (steamed meat dumpling), *erduoyan* (fried cake), and *shibajie* (deep-fried dough twist).

Dengyinglou Restaurant 登瀛楼饭店 □ *94 Binjiang Dao; tel. 23594* □ Shandong.

Friendship Club □ *268 Machang Dao; tel. 36425* □ Chinese and Western food.

Hongqiao (Red Bridge) Restaurant 红桥饭庄 □ *62 Beimenwai Ave.; tel. 50837* □ Tianjin dishes.

Tianjin Baozi Restaurant 天津包子铺 □ *near the Friendship Hotel* □ Famous for dumplings.

Tianjin Roast Duck Restaurant 金聚德烤鸭店□ *142 Liaoning Rd.; tel. 22660, 22664* □ Tianjin's roast duck is like Beijing's.

Qishilin (Kiessling) Restaurant 起士林餐厅 □ *33 Zhejiang Rd.; tel. 32020, 32561* □ European.

Hotels

Bohai Guest House 渤海宾馆 □ *in Xingang, next to the Economic and Technology Development Region.*

Crystal Palace Hotel   □ 1986. Joint venture. This should be one of the top hotels in the city.

Tianjin Guest House, a.k.a. Tianjin Grand Hotel 天津宾馆 □ *Youyi Rd., Hexi Dist.* □ 1960. 1070 beds. This giant of a hotel is on an immense lot and is surrounded by parks in the southern edge of the city, close to the Friendship Club. The hotel has two main buildings for foreign tourists, the tallest seven stories, 1057-seat theater. Huge dining room seating 1700 people. Chinese and Western food.

Tianjin (Tientsin) Hotel 天津饭店 □ *219 Jiefang Bei Rd.; tel. 34325* □ 1900; expanded in 1924, renovated in 1985. Formerly known as the Astor Hotel. 74 rooms, four suites, three stories. Mahogany-paneled lobby. British-built. Located very close to the Hai River and Friendship Store. Relatively close to the railway station. Joint venture.

Tianjin No. 1 Hotel □ *198 Jiefang Bei Rd.; tel. 36438* □ Mainly for Overseas Chinese. Formerly Talati Hotel. 74 rooms and 12 suites. Close to the Tianjin Hotel and the Friendship Store. Sichuan, Guangzhou, Chaozhou, Russian, British, and American dishes. Recent renovations and extension with foreign management. China Travel Service on premises.

Yanyuan International Hotel □ 1986. 300 rooms. Joint venture.

Yingbin Guesthouse, a.k.a. Tianjin Garden Hotel □ *337 Machang dao, Hexi Dist.; tel. 24010* □ A posh state guesthouse with 93 beds, mostly in suites. Four villas. It has a lake, apple orchard, and gardens, and is on the southern edge of the city near the Friendship Club. Tianjin and Sichuan food.

Youyi (Friendship) Hotel 友谊宾馆 □ *Shengli Rd.* □ 1975. 209 rooms, nine stories. Second-floor restaurant specializes in Tianjin food. Western, Cantonese, and Fujian food. Located close to the Foreign Trade Building and some good restaurants, in residential district. C.I.T.S. office on premises.

Other Important Addresses

Airport 飞机场
Bank of China: 80 Jiefang Bei Rd.; tel. 32559. Foreign exchange desks in most hotels, Friendship Club, Yilinge Antique Store, etc.
CAAC 中国民航售票处 : 290 Heping Rd.; tel. 24045.
C.I.T.S.: Friendship Hotel, Shengli Rd.; tel. 35663 X577. Also: 55 Chongqing Dao, Heping Dist.; tel. 34831.
C.T.S.: Tianjin No. 1 Hotel, 198 Jiefang Bei Rd.; tel. 36438, 36040.
Domestic Tourist Service: 52 Chifeng Dao; tel. 23353. Organizes tours of Beijing, Qing Tombs, Jixian County, Beidaihe, and Chengde.
Hospitals: In case of emergency, if convenient, contact your guide or hotel attendant. Otherwise: No. 1 Central Hospital (at entrance to Munan Dao), Heping Dist.; tel. 34646.
International Seamen's Club: Xingang; tel. 3897.
Taxis: Check first with a hotel. Otherwise the **Tianjin General Tourist Corporation** (Friendship Guesthouse, Shengli Rd., tel. 35647, 35664) provides chartered vehicles or sells individual tickets for sightseeing in the area.
    Tianjin Taxi Co.: 383 Heping Rd.; tel. 35221 (for charters), 35771 (for taxis).
    Tianjin Tourism Car Hire Company: Youyi Rd., Hexi Dist.; tel. 37175.
    Tianjin General Tourism Corporation: 55 Chongqing Dao; tel. 32619; cable 3266.
Tianjin Passenger Terminal
Tianjin Railway Station 火车站 : Xinwei Rd. Ticket offices at Dong Ma Rd., Heping Rd., and Harbin Dao.
Xingang (New Harbor) 新港 : 50 km from Tianjin. Has Friendship Store, hotel, and Seamen's Club. Accessible by train or road.

Turpan 吐鲁番

(Turfan). Northwest China. Northeast Xinjiang province, roughly 198 km SE of the capital Urumqi. It can be a 2-day trip by road or train from the capital, which should include Gaochang, Jiaohe, the Baziklic Caves, Astana Tombs, Imin Minaret, Karez Wells, and Valley of Grapes. It can also be reached from Lanzhou by road or rail. Weather: The hottest in China! Turpan is in the Turpan Basin, which is known as "the oven." Temperatures reach over 40°C in summer. Rainfall averages 16.6 mm a year, and in very dry years, it has been 4 mm. Strong winds blow more than 30 days a year. The hot air from

*the basin and cold air from the north create violent storms. In winter, people could wear fur coats in the morning, light clothes at noon, and dine in the evenings around hot stoves. For summer nights, one needs a sweater. It is an area of extremes. Weather people and geographers would love it. The lowest point of the basin is Aydingkol Lake, its water surface 154 meters below sea level. It is second only to the Dead Sea as the lowest body of water in the world. Nearby is Bogda Mountain with an altitude of 5445 meters. **But wait! Don't stop reading!** Some of the people who have been there say the dust and the bumpy roads are worth it!*

Turpan was once an oasis on the Silk Route. An oasis? Yes, an oasis! It existed then and now because of subterranean water from the 2000-year-old **Karez wells** 坎儿井 . During the Western Han (206 B.C.– A.D. 24), soldiers were sent to develop agriculture here. Some sources say the technology for the wells came from Shaanxi province. Other historians say farther west. In any case, the wells are most common in Turpan and nearby Hami, to the east.

In spring, snow from the Tianshan Mountain melts, and this water flows into the Turpan Basin. While a lot of this evaporates, some water does soak into the ground and is stored in vast natural underground reservoirs reached by sloping channels tapped in turn by the wells.

Modern irrigation methods based on these wells have transformed Turpan into an agricultural area. Californians, and anyone else who has made deserts produce food, should be fascinated. Cultivated here are grain, grapes, cotton, and the famous Hami melons   . Grapes have grown here for 2000 years. The vineyards are north of the city. The wooden huts with the holes are for drying the September-harvested seedless raisins in the hot, dry air. Ask to see the drying process. Hami melons cost more than US$10 each in Hong Kong, they are so much in demand. So feel privileged if you are offered any, even though the market sells them for one yuan each. They have a sweet perfume somewhat like face powder, with the texture of cantaloupe and taste of honeydew.

Turpan is also a good place to experience the different cultural minorities. **Uygur (Uighur)** 维吾尔族 and **Hui** 回族 nationalities live here with the Han.

The dry climate has meant the preservation of historical monuments. The area has many ancient tombs, Buddhist grottoes, and the ruins of ancient cities. The best grottoes in the area are in Dunhuang, so you may want to wait until you go there.

The ghost city of ***Gaochang** 高昌故城 , 40 km SE of Turpan, was capital of the State of Gaochang (500–640) and reached its peak in the ninth century, with a population of more than 30,000. Try to imagine it then. It was on the Silk Road and flourished for 1500 years, from the first century B.C. Here were once over 30 to 40 monasteries! The buildings were made of mud bricks and are now without roofs. The town covers 2 million square meters and a stop here takes about 30 minutes. Did it only decline with the Silk Road or was there another reason?

Close to Gaochang are the **Astana Tombs** 阿斯塔娜古墓 , dating from the third century to about the eighth A.D. This is where 500 mummies, plus their belongings, were found, along with 2100 documents and books. Take a flashlight. Visitors routinely see only a couple of mummies in a dark room. Where are the others? The dry weather preserved the bodies with still discernable eye lashes and eyeballs. Was Astana the Uygur capital? Astana means capital in Uygur.

*Jiaohe (a.k.a. Yarkhoto, and possibly Yaerhu) 交河故城 , 10 km west of Turpan, existed from the second century B.C. to the 14th A.D. Its mud brick buildings are better preserved than Gaochang's and were encompassed in an area 1 km by 300 meters. In the northwestern part are temple ruins with the remains of Buddhist images. There is also a rare brick Buddhist temple.

The 44-meter-high **Imim Minaret** 额敏塔 , 200 years old, stands 2 km east of Turpan, its geometric patterns in the Uygur style. However, its smooth inverted-cone shape with rounded top is reminiscent of those towers south of New Delhi on the road to Agra. The ***Pazikelik (Baizeklik) Thousand-Buddha Caves** 柏孜克里克千佛洞 are 50 km NE of Turpan by dusty road on a cliff of the Flaming Mountains. About 60 of the grottoes are still intact. They were built over a period of 1400 years, starting in the Southern and Northern Dynasties (A.D. 420–550). Dunhuang's is more interesting and younger, but it is good to compare the two. The **Flaming Mountains** 火焰山 themselves are historical and cover a territory 100 km by 10 km. They are so named because the incessant sun is supposed to make the red rocks seem to be on fire from a distance. Perhaps this happens at sunset or at dawn or just in the classic tale *Pilgrimage to the West*. In that story, the monkey king pushes a hot brick from the furnace of one of the Taoist immortals to stop Monk Xuanzhang from going to India. The mountains are 100 km long and 10 km wide, their highest peak 800 meters above sea level. Unless you know the story, this is just another set of hills and may not be worth a special visit.

Turpan grows grapes with a 15 to 20% sugar content, among the best in China. Grapes grow almost everywhere, along streets and beside private homes. A 2.5-km grape corridor is between the center of the city and the Imam Minaret. Grapes have been grown here for 2000 years.

Visitors can stay in the **Turpan Tourist Hotel.**

Urumqi 乌鲁木齐

*(Urumchi) Pronounced Oo-roo-**moo**-chi. Northwest China. This capital of Xinjiang (Sinkiang) Uygur Autonomous Region, an area one sixth of China's total, borders on the Soviet Union and Mongolia. It can be reached by plane from Beijing (over 3 hours), Lanzhou (3 hours), Shanghai (4½ hours), and Guangzhou (via Lanzhou). It can also be reached by train from Xining and Lanzhou, but from the Qinghai capital, it is about 1600 km. The Beijing-Urumqi express covers almost 4000 km, the longest train ride in China. Urumqi is at an altitude of 650 to 910 meters and is surrounded by mountains. Weather: Hottest in August, 40.9°C. Coldest in December, ⁻41.5°C. However, the coldest in August has been .5°C. Pack for cold summer nights. In May and June, the coldest has been ⁻8.9°C and ⁻4.2°C! Consider yourself warned. Maybe you can use the weather as an excuse to buy a fur jacket! The annual precipitation is 200 mm. There is snow between mid-November and March. The best time to visit is May–September. Population: 950,000 urban, mainly Uygurs, but also Hans, Kazaks, Mongolians, and Huis. The city has 13 nationalities, the province 47.*

Urumqi dates from the Han, but its attractions are its people and the scenery. **Tianshan (Heaven Mountain)** 天山 and **Lake Tianzi (Heavenly Lake)** 天池 , 115 km south of the city, is about 1950 meters above sea level and colder than Urumqi. Count on half a day at least at these, and take something extra for warmth, especially if you want to climb. Tianzi is worth the trip for the scenery. The lake is 5 square km and 100 meters deep, and can be reached by horseback if you wish. Most visitors, however, go by bus or taxi. An ancient **glacier** 冰山 , about 100 meters thick, 5000 meters by 2000 meters, sprawls near ice caves and valleys. But visitors are frequently too cold to stay to explore. It is interesting to compare this area with the Rockies or Switzerland. But did you ever see a yurt and prancing camels at Lake Louise?

About 65 km south of Urumqi is the **Nanshan Pasture** 南山草原 —mountains, valleys, fountains, waterfalls, and cypress and pine trees. Why do you think the pasture is a symbol of longevity? The pasture is in Kazak country (not related to Cossacks). Horseback riding, mountaineering, and digging for valuable ginseng roots are listed among the attractions. Here, if you are lucky—or unlucky—you might find a game of polo played with an initially live goat instead of a ball! Shades of Afghanistan! You might be able to dine and/or sleep in a yurt. Barbecued mutton drowned by tea with mare's milk has been offered to some groups. Here it is impolite to show the soles of your feet.

In the city itself, one usually visits the nine-story **Hong Ding Shan Ta (Red Hill Pagoda)** 江顶山塔 , founded in the Tang, the current building finished in 1788. From the design of the pagoda here, you should be able to see a resemblance to Indian stupas. This is about a 5-minute stop. The excellent **Xinjiang Museum** 新疆博物馆 has a collection of historical relics of the various nationalities living in the region, and has documented for regional protection 119 historical sites. Exhibits include gold Roman coins, silver Persian coins, and other relics of the Silk Road. One hall contains murals; another displays 3200-year-old mummies in case you haven't seen enough of them in Turpan. A special new exhibition hall displays ancient artifacts and the customs of 12 minorities in Xinjiang. The museum is good for 2 hours and is close enough to the hotel for visitors to go there on their own. Titles are in Chinese and English!

The **National Minorities Palace** 少数民族宫 is a good place to visit, as it has a museum with costumes of the different groups, as well as a shop.

One of the highlights of Urumqi is the **Free Market/Bazaar** 自由市场 , which is near the hotel. You should find handicrafts there. Don't forget to haggle over prices! And close your eyes to the tempting fruit, "bing" pancakes, and spicy and delicious shish-kebobs there, unless you can see them being cooked. Tourists before you have gotten sick from eating from these stalls.

The different minority groups make for an interesting city. The Ugyurs (Uighurs) are the majority in the province. They controlled NW China during the Tang. In A.D. 788, a Tang princess married a Uygur khan, by no means a love match. In subsequent years, Chinese silk and sugar were exchanged for Uygur horses and furs. Uygur cavalry often helped the Tang. Strangely enough, the Uygurs were the main supporters of the Manichaean religion (see "Quanzhou"). The power of the Uygurs declined after their capital was sacked by the Kirghiz of Western Siberia. In 842, a food shortage turned the Uygurs into very aggressive raiders and China retaliated with force and the execution of Uygurs in Xi'an.

Other Important Destinations in Xinjiang: This is a huge region, the largest in China. It is much less populated than other parts of China, as a great deal of it is desert and mountain. Two cave temples, not otherwise described in this book, are listed as historical monuments under State Council protection. They may not be open yet for tourism, but you can ask about them. They are at **Baicheng** 拜城 and **Kuqa,** almost halfway in between Kashi and Urumqi, and are said to be from the third century. Kuqa already has an airport.

For other caves and tourist attractions in the region, see "Silk Road," "Turpan," and "Kashgar."

Planned for Urumqi is a tourist village with a Uygur theme and hotel. Also planned is a 21-story hotel and hopes for direct flights from Guangzhou.

Shopping

Urumqi is just about the best place on the Silk Road to shop for minority handicrafts. These include carpets, jade carving, embroidery, musical instruments, and fur and leather articles. Embroidered caps and hand-knotted wool carpets in Persian designs are especially good buys.

Urumqi Rug Factory 乌鲁木齐地毯厂 (64 Jinger Rd.; tel. 25825); the **National Minorities Palace** also sells costumes, hats, and vests.

Food

Local specialties include roast whole sheep, kebabs, thin-skinned steamed buns with stuffing, fried rice (eaten with bare hands), deep-fried *nang,* mare's milk, and dried sour cheese. Local fruits include seedless white grapes, pears, Hami melons, apples, and raisins.

Hotels

Friendship Guesthouse 新疆友谊宾馆 □ *Yan'an Rd., Urumqi, 28 km from airport* □ Some visitors have found the food here poor, and there hasn't been a choice of Western food, but things may have improved. The meat in Xinjiang is mainly mutton, because Moslems do not eat pork. But the hotel was clean and adequate and the staff had parties for visitors, with dances and songs in the evenings. Be prepared to perform with them. This is the main tourist hotel.

Kunlun Hotel □ *Youhao Rd.* □ Recently, standards were not so good, but the hotel is being renovated.

Tian Shan Mansion □ *Dongfeng Rd.*

Urumqi Guest House □ *S. Xinhua Road.*

World Plaza Hotel □ 400 rooms, 24 stories. Joint venture. Probably will open in 1988 Aiming for four stars.

Xinjiang Guest House □ *Yan'an Road.*

C.I.T.S. 中国国际旅行社 : People's Square; tel. 25794, 25913; cable 2464.
CAAC 中国民航 : Youhao Rd.; tel. 42942.
See also "Silk Road."

Weifang 潍坊

North China. Almost in the center of Shandong province, it is noted for its annual international kite festival (the first 10 days

*in April). Weifang is also known for its handicrafts: woodblock
prints, kites, lacquer inlaid with silver, and cotton toys.*

In the city is the small, classical Chinese **Shihuyuan Garden** 十笏
园 and in the outskirts the **Tuoshan Grotto** 驼山石窟 and the **Yun-
menshan Grotto** 云门山石窟 with Buddhist sculptures from the Sui
and Tang dynasties. **Shanwang** 山旺 , south of the city, is where prehistoric fossils have been and are still being found. **Mount Yimeng**
has high cliffs and waterfalls; **Laolongwan Bay**   boasts hot
spring baths.

Tourists can eat and work with local farming families in Shijiazhuang in Anqiu County.

Students of modern history might be interested in the Second Middle School, a little over a kilometer from the Weifang Hotel. This was
once the Weihsien Concentration Camp. British, Canadian, and American prisoners of the Japanese there in the 1940s included Eric Liddell,
the hero of the movie *Chariots of Fire*. A gold medalist in the 1924
Olympics for winning the 400 meters, this Scottish athlete refused to
race on Sundays. He later became a Congregational missionary in China
and died of a brain tumor in 1945. He was buried near the prison camp
six months before the end of the war. The site is now covered by a
housing development. In 1985, some of the original prison-missionary
buildings were still standing.

Weihai 威海卫

*A.k.a. Wei-hai-wei North China. Northern Shandong province
on the Bohai Sea east of Yantai and NE of Qingdao*

Weihai was developed in the Ming because of its excellent harbor.
Some of the funds to strengthen the navy base here were squandered by
Empress Dowager Cixi on her Summer Palace in Beijing. In 1894, the
Japanese won a naval battle here and occupied the city. In 1898, it
became a British naval base on a 25-year lease, and was used to keep
an eye on the Russians at Port Arthur (now Dalian), 100 km north. For
the American navy and other imperialists, it was a summer resort with
good beaches.

Weihai has one of the three most famous **hot springs** in China. It
is not as developed as Japanese hot springs, but the yellowish, 85°C
water can be cooled, and is said to be good for skin diseases, rheumatism, etc.

Liugong Island has a museum, and the wreck of a warship from
the Sino-Japanese war is being put into it. It could be ready by the time
you go there.

Wuhan

Southwest China, almost halfway on the main railway line, 18 hours by train south of Beijing and 18 hours north of Guangzhou. The capital of Hubei province can also be reached by air or by ship. Weather: Hottest—39°C (July and August); coldest—⁻5°C (January and February). Annual precipitation 1200 mm, mainly February to May. Population: 4.1 million, the fifth largest in China.

Wuhan, the capital of Hubei, is really three cities **Hankou (Hankow)** 汉口 **, Hanyang** 汉阳**, and Wuchang** 武昌 , separated from each other by the Changjiang (Yangtze) and Han rivers, and joined by bridges. It is the most important site of the republican revolution, and is noted for its industries, its ancient chime bells, and as a gateway to the Wudang Mountains and Yangtze Gorges.

The city itself dates from the 11th century B.C. (Shang). The city wall in Hanyang, no longer standing, was first built in the Han, almost 2000 years ago. The Wuchang wall was built during the Three Kingdoms (220–265), by Sun Chuan, king of Wu, and can still be seen at the **Small East Gate** 小东门 . The city was known then as Jiangxia. Hankou and Hanyang were originally one city, but in the 15th century, the Han River changed its course. It has been an important port for at least 2000 years.

Several foreign nations forced concessions here after the Opium War, and some of the architecture still reflects old Europe. Wuchang is especially famous because on October 10, 1911, the first victory of the Sun Yat-sen revolution against the Manchus took place here, although Sun himself was absent. Wuhan became the headquarters of the left wing of the Nationalist party. In 1923, the Communists led a successful railway workers' strike; in 1927, Mao Zedong set up a Peasant Movement Institute in Wuchang.

The city was liberated in May 1949. The three cities merged administratively shortly afterward. During the Cultural Revolution, it experienced some of the heaviest fighting between factions.

Wuhan is the home of the huge Wuhan Iron and Steel Works. Other industries include metallurgy, machine building, electric power, electronics, chemicals, textiles, and food.

The **Museum of Hubei Province** 湖北省博物馆 displays some of the world's most exciting recent archaeological discoveries. In 1978, 7000 articles were excavated from the **Zenghouyi Tomb,** located just outside of Suizhou city. Dating from the Warring States period 2400 years ago, the tomb of Marquis Yi of Zeng contained bronzes, weapons, lacquer, musical instruments, gold, and jade. The contents were found in water in which oxidized copper was accidentally dissolved. This saved most of the pieces from decay. Some of the lacquer is still preserved in water that shows the original brilliant red at its best.

Most important in the find is a complete set of 65 ritual bells of different sizes. When struck, they emit a perfect 12-tone system covering five octaves. Each bell also has two tones depending on where it is struck, a quality that has not yet been found in any other bell anywhere else in the world. In addition, the name of the tone and the date were inscribed on each bell in both the Zeng and Chu scripts. The two languages side by side here are as valuable to linguists as the Rosetta stone.

The bells were a gift from the king of Chu to the music-loving nobleman on the occasion of a royal visit. Since their reigns overlapped by only a few years, the technology to produce them must have been at an astoundingly high level. Not only are their tones precise, they were probably cast in a short length of time. The heaviest is 203.6 kg and 1½ meters high. Imagine pouring hot metal into a mold that size! And of the exact mixture and amount to produce the prescribed tone!

Ritual bells were only played for ceremonies, not for pleasure. Only aristocrats and royalty were allowed to possess them, and only in certain numbers. Reproductions have been played for visitors, who have heard *Jingle Bells* as well as ancient Chinese music. They sound crisper than other bells because of the bosses.

Students of modern Chinese history must visit the site of the first victory of the republican revolution, on Shouyi Road in Wuchang. There, revolutionists accidentally exploded some ammunition, and this point of no return started the lightning that led to the takeover of the city. A statue of Dr. Sun Yat-sen dominates the front of the **Hubei Military Government Building** 武昌起义军政府旧址（红楼） , now a museum. Republican troops broke through the **Qiyi Men (Uprising Gate)** 起义门 and seized Wuchang. Originally named Zhonghe Gate, the Qiyi Gate is one of the 10 original gates of Wuchang.

If you have more time the **Guqing Tai (Platform of the Ancient Lute)** 古琴台 in Hanyang dates from at least the fifth century, a monument to a deep friendship between a woodcutter and a musician. **Baotongsi Temple** 宝通禅寺 on Hongshan Hill was originally built in A.D. 630. Important is the **Iron Buddhas' Hall,** with six iron buddhas said to be from the Tang. The temple of the **Xingfusi Pagoda** 兴福寺塔 on the western base of Hongshan Hill in Wuchang was originally built in A.D. 554, the 11.5-meter-high pagoda in 1270.

The 45-meter-high, seven-story **Hongshan Pagoda** 洪山宝塔 in Wuchang dates from the Yuan (1279). The **Guiyang Temple (of Original Purity)** 归元禅寺 , started at the end of the Ming over 300 years ago, is the most important Buddhist temple in the city, and one of the 10 biggest in China. It contains 500 clay arhats, each life-size, distinctive, and 250 years old.

The five-story, 51-meter-high, **Huang He Lu (Yellow Crane Tower)** 黄鹤楼 , first built in A.D. 223 on top of the Yellow Swan riverside rock, inspired many famous poets, including Li Bai. It was destroyed by nature or war and rebuilt several times. It was reconstructed in cement and expanded on its present site on Snake Hill starting in 1981, forced out by a bridge. The design is based largely on the Qing version that lasted from 1868–84, but is 20 meters taller. It also has elements of the previous versions, pictures of which are inside. The tower gives a good view of the Yangtze and the city.

The poets were inspired by the legend of the wine shop on the original site. Here, the owner used to give free wine to an old man who drew a picture of a yellow crane on the wall in gratitude. After the old man left, the crane came to life and danced for the customers, and the owner became rich. When the old man returned decades later, he mounted the crane and flew off into the sky.

Nearby are the White Tower, the Tablet Corridor, and gardens. Wuhan will be rebuilding 20 historical buildings in the vicinity.

Chibi 赤壁 is the site of a famous Three Kingdom's battle. The approximately 33-square-km **Donghu (East Lake) Park** 东湖公园 has the Muse-humming Pavilion, commemorating Qu Yuan, the famous Warring States (B.C. 475–221) poet and patriot. The pavilion was built in the 1950s. The **Jiu Hun Ding (Nine Heroines' Mound)** 九女墩 was the 1855 burial site of nine women who drowned themselves in the lake while fighting the Manchus during the Taiping Heavenly Kingdom rebellion.

The **Bridge over the Yangtze** 长江大桥 is smaller than Nanjing's. Completed in 1957, it is 1670 meters long.

Outside the city are the **Wuzu Temple** 五祖 in Huangmei county, originally built in the seventh century, and **Jingzhou City** 荆州城 , whose 1187 city wall was rebuilt in 1646, nine meters high and nine km in circumference, with six gates. The museum here contains a 2100-year-old male cadaver. **Jinan City** 纪南城 is 5 km north of Jingling

County and was the capital of the Kingdom of Chu from 689 to 278 B.C. Each of these is a full day's excursion, and the most important is Jingzhou.

Yuquan Temple 玉泉寺 , at the eastern base of Yuquan Mountain, near Dangyang county city, was built in the Eastern Han. It has an iron pagoda dating from 1061 and a temple from the Southern Song.

The **Wudang Mountain** 武当山 is important as a Taoist center, with an impressive collection of religious buildings. Mostly built in the Ming, it includes eight palaces, two temples, 36 nunneries, and 62 grotto temples, all along a 30-km-or-so mountain path. The highest of its 72 peaks, Tianzhu, is over 1600 meters. On top is the ***Golden Hall** (Yuan and Ming) of gilded copper. Wudang needs 5 days and is not as strenuous as other mountains. New hotels are at the foot.

The museum at the ***Ancient Copper Mine in Tonglushan** 古铜矿 铜绿山 , Daye county, has been described by a Canadian metallurgist as "incredible." One hour by road from Wuhan, it takes another half hour to explore. It is now an open pit with mining tools, shaft, ropes, and baskets, started in the Zhou about 3000 years ago. Nowhere else in the world at the time was mining technology so far advanced. The mine here is of interest primarily to miners, historians, and scientists.

Wuhan is also planning a 200 meter-long street halfway up Sheshan Hill, with old-style shops and attendants in period dress selling souvenirs and local products.

For other destinations in the province see "Gezhouba" and "Yangtze Gorges." From Wuhan, one can take a regular ferry or one of the luxury tourist ships through the Yangtze Gorges to Chongqing. See separate listings.

Cultural Events

Noteworthy are the Wuhan Acrobatic Troupe, Beijing Opera Troupe of Wuhan, the Wuhan Song and Dance Drama Troupe, and, of course, the Zenghouyi Chime Bells. All of these have performed abroad.

Shopping

Made locally are gold and silver jewelry, lacquerware, carpets, shell carvings, carved turquoise, boxwood carving, feather fans, colored pottery, and paintings.

Hubei Antique Shop 武汉古玩店 (Provincial Museum, East Lake Scenic Spot Area; tel. 75336); **Wuhan Antiques and Curios Store** 武 汉古玩店 (1039 Zhongshan Ave., Hankou; tel. 21453); **Wuhan Carpet Weaving Mill** (14 Hankou Ruixiang Rd.; tel. 22803, 22003): this factory can be visited; **Wuhan Emporium** (208 Liberation Thoroughfare; tel. 52991); **Wuhan Friendship Store** 友谊商店 (Liberation Thoroughfare, Hankou; tel. 25781 and 25794); **Wuhan Service Department of Arts and Crafts** 工艺美术店 (Minshen Rd., Zhongshan Ave., Hankou; tel. 53478).

Restaurants

Among the well-known Hubei dishes are: mianyang three steamings of fish, pork, and chicken; grilled meats of five kinds of poultry; fish balls soup with egg white in the shape of the Three Gorges; stir-fried sliced pork kidney in phoenix-tail shape; fried boneless eel; braised wild duck in brown sauce; steamed catfish; lotus seeds with white fungus in sweet soup.

Guanshengyuan Restaurant □ *115 Jianghan No. 1 Rd., Hankou; tel. 23575* □ Cantonese.

Laohuibin Restaurant □ *50 Sanmin Rd., Hankou; tel. 51971* □ Hubei food.

Laotongcheng Restaurant □ *Dazhi Rd., Zhongshan Ave., Hankou; tel. 21562.*

Sijimei (Good in All Seasons) Restaurant □ *Jianghan Rd., Zhongshan Ave., Hankou; tel. 22842.*

Hotels

Shengli (Victory) Hotel 胜利饭店 □ *11 Siwei Rd., Hankou* □ French, British, and Russian dishes. Top class.

Xuangong Hotel □ *45 Jianghan No. 1 Rd., Hankou* □ High ceilings. Chinese and Western food.

Jianghan Hotel □ *211 Shengli St., Hankou* □ Special Hubei dishes. Old European architecture.

Qingchuang Hotel 晴川饭店 □ 1983. 24 stories, roof garden.

Hongshan Guest House

Important Addresses

CAAC 中国民航 : 209 North Liji Rd., Hankou; tel. 51248.

C.I.T.S. 国际旅行社 : 1395 Zhongshan Ave., Hankou; tel. 25018 and 24109. Try also Xuangong Hotel.

C.T.S. 中旅社 : 1395 Zhongshan Ave., Hankou; tel. 21666.

Hubei Travel and Tourism Administrative Bureau 湖北省旅游局 : 1395 Zhongshan Ave., Hankou; tel. 23505.

Hospitals: In case of emergency, try your hotel first if convenient. Otherwise: **No. 1 Hospital, Wuhan Medical College** 武汉医学院附一院 : 389 Liberation Thoroughfare; tel. 51171.

No. 2 Hospital, Wuhan Medical College 武汉医学院附二院 : 130 Liberation Thoroughfare; tel. 54191.

Taxis

Hubei Travel and Tourism Bureau: tel. 22692. 24 hours.

Wuhan Taxi Corporation 武汉市出租汽车公司 : tel. 55772, 55670. 24 hours.

Wuhan Port Passenger Transport Station 武汉港客运站 : Yianjiang Ave., Hankou; tel. 53875.

Wuxi 无锡

(Wisih) East China. Between the northern shore of Lake Taihu and the Yangtze River, in southern Jiangsu province, this industrial and resort city also straddles the ancient Grand Canal. It is less than an hour by train from Suzhou, and just west of Shanghai. It is a 2-hour flight south of Beijing. The urban population is 800,000. Weather: Hottest—in July, 38°C; coldest—in January, ⁻4°C. Annual precipitation 1056 mm, mainly in June.

Wuxi is one of the oldest cities in China, founded over 3000 years ago, during the Zhou. After deposits of tin became depleted, its name was changed to Wuxi, meaning ''no tin.'' It is known as a beauty spot, with classical Chinese gardens and a famous lake from which many of the best gardens get their rockery. Notable are the **Liyuan (Li Garden)** 蠡园 and **Meiyuan (Plum Garden)** 梅园 . The Liyuan has a ''thousand-steps veranda,'' with 89 windows on the inside wall. At the Meiyuan, the plum blossoms are best seen in the early spring. In 2213-square-km **Lake Tai** 太湖 is the **Yuantouzhu (Turtle Head) Islet** 鼋头渚 , with a bridge, temple, and pavilions.

The Liyuan is close to the Shuixiu and Hubin hotels; the Taihu Hotel is close to Meiyuan and Yuantouzhu.

Historical sites include **Xihui Park** 锡惠公园 , west of the city, with its **Tianxia Di'er Quan (Heavenly Second Spring)** 天下第二泉 (Tang), **Jichang (Relaxing the Mind) Garden** 寄畅园 , and the **Longguang (Dragon Light) Pagoda** 龙光塔 (great view), both from the Ming. Jichang Garden is one of the best-known South China gardens, uniting the distant hills with the intimacies within the walls. A copy of this garden is in the Summer Palace in Beijing. Do you see the similarity?

Wuxi is also a silk-producing center, the hills around it filled with mulberry trees. Tourists can see the local **silk industry,** from silkworm-rearing through the printing and dyeing process at a silk factory 丝织厂 . The best time is May through October. There are also the **Hui Shan Clay Figures Factory** 惠山泥人厂 boat trips with lunch on Lake Tai and trips on the **Grand Canal** 大运河 (3½ hours to Suzhou, for example, with lunch, or seven days, also visiting Suzhou, Changzhou, and Zhenjiang). A trip across Lake Tai can also involve a tour of **Huzhou** (ancient writing brush factory) before you go to Hangzhou. 湖州 A good time to visit is the Mid-Autumn festival, 15th day of the 8th month (lunar calendar), with lots of colored lanterns, moon cakes, an evening cruise on the lake and, one hopes, a full moon.

Excursions can be made to nearby (69 km) Yixing (purple sandware porcelain factory and caves), and to **Jiangyin** 江阴 (home of Ming dynasty scientist and traveler Xu Xiake). Trips also can be arranged to Changzhou, Zhenjiang, Yangzhou, Suzhou, Nanjing, and Shanghai. See separate listing.

C.I.T.S. can arrange for groups and individuals to visit schools and recreation centers. Honeymooners, cyclists, gourmets, and anglers are given special treatment. Anglers are provided with rods, bait, transportation, and rubbings of your catch. Classes in Wuxi cooking and in Taiji. Medical treatment (acupuncture, moxibustion, and massage) is available for chronic problems.

Shopping

Locally made and good are clay figurines and silk. Made in the province are porcelain and Yixing pottery. Look for freshwater pearls.

Restaurants

Local specialties include freshwater fish, crabs, and shrimp.

Zhongguo (China) Restaurant 中国饭店 □ *Hanchang Rd.; tel. 23438.*

Jiang Nan Restaurant 江南菜馆 □ *435 Zhongshan Rd.; tel. 27483.*

Ying Bin Lou (Greeting Guests) Restaurant 迎宾楼

Hotels

Off-season rates from Nov. 15 to Mar. 15 (20%).

Taihu Hotel 太湖饭店 □ *Houwan Hill by Lake Tai* 1950; 1984, 1985. One of the main tourist hotels.

State Guest House 国宾馆 □ 1985. Lakeshore villas.

Hubin Hotel 湖滨饭店 □ 1979; renovated 1984. Good view of the lake. 300 beds. One of the main tourist hotels. Taihu Hotel is considered better.

Shuixiu Hotel 水秀饭店 □ *near Li Garden, by Lake Lihu* □ 1980. 200 rooms. One of the main tourist hotels.

Wuxi Hotel 无锡饭店 □ *near the new canal* □ 1987. 800 beds.

Other Important Addresses   中国国际旅行社无锡支社

C.I.T.S.   7 Xin Sheng Rd.; tel. 25416. (新生路七号)
Flight to Beijing: Ticket office—Bureau of Communications, Renmin Rd.; tel. 29326. Bus service to military airport 22 km away. From Beijing, ticket office in West Building of Beijing Hotel; tel. 507766X596. Nanyuan Airport. Flights every Tuesday and Friday.

Xiaguan 下关

*Southwest China. At an altitude of 1000 meters, this is the
capital of Dali Bai Autonomous Prefecture, Yunnan province,
with most of the population of the Bai nationality. Located at
the southern tip of 41-km-long Lake Erhai, it is a 12-hour,
400-km drive (with rest and lunch stops), west and slightly north
of Kunming. Part of it lies on the famed Burma Road. The Dali
Prefecture merits a visit because of its colorful national minorities, old cities, historical monuments, and views of snow-capped
mountains, most of the year round.*

Northwest Yunnan is a lovely off-the-beaten path experience discovered mainly by foreign backpackers and social scientists. The government is making a special effort to control drug abuse by foreigners
in this area.

The history goes back over 2000 years. In the eighth century, this
area was part of the vast Nanzhou empire, which refused to submit to
the Tang. It was later subdued by the Mongols, though. Before you go,
read C. P. Fitzgerald's *Tower of Five Glories,* about his experiences in
this area in the 1930s. One recent visitor didn't think much had changed
since then. Public buses stop running after 4:30 p.m., but you can usually hitch a ride on a horse cart. There is a tendency to confuse the
names Dali and Xiaguan. Xiaguan was the old term for greater Dali,
and the name is still used.

The city has a tea brick factory 茶砖厂 worth visiting and a temple
to the Tang general who failed to conquer it.

Two of the guesthouses here have no private toilets, no showers or
baths. You wash from basins. The bathing is great at the hot springs 4
km away. The Erhai Hotel does have private baths and a good reputation. Boat trips on the lake can be boarded nearby for great views of
3800-meter-high Cangshan Mountain. **Erhai Lake** was believed to be
manmade in the Han, over 2000 years ago. The islands here are inhabited by Bai fisherfolk.

Among the day trips, **Dali** 大理 is 10 km north, an old walled town
with marble factories and some of the best marble in China. The houses
are made with marble. Look for a large obelisk erected by conquerer
Kublai Khan in the 13th century. Dali is also on the lake and appears
to be connected with Xiaguan.

Dali has the **Sanyuejie (Third-Moon market)** 三月街 , the 15th
to 20th day of the third lunar month, with caravans of horses and mules
arriving to be traded. It is also an important market for traditional medicines. About 60,000 people take part in the market, from Burma, Laos,

and all provinces except Taiwan. Enlivened by races and, perhaps, gambling, the site west of Dali at the foot of the mountain is a former Nationalist execution grounds.

Xizhou, just north of Dali, has especially remarkable architecture, incorporating marble. Bai architecture is characterized with white-washed walls and black trim. The much-decorated houses have court-yards in the middle and living quarters on three sides, with the entrance in a painted wall. The women's dress is basically white with red or black vests and a colorful bonnet. The women sing easily on request here. In addition to courtship rituals, the songs also relate local history, and are sung at work and during ceremonies such as weddings and fu-nerals.

Shizhong Shan 石钟山　石窟　, near Jianchuan (a long, one-day excursion north), has a unique Buddhist grotto reached by a steep 45-minute climb. It has a 1-meter-high female genitalia, which women rub for fertility and boys for courage. It also has some of the earliest Bud-dhist carvings in China—several styles, including some humans pic-tured with long curly hair, probably ancient foreigners. Indians, perhaps? At the base of this mountain lies an exotic old monastery.

Shibao Shan 石宝山　, nearby, also has temples and an annual singing contest in late August or early September by young people of many minorities. During the festival, thousands sleep under the trees or in temples, talents are discovered, and friendships and romances blos-som. The singing is a courtship ritual. Currently, no public transporta-tion exists in this area, and roads are unpaved. Fish is the local specialty, but the cooking is not outstanding.

San Ta Si (Three Pagoda Temple) 三塔寺　, on the west shore of Lake Erhai, outside the NW gate of Dali, was built in the Nan-zhao/Tang period, over a 1000 years ago, and recently renovated. The view of the lake, the three towers (70 meters and 43 meters high), and the mountains behind are famous.

Butterfly Pool 蝴蝶泉　, on the northern tip of the lake, is a natural spring with one huge tree covering it. In May strings of different kinds of butterflies appear.

Check with C.I.T.S. in Kunming for dates. See also "Kunming" for **Lijiang** and **Zhongdian,** in other prefectures farther north toward the Tibetan border.

Xiamen

(Hsiamen, Amoy) East China. SE coast of Fujian (Fukien) province, over 200 km across the straits from Taiwan, but 2½ km from Quemoy (Jinmen/Kinmen), the Nationalist-held island. Xiamen can be reached by sea or air-conditioned bus from Guangzhou and Hong Kong. The passenger ships Gulang-yu *and* Jimei *sail every Tuesday and Friday between Hong Kong and Xiamen, a journey of 22 hours. If you go by train from Guangzhou, change at Yingtan. It is a 1½-hour flight SW of Shanghai and 1 hour flight NE of Guangzhou. It is also linked with Fuzhou, Manila, and Hong Kong by air. Weather: hottest—38°C, July–Aug.; coldest—2°C, Feb. Annual precipitation is 1206 mm, mainly from May to July. Population: urban 267,000.*

Xiamen was the homebase of General Zheng Chenggong (Cheng Cheng-kung), a.k.a. Koxinga, who repelled the Manchu invaders for a while and then rid Taiwan of the Dutch in 1662. Xiamen was a relatively minor trading port until it was seized by the British in 1839. In 1842, the Treaty of Nanking allowed foreigners to build residences and warehouses here. For many years, especially in the late 1950s, both explosives and propaganda shells have been lobbed to China from Quemoy 厦门, off the SW coast of Xiamen. The shells no longer fall, but propaganda balloons still occasionally blow over, and powerful loudspeakers blast away—in both directions.

Xiamen is one of the Special Economic Zones and in recent years appears to be booming.

While the national language is also spoken, local people here speak Fukienese, which is different from both Cantonese and Mandarin. Fukienese is also spoken by the majority of people on Taiwan.

The ride in from the airport passes the Special Economic Zone, where a great deal of industrial development has been taking place in the 1980s. Yes, those are granite fences.

Xiamen is basically four distinct areas: the economic zone, the southeastern part of Xiamen Island, Gulangyu Island, and Jimei Island. The economic zone has factories and one of the better hotels, the Mandarin, but the location is not the best for tourists.

If you only have one day for sightseeing, take in Gulangyu, South Putuo Temple, and hurry through Jimei.

The southeastern part of the 123-square-km island contains the downtown shopping area, the **botanical gardens** 万石植物园 (where among the tropical and subtropical plants is a redwood tree brought by then U.S. President Richard Nixon). Also in this area are the South Putuo temple, Xiamen University (built by Tan Kah Kee in 1921), and the ferry pier to Gulangyu. Staying at the Lujiang Mansion is convenient to these places.

The 1000-year-old **Nan Putuo (South Putuo) Temple** 南普院 is named after Putuo Island in Zhejiang province, the home of Guanyin, the Goddess of Mercy. Most of the current buildings are from the 1920s and 1930s, but the tablets, scrolls, sculptures, bells, etc., were made in the Song and Ming. In front of the temple is a fish pond. On the lotus base of the statue of Buddha is carved the biography of Sakyamuni, and the story of the monk Xuanzang who went to India. The eight 3-meter-high "imperial tablets" in Mahavira Hall tell about the Qing suppression of an uprising and are written in Manchu and Chinese. Most famous is the stunning, three-faced, multiarmed statue of Guanyin. Thirty or so monks are now studying Buddhism here.

Behind the temple is **Five Old Men Peaks,** which can be climbed for a good view of the Taiwan Straits. The famous Chinese writer Lu Xun taught at **Xiamen University** 厦门大学 in 1926–27 and a five-room memorial hall on his life is here, including the room in which he lived and worked. He helped to found the **Museum of Anthropology** 人类博物馆 , with exhibits from prehistoric man to the Qing, and relics from the national minorities. Look also for the Australian boomerang and the 700-year-old Japanese sword.

At the foot of Five Old Men Peaks is the **Overseas Chinese Museum** 华侨博物馆 , outlining the contributions of natives who emigrated overseas. It also has souvenirs from Thailand, Burma, Cambodia, Malaysia, etc.

One can charter a tour boat around the islands.

Gulangyu (Drum Wave) Island 鼓浪屿 is 1.7 hilly square km, seven minutes across the "Egret River" by ferry. Formerly the foreign ghetto, it is good for another half day unless you want to hike or go swimming too. It has the best beach (Gangzi Hou), frangipani, flame trees, magnolias, and other heavily scented bushes and trees, and tiny shops. A very charming collection of old mansions built for foreigners have now been converted into guesthouses. Gulangyu is a car- and bi-cycle-free resort area, great for children and relaxing. It is cleaner and more prosperous-looking than the fishing villages of Hong Kong's out-lying islands, to which it bears some resemblance. Kodak film for sale here. Staying here, however, makes it difficult for hectic sightseeing and shopping unless a special ferry to the guesthouses is laid on. The dominating new statue is of Koxinga.

Everyone *must* climb 90-meter-high **Riguang Yan (Sunlight Rock)** 日光岩 , the highest peak here, for the view and the story of the two devoted egrets, the male killed by a greedy, unromantic goshawk. Also here is the **Lotus Flower Nunnery** (a.k.a. Sunshine Temple), the camp where Koxinga stationed his men, and **Zheng Chenggong Memorial Hall** 郑成功纪念馆 , with souvenirs of his life, including a history written by a Dutchman about the fall of Taiwan/Formosa. The **Shu-zhuang Garden** was built by a Taiwan resident who moved here after the Japanese took over that island in the late 1890s. It has bridges, 12 caves, pavilions, and rockeries from Lake Taihu. Unlike most gardens of China, it incorporates the sea into its design. "The garden is in the sea and the sea is in the garden."

Jimei Island 迷宫 , 2.83 square km, is worth an hour and is over 10 km north of downtown. It is reached by a 2.8-km granite causeway from Xiamen Island, built in 1953–55, and is on the road to Quanzhou. Eighty percent of the people here have relatives abroad. On Jimei is a most interesting monument built by an Overseas Chinese philanthropist, Tan Kah Kee, who made his money from rubber, rice, and pineapples in Singapore and put a lot of it into education in his hometown, origi-nally a farming community. **Turtle Garden** 鳌园 , built in 1950, is an encyclopedia in stone, full of pictures of the things Mr. Tan wanted to teach people: factories, machinery, exotic animals, Chinese literature, history, and culture. How many scenes can you identify? His elaborate tomb is typically horseshoe-shaped, a form of tomb seen more now in other parts of Asia than in China. His biography is in pictures around the tomb. The turtle is a symbol of longevity, and Liberation Monument is set on a statue of a turtle here.

Nearby is the huge **Jimei Middle School,** which he also financed. Here, mainly Overseas Chinese students from all over the world come to study. It faces a sheltered harbor where dragon boat races are held every year. It is only one of the many schools Mr. Tan built in Jimei. For those curious about the man, a tiny museum nearby also shows pictures of his life.

Excursions

In the vicinity of Xiamen, closer to Fuzhou, is the tomb of Kox-inga. Reached by road is also the town of Zhangzhou and the historical city of Quanzhou. See separate listings.

Shopping

Locally made are Caiza silk figures, lacquer thread–decorated vases, colored clay figures, and bead embroidery. You may want to try the *Yupi* peanuts, the *gongtang* crisp peanut cakes, dried longan fruit, and preserved olives. Locally grown are longan, litchis, peanuts, sugarcane, and, of course, rice. The main shopping street is Zhongshan Road.

Lujiang Emporium (Xiahe Rd.; tel. 23810); **Huaqiao Shangdian (Overseas Chinese Store)** (7 Zhongshan Rd.; tel. 24163); **Xiamen Antiques and Curios Store** 厦门文物店 (211 Zhongshan Rd.; tel. 23363);

Friendship Store 友谊商店 ; **Tourist Shopping Center** (111–117 Si Ming Bei Rd.; tel. 25965); **Lacquer Thread Sculpture Factory** 漆绒雕厂 ; **Arts and Crafts Factory** 工艺美术厂 .

Restaurants

Fujian food is much like Cantonese, and heavy on seafoods, of course, with some distinctive dishes. See "Food" for recommended local dishes.

Hao Qing Xiang Restaurant 好清香饮食店 □ *3240 Dayuan Rd.; tel. 22973* □ Snacks.

Lu Dao Restaurant 绿岛饭店 □ *230–232 Zhong Shan Rd.; tel. 22264* □ Xiamen food.

Moslem Restaurant 清真牛肉店 □ *205 Zhong Shan Rd.; tel. 24348.*

Seafood Restaurant 海味大厦 □ *No. 1 Fengchao Shan Rd.; tel. 25561.*

Vegetarian Food Restaurant 南普陀寺素菜部 □ *South Putuo Temple; tel. 22908.*

Xinnan Xuan Restaurant 新南轩酒家 □ *17 or 35 Siming South Rd.; tel. 23968, 23979.*

Hotels

Grand Palace Hotel 帝苑大酒店 □ *Zhen Hai Rd.* □ 1987.

Holiday Inn Xiamen □ 1987. 316 rooms.

Hulisan Hotel 胡里山大酒店 □ *Hulisan area* □ 1987.

Jinbao/Zhin Bao Hotel 金宝酒店 □ *Xingang Rd., Dong Du; cable: 2888; between town and the airport, next to the Friendship Store* □ 1985. Outdoor swimming pool, nightclub, bar, roof garden. Chinese and Western food. Refrigerators, bedside controls, and good reading lights in guest rooms. Toyota vans. Free shuttle buses downtown. Hong Kong joint venture.

Lujiang Mansion 鹭江宾馆 □ *54 Lujiang Rd.; telex 92423 LUTEL CN* □ 1958; renovated 1984. Among best hotels in town and the main tourist hotel, with C.I.T.S. booth. Best location downtown, near ferry pier. Charming. Joint venture.

Overseas Chinese Mansion 华侨大厦 □ *444, Zhongshan Rd. and Xin Hua Rd.; central* □ 1982.

Ruihua Hotel □ 1985. Luxury class.

Seaview Garden Tourist Village 观海园旅游村   **a.k.a. Gulang-yu Guesthouse** □ *8 Tian Wei Rd.; south side of Gulangyu Island. From the ferry, follow the signs to "Sunlight Rock" and then turn left before the base of the hill* □ 1930; renovated 1985. About 20 beautiful old mansions on Gulangyu Island near beach and International Club. Great for family vacations, but 25-minute walk to ferry. Hotel might have own ferry service in future. Restaurant in one of the buildings.

Xiamen Bridge Hotel 金桥大酒店   □ *Hubin North Rd.* □ 1987. 500 rooms.

Xiamen Mandarin Hotel 厦门悦华酒店   □ *Huli District; telex: 93028 MANDA CN; cable 0385* □ 1984. Among best in town, but far (20 minutes by car) from downtown, 5 minutes from airport. Bathroom telephones! Bar, disco, sauna, jacuzzi, massage, health club, French restaurant, outdoor swimming pool, billiards, tennis, villas, shuttle bus to city. Hong Kong joint venture, but no connections with Mandarin International Hotels Ltd.

Other Important Addresses

C.I.T.S. 中国国际旅行社   : 7 Hai Hou Rd., 3/F; tel. 25277, 25557; cable 8381.

C.T.S. 中旅社 : Xinhua Zhong Rd.; tel. 25602.

CAAC 中国民航 and **Xiamen Airlines:** Hubin South Road; tel. 25942, 25902 X394.

Ferry Quay 轮渡码头 : Lujiang Rd.; tel. 23493, 23494. Ferries to Gulangyu every 5–15 minutes. Passengers usually stand up. No porters. Tickets paid for on Gulangyu.

Foreign Affairs Dept. of Public Security Bureau 公安局外事处   : Xinhua Rd.; tel. 22329.

International Seamen's Club of Xiamen 厦门国际海员俱乐部   : Dongdu Xingang Rd.; tel. 25763.

No. 1 Hospital of Xiamen 厦门第一医院   : Zhen Hai Rd.; tel. 22280.

Ticket Office for Ships to Hong Kong 客运轮船售票处   : Dongwen Rd.; tel. 24458.

Xiamen International Airport 厦门国际机场   : Gao Qi; tel. 25902.

Xiamen Railway Station 火车站 Wuchun; tel. 23480.

Xiamen Tourism Bureau: 7, 3/F, Haihou Rd.; tel. 25557, 25355; cable 6031.

Xi'an

(Sian; Western Peace) Northwest China. 1¾-hour flight or about 22-hour train ride SW (1165 km) of Beijing; 8-hour train ride west of Luoyang. Capital of Shaanxi province on the Guanzhou Plain, it borders on the Loess Plateau to the north and the Qinling Mountains to the south. Altitude: 400 meters. Weather: Hottest—40°C—July; coldest—⁻10°C—two weeks in January. Rain all year round, but especially July through early September. Annual precipitation 550–770 mm. Fog in winter might affect plane flights. Population: urban 1.46 million.

Next to Beijing, Xi'an is the best city to visit in China, especially if you are interested in ancient Chinese history, traditional culture, and archaeology. It is one of the 24 historical cities protected by the State Council.

Just to glimpse all it has to offer takes a full week. To savor Xi'an slowly, to study it deeply, reading about Empress Wu and her lover-protector-henchman while sitting in the shadow of a Tang pagoda—or even reading about that crafty fictional Tang detective Judge Dee, two giant silk-flower petals sticking sideways out of the back of his magisterial cap—even that kind of depth could take months.

Ancient Xi'an is the setting for many Chinese operas, their sweet young heroines waving flowing ribbon sleeves and their flag-pierced generals galloping away to battle amid the clash of cymbals. Here the real camels, caravans, and traders were involved in the exchange of silver, furs, horses, and sesame for Chinese silk and porcelain. Here that egomaniac of an emperor ordered the burning of all books except those he liked, and demanded that his subjects create an army of life-size soldiers so he could maintain his empire after his earthly death.

Xi'an was the capital intermittently for 1087 years and 11 dynasties, including the Zhou (of the ritual bronzes), the Qin (of the Great Wall and ceramic army), the Han (of the jade burial suits), the Sui (of the Grand Canal), and the Tang—ah, the Tang! This city was the center of China's world from the 11th century B.C. to the early 10th A.D. Commerce on the Silk Road thrived west of here to the Mediterranean and beyond. (See "Silk Road.") Thousands of foreigners lived in the Western Market then.

In spite of the occasional invasions and sackings by rebels and tribesmen, Xi'an, then named Chang'an (Everlasting Peace), reached its highest peak in the Tang, the population then almost two million. It was one of the largest cities in the world, with walls measuring 36 km in circumference. It declined because of late Tang debauchery and corruption, the eunuchs ruling the court and increasingly powerful governors-general controlling the provinces. In 906, the last of the Tang emperors allowed one of his generals to take complete charge while he enjoyed his lady love. Xi'an rolled downhill from there on, following the fortunes, also, of the Silk Road.

A short-lived peasant regime made Xi'an a capital again in the 17th century, but it never regained its past glory. Xi'an did, however, continue to be a tourist resort and destination for religious pilgrimages because of its Buddhist roots. In 1900, when the Empress Dowager fled the international force sent to rescue the foreign legation from the Boxers, she went to Xi'an.

During the Xi'an Incident, Generalissimo Chiang Kai-shek was kidnapped. One of Chiang's own officers thus forced him to cooperate with the Communists against the Japanese. (See 1936 in "Milestones in Chinese History.") After Chiang agreed to his captors' demands, the Communists set up a liaison office here, which is now the *Museum of the Eighth Route Army 八路军西安办事处博物馆 . On May 20, 1949, the Communists took over the city.

Today, Xi'an is a textile and manufacturing center. It also produces Chinese and Western medicines, and watches. It is an educational center, with about 20 colleges, universities, and research institutes. Xi'an Jiaotung (Communications) University is the best known, and one of the 11 "super-key" universities in the country.

Xi'an's agricultural areas grow cotton, maize, wheat, vegetables, pomegranates, and persimmons. Many houses and walls have been made of loess soil mixed with straw. If cared for properly and protected with bricks on top, mud walls can last 100 years. Cheap too! But today many farmers are rebuilding in brick.

The walled city is laid out in the classic Chinese style in a rectangle, most streets parallel, the bell tower almost in the center. If you only have one day, try to see the Qin Army Vault Museum, Bronze Chariots, Banpo Village, the Big Wild Goose Pagoda, the Provincial

Museum, the Bell Tower, and the City Wall and gates. If you've never seen a Chinese-style mosque, try to fit in the Great Mosque too. This is a very rushed itinerary.

The standard 3-day tour is:

—Qin Tomb and Terracotta Warriors, Bronze Chariots, Huaqing Hot Spring, and Banpo Neolithic Village.

—Qianlong Tomb, 75 km west of Xi'an.

—Shaanxi Provincial Museum, Big Wild Goose Pagoda, Bell and Drum Towers, and the Great Mosque.

If you have more than three days, you might want to sightsee according to geographical groupings. Alien permits may be needed for some of the outlying places.

In Xi'an and its immediate vicinity: Wild Goose Pagodas, Bell Tower, Drum Tower, City Wall, Great Mosque, Shaanxi Provincial Museum, Xianqing Palace Park, Banpo Museum, remains of Daming Palace, Memorial Museum of the 8th Route Army.

West and South of Xi'an: Chariot and Horse Pits (permit needed), Xiangjiao Temple, Xiangji Temple, Qinglong Temple, Temple of Du Fu, Cao Tang Temple, Peasant Painting of Hu County.

East of Xi'an: Huaqing Hot Springs, Qinshihuang's Tomb, Qin Army Vault Museum, Bronze Chariots and Horses.

North and Northwest of Xi'an: Xianyang Museum, Maoling Tomb, Zhaoling Tomb, Qianling Tomb.

The Essentials

*The Qin Army Vault Museum 秦俑坑博物馆 (40 km NE of the city) is the most spectacular and important place to visit here because of its 2180-year-old painted-ceramic army of more than 8000 soldiers buried to "protect" the tomb of the first Qin emperor. **If you take a photo here, you pay a high fee, or have your film confiscated!** Slides of reasonable quality can be purchased at the souvenir shops.

The relics were discovered in 1974 by local peasants digging a well. The army is a puzzle because the emperor left no record of its existence. It would be hard to hide a project of this magnitude! Excavation started in 1976. A permanent building protects the army and tourists from most of the elements, and visitors are able to walk around the periphery of the once-buried relics. If you look carefully, you might see signs of oxidation and the loss of original colors.

There are three vaults. **No. 1,** opened to the public in 1979, is 62 by 230 by 5 meters deep. Most of the army was found facing east, toward the tomb, 1½ km away. The soldiers were in lines of roughly 70 across and 150 deep, separated by 10 partition walls and 11 corridors.

The men are hollow from the thigh up and made in two parts; they are 1.78–1.87 meters tall. The soldiers in front hold crossbows; also in front were bells and drums. Charioteers hold their hands out before them as if clutching reins. The horses originally wore harnesses with brass ornaments and have been identified as a breed from Hechu in Gansu. Officers can be distinguished from soldiers by their clothing and armor. Are every one of the 6000 faces different? Judge for yourself.

Researchers believe that kilns were built around the molded figures (probably two horses at a time) and destroyed after firing. There are remains of 30 wooden chariots.

Vault No. 2, 20 meters north of No. 1, contains about 1400 figures. **Vault No. 3** has 68 officers and was probably the "command post."

In the main museum are one of the **two bronze chariots,** each with four half-size horses and one half-size charioteer, the earliest such chariots found so far in China. These are also outstanding and can be seen at closer range.

*Tomb of Emperor Qinshihuang (Chin Shih Huang-ti) 秦陵 is in Lintong County. The first emperor of the Qin Dynasty, the builder of the Great Wall, and first unifier of the Chinese nation, lived from 259 to 210 B.C. and became king of Qin at age 13. What he achieved in so short a reign is incredible, and it is no wonder that he searched his empire for pills of longevity. Over 700,000 people worked on his tomb recorded through history as a deep and magnificent underground palace begun in 246 B.C.

Preliminary explorations at this site have started, and so far archaeologists believe that the tomb has not been robbed, and that the ancient records are correct. "Rivers of mercury" probably flow through it. Tourists on the spot when it is opened to the public will be able to share in the excitement of being among the first to see it. At press time, all that can be seen is a tumulus 6 km in circumference and 40 meters high, covered with pomegranate trees.

The **Huaqing Hot Springs** 华清池 , the *site of the Xi'an Incident, have been so overshadowed by modern events that their ancient history is frequently overlooked. They are at the base of Lishan Hill, 30 km NE of Xi'an. A stop here can be combined with the Qin Army Vault, the Tomb of Qinshihuang, and Banpo village, in a quick half-day excursion. Huaqing has been an imperial resort for the last 3000 years, its most famous tenants Emperor Xuanzong (Hsuan-tsung), the last Tang emperor, and the woman blamed for his downfall, his favorite concubine Yang Guifei (Kuei-fei). The influence of Yang Guifei and her relatives at court caused much dissatisfaction. In 755, an adopted son of hers rebelled, and the emperor's troops refused to fight as long as she remained alive. She had to hang herself. The troops rode out to victory over her dead body. The emperor lived on even though they had vowed to die together. Promises! Promises!

The imperial couple used to winter here because it was warmer than Xi'an. They bathed in the Jiulong (Nine Dragons) Hot Spring and the Guifei Hot Spring. And now, so can you! You pay very little for a 40-

minute soak in 43°C mineral water (sodium, sulfur, and magnesium), said to be good for rheumatism and skin disorders. The original buildings were all destroyed, and most of the current ones were built since Liberation in the old Tang style.

You can also trace the flight from his bedroom of Chiang Kai-shek, the Chinese Nationalist leader, as he panicked at the sound of gunfire at 5 a.m. on a cold December morning in 1936. He left behind his false teeth and wore only one shoe. A pavilion today marks the spot up the hill where he was captured.

Tourists have been accommodated at some small hotels here, giving them more time to enjoy the Tang architecture and the baths. But it is a long way from the city and is not as pleasant in the wintertime.

The *Dayan (Big Wild Goose) Pagoda 大雁塔 of the Da Chi Eng Temple, along with the Little Wild Goose Pagoda in Jianfu Temple, are the most famous pagodas in China because of their age and their important historical connections. They are not, however, the most beautiful or spectacular. The bigger pagoda was built to house the sutras brought back from India in A.D. 652 (Tang) by the famous monk Xuanzang (Hsuan-Tsang). It was probably named in memory of the temple in India where the monk lived, on a goose-shaped hill. Or it could have acquired its name because some monks were starving and Buddha, in the form of a wild goose, dropped down close to them. The monks, being vegetarians, refused to eat it.

The pagoda has seven stories, 248 steps, and a great view from the top. In adjoining Da Cien Temple (A.D. 647) are painted-clay statues of 18 lohan (Ming), most with strong Indian rather than Chinese features. One gets the impression that the painter must have been playing a joke, the faces are so funny. The Japanese lantern was presented in 1974 in honor of the first Chinese monk who went to Japan in the eighth century. While both pagodas are historical monuments protected by the State Council, only a stop at one is really necessary.

The **Shaanxi Provincial Historical Museums**   省历史博物馆 are in an old (Qing and Ming) Confucian temple and its extensions. The collection is one of the best in China and covers the period from the Zhou to the end of the Tang. It has some outstanding pieces, all labeled in English and Chinese. Among them: (1) an eighth-century B.C. stone drum, believed to be the earliest stone tablet in China, with writing (about a hunting expedition); (2) a bronze gate hinge from the Qin; (3) the standardizations of weights, measures, and currency by the first Qin emperor; (4) a wooden model of a bronze seismograph (eight dragons) from the first or second century B.C.; (5) giant stone carvings, the largest from the eastern Han, including a life-size rhinoceros and ostrich (inspired by live animals given as tribute). Four of the bas-reliefs of horses from the Zhaoling tombs are on one of the walls. Two others are in Philadelphia, part of the archaeological loot taken from China between 1900 and 1930; (6) gold- and silver-inlaid dishes and ancient

Byzantine and Persian coins found in the Western Market. A most recent and very celebrated find is the 62 cm-high Gilded Bronze Horse, from the 2000-year-old tomb of Han Emperor Wu Di. Artistically, it is not as beautiful as the Flying Horse of Gansu, but it is one of the largest, oldest, and best-preserved art objects found so far in China.

The museum also has the most important *collection of steles in China, with over 1000 from the Han through the Qing, including 12 Tang engravings of the Confucian classics. These have been used by centuries of scholars to copy and study for content as well as calligraphy.

Important here is the seventh-century Nestorian stele, written in Syriac with a cross at the top. You really have to search for it in this forest, but it is a rare piece of Christian history, the commemoration of the establishment of the church in Xi'an. Rubbings of this and other steles can be obtained in the souvenir shop. The Nestorian sect started in the fifth century but was declared heretical by Rome in A.D. 431. The sect flourished in west Asia, reaching into China, Egypt, and India.

The City Wall and South Gate can be seen near the museum.

The *Bell Tower 钟楼 was first built in 1384 (Ming) in another location, and moved here 200 years later. It has been renovated several times. Three sets of eaves weaken ''the force of the rainfall,'' and actually only two stories are here. The tower is 36 meters tall and made of brick and wood, with no nails. Glass windows were installed in 1950, replacing paper. The furniture is gorgeous (Qing) and the very fancy traditional ceiling is Ming. From the second story you can see all four gates of Xi'an.

The nearby **Drum Tower** 鼓楼 is also impressive and contains a large antique store, where paintings, porcelain, and jade can be purchased. The tower was built in 1384 and is original. Drums were beaten about 800 times in 10 minutes before the city gates were closed for the night.

The *Great Mosque 大清真寺 , the largest in Xi'an, is on a back street north of the Drum Tower. It was founded as a mosque in 742 (Tang), but the present buildings are mainly Ming, with some subsequent construction. The buildings are a good example of the Sinification of foreign architecture. The minaret is pagodalike, with Chinese eaves. The interiors are Chinese right down to the bats, dragons, unicorns, marbletop tables, and mother-of-pearl-inlaid furniture. The Great Hall (Ming) is, however, more west Asian, the writing Arabic, the arches and flowers more like Istanbul or Baghdad. Shoes must be removed. Prayers are said five times a day. Moslems first came here from Xinjiang and Guangzhou, and they founded this mosque with encouragement from the Tang emperors. Today in Xi'an, 14 other mosques and this one serve 30,000 or so Moslems here. See also ''What Is There to See and Do?''

Banpo (Panpo) Museum 半坡博物馆 , in the eastern suburbs of

the city, 10 km from the Renmin Hotel, is the actual archaeological site of a 6000-year-old neolithic village. The site covers 50,000 square meters, of which the museum encloses 3000. There you see living quarters, one of the oldest pottery kilns in the country, and a graveyard.

The artifacts were discovered in 1953, and the museum was opened in 1958, encompassing a communal storage area, moat, graveyard (skeletons under glass), and fireplaces. In the museum are also a bow drill, barbed fish hook, clay pots, and pottery whistle believed to be the earliest musical instrument in China. Among its other artifacts are hairpins, stone axes, and a pot with holes in the bottom, probably used as a steamer. Its narrow-necked, narrow-based water jugs, with two handles, look surprisingly like amphoras also used by the ancient Greeks and Romans! Is there a connection? The exhibits are labeled in Chinese and English.

This culture is believed to be matrilineal (1) because of the burial customs. Most of the 174 graves had one skeleton each; the few graves that contained more than one skeleton had no male-female couples; (2) the women gathered wild food at first while the men hunted. After the women discovered how to plant seeds, land became valuable and it was passed on from mother to daughter; (3) because of the burial system (with no couples) and knowledge of an existing culture in Yunnan with similar implements, village layout, customs, etc., scientists concluded that there were no fixed marriages. Besides, did neolithic people know where babies came from? (4) the village consisted of one big house in the center for old and young, and smaller houses for visiting males. The men kept their belongings in their native villages, where they were later buried. Farming tools were kept in the communal storage pit and were not buried with the dead.

As agriculture developed, men started pursuing it too. As surpluses grew (and probably the basic principles of physiology were discovered), fixed families started. In a later neolithic grave site in Gansu, a male skeleton was found lying straight and a female kneeling in the same grave. In another, a male was in the middle and two females were kneeling toward him. Since the women were bound, they were probably buried alive with him. So much for early women's lib!

Now, what is *your* theory?

*Maoling 茂陵 , on a plateau north of the Wei River, 40 km NW of Xi'an, has more than ten tombs, small grassy pyramids, about 46.5 meters high. The main tomb is that of the fifth Han emperor, built 139–87 B.C. According to records, it contains a jade suit with gold threads (seems to be a Han fad), and, in a gold box, more than 190 different birds and animals, jade, gold, silver, pearls, and rubies. The other identified tombs are of the emperor's favorite concubine Madame Li; ***General Ho Qubing,** who fought the Xiongnus/Huns, and strengthened the dynasty from the age of 18 until he died of disease at 24!; General Wei

Qing; his horse breeder Jing Min Ji, who remained faithful even after Jing's tribe was defeated by the emperor; and General Ho Guang.

Some of the earliest and, therefore, most primitive massive stone carvings, originally placed in front of the tombs, can be studied here. Look for the horse stomping a Hun aristocrat. Each stone has a few lines added to the natural shape of the rock. Also in the museum are Han artifacts found by local peasants, including an irrigation pipe and ceramic animal figures. Look also for metal mirrors, coins, pavement bricks notched to fit together, a bronze rhinoceros wine container (reproduction?), and a bear-shaped ceramic brush holder. Near Maoling is the **Xianyang Museum,** containing 3000 painted terracotta warriors and horse figures from the Western Han (206 B.C.–A.D 24). They are each between 55 and 68 cm high.

Also near Maoling is the **Tomb of Yang Guifei,** 杨贵妃墓 , the beautiful, tragic imperial concubine.

*Xingjiao Temple (a.k.a. Xiangjiao Temple), about 25 km east of the Renmin Hotel, is on a sylvan hillside, which, with a little mist, could look like the lonely setting of the famous Japanese movie *Rashomon*. The place oozes with atmosphere, although the buildings are recent. It was founded by Tang Emperor Gaozong in A.D. 669, but destroyed and rebuilt several times. The religious statuary tends to be eclectic in style: a white jade buddha from Burma, an eight-arm Guanyin, a Ming Guanyin with a bird on her/his shoulder, a Sui Guanyin in stone, etc. The remains (at least some of them) of monk Xuanzang, who first walked to India "day and night" and brought back the sutras, are buried in the small, five-story pagoda here. A map shows his route. The temple also has six palm-leaf pages of a Song copy of the original Buddhist scriptures.

The ***City Wall** was built from 1374 to 1378 (Ming), probably with material from the old Tang wall, which by then had decayed: 3.4 (north-south) by 2.6 km (east-west); 12 meters high. The walls follow the boundaries of the Tang imperial city. The gates open to the public are the imposing **Ximen (West) Gate** 西城门 and the **South Gate.** The wall, gates, and moat are being restored, and the whole complex is being made into a public park. Six new gates have been added to the original four to facilitate the flow of traffic. Eventually the whole wall will be open to all joggers, taiji people, and tourists.

If you have more time or specialized interest:

*Qianling 乾陵 Tomb of Tang Emperor Gaozong (Kao-tsung) and the Empress Wu: She was as ruthless and outrageous as Qing Empress Dowager Cixi, but a more successful ruler. He died in A.D. 683 and she in 705. This unexcavated tomb is 85 km NW of the city, a worthwhile full day's excursion that can include other tombs as well. While earlier tombs were built to create their own artificial hills on the plains, the Tang tombs were built into existing hills. This one is 400 meters high, 1049 meters above sea level.

Approaching the hill, one passes statues of horses and ostriches, and 10 large guardian figures holding swords. Then on the left are the life-size statues of guards, tribal heads, and foreign diplomats who paid their respects at the funeral. The statues are now without heads, alas; look for names on their backs. One is labeled Afghanistan. The wall around the tomb is 4470 meters. Some of the minor tombs are excavated, and visitors can go underground to see the coffin and fine murals of court scenes in the tombs of **Princess Yong-tai** and **Prince Yide.**

Although many of the structures at Qianling were destroyed in the war at the end of the Tang, the museum here contains about 4000 pieces—three-colored Tang porcelain, pottery utensils and animals, gold and jade carvings, bronze mirrors, etc.

**Zhaoling 昭陵 70 km NW of Xi'an, is the tomb of the second Tang Emperor Taizong. It is built against a mountain near Lichuan. The 20,000-hectare cemetery contains 167 minor tombs (children, wives, generals) and took 13 years to build. A small museum with Tang pottery, stone tablets, and murals can be visited. This tomb is not worth visiting unless you can read classical Chinese. The six famous bas-reliefs of the emperor's favorite horses came from here. They are now in the Provincial Museum and in Philadelphia.

The **Xianyang Museum,** 17 km or so NW of Xi'an in the Qin capital, is important because of its 3000 items from the Qin and Han dynasties, including 2000-year-old ceramic tomb figures found in Yangjiawan Village.

If you're tired of tombs by now, head SW of Xi'an to **Huxian County Town** 户县 . Here you can visit the Huxian Peasant Painting Exhibition Hall. Some of the 2000 painters in the county have also exhibited abroad these recordings of their everyday lives and achievements in gay colors.

About 15 km away is the thatched-cottage **Caotang Temple** 草堂室 (Tang), where Indian monk Kumarajiva (Chi Mo Lo Shi) translated the sutras into Chinese. He died in A.D. 413 and was buried here in 855. The current buildings are recent, with a fine rose garden. Japanese Buddhists have presented a modern wooden statue of the monk.

The 2-meter-high stupa has some elaborate carvings and, from a well in the ground, a cloud used to come out at dawn, travel to Xi'an, and return at evening, said the guide. But this hasn't happened since the Cultural Revolution!

The **Horse and Chariot Pit** 车马坑 , Zhangjiapo, Chang'an county, can be combined with Huxian county for a half-day tour. It is the burial site of two chariots, six horses, and one slave (11th century B.C.— Western Zhou) and is the best of seven such pits found. It is of special interest to archaeologists. A permit is needed to visit it. Ask at C.I.T.S.

Back around town, the ***Little Wild Goose Pagoda** 小雁塔 , outside the south wall, is 45 meters high and was constructed of brick in A.D. 684. Thirteen stories high, it is minus two of its original stories, destroyed during earthquakes in 1444. This is all that remains of the great Da Jianfu Temple, so important in the Tang.

Xingqing Park 兴庆公园 , east of the city, was the site of one of the palaces of Tang Emperor Xongzong. The original pavilion was of sandalwood. A post-Liberation copy of the tower, where the emperor flattered his brothers out of rebelling against him, stands in the 50-hectare park. There is also a modern memorial of the Japanese monk Abe no Nakarone, who visited the city during the Tang. The park was built in 120 days in 1958 by groups of Xi'an citizens.

The ruins of ***Daming Palace,** built in A.D. 634 (Tang), are for those people who prefer to figure out their own facts and to decide just where the vast banquets were held and where the throne room was. Clue: The hall must have been large enough to seat 2000 officials in A.D. 819. The foundation of the throne room, where the emperor consulted with officials and granted audiences, can still be seen; 164 pillars held up its roof. Artifacts found in the palace can be studied in the Provincial Museum.

One visitor described the Buddhist **Xiangji Temple** as "not very interesting," but people who like to compare temples may want to include it if time permits. With its 33-meter-high pagoda, the temple honors a famous monk, Shandao. It is 20 km SW of Xi'an in Xiangji Temple village.

Other sights include the **Qinglong Temple,** in the Tang-dynasty Chang'an city in the southern suburbs at Tian Lumiao. Six famous Japanese monks were initiated into Buddhism here between A.D. 794 and 1192, and links with Japan still exist. The modest **Temple of Du Fu** is a memorial to the famous Tang poet, built in 1526, and is east of Weiqu Zhen in Chang'an county.

The **Louguan Taoist Temple** has now been restored. It is beyond Huxian, about 70 km west of Xi'an, and may require a permit to visit. It is said to be the place where Lao Tzu, founder of Taoism, taught. The temple has resident monks and makes traditional medicines. The setting and especially the entrance gate are very fine. A big yearly fair is held here.

Binxian 彬县 is about 130 km NW of the city, and is a two-day trip. It is famous for its caves of Tang Buddhist statues, the largest about 25 meters tall.

*Huangling County: Tomb of the Yellow Emperor. See "Yan'an."

Huashan Mountain 华山 , 150 km east of Xi'an, peaks to 2100 meters. Cable cars and a small hotel are being built. Until then, it is mainly for serious climbers because of its 80-degree cliffs (there *are* iron chains to hang on to) and a "1000-foot-long Flight of Stone Steps."

One also squeezes through the "100-foot-long Gorge." Famous as one of the Five Sacred Mountains, it is dotted with old temples.

Also in Shaanxi is "Yan'an." See separate listing.

Many **arts and crafts factories** in Xi'an can be visited.

Shopping

The main shopping area is east of the Bell Tower on Dong Ave. Most stores are open 7 or 9 a.m.–8 or 9 p.m. Made locally or in the province are: rubbings, reproductions of three-color Tang camels and horses, Qin Army soldiers, and murals. Also made are inlaid lacquer, cloisonne, stone and jade carvings, gold and silver jewelry, new year's pictures, paper cuts, and celadon.

At stalls outside many tourist attractions, you will find red felt vests with appliqued snakes, scorpions, lizards, and pandas. These are very popular with tourists. At about four or five yuan, they are the cheapest in China here. While they are not traditionally Chinese as far as can be ascertained, they are good souvenirs, especially at that price. The yucky bugs are to frighten away the evil spirits.

Xi'an Friendship Store 友谊商店 (Nanxin St., near Dong Da St.; tel 28301); **Xi'an Arts and Crafts** (almost opposite the Friendship Store on Nanxin St.); **Xi'an Art Ceramics Factory** (Puzi Cun; tel. 39942) and **Qianxian Art Handicraft Workshop** (Qianxian) make Tang and Buddhist art reproductions; **Xi'an Antique Store** (Drum Tower; tel. 17187); **Xi'an Jade Carving Workshop** (173 Xi-1 Rd.; tel. 22570); **Xi'an Special Arts and Crafts Factory** (138 Huancheng Xi Rd.; tel. 28891).

Restaurants

Xi'an food is similar to that of Beijing: somewhat bland. Its famous local dishes are crisp fried chicken or duck, and dried fish shaped like grapes. Much of its food has been inspired by imperial tastes. Two celebrated wines are made here—one thick and sweet with the appearance of milk. Served hot, Chou Jiu wine inspired Tang poet Li Po, who drank 1000 cups and wrote more than 100 poems. The other wine is Xifeng Jiu (55% alcohol), a blend of sour, sweet, bitter, and spicy. It is one of the Eight Most Famous Wines in China. For some local dishes, see "Food."

In season, try the persimmons, which are not stringent like American ones.

Dongya Restaurant 东亚饭店 □ *46 Luoma Shi; tel. 27396, 28410* □ Suzhou.

Sichuan Restaurant □ *151 Jiefang Rd.; tel. 24736.*

Wuyi Restaurant 五一饭店 □ *351 Dong Ave.; tel 23824, 28665* □ Yangzhou.

Xi'an Restaurant 西安饭店 □ *298 Dong Ave.; tel. 23053, 22037* □ Xi'an, Beijing, and Western food. Capacity: 1800 people.

Hotels

Xi'an has been notorious for its poor hotels. Its standards are rising daily, however, and should you arrive on the late flight hungry and without any place to eat, try the Golden Flower Hotel.

Bell Tower Hotel □ see Zhonglou.

Chang'an Hotel 长安宾馆 □ *Weiqu Town, Chang'an county.* □ 1982. 48 rooms, two stories. Ancient Chinese architecture.

Chang'an International Hotel □ *SW corner outside South Gate* □ 1987. 350 rooms.

Efang Palace Hotel □ 1987. 650 rooms. Too early to judge quality.

Golden Flower Hotel 金花饭店 □ *8 Changle Xi Rd.; telex 70145 GFH CN.* □ 1985. 205 rooms and 5 suites. 400 rooms to open in 1987–88. Two restaurants with continental and Sichuan food, open daily to 11 p.m. International standards. Managed by Swedish SARA Hotels. Aiming for five stars.

Huashan Hotel 华山饭店 □ *Jixiangcun* □ 1987. 150 rooms. Too early to judge quality.

Huaqing Hot Spring Guesthouse 临潼温泉旅馆 □ *Lintong County* □ 1982. 19 rooms. Closer to Qin Army Museum. See Huaqing Hot Spring, above.

Jiaotung University Guest House 交通大学招待所 □ 35 rooms. Book through C.T.S. Modest but good.

Renmin (People's) Hotel 人民大厦 □ *319 Dongxin St., inside walled city* □ Front section built 1953; back section, 1957. Uninspired architecture. Five buildings. Shipping office. 1800-seat auditorium. Within walking distance of main square and Friendship Store. On my last inquiry, I found it filthy and badly managed.

Shaanxi Guest House 陕西宾馆 □ *Zhangbagou, 15 km from city* □ Old hotel, built 1958, renovated 1979, on 26.7-hectare lot with lake. 122 rooms, indoor swimming pool, banquet hall. One of the better hotels.

Tangcheng Hotel 唐城饭店 □ *Ji Xiang Cun* □ 1987. The largest in the city, with 812 beds, has Tang-inspired courtyards and gardens. Wide function hall. Too early to judge quality.

Xi'an Hotel 西安宾馆 □ *Caochangpo, Chang'an Rd.* □ 1981–82. 277 rooms, 14 stories. Open-air rooftop bar. Four restaurants serving Chinese and Western food. Billiard room. Next to the Small Wild Goose Pagoda. One of the better hotels; 160 rooms added in 1986.

Zhonglou (Bell Tower) Hotel 钟楼饭店 □ *SW corner of Bell Tower* □ 1983. 100 rooms.

Other Important Addresses

Airport 飞机场 : Xishaomen; tel. 41989.
Bank of China: 833 Jiefang Rd.; tel. 25111. Foreign exchange counters at major hotels, Friendship Store, and Xi'an Antique Store.
China International Travel Service: 272 Jiefang Rd.; tel. 21191. Try also Xi'an Hotel.
China Travel Service and Overseas Chinese Travel Service: Xi-4 Rd.; tel. 21309.
Hospitals
  C.I.T.S., above, has a clinic.
  Fourth Army Hospital
  Shaanxi Provincial People's Hospital: Huangyancun; tel. 25991.
Post Offices: at major hotels. The main post office is on NE side of Bell Tower circle.
Railway Station 火车站 : Jiefang Rd.; tel. 26911. (Traditional Chinese architecture, built in 1933 and extended in 1958.)
Taxis: at major hotels.
  Also Friendship Motor Car Co.: Caochangpo; tel. 52505
  Taxi Station: 12 Xi Da Street; tel. 23417. At night, try 11A Xing-qing Rd.; tel. 32288.
  Travel and Tourism Bureau of Shaanxi Province: Caochangpo, Chang'an Rd.; tel. 53201 X252; cable: 2464. Also 272 Jiefang Rd.; tel. 26242.

Xinhui 新会

(Hsinhui; Cantonese, Sunwai) South China. This county, about 130 km SW of Guangzhou in Guangdong province, is in the heart of fan-palm country, from which many Chinese emigrated to America and Australia. Every spare inch seems to have these trees, whose leaves are woven into baskets, fans, and mats. The county seat, **Huicheng,** *has a population of about 80,000. The city is sometimes combined with Jiangmen in a two- or three-day tour. Both are about a three-hour air-conditioned bus ride from Guangzhou, or a four-hour boat ride from Hong Kong or an overnight boat ride from Guangzhou, both to Jiangmen, and then a half-hour bus ride to Xinhui. The easiest way of all is the 4-hour ferry from Hong Kong, which brings you directly into this part of the province.*

Visitors can see the fan-palm factory or relax on a very pretty nearby hill on top of which is **Yuhu Lake.** This artificial lake has a changing room for swimming, the usual pavilions, and a restaurant. In another direction from the city and 7 km away, a magnificent old tree called **Birds' Paradise** is home at night to thousands of cranes.

In the area also is the **Yutai Temple** (Tang), and the **Zhenshan Pagoda.** In the southeastern part of the county is the **Yamen Fort,** a modest building used by the Qing administrators, and the remains of **Ciyuan Temple.**

The **Overseas Chinese Hotel** is on the main street of the town and the **Yu Hu Guest House** is at the foot of Guifeng Hill.

Xining   西宁

Northwest China. Capital of Qinghai (Tsinghai) province. A little over 7 hours by small plane from Beijing (three stops), or 55 minutes NW from Lanzhou. A highway was built in 1954 from here to Lhasa, and is now asphalted, the highest highway in the world. The railway joins Xining with Golmud in the western part of the province and also with Lanzhou and Xi'an, eastward. Currently being built is a 1200-km line from Golmud to Lhasa. When it is finished, it should be one of the most spectacular train rides in the world. Qinghai is the source of both the Yellow and Yangtze rivers and has a lot of hydroelectric power. It is rich in aluminum, coal, and oil. Weather: Hottest—less than 32°C in July and August; coldest—⁻16°C in January and December. Annual precipitation is 450 mm in July and August.

This province has only recently opened to tourists. A one-day visit to Xining can include the Taer Lamasery, Dongguan Mosque, and North Mountain Temple. The ***Taer Monastery** 塔尔寺 (Ming), the center of the yellow-hat sect of Tibetan Buddhism, is at Huangzhong, about 30 km from the Xining Guest House and the Qinghai Hotel. Built in 1397 (or 1577, depending on the source), it is worth a visit. Its kitchen has three bronze cauldrons that are said to cook 13 cattle at one time to serve 3600 people. Ask why meat is served in this Buddhist monastery! In the winter, frozen butter, two meters high by 26 meters long, is sculptured into Buddhist scenes and displayed on the 15th day of the lunar New Year. It also has 20,000 religious paintings and embroideries.

The **Dongguan Mosque** 东关，清真寺   , one of the biggest in Northwest China, was built in 1380 and is 2 km from the Xining Guest House. The **North Mountain Temple** 北禅寺 is also 2 km from the hotel.

Qinghai Lake 青海湖 (China's largest saltwater lake) is 3196 meters above sea level and is 130 km from the capital. A bird sanctuary,

Bird Island 鸟岛 , is about 350 km away from Xining. The .8-square-km island attracts 100,000 migrating geese and gulls each summer and autumn, and has bird-watching pavilions and Tibetan-style hotels.

About 60 km east is another temple also under State Council protection, the ***Qutan Temple** (Ming).

The province has wild antelope, yak, donkeys, camels, lynx, deer, and pheasant, all protected.

Golmud 格尔木市 is a new industrial city in the Gobi Desert, in the west of the province. It has a population of 130,000, is 800 km from Xining, and is a trans-shipment point for Tibet. Between Xining and Golmud is the Salt Bridge and Salt Pond.

The province is huge, covering one thirteenth of China, and is in the Qinghai-Tibet Plateau. It has less than four million people, mainly Han (60%), the rest Tibetan, Hui, Mongolian, Kazak, Sala, and Tu. Many of these are nomadic herdsmen. Ninety-six percent of its land is pasture for 22 million horses, yak, and sheep. Livestock breeding has been practiced here for 4000 years, and cow dung is used for fuel. Half of China's yak and one third of all the world's yak are in Qinghai.

Times are changing however: recently, a 3500 gm gold nugget was found, and a gold rush is on. The national government is focusing its economic development on the NW region. Pastureland is now contracted to herdsmen for 30 years, thus encouraging the users to manage it more wisely. Bonuses are given in some counties for families who send children to school, not an easy task for nomads. The government is building railways and highways.

Lindblad has a tour that includes Xining, Qinghai Lake, and Golmud, which goes on to Lhasa and then to Kathmandu in Nepal.

Shopping

Good buys are handicrafts made by the minorities.

Restaurants

Rong Yuan Restaurant 蓉苑餐厅   □ *1 Xiao Qiao (Small Bridge) Ave., Xining; tel. 54725* □ Sichuan and local dishes.

Hotels

Qinghai Hotel 青海宾馆   □ *20 Huang He Rd.* □ The New Qinghai Hotel should be completed in 1987.

Xining Guest Hotel 西宁宾馆   □ *Qiyi Rd.* □ 1957; renovated 1985. 12 km from airport. Main tourist hotel.

C.I.T.S. 国际旅行社 : Qiyi Rd.; tel. 23901 C.O. 700.
CAAC 中国民航 : 74 Xining East Ave.; tel. 77434.

Xiqiao Mountain 西樵山

South China, 70 km SW of Guangzhou via Foshan in Guang-dong province. A good place for a leisurely family vacation relatively close to Hong Kong. With two resort areas, one at the base and the other on top of a 400-meter-high mountain, hikers have an area 10 km in circumference to explore. The mountaintop has three lakes (one in an extinct volcanic crater) with bicycle paddle boats, 44 caves and grottoes, 72 peaks, 207 springs, and innumerable waterfalls. The eight villages are home to 600 people, their houses very traditional. Partway up the mountain is a layer of clam shells near which archaeologists have found 2000-year-old pottery shards. The weather at the base of the mountain is hottest, 32°C, from July to September; it is coldest, 7°C, in January and February. Precipitation is 1150 mm, mainly March to June.

The resort at the base of Xiqiao Mountain seems noisy partly because the area makes firecrackers that are frequently set off by firecracker-deprived Hong Kong tourists. Guangzhou swingers have come here to learn dancing, and schoolchildren come on excursions to visit the three-story Ming tower and the Qing Taoist temple. Also at the base is a 1-km-long artificial lake, horses, shooting gallery (machine guns!), waterfalls, electronic games, basketball court, badminton, roller-skating rink, and amusement park.

Hotels

Baiyun Lou Guest Hotel 白云楼宾馆 □ 1959. Restaurant. On top of the mountain. 26 air-conditioned rooms. Hot water, but no heat. Near one of the villages.

Handan Biedi 邯郸别邸 □ 1948. Restaurant.

Sanhu (Three Lakes) Guest House 三湖宾馆 □ is the main tourist hotel. 1978; renovated 1982. 70 km from Guangzhou airport. Coffee shop, restaurant, dance hall. Spanish style.

Xiqiao Great Hotel 西樵山大酒店 □ 1986. Coffee shop, dance hall, Chinese and Western food. Aiming for four stars.

C.I.T.S. 国际旅行社 : White Cloud Cave, Xiqiao Mountain, Nanhai County; tel. 230 or 56799. It can arrange for taxis to meet you anywhere in the area, such as the Guangzhou airport or railway station.

C.I.T.S. Market 国旅商场 : tel. 582.

Taxi: tel. 661.

Xuzhou 徐州

East China. Northwest Jiangsu province, conveniently located on two railway lines. Three pits containing 3000 terracotta horses and warriors 27–54-cm-high were recently unearthed here, believed connected with the tomb of a Western Han duke. The Han Dynasty Museum is at the site of the discovery, the mausoleum of Prince Chu, ruler of Xuzhou, during the reign of Emperor Wu Di (156–87 B.C.)

Yan'an 延安

(Yenen) Northwest China. 2½ hours by air SW of Beijing (with one stop); 1 hour by air or 8½ hours by road north of Xi'an. No rail connection. Northern Shaanxi in the Loess Plateau. Weather: Hottest—35°C in July; coldest—⁻25°C in January. Rainy season: August–September. The altitude in the city is 800–1000 meters. During the rainy season, planes may be postponed or canceled. Urban population: 50,000.

Yan'an was a small administrative town 1000 years ago. In 1936 it had a population of 3000. It became the most important Communist revolutionary site in China in January 1937 after the end of the Long March. The Communists chose to settle here because of the rugged mountain terrain, a wise choice because the Nationalists failed to dislodge them for 10 years. Yan'an was also chosen because it was the only existing Communist base big enough to accommodate so many people, and it was close enough to inflict damage on the Japanese. Here, the Communists trained leaders, developed policies, organized the peasants, and planned strategy against the Nationalists and Japanese. In 1945 the population was 100,000. Chiang Kai-shek finally succeeded in capturing the city without a fight in March 1947 and held it until April 1948, while Mao Zedong (Mao Tse-tung) went on to take the whole of China.

Today Yan'an is primarily of interest to revolutionists and students of modern history and architecture. For others it has only a Tang pagoda famous primarily because of the revolution, and a tiny cave of 10,000 Buddhas. This is an interesting off-the-beaten-path destination now.

The city, clinging to the mountainside, stretches along both sides of the Yan River and the South and Dufu streams. In July 1977 the river flooded the lower parts of the city. The soil is loess, excellent for construction. Most of the area houses are quonset-hut-shape "caves," either freestanding or dug into a mountain. They are said to be cozy and dry in the winter and cool in the summer. Even the university was built in this style, and the villages are fascinating. Originally of loess soil, many buildings are converted to brick as income increases.

The city is now largely industrial. Nearby are oil wells and coal mines. Meter-high mounds of huge black chunks of coal piled haphazardly in the streets are a little startling.

The middle school rates a visit insofar as it was started after the Long March, whose leaders visited often to oversee the curriculum. Now it is like any other school. See also "Milestones in Chinese History."

Yan'an Revolutionary Memorial Hall 延安革命纪念馆 : This excellent museum has a giant map outlining the route of the Long March in neon. Titles are in English and Chinese. Exhibits also include a fascinating model of tunnel warfare, Communist bank notes, and Chairman Mao's horse (stuffed).

Residences of Chairman Mao 毛主席旧居 are also museums, furnished as simply as they were then, all of them "caves":

(1) Foot of Fenghuang (Phoenix) Hill 凤凰山麓 : January 1937–November 1938. Here Mao wrote his important articles on "contradiction" and "protracted war." The photo in front of the cave was taken in 1937, just after Zhou Enlai (Chou En-lai), who lived nearby, returned from settling the Xi'an Incident. Mao left this cave because of Japanese bombing.

(2) Yangjialing 杨家岭 : November 1938–January 1943. The auditorium was the site of several party Central Committee meetings and a national congress (1945), delegates risking their lives to come from and return to Nationalist-held areas. This is where Mao made his "Foolish Old Man Who Removed the Mountains" speech. Here also was the site of the Yenan Forum on Arts and Literature to encourage musicians, writers, and painters to "make art and literature serve the workers and peasants better."

(3) Zaoyuan (Date Orchard) 枣园 : January 1943–end of 1945. The Secretariat was close by. The lilac tree in front was planted by Mao. Mao wrote 28 articles and several other works here. On his desk is the first iron bar made in the local foundry. He exercised his hand with the bar to avoid writer's cramp. From here Zhou Enlai flew to Chongqing to negotiate with Chiang, an American-instigated effort to avoid civil war.

(4) Wangjiaping 王家坪 : January 1946–March 1947. Headquarters of the Eighth Route Army. Dances were held in the garden. The civil war resumed, and here Mao argued with his military commanders about withdrawing from Yan'an in the face of an enormous Nationalist campaign in March 1947. While his commanders wanted to defend the city, Mao argued, "We must not concentrate on hanging on to places. Our main purpose is to wipe out the enemy's effective forces . . . there are only a few caves here. If they destroy the caves, it is good. We can build high buildings when we come back.'' The Communists regained the city on April 22, 1948, but Mao did not return then. The guides here might insist that the Nationalists at this assault were backed by U.S. imperialism, but President Truman had stopped all aid to the Nationalists in 1946 after his failure to reconcile the two.

Baota (Precious Pagoda) 宝塔 (延安宝塔) a.k.a. Yan'an Pagoda: 44 meters, nine stories; 1300-year-old (Tang) building. Can be climbed.

Wangfo Dong (Cave of the 10,000 Buddhas) 万佛洞 is right in town below the pagoda and relatively close to Wangjiaping. It dates from the Song and Jin. Most of the Buddhas are tiny; some are in good condition. The cave was used to house the printing presses of the Central Committee. Up the hill is a Laughing Buddha carved on the hillside, now the back wall of a house. The god can be seen through the front window. During the Cultural Revolution, it was hidden by a cloth, which saved it from the Red Guards.

If you have more time: **Nanniwan** 南泥湾 , 45 km south, was turned from a wasteland into a productive area in 1941–43 by the 359 Brigade of the revolutionary army. It is now a village with a small museum.

Liu Lin Village has been documented by visitors as far back as the '60s. Read Jan Myrdal's *Report from a Chinese Village* if you want to compare progress then and now.

Huangling County 黄陵 , just about halfway on the road between Xi'an and Yan'an, 4 hours' drive from each. Huangling makes an interesting break and, for ancient Chinese history buffs, is a very important stop. There is a hotel, built 1978.

The ***Tomb of the Yellow Emperor Xuan Yuan:** 3.6 meters high and 50 meters in circumference, originally built in the Han but moved here to its present site in the Song. The Yellow Emperor is the legendary ancestor of the Chinese people believed to have lived about 2000 B.C. The tomb is at the top of Qiaoshan (hill), 1 km north of Huangling town. At the base is Xuan Yuan temple. Of its 63,000 cypress trees, one is said to have been planted by the Yellow Emperor himself. It is the largest known ancient cypress in China. In front of the tomb is the Platform of Immortality built by Emperor Han Wu (156–87 B.C.) to announce his victory over his enemy and to pray for longevity. The temple of Xuan Yuan was built in the Han, the many steles here recording the sacrifices offered, memorials about repair work, etc. The throne stands in the middle with information about Xuan's life on both sides. In ancient times, travelers had to dismount from their horses and pay respect to their First Ancestor as they passed by.

The **Cave Temple of a Thousand Buddhas** (Tang) is halfway up Ziwu Hill in the western part of Huangling county.

In **Luochuan County,** 120 km south of Yan'an, one can sleep in a guesthouse made of 40 "caves" and see local folk arts—embroidery, animal-head slippers and hats for children, cloth articles, paper cuts, and paintings (based on paper-cut designs). Embroidered aprons are for men to keep bellies warm, not for cooking or cleaning.

See "Food" for local dishes.

Hotels

Yan'an Guest House 延安宾馆 □ 1965. 110 beds, three stories. Expanded 1980 with 250 additional beds. 10 km from airport. Short walk to shopping, downtown, cinema, pagoda. Next door to No. 1 Mao Residence. The hotel has some documentary films showing Mao giving a lecture, available on request.

Being constructed are the 200-bed **Jialing Hotel** and 500-bed **Fenghuang.**

See also "Jinggang Shan" and "Shijiazhuang."

Yangtze Gorges 长江三峡

(a.k.a. Yangzi or Changjiang River Gorges) The boat trip through the gorges and on the great river itself to or from Chongqing is highly recommended not just for its relaxed sightseeing of spectacular scenery but also for its history. Do bring binoculars, a telephoto lens if you're a camera bug, and reading material. The scenery includes sheer cliffs rising up to 400 meters on either side of narrow, rushing water, mountains up to 1000 meters, old towns cut by slender lines of stone steps, and a mountain lined from top to bottom with a pagoda. The Yangtze River is also a busy highway now being harnessed even more for flood control, irrigation, and hydroelectric power.

The history is still alive in some of what you experience here: the chant of men pulling heavy loads: "wei wei li hou"; the towpaths cut out of the sides of sheer cliffs; the towing of boats upstream by manual labor; the lives lived on the water; the 12-man-powered sampan-junks, and the architecture. Guides will tell you stories of the Three Kingdoms, but do bring your own history books along, or a copy of *The Sand Pebbles* or *Yangtze Patrol: The U.S. Navy in China.* The *Romance of the Three Kingdoms* has been translated into English, and the names of the heroes of this great military story will keep coming up almost anywhere you go in central China. If you don't have a guide with you, maybe the steward or cook can point out landmarks. The Yangtze was also central to the foreign merchants, gunboats, and missionaries in the late 1800s and early 1900s, but guides will not give you much information about this embarrassing period.

There are several ways of sailing the Gorges. The cheapest are the **passenger ferries,** where tour groups get first crack at the top second-class accommodations with a lounge and the best view. Second-class has two bunks. No one gets private toilets, baths, or air conditioners. Individual travelers with second-class tickets might even get down-graded to third, fourth, or fifth class, where you share a room with an increasing number of people, or sleep in hallways. You might get bumped off the boat entirely by tour groups. Try for an outside cabin. The inside ones can get pretty stuffy in summer, and you might find other passengers gambling noisily on the floor outside your room.

Stops are prescheduled and not necessarily at tourist sites like Shibaozhou (Shibao Block), nor can you be sure your ship will get close enough to get a photo of that lovely 11-story pagoda unless you have a lens at least 200 mm long. But you only pay for passage to where you want to get off. And, by ferry, you can get closer to Chinese people, and experience with them the loudspeakers blaring announcements at 6 a.m. and queues for showers. After all, didn't you come here to meet the people?

Currently, seven air-conditioned ships for tourists ply the Yangtze and can be booked for groups through tour agents. On these you are isolated from Chinese people, but **tourist ships** are more comfortable. Individual travelers showing up at C.I.T.S. ticket counters cannot always ride them, though. Some branches of C.I.T.S. will not sell tickets to you. Shanghai C.I.T.S. said it could. Lindblad, Pacific Delight, Silk-ways, and other agencies will book them.

Itineraries differ depending on which way you are going—up- or downriver, and which ship you book. The most luxurious ships are frequently chartered by Lindblad: the 36-passenger M.S. *Kunlun* has been offering 10-day cruises between Nanjing and Chongqing. The M.S. *Goddess* and the M.S. *Bashan* take a week to sail between Chongqing and Wuhan. The M.S. *Goddess* is cheaper; the *Bashan* has a swimming pool. Both go between Chongqing and Wuhan. The M.S. *Great Wall* has 200 beds, a swimming pool, dance hall, bar, canteen, gym, and solarium.

These three and other tourist ships stop for sightseeing at some but not all of the following: Lake Dongting, Fengjie, Jingzhou, Jiujiang, Nanjing, Lushan, Shashi, Shibao Block, Wanxian, Wuhan, Yangzhou, Yueyang, Yichang, and Zhenjiang. Their services include guide-in-terpreter, double rooms with private baths, laundry, doctor, currency exchange, post and telegraph, beauty salon, library, lounge (with evening movies), a bar, Chinese and Western food, and a store—none of which the public ferries have. Depending on class, you would be lucky to get a seat for eating on a passenger ferry. Lindblad has offices in

Hong Kong and Beijing; Pacific Delight and Silkways have offices in the United States and Hong Kong.

In addition to the above three, the other ships are the M.S. *Emei* (with swimming pool), the M.S. *Sanxia* (Three Gorges), and the M.V. *Yangzijiang* (Yangtze River). Pacific Delight has chartered the M.V. *Three Gorges*. Five of the ships belong to the Chongqing Changjiang Shipping Company and can be chartered through C.I.T.S. Changjiang-Chongqing Sub-branch. The M.V. *Yangzijiang* belongs to C.I.T.S. Hubei in Wuhan. In 1986, more cruise ships went into service.

Meanwhile back at the **public ferry,** going downstream from Chongqing to Wuhan, which is the best way to go—faster—the trip takes two nights on board ship and three days on the water. The ferries stop at towns along the way for a few minutes up to several hours. Take your own soap and towel. Each ferry has about 24 second-class cabins. The third class has four to a room, no curtains. None have much privacy. It is better, if you are on a ferry, to ride only to Chenglingji (Yueyang) because the stretch between Yichang and Wuhan, a whole day's ride, isn't all that interesting. After a day of sightseeing around Dongting Lake (Candice Bergen was a missionary there in *The Sand Pebbles*—see "Yueyang"), you can go on to Changsha or Wuhan by train.

Ferry Downstream —Day 1: Leave Chongqing early (about 7 a.m.). Note white pagoda on north bank at Changshou. At about 3 hours out, Fuling. At 8½ hours out, Zhongxian. At 10 hours out, look for **Shibaozhai (Precious Stone Village),** a.k.a. Shibao Block, on the north bank, with its 11-story Qing pagoda. It is built on a limestone rock hill, Yuyin Shan (Jade Seal Hill), that rises to 160 meters above the river. In the main temple are statues of Liu Bei, Zhuge Liang, Guan Yu, and Zhang Fei, historical personages. Three of these swore oaths in a peach orchard to support each other. They are immortalized in *The Romance of the Three Kingdoms*. Emperor Liu Bei, who led an unsuccessful army to avenge the death of Guan Yu, retreated here and died of sorrow.

At 12½ hours, overnight stop at 2000-year-old **Wanxian,** the site of one of the first successful assertions of Chinese power against the imperialist gunboats during the Northern Expedition. There was a lot of shooting here in the late 1920s. Tourists climb about 85 steps to the 700,000-population town for a tour of a silk factory. There is a Friendship Store.

Day 2: The ship leaves early (about 2:30 a.m.), depending on the current, to reach the first gorge 4½ hours later, at daylight. Near the entrance on the north bank is a two-story pavilion with red lacquer columns, which marks the beginning of the gorges. On the south side of Kui Men Gate are two stone towers and five Chinese characters, which mean "The Kui Men Gate is an unmatched pass."

The **Qutang (Chutang) Gorge** is 8 km long and takes about an hour to pass through. It is the "most imposing" of the gorges, only 100–150 meters wide. Prepare for a very windy passage, as the wind as well as the water is funneled between the cliffs.

The **Wuxia (Wuhsia),** or just Wu Gorge, starts 30 minutes after you leave the Qutang. It is 44 km long and takes about 1½ hours to pass through. Look for the Twelve Peaks Enshrouded in Rain and Mist, of which you can see six on the north bank and three on the south. Of these, the Peak of the Goddess is the highest, at over 1000 meters. It has a tall stone column on top that looks like "a strongly built young woman gazing from high up in the sky at the waterway down below." Look for a tablet-shaped rock with six Chinese characters meaning "The Wu Gorge boasts craggy cliffs," said to be written by a prime minister of the Shu Kingdom in the third century. Ask also about Xiang Xi (Fragrant Stream), where a lady-in-waiting of a Han emperor dropped her pearls accidentally. The water here is said to be "limpid and fragrant" as a result.

About 20 minutes after leaving the Wuxia Gorge at the town of Badong, pomelos, oranges, and persimmons are for sale on shore, if in season. Look for a temple high on a hill. You are now in Hubei province. At this border is being built the largest dam in the world, which will also raise the water level in the gorges 150 meters.

About 1 hour from Badong is the 75-km-long **Xiling (Hsiling) gorge,** which takes about 1½ hours to pass through. It is the longest and most treacherous of the three. Oranges grow on some of the hillsides. Thirty minutes beyond the entrance, on the south side, is Kuang Ming village, with a large temple, Huang Ling Miao. Then comes Five Sisters Peaks, Three Brothers Rocks, and the Needle. Toward the end of this gorge are unsightly sandstone quarries, and then the locks at Gezhouba dam. After that is Ichang, an industrial city in the plains. This is the end of the spectacular scenery. From here read or get to know some of the 500 other passengers. If you stay on board, you arrive late afternoon the next day in Wuhan.

See also "Gezhouba."

Jingzhou has a well-preserved 2000-year-old mummy, an ancient gate, walls from the Three Kingdoms period (A.D. 220–265), a factory for thermos bottles and bedspreads, and a museum.

Fengjie was the capital of the state of Kwei during the Spring and Autumn Period (722–481 B.C.), the time of Confucius. The tomb of Liu Bei's wife is here. See *Romance of the Three Kingdoms*. Temples and pavilions here are dedicated to famous poets and warriors. The ancient wall and gate still stand. Fengjie is near the western entrance to the gorges. The White Emperor City, close by, was built in the Western Han. Here Emperor Liu Bei gave his state and his retarded son to Zhuge Liang, prime minister of the Shu Kingdom during the Three Kingdoms.

If you miss the boat at any of your stops, C.I.T.S. can arrange transport for you to catch up.

Yangzhou 揚州

(Yangchow) East China. North of the Yangtze on the Grand Canal in Jiangsu province, Yangzhou is 2400 years old and famous for its gardens and pavilions. Because of its location, it was a very prosperous port after the Sui emperors had the canal built. At one time it was the residence of many Persian merchants. One of Prophet Mohammed's descendants is buried here, and Marco Polo is said to have spent three years as governor-general. Yangzhou's wealth declined with that of the canal, and by the Qing, it was famous only as an imperial resort city. It is one of the 24 historical and cultural cities protected by the State Council. It can now be reached by ferry and bus from Zhenjiang on the south shore, 2 hours by road from Nanjing, or by boat along the Yangtze or the Grand Canal. Its population is 370,000. Its hottest temperature is 38.6°C in July–August; its coldest is ⁻12°C in January–February. Annual precipitation is about 1000 mm, mainly from June to September.

If you only have one day in Yangzhou, C.I.T.S. recommends hurrying through Shouxi Lake, Daming Temple, Geyuan Garden, Heyuan Garden, and the city museum. You have to choose between a lacquerware, jade-carving or paper-cutting factory. If time permits, there's shopping and the Free Market.

The **Shouxi (Slender West) Lake** 瘦西湖 , in the NW suburbs, is 4.3 km long and surrounded by lovely, peaceful scenes: curled-roof pavilions, the Five Pavilion Bridge, and the imposing White Dagoba (Qing), all packaged in the South China garden style. At the Diaoyutai (Fishing Terrace), Qing Emperor Qianlong is supposed to have fished once. He sounds like a good politician. The Five Pavilion Bridge was built on the occasion of his visit. It is best seen on the night of a full moon, when 15 moons are supposed to reflect from the water under the arches, a Chinese puzzle that must be seen.

The **Daming Temple** 大明寺 , in the northwestern suburbs, was founded in the fifth century. An impressive arch commemorates a famous nine-story pagoda that used to be here but was destroyed by fire in 843. The Daming has 138 carved Buddhist statues.

The **Jian Zhen Memorial Hall** 鉴真纪念堂 , near Daming Temple, was built recently to commemorate the 1200th birthday of Monk Jian Zhen. It, too, is lovely in spite of its youth; it is a copy of the Toshodai Temple in Nara, Japan. This abbot of Daming Temple persisted in going to Japan to teach Buddhism in spite of five unsuccessful efforts and his blindness. He succeeded at age 66. Because he and his disciples also introduced Tang literature, medicine, architecture, sculpture, and other arts to Japan, he is highly honored in that country, where he died and is buried. An over-1000-year-old statue of Jian Zhen, now a national Japanese treasure, was brought back for the anniversary ''because it looked homesick.''

The **Yangzhou Museum** 扬州博物馆 is small, informal, and pleasant. It is near Daming Temple and Jianzhen Memorial Hall and built on the site of the seventh-century pleasure palace of Sui Emperor Yang Di.

The **Geyuan Garden** 个园 (Qing) was started as a private garden and later became the home of the Ye Chun Poet's Society in the Qing. It is full of gnarled rockeries, moon gates, bamboo, latticed doorways, wavy walls, and real picture windows. The rockeries are built around a spring-summer-autumn-winter theme. Do these inspire you, too, to poetry?

The **Heyuan Garden** 何园 (Qing), in the SE part of the city close to the Geyuan, is typical of Yangzhou's gardens. The Arabic-styled **Tomb of Puhaddin** is between the Geyuan and Heyuan in the east side of the city, by the Grand Canal. Built in the 13th century, it contains the remains of this 16th-generation descendant of Mohammed, the founder of Islam. Puhaddin (Burhdn Al-Dan) came to China as a missionary in the Southern Song. The 700-year-old **Xianhe (Crane) Mosque** is one of the four most famous in China, and was built between 1265 and 1275.

If you can squeeze in time between the factories, just walking the back alleys and looking into houses is fun. People are friendly and relaxed.

If you have more time, Yangzhou has enough tombs, pagodas, and the very interesting Grand Canal to keep you busy another day. The most impressive pagoda is the seven-story **Wen Fang Pagoda** 文峰塔 by the Grand Canal, first built in the Ming. The **Wen Chang (Flourishing Culture) Pavilion** 文昌阁 has a roof like the Temple of Heaven, but that's as far as the resemblance goes. A small, five-story stone Tang pagoda may be of interest, with carvings of Buddhas on each of its sides and layers.

Jiaochang 教场 , an area of traditional shops, will be set up especially for visitors to stroll around and meet local people, in time for your visit. Two more gardens, a traditional one called **Xiaopangu** and a modern one, named **Zhuyuxan Garden** 朱鱼湾公园 , are expected to be open soon.

Day trips go from here to Zhenjiang and Nanjing; there are longer excursions along the canal to Suzhou.

Shopping

Locally made are lacquerware, red lacquer carving, jade carving, paper cuts, and silk lanterns. At the paper-cutting factory, a master craftsman can cut lacy paper chrysanthemums for you. Yangzhou also exports potted landscapes, miniature trees and mountains. Ask also about visiting the silkworm farm in the NW of the city, next to the Grand Canal.

Arts and Crafts Building 工艺美术大厦 (22 Yanhe Road; tel. 24195); **Antique Shop** 文物商店 (1 West Yanhe Rd.; tel. 24987); **Friendship Store** 友谊商店 (454 Guoqing Rd.; tel. 21842).

Restaurants

Thousand-layer oily cake may sound awful, but it is delicious, like layered French pastery. People also go to Yangzhou from Nanjing just for the dumplings.

Caigenxiang Restaurant 菜根香饭店 ☐ *115, Guoqing Rd.; tel. 22079.*

Fuchuan Garden Tea House 富春花园茶社 ☐ *15 Yanhe Rd.; tel. 23748.*

Fuchuang Tea House 富春茶社 ☐ *35 Desheng Bridge; tel. 22314* ☐ Air-conditioned.

Hotels

Yangzhou Hotel 扬州饭店 ☐ *5 Upper Fengle St., 125 km from closest airport* ☐ 1984. Traditional Chinese style. Swimming pool, roof garden, coffee shop, theater, dance hall. Joint venture. Chinese and Western food. Yangzhou food specialties here include Yangzhou fried rice, lion head, Fuchun pastry, pearl-in-palace lantern, Mandarin fish rolls, Yangzhou dried bean curd. Within 5 km of important tourist attractions.

Xiyuan Hotel 西园饭店 ☐ *1 Upper Fengle St.* ☐ 1976; renovated 1984. Very pleasant.

Xilinmen Hotel 喜临门酒店 ☐ *1 Upper Fengle St.* ☐ 1986.

C.I.T.S. 中国国际旅行社 : 1 Upper Fengle St.; tel. 21915 or 22611 X380.
CAAC 中国民航 : Zhenyuan Hotel, Sanyuan Rd.; tel. 24619.
Taxi: 1 Upper Fengle St.; tel. 22611 X371 and X372.

Yantai 烟台

A.k.a. Zhifu (Chefoo, Cheefoo) North China. On the northern coast of Shandong province, about 235 km NE of Qingdao by train. It can be reached by small plane in 2 hours from Beijing or 2½ hours from Shanghai. It can also be reached by ship and by direct 20-hour train from Beijing. An international airport should be open by the end of 1987. Weather: Coldest—

⁻30°C in January; hottest—28.3°C in July and August. Annual precipitation about 700 mm in June.

Inhabited almost 2200 years ago, this fishing village was visited by the first Qin emperor early in its existence. That egomaniac really got around! In 1398, during the Ming, a military post was set up, and beacon towers built for transmitting messages. Yantai means "smoke tower."

Yantai was opened to foreign trade in 1862. It was a summer resort for the U.S. Navy's Yangtze Patrol (with White Russian bar girls). The China Inland Mission operated a school here for missionary children; the buildings now are used by the Chinese Navy. Yantai's harborside area and Chaoyang Street still reflect the old architecture. Yantai Hill once housed 10 foreign consulates.

Yantai is one of the 14 Coastal Cities recently opened to trading and accelerated industrial development. The urban population is now about 330,000.

Today, Yantai is an important icefree port that has received international cruise ships like the *Pearl of Scandinavia, Sagafjord,* and *World Discoverer.* It also claims one third of China's prawn catch, and one tenth of its total aquatic harvest. It farms prawns, abalone, scallops, and jelly fish. It grows peanuts (one fifth of China's crop), cherries, grapes, and apples, and grows and cans white asparagus. It mines one quarter of China's gold. The closest mine is about 80 km from the city.

Yantai is looking for a sister city abroad for cultural and economic exchanges.

Yantai is one of the prettiest little cities in China, nestled between the sea and, on three sides, gentle hills. Many of its buildings are topped with orange tiles, and some are of rose-colored stone. It does not have the depressing look of neglected structures that many Chinese cities unfortunately have. It has a cheerful atmosphere of vitality and prosperity. Off the main tourist track, it is more for relaxed family sightseeing and swimming than hectic tourism.

Penglai Pavilion 蓬萊閣 is the most important tourist attraction here and is 83 km NW of the city, past the Yantai Economic and Technology Development Zone. A visit to Penglai can take half a day. Chinese-speaking guides are available on site.

Penglai Pavilion was a favorite place for centuries of scholars and poets, for it was from here, legend says, that the Eight Taoists Immortals flew across the seas. After getting drunk, each tried to compete with the other using his-her own treasure. (See *Attributes of the Eight Taoist Genii* in "What Is There to See and Do?") Some people say they flew to Japan, fighting on the way with the dragon king of the sea. A Japanese legend speaks of seven ferries. But some people say these ferries achieved immortality or arrived in paradise. Myths vary. The pavilion was first built in the Northern Song (1056–63) and extended in 1589. The buildings themselves cover 19,000 square meters.

From the Penglai Pavilion, mirages have been seen on the calm summer surface of the sea by many people. The last one, in 1981, lasted 45 minutes near Long Island, but defied photography. Natives have conflicting opinions about the ideal conditions for mirages, but they seem to be spring and summer with the east wind blowing shortly after a gentle rain, between 2 and 3 p.m. The mirage is of a high mountain, or old city, which some people believe to be Dalian across the straits. But sometimes, it is of another city!

The pavilion with the tables and chairs has a chair of longevity. If people sit on it, they will live a long time. It was in this room that the immortals had their party! Oh, come on!

Movies about the Taoist ferries have been shown regularly on television. Ask about them, but remember, the ferries were each from different periods of history—but legend says they did get together during the Song! Ferries can do anything!

Among the other buildings nearby are the Temple of the Sea Goddess Tian Hou, a Taoist temple, and the Wind Protection Hall, where lighted matches will not blow out even if the wind is from the north. Important is the room full of calligraphy by a famous Ming calligraphist who lived here for three years waiting unsuccessfully to see a mirage. Let that be a lesson to you!

The *Penglai Water Town (a.k.a. Beiwocheng), immediately to the south of the pavilion, was built as a fortress, particularly against Japanese pirates. The Song and Ming navies trained here, and the Ming expanded the defenses. Intriguing is the water gate. In the old days, pirates were lured inside and the gate closed behind them. Then, after the water level rose, the gate was opened and the dead pirates flushed out. Originally built in 1376, the gate was rebuilt in 1596.

A replica of the Ming town **Dengzhou** 登州 , including an old-style bazaar, is currently being built on the way from the bus stop to the pavilion. Staff members wear ancient costumes and musicians play rarely heard period music—if notified in advance. Penglai has a small hotel. Two recently built warships take visitors for rides.

Also important to see in Yantai is the **Museum** 烟台博物馆 (2 Yulan St.; tel. 2814, 2877). Open daily, except Mondays and Thursdays, in the middle of town. It is in a gaudy Fujian-style guild hall with a temple dedicated to the sea goddess. The beautifully restored building was constructed from 1884 to 1906 in Fujian, and brought in three sections here. Note the jawbone of a whale and the remains of a giant sea turtle. A statue of the goddess, destroyed during the Cultural Revolution, has not yet been replaced. The museum has a few relics from 8000 B.C. to more recent times, with labels in English. It can be seen in 30 minutes. Antique store on premises.

Pleasant to visit is the 600-year old **Yuhuang (Jade Emperor) Temple,** at 70 meters above sea level, with a good view of the city. The temple building is original, the tower built in 1984, and the memorial arch in 1876. A 600-year-old pomegranate tree here still bears fruit. Nearby is another garden, "Little Penglai," inspired by the real one to the north.

A visit to the **Zhang Yu Wine Company** 张裕葡萄酒厂 and the **Woolen Embroidery Factory** 绒绣厂 are also recommended if you are interested. The wine-making and the embroidery date from imperialist days, the needlepoint probably taught by missionaries. Some of the patterns are European. The woolen embroidery of China's mountains in Chairman Mao's Mausoleum in Beijing was made here.

If you have more time: On **Yantai Hill** 烟台山 a lighthouse was built on top of a Ming dynasty beacon tower. It has a good view of the harbor.

Yangma Dao (Horse Racing Island) (a.k.a. Elephant Island, because of its shape) is 11 km by ship or 1 hour by road away. Here the first Qin emperor raised horses and visited three times. A 4-km horse-racing track with bleachers is scheduled to open soon, but no gambling at this time. The island is being developed for tourists, with bathing beaches and hotels (including one owned by Xinhua News Service and People's Daily). It already has farms for raising prawns, harvested in October.

Yantai has two bathing beaches in the city proper: **No. 1 Bathing Beach** 海水浴场 , in central Yantai, and **No. 2 Bathing Beach** farther east (tel. 5440). Both have all facilities. C.I.T.S. here claims that Yantai has no sharks, but rival summer resort Qingdao does! In addition to the beaches on Horse Racing Island, a summer resort is planned 120 km from the city in Haiyang County, incorporating a 10,000-meter-long beach of golden sand. Currently, there is a small hotel. The swimming season goes from June to early September.

Shandong is a pioneer in **home-stay** programs "for tourists bored by temples." Visitors can pay to live very comfortably in the relatively substantial homes of rich peasants or fishermen, and learn about life in the countryside (usually two days and one night). Visitors can also sail with fishermen. Much of the fishing here is done with fixed nets, which are checked every one or two days.

By Chinese standards, some of the rural villages here are incredibly wealthy, and a visit will explain why. **Xiguan Village** 西关村 , 23 km away, is one of the places where you can spend the night with a family (usually part of a package, and not cheap).

Kongtong Isle 崆峒岛 is 4.5 nautical miles off Yantai. Local people catch the wild rabbits here, but this is not officially permitted. **Kunlun Mountain,** 30 km away, should have, by 1987, 33 square km set aside for hunting wolves, foxes, rabbits, geese, and badgers. Guns and mopeds are available for rent. **Yunfeng (Cloud Peak) Mountain,** 207 km away, has a calligraphy center with one of the most important collections in China.

C.I.T.S. here seems to try harder because it doesn't have all that many attractions. It says it can organize Wedding Tours complete with a traditional red Chinese gown and the bridal chamber at the Zhifu Hotel. It also has tours for bicycles and mopeds, fishing (small ones only), picking your own apples, and visits to vineyards. At press time, it was allowed to organize tours more cheaply than other travel organizations in China if the tours are confined to Shandong, Beijing, Shanghai, and Hangzhou.

Yantai is building some institutions of higher learning, where students pay fees and find their own jobs. It would be a good place for visitors to glimpse the latest developments of education. Yantai has a teacher's college that is looking for a sister college abroad for cultural exchanges.

See also "Weihai," "Qingdao," and "Jinan."

Entertainment

Evening dance parties near Yantai Hill Guest House. Best arranged through C.I.T.S., but you can find it from the noise. Cheap.

Shopping

Riesling wines, vermouth, Gold Medal Brandy, lace, tablecloths, wooden-framed clocks, and partially completed woolen needlepoint pieces (very cheap). Yantai may be selling gold by the time you get there, but make sure before you buy that you may take it out of China.

Yantai Tourist Products Service, near the museum, has a limited selection of locally made products.

Friendship Store.

Food

Seafood, of course! Shandong food is not peppery hot or overly sweet. Lots of garlic, onions, and salt. Yantai people say that Beijing duck originated when two indigent Shandong peasants went to Beijing and found a dead duck on the road. Improvising an earthen oven, they cooked the duck. An official happened by, liked the smell, and asked for a taste. Pleased, he presented the dish to the emperor, who rewarded the official and the poor peasants. See Shandong section under "Food" for some dishes.

Huibinlou Restaurant 会宾楼 □ *268 Shengli Rd.* □ Mainly seafood. Big scallops and prawns.

Hotels

Dongshan Hotel 车山宾馆 □ *tel. 24501* □ 1968. 150 beds. Billiards. Quiet hotel in garden setting. Six villas, near beach and pier. Good for joggers. Some rooms upgraded (joint venture) to top quality.

Huaqiao (Overseas Chinese) Hotel 华侨宾馆 □ *eastern suburbs* □ 1983. 250 beds. Only partially air-conditioned. Zhifu Hotel better.

Nanyuan Hotel □ probably 1987. About 300 beds.
Wang Hai Lou (Sea-viewing) Hotel 望海楼 □ 1986. 350 beds.
Joint venture.
Wenhua Hotel □ 1986. 400 beds. Joint venture.
Yantai Shan Hotel 烟台山宾馆 □ *Haian Rd.* □ 1984. Dismal,
but will be renovated. Best location in old city for people-watching and
evening walks by the seashore and up into Yantai Hill.
Zhifu Guesthouse □ *eastern suburbs* □ 1981. 250 beds. 20 km
from airport. This is the main tourist hotel. Well-trained, uniformed
staff. Pleasant atmosphere. Near beach #2. A little far from downtown
area.

Other Important Addresses
Bank of China: Currency exchange offices in the main hotels, the De-
partment Store, and embroidery factory.
C.I.T.S. 国际旅行社 : 10, Shuntai Rd.; tel. 25626
C.T.S. 中国民航
CAAC 中旅社 : western suburbs; tel. 26605.
Passenger Ship Quay
Ticket Office for Passenger Ships

Yinchuan 银川

*Northwest China. Capital of the Ningxia (Ningsia) Hui Auton-
omous Region, which lies between Inner Mongolia and Gansu
on the north central border of China. It is linked by air with
Beijing (4 hours), Xi'an (2 hours), Baotou, and Lanzhou. It is
also linked by train with Beijing and is on the Lanzhou-Baotou
line. Yinchuan is in the northern part of the province, a few
km west of the Huanghe (Yellow) River. It is in the middle of
a mesh of irrigation canals in the plains, but close to mountains and classic sand deserts. Weather: In the province the
coldest temperature ranges from ⁻13°C to ⁻7°C in January;
the hottest is 17°C to 26°C in July. Very little rain. Sandstorms, which blow hard in spring and autumn, mean having
to take some cloth to cover your nose and eyes. At times,
everything appears covered with sand.*

Yinchuan has only recently been opened to tourists, and whoever
goes there has to be adventurous. It is not as far from Beijing as the
Silk Road, but the weather is severe, and it is still in the early stages
of being developed for tourists.
Ningxia was inhabited 30,000 years ago, and 8000-year-old neolithic relics have also been found here. It was home to the Yong and Di

tribes in the Western Zhou. The first Qin emperor conquered the tribes and connected parts of the Great Wall here. He sent thousands of men to settle and defend this area.

Ningxia was close enough to the trade routes for Persian coins to be found in its Northern Wei tombs. It exists because parts have been irrigated by the Yellow River for the last 2000 years. Its fight against the relentless sands is admirable, and visitors from areas like California should be especially interested in how the Chinese here manage. A great deal of the region is covered by the Liupan Mountains, through which the Long March passed in 1935.

Ningxia Hui Autonomous Region was founded in 1958, and many people were moved here from other parts of China in the '60s during the Cultural Revolution. Today, it has many national minorities, including the Huis (31.7%), Mongolians, Manchus, Turfans, and others. The provincial population is 3.89 million.

Ningxia now produces rice, wheat, melons, fruit, and the black hairlike moss called *facai*. The region exports coal and also produces petroleum, mica, asbestos, and lime.

Yinchuan (formerly Xingqing) was founded in the Tang and had a variety of other names until 1947. It was the capital of the Western Xia during the early part of the Song (1038) when it was known as Xing-qing. The Xia kings reigned for about 190 years, but the dynasty was destroyed by Genghis Khan. Very little is known about the Western Xia, as there are no records.

Today, 370,000 people live in the urban part of Yinchuan, about 20% Huis, Moslem descendants of those who came 700 years ago to develop this region.

Of importance to visitors is the **Chengtian Monastery Pagoda** 承天寺宝塔 built in A.D. 1050 (Western Xia) and renovated in the Qing. Like many of the area's pagodas, it is unusually plain. The old **Tanglai Canal** 唐徕古渠 (Tang) and **Hanyan Canal** 汉延古渠 (Han) should be seen as examples of ancient irrigation efforts. Note the old water-wheels. The **South Gate Mosque** 南关清真寺 is recent, with an onion dome. The **Zhongda Mosque** 中大寺 is more in the Chinese style.

The **Tongxin Mosque** 同心清真寺 is from the early Ming and was repaired in the Qing. It is one of the largest mosques in the region. The imposing **Jade Emperor Pavilion** 玉皇阁 (Ming) is good for photographs, with its delicate towers, as is the unusual **Drum and Bell Tower** 钟鼓楼 . The ***Haibao (Sea Treasure) Pagoda (a.k.a. North Pagoda)** 海宝塔 is also unusual, a naked structure without fancy eaves, and appearing more like a strange sort of Masonic temple. Dating from the early 5th century, it was destroyed by an earthquake but rebuilt in the 18th century in its original style. It is 1 km north of the city.

The **Twin Pagodas at Baizi Pass on Mt. Holan** 拜寺口双塔 and the **Western Xia Mausoleum** 西夏王陵 are at the base of Mt. Holan, just west of Yinchuan. The mausoleum is rather crude and of interest primarily to people keen on history. In treeless surroundings, it has a stark kind of primitive beauty. The founder of the Western Xia kingdom built over 70 tombs, all but one as decoys.

Adventurers can also take rides on the river on rafts buoyed by inflated pig skins. How many of your friends at home have ever, ever done that! Normal watercraft are also available. At **Qingtongxia** 青铜峡 , south of the city, is a gorge and an impressive dam. Nearby on a barren hill, the mysterious 108 white dagobas are arranged in the shape of a triangle in 12 rows from one to 19 in odd numbers. The smallest one is about six feet and three arm-spans around. No one seems to know the significance of the site and the layout. They do look magnificent from a distance.

The city also has a **museum** 博物馆 and a Russian Orthodox Church. The Guyuan grottoes, the mosque in Tongxin county, the Kangji Buddhist Pagoda in Tongxin County, and the Wanshou Pagoda (the latter two both dating from A.D. 1038 to 1227) are among the attractions being renovated for Ningxia's 30th anniversary in 1988.

Also in the region: **ancient rock paintings on Holan Mountain** 贺兰山古石画 ; the ruins of the **Great Wall** 长城 (Warring States: 475–221 B.C.) are mainly earthen mounds, no stone. Especially important are the *****Buddhist grottoes on Mt. Xumi** (a.k.a. Sumeru) 须弥山 in Guyuan County. They are Northern Wei to the Tang (A.D. 618–907) and have a 19-meter-tall bust of Buddha rising from the floor of a cave. In the south of the province, these caves are impressive, although many of their 300 statues are damaged. Unless they have been recently built, few, if any, sidewalks and stairs connect the 132 caves. This cave temple covers an area 1 by 2 km and the trip is rugged.

The **Gao Temple,** in Zhongwei County in the western part of the province, is striking because of its sandy monotone. A temple for Confucianism, Buddhism, and Taoism, it also has statues of the Jade Emperor, the Holy Mother, and Guan Yu, the god of War. These point to the eclecticism of Chinese religion. Multipurpose temples of this broad range, however, are rare.

C.I.T.S. can make arrangements for tourists to visit Moslem homes.

Shopping
The region produces sheepskin garments, licorice root, Holan inkstone carvings, rugs, and blankets.

Food is mainly Moslem (mutton, no pork). Corn on the cob and oil sticks (like long donuts) are delicious.

Restaurants
Yinbinlou Restaurant □ *Jiefang Xi St.* □ Moslem food.
Wu Yi Restaurant □ *204 Jiafangdong St.* □ Han food.

Hotels
Ningxia Hotel □ *3 Gongyuan St., Yinchuan.*
Yinchuan Hotel □ *25, Jiefang Xi St.*
Zhongwei Hotel □ *Zhongwei County.*

CAAC: 14 Minzu Bai St.; tel. 2143.
C.I.T.S.: 150, Jiefang Xi St.; tel. 4720, 4709.

Yixing 宜兴

(Yihsing, Ihsing, Yising) East China. Due west of Shanghai and Suzhou, on the west side of Lake Tai (Taihu) in SE Jiangsu province, Yixing is best known for its purple stoneware pottery and limestone caves. Population: one million.

If you like caves and pottery, this can be a two-day trip. **Shanjuan Cave** 善卷洞, 25 km SW of the city, is named after a poet who lived here 4000 years ago after refusing to accept political responsibilities. Historical records mentioned the cave 2000 years ago (Spring and Autumn Period). It totals 5000 square meters and is divided into three layers with four caves all joined together: a foggy (23°C) upper cave, and a spacious middle cavern with a 50-by-20-meter chamber and a ''lion'' and ''elephant.'' In the lower, narrow cavern, one can hire a rowboat on a 120-meter-long underground river. At the entrance to the middle cave is a stalagmite seven meters high, probably 35,000 years old. The rocks are shaped like dragons, horses, sheep, cats, and fruit, and are bathed in colored lights. A waterfall outside adds to the sound effects. Tourists walk less than 700 meters and a visit takes about an hour.

Near the entrance is a hotel, a stone monument telling about the ''Bixian Nunnery,'' and the tombstone of Zhu Yingtai's musical instrument and sword. The nunnery existed in A.D. 345. It was once rented by Zhu Yingtai, an early feminist, as her study room in the Jin (A.D. 265–420). One old legend says that Liang Shanbo and Zhu were star-crossed lovers. Liang died and Zhu was allowed to visit his tomb before her forced marriage to another man. Amid thunder and lightning, the tomb opened and she jumped in. The two became butterflies!

The **Zhonggong Cave** 张公洞 in Yufeng Hill, 22 km SW of Yixing, goes back over 2000 years in mythology, the home of an old hermit, Gengsang Chu. Zhang Daoling, one of the founders of Taoism, lived here in the Han, as did Zhang Guolao in the Tang. Zhang Guolao was one of the Eight Taoists Immortals. Zhanggong consists of 72 small, interconnected caves, of varying sizes and temperatures, totaling 3000 square meters. Tourists can walk 1 km, and up and down 1500 stone steps, but most do not. Look for the Dragon King Hall and "Carps Frolicking in the Water."

All the **pottery factories** are in **Dingsu** 鼎蜀镇 , the most famous being the Purple Sand 紫砂陶工厂 . Made here also are celadon, and Jun-glazed 均陶厂 . Dingsu claims to be the pottery capital of China, but some people might argue in favor of Jingdezhen. Arrangements to visit must be made through C.I.T.S. The huge **Pottery Exhibition Hall** 陶瓷陈列馆 (tel. 411) shows 10,000 pieces.

Other places of interest include the **Yiangxian Tea Plantation** 阳羡茶园 , 4 km from Zhonggong Cave, where visitors can see tea being grown and processed. Takes about an hour. The **Bamboo Ocean** 竹海 , near the tea plantation, is a garden of various kinds of bamboo, with toilets and rest houses.

The **Linggu Cave** 灵谷洞 , 30 km SW of Yixing, is in a tea plantation, 8800 square meters. Walk of 1200 meters. Some of the graffiti dates from the Tang.

The **Free Market** here is different from that of other cities. C.I.T.S. can also arrange for you to see fish hawks catching fish.

The **Friendship Store** is in the Yixing Guest House (tel. 2880).

Local specialties include spiced wild duck 香酥野鸭 , diced chicken with ginkgo nuts 白果鸡丁 , lily-bulb soup with sweet osmanthus flower 桂花百合羹 , and Xushe sweet pastry 徐舍酥糖 (sent as tribute to the Qing emperors).

Hotels

Yixing Guest Houses 宜兴宾馆 □ *1 Renmin Nan Rd.* □ 1980. An extension was completed in 1985.

C.I.T.S. 中国国际旅行社 : Yixing Guest House; tel. 2559, 2493.
Taxis: Yixing Guest House; tel. 2560.

Yueyang 岳阳

(Yoyang, Yochow) South China. On the north shore of Lake Dongting 洞庭湖 *in northern Hunan, just south of the Yangtze, 2000 year old Yueyang is sometimes a side trip from Changsha, 140 km south. It can be a pleasant, relaxing day's visit.*

Yueyang Tower 岳阳楼 was first built in A.D. 716 in the Tang as a place for officers to train the navy. The site was a Warring States military burial ground. The tower was destroyed and rebuilt many times, the latest time in 1867 in the original Tang style. At that time it became the west gate of the city. It is made of wood, is 19 meters high, and covers 240 square meters. One of the eight Taoist genii—Lu Tung-pin, with the supernatural sword—was a Tang scholar who became a priest after failing the imperial examinations. He is said to have magically saved the original tower from collapsing. He is also said to be responsible for the creation of the long, silver-white fish in Lake Dongting. On the right of the tower is the Drunk Three Times Pavilion, named after the occasions Lu became drunk here; on the left is the Fairy Plum Pavilion, named because a stone slab with imprints was found under the foundation during renovations in the Ming. The main tower is now a museum. Around the tower are 40 stone tablets inscribed with ancient poems praising the building.

In 1962 a pavilion was built nearby to commemorate the 1250th birthday of famous Tang poet Tu Fu. Look for a finger-painting demonstration. A hotel for tourists was built in Yueyang in 1981.

Junshan Island 军山岛 , 15 km west across the lake, has 72 hills on 247 acres of land. The highest hill has a celebrated view of the 740,000-acre lake, which is one of the settings of the novel and movie *The Sand Pebbles*. The island grows the famous Junshan Silver Needles Tea, many species of bamboo, and a tree with red leaves on one side and green on the other. It is a bird-watcher's paradise. The island also abounds in myths, so expect your guide to tell you many of the stories as you sip tea made from Liu Yi well water. Try to imagine the time during the Song when 10,000 troops were stationed here.

Zhangzhou (Chengchow) 漳州

South China. In southern Fujian reached by road west from Xiamen, Zhangzhou is in the best rice-growing area in the province. It is famous for its narcissus flowers, streets lined with magnolia trees, and its many plants for industrial and medicinal use. Zhangzhou also grows a lot of fruit and makes fruit wines. The Zhangzhou Arts and Crafts Factory produces the famous Longxi puppets. Zhangzhou was first recorded over 1200 years ago. Its hottest temperature has been 37°C in July or August, its coldest 3°C in February or March. The annual precipitation is 1500 mm, mainly from February to April. It is off-the-beaten-track and for this reason may appeal to people looking for something unusual.

Most important are Nanshan Temple, the Zhangzhou Arts and Crafts Factory, and Baihua Hamlet.

The **Nanshan Temple** 南山寺 , 2 km from the O.C. Hotel in the southern suburbs, has a large Tang Buddha, a copper bell from the Yuan, and a white jade Buddha. Flower lovers should be interested in

Baihua (Hundred Flower) Village 百花村 and the **Home of Narcissus** 南山寺 , which specializes in growing these spring flowers. The **Zhangzhou Arts and Crafts Factory** is half a kilometer and the **Mu Mian pavilion** 14 km from the O.C. Hotel.

In the northern suburbs, **Mysterious Pond** 仙字潭 has some writing on a cliff no one has been able to decipher completely. **Yundong Rock** 云洞岩 is in the eastern suburbs.

Local specialties include Jiangdong perch, fried oysters, rice noodles, and noodles with fried bean curd.

Shopping

Narcissus bulbs, Pian Zai Huang tablets, cotton patchwork, and fruit. **Friendship Store** (tel. 3976); **Department Store** (tel. 3320); **Arts and Crafts Service Department** (tel. 3657); **North Yan'an Drug Store** (tel. 4970).

Hotels

Fujian Zhangzhou Overseas Chinese Hotel 华侨饭店 ☐ *38 North Yan'an Rd., 69 km from Xiamen Airport, 1.5 km from railway station, and within view of central bus station* ☐ 1951; renovated 1984. Central location close to shops, post office, and theaters.

Zhangzhou Guest House 漳州宾馆 ☐ *4 Shengli (Victory) Rd.* ☐ 1956; renovated 1983.

Zhangzhou New Times Hotel 漳州新时饭店 ☐ *4 Victory Rd.* ☐ 1986.

CAAC: 38 North Yan'an Rd.; tel. 3643.
C.I.T.S. 国际旅行社 and **C.T.S.** 中旅社 : 38 North Yan'an Rd.; tel. 3614
Taxi: Overseas Chinese Hotel; tel. 3643.
Bus Station: 汽车站

Zhanjiang 湛江

(Chanchiang) a.k.a. Ft. Bayard, Kwangchow-wan. South China. This deepwater port is in a bay on the little hook-shaped peninsula on the SE Guangdong coast just north of Hainan Island. Reached by plane from Guangzhou in a little over an hour, it is also a direct 486-km air-conditioned bus ride from Guangzhou, the terminal beside C.I.T.S. and the train station there. It is a 22-hour train trip from Guangzhou via Guilin and Luizhou in Guangxi province, and also a 16-hour sea voyage from Haikou. On the same latitude as Hanoi in Vietnam, about 500 km west of here, it is subtropical too. The population of Zhanjiang

is 880,000. It is one of the 14 Open Coastal Cities, one of the centers of oil exploration, and a naval base.

Zhanjiang was leased to the French in 1898, at which time it was a coaling station.

If you only have one day in the city, C.I.T.S. recommends: **Huguanyuan Garden** 湖光岩公园 , **Friendship Store, Haibin Garden** 海滨公园 , **Cunjin Qiao (Inch of Gold Bridge) Park** 寸金桥公园 , and **museum** 博物馆 , and the **tropical plant experimentation station** 热带植物园 .

If you have more time, there's the **Hedi Reservoir Resort of Lianjiang** 廉江鹤地水库 , 75 km away in Haikang, with a hotel and swimming. At the **Leizhou Ancient Town** 雷州古镇 , 80 km away, is the old **San Yuan Pagoda** 三元塔 , **Pavilion of Su Dong-po** 苏公亭 , Sihu Garden 西湖公园 , Yuansi Academy 阳生师院 , and **Siyi Temple** 十览寺 . The rocky **Fangji Islet** 放鸡岛 (120 km away) is for scuba diving, with parrot fish, pomfret, and lobsters. Also of interest are the **Yangchun resort area** 阳春风景区 (245 km) and **Xie Lu Villa** of Luchuan 陆川榭鲁山庄 .

The **Tachun Island** scenic spot 特星岛风景区 (1½ nautical miles away from Zhanjiang) has a bathing beach, diving service company (rentals), pine tree forest, holiday village, amusement park, and rifle range. The **Huguang Village Club** 湖光乡村俱乐部 (20 km away) has a hotel, holiday village, golf course (being built), shooting and hunting ranges, and archery field.

Haikou, on Hainan Island, is 185 km away, and a half-hour's plane ride. See separate listing.

Food

Seafood, of course! These taste better than they sound.

Crab meat roasted with fish maw; steamed crab roe; braised northern mushroom with duck feet; steamed fish with only delicious vegetables; savory and crisp duck; fragile skin deep-fried chicken 脆皮炸子鸡 ; deep-fried chicken with four nice colors 四彩大拼盆 ; fried shrimps with chicken and vegetables 碧绿麒麟鸡 ; fried rice Yangzhou style 杨州炒饭; steamed lobster 清蒸龙虾 ; sea warfare with cold vegetables

Hotels

Haibin Hotel 海滨宾馆 □ *Haibin Rd., Sashan, 11 km from airport.*

Overseas Chinese Hotel 中国华侨旅社 □ *22 Renmin Ave.*

Youyi (Friendship) Hotel 友谊宾馆 □ *Renmin Ave., Sashan, 9 km from airport.*

Zhanjiang Hotel 湛江宾馆 □ *Second Rd. of Haibin, Sashan, 10 km from airport.*

International Hotel 国际大酒店 and the **Friendship Building**
友谊大厦 □ both currently being built on Renmin Road.

Other Important Addresses
Bank of China 中国银行
CAAC 中旅社 : tel. 24415.
C.I.T.S. 国际旅行社 : 22 Renmin Rd.; tel. 23688.
Friendship Store

Zhaoqing 肇庆

*(Chaoching) East China. About 110 km west of Guangzhou on
the west bank of the Xijiang River, Zhaoqing is famous for its
scenery and Duan inkstones. It can be reached by ship or bus
from Hong Kong or Guangzhou. A railway is being built from
Guangzhou. The population is about 200,000. The weather is
subtropical, with an annual precipitation of 1599 mm, mainly
from April to August.*

Seven Star Crags, so named because they appear placed like the
seven stars of the Big Dipper, has been described by one tourist as
"prettier than Hangzhou." The mountains are very much like those of
Guilin, including caves with grotesque limestone formations and an underground stream for boat riding. Seven Star Crags (or Cliffs) is like a
potted miniature garden.

Known since ancient times, Zhaoqing was the home for six years
of the Italian Jesuit missionary Matteo Ricci, his first in China. He lived
in "Shuihing" in the 1580s. Zhaoqing was also one of the starting
points of the Northern Expedition in 1926, and was not really developed
as a resort until 1955. Then, 460-hectare Star Lake was created for
irrigation, fish breeding, and scenery. Walkways, bridges, and lights
were set up in the caves.

The seven crags are named Langfeng (Lofty Wind), Yuping (Jade
Screen), Shishi (Stone Chamber), Tianzhu (Pillar of Heaven), Chanchu
(Toad), Shizhang (Stone Palm), and Apo (Hill Slope). The biggest cave
is at the foot of Apo Crag and can be entered by boat. If you hit the
rocks at Music Instrument Rock, you get different musical notes. Zhaoqing
also boasts the **Baiyun (White Cloud) Temple,** built in the Tang (618–
907) and the **Chongxi, Yuanku, Wenming, and Xufeng pagodas.**
Qingyun Temple is at the foot of 1000-meter-high Tripod mountain,
18 km NE of Zhaoqing. You could also look for the **Yuejiang Tower,**
and the **Water and Moon Palace,** from the Ming. These were damaged
during the Cultural Revolution but are now renovated.

The mountain, which is a nature preserve, has a 30-meter-high waterfall on its NW side.

The **Xinghu Amusement Park** is near Xinghu Lake. The city also has restaurants, swimming pools, and an art gallery. Golf is planned.

Shopping

In addition to the famous inkstones, locally made are ivory and bone carvings, sandalwood fans, paintings, straw products, umbrellas, and jewelry. Ginseng Cola will soon be made here. **Guangdong Zhaoqing Duanxi Factory of Famous Ink Stones** (Gongnong Rd.; tel. 23975. Cable 4551).

Hotels

Xinghu (Star Lake) Hotel □ 1987. Joint venture. 400 rooms. 29 stories. The upper two stories revolve.

Songtao (Pine Wave) Hotel □ *cable 9038* □ is one of the best in town now. Joint venture. 200 rooms, four dining rooms, and ballroom. On the lake.

Guangdong Zhaoqing Tourist Trade Development General Corporation: 53 Qixingyanpaifang Dongjie; tel. 23952, 24627; cable: 8888.
Recommended reading: *The Wise Man from the West—Matteo Ricci and His Mission to China* by Vincent Cronin.

Zhengzhou 郑州

(Chengchow) Northwest China. On both the Beijing-Guangzhou and the Shanghai-Xi'an railway lines, this capital of Henan province is also a 2-hour flight south of Beijing. It is about 20 km south of the Yellow River on the main railway line between Luoyang and Kaifeng. In the province, the coldest average temperature is ⁻3°C in January; the hottest is 29°C in July. Annual rainfall is 500–900 mm, especially July through September. Population: urban 850,000.

Zhengzhou is historically important as one of the first cities to be built in China. This was during the Shang dynasty 3500 years ago. It is also important because of its proximity to Shaolin Monastery, known to every *kung fu* fan.

For historians, Zhengzhou has one of the best museums because Henan was a big part of the cradle of Chinese civilization. It was in Anyang that the oracle bones with one of the first Chinese writings were found. The capitals of the Eastern Zhou, Han, Wei, Jin, Northern Song, Tang, and Liang were in this province. At least one of the capitals and possibly four of the five other capitals of the Xia dynasty were also in this province. The Xia was China's first dynasty, and until recently was clouded in legend, traditionally dating from the 16th century B.C. China's first Buddhist temple, the Luoyang Grottoes, and the earliest astronomical observatory are also located here.

Zhengzhou was the site of the February 7th Beijing-Hankou Railway Workers' General Strike of 1923, part of a larger workers' movement for better wages and conditions. Over 100 railroad workers were killed. The strike is commemorated with a modern 14-story double pagodalike clock tower in February 7th Square, built in 1971.

If you only have one day in Zhengzhou, you have a hard choice to make. One day is only time for sightseeing along the Yellow River, hopefully from the top of **Mangshan Mountain** 邙山 (28 km from the International Hotel). There is time also for the Provincial Museum and nearby Shang palace ruins and old city walls.

Near the Provincial Museum is also the **Yellow River Museum,** which gives detailed geological data on that monstrous yet beloved river, recordings of floods, construction work, etc. It will help you understand the regard the Chinese people have for it. The government has done an outstanding job of making dams and reservoirs for irrigation and flood control.

Dahecun Village 大河村 , a 5000-year-old site for Yangshao and Longshan neolithic cultures and Shang ruins, is NE about 12 km and can also be included.

Songshan Mountain takes at least one day, and if you have a third day, then there are Mixian and Gongxian counties.

Songshan Mountain 嵩山 is about 75 km SW of Zhengzhou in **Dengfeng County** 登封层 It stretches more than 60 km east to west. The highest peak is 1512 meters above sea level. It is one of China's Five Sacred Mountains, and emperors came here to worship. During the Southern and Northern Dynasties (A.D. 420–589), 72 temples and monasteries flourished here.

Songshan is the home of **Shaolin Monastery** 少林寺 , world famous because of the popularity of China's martial arts. Here is where one of the better kung-fu movies was filmed in the early 1980s. If you have a chance, see *Shaolin Monastery.* This Hong Kong-China production should make ancient China seem more vivid to you.

Shaolin was first built in A.D. 495–496 and became famous because 13 fighting monks from here supported the first Tang emperor. (There is a famous story about a group of monks from Shaolin involved in a conspiracy against the Manchus, but they were from a lesser-known Shaolin Monastery in Fujian.)

At this Shaolin temple 13 km NW of Dengfeng County town, you can see the depressions in the floor worn by generations of monks practicing martial arts. Among the murals and frescoes are some of 500 arhats (Ming), but also some depicting fighting monks. At one time, 2000–3000 monks lived here. The **Ta Lin (Forest of Pagodas)** 塔林

is the largest group of memorial pagodas in China. A cemetery for abbots, it has over 230 miniature pagodas grouped here, dating from the Northern Wei.

Northwest of the temple is a cave where the sixth century Indian missionary Bodhidharma, was reputed to have spent nine years in meditation before achieving Nirvana. He was the founder of Chan Buddhism, more popularly known as Zen, and is frequently depicted in art in his robes, crossing the Yangtze River standing on a reed. The cave is marked with a memorial arch.

The 40-meter-high ***Songyue Pagoda** 嵩岳寺塔 at **Fawang Temple** 法王寺 is the oldest proven extant pagoda in China. Built of brick in about A.D. 520 (Northern Wei), it is also unusual because it has 12 sides and is curved like an Indian *sikhara* tower. It is of extreme importance to those studying pagoda architecture. The **Songyang Shuyuan (Songyang Academy of Classical Learning)** 嵩阳书院 at the foot of the mountain has two cypress trees said to be over 2000 years old, each measuring 12 meters in circumference. The school was one of the four imperial academies preparing students for the imperial examinations.

Zhongyue Miao (Central Mountain Temple) 中岳庙 , at the base of Taishi Peak and 4 km east of Dengfeng County, was founded in the Qin and moved here in the Tang. It has four feisty 3½-meter-high iron figures (Northern Song) guarding it. One of the earliest Taoist temples, it is huge, the largest extant monastery in the province. It was enlarged during the Qing, along the lines of the Forbidden City in Beijing. The ***Taishi Tower** 太室阙 is from the Eastern Han. One can climb to the top of Huanggai Peak for an overall view of the 400 or so buildings and the 300 Han cypresses.

The ***Shaoshi Tower** 少室阙 and the ***Qimu Tower** 启母阙 , also on the mountain, are from the Eastern Han too. The ***Astronomical Observatory** 观星台 was built early in the Yuan and is the oldest in China. Located in Dengfeng, it was able to prove that the earth revolved around the sun once every 365.2425 days, 300 years before the Gregorian calendar.

A search for the first Xia capital, China's oldest dynasty, has been centered in Dengfeng County, ½ km west of the town of **Gaocheng** 告城 at **Wangcheng Gang (Royal City Mound)** 皇城岗 . The search started in 1975, and this site is not usually included in a tour, but people interested in archaeology might ask about it. Uncovered have been city walls, skeletons (probably of slaves, buried alive in a foundation pit), wine vessels, bronze fragments, and ceramic pots. However, Wangcheng Gang was found to be of a later date (5th century B.C.)

Across the river and ½ km NW of Gaocheng is another site where the earliest bronze vessels in the province were found and carbon-dated to 2000 B.C. This is now thought to be the earliest Xia capital. These sites are about 40 km SW of Zhengzhou.

Also SW of Zhengzhou, but closer to the city, are the **Han Tombs at Dahuting (Tiger-hunting) Pavilion** 打虎亭村汉墓 in **Mixian County** 密县 . They are worth a short stop for their paintings and stone carvings. A few km north of Mixian is the ***Gongxian County Cave Temple,** dating from A.D. 517 (Northern Wei) to Song, some of its 7743 Buddhist sculptures in an excellent state of preservation. They are not as big or as impressive, though, as Luoyang's, but they are certainly worth a look.

The ***Song Tombs,** 75 km west of Zhengzhou and also in Gongxian, are from the Northern Song, when that illustrious dynasty had its capital in Kaifeng. They are impressive for their huge stone guardians, among them foreign envoys wearing turbans. The tombs themselves have so far proved less spectacular than those of the later Ming and Qing emperors and are spread over an area 15 km long. They were built in a much shorter time than those of their successors, and without the personal supervision of the emperor who was going to reside there. One of the imperial tombs is expected to be opened in the near future.

Gongxian was also the home county of Tang poet Du Fu (Tu Fu). **Du Fu's Native Place,** the cave where he was born, has been embellished with brick walls and can be visited. The famous three-color Tang porcelain (horses, camels) of which you see reproductions in every Friendship Store in the area, were first made in a kiln at **Xiaohuangye.** One can also visit the 300-year-old **Manor of Landlord Kang Baiwan** for a good insight into how the aristocracy lived then. Just imagine yourself living here as a servant! In what did you cook? Where did the sewage go? How could you deliver clandestine notes to the young mistress from her secret lover?

In Yanshi county are the ruins of a capital of the early Shang dynasty, at least 3000 years old, one of the earliest, largest, and best-preserved ancient cities.

If you have more time, there's a lovely stone dragon at **Huishan Temple** and one of the oldest extant octagonal brick pagodas in the country built in A.D. 746 (Tang). The **Fengxue Temple** 9 km NE of Linru county, is from the Wei. It has a 22-meter-high pagoda. Can you tell just by looking how old it is?

A Central Land Tourist Center is being constructed 30 km west of Zhengzhou. And in the province, there's also Kaifeng (70 km away), Luoyang, and Anyang. For destinations close by in Shanxi province, across the Yellow River, see "Taiyuan." For Hebei province, see "Shijiazhuang."

Shopping

Made here are reproductions of three-color Tang porcelain figures, jade and lacquerware, calligraphy and paintings. It's a good place to buy Chinese writing brushes, paper, inkstones, and inkbars. Made in the province are also Jun porcelain and embroidery from Kaifeng.

Restaurants

A suggested specialty is mentioned. The following have other dishes too.

Restaurant on the Water □ *tel. 23317* □ for live Yellow River carp (cooked, of course).

Zhengzhou Roast Duck Restaurant 郑州烤鸭店 □ *tel. 24582* □ for Zhengzhou's version of this favorite dish.

Shaolin Restaurant 少林餐厅 □ *tel. 22441* □ for fried monkey head-shaped fungus.

Hotels

International Hotel 国际饭店 □ *East Section, Jinshui Rd.* □ 1982. 8 km from airport. This is the main tourist hotel.

Zhengzhou Hotel 郑州饭店 □ *Jinci, south suburbs.*

Henen Hotel □ *west section of Jinshui Rd.*

Friendship Hotel □ *Xintongqiao.*

February 7 Hotel □ *Jiefang Rd.*

Several new hotels should be opened in 1987.

C.I.T.S. 国际旅行社 : 16 Jinshui Rd.; tel. 25396.
CAAC 中国民航 : tel. 24517.

Zhenjiang 镇江

(Chinkiang, Chenchiang, Chenkiang: to pacify the river) East China, in central Jiangsu province, where the Grand Canal meets the south bank of the Yangtze. About 1 hour by train (63 km) east of Nanjing, and about 4 hours (220 km) NW of Shanghai. The closest airport is at Nanjing. It is a historic old city, its streets lined with plane trees, some of its houses small and whitewashed like Suzhou's, others black brick with courtyards. It is bound on three sides by hills and on the north by the Yangtze River. Weather: Coldest—⁻8°C from the mid to the end of January; hottest—38°C, July and August, with breezes from the Yangtze. Annual precipitation 1000 mm, mainly in July. Population: 390,000.

Zhenjiang was founded in the Zhou, when it was called Guyang, and then Dantu. It boasts 2500 years of history, including seven as capital of the Eastern Wu (third century), when it was called Jingko (entrance to Nanjing). Many battles were fought in the area and the city is mentioned in *The Romance of the Three Kingdoms*.

During the Yuan, Zhenjiang was visited by Marco Polo. The first British missionaries arrived in the 17th century. Toward the end of the

First Opium War, it was the only city that strongly resisted the imperialists. After that failed, however, about 1000 foreigners, mainly merchants and missionaries from Britain, Germany, and the United States lived here. The foreigners left their mark on some of the architecture.

In 1938, Marshall Chen Yi's New Fourth Army was stationed about 50 km away, and some skirmishes with the Japanese took place in the area. In April 1949, the British warship H.M.S. *Amethyst,* while rescuing British citizens upriver, was caught in the crossing of the Yangtze by the People's Liberation Army and held for over three months here. The captain refused to cooperate or admit his ship fired first. Under cover of a passing passenger boat, the *Amethyst* finally escaped.

Today, Zhenjiang has 500 factories and mines, and makes industrial chemicals, textiles, silk, and paper (from rice stocks) for export.

If you only have one day, C.I.T.S. suggests Jinshan Hill, Jiaoshan Island, the museum, and the Thousand-Year-Old Street. This street, which is 4 km from the Jinshan Hotel, has an unusual stupa built above the sidewalk.

Jiao Hill 焦山 (150 meters high) on Jiao Shan Island, less than ½ km from the city (13 km from the Jinshan Hotel), is named after an Eastern Han scholar, Jiao Guan. A slightly larger than life-size white statue of the hermit meditating in the dim light of his actual cave is at the base. Up 250 steps later is a magnificent view of the Yangtze—all three of Zhenjiang's hills have magnificent views of the Yangtze—and one can see the place where the *Amethyst* was held. What would you have done if you were captain?

Back at the base of Jiao Hill, you can look at the **Battery,** which was used against the British in 1842. It was originally on the river. Also below is a garden with steles of many calligraphers, including that of the father of modern calligraphy, Wang Hsi-chih of 1500 years ago. The original tablet was broken, but it was retrieved from the river in 1713. At the loquat orchard and the **Din Hui Buddhist Temple** most of the Ming statues were destroyed by the Red Guards. The existing statues were made in 1979.

Jinshan (Golden Hill) 金山 , 1 km from the Jinshan Hotel, looks better from afar than close up. The temple here was first built 1500 years ago (Jin) and rebuilt several times since, a victim of lightning, fire, and weather. The current pagoda was finished in 1900 with animal carvings, in time for the Empress Dowager Cixi's birthday. It reflects her crude tastes. Seven stories tall, 30 meters high, it is easier climbing up the 119 steps than down because of the shallow steps.

But there are some fun **caves,** all the more interesting because of the presence in one of the white, ghastly-looking, life-size figure of the monk Fa Hai, and in another the two beautiful women said to be the White Snake and the Blue (sometimes Green) Snake, both fairies. The cave is said to reach Hangzhou!

Guides avoided telling such traditional stories in the 1960s, and it has only been since the late 1970s that one has heard them again. The White Snake's is also the plot of a famous Beijing opera. Briefly, the several-thousand-year-old White Snake from Mount Emei (the Blue Snake is the maid) becomes a beautiful woman and goes to Hangzhou. There at the Tuanqiao (the Bridge of Breaking Up), she falls in love with a scholar, and eventually the two marry. The White Snake, using her magic powers, takes money from a government official to build a house, but because the official's seal is still on the money, the young man is arrested and ordered beaten for theft. The White Snake again uses her magic so that whenever her husband is beaten, the official's wife feels the pain. Consequently, the young man is expelled to Zhenjiang. After his arrival, the monk master Fa Hai, jealous of their happiness, tries to separate the couple, but the White Snake floods the area, including Jin Shan temple. They are reunited at the Tuanqiao. The unrelenting monk master retaliates by imprisoning the White Snake under the Leifeng pagoda in Hangzhou. There she is rescued by the Blue Snake. The White Snake, her husband, and her son are reunited and live happily ever after.

This is a popular Chinese tale and a study of the significance of its symbolism and the psychology of its popularity could keep a folklorist busy for years.

Museum 博物馆 : Housed in the former British consulate building next door to the former Southern Baptist Convention buildings, this museum was opened in 1958. It is 4 km from the Jinshan Hotel. Its permanent collection includes an anchor from the British ship *Amethyst* and a land lease dated 1933 referring to the "former British Concession lot." It has the well-preserved 720-year-old corpse of a scholar, buried with his precious Imperial University entrance certificate in hand. A tiny silver coffin found under the nearby Iron Pagoda contains two gold coffins and the ashes of a Buddhist saint. Charming is the Song porcelain pillow in the shape of a sleeping child.

If you have more time, the **Bei Gu (North Consolidated) Hill 北固 山**, 9 km from the Jinshan Hotel, is the site of the temple where Liu Pei, founder of the Shu Han dynasty and hero of *The Romance of the Three Kingdoms,* was married to the sister of Sun Chuan. After he died, his wife mourned for him at the pavilion on top of the hill now called Mourning over the River Pavilion. On this hill also is an 11th-century Iron Pagoda (Northern Song), originally nine stories high. Struck by lightning several times, it was repaired in 1960 and now has only its first, second, fifth, and sixth stories.

Zhenjiang also offers **boat tours** on the Yangtze 扬子江 and the Grand Canal 大运河 , a **Children's Palace** (6 km away), and a **Silkworm and Mulberry Research Institute** (6 km away).

Yangzhou, a pleasant, cultured city, is 25 km away by road and ferry across the Yangtze. **Yixing,** 150 km away, has famous caves and ceramics. See separate listings.

Shopping

Dashikou 大市口 is Zhenjiang's main shopping area—department store, antique stores, arts and crafts, and Friendship Store. Zhenjiang's factories make elaborate palace lanterns and are famous for their ''crystal'' meat and vinegar. Also made in the city are silk, jade carvings, paper cuttings, and silk birds.

Restaurants

A local specialty is crab cream bun, a steamed meat pastry. Make a hole first and slurp out the soup inside. Food here is concerned with fragrance, shape, and color, and is neither too sweet nor too salty. You might find your hors d'oeuvres looking like butterflies, peacocks, or fans. Everything can be dipped in vinegar.

Jingjiang Restaurant 京江饭店 □ *111 Jiefang Rd.; tel. 22842.*

Tongxinglou Restaurant 同兴楼饭店 □ *218 Zhongshan Rd.; tel. 23942.*

Hotels

Jinshan Hotel 金山饭店 □ *1, Jinshan Rd. West; 5 km from railway station* □ 1979; renovated 1985. Tennis courts, swimming pool, joint-venture coffee shop, theaters, dance halls, Chinese and Western food.

No. 1 Spring Hotel 一泉饭店 □ *1 Yiquan Rd.* □ 1981; renovated 1984.

C.I.T.S. 中国国际旅行社 : 22 Jiefang Rd.; tel. 23281.
Taxis 计程车 : 1 Jinshan Rd. W.; tel. 22142.
Railway Station 火车站

Zhongshan 中山

(Chung Shan) South China in Guangdong province. Close to the Portuguese colony of Macao, across the Pearl River delta south of Hong Kong, this county can be directly reached by 1-hour Hovercraft from Hong Kong or via Macao. It is 2 hours by road SW of Guangzhou.

A 1-day tour from Hong Kong usually includes a visit to the former residence of Dr. Sun Yixian (Sun Yat-sen) 孙中山故居 in Cuiheng village 翠亨村 . The house was designed by the father of the Chinese republic himself and is an adaptation of the local style. The Sun Yixian Memorial Middle School is a couple hundred meters away. Tourists have taken lunch in **Shiqi** 石岐 and visited the Long Rui Village before returning to Macao or Hong Kong, or going on to other places in the area.

The county also has two hot spring resorts. The **Shi Ching Shan Tourist Center** is booked through the Golden Star Tourism Corp. (469 Nathan Rd., Sun Beam Commercial Bldg., No. 1009, Yaumati, Kowloon). The center, which is a 20-minute drive from the Macao border, has boating, tennis, shooting gallery, horses, and a swimming pool.

The **Zhongshan (Chung Shan) Hot Spring Resort** 中山温泉 is 30 km from the border. Sintra Tours, which can book it from Macao, lunches its tours here. The resort has 200 rooms, tennis, shooting gallery, a swimming pool, and a fishing lake.

The **Zhongshan (Chung Shan) Hot Spring Golf Club** 中山温泉 高尔夫球会 is close to the Zhongshan Hot Spring Resort. The 18-hole, par 72 golf course was designed by the Palmer Course Design Company, named after Arnold Palmer. For those coming from abroad, the club can arrange visas. The address is: Sanxiang Commune, Zhongshan City; tel. 22811; cable: 3306; telex: 44828 CSHS CN. In Hong Kong, telephone 5–210377 or 5–210378. In Macao, tel. 71702. Bookings also from major hotels in Guangzhou.

Shiqi (Shekki, Shekket), the county seat, has a 180-room hotel built by C.T.S. in 1980, and a 392-room hotel built by C.I.T.S. in 1986. Its Jumbo Restaurant is a smaller version of the floating restaurant in Hong Kong.

Zhuhai 珠海

South China, Guangdong Province. Adjacent to the Portuguese colony of Macao across the Pearl River delta south of Hong Kong, this county can be directly reached by ferry from Hong Kong or Shekou, and by road via Macao. It is a 2-hour drive from Guangzhou. Zhuhai is a Special Economic Zone, also developed as a resort area especially for crowded, wealthy Hong Kong. Heliport. An international airport is planned.

Zhuhai says it is the fourth largest tourist destination after Shanghai, Beijing, and Guangzhou, with 478,000 visitors in recent years, mainly from Hong Kong and Macao, but also many from abroad.

In the vicinity are the Lienchien cave and the birthplace of Dr. Sun Yat-sen. See "Zhongshan." Population is 405,400.

The architecture of the Jiu Zhou Cheng shopping center (Jing Shan Rd.; tel. 22959, 22958; cable 3188) was inspired by Beijing's Forbidden City.

Hotels and Resorts
Zhuhai has at least 83.

The 295-room **Zhuhai Resort** can be booked in Hong Kong. It looks plush, covers 800,000 square feet, and is a 10-minute drive from the Jiuzhou Pier in Zhuhai. The resort was built in 1985–86 and has two swimming pools, billiard room, tennis court, sauna, disco, children's playground, game room, convention center with simultaneous translation equipment, restaurants, coffee shop, shopping mall, Chinese-styled suites.

Zhuhai Holiday Resort □ *Shihuashan; cable 3988* □ Villas, hotel, restaurant, bowling, billiards, swimming pool, tennis, racecourse, and shooting range.

Shi Ching Shan Hotel □ *Ching Shan Rd.; cable 2828; telex 44517 SCST* □ is 20 minutes from Jiuzhou; 20 minutes from Macao. Near Shi Ching Shan Tourist Centre. Banquet hall, bars, direct telephone lines with Hong Kong, Macao, and Guangzhou. Telefacsimile, shuttle bus, and limousine services. Can arrange tourist visas.

Shi Ching Shan Tourist Centre □ *cable 2828* □ 20 minutes from Macao. 115 rooms. 24-hour hot water. Restaurant, coffee shop. Swimming pool, tennis court, riding stable, game room, boating. Live-ammunition shooting range. Limousines, vans, and buses.

Gong Bei Palace Hotel □ *Gongbei* □ 62 rooms, 53 villas. Cantonese and Western food. Swimming pool, billiards, sauna, massage room, coffee shop. Main building inspired by the Efang Palace of the Qin dynasty.

Zibo 淄博

North China. In Shandong, on the Beijing-Shanghai express-train route, it can also be reached by air via Jinan. Zibo is near **Linzi,** *the capital of Qi (859–221* B.C.*), where 150 ancient tombs have yielded a large mirror, horse skeletons, bronzes, crossbows, and bronze coins from that era. Zibo itself makes good porcelain, artistic pottery and glassware, and silk.*

Zunhua 遵化

(Tsunhua) North China. Hubei province, about 125 km NE of Tianjin and 135 km east of Beijing. It takes 3 or 4 hours to get there because the road is congested with donkey and horse carts, trucks, and creeping tractors. Several checkpoints along the road may or may not stop your car for your alien travel permit.

Among the imperial Qing tombs at nearby **Dongling** (Eastern Tombs) are those of Qianlong (Chien Lung) at Yuling. Qianlong is the emperor who snubbed Britain's envoy. He is buried with his five wives. A devout Buddhist, his tomb is covered with religious statues and sutras in Indian, Tibetan, Chinese, Manchurian, and Mongolian.

The tombs of Empress Dowager Cixi (Tzu Hsi) and Empress Ci'an are together at **Dingdongling.** The empress dowager was the fascinating, outrageous, scheming, brilliant, scandalous but short-sighted woman who built the Summer Palace in Beijing. Her tomb, covered with phoenixes deliberately and arrogantly placed *above* the dragons (symbolizing the emperor), was completed in 1881 and renovated in 1895, with an additional 4590 taels of gold as decoration. She died in 1908. Both mausoleums can be entered. The carving is more elaborate than that in the Ming tombs, with Buddhist sutras (in Tibetan and Sanskrit) and figures inside. You can see an exhibition of her clothes, utensils, and photos. Her tomb was robbed in 1928 by a Nationalist warlord who used explosives to open it. He stripped over 500 pearls off her clothes.

Like the Ming tombs, there is also an animal-lined Sacred Way, the figures here smaller but more elaborately carved. It seems each dynasty tried to outdo its predecessors, the Ming being more elaborate than the Song (see "Zhengzhou"). The tombs of the emperors and empresses have yellow glazed roofs. Those of persons of lesser importance have green roofs.

The attendants here are dressed in Qing imperial costumes with eye-catching Manchu hats, and high heels attached to the center of their shoes. Some heels are in the shape of vases or bells. Some of these women have been surprisingly shy about having their photos taken, so do it on the sly.

Another word of warning: No decent bathrooms nor running water exist except in the guesthouse in the courtyard to the right of Qianlong's Tomb. The roads in the area are unpaved.

The **Xiling (Western Tombs),** 120 km SW of Beijing at **Yixian** are not as illustrious. They hold the remains of emperors Yongzheng (Tailing), Jiaqing (Changling), Daoguang (Muling), and Guangxu (Chongling), plus the usual retinue of wives and children. They may not be open all the time because of nearby military exercises.

SPECIAL FOR OVERSEAS CHINESE

Overseas Chinese who speak no Chinese should take C.I.T.S. tours if they are interested primarily in getting the best accommodations and facts in English while sightseeing. If you want to be treated more like family, sometimes taking second place to foreign guests, but getting cheaper rates, go C.T.S. If you want to learn about China, try to find a family, especially yours, to live with.

I have gone to China all three ways. Emotionally it's a strain, because with a C.I.T.S. group, I get annoyed at the higher prices and furious with foreigners joking about *my* people. With one C.T.S. Hong Kong group, our tour director had a lot of *guanxi,* and we were met not just by a guide, but by the manager of C.T.S., and given the same rooms as Foreign Friends for cheaper prices. Our trip down the Yangtze was a riotous floating poker game, interrupted only by glances at the Three Gorges. I missed much of the commentary because it was all in Cantonese and Mandarin, but we had a ball!

With relatives, I learned more about China than any of the group tours, but in a different way. The first time we met, they pointed out a long-forgotten photograph on the wall of my Canadian family taken 20 years before. My aunt knew everyone by name. Until I started planning a trip to China, I didn't know she existed. In her home, I saw how a six-course meal could be cooked in one wok in one hour. I learned how politeness smooths over a multitude of sins, all ignoring my embarrassing encounter with a naked nephew who was bathing behind a screen in the kitchen (there was nowhere else to bathe). On the streets they pointed to the strange-looking foreigners, *my* fellow Westerners, who had then just started to invade Xinhui. I didn't learn much about the history of the city, but I sure learned a lot about Chinese people and myself.

I think people of Chinese ancestry in particular should visit China. If you feel this bicultural conflict as many of us do, it would be good to explore the Chinese part of your roots. If nothing else, it will help you understand your parents, your grandparents, and your great-grandparents. It might even help you understand things about yourself.

In my father's village in Taishan, I was shocked to learn he had been born in a mud house. I found the watch towers where he used to look out for bandits, and imagined him riding the water buffalo. My grandfather's grave was a simple mound. I expected something more elaborate, considering the money my father said he sent back to the village.

I highly recommend a visit to your ancestral village. Even if you have no relatives there, at least you can look around and see how you would have lived if your ancestors had not emigrated. If you find relatives, you might find your name, if you're male, in a family history book. Part of my novel *Beyond the Heights* is about this experience, which can be traumatic.

But you don't have money to take expensive presents? Don't be silly! People outside China send back presents to family partly to show off. They also send because they feel a strong family obligation. People in China ask for expensive luxury presents like Omega watches because they do not really know how much these things cost outside. And they want to keep up with the Wongs. Remittances have supported a few idlers. If you don't want to contribute to idleness and foolish pride, don't give an expensive gift.

So what do you think will happen if you don't take them a video? Do you think your relatives are going to be rude to you? Of course not. If they ask, tell them you couldn't afford it. My relatives were pleased with the U.S.$20 watch I took in once, especially after I showed them the U.S.$16 Timex I wore myself. Making friends and learning about China are much more important.

You should take some presents, of course. You'd take a bottle of wine to a hostess in the United States, wouldn't you? If you're arriving from Hong Kong, exotic gifts like American delicious apples, Sunkist oranges, and Danish butter cookies can be bought there. In China, you and your F.E.C.s are in a privileged position. You could accompany aunts, uncles, and cousins to the Overseas Chinese store and buy them what they want, in exchange for R.M.B. Then you could use the R.M.B. to treat them to dinner at a restaurant, a nice gesture, especially if you're staying with them.

You may find you have nothing in common with Chinese people. On the other hand, you may find that you do. You may have no feelings of obligation to help, dismissing their comparative poverty as their, not your, bad luck. So be it. At least you went and had a look.

For those who do feel pangs of conscience, I think you should be sensitive to opportunities to help. They would trust you more than any other foreigner and would be less reticent to ask you for help.

You can teach—simple skills like English. The children, especially, are learning. You can teach swimming! Imagine my surprise at finding that no one in my village knew how to swim! You can inspire them with technical advances in your home country, drawing pictures if you can't speak the language.

Developing industries and markets have high priority, and never before have the opportunities been so ripe. Every rural village in Guangdong and Fujian seems to be building a hotel for visiting relatives. And restaurants! You may be asked your opinion. The handicraft industry, especially tourist souvenirs, is flourishing. They need ideas on cottage industries that would appeal to foreigners.

New enterprises no longer need approval from Beijing, and you could help them with foreign exchange and expediting imports of machinery and materials from abroad. But do read something about appropriate technology, spare parts, and maintenance before you do. Photocopy machines have lain idle for years because no one knew how to fix them. You may want to set up a joint venture as many other Overseas Chinese and compatriots have done.

Paying for education is also important. Government schools have been free, but a very small percentage of students have been able to qualify. Private schools, including universities, have now sprung up, but fees are needed, of course. These are much cheaper than schools in your home country, and may be more relevant to China's needs. You may want to invest in a private school yourself. Or stay and teach. Of course, living in China takes a special kind of person, one with a great deal of patience and, particularly, a good sense of humor. It is not easy for someone used to Western affluence and efficiency to adapt to Chinese standards, but many do.

Sponsoring a Chinese student to study abroad is also helpful, but only if the student returns to apply his knowledge in China. Nothing is really solved if the student sends back only foreign exchange to an increasingly greedy family. China needs scientists and technicians *in China*.

Help to emigrate is of debatable value. China cannot modernize if her best brains leave the country.

SPECIAL FOR BUSINESS PEOPLE

Advice: Trading with China is not like trading with other countries. As one trade official put it, "If you want to play in the Chinese sand pile, you have to play by Chinese rules."

These rules are much too complicated to put into a travel guide. There are lots of books, business guides, and experienced people to give advice. But to get you started: Trading with China is done primarily through foreign trading corporations, a list of which can be obtained from a Chinese mission. Joint ventures are negotiated through the China International Trust and Investment Corporation.

K. G. Ramsay, former Commercial Counsellor at the Canadian embassy in Beijing also says:

1. It is possible sometimes for a member of a tour group to get a business appointment.

2. Don't come with the attitude, "We're going to liberate the Chinese." These aren't Chinese laundrymen you're talking to. They'll ask you questions like "Why did you reduce the number of your employees from 500 to 200 last year?" Be prepared. The Chinese know b.s. when they hear it.

3. The Chinese want specific proposals. Don't give them general statements. However, whatever proposal you make won't be accepted anyway. Do not quote rock-bottom figures. The Chinese like to negotiate.

4. Be patient. If you lose patience, you've lost the negotiating battle.

5. Keep accurate notes. The Chinese do. But no tape recorders. The Chinese use interpreters even though they can speak good English. There is plenty of time to make notes. Record who is present, dates, and what was said. Later the Chinese may say to you, "On such a date you said . . . Why are you now saying . . . ?"

6. There is no need to take your own interpreter—too expensive. Chinese interpreters are competent.

7. A Memorandum of Understanding means two parties have identified a field where there is reason to believe there are grounds for pos-

sible future negotiations, which, if exploited should lead to a possible contract. It is not a contract, even if it mentions prices.

8. If the Chinese give you a welcoming banquet, you should return a banquet. Get advice from your embassy.

9. Gifts must be modest: an appointment calendar or a small calculator. You may want to say, "Would it cause you any embarrassment if I gave you a small token of my esteem . . . ?" Cash is out, but the Japanese have been giving television sets and computers.

To this, let me add that the atmosphere in China among foreign traders is very informal and friendly. Fairs are among the best places to get advice from fellow traders unless you happen to meet a competitor. Try also the Chinese consulate nearest you or, in Hong Kong, China Resources. Your own government's department of trade probably has a free booklet on the subject. If you are in Hong Kong or Beijing, contact the trade representative at your country's mission.

Do take a pile of your business cards. Exchanging them with both hands is now part of the ritual when people meet for business.

China has been improving its communications and constructing industrial buildings, especially in the Special Economic Zones and 14 Coastal Cities. IDD telephone communications, luxury hotels, international airports, branches of foreign banks, new labor regulations, tax breaks, and decentralized decision making are among China's efforts to encourage foreign investment.

Best News Sources on Trade with China: *Asian Wall Street Journal* (daily); *South China Morning Post* (Hong Kong daily); *Asian Wall Street Journal Weekly; Far Eastern Economic Review* (weekly).

Very Helpful: "China Trade Report" (monthly), *Far Eastern Economic Review; The China Business Review* (bimonthly), National Council on U.S.-China Trade; *Business China* (bimonthly); *China Trader Weekly Bulletin; China Briefing* (quarterly and free), Hongkong Shanghai Banking Corporation; *Amcham Magazine* (of the American Chamber of Commerce, Hong Kong, a monthly that focuses several times a year on China); *China Trader,* and *China Daily.*

Also Helpful: *Economic Reporter,* English Supplement; *China's Foreign Trade; Ta Kung Pao Weekly.*

Guides: *China,* Business Profile Service. The Hong Kong and Shanghai Banking Corporation, Hong Kong; anything from the National Council for U.S.-China Trade. Edith Terry's *The Executive Guide to China,* and *China,* by Robert Delfs and Thomas D. Gorman, published in Hong Kong by the Far Eastern Economic Review.

Trade Councils: Established in 1973, the National Council for U.S.-China Trade is a private, not-for-profit membership association of more than 400 American firms engaged in trade and investment with the People's Republic of China. The Council's primary objective is the promotion and facilitation of bilateral economic relations, and its activities include delegations, seminars, and briefings on various topics related to trade with China. Other services provided member firms include practical business assistance, advice on the development and expansion of their trade with China, and up-to-date information through the resources of its library in Washington and offices in Beijing.

The Canadian equivalent is the Canada-China Trade Council, and for the British, the Sino-British Trade Council.

For Australian and other business addresses, see "Important Addresses."

See also *Individually as a Business Person* in "The Basics" and "Introduction."

USEFUL PHRASES

These are designed so you will be able to communicate with people who speak only Chinese. In most cases you need only point to the Chinese and you will get a "yes" (shi de) or "no" (bu shi) answer or a reassuring smile or an attempt to look up an answer from this book.

Read through the phrases at your leisure so you will know what is available. If you think you need other phrases, get a Chinese-writing friend to do them for you.

TRAVEL

Arrivals

I am looking for the interpreter who is supposed to meet me.

我正在找一位翻译，他是来接我的。

He is from————. 他是 ＿＿＿＿＿＿＿＿ 的人。

    C.I.T.S.   中国国际旅行社。

    the Foreign Ministry   外交部

    Foreign Trade Corporation   外贸公司

    Academy of Sciences   科学院

    All-China Sports Federation   中华全国体育总会

    Committee for Cultural Relations with Foreign Countries

        对外文委

    Chinese People's Association for Friendship with Foreign Countries

        对外友协

    People's Institute for Foreign Affairs

        中国人民外交学会

When do I get my passport back?

什么时候能将护照还给我？

Where do I get my checked luggage?

我托运的行李在那里取？

That bag is mine. Please give it to me.

那个手提包是我的。请递给我。

Is there someone here who can carry my bag for me?

有没有人可以帮我拿手提包？

Please call a taxi for me.

请代我叫一辆出租汽车。

How long will it take for the taxi to get here?

出租汽车要多久才能到达这里？

minutes 分钟   hours 小时

Is there a bus I can take to the city?

有进城的公共汽车吗？

How can I get to the city?

我怎样可以到城里去？

City Travel

Do you have a map of this city in English?

你有一张这个城市的英文地图吗？

. . . with city bus routes?   有公共汽车路线图的？

I want to go to ———.   我要去————。

China International Travel
              Service 中国国际旅行社

CAAC office   中国航空公司

Bank of China   中国银行

hotel   旅馆

hovercraft terminal 气垫船终点站

train station   火车站

ferry terminal   渡船码头

airport   飞机场

bus station   公共汽车站

trade center (as planned for
            Beijing) 商业中心（像为北京设计的）

Guangzhou (Canton) Export
       Commodities Fair 广州出口商品交易会

Where can I get a ———? 我在哪里可以叫／乘————？

taxi 一辆出租汽车   motorscooter 摩托车

bicycle rickshaw 三轮车   city bus 市内公共汽车

subway 地下铁道列车

About how much would it cost? 大约要多少钱？

City Bus

What number city bus do I take to go from here to ———?

我从这里到_____应该乘那一路公共汽车？

Please show me where I can get that bus.

请告诉我在那里上车。

Across the street?

过街？

This side?

这一边？

Please tell me where I get off for ———.

请告诉我到_____去应该在那儿下车。

Do I need to change to another bus?

我要不要换车？

What number?

几路？

Taxi

Please drive more slowly.

请开的慢一些。

Please drive faster.

请开的快一些。

Please wait for me.

请等我一会。

I will be about ——— minutes.

我要耽搁_____分钟。

How much does it cost for you to wait?

等我得付多少钱？

An hour?

一小时？

Where will you wait?

你在哪里等我？

I want to be sure there is a taxi for me early tomorrow morning at ———
o'clock. 我要确定能在明天早晨____点种叫到一辆出租
汽车。

Could you order a taxi for me for that time?

你能为我订一辆那个时候要的出租汽车吗？

Buying a Ticket (see also Permission)

I want to buy a ticket to go to ———.

我要买一张到_____去的车票。

One-way   单程   Return 来回

Can I make the return reservation now?

现在我能订回来的票吗？

I want to go ——. 我要在_____走。

in the morning	早晨	in the afternoon	下午
in the evening	晚上	today	今天
tomorrow	明天	the day after tomorrow	后天
next week	下星期	earlier	早一些
later	晚一些	as soon as possible	尽早地
soft class	软席	hard class	硬席
berth	卧铺	seat	座位

What times does it leave?

什么时候开车？

What time does it arrive?

什么时候到？

Where does it leave from?

车从哪儿开出？

Please write that address here.

请你把地址写在这里。

What time should I be there?

我应该在什么时候到那里？

How much is it?

多少钱？

Do you have a schedule in English?

你有一个英语时间表吗？

Cancellations

Do you think someone might cancel a ticket later?

你想等一等会有人退票吗？

Could I take his place?

能把他的位子给我吗？

When should I try again?

我应该什么时候再来问？

Can I exchange this reservation for another time?

我能把订的这张票换一个别的时间的吗？

Is there a service charge?

要付服务费吗？

I would like to cancel this ticket and get a refund.

我想把这张票退掉。

If I wait here, is there a possibility I can get a ticket?

如果我等在这里，有可能买到一张票吗？

Someone may not show up.

可能有人不来。

It is an emergency.

这是一个紧急情况。

(For waiting list, see Hotel section of this chapter.)

Private Car

Checkpoint 检查站

Do you have permission to pass here?

你有通行证吗？

I didn't know we needed permission.

我不知道我们需要办通行证。

I didn't see a sign.

我没有看见牌子。

We are only sightseeing.

我们只是在观光。

We are traveling from —— to——.

我们是从 _____ 旅行到_____ 。

We are lost.

我们迷路了。

Could you please tell me how to go from —— to ——?

请告诉我从_____到_____怎么走。

How far is it from here?

从这里去有多远？

Please mark where we are now on this map.

请在地图上把我们现在所在的地方做个记号。

Please draw a map for us.

请给我们画个地图。

here   there

这里   那里

Do you have a telephone?

你有电话吗？

We are ——. 我们是。_____。

　　　diplomats 外交官
　　　guests of the China International Travel Service

　　　　　　　中国国际旅行社的客人

　　　Overseas Chinese 华侨
　　　foreign experts 外国专家

Where can we find a(n) —— 哪里有_____?
　　　gas station? 加油站
　　　restaurant? 饭馆

lavatory?　　　厕所

hotel?　　　　旅馆

English-speaking person? 会说英语的人

Please circle the location on this map.

请在这个地图把那个位置圈一下。

Permission

Is permission necessary?

需不需要先申请？

Do I need permission to come back to this city?

再回这个城市我还需要先申请吗？

Where do I get permission to go there?

到哪里办申请？

Please write that address down here.

请把地址写在这里。

Alien Permit

Where is the office of the Security Police? I want to get permission to go to the following cities:

公安局在哪里？我要申请到以下几个城市去：

When?　　　什么时候？

Passport?　护照？

What hotel are you staying in? 你住在哪一个旅馆？

Who invited you to China? 谁邀请你来中国的？

Come back tomorrow.　请明天再来。

Come back in two days.　两天后再来。

What time?　　　什么时间？

Is there any charge?　要付钱吗？

Departures (see also City travel)

Is it time to board yet?

还不该上车吗？

Which platform?

哪一个站台？

Which coach?

哪一辆车箱？

Where is the ———?

_____在哪里？

waiting room　　　候车室

schedule in English 英语时间表

restaurant　　　　餐馆

retail store   商店

ticket   车／船／飞机票   passport   护照

customs declaration form

海关报税单

foreign exchange receipt

外汇兑换收据

identification badge

身份证章

Lost and Found

I have lost my———,

我的_____丢了。或：我找不到我的_____。

spouse	丈夫／妻子	luggage	行李
tour group	旅行团	watch	手表
glasses	眼镜	wallet	皮夹子
umbrella	伞	camera	照像机
purse	钱包	tape recorder	录音机
typewriter	打字机	shoe	鞋
luggage wheels	推行李的小车	package	包裹

Have you seen it? 你看见了吗？

Is there a lost-and-found here? 这儿有失物招领柜吗？

If someone finds it, could you

please mail it to me at this address?   如果有人找到了，
请寄到这个地址给我。

HOTEL

General Information

Where do I register? 我在哪儿登记？

I have a reservation for today. 我已经订了今天的房间。

single 单人房   double 双人房   suite 套房

——— persons_____个人。

cheapest   最便宜的   whatever is available

most expensive   最贵的   不管有什么都行

old wing   老厅   in between 中间的

private bath or shower 私人浴室或淋浴   new wing   新厅

air-conditioned   有冷气的   not air-conditioned 没有冷气的

better view   看出去风景较好的。

Can I wait in the lobby until a room is available?

我在前门大厅等到有房间空出来行不行？

Please put me on the waiting list.

请把我的名字登记上。

I will check with you tomorrow morning.
明天早上我再来问。

I would like to make a reservation for a future date.
我想订一个房间。

I am looking for a friend.
我在找一个朋友。

Please show me the registration forms so I can find his room number.
请将登记本给我查一下他的房间号数。

His nationality?
他的国籍？

Is there someone to carry my bags to my room?
有人帮我把行李拿到房间里去吗？

Where is ———?
_____ 在哪儿？

barber shop	理发店
hairdresser	理发师
masseur	按摩师
bank	银行
post office	邮局
cable office	电报局
Telex	用户电报
clinic	诊疗所
retail store	零售商店
bar	酒吧间
coffee shop	咖啡馆

When does it open? 什么时候开门？
When does it close? 什么时候关门？

Do you have ———? 你有_____吗？ Where? 在那里？

ping-pong	乒乓
billiards	台球
badminton	羽毛球
racket	拍子
bird	羽毛球
net	球网
volleyball	排球
swimming pool	游泳池
hot spring	温泉
nearby park for jogging	附近可供步行锻练的公园
scales for weighing luggage	秤行李用的磅秤

English-language newssheet (Xin Hua)

新华社英语报纸

Chinese newspaper

中国报纸

typewriter

打字机

meeting room for ——— people

———人开会用的会议室

professional photographer

职业摄影师。

simultaneous translation equipment

同声翻译设备

interpreter

翻译

movie projector   放影机

    35 mm.   35 毫米

    8 mm.   8 毫米

    super 8   超 8

  slide projector   幻灯机

  tape recorder   录音机

    spool   录音胶带

    cassette   暗盒

    8-track   八声道

  microphone   扩音机

  megaphone   传声筒

  refrigerator   冰箱

  freezer   致冷器

What is the rental price?

租金多少？

Can you organize a cocktail party for ——— people?

你能为———人安排一个鸡尾酒会吗？

Please show me the room.

请你让我看看那个房间。

How much for hors d'œuvres and canapes?

小吃多少钱？

How much for liquor?

酒多少钱？

How much if we supply our own liquor and you supply the ice and glasses,
waiters, and bartender? 我们带自己的酒，你供应冰块、
玻璃环、服务员和酒吧间招待员，要多少钱？

What is your cable address?

你的电报挂号是什么？

What is your telephone number?

你的电话号码是什么？

Dining Room

Where is the dining room?

餐厅在哪里？

Chinese food

中餐

Western food

西餐

upstairs?

楼上

downstairs?

楼下

What time does it open? close? 餐厅什么时候开？关？

Laundry

If I give you my laundry now when will it be done?

如果我现在把要洗的东西给你，什么时候可以洗好？

I must have it by tomorrow morning. I am leaving at ———.

我明天早上一定要。我＿＿＿＿点钟动身。

Where is my laundry? I gave it to the attendant yesterday and he promised to have it done now. 我交去洗的东西在哪里？

我是昨天交给服务员的，他答应我现在可以洗好。

man's	男人的
woman's	女人的
child's	小孩的
shirt	男式衬衫
trousers	长裤
blouse	女人衬衫
underpants	内裤
undershirt	内衣
socks	短袜
dress	衣裙
pajamas	睡衣
tie	领带
suit (man's)	西装
dry cleaning	干洗

I am leaving this morning.	我今天早上走。
I don't have anything else to wear.	我没有别的衣服可穿了。
I need it today.	我今天要。
I need it right now.	我现在就要。

Rooms

There are mosquitoes in this room. Can you give me an incense coil to burn?

这个房间里有蚊子。你能给我一盘蚊香吗？

Do you have a mosquito net?

你有蚊帐吗？

extra blanket?

你还有毯子吗？

Please give me some hot water in a thermos.

请给我一暖瓶热水。

I need enough hot water for a bath.

我需要足够洗一个澡的热水。

Please bring me ———. 请给我拿＿＿＿＿来。

ice	冰	beer	啤酒	tea	茶
orange soda	橘子汽水	Coke	可口可乐	glasses	玻璃杯
cup	杯子	towel	毛巾	soap	肥皂
clean	干净的	fan	电风扇／扇子		

Something is broken in my room. 我房间的＿＿＿＿坏了。

toilet	厕所	light	电灯
telephone	电话	chair	椅子
bed	床	air conditioner	冷气机
fan	电风扇	mosquito net	蚊帐
television	电视机	radiator	暖气

There isn't enough heat. 不够热

This is dirty. 这个不干净

Could someone fix it immediately?

能叫人立刻来修吗？

No. 不能   Yes. 能   I will try. 我试试看

I will ask my director.

我问一下主任。

Can I get a discount on my room if it is not fixed before I leave?

如果在我离开以前没有修好，我是否可以少付房钱？

Can I have a hot water bottle?

能给我一个热水袋吗？

Telephones

How do I get an outside line on the telephone?

我怎样打外线电话？

Please telephone this person and ask him/her to meet me at the hotel

请你给这个人打一个电话，让他／她在_____点钟到

at ——— o'clock. My name is ——— and my room number

旅馆来找我。我叫_____住在_____号房间。

is———.

I would like to make an international telephone call.

我想和国外通一个电话。

I would like to call long distance in China.

我想打个中国国内的长途电话。

Can I take it in my room?

我能在我房间里接吗？

Can I pay for it with a credit card?

我能用信用卡付款吗？

collect call

收话人付款的长途电话。

FOOD

Banquets 宴会

(Arrangements can be made at service counter at hotel.)

Can you recommend a good restaurant for me?

你能推荐一家好的餐馆吗？

One noted for good food, moderate prices. I don't care what it looks like.

一家菜闻名，而价钱公道的，我不在乎餐馆的样子
如何。

One noted for beautiful surroundings and good food.

一家环境优美，菜又好的餐馆。

Could you please make a reservation for me for ——— people

a. at ——— each. b. The chef can decide the menu.

请你代我订_____人一桌的菜。每人_____元的。
菜单由厨师决定。

Yes, I understand we have to pay extra for drinks.

对，我知道喝的要另外算。

Can we bring our own bottles of liquor?

我们能自己带酒吗？

Is it possible to include one dish of ——— for that price?

这个价钱能不能有个_____菜？

Please make the reservation for ——— o'clock
请代我订在＿＿点钟。

today.	今天
tomorrow	明天
the day after tomorrow.	后天

Please write down the name and address for the taxi driver.
请将名字和地址写给司机。

Small Noodle or Bun Shops (food is usually in sight)

I understand Foreign Friends and Overseas Chinese do not have to give ration coupons.
我听说外国朋友和华侨不需要给粮票。

Please, I would prefer to stand in line with everyone else.
啊，我愿意和大家排在一起。

Hotel Dining Rooms and Other Restaurants

I am in a hurry.   我有急事，请你快一点。

Please bring me ———.请给我＿＿＿＿＿。

a bowl of noodle soup	一碗汤面
fried noodles	炒面
fried rice	炒饭
an assortment of meat dumplings	肉馅饺子／馄饨
a dish of meat	一盘肉菜
anything that can be	
prepared quickly	任何快餐都行。

I would like a Chinese breakfast. 我要一份中式早餐

rice congee	大米粥	baked buns	烧饼
pickles	泡菜	oil sticks	油条
salted eggs	咸蛋	dim sum	点心
peanuts	花生米	soy milk	豆浆
tea	茶		

I would like a Western breakfast. 我要一份西式早点

fruit or juice	水果或水果汁		
toast or buns	烤面包或小园面包		
eggs	鸡蛋	butter	黄油
bacon or ham	咸肉或火腿	coffee	咖啡
jam	果酱	milk	牛奶
sugar	糖		

If you have a menu in English, please bring it.
如果你有英语菜单，请拿给我看一看。

What do you recommend that is good but not expensive?

你可以介绍什么好而又不贵的菜吗？

What is the specialty of this restaurant?

这里的特菜是什么？

Please bring enough food for one person.

请你给够我一个人吃的饭菜。

Please bring enough food for all of us. Total cost no more than ——— per person.

请你给够我们大家吃的饭菜，每人不超过_____。

Please bring me one order of———.

请你给我一份_____。

beef	牛肉	vegetables	菜蔬
chicken	鸡	celery cabbage	芹菜
pigeon	鸽子	green beans	青豆
goose	鹅	green onions	葱
pork	猪肉	bean sprouts	豆芽
fish	鱼	bamboo shoots	竹笋
crab	螃蟹	water chestnuts	荸荠
lobster	龙虾	watercress	水芹菜
shrimp	虾	cabbage	白菜
sea cucumber (or slug)	海参	mushrooms	蘑菇
bean curd	豆腐	cloud's ears (fungus)	银耳
Beijing (Peking) duck	北京鸭	pine nuts	松子
duck	鸭子		
monkey	猴子	cashews	槚如树果
snake	蛇	peanuts	花生
dog	狗	walnuts	核桃
frogs' legs	蛙腿	eggs	蛋
civet cat	香猫	caviar	鱼子
turtle	甲鱼	hors d'œuvre	小吃
lotus seed	莲子	black or yellow bean	黑或黄豆
heart	心	gizzard	胗
liver	肝	kidney	腰子
brains	脑	spareribs	排骨
hocks	蹄膀	tongue	舌
steak	牛排	fillet (boneless)	里几子
slices	肉片	balls	丸子
soup	汤	stomach	肚子

minced	剁碎的	shark's fins	鱼翅
bird's nest	燕窝		

stir-fried	快炒	roasted	烤
deep-fried (in batter)	炸(裹鸡蛋面)	cooked in wine	酒焖的
poached	烫熟的	barbecued	烧烤
steamed	蒸的	baked	烘烤
fried in paper	包纸炸的	baked in mud	泥烤
scrambled	炒	baked in salt	盐烤
boiled (hard)	煮（老的）	boiled (soft)	煮（嫩的）

sweet and sour sauce	糖醋汁		
hoisin sauce	甜面酱	bland	淡的
oyster sauce	牝蛎酱	no salt	无盐的
soy sauce	酱油	sour	酸
mustard	芥茉	spicy hot	麻辣
hot pepper	辣椒	sweet	甜糖
plum sauce	梅子酱	no sugar	无糖
sesame oil	芝麻油／香油	salty	咸
peanut oil	花生油	1000-year-old eggs	皮蛋
coriander	芫荽	white rice	白米饭
honey	蜂蜜	ginger	薑
salt	盐	garlic	蒜
vinegar	醋		

canned	罐头的	fresh	新鲜的
sweet cakes	甜饼	apples	苹果子
bananas	香蕉	oranges	橘子
apricots	杏子	plums	李子
olives	橄榄	kumquats	金橘
pomelo	柚子	lichees	荔枝
pineapple	菠萝		

What kind of tea do you have?

你们有什么茶？

jasmine	茉莉花茶	lung ching	龙井茶
woo lung	乌龙茶	bo ni	普洱茶
chrysanthemum	菊花茶	ginseng	人参茶

milk (hot)	热牛奶	milk (cold)	冷牛奶
unsweetened	未加糖的	soft drink	
beer	啤酒	Coca Cola	饮料
red wine	红酒	fruit juice	可口可乐
white wine	白酒	fermented	果子汁
mao tai	茅台酒	mare's milk	发酵的马奶
mineral water	矿泉水	buttered tea	油茶
cold drinking water	冷开水	cocoa	可可

This tastes terrible. Please bring me something else.

这个很难吃／喝。 请给我来点别的。

Enough! 够了！

We cannot eat any more. Please cancel the other dishes.

我们吃不下了，请把别的菜取消罢！

Western food

西餐

bread	面包	hot dog	热狗
sandwich	三文治	hamburger	面包夹牛肉饼
ice cream	冰淇淋	popsicle	冰棍

Please write down the name of this dish so I can order it again.

请将这个菜名写下来，我以后好再要。

I am a strict vegetarian. I would like to order a dish of only vegetables, cooked in vegetable oil. What do you recommend?

我是一个真正的素食者。我想要一个素油炒的蔬菜。你能给我介绍几个这样的菜吗？

I am a Moslem. I do not eat pork or anything cooked in lard. What do you recommend?

我信伊斯兰教。我不吃猪肉或猪油烧的东西。你有什么我可以吃的呢？

I am a diabetic. I cannot eat anything with sugar in it.

我有糖尿病，我不能吃任何有糖的东西。

TELEPHONE (see also Hotel Telephones)

Finding a Public Telephone

Please show me where I can find a telephone.

请告诉我哪里有电话？

How much for using the telephone?

打一次电话多少钱？

Can you find out the telephone number for ——?

你能帮我找一找 _____ 的电话号码吗？

the China International Travel Service in this city?

这里的中国国际旅行社？

the CAAC office in this city?

这里的中国航空公司？

someone who speaks English?

会说英语的人。

Please telephone this person. I want to talk to him.

请给这个人打一个电话。我要和他说话。

I want to make ——.   我要一个 _____ 。

a long-distance call in China 中国境内的长途电话。

an international telephone call 国际长途电话。

Can I take the call in my room?

我能在我房间里接吗？

Can I pay for it with a credit card?

我能用信用卡付款吗？

collect call

收话人付款的长途电话。

How long will it take?

要多久可以接通？

EMERGENCIES

If Lost

Help!   救命！

Excuse me. 对不起。

I am lost. Which way to this
address?

我迷路了，到这个地址去走那一条路？

the closest hotel?

最近的旅馆在哪里？

the nearest English-speaking person?

在哪个最近的地方可以找到会说英语的人？

Can you ask someone to take me there?

你能叫人带我去吗？

I am very tired.

我很累。

Please don't push me.

请不要推我。

Where can I find a telephone?

哪里有电话？

Embassies

Please contact the embassy of ———.

请你和_____大使馆接个电话。

I will speak to them on the telephone.

我要和他们说话。

Please tell their representative to come here.

请告诉他们的代表到这儿来。

Australia	澳大利亚
Belgium	比利时
Britain	英国
Canada	加拿大
France	法国
India	印度
Indonesia	印尼
Italy	意大利
Japan	日本
Malaysia	马来西亚
Mexico	墨西哥
Netherlands	荷兰
New Zealand	新西兰
Pakistan	巴基斯坦
Philippines	菲律宾
Portugal	葡萄牙
Singapore	新加坡
Spain	西班牙
The Federal Republic of Germany	德意志联邦共和国
The German Democratic Republic	德意志民主共和国
Switzerland	瑞士
Thailand	泰国
U.S.A.	美国

Miscellaneous Emergencies

Stop, please.

请停下来。

I need a lavatory. Please show me the closest one.

我需要上厕所。请告诉我最近的一个在哪里。

women's	女人的 （如指厕所则是：女厕）
men's	男人的　　　　　　　　　男厕
Stay away!	站开点！
Danger!	危险！
Run away!	跑开！
Follow me!	跟着我！
Please hurry!	快些！
air attack	空袭
air-raid shelter	防空洞
boat sinking	船在沉
Fire!	失火了！
Explosion!	爆炸了！
Earthquake!	地震了！

Get outside, away from falling debris.

到外面去，躲开掉下来的碎砾。

Riot!	暴动！
accident	意外。
flood	水灾。

Please call someone who speaks English.

请叫一位能说英语的来。

Please call the China International Travel Service.

请叫中国国际旅行社的人来。

Medical Emergencies

Is anyone hurt? 有人受伤吗？

Is there someone here who can help us?

这里有那一位能帮助我们吗？

Please ask people to stand back and give us some air.

请你叫人们靠后站，使我们能吸到些空气。

Please call a doctor.

请叫一位医生来。

Please bring ———. 请你拿＿＿＿＿来。

blanket	一床毯子
stretcher	一个担架
oxygen	氧气
ice	冰
splints	夹板
bandages	绷带
drinking water	喝的水

Stop the bleeding.	止血
Call an ambulance.	叫救护车来
Get him to a hospital.	送他去医院
Hurry.	快！
Help him breathe.	帮助他呼吸
A bone caught in the throat.	喉咙里卡了一根骨头。
Help him lie down.	帮他躺下。
Raise his head.	把他的头抬起来。
Lower his head.	把他的头放下去。
Raise his feet.	把他的脚抬起来。
Give heart massage.	给他按摩心脏。
Give mouth-to-mouth resuscitation.	做口对口的呼吸急救。
Get him cool.	让他凉快凉快。
Fan him.	给他扇一扇。
appendicitis	阑尾炎
bleeding	流血
Broken bone. Do not move it.	骨头断了，不要挪动。
burn	烧伤
diabetic	糖尿病
drowned	淹了
drunk	喝醉了
epileptic fit	癫痫发作
heart attack	心脏病发作
high fever	高烧
insect bite	虫咬了
poisoned	中毒了
snake bite	蛇咬了
stroke	中风
vomit	呕吐

Medical (see also Medical Emergencies)

Where can I find a doctor to treat this ———?

在哪里能找到一位医生治这＿＿＿？

itch	痒
pain here	这儿痛
bleeding here	这儿流血
common cold	受凉感冒
diarrhea	腹泻
cough	咳嗽
headache	头痛

fever 发烧
difficulty in breathing 呼吸困难
hives 荨麻疹
sore throat 喉咙痛

acupuncture 针刺治疗
compress 纱布垫
injection 打针
soak 浸湿
bandage 用绷带包扎
Go to the hospital. 去医院
How long bed rest? 要卧床多久？
When can he continue on his
journey? 他什么时候可以继续旅行？
What is his temperature? 他的体温是多少？
What is that in Fahrenheit? 华氏多少度？
Is it a high fever? 体温高吗？
Is it normal? 正常不正常？

Dental

dental 牙齿的。
I have a pain here. 我这儿痛。
I think I have lost a filling. 我想我有一个牙齿的充填物掉了。
Can you give me a temporary
filling? 能给我临时补一下吗？
Please do not pull out the tooth. 请不要把那个牙拔掉。
Please pull out this tooth. 请把这个牙拔掉。
Can you give me something to ease
the pain? 你能给我什么止痛的药吗？

Pharmacy (see also Medical)

traditional Chinese herbal medicine 中国草药
Western medicine 西药
allergy to antibiotics 对抗生素过敏
aspirin 阿司匹灵
insulin for diabetic 治疗糖尿病的胰岛素。
How many teaspoons a day? 一天服几匙？
How many times a day? 一天服几次？
How many pills? 几丸？
For how long? 服多久？
How much water? 多少水？

Boil and drink like tea?	熬后像喝茶一样喝下去吗？
All of it?	全喝吗？
With sugar?	加糖吗？
Is it bitter?	苦不苦？
Any more injections?	还要打针吗？
aphrodisiac	催欲剂
ginseng	人参
sea horse	海马
pearl	珍珠
sleeping pill	安眠药
snake	蛇
insects	昆虫
herb	草药
mineral	矿石
animal	动物
deer horn	鹿角

WEATHER

What is the temperature today?	今天的温度是多少？
Is it hot?	今天热吗？
cold?	冷
rainy?	有雨
snowing?	下雪
sunny?	晴
Do I need to take a ———?	我需要带_____。
coat	一件外套
sweater	一件毛衣
umbrella	一把伞
swimming suit	游泳衣
suntan lotion	一瓶防晒油

RENTALS

Where can I rent a ———?	哪里可以租_____？
bicycle	一辆自行车
rowboat	一条划艇
tennis racket	一个纲球拍
car (with driver)	一辆有司机开的汽车

How much for an hour? 多少钱一小时？

    a day? 一天？

    deposit? 押金多少？

I will return it in about ——

hours. 我大概在＿＿小时后送还。

CONVERSATIONS

Courtesies

Hello!	你好！	Ni hao.
Good-bye!	再见！	Zai jian.
I'm sorry. (or) Excuse me!	对不起（或）请原谅！	Dui bu qi (or) Qing yan liang
Please.	请	Qing.
Thank you.	谢谢你！	Xie xie ni.
You're welcome.	不客气。	Bu ke qi.
Yes.	是。	Shi de.
No.	不是。	Bu shi.
Maybe.	可能。	Ke neng.
Wait awhile.	等一会。	Deng yi hui.

Please tell me how to say this in Chinese.

请告诉我这个用中国话怎么说。

Please say it again slowly.

请再慢一些说一遍。

Would you feel offended if I gave you a small token of my appreciation?

如果我送你一件小纪念品以表示我的谢意，你会不会不高兴？

It is not necessary.

你不需要这样做。

But you have been so kind and I feel I will be indebted to you for the rest of my life. 但是你对我这样好，使我觉得此生欠了你很大的情份。

It is not convenient.

我不便接受。

In that case, I will not feel offended.

如果是这样的话，我就不会不高兴了。

Meeting Strangers (Please have someone fill in the blanks beforehand in Chinese.)

Hello.

I am sorry, I do not speak Chinese. 对不起，我不会说中文。

I speak English. 我说英文。

My name is ———.	我的名字是_____。
I am from ———.	我是_____人。
I am in China for ——— weeks.	我要在中国_____周。
——— months.	_____个月。
I arrived ———.	我是在_____到的。
I expect to leave ———.	我预定在_____离开。
Please write that down and I will have someone translate it later.	请把它写下来，以后我再找人翻译。
I am visiting ———, ———, ———, ———, ———, and ———.	我将到_____ _____去观光。
Where do you work?	你在哪里工作？
factory	工厂
commune	公社
hospital	医院
office	办公室
restaurant	饭馆
transportation	运输部门
hotel	旅馆
school	学校
cultural organization	文化机构
government organization	政府机构
I am a ———————. (profession)	我是一个_____（职业）
Do you work in this city?	你在这个城市工作吗？
Where were you born?	你出生在哪里？
How many children do you have?	你有几个孩子？
Are they all in school?	他们都进学校了吗？
How old are they?	他们多大？
How much money do you make a month?	你一个月赚多少钱？
How much do you pay for rent?	你的房租多少？
for food?	你吃饭花多少钱？
What hours do you work?	你什么时间上班和下班？
Do you have any relatives in my country?	你有亲属在我的国家吗？
Do you have any friends in my country?	你有朋友在我的国家吗？
How many years of schooling have you had?	你曾在学校读过多少年书？

How much time have you spent doing manual labor in the countryside?

你下乡干体力劳动的时间有多久？

When was the last time and for how long?

你最后一次是什么时候去的，去了多久？

Expecially for People with Chinese Relatives

I am very happy to meet you.

见到你我很高兴。

Could you join me for a meal?

你能和我一起吃饭吗？

For tea? 你能和我一起喝茶吗？

In the hotel? 我们在旅馆里吃好吗？

Then follow me. 那么，咱们去吧！

In a nearby restaurant? 到附近的饭馆去吃好吗？

Do you know of a good place? 你知道有什么好饭馆吗？

Please lead the way, but you are my
guest. 请你带我去，不过让我请客。

Could you please order? 你点菜好吗？

Anything you like. 随便什么你喜欢吃的菜都行。

I don't know how to do it in
Chinese. 我不知道怎样用中国话说。

Not too much. I don't like to waste
food. 不要点太多菜。我不愿意浪费。

Did you know my father? 你认识我的父亲吗？

Did you know my grandfather? 你认识我的祖父吗？

Have you visited my ancestral
village lately? 你最近去过我的家乡吗？

How is it? 那儿怎么样？

Poor? 挺穷吗？

Prosperous? 富裕吗？

Far away? 很远吗？

Just getting along? 还过得去吗？

Can you take me there for a short
visit? 你能带我去看一看吗？

One of your children? 你的孩子？

Can you help me make
arrangements? 你能帮我安排吗？

As soon as possible. 愈快愈好。

When I get back from my tour. 我参观回来的时候。

Should I make the application now? 我要不要现在就申请？

Tomorrow?　明天？

I am sorry I know so little about
you.　我很遗憾对你不够熟悉。

What do you do for entertainment?　你参加什么娱乐活动？

sports?　运动？　　　movies?　看电影？

parks?　去公园？　　visiting friends?　看朋友？

no time?　没有空？　television?　看电视？

How many ration coupons do you
get a month for ———?　你一个月有多少_____？

肉票　meat　　　　　　　　公斤　kg.
粮票　grain　　　　　　　　斤　catties
布票　cotton cloth　　　　　米　meters
油票　cooking oil　　　　　两　ounces
肥皂　soap　　　　　　　　块　bars

Is it sufficient for your needs?　它够不够？

Do you have ———?　你有_____吗？

　　a bicycle　　　　　一辆自行车
　　a sewing machine　一架缝纫机
　　a television set　　一个电视机
　　a fan　　　　　　　一个风扇
　　a radio　　　　　　一个无线电
　　your own kitchen　一个自己的厨房
　　a refrigerator　　　一个冰箱
　　a gas stove　　　　一个煤气炉

Where is the closest school to your
house?　离你家最近的学校在哪里？

　　primary　小学
　　middle　中学

Do your children walk to school?
你的孩子是不是步行去学校？

Do your children take a public bus?
你的孩子是乘公共汽车去吗？

How much does it cost for ———?　_____是多少钱？

　　tuition　　　　　学费
　　room and board　膳宿费
　　university　　　　大学

How many people are there in your household who make money?
你们家里有几人赚钱？

How much money did you all make last year?
去年你们全家的收入是多少？

Do you have any savings?

你们有储蓄吗？

How much did you spend for ———?

你（你们）_____化多少钱？

    clothing   穿

    food   吃

    rent   房租

    entertainment 娱乐

    transportation 交通

    medical expenses 医药

    per month?   一个月？   per year? 一年？

May I see your house?

我能看看你的房子吗？

How many people sleep here?

多少人睡在这里？

Where do they all sleep?

他们都睡在哪里？

Who does the cooking?

哪一位烧饭？

Who takes care of the children while you are working?

你上班的时候，谁照顾孩子？

Do you have a clinic with a full-time doctor nearby?

你们附近有没有一个长驻大夫的诊所？

How much does it cost for a visit if you are sick?

每看一次病要付多少钱？

Do you get your salary if you are sick and cannot work?

如果你病了不能上班，工资是不是照发？

How much does it cost per day in the hospital?

住院一天要多少钱？

How many days maternity leave does a woman get with pay?

有工资的产假是多少天？

If she is nursing her baby, how many hours with pay does she get a day to
feed it? 如果自己照顾婴儿，不扣工资的喂奶时间一天
    有几小时？

How many years of school have you had? 你上过几年学？

    primary   小学

    middle   中学

    university   大学

    technical school   技术学校

    on-the-job training 在职训练

Please forgive me if I am asking too personal questions,

如果我的问题太冒昧，希望能得到你的谅解。

but I am very curious about the way of life in China.

但是我很想知道中国的生活情况。

Are you happy here?

你在这里幸福吗？

Do you like the government?

你喜欢这个政府吗？

Do you want your children to study abroad?

你想让你的孩子到国外去读书吗？

I think I can help you.

我想我可以帮你的忙。

I am sorry I cannot help you.

很抱歉，我不能帮你的忙。

It is very expensive to travel abroad.

出国路费很贵。

It is very expensive to go to school abroad.

到国外读书要化很多钱。

I am not wealthy.

我不是一个富裕的人。

Especially for Villages

What is the name of this ———? 这个＿＿＿＿＿叫什么？

How many people are there in this ———? 这个＿＿＿＿有多少人？

commune	公社？
production brigade	生产大队？
production team	生产队？
live here	在这里生活。
work here	在这里工作。

How much money did you make last year?

你去年的收入是多少？

Can a woman make the same amount as a man if she does the same job—like drive a truck?

男女是否同工同酬？例如驾驶卡车。

How big is your private vegetable plot?

你的蔬菜自留地有多大？

(1 hectare = 15 mou; 1 mou = 10 fen)

Do you raise for your own use ——?

你饲养的＿＿是给自己吃的吗？

    pigs   猪

    poultry   鸡

Did you raise enough meat to sell some on the free market?

你饲养的家畜和家禽除自己食用，还有没有多余的拿到自由市场去卖？

Did you sell vegetables on the free market?

你在自由市场卖过蔬菜吗？

If so, how much money did you make selling your surplus?

你卖了多少钱？

Your household?

这是你的家吗？

How many earners are there in your household?

你家里有几个人赚钱？

How many people are there in your household?

你家里有几口人？

Is there a barefoot doctor in this production brigade?

这个生产大队有赤脚医生吗？

Are there any urban-educated youth living and working here?

有没有城里的知识青年在这里住和工作？

Is there anyone here who speaks English?

这里有人会说英语吗？

Can I meet them?

我能见见他们吗？

Are your grown-up children living in this village?

你的成年子女住不住在这个村里？

If you are sick and unable to work, does the commune take care of you?

如果你病了不能工作，公社照顾你吗？

Your family?   你家里的人？

What if you have no family?   如果你没有亲属怎么办？

Is there a pension when you get too old to work?

你们有养老金吗？

Do you still have ———?　你们还有＿＿＿＿＿吗？
　　　ancestral tablets　　　　　　　祖宗牌位
　　　ancestral temple　　　　　　　祖庙
　　　ancestral family book　　　　　家谱
Do you decorate the graves during the Ching Ming still?
　你们清明还去上坟吗？
Is this pond for fish?　这是养鱼池吗？
　　　　　　　　ducks?　这是养鸭池吗？
May I see your ———?　我能看看你们的＿＿＿＿＿吗？
　　　composting techniques　　　　堆肥技术
　　　irrigation system　　　　　　　灌溉系统
　　　old watchtower　　　　　　　　老的守望塔
　　　retail store　　　　　　　　　　零售店
　　　tractor　　　　　　　　　　　　拖拉机
　　　school　　　　　　　　　　　　学校
　　　house　　　　　　　　　　　　房子
　　　private plot　　　　　　　　　自留地
　　　pigs　　　　　　　　　　　　　猪
　　　source of drinking water　　　饮水源
　　　latrine　　　　　　　　　　　　厕所
　　　clinic—for family planning　　诊所——负责节育的
　　　motorized water pumps　　　　机器水汞
Who takes care of the children while you work?
　你工作的时候谁照顾孩子？
What is the name of that ———?　＿＿＿＿＿叫什么？
　　　tree　　　　　　　　那棵树
　　　vegetable　　　　　　那种菜
　　　building　　　　　　　那幢房子
Please write down the name here in Chinese so I can have it translated later.
　请用中文把名字写在这儿，以后我再让人翻译。

Especially for Factories

How many people work here?
　有多少人在这儿工作？
Salary range a month, i.e., lowest–highest?
　最高和最低的月工资是多少？
How much do most workers make?
　大多数工人的收入是多少？
What is the age range?
　最年轻和最老的工人的年纪有多大？

How long does it take to make one
of those?
　　做一个那样的东西需要多长时间？
　　　　days　　　天
　　　　months　　月
　　　　weeks　　　星期
cooperative?　合作社？
state-owned?　国有的？
Where do you get your raw
materials?　你的原料是从那里来的？
Where do you sell most of your
products?　你的产品大多在那里出售？
Do you have a store where I could buy something like this?
　　你们有出售这样产品的商店吗？
How old are you?
　　你多大岁数啦？
How many years have you worked here?
　　你在这里工作几年啦？
How much money do you make a month?
　　你一个月赚多少钱？
How many hours do you work a week?
　　你一星期工作多少小时？
Do you live in factory-provided housing?
　　你住在厂里给的房子吗？
How much rent do you pay?
　　房租多少？
How many years of training have you had to do this?
　　你经过多少年的训练才能做这个工作？
It is interesting.　　很有趣
　　　　beautiful.　　漂亮
　　　　very difficult.　很难

SHOPPING

For Daily Necessities

What do you recommend for ——?
　　——你说吃什么好？
motion sickness　晕船（晕车）
Do you have any ——?　你有＿＿＿＿吗？
aspirin　　　　　　　　阿司匹灵
toothpaste　　　　　　牙膏

toothbrush	牙刷
razor	剃刀
razor blades	剃刀刀片
toilet tissue	卫生纸
mild soap	咸性不大的肥皂
hand soap	肥皂
laundry detergent	洗衣粉
shampoo	洗头水
sanitary napkins	卫生巾
sanitary belt	卫生带
ball-point pen	圆珠笔
notebook	笔记本
letter-writing paper	信纸
airmail paper	航空信封
envelopes	信封
foreign film	外国胶卷
something to cover this	可以包扎这个＿＿＿的东西。

cut	伤口
blister	水疱

something to keep my shoe from hurting
有什么东西可以防止我的鞋子把这儿磨疼。

an antiseptic ointment or cream
消灾药膏或软膏

menstrual cramps
月经痛

Mending

Where can I get this mended?	这个在什么地方可以修理？
How soon will it be finished?	多快能修好？
Can it be done faster?	能够快一些吗？
I will have it done later.	我以后再修。
Please do it now.	请你现在就修。
How much will it be?	要多少钱？

You may not be here when I come to get it. Please write down here what I should ask for. 我来取的时候你可能不在。请将我要取的
东西写在这儿。

Shopping in General

Please show me on the map where there is a ———.
请指给我看地图上哪里是＿＿＿＿＿。

Please take me to a ——.

请带我到一个_____去。

Please point the way to a ——.

请指给我看到_____怎么走。

How many blocks is it?

要过几条街？

left	左面
right	右面
department store	百货商店
foreign-language bookstore	外文书店
cloth store	布店
Arts and Crafts Store	手工艺品商店
Friendship Store	友谊商店
Chinese traditional medicine store	中国药店
antique store	古董铺
more expensive	更贵一些的
less expensive	便宜一些的
bigger	大一点的
smaller	小一点的

Do you have others the same as this?

你还有这样的东西吗？

Different color?

不同颜色的？

Different design?

不同图案的？

How old is this?

这个有多少年了？

Will I be able to take it out of China?

我能把它带出中国吗？

What dynasty?

什么朝代的？

Can you wrap it so it won't break when I mail it?

能不能把它包好免得会在邮寄时打破。

Where can I have this wrapped and shipped?

哪里可以包装及运出这个？

I'm sorry, I don't have ration coupons.

很抱歉我没有布票。（粮票、工业券）

I was told I didn't need ration coupons.

人家告诉我我不需要给布票。

Will you be getting more within the next three days?

三天之内你们会有更多的来货吗？

Can it be washed in soap and water without damage?

这能用肥皂和水洗吗？

Should it be dry-cleaned?

需要不需要干洗？

Arts and crafts—also for Sightseeing

What is it made of? 这是用什么东西做的？

bamboo	竹子	marble	大理石
bone	骨头	metal alloy	合金
brick	砖	mother-of-pearl	螺母
bronze	铜	palm straw	棕榈
carved	雕刻的	(for baskets and mats)	（编篮子和席子用）
celadon	青瓷		
ceramic	陶瓷	paper	纸
clay	泥	pearl	珍珠
cloisonné	景泰兰	plastic	胶料
coconut	椰子	rattan	藤
coral	珊瑚	rayon	人造纤维
cotton	棉花	rice husks	谷壳
dough (flour mixture)	揉面	rice paper	宣纸
eiderdown	绒毛	satin	缎子
enamel	搪瓷	silk	丝
filigree	金丝	silver	银子
glass	玻璃	soapstone	皂石
glaze	釉料	stone	石头
iron	铁	turquoise	松石
ivory	象牙	wire	铁丝
gold	金子	wood	木头
jade	翡翠	wool	羊毛
lacquer	漆器	animal	动物
lapis lazuli	青金石	vegetable	蔬菜
leather	皮子	mineral	矿石
malachite	孔雀石		
(Animate objects)			

What is it? 这是什么？

banyan tree 榕树

bird 鸟

bodhisattva (Lohan)	罗汉
Buddha	佛
camel (two-humped)	骆驼（双峰）
cypress tree	柏树
dragon	龙
(five-toed imperial)	五爪金龙
dromedary (one-humped)	单峰骆驼
emperor	皇帝
empress	皇后
fairy	仙女
god	神
goddess	女神
goddess of mercy	观音
flames	火焰
horse	马
imperial family	皇室
lion	狮子
leaders	领袖
Mao Tse-tung	毛泽东
Chou En-lai	周恩来
lotus	莲花
Lu Hsun (author)	鲁迅（作家）
mandarin	橘子
monkey	猴子
mountains	山
mountains of Kweilin	桂林的山
mythical animal	神兽
peach	桃子
phoenix	凤凰
poet	诗人
revolutionary hero	革命英雄
Soldier Lei Feng	战士雷锋
Dr. Norman Bethune	白求恩大夫
revolutionary theme	革命题材
e.g., episodes on the Long March	如长征组歌
scales of the dragon	龙鳞
scholar	学者
temple guardian	庙祝
tiger	老虎
tortoise	龟

What language?　哪一国文字？
　　ancient Chinese　中国古文
　　Arabic　阿拉伯文
　　Chinese　中文
　　Manchu　满族文

　　Mongolian　蒙文
　　Sanscrit　梵文
　　Tibetan　藏文

(Inanimate objects)

What is it?　这是什么？
bell　钟、铃
Buddha's footprint　佛的脚印
chariot　战车
cooking utensil　炊具
cosmetic box　化妆品盒
costumes—theatrical　戏装
drum　鼓
fan　扇子
food-serving utensils　餐具
funeral objects (buried with deceased)　陪葬品
gong　锣
house　房子
incense burner　香炉
inkstand　墨水台
jar　坛子
jewelry　手饰
jug　盂
mask—theatrical　戏台用面具
mirror　镜子
moon　月亮
musical instrument　乐器
ornament　装饰品
paperweight　纸镇
pearl (flaming usually)　夜明珠
pillow　枕头
poem　诗
　　by Chairman Mao　毛主席的诗
snuff bottle　鼻烟壶
spirit screen　招魂幡
toilet box　梳妆盒

tool	工具
toy	玩具
vase	花瓶
water buffalo	水牛
weapon	军器
wheel of the law	法轮
wine goblet	酒杯
yin-yang symbol	太极图
calligraphy	书法
carving	雕刻
copy	抄本、摹本、复制品
drawing	画
embossing	浮雕
embroidery	刺绣
engraving	雕刻
etching	蚀刻画
fresco	壁画
handmade	手工的
ink	墨水
machine-made	机制的
original	原本
print	印刷
rubbing	摹拓
scroll	卷轴
sculpture	雕塑品
sketch	速写
watercolor	水彩
woodcut	木刻
woven photograph	丝织像
hand loom	手织机、纺车

Paying

How much does that cost?

那个多少钱？

Please write down that price here.

请你将价钱写在这儿。

That's too expensive

太贵了。

How about half the price?   Na ge do shao qian?

半价怎么样？

How much then?

那样是多少钱？

yuan/kwai/renminbi

元／块／人民币

mao (1/10 of a yuan)

毛（１／１０元）

fen (coin)

分（硬币）

Do you know how much that is in U.S. money?

你知道合成美金是多少？

Please bring my bill.

请把帐单给我。

Do I pay you or the cashier?

我把钱付给你还是付给出纳员。

I am leaving early tomorrow morning. Can I pay the bill tonight?

我明天一早就走。我可以不可以在今晚付帐？

May I have a receipt, please?

能给我一个收据吗？

Can I pay with ———?   我能用_____付款吗？

    a Bank of China traveler's check　中国银行的旅行支票

    a foreign traveler's check　外国旅行支票

    a personal check　私人支票

    a company check　公司的支票

    a credit card　信用卡

BUILDINGS

What is the name of this place?

这个地方叫什么名字？

Please write it in Chinese.

请把它用中文写下来。

What was it before Liberation?

解放前这个地方是做什么用的？

What dynasty was it built in?

它是那个朝代建造的？

What date?

什么年代？

How high is it? 它有多高？

    stories? 多少层？

    meters? 多少公尺？

Can I get a closer look?	我能走近一些看看吗？
Can I go inside?	我能进去吗？
What direction is it?	这是什么方向？

north	北	bei		south	南	nan
east	东	dong		west	西	xi

ancient?	古代的？
minorities?	少数民族的？
imperial?	宫殿式的？
modern?	现代的？
post-Liberation?	解放后的？
revolutionary?	革命的？
for children?	为孩子的？
for workers?	为工人的？
Is it religious?	是不是宗教性的？
ancestral	祖先的
atheistic	无神论的
Buddhist	佛教的
Christian	基督教的
Confucian	孔教的
Lamaist/Tibetan	喇嘛的／西藏人的
Moslem	伊斯兰教的
Taoist	道教的
Is it any of these?	它是这其中的一种吗？
air-raid shelter	防空洞
apartment building	公寓
aqueduct	沟渠
aquarium	水族馆
archaeological site	考古现场
bridge	桥
cemetery	公墓
church	教堂
cinema	电影院
dagoba (Indian stupa)	舍利子塔（印度神龛）
democracy wall	民主墙
drum or bell tower	鼓或钟楼
exhibition hall	展览馆
fort	堡垒
factory	工厂
garden	花园
gate	大门

hotel	旅馆
house	房子
kiln	窑
library	图书馆
military camp	军营
moat	护城河
monastery	寺
monument—commemorative	纪念碑
mosque	清真寺
museum	博物馆
observatory	天文台
office building	办公大楼
pagoda	塔
palace	皇宫
park	公园、楼阁
pavilion	馆、场
playground	操场
restaurant	饭馆
resort	胜地
school	学校
primary	小学
middle	中学
university	大学
shipyard	船坞
shrine	神龛
sports stadium	运动场
stele	石碑
grave	墓
historical event	历史性的
poem	诗
subway	地下铁道
temple	庙
theater	戏院
tomb	墓
train station	火车站
wall	墙
watchtower	瞭望台
water tower	水塔
zoo	动物园

PHOTOGRAPHY

May I take a photo of you?
我能给你拍张照片吗？

Please smile.
请微笑。

Can I have a photo of you and me together?
我能和你合拍一张照片吗？

I would like to show my friends what nice people there are in China.
我想让我的朋友看看在中国有多么友好的人。

I would like to show my friends who cannot visit China what things look
like here. 我想让我那些不能来访问中国的朋友看看中国
是什么样子。

Could you please take my photo in front of this place with my camera?
请用我的照像机给我在这里拍一张照。

It is all set. Just press here. 都对好了，你只要在这里按一下。

Closer 靠近一些。   Back up. 退后一些。

I'm sorry, I don't have any more film.
对不起我没有胶卷了。

I'm sorry, I didn't know I couldn't take photographs here.
对不起，我不知道不许在这儿拍照。

May I have my camera back?
能将我的照像机还给我吗？

Where can I get film developed?
哪里可以冲洗胶卷？

Black and white?
黑白的。

Color slides?
彩色幻灯片？

Color prints?
彩色照片？

Do you cut the film and mount the slides?
你们切装幻灯片吗？

How much for each print?
印一张多少钱？

How long will it take?
要多长时间？

What size film do you have?
你们有几号胶卷？

Do you have any foreign film?

你们有外国胶卷吗？

ENTERTAINMENT

Is there a good cultural presentation on now in this city?

现在这里有没有一个好的文艺节目在上演？

movie	电影	ballet	芭蕾舞
acrobats	杂技	traditional opera	京戏
play	话剧	martial arts	武术
puppet	木偶戏	concert	音乐会
Chinese	中国的	foreign	外国的
English subtitles	英文字幕	sports competition	运动比赛

Where can I buy tickets? 在哪里买票？

What is the address?

什么地方？

I would like tickets ———. 我要_____票。

　　　　for today　　　　　　　今天的。
　　　　for tomorrow　　　　　明天的。
　　　　for the day after tomorrow　后天的。

What are the times? 有那些时间的？

How much do the best seats cost? 最好的座位多少钱一张？

Do you have seats close to the stage so I can take photographs?

有没有靠近舞台可以让我拍照的位子？

How about an aisle seat?

侧厢的座位怎么样？

Is the theater air-conditioned?

戏院有冷气吗？

Is the theater heated?

戏院有暖气吗？

What time is the performance over?

演出什么时候完？

Will you be my guest?

我请你看好吗？

Can you buy the tickets for me?

你能代我买票吗？

Where will I meet you?

我们在哪里碰头？

What time?

什么时候？

I have to cancel my tickets.

我得退票。

Can I have my money back?

能把钱退给我吗？

Would you like to use my tickets instead?

你愿意要我的票吗？

Can we go backstage to meet the performers?

我们能去后台看看演员吗？

I must tell you how very much I enjoyed the performance.

我一定要告诉你我是多么欣赏你的演出。

I hope someday you can come to perform in my country.

我希望有一天你能来我的国家演出。

May I touch your costumes?

我能摸摸你的戏装吗？

May I touch your musical instruments?

我能摸一摸你的乐器吗？

May I take a photograph with you?

我能和你合拍一张照片吗？

Can you show me how this works?

你能告诉我这个怎么用？

How much training have you had?

你受过多久的训练？

At what age did you start?

几岁开始的？

Will you be giving another performance here?

你在这里还将再演出一次吗？

When?

什么时候？

Will it be the same?

还是这个节目吗？

Where is there a dance party in this city?

这个城市里什么地方有午会？

When? What day and time?

什么时候？那一天？几点钟？

How much does it cost?

多少钱？

MISCELLANEOUS

Colors

red	红色	hong se	blue	蓝色	lang se
orange	橙色	cheng se	purple	紫色	zi se
yellow	黄色	huang se	black	黑色	hei se

| green | 绿色 | li se | brown | 褐色 | he se |

Directions

near	近		far	远	
up	上		down	下	
above	上面		below	下面	
inside	里面		outside	外面	
right	右		left	左	
center	中间				

Months of the Year

January	一月	July	七月
February	二月	August	八月
March	三月	September	九月
April	四月	October	十月
May	五月	November	十一月
June	六月	December	十二月

Days of the Week

Sunday	星期天	Thursday	星期四
Monday	星期一	Friday	星期五
Tuesday	星期二	Saturday	星期六
Wednesday	星期三		

Today, Yesterday, and Tomorrow

today	今天	jin tian
yesterday	昨天	zo tian
tomorrow	明天	ming tian

Seasons

| spring | 春 | cheung | summer | 夏 | xia |
| autumn | 秋 | qiu | winter | 冬 | dong |

Terms and Names

attendant (term used for room boy, waitress)

      fu wu yuan   服务员

interpreter (term used for guide)   翻译

cadre (also leading member)   干部

management committee   管理委员会

party member   党员

Communist Party of China   中国共产党

Politburo	政治局
State Council	国务院
peasant	农民
worker	工人
People's Liberation Army	中国解放军
Four Modernizations	四个现代化
agriculture	农业
national defense	国防
technology	技术
science	科学
Is there a campaign on now?	现在有运动吗？
Chairman Mao	毛主席
socialism	社会主义
dictatorship of the proletariat	无产阶级专政
democratic centralism	民主集中制
Gang of Four	四人帮

Numbers

one	一	yi
two	二	er
three	三	san
four	四	si
five	五	wu
six	六	liu
seven	七	qi
eight	八	ba
nine	九	jiu
ten	十	shi
eleven	十一	shi yi

twelve	十二	shi er
twenty	二十	er shi
twenty-one	二十一	er shi yi
thirty	三十	san shi
forty	四十	si shi
fifty	五十	wu shi
hundred	百	bai
thousand	千	qian
ten thousand	万	wan

MILESTONES IN CHINESE HISTORY

The Chinese interpret history in Marxist terms, pointing out that dynasties fell primarily because of peasant unrest and uprisings. Roughly, this is how they see history (here with place names in the new spelling and historical names in the old). See "Quick Reference" for new spellings of dynasties.

c. 1,000,000–4000 years ago—primitive society.

c. 21st century–476 B.C.—slave society. Slave holders owned all the means of production including slaves captured in wartime. Slaves were killed and buried with their deceased owners supposedly to continue their work of servitude in the afterworld.

475 B.C.–A.D. 1840—feudal society. While slaves were kept after the end of the 5th century, slave holders ceased to own all the means of production. A new class of landowners found that giving slaves some freedom resulted in better production. Land was contracted to them as serfs in return for a large part of the harvest. If the serf did not produce, the fields were contracted to someone else. The transition to feudal society took place in the Warring States period, and after 476 B.C. slaves were no longer sacrificed.

1840–1919—semi-colonial and semi-feudal society. Pure feudalism ended with the Opium Wars and the advent of foreign domination. In 1919 the May 4th Movement marshaled anti-imperialist and nationalistic sentiments.

The Chinese also call *1912–1927* the period of the First Revolutionary War, which failed when Chiang Kai-shek betrayed the revolution and massacred the Communists. They also consider this war a failure because of the divisions within the Communist Party itself.

August 1927–July 1937 was the Second Revolutionary War, a period of armed struggle against the Nationalists and the warlords from the first armed Communist uprising to the beginning of the Japanese war.

In July 1937 the Japanese invaded China and there was some attempt at cooperation between the Communists and Nationalists again. After the Japanese surrender in 1945, the civil war resumed. That war and the semi-colonial and semi-feudal society ended with Liberation in 1949. Now is the socialist society.

With earlier dates approximations, the milestones are:

c. 8,000,000 years ago—Ramapithecus (Lufeng, Yunnan).

c. 1,000,000 years ago—Yuanmou Man.

c. 600,000–700,000 years ago—Lantian Man.

c. 400,000–500,000 years ago—Peking Man. (See Zhoukoudian under "Beijing.")

c. 20,000–30,000 years ago—Liuchiang Man (Guangxi), Hotao Man (Inner Mongolia), and Upper Cave Man (Zhoukoudian).

c. 5,000–7,000 years ago—Lungshan Culture (Shandong) and Yangshao Culture (Henan). (See "Xi'an"—Banpo Museum.)

Dynastic dates overlap because different dynasties controlled different parts of China at the same time. Eastern and Western usually refer to periods of the same dynasty with different capitals, e.g., Changan or Luoyang. Northern and Southern Sung refer to the Kaifeng and Hangzhou capitals.

c. 21st–16th centuries B.C.—HSIA: beginning of the slave system; irrigation and flood control work; rudimentary calendar; the earliest form of writing.

c. 16th–11th centuries B.C.—SHANG: earliest glazes, wine, and silk; highly developed bronze casting primarily of ritual vessels; jade handles on swords and spears; ivory cup inlaid with jade; iron; cowry shells used for money; trade outside of China; development of writing; ancestor worship; divination by tortoise shells; beginning of cities (Zhengzhou and Anyang).

c. 11th century–771 B.C.—WESTERN CHOU and 770–249 B.C.—EASTERN CHOU: welded bronze; flat building tiles; first lacquer; copper coins; crossbows; walled cities; elaborate rituals and music using jade as well as bronze vessels.

770–476 B.C.—SPRING AND AUTUMN PERIOD: warring states fighting for power; Confucius preached a return to the Chou rituals and tried to stabilize society by insisting on obedience to the emperor, father, husbands, older brothers, etc. Beginnings of feudalism; cylindrical tile sewer pipes; iron implements and oxen for plowing; steel; metal spade-shaped coins; knowledge of multiplication tables, mathematics, astronomy; medicine.

475–221 B.C.—WARRING STATES: transitional period to feudalism; *Master Sun's Art of War* written; Taoism, Mohism, and Mencius; first large scale irrigation and dams including erosion control; iron farm tools widely used; mining; use of arch in tomb and bridge building; discovery of magnets; carpenter's saw, plane, and square; manure for fertilizer; salt production; medical diagnosis through feeling the pulse; the first books on astronomy.

221–206 B.C.—CHIN: unification of China for the first time; building of Great Wall; standardization of weights and measures; strict legal code; unification of currency; standardization of writing; first clay burial figures; the burning of all historical records except those dealing with the Chin, medicine, and agriculture; the execution of some scholars.

206 B.C.–A.D. 220—EASTERN AND WESTERN HAN: water wheel, windmill, the first plant-fiber paper, seismograph, water-powered bellows for smelting; first important Chinese medical text; the first armillary sphere; the discovery that moonlight comes from the sun; the use of general anaesthesia in surgical operations, and acupuncture and moxibustion; jade burial suits and gold-coated bronze; Szuma Chien, China's first historian.

2nd century B.C.—14th century A.D.—The Silk Road: The Chinese exchanged silk, tea, iron and steel, knowledge of deep-well digging, paper making, peach and pear trees. They received grapes, pomegranate and walnut trees, sesame, coriander, spinach, the Fergana horse, alfalfa, Buddhism, Nestorianism, and

Islam. Trade was with India, West Asia, and even Rome, and the main stops in China west from Xi'an were Lanzhou, Wuwei, Dunhuang, north through Turpan or south through Ruoqiang. Arab and Persian traders settled in Xi'an and Yangzhou (Yangchow).

A.D. 68—First Buddhist temple built by Emperor Han Ming-ti in Luoyang.

220–265—THREE KINGDOMS (Wei, Shu, and Wu): development of a water pump, celadon, and ships big enough to carry 3,000 men.

265–420—WESTERN AND EASTERN TSIN and 420–589—SOUTHERN (Sung, Chi, Liang, Chen) and NORTHERN (Wei, Chi, Chou) DYNASTIES: first arched stone bridge, widespread use of celadon, two crops a year. Northern Wei dynasty started Buddhist statues at Luoyang and Datong.

581–618—SUI: built the Grand Canal (2,000 km. long), ships up to 70 meters long, and an arched stone bridge still in use today (Zhaoxian county, Hebei).

618–907—TANG: one of China's most prosperous and culturally developed dynasties; three-color glazes, snow-white fine porcelains, inlaid mother-of-pearl, gold and silver, wood-block printing, fine silks, the weaving of feathers; water wheel and adjustable curved-shaft plow; attempt at land reform; the most prosperous period of the Silk Road and the opening of a special office for foreign trade in Guangzhou, a city where a mosque was built by Arab traders; cultural expansion—Tang princess took Buddhism to Tibet; Chinese monks took Buddhism to Japan and Korea (Kyoto is modeled on Xi'an); Chinese monk Hsuan Tsang went to India 629–645 to obtain Buddhist sutras. Chinese travelers also went to Persia, Arabia, and Byzantium; Tang poets still the most famous. Look for fat faces in paintings and sculptures—they are most likely Tang.

907–960—FIVE DYNASTIES (Liang, Later Tang, Later Tsin, Later Han, Later Chou): a transitional warring period.

916–1125—LIAO: controlled Inner Mongolia and part of southern Manchuria; invaded China and occupied Beijing; built extant 66.6-meter wooden pagoda, Ying Xian, Shaanxi.

960–1279—NORTHERN AND SOUTHERN SUNG: another of the most prosperous and culturally developed dynasties; first paper money, moveable type, compass, gunpowder, rocket-propelled spears; fine porcelains; red lacquer; the development of acupuncture and moxibustion; progress in mining and metallurgy; Hangzhou, then known as Qinsai, was the largest, richest city in the world.

1038–1227—WESTERN HSIA: controlled today's Gansu and western Inner Mongolia.
1245—Franciscan friars arrived at Inner Mongolia.

1115–1234—KIN (a.k.a. CHIN): captured Beijing and controlled Kaifeng, the Wei River valley, Inner Mongolia, and northwestern China.

1271–1368—YUAN (a.k.a. Mongol): water clock; improved cotton spinning and weaving; developed blue-and-white and underglaze red porcelain; cloisonne; controlled all of today's China and areas north and east including Moscow, Kiev, Damascus, Baghdad, and Afghanistan.

1275–92—Marco Polo visited China, serving in court of Kublai Khan.

1368–1644—MING: imported corn, potato, tobacco, peanut, sunflower, tomato (seeds that is) from America; refined blue-and-white porcelain; polychrome porcelain; sea links with Malacca, Java, Ceylon, East Africa; opium first introduced as a narcotic.

1513—First European to south China—Jorge Alvares of Portugal.

1557—Macao "lent" to the Portuguese.

1582—First Christian missionary, Matteo Ricci, S.J., to Macao and then in *1601* to Beijing.

1623—Dutch colony in "Formosa," a.k.a. Taiwan—until 1662.

1644–1911—CHING (a.k.a. Manchu): made some of the best porcelains in early part of dynasty; had to cope most with foreign powers; Cheng Cheng-kung, a.k.a. Koxinga, drove out Dutch from Taiwan; expanded into Russia, Korea, Vietnam, Burma, Sikkim at first, but later lost a great deal of territory.

1683—Taiwan became part of China.

1757—All foreign trade in south confined to Chinese trading associations (Cohongs) in Guangzhou (Canton). Families of foreign traders live in Macao.

1784—First U.S. trading ship, *Empress of China*—Guangzhou.

1793—First British mission—Lord Macartney.

1807—First Protestant missionary, Robert Morrison of Britain.

1830—First U.S. missionaries.

1839—Chinese attempted to stop opium trade. Burned 20,000 chests near Guangzhou, more than half one year's trade.

1840–42—Opium War, mainly over freedom to trade with China and of course British objection to the government's opium policy. Britain needed to sell China opium to balance trade. British forces with French help seized a few cities along the coast and threatened Nanjing. The Chinese gave in, ceding Hong Kong to Britain and opening to foreign trade Guangzhou (Canton), Xiamen (Amoy), Fuzhou (Foochow), Ningbo (Ningpo), and Shanghai. This was the beginning of the foreign exploitation of a militarily weak, and badly-led China until 1949. Also involved were Germany, Italy, Japan, Belgium, Russia and the U.S.

1841—Uprising of people of Sanyuanli, Guangzhou, against the foreign imperialists.

1844—Treaty of Wang-hsia. First U.S. treaty with China.

1844—Emperor agreed to tolerate Christian churches.

1848–50—Chinese emigration to America and Australia started.

1851–64—Taiping Heavenly Kingdom, a rebellion against the Manchus led by a Christianity-inspired Cantonese who believed himself the younger brother of Jesus Christ. Starting in January 1851 in Jin Ting Village, Guangxi. This was the largest peasant movement in Chinese history. At one time or another it occupied most of China, including Zhejiang (but not Shanghai), Guilin, Suzhou, and almost Chongqing. It established a capital at Nanjing for eleven years, where there is now a Taiping museum. It was defeated in part by a foreign mercenary army led by a British officer Charles Gordon, known as Chinese Gordon, who was later killed in the Sudan. "Taiping" means "great peace."

1856–60—Second Anglo-Chinese War, a.k.a. Arrow war, and more unequal treaties. British took Kowloon.

1860—British and French sacked Beijing, burned down Summer Palace.

1870—China started to send thirty students a year to U.S. to study. Students also to Britain and France.

1870—Tientsin Massacre of French missionaries (see "Tianjin").

1885—French took Vietnam (then a tributary state of China) and turned over Taiwan and Pescadores to China.

1886—British took Burma.

1895—Sino-Japanese War. Japan took Taiwan, the Pescadores, and the Liaoning peninsula from China.

1898—Britain leased area north of Kowloon and about 235 islands around Hong Kong for 99 years.

1898-1908—The Kuang Hsu Emperor kept under house arrest by Empress Dowager Tzu Hsi for defying her and passing reforms that attempted to modernize China.

1899—"Open Door" notes on China, whereby the U.S. unilaterally declared that foreign powers should not cut up China into colonies, that all nations should be free to trade with China. Only Britain bothered to reply, but because of these notes, China looked for a while to the U.S. as its only foreign friend.

1900—Boxer Rebellion, a.k.a. the Rebellion of the Society of the Righteous and Harmonious Fists, a reaction, at times encouraged by the Manchu Empress Dowager, against the increasing foreign domination of China. Attacks on foreigners and Chinese Christians. (See "Beijing.") Foreign powers, including the Americans, responded by capturing Beijing, sacking it, and forcing another humiliating treaty on China.

1904—Russian-Japanese War fought on Chinese soil. A year later southern Manchuria taken by Japanese.

1908—Death of Empress Dowager. Succeeded by two-year-old Pu-yi.

April 1911—Most important of several small abortive attempts by Dr. Sun Yat-sen against the Qing. Huanghuagang Insurrection, Guangzhou.

October 10, 1911—First victory of Sun Yat-sen's republican revolutionists following an accidental explosion in one of their bomb factories. Hankou.

January 1, 1912—Dr. Sun Yat-sen declared provisional president of the Chinese Republic, with its capital at Nanjing.

1912—Outer Mongolia with Russian help declared independence from China.

1913—Yuan Shih-kai elected president of the new republic.

August 27, 1914—Japan declared war on Germany. Under guise of attacking German concession at Kiaochow Japanese troops gained foothold in China, also taking over naval base at Qingdao (Tsingtao).

1915—Yuan agreed to many of Japan's Twenty-one Demands. Much protest. More protest after Yuan proclaimed himself emperor.

June 11, 1916—Death of Yuan in Beijing of heart attack. Warlords controlled country.

1917—China sent coolies to France to dig trenches along Western Front.

1919—Versailles Treaty concluding World War I. Japanese kept gains in China. Western powers retained their pre-war concessions.

May 4, 1919—Student demonstrations against the Versailles Treaty mark the beginning of the nationalistic and cultural upsurge known as the *May Fourth Movement,* the training ground for many Communist revolutionaries.

July 1, 1921—Founding of the Chinese Communist Party in Shanghai with Russian Communist help, although the Soviets, for tactical reasons, preferred to support Sun Yat-sen.

1923—Sun Yat-sen agreed to cooperate with Russian and Chinese Communists. Chiang Kai-shek sent to Moscow for military training. Mikhail Borodin and General Vassily Blucher arrived as advisers. Communists were allowed to join the Nationalist Party as individuals. Sun Yat-sen could not be sure of help from Britain and America.

1924—Chiang Kai-shek established Whampoa Military Academy, Guangzhou, with Chou En-lai in charge of political indoctrination. The Soviet Union voluntarily gave up privileges and concessions in China and recognized Outer Mongolia as part of China.

March 12, 1925—Dr. Sun died of cancer in Beijing.

May 30, 1925—Demonstrations in the International Settlement in Shanghai.

1926—Northern Expedition started out led by Generalissimo Chiang Kai-shek and Whampoa-trained officers with Communist cooperation and Soviet supplies. It attempted to unify China, wrest control from the warlords, and fight the unequal treaties. The Nationalists aimed for support from merchants, landlords, and warlords; the Communists concentrated on the peasants and urban proletariat.

March 1927—The Northern Expedition took Nanjing.

April 12, 1927—Chiang purged Communists in Shanghai. Chou En-lai escaped. Chiang later killed Communists in other cities.

August 1, 1927—Nanchang Uprising. Founding date of the Chinese Red Army. (See "Nanchang.")

April 18, 1927—Chiang declared Nanjing his capital.

September 8, 1927—Autumn Harvest Uprising led by Mao. Miners from Anyuan, some students, peasant cadres, and a peasant militia set out to take Changsha. Ill-prepared, they withdrew to Jinggang Shan (Chingkang Mountains), Jiangxi (Kiangsi), where they met up with the army from the Nanchang Uprising and established the first Chinese soviet, distributing land to the peasants in the area.

June 4, 1928—Nationalists took Beijing, renaming it Peiping (Northern Peace).

1930—Communists unsuccessfully attacked Nanchang and Changsha. Chiang retaliated with three "extermination" campaigns which almost succeeded against Jinggang Shan.

September 18, 1931—Japanese invaded Manchuria and set up puppet government under Pu-yi. Chiang returned to Nanjing to head the defense. With no international help available, Chiang accepted a humiliating truce in 1933.

1933—Chiang renewed attack on Communists on Jinggang Shan with a "scorched earth" policy.

October 16, 1934—The Communists, aware they could no longer hold their base on Jinggang Shan, started out with 80,000 troops on what is now known as the *Long March*. It was not until they arrived three months later in Xunyi (Tsunyi), Guizhou (Kweichow), that they decided on northern Shaanxi as their goal, since that was the only Communist base big enough. In addition, there was the added incentive of being able to fight the Japanese invaders in that area. At that meeting also, Mao Tse-tung took over as leader of the March.

From Xunyi, the march continued in spite of Nationalist bombs and persistent Nationalist pursuers. The major battles were fought at Loushan Pass (February 1935) and Luting suspension bridge over the Tatu River, which forward units had to cross on its three chains under fire, the enemy having ripped up most of the wooden floor boards. There were uninhabited grasslands, snow-capped 16,000-foot mountains, and hostile tribesmen. Edgar Snow gives a good account of the march in *Red Star Over China*. Some of the important battles have been immortalized in ivory or porcelain.

During the Long March, the original Central Army was joined by other Communist armies. It officially ended in Wuqi in northern Shaanxi on October 20, 1935. For the original marchers now reduced to 8,000, including thirty women, it had been a journey of 12,500 kilometers.

From Wuqi, the Communists eventually moved to Bao An where Edgar Snow visited them and researched his classic book. The move to Yan'an was made in January, 1937 (see "Yan'an").

1934—Chinese Communists declared war on Japan but Chiang concentrated on eliminating the Communists.

1936—Xi'an Incident. Chiang kidnapped by one of his own officers at Huaqing Hot Spring and forced into a wartime coalition with the Communists against the Japanese.

July 7, 1937—Marco Polo Bridge Incident. Killing of Japanese soldiers near Beijing set off *1937–45* war between Japan and China. Japan occupied most urban areas. Chiang moved capital to Hankou and finally to Chongqing (Chungking). Western powers remained neutral. Many warlords with their private armies rallied in fight against Japanese. Badly armed, the warlords were destroyed.

Although Nationalists blocked supply routes, Communist Eighth Route Army and New Fourth Army waged guerrilla warfare against Japanese, engaged in political and economic work among peasants, and developed strategy, discipline, and plans for takeover of rest of China. (See "Yan'an.")

1938—Canadian surgeon Dr. Norman Bethune joined Eighth Route Army and died the following year of blood poisoning while operating without antiseptics. Because of his skills at improvisation and selfless devotion to duty, Bethune later became a Chinese national hero. (See "Shijiazhuang.")

December 7, 1941—The U.S. declared war after Japan's attack on Pearl Harbor. It increased aid to Chiang via the Burma Road until 1942, and then via transport planes over the Himalayan "hump" to Chongqing and Kunming. U.S. tried to reconcile Mao and Chiang against the Japanese.

1943—Treaties with U.S. and Britain abolishing concessions and extraterritorial rights. At the Cairo Conference, Chiang promised to make more effort to fight Japan; Roosevelt and Churchill promised more military aid and China's repossession of Manchuria, Taiwan and the Pescadores after Japan's defeat.

February 1945—Yalta Conference declared Outer Mongolia to be independent, Manchuria to be under Russian sphere of influence.

August 6 & 9, 1945—U.S. dropped atomic bombs on Hiroshima and Nagasaki, Japan. Russia invaded Manchuria.

August 14, 1945—Japanese surrender. Lin Piao, leading Communist Army, advanced into Manchuria to receive Japanese surrender. Chou En-lai and Mao Tse-tung met with Chiang in Chongqing.

October 1945—Nationalists and Communists clashed in Manchuria.

November 1945—Chongqing talks broke off. U.S. President Truman ordered end of all aid to Nationalists, because the U.S. would otherwise be involved in a civil war. Civil war continued. Communists advanced because of severe inflation, Nationalist government corruption, breakdown of law and order, mass Nationalist troops defections, and the Communists' exemplary work in winning the hearts and minds of the peasants.

October 1, 1949—Known as *Liberation*. Chairman Mao proclaimed the birth of the People's Republic of China from the Gate of Heavenly Peace in Beijing.

Later Chiang and troops and officials loyal to him fled to Taiwan. Refugees flooded Hong Kong. Communists tried but failed to take offshore islands of Matsu and Quemoy across from Taiwan.

December 1949—Mao visited Moscow.

February 1950—Sino-Soviet Treaty of Friendship and Alliance.

1950—Trials started against landlords. Two million people believed executed. Social reforms instigated. Remolding of intellectuals.

January 5, 1950—Britain resumed diplomatic relations.

1950–1953—Land reform. .15–.45 acres per peasant.

1950–51—Campaign to assert control over Tibet opposed by Khamba tribesmen. People's Liberation Army (PLA) took Tibet, September 1951.

1950—North Korea invaded south. In October, Chinese forces joined North Koreans after United Nations and South Koreans counterattacked north of 38th parallel border and threatened China.

In China, many foreign missionaries, teachers, and scholars jailed and then expelled as imperialist spies. China accused U.S. of poison gas and germ warfare and circulated maps showing American bases surrounding China. U.S. and Canada decided against resuming diplomatic relations.

1951—Americans began an embargo which wasn't lifted until the 1970s.

1953—China started to use Hong Kong and Macao as trading centers and sources of foreign exchange.

1954—Chiang signed mutual defense treaty with U.S.; French defeat and beginning of U.S. involvement in Indochina.

1954–55—Countryside reorganized into cooperatives with pooling of labor and land.

1955—Bandung Conference of nonaligned nations of Asia and Africa to continue "struggle against imperialism and colonialism" and to assert idea of peaceful coexistence. Attended by Chou En-lai.

1955—Khamba rebellion in Tibet.

1956–57—*Hundred Flowers Movement*. Free expression of opinion temporarily encouraged.

1957—*Anti-Rightist Campaign*. Public criticism and jailing of "Rightists," many of whom were not released until 1978.

1958–60—*Great Leap Forward*. Mobilization of masses to increase production; communes established; backyard furnaces smelted scrap metals. Mao resigned presidency to concentrate on this campaign, which apologists claim succeeded because it mobilized the masses. In 1979 the Chinese leadership admitted it was an economic disaster.

August 1958—Chinese attempted to capture Quemoy. Russia refused to give help, except to threaten retaliation if the Americans intervened. Nationalist air force outfought the Communists.

1959—Mao accused Russians of being revisionists, or giving in to capitalism and to nuclear blackmail. Chinese rejected Russia's offer of nuclear weapons in exchange for bases in China. Dalai Lama fled to India.

June 1960—Bucharest Conference. Rift between Russia and China became extremely bitter.

1959–62—Period of extreme economic difficulties due to "natural calamities." Some scholars also blame bad planning. Government insisted on repaying Russians for military aid immediately.

August 1960—Khrushchev ordered end of all Soviet aid to China. Advisers left many unfinished projects and took the plans back to Russia.

1962—Liu Shao-chi became president. Mao chairman of the Communist Party.

October 1962—India asserted control of disputed border territory. China sent punitive invasion force into India. It defeated the Indians and then unilaterally announced ceasefire in November and withdrew.

1963—China started to supply Hong Kong with fresh water.

October 1964—First atomic bomb exploded at Lop Nor testing grounds in Xinjiang (Sinkiang).

1964—Chiang Ching, wife of Mao Tse-tung, started campaign to make culture serve the revolution. Traditional Peking opera abolished. From this time until her downfall, only eight revolutionary operas allowed, all written by committees.

1965—PLA under Lin Piao abolished all outward display of rank.

November 1965—Publication of article instigated by Mao in a Shanghai daily *Wen Hui Pao* brought the Cultural Revolution into the public eye for the first time.

May 25, 1966—First important "Big Character Poster" put up at Beijing University.

July 29, 1966—Chairman Mao swam the Yangtze River at Wuhan (9 miles) to show he was still powerful.

August 18, 1966—First of many Red Guard rallies in Tian Anmen Square, Beijing, in support of Chairman Mao with PLA Commander Lin Piao at his side. Schools closed so that students could travel and learn how to make revolution. From this time until the end of the Cultural Revolution, much violence took place; the British embassy was sacked (August 22, 1967) by a group of extremists called the May 16th Detachment, which also took over the Foreign Ministry and the media at the same time.

The *Great Proletarian Cultural Revolution* was started by Chairman Mao to regain lost power, an attempt to return to his ideals of the Chinese Communist revolution. Supporters of "revisionism" as propagated by President Liu Shao-chi had been promoting, among other things, an intellectual elite and an urban base. One big quarrel was over which incentives to use to increase production: bonuses versus pure political idealism. Liu wanted bonuses. (He was to succeed in 1978.)

Chairman Mao had always taught that the workers and the peasants, not the intellectuals, are the basis of the Chinese revolution. So as Mao regained his power with Red Guard and army help, many party cadres were sent to May Seventh Cadre Schools to be reeducated in the "correct" political thinking by learning to respect and love physical labor. Police chiefs pounded beats; doctors swept floors to help them identify with the masses and understand their problems. Officials who took privileges like personal use of office cars and the acceptance of "gifts" were violently attacked.

Red Guards, riding free on the trains and sleeping in school dormitories while fed by the municipalities, traveled around the country taking part in revolutionary movements such as the "Four Olds." In this, they physically destroyed many religious statues, buildings, ancestral tablets, and opposed many of the old virtues like long life, happiness, and personal wealth. They changed the names of streets and parks from old dynastic names to "The East Is Red" and "Liberation," stripped some women of their tight trousers (it was the style then), and cut off long "bourgeois" hair. They sought to eliminate "old ideas, old culture, old customs, and old habits.'' They also attacked elements of foreign influence. They believed all these were obstacles to completing the course of the revolution. Teng Hsiao-ping was denounced. Liu was deposed in 1968 and has since died. He was officially rehabilitated in 1979.

1967—Communist-inspired riots in Macao and Hong Kong.

1969—Border clashes with Soviet Union. Schools reopened with emphasis on "more red than expert.'' Students were chosen for university, after they completed at least two years of manual labor, by fellow peasants and workers according to level of political consciousness—how well they knew Maoist theory and how enthusiastic and selfless they were in serving the people.

1970—First Chinese satellite launched.

1971—U.S. Secretary of State Dr. Henry Kissinger and U.S. table tennis team visited China. Lin Piao accused of plotting to overthrow Mao, killed in plane crash while fleeing to Soviet Union. Death announced in 1973. China took United Nations seat from Taiwan. Canada resumed diplomatic relations.

1972—President Richard Nixon's historic visit.

1973—Campaign criticizing Lin Piao and Confucius. Teng Hsiao-ping rehabilitated and became Vice-Premier in charge of planning.

1974—Chinese aided Frelimo guerrillas in Mozambique and Angolan guerrillas against Portuguese. Asserted control in Paracel Islands. Seized stray Russian helicopter. One million Soviet troops along border. Russian tanks within 600 miles of Beijing. Teng Hsiao-ping announced Three Worlds policy in speech of United Nations.

1975—Death of Chiang Kai-shek in Taiwan.

January 1976—Death of Premier Chou En-lai. Succeeded by Teng Hsiao-ping (Deng Xiao-Ping) as acting premier.

April 1976—Tian Anmen incident (see "Beijing"). Supporters of Chou put wreaths on monument honoring former premier. Chiang Ching, Mao's wife, ordered removal. Clash ensued. Teng blamed.

July 1976—Tangshan earthquake. China refused all outside help.

September 9, 1976—Death of Mao Tse-tung. Hua Kuo-feng succeeded.

October 6, 1976—Gang of Four arrested. *The Gang of Four,* along with Lin Piao, are blamed for many of the country's ills. They are Chiang Ching, widow of Chairman Mao, and three leaders from Shanghai who rose to prominence during the cultural revolution.

1977—Split with Albania, for many years China's only ideological friend.

August 1977—Teng completely rehabilitated. Resumed previous posts.

1978—Democracy walls flourished for four months.

January 1, 1979—The U.S. and China resumed full diplomatic relations.

February 1979—Vice-Premier Teng visited U.S.

February 17–March 16, 1979—Because of continued Vietnamese "armed incursions'' Chinese forces invaded Vietnam. Border clashes since then.

March 1979—Government bans posters critical of Communists. See "Local Customs.''

January 1, 1980—First of series of new laws on crime and judicial procedures officially came into effect.

1980–81—Multicandidate county-level elections.

1980—Zhao Ziyang succeeded Hua Guo-feng as premier. Leaders tried to improve living standards and eliminate "left deviation, i.e. over-rigid and excess control of economic system, the rejection of commodity production, and the mistaken attempt to transfer prematurely the ownership of all enterprises to the

state.'' Admitted financial deficit. Began economic reassessment and retrench-
ment. Banned all Democracy Walls.
December 1980—Pan-Am flew first direct U.S.-China flight in 30 years. China
protested Netherland's plan to sell two submarines to Taiwan.
1981—Chinese officials stated that Mao Tse-tung's contribution to China out-
weighed his mistakes. China modified the commune system, making the family
the basic economic unit, and diminished the role of the Communist Party in just
about every aspect of life. Chiang Ching (Jiang Qing) and one other member
of the Gang of Four were given suspended death sentences following trials the
previous November. Hua Guo-feng, Mao's chosen successor, was replaced by
Hu Yaobang as Chairman of the Communist Party.

1982—Hua Guo-feng was ousted from the Politburo. The United States agreed
not to increase arms sales to Taiwan; China reiterated that she would use force
to regain Taiwan only if all else failed. British Prime Minister Margaret Thatcher
visited Beijing to discuss Hong Kong's future.

Relations with the Soviet Union started to improve again but China restated
objections to Soviet intervention in Afghanistan and Indochina, and to the large
numbers of Soviet troops near Chinese borders. Relations with the Netherlands
deteriorated even more with a Dutch airline flying to Taipei.

China announced centralized economic controls only for some essential
commodities, and gradual changes in prices based on market forces. Its foreign
trade surplus build-up resulted largely from restrictions on imports. The Chinese
fiancee of a French diplomat was arrested (and later released).

1983—Beijing ordered the round-up of 50,000 criminals and executions of 10%,
in its campaign against the increase in crime. Public sentencing rallies, marches
of condemned criminals through the streets, and posting of photos of executed
prisoners continued the following year.

U.S. Defense Secretary Caspar Weinberger visited, and permitted the sale
of some U.S. military technology to China. The United States grant of political
asylum to a visiting Chinese tennis player disrupted cultural and sports exchanges between the two countries. The American restriction of several categories of textile imports led to Chinese cutbacks on purchases of U.S. cotton,
synthetic fibers, and wheat. Hijackers forced a CAAC plane to fly to Seoul.
Marriages between most Chinese and foreigners were now permitted with one
month's notice. The campaign against ''spiritual pollution'' (immoral foreign
influences) was vigorously pursued and gradually slowed down.

Record harvests took place in spite of a decrease in agricultural lands.
These, along with a sharp increase in cash crops, encouraged the continuation
of the new economic policies. All state-owned companies were ordered to make
a profit and pay taxes. Authorities began to question the decentralization of
economic decision making. Foreign oil companies under joint ventures started
drilling in Guangdong province and the Yellow Sea area.
1984—another abundant harvest, the fourth in a row. Foreign exchange reserves
hit a record high, and China went on an importing spree. The Cultural Revolution was denounced completely. The Communist Party booted out thousands
of leftists. Intellectuals started being sought out and encouraged to contribute to
modernization. Lounges and bars, even in previously foreigners-only hotels,
were opened to all Chinese citizens. The Italian correspondent for *Der Spiegel*
was expelled.

Factories became independent, making their own production and marketing decisions. An American demographer reported 250,000 female infanticides in China since 1979. U.S. President Ronald Reagan visited. China protested the release to Taiwan of Chinese hijackers imprisoned in Seoul. Clashes continued with Vietnam.

Britain and China agreed on Hong Kong's future: It will all revert back to China in 1997. Deng proclaimed a one-country, two-systems policy in dealing with Taiwan and Hong Kong. The Japanese prime minister visited. Premier Zhao Ziyang toured the United States, Canada, France, and Belgium. The rift with the Netherlands was patched up. Foreign Minister Wu Xueqian met with Soviet Foreign Minister Andrei Gromyko at the United Nations.

The Communist Party spelled out its plan for the next three to five years and explained "socialism with Chinese characteristics." China started drafting up bankruptcy laws. The chronic shortage of electricity continued. Local governments and other enterprises were encouraged to build railway lines up to 200 km long.

1985—The riot following China's loss to Hong Kong in a soccer match in Beijing left 30 policemen hurt, 25 vehicles damaged, and 127 arrested. An end-of-1985 deadline was set for firing incompetent managers of state enterprises. Two-hour lunch breaks were reduced to one hour. (Government offices closed one hour earlier, instead.)

A Chinese demographer pointed out that sex ratios in demographic figures do not necessarily mean infanticide, and admitted to a few isolated cases.

Nine aging members of the Politburo resigned to make way for younger leaders, whose average ages are 50–59. Over one million elderly party members also resigned. President Li Xiannian visited the United States and Canada. Unauthorized resale of imported motor vehicles in Hainan Island created a big corruption scandal. Such shopping sprees helped to deplete foreign exchange reserves, and restrictions again were imposed for a few months.

1986—Taiwan negotiated release of its cargo plane hijacked to Canton. Sweden became the first customer for China's satellite launching service. China joined the Asian Development Bank. Some government-owned factories allowed to isue stock.

See also "Introduction."

IMPORTANT ADDRESSES AND INFORMATION

SOME CHINESE MISSIONS ABROAD

	Telephone
Australia	
Embassy of the People's Republic of China	412447
247 Federal Highway	412446
Watson, Canberra, A.C.T. 2602	
Canada	
Embassy of the People's Republic of China	(613) 234–2706
515 St. Patrick St.	234–2682
Ottawa, Ont., K1N 5H3	234–2718
Consulate General of the People's Republic of China	
240 St. George St.	
Toronto, Ont., M5R 2P4	(416) 964–7575
Consulate General of the People's Republic of China	
3380 Granville St.	
Vancouver, B.C. V6H 3K3	
England	
Embassy of the People's Republic of China	(01) 636–5726
31 Portland Pl.	
London, W1.	
France	
Embassy of the People's Republic of China	256.04.24
11, Ave. Georges V	256.20.30
75008, Paris	256.04.25
Federal Republic of Germany	
Embassy of the People's Republic of China	(Bonn) 345051
Konrad Adenauer Allee 104	
5307 Wachtberg-Niederbachem	

519

Italy
Embassy of the People's Republic of China
Via Bruxelles, 56
00198 Roma

Japan
Embassy of the People's Republic of China
4-33, Moto-Azabu 3-chome
Minato-ku, Tokyo   (03) 403–3389

Malaysia
Representative of the People's Republic of China
229, Jalan Ampang
Kuala Lumpur   428495

New Zealand
Embassy of the People's Republic of China   721382
22/6 Glenmore St.   721383
Wellington

Norway
Embassy of the People's Republic of China   44 96 74
Inkognitogt. 11   (Oslo) 44 74 91
Oslo 2, Norway

Philippines
Embassy of the People's Republic of China
2038 Roxas Blvd. (Visa Office), Metro Manila   57.25.85
or 4896 Pasay Rd., Dasmarinas, Metro Manila   86.77.15

Singapore
Office of the Commercial Representative of the People's Republic of China
70–76 Dalvey Rd.
Singapore 1025   7343360

Switzerland
Embassy of the People's Republic of China
Kalcheggweg 10   (31) 447333

U.S.A.
Embassy of the People's Republic of China
2300 Connecticut Ave., N.W.   (202) 797–8909 (visa)
Washington, DC 20008   (202) 797–9000 (chancery)

Consulate General of the People's Republic of China
3417 Montrose Blvd.
Houston, TX 77066

Permanent Mission to the People's Republic of China to the United Nations
520 12th Ave.
New York, NY 10036

Consulate General of the People's Republic of China
1450 Laguna St.
San Francisco, CA 94115

Bank of China
Overseas Offices in London, New York, Singapore, Luxembourg, and Hong Kong.

China International Travel Service
China Tourist Office, 4 Glentworth St., London NW1, England
Office Du Tourisme de Chine, 51 Rue Sainte-anne 75002, France
China Tourist Office, Eschenheimer Anlage 28, D-6000 Frankfurt am Main-1, Federal Republic of Germany
China Tourist Office, 6F Hachidai Hamamatsucho Bl. 1-27-13, Hamatsu-cho, Minato-ku, Tokyo, Japan
China Tourist Office, Lincoln Building, 60 E. 42nd St., Suite 465, New York, N.Y. 10165, U.S.A.

TOUR ORGANIZERS AND TRAVEL AGENTS

Australia

Bannink's World Tours, 11 Hamilton Pl., Mt. Waverley, 3149, Victoria.
Cathay Pacific Airways, Swire House, 8 Spring St., Sydney 2000.
Marco Polo Travel, 45 Dixon St., Sydney 2000.

Canada

Blyth & Co., 68 Scollard St., Toronto, Ont. M5R 1G2.
P. Lawson, 5353 Dundas St. W., Suite 400, Toronto, Ont., M9B 6J3.
Pan-Pacific Travel Service, 166 East Pender St., Vancouver, B.C., VGA 1T4.
Tin-Bo Travel Service Ltd., 123 Edward St., Toronto, Ont., M5G 1E2.

China

China International Travel Service, Head Office, 6, East Chang'an Ave., Beijing. Telex: 22350 CITSH CN. Cable: LUXINGSHE BEIJING. Addresses of domestic branches in "Destinations."
China International Travel Service, FIT Division, Room No. 1302, Chongwenmen Hotel, Beijing. Telex: 22004 CIFIT CN. Cable: LUXINGSHE BEIJING.
China Travel Service and Overseas Chinese Travel Service, 8 Dong Jiao Min Xiang, Beijing. Tel. 550031–271. Telex: 22487 CTSHO CN. Cable: 2464. Try also China Travel Service in Hong Kong.
China Sports Service, 9 Tiyuguan Rd., Beijing. Tel. 754250. Telex: 22238 CSS CN. Cable: SPORTSCHINE BEIJING.

Hong Kong

China International Travel Service (H.K.), 6th Fl., Tower II, South Seas Centre, 75 Mody Rd., Tsimshatsui, Kowloon. Tel. 3–7215317. Telex: 38449 CITC HX. Cable: 2320 Hong Kong.

China Travel Service (H.K.), 77, Queen's Rd. C., Hong Kong. Tel. 5–259121. Cable: TRAVELBANK. *Branches:* 27–33, Nathan Rd., 1/F (entrance on Peking Rd.), Kowloon, tel. 3–667201; 24–34 Hennessy Rd., Wan Chai, Hong Kong, tel. 5–280102; Hung Hom Railway Station, Kowloon, tel. 3–330660; Tai Kok Tsui HK/Guangzhou Pier, tel. 3–929403.

China Youth Travel, Rm. 606, Wing On House, 71, Des Voeux Road, C., Hong Kong. Tel. 5–410975, 5–259075. Telex: 61679 YOUTH HX. Cable: HONSHANC.

Club Med, 3/F, BCC House, 10 Queens Rd. Central, Hong Kong.

Crosspoint Tours, 1101 Bank of America Building, Peking Rd., Tsimshatsui. Tel. 3–7234342. Telex: 50340 XPLOT HX. Cable EXPLORETVL.

Hong Kong Student Travel Ltd., 8/F Tai Sang Bank Bldg., 130 Des Voeux Rd., C, Hong Kong. Tel. 5–414841. Telex: 66347 HKSTB. Cable: HKFSSTB.

International Tourism, 2/F Floor, Burfield Bldg., 143, Connaught Rd. C., Hong Kong. Tel. 5–412011.

Rosalind Henwood, 701 William House, 46 Wellington St., Hong Kong. Tel. 5–232237 or 5–260623.

Silkway Travel Ltd., Rm. 611 Silvercord, Tower 1, Canton Rd., Tsimshatsui. Tel. 3–7241661; 1227A Star House, Tsimshatsui, Kowloon. Tel. 3–7243322; Telex: 36662 SILK HX.

The Travel Advisers Ltd., Room 1006, 10/F, Silvercord, Tower One, 30 Canton Rd., Tsimshatsui, Kowloon. Tel. 3–698321. Telex: 44430 ADVSR HX. (Across from Marco Polo Hotel.) Branches in Swire House and Hotel Regal Meridien.

Travellers Hostel, 16th/F, Chungking Mansions, 40 Nathan Rd., Kowloon. Tel. 3–687710, 3–682505.

United (Tai Shan) Travel, P.O. Box 80748, Cheung Sha Wan P.O., Kowloon. Tel. 3–849269 (office hours); 3–7285267 (mornings and evenings). Sidney Chee.

Voyages Jules Verne, Lee Gardens Hotel, Hysan Ave., Causeway Bay, Hong Kong.

Zhuhai Tours (HK) Ltd., Room 3207 New World Tower, 16–18 Queen's Rd., C., Hong Kong. Tel. 5–232136, Telex: 74493 HMHCO–HX.

Macao

China Travel Service, 33 rua Vis. Paco de Arcos. Tel. 88922.
International Tourism, Rua Da Praia Grande 10B. Tel. 86522, 86298.

New Zealand

Thomas Cook Travel, P.O. Box 24, Auckland.
Globetrotter Tours (NZ), Chelsea House, 85 Fort St., Auckland.
Viva Holidays, West Plaza Building, cnr. Albert and Fanshawe sts., Auckland.

U.S.A.

American Youth Hostels, 132 Spring St., New York, NY 10012
China Passage, Inc., 302 Fifth Ave., New York, NY 10001
Club Med, 40 W. 57 Street, New York, NY 10019
Kuo Feng Corporation, 2 East Broadway, New York, NY 10013; 722 Sacramento St., San Francisco, CA 94108.

Lindblad Travel, Inc., 1 Sylvan Rd. N., P.O. Box 912, Westport, CT 06881.
Mountain Travel, 1398 Solano Ave., Albany, CA 94706.
Pacific Delight Tours, Inc., 132 Madison Ave., New York, NY 10016. (Offices also in Los Angeles, San Francisco, Minneapolis, and Seattle.)
Silkway Travel and Trading, 927 Kearny St., San Francisco, CA 94133.
Society Expeditions, 723 Broadway East, Seattle, WA 98102.
Special Tours for Special People, Inc., 250 W. 57th St., New York, NY 10019.
Voyages Jules Verne, Great Journeys Ltd., 2 W. 45th St., Suite 1009, New York, NY 10036.

SOME CHINESE ORGANIZATIONS WHO INVITE PAYING GUESTS TO CHINA

All China Sports Federation, Beijing.
Chinese Medical Association, c/o Academy of Sciences, Wen Ching Chieh No. 3, Beijing.
Chinese Mountaineering Association, Beijing.
Chinese People's Association for Friendship with Foreign Countries, Beijing.
Chinese People's Institute for Foreign Affairs, Beijing.
Committee for Cultural Relations with Foreign Countries, Beijing.
Foreign Affairs Department, Academy of Sciences, Wen Ching Chieh No. 3, Beijing.
Foreign Affairs Dept., Scientific and Technical Association, Beijing.
Information Department, Ministry of Foreign Affairs, Beijing.

CHINA FRIENDSHIP ASSOCIATIONS

Australia-China Society, 226 Gertrude St., Fitzroy 3065, Victoria, Australia.
Federation of Canada-China Friendship Associations, Box 984, Station "K", Toronto, Ont., M4P 2V3, Canada.
Society for Anglo-Chinese Understanding, 152 Camden High St., London, NW1, England.
Associazione Italia-Cina, 00186 Roma–Via del Seminario, 87, Italy.
New Zealand-China Friendship Society, 22 Swanson St., P.O. Box 3460, Auckland, New Zealand.
U.S.-China Peoples Friendship Association, National Office, 2025 Eye St. N.W., Washington, DC 20006, U.S.A.

FOR SCHOLARS, STUDENTS, AND FOREIGN EXPERTS

Australia

Australia-China Council, c/o Department of Foreign Affairs, Canberra, ACT 2600, Australia.
Australian Teachers' Federation, GPO Box 1891, Canberra, ACT 2601.
Department of Education, P.O. Box 826, Woden, ACT 2606.

Canada

Association of Universities and Colleges of Canada, 151 Slater St., Ottawa, Ont. K1P 5N1.

Canadian Executive Service Organization, Operations Centre, 1867 Yonge St., Suite 200, Toronto, Ont., M4S 1Y5.
Ontario Teachers' Federation, 1260 Bay St., 7/F Toronto, Ont. M5R 2B5.
Social Sciences and Humanities Research Council, 255 Albert St., Ottawa, Ont., K1P 6G4.

China

Foreign Experts Bureau, Foreign Affairs Department, Ministry of Education, 37 Da Mu Cang Hu Tong, Beijing. Tel. 66–1758. It is quicker to write directly to the Office of the President or the Foreign Affairs Office of the school where you wish to teach, as the Foreign Experts Bureau is primarily a central clearing house. Foreign Affairs Division, **Arts Education Bureau,** Ministry of Culture, Beijing. Tel. 44–6571X515 (for teachers in the performing arts).
Foreign Student Affairs Division, Foreign Affairs Dept., Ministry of Education, Beijing. Tel. 66–1917.
International Liaison Dept., **State Science and Technology Association,** Beijing. Tel. 86–8361X714 (for teachers of science and technology.)

England

Education Office of the **British Council,** Clarendon House, Spring Gardens, London SW1.
Great Britain-China Centre, 15 Belgrave Square, London SE1K 8PG.

Hong Kong

University Service Center, 155 Argyle St., Kowloon.

U.S.A.

China Affairs Division, United States Information Agency, Washington, DC 20547.
Committee on Scholarly Communication with the People's Republic of China, National Academy of Sciences, 2101 Constitution Ave., NW, Washington, DC 20418.
Council for International Exchange of Scholars (CIES), 11 Dupont Circle, Suite 300, Washington, DC 20036. (Fulbright).
National Association for Foreign Student Affairs, 1860 19th St. NW, Washington, DC 20009.

OTHER IMPORTANT ADDRESSES

Australia

Australia-China Business Co-operation Committee, P.O. Box 14, Canberra, ACT 2600. Independent body for the promotion of trade between Australia and China and to provide a forum for the exchange of up-to-date material on China.
Australia-China Chamber of Commerce and Industry, c/o Melbourne Chamber of Commerce, 60 Market St., 21st Floor, Melbourne, Victoria 3000. A nonprofit organization to promote trade; to serve as liaison between governments

on trade matters; to assist counterpart organizations in China; to promote social and cultural contacts between the two countries, etc.

Department of Trade, Edmund Barton Building, Kings Ave., Barton, ACT 2600. Ask for booklet.

NSW-ACT Chamber for China Trade and Commerce, Suite 69, 6/F, 104 Bathurst St., Sydney, NSW 2000.

Canada

Canada-China Programme, Canadian Council of Churches, 40 St. Clair Ave. East, Toronto, Ont. M4T 1M9.

Canada-China Trade Council, Suite 900, 199 Bay St., Toronto, Ont. M5J 1L4.

Convention Administrator, Canadian Wildlife Service, Environment Canada, Ottawa, Ont. K1A OE7.

Customs Office, 360 Coventry Rd., Ottawa, Ont. K1K 2C6.

Department of Regional and Industrial Expansion, First Canadian Place, Toronto, Ont. Branches in all provinces.

China

CAAC, 155 Dongsi St. West, Beijing. Tel. 558861.

China Daily, 2, Jintai Xi Rd., Beijing. Tel. 596231.

China Travel and Tourism Press, Room 304, Chongwenmen Hotel, Beijing.

For other addresses in China, see each city under "Destinations," especially "Beijing," "Guangzhou," "Shanghai," and "Shenyang."

England

Sino-British Trade Council, 5/F, Abford House, 15 Wilton Rd., London SW1V 1LT.

Hong Kong

American Chamber of Commerce, 1030 Swire House, Hong Kong.

Asia Travel Trade, Interasia Publications, Ltd., 200 Lockhart Rd., 13/F, Hong Kong.

Asian Wall St. Journal, G.P.O. Box 9825, Hong Kong.

Australian Commission, Hong Kong Harbour Centre, 25 Harbour Rd., Hong Kong.

Bank of China, 2A Des Voeux Rd. Central, Hong Kong.

CAAC, G/F Gloucester Tower, Pedder St., Hong Kong.

Canadian Commission, 14/15/F, Asian House, 1 Hennessy Rd., Hong Kong.

China Resources Co., Causeway Center, Gloucester Rd., Hong Kong.

Chinese Arts and Crafts (H.K.) Ltd. *Branches:* Star House (at Star Ferry Terminal), Kowloon: 233 Nathan Rd., Kowloon; Shell House, Queen's Rd., Central, Hong Kong.

Far Eastern Economic Review, G.P.O. Box 160, Hong Kong.

Holy Spirit Study Center, 6 Welfare Rd., Aberdeen.

Hongkong China Liaison Office, World Division, Board of Global Ministries, The United Methodist Church, 2 Man Wan Rd., C–17, Kowloon.

Hong Kong Tourist Association, Connaught Centre, 35/F, Hong Kong. (Represented abroad by offices in San Francisco, New York City, Chicago, Sydney, London, Rome, Paris, Frankfurt, Singapore, Tokyo, and Osaka, and by Cathay Pacific Airways.)
Joint Publishing Co., Reader's Service Center, 98 Granville Rd., Tsimshatsui East.
South China Morning Post, G.P.O. Box 47, Hong Kong.
Ta Kung Pao—Weekly supplement, 342 Hennessy Rd., 7/F, Hong Kong.
Tao Fong Shan Ecumenical Center, P.O. Box 33, Shatin, N.T.
United States Consulate, 26 Garden Rd., Hong Kong.
Visa Office, Ministry of Foreign Affairs of the People's Republic of China in Hong Kong. 5/F, Lower Block, 26 Harbour Rd., Wanchai. Tel. 5–744163. 9 a.m.–noon and 2–5 p.m. daily. Saturdays 9 a.m.–noon.
Yue Hwa—Chinese Products Emporium Ltd., 301–309 Nathan Rd., Kowloon; 54–64 Nathan Rd., Tsimshatsui.

U.S.A.

Asian Wall St. Journal Weekly, 200 Liberty St., New York, NY 10281.
Bank of China, 410 Madison Ave., New York, NY 10017.
CAAC, 45 E. 49th St., New York, NY 10017; 51 Grant Ave., San Francisco, CA 94108; 2500 Wilshire Blvd., Los Angeles, CA 90057.
China Books and Periodicals, 2929 24th St., San Francisco, CA 94110 (retail and mail orders); 125 Fifth Ave., New York, NY 10003; 37 S. Wabash, Suite 600, Chicago, IL 60603 (hours are irregular—call first, (312) 782–6004).
China Daily Distribution Corp., 15 Mercer St., Suite 401, New York, NY 10013.
Federal Wildlife Permit Office, United States Department of the Interior, 1000 North Glebe Rd., Room 611, Arlington, VA 22201.
National Committee on U.S.-China Relations, 777 United Nations Plaza, New York, NY 10017.
National Council for U.S.-China Trade, 1050 Seventeenth St., NW, Washington, DC 20036.
National Council of Churches, China Program Administrative Committee, 374 Riverside Dr., 6/F, New York, NY 10115.
United States Customs Service, Public Information Division, Washington, DC 20229.

CHINESE CUSTOMS REGULATIONS

Upon entrance every tourist is requested to fill in a Baggage Declaration in duplicate to be handed in to Customs.

Articles for personal use carried by a tourist including foodstuffs to be consumed during the trip, 2 bottles of wine (not exceeding 750 grams each) and 400 cigarettes may be imported duty free. Wristwatches, recorders (including multi-purpose combination sets), cameras and cinecameras for personal use may be imported but may not be transferred or sold privately and are to be taken out of the country at the time of exit. Gifts for friends and relatives or articles carried on behalf of others are to be declared to the Customs.

Tourists should retain the duplicate copy of the baggage declaration issued by the customs at the entry port. Upon exit tourists should fill in the blanks for exit declaration which is to be submitted to the customs for inspection.

Invoices for purchases made in China in reasonable quantities for personal use should be produced to the customs upon exit. Shipped goods are exportable with the export permit which is obtained upon application.

Import of the following articles is prohibited:

(1) Arms, ammunition and explosives of all kinds;

(2) Radio transmitter-receivers and principal parts;

(3) Renminbi;

(4) Manuscripts, printed matter, films, photographs, gramophone records, cinematographic films, loaded recording tapes, video-tapes, etc. which are detrimental to China's politics, economy, culture and ethics;

(5) Poisonous drugs, narcotics and opium, morphia, heroin, etc;

(6) Animals, plants and products thereof infected with or carrying disease germs and insects pests;

(7) Insanitary foodstuffs and germ-carrying foodstuffs from infected areas; and

(8) Other articles the import of which is prohibited by state regulations.

Export of the following articles is prohibited:

(1) Arms, ammunition and explosives of all kinds:

(2) Radio transmitter-receivers and principal parts;

(3) Renminbi and securities, etc. in RMB;

(4) Foreign currencies, bills and securities in foreign currencies (with the exception of those allowed to be taken out);

(5) Manuscripts, printed matter, films, photographs, gramophone records, cinematographic films, loaded recording tapes, video-tapes, etc. which contain state secrets or which are otherwise prohibited export;

(6) Valuable cultural relics and rare books relating to Chinese revolution, history, culture or art;

(7) Rare animals and rare plants and their seeds;

(8) Precious metals and articles made thereof, jewelry, diamonds and ornaments made thereof (with the exception of those which have been brought in and declared to the Customs); and

(9) Other articles the export of which is prohibited by state regulations.

Overseas Chinese with foreign passports can import, duty-free, to be left in China once a year, gifts like 100 pieces of clothing, four bottles of wine, 600 cigarettes, ¥200 worth of medicines, one watch, radio, TV, electric fan, refrigerator, small computer, sewing machine, bicycle, 30 meters of cotton cloth, and ¥300 worth of food stuffs and daily necessities. A Chinatown or Hong

Kong travel agent specializing in Overseas Chinese tours can give you more details.

Duty if levied, is high. You pay ¥600 on a Rolex watch; ¥275 on a Chinese-made 12–15-inch color television, ¥350 on a similar foreign-made one. If you don't want to pay the duty, leave the item with Customs and pick it up on the way out.

BIBLIOGRAPHY

Ahrens, Joan Reid and Malloy, Ruth Lor. *Gems & Jewellery in Hong Kong—A Buyer's Guide*. Hong Kong: South China Morning Post, 1984.

Barber, Noel. *The Fall of Shanghai*. New York: Coward-McCann and Geoghegan, Inc., 1979.

Barr, Pat. *To China with Love—the Lives and Times of Protestant Missionaries in China, 1860–1900*. New York: Doubleday & Co., Inc., 1973.

Bonavia, David, and Bartlett, Magnus. *Tibet*. Hong Kong: Shangri-la Press. China Guides Series. 1981.

Bredon, Juliet. *Peking*. Shanghai: Kelly and Walsh, Ltd., 1931; Hong Kong: Oxford University Press. 1982.

Buck, Pearl S. *The Good Earth*. New York: J. Day, 1977.

Buckley, Michael, and Samagalski, Alan. *China—A Travel Survival Kit*. Victoria and Berkeley: Lonely Planet, 1984.

Catchpool, Brian. *A Map History of Modern China*. London: Heinemann Educational Books Ltd., 1977.

Chen, Jack. *A Year in Upper Felicity*. New York: Macmillan, 1973.

Chen, Jerome. *Mao and the Chinese Revolution*. Oxford, 1976.

Chen Yuan-Tsung. *The Dragon's Village*. New York: Pantheon, 1980.

Coye, Molly Joel, etc., editor. *China, Yesterday and Today*. New York: Bantam Books, 1984.

Cronin, Vincent. *The Wise Man from the West, Matteo Ricci and His Mission to China*. London: Collin, Fount Paperbacks, 1984.

Daubier, Jean. *A History of the Chinese Cultural Revolution*. New York, Toronto: Vintage Books, 1974.

Dawson, Raymond. *Imperial China*. New York: Pelican Books, 1976.

Fairbank, John K. *The United States and China*. Cambridge: Harvard University Press, 1983.

Fitzgerald, C. P. *The Tower of Five Glories—A Study of the Min Chia of Ta Li, Yunnan*. West Point, CT: Hyperion Press, 1973.

Gernet, Jacques. *Daily Life in China on the Eve of the Mongol Invasion. 1250–1276*. Stanford, Ca.: Stanford University Press, 1973.

Gottschang, Karen Turner. *China Bound: A Handbook for American Students, Researchers and Teachers*. Washington: Committee on Scholarly Communication with the People's Republic of China.

Haldane, Charlotte. *The Last Great Empress of China*. New York: Bobbs-Merrill, 1965.

Han Suyin. *The Crippled Tree*. New York: Bantam, 1972.

————. *A Mortal Flower*. London: J. Cape, 1966.

————. *Birdless Summer*. New York: Putnam, 1968.

Harrer, Heinrich. *Return to Tibet*. London: George Weidenfeld & Nicolson Ltd., 1984.

————. *Seven Years in Tibet*, London: The Adventure Library, Rupert Hart-Davis, 1957; London: Granada, 1984.

Hollingworth, Clare. *Mao and the Men Against Him*. London: Jonathan Cape, 1985.

Latsch, Marie-Liuse. *Peking Opera as a European Sees It*. Beijing: New World Press, 1980.

Li Nianpei, *Old Tales of China—a tourist guidebook to better understanding of China's stage, cinema, arts and crafts*. Beijing: China Travel and Tourism Press, 1981.

Li Xueqin, *The Wonder of Chinese Bronzes*. Beijing: Foreign Languages Press, 1980.

Liang Heng and Shapiro, Judith. *Son of the Revolution*. New York: Vintage Books, 1984.

Lin Yutang. *Moment in Peking*. New York: John Day, 1939.

Ling, Ken. *The Revenge of Heaven*. New York: G.P. Putnam's Sons, 1972.

Lo Kuan-chung. *Three Kingdoms*. Robert Moss, trans. & ed. New York: Pantheon, 1976.

Malloy, Ruth Lor. *Beyond the Heights*. Hong Kong: Heinemann Educational Books Ltd. (Asia), 1980.

McKenna, Richard. *The Sand Pebbles*. Greenwich, Conn.: Fawcett, 1962.

Medley, Margaret. *A Handbook of Chinese Art*. New York: Icon Ed., 1974.

Schram, Stuart. *Mao Tse-tung*. New York: Penguin, 1967.

Seagrave, Sterling. *The Soong Dynasty*. New York and Sydney: Harper & Row.

Sharman, Lyon. *Sun Yat-sen, His Life and Its Meaning*. Stanford: Stanford University Press, 1978.

Snow, Edgar. *Red Star Over China*. New York: Penguin, 1977.

Spence, Jonathan. *To Change China: Western Advisers in China. 1620–1960*. Boston, Toronto: Little, Brown, 1969.

Sullivan, Michael. *The Arts of China*. Los Angeles, Berkeley, London: University of California Press, 1977.

Terry, Edith. *The Executive Guide to China*. New York: John Wiley & Sons, 1984.

Tolley, Kemp. *Yangtze Patrol: The U.S. Navy in China*. Annapolis, Md.: Naval Institute Press, 1971.

Tsao Hsueh-Chin. *The Dream of the Red Chamber* (Hung Lou Meng). New York: The Universal Library, Grosset & Dunlop, 1973.

Tsao Hsueh-chin and Kao Ngo. *A Dream of Red Mansions*. Beijing: Foreign Languages Press, 1978. (Three volumes.)

Tung Chi-ming. *An Outline History of China*. Hong Kong: Joint Publishing Co., 1979.

U.S. Government. *Post Report on China*. Government Printing Office, Washington, DC.

Warner, Marina. *The Dragon Empress: The Life and Times of Tz'u-Hsi, Empress Dowager of China, 1835–1908*. New York: Macmillan, 1972.

White, Theodore. *In Search of History*. New York: Warner, 1978.

Williams, C.A.S. *Outlines of Chinese Symbolism and Art Motives*. New York: Dover Publications, 1976.

Witke, Roxanne. *Comrade Chiang-Ching*. Waltham, MA: Little, Brown, 1977.

Woodcock, George. *The British in the Far East*. New York: Atheneum, 1969.

Wu Zuguang. *Peking Opera and Mei Lanfang*. Beijing: New World Press, 1981.

————. *Doing Business in Today's China*. The American Chamber of Commerce in Hong Kong.

————. *Zhonghua Renmin Gongheguo Fen Sheng Dituji*. (Atlas of China). Beijing: Xinhua Shudian, 1971.

————. China City Guide Series. Beijing: Travel and Tourism Press. 1983. Guides of Beijing, Guangzhou, Guilin, Hangzhou, Kunming, Nanjing, Shanghai, Taiyuan, Tianjin, Xiamen, etc.

QUICK REFERENCE

Official Chinese Holidays

January or February	Spring Festival/New Year, the date depending on lunar calendar (3 days).
May 1	Labor Day
October 1 and 2	National Day, celebrating the founding of the People's Republic of China in 1949.

In addition, the following are celebrated with special programs, but offices and schools are open.

March 8	International Working Women's Day
May 4	Youth Day (May 4th Movement)
June 1	Children's Day
July 1	Founding Day of the Communist Party of China
August 1	Founding Day of the People's Liberation Army

The Chinese also celebrate several other traditional holidays. The Lantern Festival is the last day of the old lunar new year celebrations. The Dragon Boat races commemorate the untimely death of an upright official. Originally, the boats raced to feed the fish so they wouldn't eat him! (But no one thinks of that now.) The Mid-Autumn Festival celebrates the most beautiful full moon of the year.

Check with C.I.T.S. about special events related to the festivals (not necessarily on the specified day).

Since the dates for the traditional festivals fluctuate (like Easter) according to the lunar calendar, the western equivalents are:

	1987	1988	1989	1990
Lunar New Year	Jan. 29	Feb. 17	Feb. 6	Jan. 27
Lantern Festival	Feb. 12	Mar. 2	Feb. 20	Feb. 10
Dragon Boat Festival	May 31	June 18	June 8	May 28
Mid-Autumn Festival	Oct. 7	Sept. 25	Sept. 14	Oct. 3
Confucius's Birthday	Oct. 19	Oct. 7		

	Old Spelling	Pinyin	Province in Pinyin
厦门	AMOY	Xiamen	Fujian
鞍山	ANSHAN	Anshan	Liaoning
安阳	ANYANG	Anyang	Henan
常州	CHANGCHOW	Changzhou	Jiangsu
长春	CHANGCHUN	Changchun	Jilin
长沙	CHANGSHA	Changsha	Hunan
肇庆	CHAOCHING	Zhaoqing	Guangdong
樟州	CHENGCHOW	Zhangzhou	Fujian
郑州	CHENGCHOW	Zhengzhou	Henan
承德	CHENGTEH	Chengde	Hebei
成都	CHENGTU	Chengdu	Sichuan
嘉峪关	CHIAYUKUAN	Jiayuguan	Gansu
景洪 (西双版纳)	CHINGHUNG, HSISHUANG PANNA	Jinghong, Xishuangbanna	Yunnan
井冈山	CHINGKANG MOUNTAINS	Jinggang Shan	Jianxi
景德镇	CHINGTECHEN	Jingdezhen	Jianxi
镇江	CHINGKIANG (also Chenkiang)	Zhenjiang	Jiangsu
秦皇岛	CHINWANGTAO	Qinhuangdao	Hebei
酒泉	CHIUCHUAN	Jiuquan	Gansu
九华山	CHIUHUA MOUNTAINS	Jiuhua Shan	Anhui
曲阜	CHUFU	Qufu	Shandong
重庆	CHUNGKING	Chongqing	Sichuan
福州	FOOCHOW	Fuzhou	Fujian
佛山	FASHAN (also Fatshan)	Foshan	Guangdong
抚顺	FUSHUN	Fushun	Liaoning
海口	HAIKOW	Haikou	Guangdong
杭州	HANGCHOW	Hangzhou	Zhejiang
邯郸	HANTAN	Handan	Hebei
哈尔滨	HARBIN	Harbin	Heilongjiang
衡阳	HENGYANG	Hengyang	Hunan
合肥	HOFEI	Hefei	Anhui
襄樊	HSIANGFAN	Xiangfan	Hubei
湘潭	HSIANGTAN	Xiangtan	Henan
新会	HSINHUI (also Sunwai)	Xinhui	Guangdong
咸宁	HSIENNING	Xianning	Hubei
锡林浩特	HSILINHOT	Xilinhot	Nei Monggol
新乡	HSINHSIANG	Xinxiang	Henan
西柏坡	HSIPAIPO	Xibaipo	Hebei

徐 州	HSUCHOW	Xuzhou	Jiangsu
黄 山	HUANG MOUNTAINS	Huang Shan	Anhui
呼 和 浩 特	HUHEHOT	Hohhot	Nei Monggol
辉 县	HUIHSIEN	Hui Xian	Henan
宜 兴	IHSING (also Yising)	Yixing	Jiangsu
开 封	KAIFENG	Kaifeng	Henan
江 门	KIANGMEN (also Kongmoon)	Jiangmen	Guangdong
吉 林	KIRIN	Jilin	Jilin
九 江	KIUKIANG	Jiujiang	Jiangxi
巩 县	KUNGHSIEN	Gongxian	Henan
昆 明	KUNMING	Kunming	Yunnan
广 州	KWANGCHOW (also Canton)	Guangzhou	Guangdong
桂 林	KWEILIN	Guilin	Guangxi
桂 平	KWEIPING	Guiping	Guangxi
拉 萨	LHASA	Lhasa	Xizang (Tibet)
兰 州	LANCHOW	Lanzhou	Gansu
连 云 港	LIENYUNKANG	Lianyungang	Jiangsu
林 县	LINHSIEN	Linxian	Henan
柳 州	LIUCHOW	Liuzhou	Guangxi
乐 山	LOSHAN	Leshan	Sichuan
洛 阳	LOYANG	Luoyang	Henan
路 南—石 林	LUNAN—STONE FOREST	Lunan—Stone Forest	Yunnan
马 鞍 山	MAANSHAN	Ma'anshan	Anhui
莫 干 山	MOKAN MOUNTAINS	Mogan Shan	Zhejiang
紫 金 山	MT. CHIKING	Zijin Shan	Jiangsu
庐 山	MT. LUSHAN	Lushan	Jiangxi
峨 嵋 山	MT. OMEI	Emei Shan	Sichuan
南 昌	NANCHANG	Nanchang	Jiangxi
南 京	NANKING	Nanjing	Jiangsu
南 宁	NANNING	Nanning	Guangxi
宁 波	NINGPO	Ningbo	Zhejiang
北 雁 荡 山	NORTH YENTANG MOUNTAINS	Bei Yandang Shan	Zhejiang
包 头	PAOTOW	Baotou	Nei Monggol
北 戴 河	PEHTAIHO (also Peitaihe)	Beidaihe	Hebei
北 京	PEKING	Beijing	
宾 阳	PINYANG	Binyang	Guangxi
三 门 峡	SANMEN GORGE	Sanmenxia	Henan

上海	SHANGHAI	Shanghai	
绍兴	SHAOHSING	Shaoxing	Zhejiang
韶山	SHAOSHAN	Shaoshan	Hunan
沙市	SHASHIH	Shashi	Hebei
沙石峪	SHASHIHYU	Shashiyu	Hebei
胜利油田	SHENGLI OIL FIELD	Shengli Oil Field	Shandong
沈阳	SHENYANG	Shenyang	Liaoning
石家庄	SHIHCHIACHUANG (also Shihkiachwang)	Shijiazhuang	Hebei
石河子	SHIHHOTZU	Shihezi	Xinjiang
西安	SIAN	Xi'an	Shaanxi
苏州	SOOCHOW	Suzhou	Jiangsu
汕头	SWATOW	Shantou	Guangdong
大寨	TACHAI	Dazhai	Shanxi
大庆油田	TACHING OIL FIELD	Daqing Oil Field	Heilongjiang
泰安(泰山)	TAIAN (Mt. Tai)	Tai'an (Mt. Tai)	Shandong
太原	TAIYUAN	Taiyuan	Shanxi
大港油田	TAKANG OIL FIELD	Dagang Oil Field	Tianjin
大连	TALIEN	Dalian (also Luda)	Liaoning
唐山	TANGSHAN	Tangshan	Hebei
丹江	TANKIANG	Danjiang	Hubei
大同	TATUNG	Datong	Shanxi
天津	TIENTSIN	Tianjin	
济南	TSINAN	Jinan	Shandong
青岛	TSINGTAO	Qingdao	Shandong
从化	TSUNGHUA	Conghua	Guangdong
遵化	TSUNHUA	Zunhua	Hebei
敦煌	TUNHUANG	Dunhuang	Gansu
吐鲁番	TURFAN	Turpan	Xinjiang
淄博	TZUPO	Zibo	Shandong
乌鲁木齐	URUMCHI	Urumqi	Xinjiang
万县	WANHSIEN	Wan Xian	Sichuan
潍坊	WEIFANG	Weifang	Shandong
温州	WENCHOW	Wenzhou	Zhejiang
武汉	WUHAN	Wuhan	Hubei
芜湖	WUHU	Wuhu	Anhui
武鸣	WUMING	Wuming	Guangxi
无锡	WUSIH	Wuxi	Jiangsu
扬州	YANGCHOW	Yangzhou	Jiangsu
阳泉	YANGCHUAN	Yangquan	Shanxi
阳朔	YANGSHUO	Yangshuo	Guangxi

延 安　YENAN　　　Yan'an　　　Shanxi
烟 台　YENTAI　　　Yantai　　　Shandong
岳 阳　YOYANG　　　Yueyang　　　Hunan
禺 县　YUHSIEN　　　Yuxian　　　Henan

DYNASTIES-pinyin (old spelling)

夏　Xia (Hsia)　　　　　　c. 21st–16th century B.C.
商　Shang (Shang)　　　　c. 16th–11th century B.C.
西 周　Western Zhou (Chou)　c. 11th century–771 B.C.
春 秋 国　Spring and Autumn Period　770–476 B.C.
战 国　Warring States Period　475–221 B.C.
秦　Qin (Chin)　　　　　　221–206 B.C.
西 汉　Western Han (Han)　　206 B.C.–A.D. 24
东 汉　Eastern Han (Han)　　25–220
三 国　The Three Kingdoms　220–265
魏　　Wei (Wei)　　　　　220–265
蜀　　Shu (Shu)　　　　　221–263
吴　　Wu (Wu)　　　　　222–280
西 晋　Western Jin (Tsin)　　265–316
东 晋　Eastern Jin (Tsin)　　317–420
南 北 朝　Southern and Northern Dynasties　420–589
　　宋　Southern Dynasties　　420–589
　　齐　　Song (Sung)　　　　420–479
　　梁　　Qi (Chi)　　　　　　479–502
　　陈　　Liang (Liang)　　　502–557
　　　　Chen (Chen)　　　　557–589
北 朝　Northern Dynasties　　386–581
北 魏　　Northern Wei (Wei)　386–534
东 魏　　Eastern Wei　　　　534–550
西 魏　　Western Wei　　　　535–556
北 齐　　Northern Qi (Chi)　　550–577
北 周　　Northern Zhou (Chou)　557–581
隋　Sui (Sui)　　　　　　581–618
唐　Tang (Tang)　　　　618–907
五 代　Five Dynasties　　　907–960
辽　Liao (Liao)　　　　916–1125
宋　Song (Sung)　　　　960–1279
　北 宋　Northern Song (Sung)　960–1127
　南 宋　Southern Song (Sung)　1127–1279
西 夏　Western Xia (Hsia)　1038–1227
金　Jin (Kin)　　　　　1115–1234

元	Yuan (Yuan)	1271–1368
明	Ming (Ming)	1368–1644
	Hongwu (Hung Wu)	1368–1399
	Jianwen (Chien Wen)	1399–1403
	Yongle (Yung Lo)	1403–1425
	Hongxi (Hung Hsi)	1425–1426
	Xuande (Hsuan Teh)	1426–1436
	Zhengtong (Cheng Tung)	1436–1450
	Jingtai (Ching Tai)	1450–1457
	Tianshun (Tien Shun)	1457–1465
	Cheng Hua (Cheng Hua)	1465–1488
	Hongzhi (Hung Chih)	1488–1506
	Zhengde (Cheng Teh)	1506–1522
	Jiajing (Chia Ching)	1522–1567
	Longqing (Lung Ching)	1567–1573
	Wanli (Wan Li)	1573–1620
	Taichang (Tai Chang)	1620–1621
	Tianqi (Tien Chi)	1621–1628
	Chongzhen (Chung Cheng)	1628–1644
清	Qing (Ching)	1644–1911
	Shunzhi (Shun Chih)	1644–1662
	Kangxi (Kang Hsi)	1662–1723
	Yongzheng (Yung Cheng)	1723–1736
	Qianlong (Chien Lung)	1736–1796
	Jiaqing (Chia Ching)	1796–1821
	Daoguang (Tao Kuang)	1821–1851
	Xianfeng (Hsien Feng)	1851–1862
	Tongzhi (Tung Chih)	1862–1875
	Guangxu (Kuang Hsu)	1875–1908
	Xuantong (Hsuan Tung)	1908–1911

HOW TO PRONOUNCE CHINESE LETTERS

Following is a table of the Chinese phonetic alphabet showing pronunciation with approximate English equivalents. Letters in the Wade-Giles system are in parentheses.

"**a**" (a), a vowel, as in far;

"**b**" (p), a consonant, as in be;

"**c**" (ts), a consonant, as in "ts" in its; and

"**ch**" (ch), a consonant, as in "ch" in church, strongly aspirated;

"**d**" (t), a consonant, as in do;

"**e**" (e), a vowel, as "er" in her, the "r" being silent; but "**ie**," a diphthong, as in yes and "**ei**," a diphthong, as in way;

"**f**" (f), a consonant, as in foot;

"**g**" (k), a consonant, as in go;

"**h**" (h), a consonant, as in her, strongly aspirated;

"**i**" (i), a vowel, two pronunciations:
 1) as in eat
 2) as in sir in syllables with the consonants c, ch, r, s, sh, z and zh;

"**j**" (ch), a consonant, as in jeep;

"**k**" (k), a consonant, as in kind, strongly aspirated;

"**l**" (l), a consonant, as in land;

"**m**" (m), a consonant, as in me;

"**n**" (n), a consonant, as in no;

"**o**"(o), a vowel, as in "aw" in law;

"**p**" (p), a consonant, as in par, strongly aspirated;

"**q**" (ch), a consonant, as "ch" in cheek;

"**r**" (j), a consonant pronounced as "r" but not rolled, or like "z" in azure;

"**s**" (s, ss, sz), a consonant, as in sister; and "**sh**" (sh), a consonant, as "sh" in shore;

"**t**" (t), a consonant, as in top, strongly aspirated;

"**u**" (u), a vowel, as in too, also as in the French "u" in "tu" or the German umlauted "u" in "Muenchen";

"**v**" (v), is used only to produce foreign and national minority words, and local dialects;

"**w**" (w), used as a semi-vowel in syllables beginning with "u" when not preceded by consonants, pronounced as in want;

"**x**" (hs), a consonant, as "sh" in she;

"**y**" used as a semi-vowel in syllables beginning with "i" or "u" when not preceded by consonants, pronounced as in yet;

"**z**" (ts, tz), a consonant, as in zero; and "**zh**" (ch), a consonant, as "j" in jump."

—from *China Reconstructs,* March 1979

CELSIUS-FAHRENHEIT CONVERSION TABLE

Centigrade (Celsius)		Fahrenheit
−40°		−40°
−20°		− 4°
0°	Freezing Point	32°
10°		50°
20°		68°
30°		86°
40°		104°
50°		122°
60°		140°
70°		158°
80°		176°
90°		194°
100°	Boiling Point	212°

To convert Fahrenheit to Celsius subtract 32, multiply by 5, and divide by 9. To convert Celsius to Fahrenheit multiply by 9, divide by 5, and add 32.

Distances Between Main Tourist Cities

(Shortest distance between cities by rail in kilometres)

City	Beijing	Shanghai	Tianjin	Guangzhou	Nanning	Changsha	Shaoshan	Wuchang	Nanjing	Wuxi	Suzhou	Hangzhou	Jinan	Qingdao	Xi'an	Kunming	Chengdu	Chongqing	Zhengzhou	Shijiazhuang	Dalian	Shenyang	Changchun
Shanghai	1462																						
Tianjin	137	1325																					
Guangzhou	2313	1811	2450																				
Nanning	2565	2063	2702	1334																			
Changsha	1587	1187	1724	726	978																		
Shaoshan	1718	1216	1855	755	1007	131																	
Wuchang	1229	1534	1366	1084	1336	358	489																
Nanjing	1157	305	1020	2116	2368	1492	1521	1229															
Wuxi	1334	128	1197	1939	2191	1315	1344	1406	177														
Suzhou	1376	86	1239	1897	2149	1273	1302	1448	219	42													
Hangzhou	1651	189	1514	1622	1874	998	1027	1356	494	275	317												
Jinan	494	968	357	2284	2536	1558	1689	1200	663	840	882	1157											
Qingdao	887	1361	750	2677	2929	1951	2082	1593	1056	1233	1275	1550	393										
Xi'an	1165	1511	1302	2129	2381	1403	1534	1045	1206	1383	1425	1700	1177	1570									
Kunming	3179	2677	3316	2216	1501	1592	1503	1950	2982	2805	2763	2488	3119	3512	1942								
Chengdu	2048	2353	2185	2544	1829	1920	1831	1887	2048	2225	2267	2542	2019	2412	842	1100							
Chongqing	2552	2501	2689	2040	1325	1416	1327	1774	2552	2729	2771	2312	2523	2916	1346	842	504						
Zhengzhou	695	1000	832	1618	1870	892	1023	534	695	872	914	1189	666	1059	511	2453	1353	1857					
Shijiazhuang	283	1266	420	2030	2282	1304	1435	946	961	1138	1180	1455	298	691	923	2865	1765	2269	412				
Dalian	1238	2426	1101	3551	3803	2825	2956	2467	2121	2298	2340	2615	1458	1851	2403	4417	3286	3790	1933	1521			
Shenyang	841	2029	704	3154	3406	2428	2559	2070	1724	1901	1943	2218	1061	1454	2006	4020	2889	3393	1536	1124	397		
Changchun	1146	2334	1009	3459	3711	2733	2864	2375	2029	2206	2248	2523	1366	1759	2311	4325	3194	3698	1841	1429	702	305	
Harbin	1388	2576	1251	3701	3953	2975	3106	2617	2271	2448	2490	2763	1608	2001	2553	4567	3436	3940	2083	1671	944	547	242

MILE-KILOMETER CONVERSION TABLES

Miles	Kilometers	Kilometers	Miles
1	1.6093	1	.621
2	3.2186	2	1.242
3	4.8279	3	1.863
4	6.4372	4	2.484
5	8.0465	5	3.105
6	9.6558	6	3.726
7	11.2651	7	4.347
8	12.8744	8	4.968
9	14.4837	9	5.589
10	16.093	10	6.21
20	32.186	20	12.42
30	48.279	30	18.63
40	64.372	40	24.84
50	80.465	50	31.05
60	96.558	60	37.26
70	112.651	70	43.47
80	128.744	80	49.68
90	144.837	90	55.89
100	160.93	100	62.1
200	321.86	200	124.2
300	482.79	300	186.3
400	643.72	400	248.4
500	804.65	500	310.5
600	965.58	600	372.6
700	1126.51	700	434.7
800	1287.44	800	496.8
900	1448.37	900	558.9
1000	1609.3	1000	621.

(Prepared by Linda Malloy)

WEIGHTS AND MEASURES

China uses both the metric system and the Chinese system

1 gong-jin (kilogram)	= 2.2 pounds
1 jin or gun (catty)	= 1.33 pounds = .604 kg.
1 dan (picul) = 100 catties	= 133 pounds or 60.47 kg.
1 mi (meter)	= 39.37 inches
1 gong li (kilometer)	= .6 mile = 1 km.
1 li (Chinese mile)	= .3106 mile = ½ km.
1 mu	= .1647 acres
1 hectare	= 2.471 acres = 10,000 sq. meters
100 hectares	= 247.1 acre = 1 sq. km.
259 hectares	= 1 sq. mile

NAMES OF CHINESE ADMINISTRATIVE REGIONS

Pinyin   *Old Spelling*

Municipalities (Shi)

Beijing	Peking
Tianjin	Tientsin
Shanghai	Shanghai

Provinces (Sheng)

Hebei	Hopei
Jilin	Kirin
Jiangsu	Kiangsu
Jiangxi	Kiangsi
Hubei	Hupeh
Shaanxi	Shensi
Sichuan	Szechwan
Shanxi	Shansi
Heilongjiang	Heilungkiang
Anhui	Anhwei
Fujian	Fukien
Hunan	Hunan
Gansu	Kansu
Guizhou	Kweichow
Taiwan	Taiwan
Liaoning	Liaoning
Shandong	Shantung
Zheijiang	Chekiang
Henan	Honan
Guangdong	Kwangtung
Qinghai	Chinghai
Yunnan	Yunnan

Autonomous Regions (Zizhiqu)

Nei Monggol autonomous region	Inner Mongolia autonomous region
Guangzi Zhuang autonomous region	Kwangsi Chuang autonomous region
Ningxia Hui autonomous region	Ningsia Hui autonomous region
Xinjiang Uygur autonomous region	Sinkiang Uighur autonomous region
Xizang autonomous region	Tibet autonomous region

LEADERS

In the mid-1980s, Li Xiannian was president, Deng Xiaoping was usually described as "leader" or "elder statesman," Zhao Ziyang was premier, and Hu Yaobang was Communist Party General Secretary.

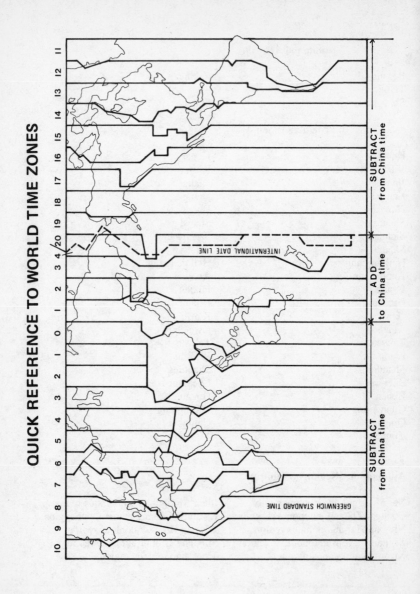

All of China is in one time zone. At 8 a.m. in China the time is 1 a.m. in West Germany or
a.m. in Singapore. The time in China is 13 hours later than in the eastern United States. F
example, 8 a.m. in China is 7 p.m. Eastern Standard Time, or 6 p.m. Daylight Savings Time, t
previous day in New York City.

Glossary

arhats—Buddhists who have attained Nirvana.

bodhisattvas—Buddhist saints who have attained Nirvana but have returned to help others. See "What Is There to See and Do?"

CAAC—formerly China's only airline. See "Getting Around."

cadre—in Chinese *kanpu,* meaning "core element." Any person who plays a leadership role.

C.I.T.S.—China International Travel Service.

C.T.S.—China Travel Service (the travel agency for Overseas Chinese and Compatriots).

dagoba—similar to an Indian stupa, a bell-shaped tower under which is buried a Buddhist relic or the ashes of a monk.

F.E.C.s—Foreign Exchange Certificates.

F.F.—Foreign Friend

feng-shui—literally, wind and water. Geomancy. The belief that the placement of buildings in relation to water, and the contours of the land, affects the fortunes of the people who live in or near them; in the case of tombs, the placement affects the fortunes of the descendants.

quanxi—connections. See "Local Customs."

H.K.—Hong Kong

joint venture—a business arrangement involving several parties. China has entered into many joint ventures with foreign businessmen.

lohan—the Chinese word for *arhat.*

Luxingshe—the Chinese name for C.I.T.S.

Manchu—the group from northeast China who ruled China under the dynasty name *Qing.*

Mongol—the group of people from north China who ruled China under the dynasty name *Yuan.*

neolithic—pertaining to the Stone-Age period in which man developed pottery, weaving, and agriculture, and worked with polished stone and metal tools.

penjing—the art of growing miniature trees and plants. Similar to Japanese *bonsai.*

P.L.A.—People's Liberation Army (currently being reorganized).

pinyin—the new system of romanizing the Chinese language now adopted as official.

pusa—the Chinese word for bodhisattva.

R.M.B.—*ren min bi*—people's money, one of the terms used to refer to Chinese currency. R.M.B. is not the same as F.E.C., above.

stele—a large stone tablet used to commemorate an event, a life, or an important piece of writing.

Wade-Giles—the most commonly used of the old systems of romanizing the Chinese language.

W.C.—water closet. Toilet.

wok—a large, round pan fitted into a stove for cooking.

work unit—every salaried worker belongs to one of these.

¥—yuan, similar to a dollar. See "Budget."

Names of People in *pinyin* and Wade-Giles

Pinyin	*Wade-Giles*
Bainqen Lama	Panchen Lama
Cixi	Tzu Hsi, (Tsu-hsi, Qing Empress Dowager)
Deng Xiaoping	Teng Hsiao-ping
Feng Yuxiang	Feng Yu-hsiang (general)
Guan Yu	Kuan Yu (Three Kingdoms)
Guo Moruo	Kuo Mo Ruo
Hua Kuofeng	Hua Guo-feng (former Party chairman)
Jiang Jieshi	Chiang Kai-shek
Jiang Qing	Chiang Ching (widow of Mao Tse-tung)
Lin Biao	Lin Piao
Liu Shaoqi	Liu Shao-chi (former president)
Mao Zedong	Mao Tse-tung
Sun Yixian	Sun Yat-sen (father of republican China)
Xuan Zang	Hsuan-tsang (Tang dynasty monk)
Yuan Shikai	Yuan Shih-kai (2nd president of China)
Zhong Shan	Chung Shan (the honorific name of Dr. Sun Yat-sen)
Zhou Enlai	Chou En-lai (former premier of China)
Zhu Yanzhang	Chu Yuan-chuan (first Ming Emperor)

BUDGET AND HOTEL QUICK REFERENCE

HOW MUCH MONEY SHOULD YOU TAKE TO CHINA?

Be aware that (a) only a few credit cards are accepted, most of them with a 4% surcharge. See "Important Addresses and Information." Find out before you go the latest regulations regarding credit card usage in China from your credit card company; (b) personal checks are not generally accepted, but some can be cashed at the Bank of China with some credit cards; (c) companies and embassies established in China can pay by check if known to the person cashing the check; (d) it takes five banking days to cable money to you in China, assuming everyone knows his job and has your passport number; (e) you might ask your embassy to cash a personal check, but I wouldn't count on it.

These all mean, of course, that you should take enough **cash or traveler's checks.** Cash brings a slightly lower foreign exchange rate than traveler's checks, leaving you with less money. Acceptable traveler's checks are listed below.

Bank of China traveler's checks might save you from the fluctuations in the exchange rate, but in Hong Kong, for example, you lose money if you change from U.S.$ to Chinese currency. (The money has to be calculated from U.S. to Hong Kong dollars and from there to Chinese.) Try Bank of China's foreign branches. These traveler's checks are good for only six months. In the mid-1980s, Chinese currency decreased considerably against U.S. and Canadian dollars. If you bought Chinese travelers checks and didn't spend them for a few months, you lost out on quite a bit of additional money.

For current foreign exchange rates, check business newspapers, your local bank, or *China Daily*. For rates at press time, see below.

Prepaid travelers booking through a travel agent usually have to pay the full price of the tour prior to their arrival in China. You may have to pay extra at the end of your trip. A final accounting is tallied toward the end of the tour. If there are to be additional expenses, you are usually consulted during the trip. For example, flights delayed by weather might mean an option of paying for an additional day or cutting out another part of the tour.

Many travel agencies cover any small additional costs themselves rather than antagonize their clients. On the other hand, you might get some money back.

So how much money should you take to China?

Read ahead and then budget in addition to the price of your China tour:

¥ _____   (a) at least ¥100 per week for "unforeseen circumstances" that one hopes won't happen. How much would it cost if you lost your passport and had to spend a couple of extra nights in a hotel in Shanghai?

¥ _____   (b) for "optional tours" that might mean you would otherwise be wandering around the city alone.

¥ _____   (c) for whatever you want for shopping. It's painful to resist buying things you've watched being made, especially if you know they are more expensive at home; don't forget film and film processing (if you can't wait to do it before you get home).

¥ _____   (d) if you socialize a lot and enjoy buying a round of drinks in the evening.

¥ _____   (e) if you take people out to dinner.

¥ _____   (f) for laundry, cheap at modest hotels; more at international standard hotels.

¥ _____   (g) for a massage at a modest hotel barber shop, or for about ¼ of that at a public bath house.

¥ _____   (h) for a barber or hairdresser.

¥ _____   (i) for miscellaneous extras—overweight luggage, telephone calls, medical expenses, postage, photography, etc.

    After you total this up, add about 20%, and you should have sufficient.

¥ _____   Total.

Pay-as-you-go travelers should budget in addition to the above:

¥ _____   (j) for a hotel room (one or two people). The highest prices are for luxury, international standard hotels. The lowest prices listed are for adequate but crude accommodations, almost always with private bath in the smaller cities. In the larger cities you may have to book an expensive hotel room.

¥ _____   (k) for food and drinks.

¥ _____   (l) for transportation (between and inside cities), permits, etc. Count on ¥10 for airport tax each time you leave China. Less energetic people tend to use taxis more, and could spend ¥10 to ¥60 a day on taxis.

¥ _____   (m) for entrance fees to most tourist attractions.

¥ _____   (n) bus or boat tours.

¥ _____   (o) C.I.T.S. charges.

¥ _____   (p) entertainment

¥ _____   (q) unforeseen circumstances like currency fluctuations, medical treatment, and price changes. Give yourself ample. Be sure you are covered by medical insurance.

¥ _____   **Grand Total.** Now figure out what that comes to in your own currency.

Overseas Chinese and backpackers should calculate 10% to 40% less on hotels and transportation if they're good at arguing.

Those who want to save money have to take much more time, and not care about the highest available standards of cleanliness and comfort.

If you go on your own, save first **before** going to China. Look for bargain airfares. Haggle with managers in travel agencies and airline offices (especially KAL, PAL, SIA, and CAL). You have nothing to lose but your pride. Read the youth travel columns in newspapers. Talk to backpackers about cutting costs. Check out People's Express across the Atlantic and then the train from London to Beijing via Moscow. Tickets on the Trans-Siberian railway are said to be much cheaper if bought in an East European country.

Or how about the special air rates between London and Hong Kong for British citizens? Or excursion fares? Across the Pacific, try OC Tours to Hong Kong from Oakland. How about via Manila? C.I.T.S. and CAAC discount from December 1 to March 31 on some routes and tours. Hotels too.

Let the Chinese pay your way, or at least part of it. Go as a **teacher or foreign expert,** or while you are in China offer to teach at a school for a few months. The Chinese will hire qualified teachers more readily if you pay your own airfare to get there, and will give you a modest bit of pocket money besides, and possibly travel discounts. You'll get a much less superficial experience than as a tourist, and teaching can be very satisfying.

Organize your own tour group. In a group of 15 persons (sometimes 10), inclusive service in China is free for one traveler, and airlines might give one free seat.

In China

At each **hotel,** do not be afraid to *ask* if there are cheaper rooms. If the clerk says no, keep trying every day, or try other hotels. The Chinese might offer you the most expensive for your own comfort as well as for the higher revenue. Rooms on the uppermost floors are usually more expensive. *Argue* pleasantly. Tell the clerk you're a student (if you have your card), or a foreign expert (even if you've just given *one* lecture). One Overseas Chinese argued successfully for 50% hotel discounts, and he didn't look Chinese! Many hotels have dorms with up to 30 or 40 beds in a room for about ¥5 and up. Try hostels. Share rooms with friends, as most rooms cost the same for one guest as for two. As hotels in big cities are more expensive, stay away from the center of the city. Or take anything you can get for the first night, and then look around.

Ask a **local Chinese** friend to buy you a train ticket (at local prices). You can always pay the difference on the train if the conductor objects—and few conductors so far have objected.

Book **hard-class train.** You might like it. If not, you can frequently upgrade your accommodations, if space is available, by paying more.

Travel with an Overseas Chinese friend and book through **C.T.S. Avoid C.I.T.S.** if you can.

Do not assume that the Chinese are giving you anything free. Always ask, ''What is the charge?''

Go by **public bus or boat.** Some of these aren't bad. Some are filthy and noisy. See ''Jiangmen'' for one kind of boat. Some buses are air-conditioned and reasonable. The price difference between the regular ferry and the luxury tour boats on the Yangtze River is considerable. So are the standards of comfort and privacy. See ''Yangtze Gorges.''

Eat in bun or noodle shops or at market stalls. These cost considerably less than hotel restaurants and some of them are clean. One backpacker spent 2½ months in China eating cheaply at market stalls and never got sick. But others aren't so lucky.

Avoid tourist restaurants. Invite one of the young people trying to practice English on you to take you to a restaurant where ordinary people eat.

If you're traveling only a few kilometers by **taxi,** it may be cheaper to have your taxi wait than to hire a car by the day or the half-day. Ask about waiting time and maximum distances for the day rate.

Ask your hotel service desk or C.I.T.S. if a **tour bus** you can join goes to the tourist attractions. For one or two people, this may be cheaper than taking taxis. You might try to hitch free rides with tour groups. Or try to interest other individual travelers in sharing taxis or minibuses. How about renting a bicycle?

Stay with friends or relatives. Courtesy demands you take them presents, but this could be anything from a bag of fruit, candy, or cookies, to a video or refrigerator. See *Gifts* in ''What to Take'' and ''Special for Overseas Chinese.''

Foreign hitchhikers have traveled around China successfully, sleeping in hostels for local Chinese (after much persistent pleading), sometimes for less than ¥1 a night. (Take your own bedding and don't be surprised at bedbugs.)

Travel during low tourist season. The south is pleasant in the wintertime.

Search out backpackers, who are usually happy to exchange travel tips. Look for them in dormitories at hotels like the Chongwenmen in Beijing, and the Chungking Mansions in Hong Kong.

1985 PRICES

These are listed primarily to help you plan. China has been allowing market forces to set prices, and many of the following will go up or down, but mainly up in 1987.

Note that tourist facilities, like Friendship Stores, taxis, and joint ventures, must be paid in F.E.C.s.

Ten percent service and 3 or 5% sales taxes are added to bills in joint-venture restaurants and hotels.

Some establishments have two sets of prices—the higher for R.M.B.; and lower for F.E.C.

Your highest prices are usually in the big cities, especially Beijing. Then there's Tibet! The more expensive the hotel, the higher the cost of other services like laundry.

Barber Shops, Hairdressers, Massages: At the expensive Mandarin Hotel in Xiamen: full body massage—¥30; haircut and wash—¥5; shampoo and fingerwave—¥10. If your hotel is charging too much, look for a cheaper hotel.

C.I.T.S: Guide-interpretor per day—¥32. Reconfirming plane tickets, or booking plane or train tickets—usually ¥1 to ¥3, but some have charged as much as ¥7, which includes long-distance telephone call to another city.

Making a reservation for a local hotel—usually ¥1 or ¥2. But Guilin charged ¥10, and Datong charged ¥7 (for the one hotel in town).

These services may not be available during busy tourist seasons.

For prices of minipackages and prepaid tours, write to C.I.T.S. or consult your travel agent. Low tourist season discount was 30%.

Drinks: Happy Hour means cheaper drinks.

Soft drinks ranged from a low of ¥.30 on the train to a high of ¥1.60 at a good hotel and ¥3 at a very posh restaurant. Beer ranged from about ¥.70 to ¥2.00. By the liter, Tsingtao beer was about ¥1.20.

Coffee at a medium-priced hotel was ¥1.00.

Entertainment: Discos at big-city hotels cost from ¥5 to ¥8, but could be cheaper in smaller cities. For foreign tourists, tickets to most cultural events ranged from ¥1 to ¥3.

Food: It is possible to fill your stomach from food stalls for ¥1 a day!

Set menus seemed to range from ¥16 to ¥28 a day, depending on the hotel. The Baiyun in Guangzhou charged ¥5 for breakfast, ¥8.50 for lunch, and ¥8.50 for dinner. The Shanghai Hotel in Shanghai charged ¥4 for breakfast, ¥8.50 for lunch, and ¥8.50 for dinner. The ¥16 was in a decrepit hotel with poor food. See "Food."

One top Beijing hotel charged the following prices, so all other hotels should be considered cheaper:

Chinese **breakfast** (congee, spring rolls, barbecue pork bun, and coconut tart)—¥10.00

American breakfast (fresh orange juice, eggs any style, toast or croissant, and tea or coffee)—¥12;

Continental breakfast—¥8; waffles and maple syrup a la carte—¥5.50.

Chinese **Dinner:** A la carte (smallest dish or ''per person'')—See *Ordering* in "Food."

soup—¥10 to ¥65;

fish—¥15 to ¥52 (in one of Guangzhou's top hotels, most were ¥5 to ¥10);

prawns, crabs, and scallops—¥14 to ¥35;

poultry—¥10 to ¥17; (in Guangzhou, most were ¥8 to ¥13);

pork—¥7 to ¥8; beef—¥10 to ¥18 (pork and beef in Guangzhou—¥4 to ¥7);

vegetables —¥7 to ¥15 (in Guangzhou, ¥4 to ¥9);

desserts—¥3 to ¥4.

Banquet—about ¥600 for 10 people. Prices flexible depending on the menu.

Buffet in top hotel in Guangzhou—¥21 a person.

—lunchtime buffet at the White Swan—¥15 including one drink.

Light lunches:

small bowl of noodles at a stall—¥.40.

small bowl of noodles at a medium-priced hotel—¥2.00

fried rice or noodles at a top-priced hotel—¥2 to ¥4.

Friendship Store Cafe, Guangzhou: hamburger ¥1.30; hot dog (of sorts)—¥.70; spaghetti—¥3.30; milk shake—¥2.60.

Train dining car: Simple Western breakfast—¥3; most dishes—¥2 to ¥6. It is best to order one or two dishes rather than the set menu at ¥10, which has too much food for one person.

Dim Sum in Guangzhou was usually ¥3 to ¥5 a person in restaurants for the masses; but in the fancy rooms with fancy dishes at the Panxi Restaurant there, it could go up to ¥15 to ¥20 a person.

Laundry: At medium-priced hotels, slacks cost about ¥1, a long-sleeved shirt ¥.50 to ¥.80, and shorts ranged from ¥.20 to ¥80. At expensive hotels, prices are double or triple.

Medical: For many years now, treatment for a cold or upset stomach at a hotel clinic, including medicines, cost from ¥2 to ¥4. In late 1985, China announced that medical prices for foreigners were going up, but Overseas Chinese would pay less than F.F. prices. A consultation at the clinic of the Great Wall Hotel or at Capital Hospital (with its high standards) was ¥20 to ¥30.

Permits: Alien permit or travel permit—about ¥8.

Photocopying: About ¥.30 or ¥.50 per sheet. The quality is often poor.

Photography: Photographs at a tourist site were about ¥4.20 to ¥5.20, including surface mail in China.

Camera film paid for in F.E.C.s was cheaper than in R.M.B. So stock up at Friendship Stores and in your hotel. Prices found in Friendship Stores were: Kodachrome 35mm, 36 X, 64 A.S.A.—¥27.30; Kodacolor 100—¥21.00; Kodacolor 100, 36 X—¥6.60. In other words, buy if the price is good, but **check the date** on the box. Best stock up before you arrive.

Porters: If you can find one, about ¥.40 a bag. Baggage carts are slightly more and are nonexistent except in the largest cities.

Postage: Airmail: postcard—¥.70; letter—¥.80. Airmail packages—¥15 per kg; seamail—¥5.40 for one kg, ¥9.00 for two. Registration—¥.50.

Shopping: Some sample prices:
Small flashlight and battery—¥1.99.
Silk—¥8 to ¥19 a meter.
Hand-knit sweaters—¥55 in Guangzhou Friendship Store: cheaper in smaller cities, but may not be as stylish. Men's silk shirts were about ¥37.
Down jackets—¥79 to ¥83, in a proletarian store.
Shanghai Foreign Languages Book Store: *Dream of the Red Chamber* (three volumes)—¥18.95 plus ¥15.00 shipping to Canada. (Cheaper than buying the Beijing edition in the U.S.) All books printed in China are one third to one half the price elsewhere.

Sightseeing: Entrance to tourist attractions—¥.10 to ¥4.50, with most below ¥1.00. Might be slightly higher for Foreign Friends. Express window for cable car up Fragrant Hills in Beijing—about ¥4.50. Slower line—a little over ¥1. The cable car at Taishan costs ¥7 round trip (even if you can only go one way because of adverse weather).
Optional tours: in tour group, ¥10 each for 3½-hour boat ride (with acrobats) in Shanghai. Fancier boat—¥15.

Telephones: Top hotel—Service charge on collect call overseas: ¥3 to ¥5; on overseas calls—10% to 15%. Baiyun Hotel in Guangzhou—¥1.40 for collect calls.
Local telephone calls—free in hotel; about ¥.04 in street.

Transportation: A few hotels offer free transportation to downtown areas and from airport.

Airplane: CAAC for F.F., Guangzhou to H.K.—¥105; Guangzhou-Beijing—¥425 (F.E.C.) Prices of domestic flights can be obtained from the CAAC schedule or from a travel agent. It should include airport transportation to or from the CAAC office.
For foreigners, Xiamen to Beijing—¥282. For Chinese—¥156.00

Bicycles: Some rented at ¥1 for 4 hours; others about ¥4 a day. A few tourist places have asked about ¥14, but that is exceptional.

Buses: Xiamen to Guangzhou for Chinese (showing i.d.)—¥54; for foreigners—¥66 (R.M.B.), ¥36 (F.E.C.), or HK$100; C.I.T.S. air-conditioned bus from Xiamen to Hong Kong or Shenzhen—¥60.

City buses: usually cost less than ¥.50 a trip, depending on destination.

Ferries: ¥.10 or so on cross-harbor or cross-river ferries.

Hydrofoil, Guangzhou to H.K.—¥43

Hovercraft, Guangzhou to H.K.—¥36

Ship from Xiamen to Shanghai—¥33.30 to ¥86. From Xiamen to Guangzhou—¥25.40 to ¥64.40, depending on class.

Taxis: Prices are per kilometer and dependent on age of vehicle, size, and air conditioning. Frequently, you have no choice. Taxis can be hired by the day, half day, or by the kilometer. Prices ranged from ¥.60 to ¥.80 per kilometer for a small, air-conditioned taxi.

Waiting time varies. In Shanghai it was ¥4.80 an hour, plus parking fee (in some places). At Dream of the Red Chamber, parking was ¥1.

One-way trips out of town usually cost an additional half of the one-way fare.

By the half day, a few cities charged ¥30 with ¥.70 a km over 30 km, or a full 8-hour day, ¥60 with ¥.70 a km over 60 km. Most taxis charged from ¥35 to ¥50 for a day, with a few as high as ¥80. Out-of-town can be ¥150 a day. Prices should be posted near the odometer.

Most minibuses that could take eight and perhaps twelve cost from ¥40 to ¥60 a day for the first 40 km. A few cities charged as much as ¥80. Ask about maximum distance. Zhanjiang charged ¥.90 per km, plus ¥8.00 an hour waiting time.

Train: (Foreign Friends) Train prices differ according to the speed of the train, as well as the status of the passenger (O.C., F.F., or local Chinese.) Train fares and schedules are available in English from C.I.T.S. or the train station.

Guangzhou to Beijing: soft berth—¥204.70; hard berth—¥108.40; hard seat—¥67.80.

Guangzhou to Shanghai: soft berth—¥168.10; hard berth—¥89.20; hard seat—¥55.90.

Guangzhou to H.K.: express—¥44.

Xiamen to Shanghai: soft berth—¥131.30; hard berth—¥38. Soft berth for Chinese—¥75.00.

Charge for extra piece of luggage—Xiamen to Guangzhou—¥10.

Hotels

Like everything else, these prices are subject to change. Most will probably increase 10–15% in 1986; for example, the Toronto-Beijing Hotel will change its prices several times from ¥170 in 1985 to ¥288 in November 1986! Other top hotels will probably do the same. Information on prices have been very difficult to obtain from China, as some hotels increased their prices a couple of times during 1985, and many cities ignored our request for information. Even a personal visit to one hotel did not succeed, as the hotel was planning on renovating and would not know its prices for a year. The following are listed to give you an idea of the price ranges and should not be considered absolute, also because of discounts for groups, Overseas Chinese (O.C.), foreign experts, Chinese, payment in F.E.C., payment in R.M.B. (higher than F.E.C.s), foreign exchange rate, old and new wings, etc., etc.

A 10% surcharge will be added to these prices in joint-venture hotels. Some hotels also add a 3 or 5% sales tax, or include it in the base rate.

Some hotels discount 20% in low tourist season.

Throughout this book, we have roughly categorized hotels as "inexpensive" if below ¥50 for a standard double, "medium" (¥50 to ¥100), "expensive" (¥100 to ¥200), and "very expensive" (over ¥200).

Most hotels only have double rooms and suites. A few hotels, especially the newer ones, have singles as well. Prices are usually the same for one as for two people.

The agency from whom you book your hotel should be able to tell you the latest price, but don't count on it. They have trouble getting information, too, except for the top hotels.

The following are some 1985 hotel prices. Please note that the telephone numbers are the latest we could possibly obtain. China is in the process of upgrading its telephone service, and is therefore changing many of its telephone numbers.

	telephone	*rate in R.M.B.*	*page*
Anshan:			
Anshan		¥35	154
Shengli		¥30	155
Anyang:			
Anyang	2157, 2244, 2239	¥36	156
Taihang	2012		156
Xiangzhou	4238	¥36	156
Baotau:			
Baotou	26612	¥30	157
Donghe	43541	¥30	157
Qingshan (Blue Mountain)	24615	¥30	157
Beidaihe: (Low tourist season: Oct. 2–April 30, 20% discount)			
Xishan (West Hill)	2678, 2768	¥34, 38	159
Zhongtan Tai (Central Beach)	2398	¥34, 38	159
Beijing:			
Beijing	5007766	about ¥130	182

Chongwenmen	757181		182
Diaoyutai	866152, 866250		182
Great Wall	5005566, 558851	US$150	182
Heping (Peace)	558841		183
Holiday Inn Lido	5006688	¥150	183
Huadu	475431, 5001166	about ¥72	183
Huaqiao Mansion	558851		183
Huaqiao Hotel	441231, 446611		183
Jianguo	5002233	¥155	183
Jinglun	5002266	¥170	183
Minzu (Nationalities)	668541	about ¥60	184
Qianmen	338731		184
Wannian Qing (Evergreen)	89133		184
Xiangshan (Fragrant Hills)	819225, 285491, 81942	about ¥150	184
Xinqiao	557731	¥60	184
Xiyuan	868821, 890721		184
Yanjing	868621, 868721		184
Yanshan	282394, 285570		184
Yanxiang	5006666		185
Yiheyuan Fandian (Summer Palace)	285398		185
Youyi (Friendship)	890621		185
Zhaolong	5002299	¥160	185

Changchun:

Changbaishan	53551	¥40	189
Nanhu	53571	¥64	189
Provincial Chun Yi	38495	¥40	190

Changsha:

Fenglin	82901	¥40	193
Furong (Hibiscus)	26246	¥45	193
Hunan	26331		193
Rongyuan		¥45	193
Xiangjiang (Xiang River)	26261	¥40	193

Chengde:

Chengde (old)	2551	¥41	199
Shanzhuang	2457	¥42	198
Xinhua	2556	¥40	199

Chengdu:

Chengdu	42312	¥38	204
Jinjiang (Brocade River)	24481	¥40	203
Jinniu	29151, 25300, 24214		204
Wanjiang	29217		204

Chongqing:

Chongqing	53158		207
Huixianlou Hotel	43808		

Renmin (People's)	53421		207
Yuzhou	23829		207

Dalian:

Bangchuidao (Ginseng Islet)	25131, 23131	¥45–150	210
Dalian Hotel	23171		210
Dalian Guest House	23111		210
Nanshan	25103	¥70	210

Datong:

Datong	33481, 32333	¥54	213
Datong Mining Co.	32431		213

Dunhuang:

Dunhung Hotel	74		217

Fushun:

Fushun	22181		220

Fuzhou:

Overseas Chinese	57603, 31386		222
Minjiang (Min River)	33492		222
Qiaolian	34944		222
Xi Hu (West Lake)	32955, 32227		222

Guangzhou:

Baitian E (White Swan)	886968	¥80 and up	235
Baiyun	67700	¥90	235
China	66888	about ¥100	235
Dongfang	69900		235
Guangdong	32950		236
Guangzhou	338168	about ¥40	236
Huaqiao (O.C.)	61112	about ¥87	236
Huayuan (Garden)	773388	¥100	236
Kuangchuan (Spa)	32540, 61334	¥34–48	236
Liuhua	68800	about ¥45	236
Nanhu (South Lake)	76367, 78052	¥60–70	236
Renmin (People's)	61445	¥58–63	237

Guilin:

Dangui (Osmanthus)	2261, 3576		242
Guilin Jiashan	2240, 2986, 4712		243
Lijiang (Li River)	2881, 3050	¥50	243
Rongcheng	2311, 5893	¥65	243
Ronghu (Banyan)	3811	¥70	243
Yangshuo	2260		243

Guiyang:

Huaxi	25973		245

Hangzhou:

Hangzhou	22921, 25928	¥132	253
Huagang	71324, 72481, 24001	¥45	253

Huajiashan	71224, 26450	¥48	253
Huaqiao (O.C.)	23401, 22665		253
Liulang	21129		254
Wanghu	71024, 71942	¥85	254
Xihu (West Lake)	26867, 21728k		254
Xiling	28301, 22921	¥132	254
Zhejiang	25601, 24483	¥48	254

Harbin:

Friendship Palace	46146, 46119		256
Guoji (International)	31441, 33001	¥60	256
Beifang (North Mansion)	33081, 33061		256
Harbin	45846		
Hepingcun (Peace Village)	33047, 33048, 32093	¥60	256
Songhua River Hotel	44642		
Swan	51006, 53728		256

Hefei:

Daozianglou	74791		258
Jianghuai	72221	¥45	258
Luyang	74791	¥50	258
Meishan	62584		

Hohhot:

Hohhot	23291	¥40	264
Inner Mongolian	41183	¥60 and ¥80	263
Xincheng (New City)	23107	¥44	264

Huangshan:

Beihai (North Sea)	241		265
Huangshan	202		265
Taoyuan (Peach Spring)	295		265
Yupinglou (Jade Screen)	303		265

Jiangmen:

Donghu (East Lake)	33611		267

Jilin:

Dongguan Hotel	3555		268
Xiguan	5545		268

Jinan:

Jinan	35351, 35352		272
Nanjiao (South Suburbs)	23931		272

Jiuquan:

Jiuquan	2943	¥38	276

Kunming:

Green Lake	22192, 23514	¥45	283
Kunming	27732, 22063	¥50	283
Xiyuan	81059		283

Lanzhou:

Lanzhou	22981, 22985		286
Ning Wozhuang	22891		286
Victory	21501		286
Friendship (Youyi)	3051		286

Lhasa:

Lhasa	23859	¥120	294
No. 1 Hotel	22500	¥120	294
Snowland	23687	¥20	294

Liuzhou:

Liujiang	25021		295
Liuzhou	24921	¥24–36	295

Luoyang:

Youyi (Friendship)	6006, 2157, 2159		299

Lushan:

Lulin	2424	¥35–50	302
Lushan Hotel	2497, 2427, 2932	¥45	302
Lushan Mansion		¥35	302
Yunzong (Amidst the Clouds)	2547		302

Nanchang:

Jiangxi	64861		305

Nanjing:

Dingshan	85931	about ¥40	314
Dongjiao	34121, 41700		314
Jinling	44141, 41121, 42525	about ¥70	314
Nanjing	34121	about ¥50	314
Shengli (Victory)	43035, 43880, 42217		314
Shuangmenlou	85965, 85535, 85931	about ¥40	315

Nanning:

Min Yuan	28923	¥36	317
Xi Yuan	29923	¥36	317
Yongjiang (Yong River)	28123	¥36	317
Yongzhou	23120	¥36	317

Ningbo:

Overseas Chinese (Huaqiao)	63175	¥42	320
Ningbo	66334	¥38	320
Yonggang	65621	¥40	320

Qingdao:

Badaguan	26800		324
The Guesthouse	26120		324
Huanghai	84215, 85965		324
Huaqiao (O.C.)	86738-9, 85738, 27738		324

Liaoning Mansions	62546		360
Youyi (Friendship)	62822		

Shenzhen:
Shenzhen International		about ¥90	

Shijiazhuang:
Hebei Guest House	48961	¥40	363
Shijiazhuang	45866		363

Suzhou:
Gusu (Ancient Suzhou)	24646		371
Nanlin	24441, 24641	about ¥45	371
New Nanlin	24641		372
Nanyuan	24641, 24441		372
Suzhou	24646, 22298	about ¥45	372

Tai'an:
Taishan Guest House	4694		373

Taishan, Guangdong:
Friendship		¥23	375
Huaqiao (O.C.)	2720	¥32	375
Hubin		¥40	375
Stone Flower Mountain		¥22	375

Taiyuan:
Bingzhou	25924		378
Jinci	29441, 29941		378
San Jin Mansions	23489		379
Yinze	23211		379

Tianjin:
Tianjin Guest House a.k.a. Grand	39213, 39288		384
Tianjin Hotel a.k.a. Astor, Tientsin	34325		384
Tianjin No. 1	36438		384
Yingbin a.k.a. Tianjin Garden	24010		384
Youyi (Friendship)	35663		384

Urumqi:
Friendship	23991, 23951, 22233	¥36	390
Kunlun	23360, 42411		390
Tian Shan	23101, 23010		390
Urumqi	24576		390
Xinjiang	22233, 23222		390

Wuhan:
Hongshan	71581		396
Jianghan	21253, 23998	¥50	396
Shengli	21241, 22531	about ¥40	396
Xuangong	21023, 24404	about ¥30	396

Wuxi:

Hubin	26712	¥47	398
Shuixiu	26591	¥50	398
State Guest House	23001		398
Taihu	23001	¥130	398

Xiamen:

Huaqiao (O.C.)	25699, 24286, 22729	¥56	404
Jinbao	26888	¥75	404
Lujiang	23234, 23232, 22212	¥70	404
Seaview Garden Tourist Village	24210, 22052	¥60	405
Xiamen Guest House	24941		405
Xiamen Mandarin	43333	¥150	405

Xi'an:

Chang'an	2461	¥48–52	417
Golden Flower	32981	US$120	417
Huaqing Hot Spring		¥48	417
Renmin (People's)	25111	¥60–80	417
Shaanxi	23831, 41813	¥60	417
Tangcheng	51427		417
Xi'an	51351	¥58–70	417
Zhonglou (Bell Tower)	28767	about ¥55	417

Xining:

Qinghai	23961	¥41–59	420
Xining	23901	¥30	420

Xiqiao:

Baiyun Lou	611	¥8	421
Handan Biedi	242	¥20	421
Sanhu	342	¥65	421

Yan'an:

Yan'an Guest House	2767, 2252		425

Yangzhou:

Xiyuan	22611, 23511 X590, 591, 593	¥40–80	431
Yangzhou	22611 or 23511 X453, 454, 455	¥56–112	431

Yantai:

Dongshan	24501	¥40	435
Huaqiao (O.C.)	24431		435
Yantai Shan	22936	¥40	436
Zhifu	24381	¥40	436

Yinchuan:

Ningxia	2131		439
Yinchuan	3053, 2615		439

Yixing:

Yixing	2559, 2493, 2179	¥38	440

Zhangzhou:

Huaqiao (O.C.)	3614	¥34	442
Zhangzhou	4714	¥34	442
Zhangzhou New Times	4687		442

Zhanjiang:

Haibin	23555	¥30–80	443
Overseas Chinese	24966		443
Youyi (Friendship)	23555, 24808	¥96	443
Zhanjiang	23888, 23788		443

Zhengzhou:

February 7	26744		449
Henan	22581		449
International	26531		449
Youyi (Friendship)	24604		449
Zhengzhou	29941, 24937		449

Zhenjiang:

Jinkou		¥30	
Jinqiao		¥28	
Jinshan	24962	¥45	452
No. 1 Spring Hotel	23422	¥45	452

Zhuhai:

Zhuhai Resort	22221, 22739		453

FINANCES

Not all foreign banks and financial institutions have relations with the Bank of China. To avoid inconvenience, always ask if their services can be used in China.

Only some **foreign currencies** are accepted for exchange in China. These are: Australian dollar (A$), Austrian schilling (Sch), Belgian franc (BF), Canadian dollar (Can$), Danish krone (DKr), West German mark (DM), French franc (FF), Japanese yen (¥), Malaysian dollar (M$), Dutch guilder (fl.), Norwegian krone (NKr), Singapore dollar (S$) Swedish krona (SKr), Swiss franc (SF), pound sterling (£), US dollar (US$) and Hongkong dollar (HK$).

Not all **credit cards** are acceptable in China. Some can be used to pay for a limited number of hotels, obtain cash, and pay for purchases in a few designated stores, with a 4% surcharge. Currently accepted are Federal Card, Visa/MasterCard, American Express, Diner's Club, Million Card, Great Wall, and JCB Card. Payment can also be made with Renminbi Travelers Letter of Credit bought with foreign currencies, drafts and other payment instruments in convertible currencies issued by the Bank of China branches in London, New York, Singapore, Luxembourg and Hongkong and the banks maintaining accounts in convertible Renminbi with the Banking Department, Bank of China, Head Office.

Some travelers, however, have found Letters of Credit difficult to convert into F.E.C.s.

The only **traveler's checks and money orders** accepted are issued by foreign banks that have concluded payment arrangements with the Bank of China. These are:

Rafidain Bank, Baghdad, Iraq. T/C	US.$, £
Arab Bank Ltd., Amman, Jordan. T/C	US.$ £
The National Bank of Australasia Ltd., Melbourne, Australia. T/C	Australian Dollar
Bank of New South Wales, Sydney, Australia. T/C	Australian Dollar
Australia & New Zealand Banking Group Ltd., T/C	$, $A
Commonwealth Trading Bank of Australia, Sydney, Australia. T/C	$, $A
MITSUI-THOMAS COOK T/C	Japanese Yen
Hankyu Express International Co. Ltd., "VISA" T/C	Japanese Yen
Yamaguchi Bank Ltd., "VISA" T/C	Japanese Yen
The Bank of Tokyo, Ltd., Tokyo. T/C	US.$, Yen
The Sumitomo Bank Ltd., "VISA" T/C, Tokyo	Yen
The Fuji Bank, Ltd., Tokyo. T/C	Yen
Barclays Bank International Ltd., "VISA" T/C and International Money Order, London	£, US.$
Lloyds Bank Ltd., London. T/C	£
Standard Chartered Bank Ltd., London. T/C	£, US.$
The Royal Bank of Scotland Group T/C, London	£
Grindlays "VISA" T/C, London	£
National Westminster Bank Ltd., London. T/C	£
Thomas Cook & Sons Ltd., London. T/C	£, US.$, Can.$, A$
The Hongkong & Shanghai-THOMAS COOK T/C	Hongkong Dollar
Standard DM. T/C Issued by 30 German Banks	Deutsche Mark
Societe Francaise Du Cheque De Voyage S.A. T/C	French Frs.
Societe Generale THOMAS COOK T/C	French Frs.
Swiss Bankers T/C, Berne, Switzerland.	Swiss Frs.
Banque Bruxelles Lambert, Brussels T/C	Belgian Frs.
Societe Generale De Banque, Brussels T/C	Belgian Frs.
Algemene Bank Nederland N.V., Amsterdam T/C	Florin
Amsterdam-Rotterdam Bank N.V., Amsterdam T/C	Florin
Nederlandsche Middenstandsbank N.V., Amsterdam. T/C	Florin
Norwegian T/C	Norwegian Krone
The Royal Bank of Canada, Montreal. World Money Order	Can.$, US.$
Bank of America, San Francisco, T/C	US.$
Citicorp, New York, T/C	US.$
Manufacturers Hanover Trust Co., New York, International Money Order	US.$
American Express Co., New York. T/C	US.$, £, F.frs., Can.$, Yen, DM, S.frs.

First National Bank of Chicago "VISA" T/C, Chi-   US.$
cago
Republic Naitonal Bank of Dallas, Texas. T/C   US.$

SALARIES

For your information, some monthly salaries in China are:

Attendants—at a top Beijing joint-venture hotel: about ¥120; at a good but small hotel in a small city in Shandong: ¥40 plus ¥5 to ¥20 bonus; attendant in the dining car on a train: ¥46 plus ¥20 bonus if business is good. (He paid ¥2.31 rent for one room); attendant at the Dream of the Red Chamber site in Shanghai: ¥80 to ¥90.

C.I.T.S. guides in Chengde—¥50 to ¥70 plus bonus.

Most Chinese salaries range from ¥70 to ¥140.

CURRENCY

Chinese money is called Renminbi (RMB)—people's money. The Chinese dollar, known as the *yuan* (or *kuai*) equals 10 *jiao* or 100 *fen*. Yuan notes are in denominations of 10, 5, 2, and 1. The smaller jiao notes are 5, 2, and 1. The coins are 5, 2, and 1 fen.

F.E.C.s are Foreign Exchange Certificates with which you must pay for tourist hotels, tourist restaurants, and some shops.

Foreign exchange rates fluctuate. There is also a slight variation for cash or traveler's checks. Please consult your bank, Bank of China, or the *China Daily*.

The following chart will give you a rough idea of Chinese equivalents. If you cannot find the exchange rate in effect when you go, draw up your own table so that you can convert easily.

DOLLAR TO YUAN CONVERSION TABLE
(Prepared by Terry Malloy)

Dollar	Yuan	Yuan	Yuan	Yuan	Yuan	Yuan	Yuan
1	2.10	2.30	2.50	2.70	2.90	3.10	3.30
2	4.20	4.60	5.00	5.40	5.80	6.20	6.60
3	6.30	6.90	7.50	8.10	8.70	9.30	9.90
4	8.40	9.20	10.00	10.80	11.60	12.40	13.20
5	10.50	11.50	12.50	13.50	14.50	15.50	16.50
6	12.60	13.80	15.00	16.20	17.40	18.60	19.80
7	14.70	16.10	17.50	18.90	20.30	21.70	23.10
8	16.80	18.40	20.00	21.60	23.20	24.80	26.40
9	18.90	20.70	22.50	24.30	26.10	27.90	29.70
10	21.00	23.00	25.00	27.00	29.00	31.00	33.00
20	42.00	46.00	50.00	54.00	58.00	62.00	66.00

Dollar	Yuan	Yuan	Yuan	Yuan	Yuan	Yuan	Yuan
30	63.00	69.00	75.00	81.00	87.00	93.00	99.00
40	84.00	92.00	100.00	108.00	116.00	124.00	132.00
50	105.00	115.00	125.00	135.00	145.00	155.00	165.00
60	126.00	138.00	150.00	162.00	174.00	186.00	198.00
70	147.00	161.00	175.00	189.00	203.00	217.00	231.00
80	168.00	184.00	200.00	216.00	232.00	248.00	264.00
90	189.00	207.00	225.00	243.00	261.00	279.00	297.00
100	210.00	230.00	250.00	270.00	290.00	310.00	330.00
200	420.00	460.00	500.00	540.00	580.00	620.00	660.00
300	630.00	690.00	750.00	810.00	870.00	930.00	990.00
400	840.00	920.00	1000.00	1080.00	1160.00	1240.00	1320.00
500	1050.00	1150.00	1250.00	1350.00	1450.00	1550.00	1650.00
600	1260.00	1380.00	1500.00	1620.00	1740.00	1860.00	1980.00
700	1470.00	1610.00	1750.00	1890.00	2030.00	2170.00	2310.00
800	1680.00	1840.00	2000.00	2160.00	2320.00	2480.00	2640.00
900	1890.00	2070.00	2250.00	2430.00	2610.00	2790.00	2970.00
1000	2100.00	2300.00	2500.00	2700.00	2900.00	3100.00	3300.00

YUAN TO DOLLAR CONVERSION TABLE
(Prepared by Terry Malloy)

	IF YOUR DOLLAR IS WORTH						
Yuan	¥2.10	¥2.30	¥2.50	¥2.70	¥2.90	¥3.10	¥3.30
1	$ .48	$ .43	$ .40	$ .37	$ .34	$ .32	$ .30
2	.95	.87	.80	.74	.69	.65	.60
3	1.43	1.30	1.20	1.11	1.03	.97	.90
4	1.90	1.74	1.60	1.48	1.38	1.29	1.21
5	2.38	2.17	2.00	1.85	1.72	1.61	1.51
6	2.86	2.61	2.40	2.22	2.07	1.94	1.81
7	3.33	3.04	2.80	2.59	2.41	2.26	2.12
8	3.80	3.48	3.20	2.96	2.76	2.58	2.42
9	4.29	3.91	3.60	3.33	3.10	2.90	2.73
10	4.76	4.35	4.00	3.70	3.45	3.23	3.03
20	9.52	8.70	8.00	7.40	6.90	6.45	6.06
30	14.29	13.04	12.00	11.11	10.34	9.68	9.09
40	19.04	17.39	16.00	14.81	13.79	12.90	12.12
50	23.81	21.74	20.00	18.52	17.24	16.13	15.15
60	28.57	26.09	24.00	22.22	20.69	19.35	18.18
70	33.33	30.43	28.00	25.93	24.14	22.58	21.21
80	38.10	34.78	32.00	29.63	27.59	25.81	24.24
90	42.86	39.13	36.00	33.33	31.03	29.03	27.27
100	47.62	43.48	40.00	37.04	34.48	32.26	30.30
200	95.24	86.96	80.00	74.07	68.97	64.52	60.60

	IF YOUR DOLLAR IS WORTH						
Yuan	*¥2.10*	*¥2.30*	*¥2.50*	*¥2.70*	*¥2.90*	*¥3.10*	*¥3.30*
300	142.86	130.43	120.00	111.11	103.45	96.77	90.90
400	190.48	173.91	160.00	148.15	137.93	129.03	121.21
500	238.10	217.39	200.00	185.19	172.14	161.29	151.51
600	285.71	260.87	240.00	222.22	206.90	193.55	181.81
700	333.33	304.35	280.00	259.26	241.38	225.81	212.12
800	380.95	347.83	320.00	296.30	275.86	258.06	242.42
900	428.57	391.30	360.00	333.33	310.34	290.32	272.72
1000	476.19	434.78	400.00	370.37	344.82	322.58	303.03

In June 1986, the exchange rates in R.M.B. yuan as printed in *China Daily* were:

Currency		*Per*	*Buying*	*Selling*
Australia	$	100	226.72	227.86
Austria	Sch	100	20.03	20.13
Belgium	Fr	10000	(c)685.79	689.23
			(f)678.96	682.36
Canada	$	100	229.95	231.11
Denmark	Kr	100	37.94	38.14
Finland	Fmk	100	61.59	61.89
F.R.G.	Dm	100	141.55	142.25
France	Fr	100	45.57	45.79
Iran	Rial	10000	376.82	378.70
Italy	Lira	10000	20.65	20.75
Japan	Yen	100000	1786.93	1795.89
Holland	G	100	124.27	124.89
Norway	Kr	100	44.48	44.70
Pakistan	Rs	100	20.00	20.10
Singapore	$	100	143.72	144.44
Sweden	Kr	100	44.11	44.33
Swiss	Fr	100	165.68	166.52
U.K.	pound	100	476.22	478.60
USA	$	100	320.63	322.23
Hongkong	$	100	40.88	41.08

¥1.00 F.E.C. = ¥1.60 R.M.B. on the black market making US$1.00 approximately = ¥5.9 R.M.B.

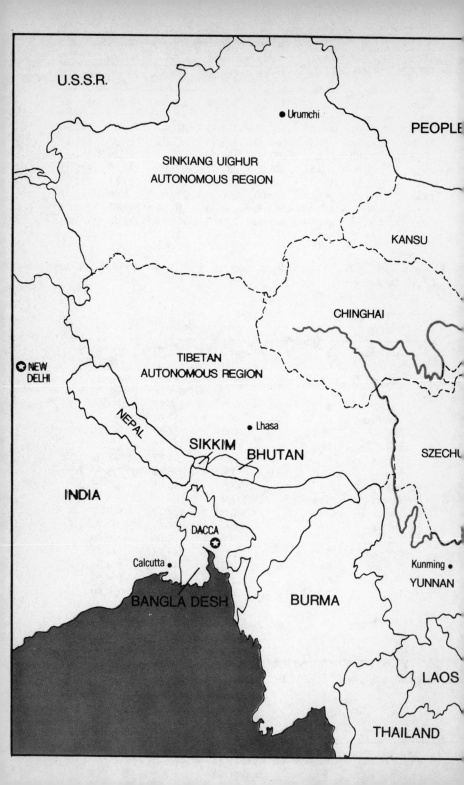

The People's Republic of China
(old spelling)

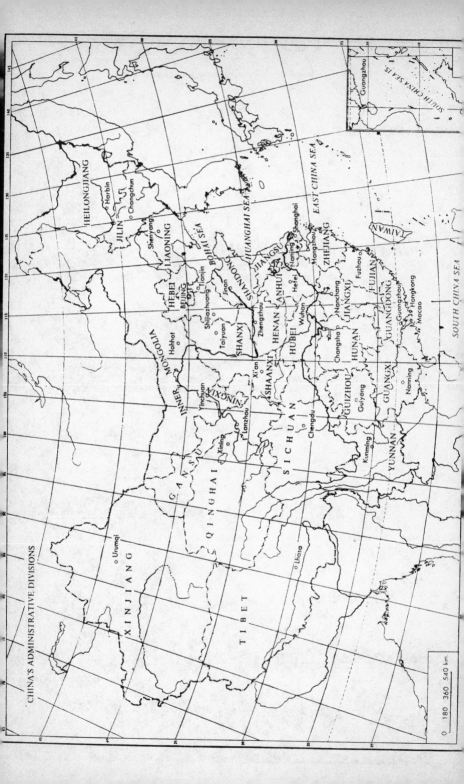

Xuzhou

JIANGSU

ANHUI

Yangzhou

Nanjing
Zhenjiang

Hefei
Wuxi
Changzhou
Suzhou
Yixing

Shanghai

Yangtze River
Hangzhou
SHANGHAI

Huangshan
Shaoxing
Ningbo

ZHEJIANG

Fuzhou

FUJIAN
Quanzhou
Zhangzhou
Xiamen

Z.M. Li

**EAST CHINA
TOURIST REGION**

NORTH CHINA
TOURIST REGION

INNER
MONGOLIA

Baotou

Hohhot

Yellow River

Datong

Hengshan

Taiyuan

Dazhai

SHANXI

Yinchuan

NINGXIA

Chengde

Zunhua

Beijing

Shanhaiguan
Qinhuangdao
Beidaihe
Tangshan

Tianjin

HEBEI

Shiziazhuang

Handan

Yellow River

Zibo

Jinan

Tai'an

Qufu

Yantai

Weihai

Qingdao

Weifang

SHANDONG

Z.M. Li

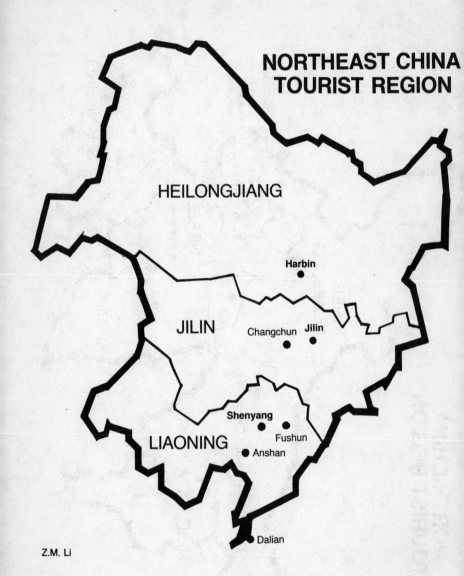

NORTHEAST CHINA TOURIST REGION

HEILONGJIANG

Harbin

JILIN

Changchun   Jilin

Shenyang

LIAONING   Fushun

Anshan

Dalian

Z.M. Li

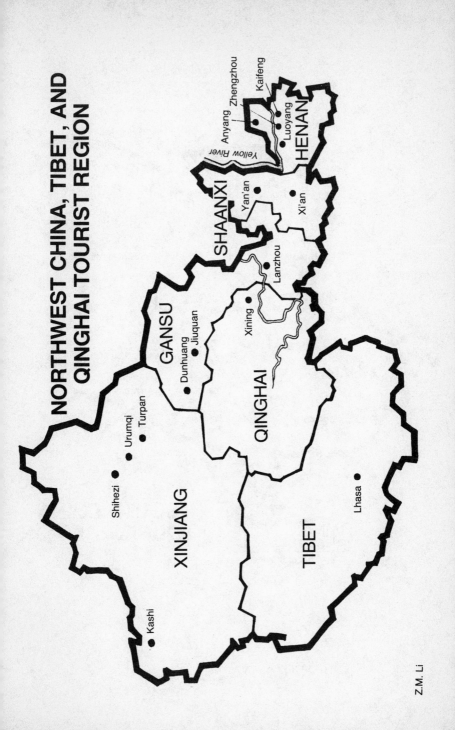

NORTHWEST CHINA, TIBET, AND
QINGHAI TOURIST REGION

HENAN

Anyang
Zhengzhou
Kaifeng
Luoyang
Yellow River

SHAANXI

Yan'an
Xi'an

Lanzhou

GANSU

Jiuquan
Dunhuang

Xining

QINGHAI

Turpan
Urumqi

Shihezi

XINJIANG

Kashi

TIBET

Lhasa

Z.M. Li

Jiujiang

Lushan

Jingdezhen

Yueyang

HUNAN **Changsha**

Nanchang

JIANGXI

Shaoshan

Hengshan

Jinggang
Mountains

Guilin

Liuzhou

Shaoguan

GUANGDONG

GUANGXI

Shantou

Foshan Conghua

Zhaoqing **Guangzhou**

Guiping

Xiqiao Shekou

Nanning Jiangmen Shenzhen

Taishan Hong Kong

Xinhui Zhuhai

Zhongshan

Zhanjiang

HAINAN Haikou

ISLAND Sanya

SOUTH CHINA
TOURIST REGION

Z.M. Li

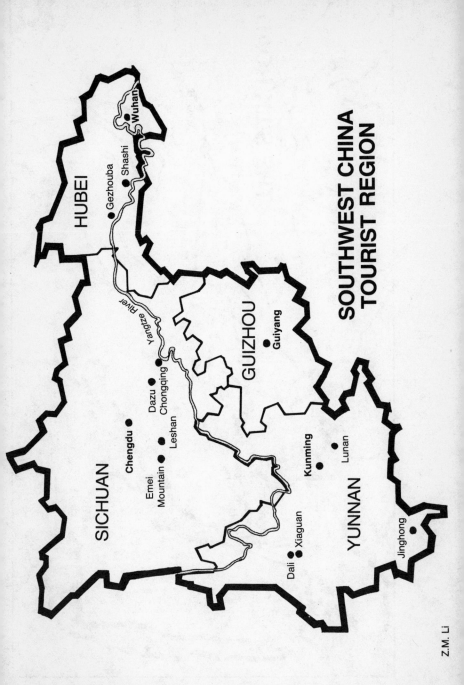

SOUTHWEST CHINA
TOURIST REGION

HUBEI

Gezhouba

Shashi

Wuhan

Yangtze River

SICHUAN

Chengdu

Dazu

Chongqing

Emei Mountain

Leshan

GUIZHOU

Guiyang

Kunming

Lunan

YUNNAN

Dali

Xiaguan

Jinghong

Z.M. Li

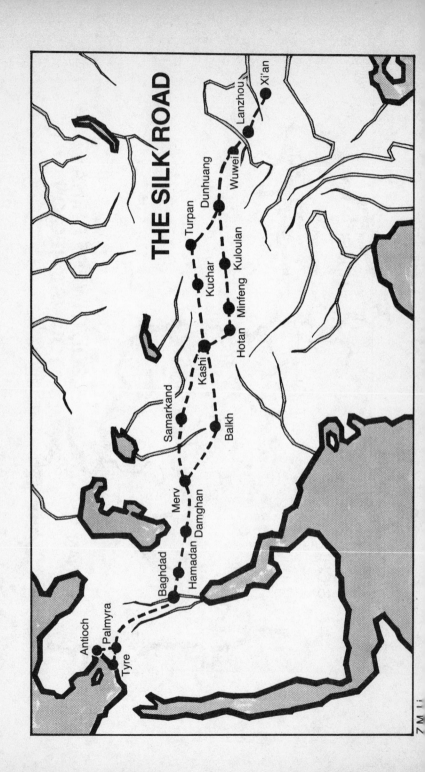

THE SILK ROAD

Xi'an
Lanzhou
Wuwei
Dunhuang
Turpan
Kuchar
Kuloulan
Minfeng
Hotan
Kashi
Balkh
Samarkand
Merv
Damghan
Hamadan
Baghdad
Palmyra
Antioch
Tyre

Z M li

THE YANGTZE GORGES

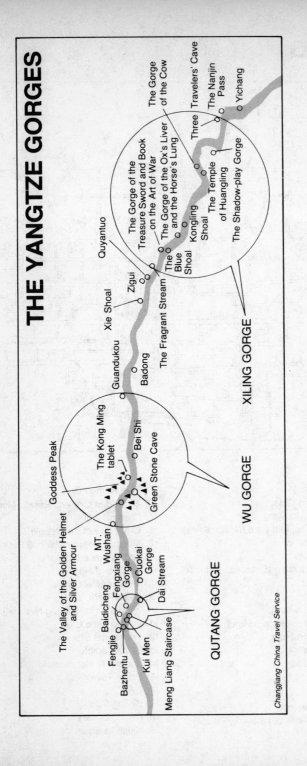

Changjiang China Travel Service

QUTANG GORGE

- The Valley of the Golden Helmet and Silver Armour
- Baidicheng
- Fengjie
- Bazhentu
- Kui Men
- Meng Liang Staircase
- Fengtu
- MT. Wushan
- Fengxiang Gorge
- Cuokai Gorge
- Dai Stream

WU GORGE

- Goddess Peak
- The Kong Ming tablet
- Bei Shi
- Green Stone Cave
- Guandukou
- Badong

XILING GORGE

- Quyantuo
- Xie Shoal
- Zigui
- The Fragrant Stream
- The Gorge of the Treasure Sword and Book on the Art of War
- The Gorge of the Ox's Liver and the Horse's Lung
- The Blue Shoal
- Kongling Shoal
- The Temple of Huangling
- The Shadow-play Gorge
- The Gorge of the Cow
- Three Travelers' Cave
- The Nanjin Pass
- Yichang

BEIJING

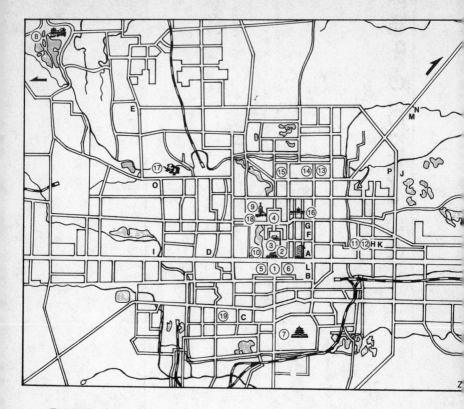

Tourist Hotels
A. Beijing (Peking)
B. Xin Qiao (Hsin Chiao)
C. Qianmen (Chien Men)
D. Minzu (Min Tzu, Min Dzu) [Nationalities]
E. Youyi [Friendship]
F. Heping [Peace]
G. Huaqiao (Huachiao) [Overseas Chinese]
H. Jianguo Hotel
I. Yanjing Hotel
J. Great Wall Sheraton
K. Jinglun (Toronto-Beijing) Hotel
L. Chongwenmen Hotel
M. Yanxiang Hotel
N. Holiday Inn Lido
O. Xiyuan Hotel
P. Huadu Hotel

Of Interest to Visitors
1. Tian Anmen [Gate of Heavenly Peace]
   Square

2. Tian Anmen Gate
3. Forbidden City and Palace Museum
4. Coal Hill Park
5. Great Hall of the People
6. Museums of the Chinese Revolution
   and Chinese History
7. Temple of Heaven
8. Summer Palace
9. Beihai Park
10. Zhongnanhai (Chung Nan Hai)
11. International Club
12. Friendship Store
13. Lama Temple
14. Temple of Confucius
15. Drum Tower
16. CAAC
17. Beijing Zoo
18. Beijing Library
19. Niujie Mosque

CHANGSHA

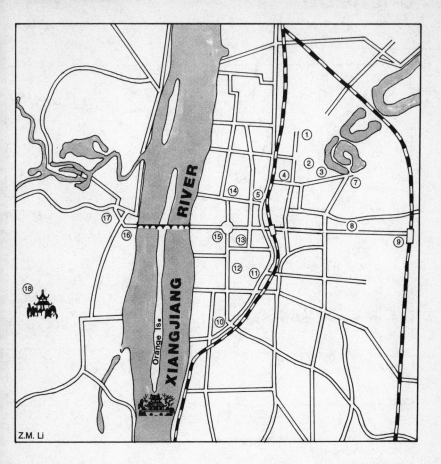

Z.M. Li

1. Hunan Provincial Museum
2. Martyrs' Park
3. Hunan Guest House
4. Hunan Exhibition Hall
5. Xiangjiang Guesthouse
6. Friendship Store
7. Rongyuan Hotel
8. Changdao Hotel
9. Railway Station

10. Hunan No. 1 Normal School
11. Tianxin Park
12. Huangxing Rd.
13. Jiefang Rd.
14. Zhongshan Rd.
15. Hunan Embroidery Building
16. Lushan Hotel
17. Fenglin Hotel
18. Aiwan Pavilion

CHENGDU

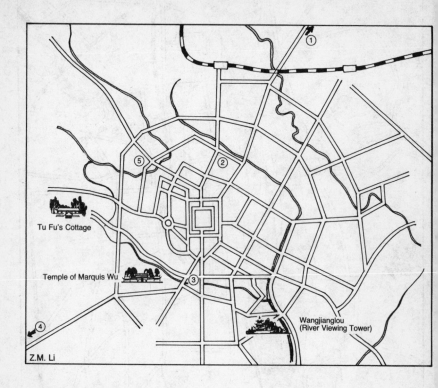

Tu Fu's Cottage

Temple of Marquis Wu

Wangjianglou
(River Viewing Tower)

Z.M. Li

1. To Zoo and Divine Light Monastery
2. Wenshui Monastery
3. Jinjiang Hotel
4. To Leshan and Emei Shan
5. Tomb of Wang Jian

CHONGQING

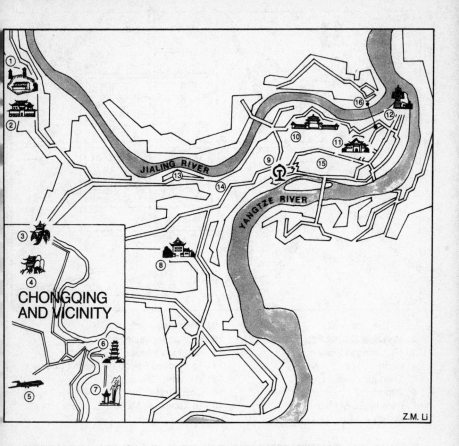

1. Jiatse Cave
2. Bai Gong Guan
3. North Hot Spring Park
4. Chingyun Park
5. Airport
6. South Hot Spring Park
7. South Mountain Park
8. Yuzhou Guest House
9. Railway Station
10. People's Guest House
11. Chongqing Guest House
12. Chaotianmen Wharf
13. Hongyancun (Red Crag Village)
14. Eling (Goose Neck Park)
15. Loquat Hill
16. Cableway
   Jinshajie Station
   Cangbailu Station

DATONG

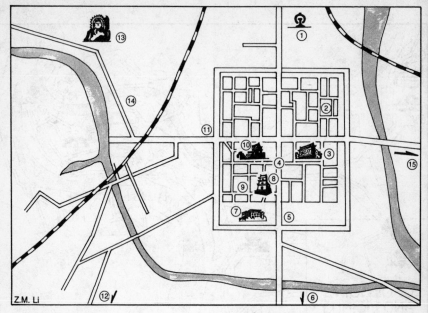

Z.M. Li

1. Railway Station
2. Municipal Carpet Factory
3. Nine Dragon Screen
4. Drum Tower
5. Yungang Guest House
6. Airport
7. Datong Guest House
8. Shanhua Monastery
9. Brassware Factory
10. Huayan Monastery
11. Red Flag Bazaar
12. To Wooden Pagoda, Yingxian County
13. Yungang Caves
14. Guanyin Hall
15. To Temple in Mid-air

GUANGZHOU

1. National Peasant Movement Institute
2. Memorial Gardens to the Martyrs of the 1927 Guangzhou Uprising
3. Mausoleum of the Seventy-two Martyrs at Huanghuagang
4. Guangzhou Zoo
5. Zhenhai Tower
6. Dr. Sun Yat-sen Memorial Hall
7. Temple of the Six Banyan Trees and Liurong Temple
8. Guangzhou Cultural Park
9. Guangzhou Trade Center
10. C.I.T.S.
11. CAAC
12. Friendship Store
13. Huai Sheng Mosque a.k.a. Guang Ta Monastery
14. Nanfang Department Store
15. Zhoutouzui (Ship Quay)
16. Qingping Free Market
17. Guangxiao Temple
18. Cathedral of the Sacred Heart
19. Folk Arts and Crafts Hall

Hotels

A. Dongang (Tung-fang) and China Guangzhou
B. Guangzhou
C. Liu Hua
D. Huaqiao [Overseas Chinese] Mansion
E. Renmin [People's]
F. Kuang Chuan [Spa Villa] Hotel
G. Bai Tian E (White Swan)
H. Baiyun and Garden Hotels

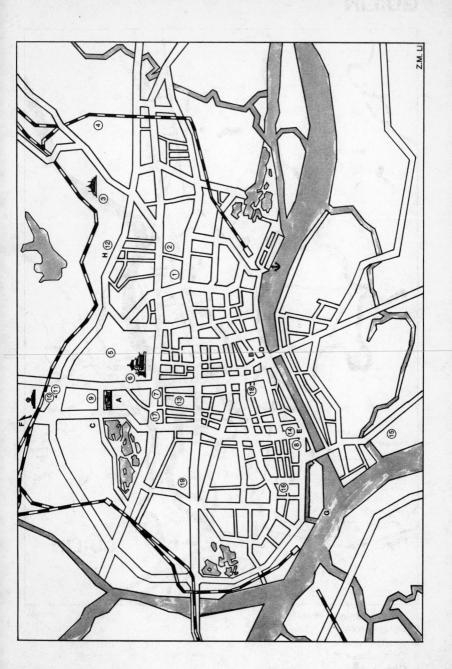

Z.M. Li

GUILIN

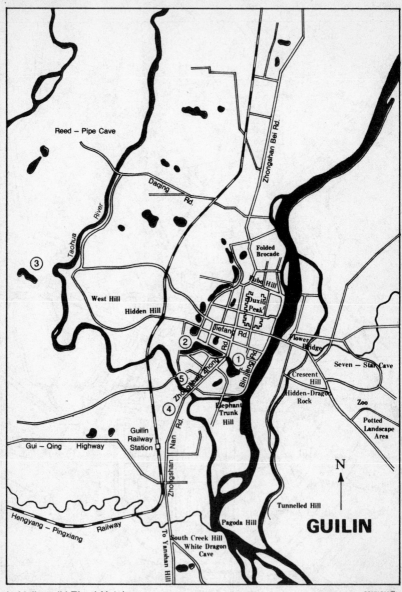

Reed – Pipe Cave

Daqing Rd.

Zhongshan Bei Rd.

Taohua River

3

West Hill

Hidden Hill

Folded Brocade

Fuba Hill

Duxiu Peak

Jiefang Rd.

2

Binjiang Rd.

1

Flower Bridge

Seven – Star Cave

Crescent Hill

Hidden - Dragon Rock

Zoo

5

Zhongshan Zhong Rd.

4

Elephant Trunk Hill

Potted Landscape Area

Zhongshan Nan Rd.

Gui – Qing Highway

Guilin Railway Station

N

Hengyang – Pingxiang Railway

To Yanshan Hill

Pagoda Hill

Tunnelled Hill

GUILIN

South Creek Hill
White Dragon Cave

ROMY PARIÑA

1. Li Jiang (Li River) Hotel
2. Ronghu Hotel
3. Jiashan Hotel
4. Osmanthus Hotel
5. Guilin Hotel

HANGZHOU

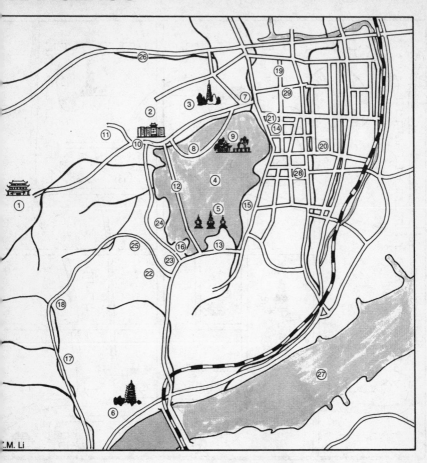

.M. Li

1. Lingyin Temple
2. Hangzhou Hotel
3. Baochu Pagoda
4. West Lake
5. Three Pools Mirroring the Moon
6. Six Harmonies Pagoda
7. Children's Palace
8. Baidi Causeway
9. Autumn Moon on Calm Lake
10. Temple of Yue Fei
11. Jade Spring
12. Sudi Causeway
13. Nanshan Rd.
14. Hubin Rd.
15. Liulangwenying Park
16. Huagang Park
17. Nine Creeks and Eighteen Gullies
18. Dragon Well
19. Yan'an Rd.
20. Jiefang Rd.
21. Overseas Chinese Hotel
22. Huajiashan
23. Huagang Hotel
24. Xihu Hotel
25. Zhejiang Hotel
26. Yellow Dragon Hotel
27. Qiantang River
28. China-Japan Friendship Hotel
29. Wanghu Hotel

KAIFENG

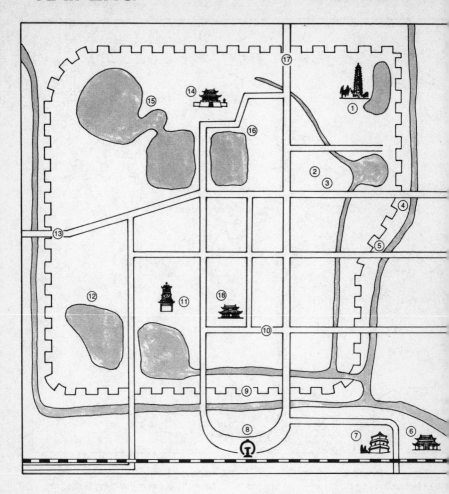

1. Iron Pagoda
2. Kaifeng Embroidery Factory
3. Painter's Studio
4. Caomen Gate
5. Songmen Gate
6. King Yu's Terrace
7. Pota Pagoda
8. Railway Station
9. South Gate
10. Guest House
11. Yanqing Taoist Temple
12. Baofu Pit
13. West Gate
14. Dragon Pavilion
15. Yangjia Lake
16. Panjia Lake
17. North Gate
18. Xiangguo Monastery

KUNMING

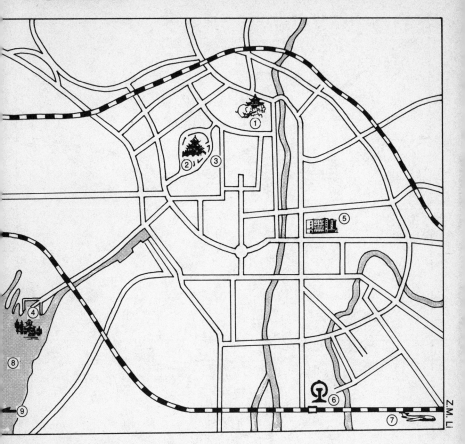

1. Yuantongshan Mountain
2. Zhui Hu (Green Lake) Park
3. Green Lake Hotel
4. Daguan Lou (Grand View Pavilion)
5. Kunming Hotel and C.I.T.S.
6. Railway Station
7. To Airport
8. Dianchi Lake
9. To Western Hills

NANJING

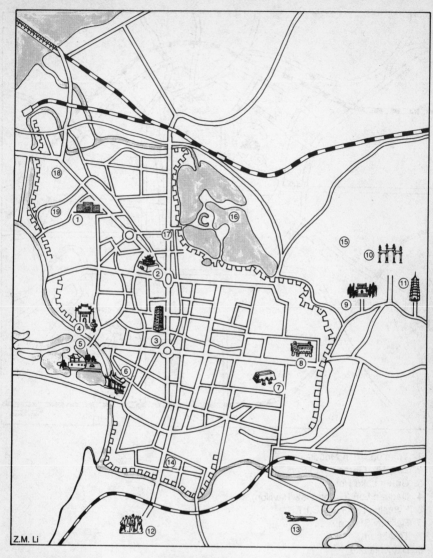

1. Nanjing Hotel
2. Drum Tower
3. Jinling Hotel
4. Stone Citadel
5. Mochou Park
6. Chaotian Palace
7. Wuchao Gate and Ming Palace ruins
8. Nanjing Provincial Museum and Zhongshan Hotel
9. Ming Tomb
10. Sun Yat-sen Mausoleum
11. Linggu Pagoda
12. Yuhuatai Mausoleum
13. To Airport
14. Museum of the Taiping Heavenly Kingdom
15. Purple Gold Mountain Observatory
16. Xuanwu Lake
17. Friendship Store
18. Shuangmenlou Hotel
19. Dingshan Hotel

Z.M. Li

QINGDAO

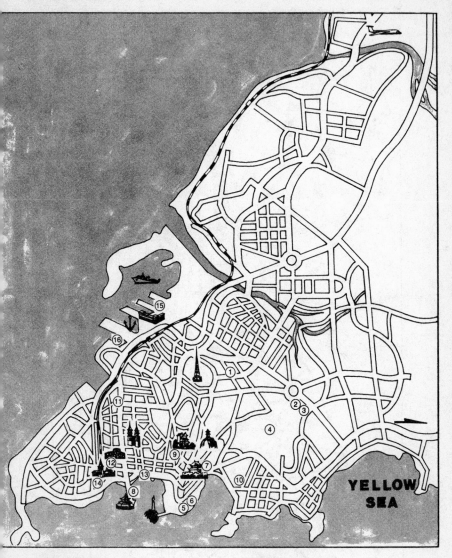

YELLOW SEA

1. Qingdao Brewery
2. Embroidery Factory
3. Jade Carving Factory
4. Zhongshan Park
5. Luxun Park
6. Qingdao Museum of Marine Products
7. Qingdao Museum
8. Pier
9. Guesthouse
10. Huiquan Guesthouse
11. Zhongshan Rd.
12. Huaqiao (Overseas Chinese) Hotel
13. Zhanqiao (Pier) Guesthouse
14. Railway Station
15. Youyi (Friendship) Hotel
16. Passenger Quay

URBAN SHANGHAI

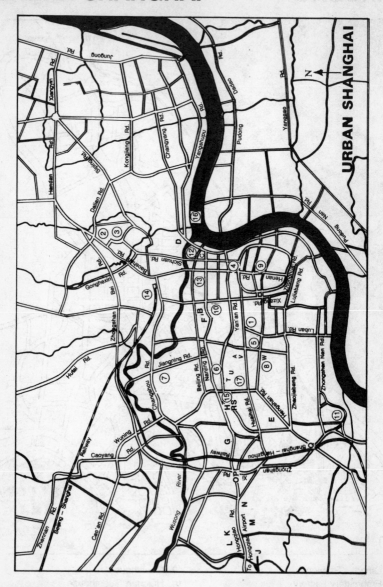

SUZHOU

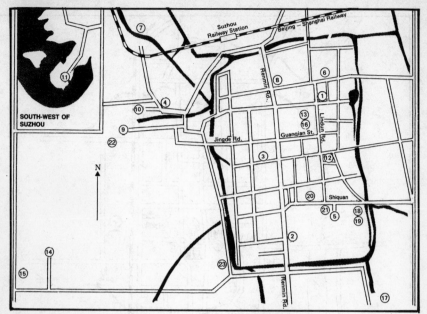

1. Shizilin [Lion Forest] Garden
2. Chang Lang [Gentle Wave Pavilion]
3. Yi [Joyous] Garden
4. Liu [Lingering] Garden
5. Wangshih [Garden of the Master of Nets]
6. Zhuozheng [Humble Administrator's] Garden
7. Hu Qiu [Tiger Hill]
8. North Temple Pagoda
9. Han Shan Temple
10. Xiyuan [West Garden] Temple
11. Purple Gold Nunnery

12. Twin Pagodas
13. Xuan Miao Guan [Taoist Temple]
14. Sky High Hill
15. Divine Cliff Hill
16. Friendship Store
17. Precious Belt Bridge
18. C.I.T.S.
19. Suzhou Hotel and Gusu [Ancient Suzhou] Hotel
20. Nanlin Hotel
21. Nanyuan Hotel
22. Grand Canal
23. Panmen Gate

14. Shanghai Railway Station
15. International Club
16. Foreign Passenger Quay
17. U.S., Japanese, and French consulates

Hotels

A. Jing Jiang (Chin Chiang)
B. Huaqiao [Overseas Chinese]
C. He Ping [Peace]
D. Shanghai Da Sha [Shanghai Mansions]
E. Heng Shan
F. Guo Ji [Park]
G. Da Hua Guest House
H. Shanghai
J. Cypress Hotel

K. Western Suburb Guest House a.k.a. Xijiao
L. Chengqiao Hotel
M. Xinyuan (New Garden) Hotel
N. Cherry Tourist Village
O. Hongqiao Hotel I
P. Hongqiao Hotel II
Q. Huating Hotel
R. Jing'an Guest House (New Building)
S. Jing'an Hilton
T. Yan'an Hotel
U. Donghu (East Lake) Guest House
V. Jinjiang New Tower Hotel
W. Ruijin Guest House

TAIYUAN

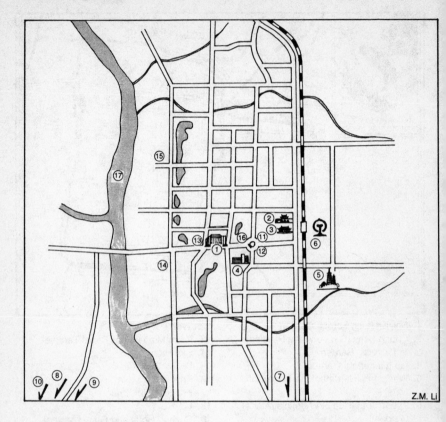

Z.M. Li

1. Yingze Guest House
2. Chongshan Monastery
3. Provincial Museum No. 1
4. Bingzhou Hotel
5. Shuangta Monastery
6. Railway Station
7. To airport
8. To Long Shan (Dragon Mountain) Taoist caves and Tian Long Shan Caves
9. To Jinci Temple
10. To Jinci Hotel (near the Temple)
11. Yunshan Hotel
12. San Jin Mansions
13. Tang Ming Hotel
14. Shanxi Hotel
15. San Qiao Mansions
16. Provincial Museum No. 2
17. Fen River

WUHAN

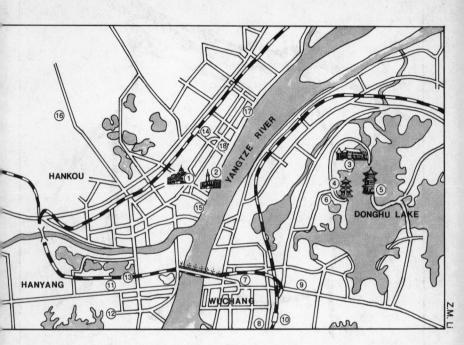

1. Xuangong Hotel
2. Wuhan Customhouse
3. Changtian Lou (Long Heaven Tower)
4. Xinyin Ge (Pavilion for Reading Poems)
5. Huguang Ge (Lake Scenery Pavilion)
6. Hubei Provincial Museum
7. Yellow Crane Tower on Snake Hill
8. Qiyi (Uprising Gate)
9. Hongshan Hill

10. Wuchang Railway Station
11. Hanyang Railway Station
12. Guiyang Temple
13. Platform of the Ancient Lute
14. Hankou Railway Station
15. Passenger Quay
16. Airport
17. Shengli Hotel
18. Jianghan Hotel

ANCIENT XI'AN

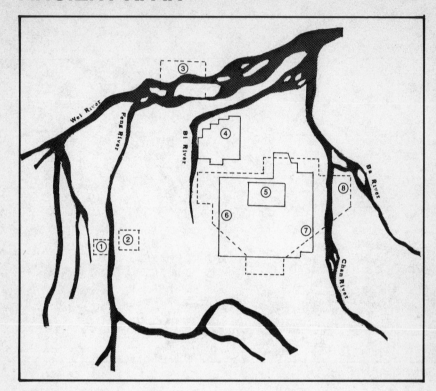

Locations in different historical periods

1. W. Han—Fengjing
2. W. Han—Haojing
3. Qin—Xianyang
4. Han—Changan

5. Ming and Qing—Xi'an
6. Sui—Daxing
7. Tang—Changan
8. Xi'an today

XI'AN

1. Shaanxi Provincial Museum
2. Big Wild Goose Pagoda
3. Little Wild Goose Pagoda
4. Bell Tower
5. Drum Tower
6. West City Gate
7. Great Mosque
8. Xingqing Park
9. Museum of the Eighth Route Army
10. Renmin Hotel

11. Friendship Store
12. Zhonglou (Bell Tower) Hotel
13. Chang'an Hotel
14. Efang Palace Hotel
15. Golden Flower Hotel (Jinhua)
16. Huashan Hotel
17. Sports Hotel
18. Tangcheng Hotel
19. Xi'an (Xiaoyanta Hotel)
20. Scarlet Bird Hotel

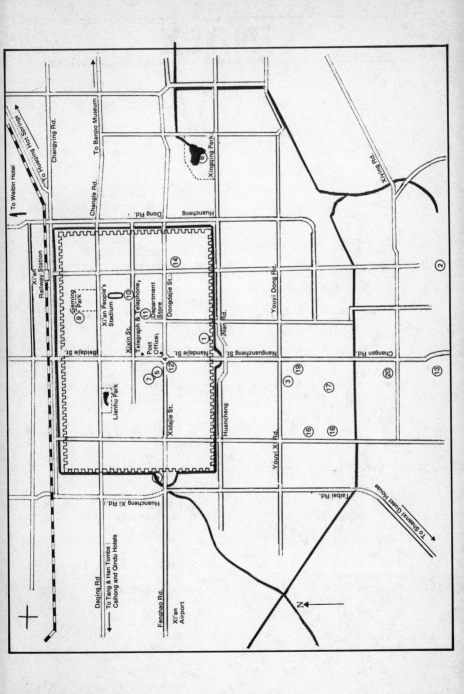

INDEX

Ruth Lor Malloy at Lama temple,
Chengde.

Priscilla Liang Hsu in Zunhua.

About the Authors

Ruth Lor Malloy is a Canadian of Chinese ancestry whose father is from Taishan in Guangdong province. Although trained as a social worker, she has been a conference organizer, freelance writer, photographer, travel columnist, wife, and mother, living and traveling in Asia for over a decade. Her first trip of many to China was in 1965. In addition to writing guidebooks on China since 1973, she has written *Post Guide Hong Kong, Gems and Jewelery in Hong Kong—A Buyer's Guide* (with Joan Reid Ahrens, G.G.). She currently lives in Toronto, making periodic research trips back to China.

She pleads guilty to first person references in the text and being overly cautious in what she eats because she has gotten sick from eating watermelon and Popsicles in China.

Priscilla Liang Hsu spent her first ten years in Shanghai and Qingdao in China. After undergraduate education in Taiwan, she did graduate study in social work at the East-West Center of Hawaii. She then worked for many years at the Children's Mental Health Center (St. Louis) and Child Development Clinic (Houston). She has also taught social work in Hong Kong. In the last couple of years, she has spent most of her time traveling. She wants to disassociate herself from Ruth's warnings about eating such things as watermelon. She is not careful about what she eats, and has rarely been sick.

Mrs. Hsu has a lifelong commitment to promoting the growth of self and those around her. She is happy to serve as a bridge for those interested in China and once helped a friend find out about his previous incarnation in China. In the next few years, she plans to write and travel more, especially to the remote areas of China, visiting minorities, and enjoying the wilderness. She maintains residences in both Houston and Beijing.

PLEASE HELP US HELP OTHER CHINA TRAVELERS

Please complete this form and mail to *Fielding's People's Republic of China*, c/o William Morrow and Co., 105 Madison Ave., New York, NY 10016. Use more paper if necessary.

I have found the following hotels to be of acceptable international standards.

I have found the following different from your book.

Other comments about my China visit:

Dates of visit:
Name:

Address: (optional—but we might want to contact you for clarification).

Telephone number: (optional):